# A CULTURAL INDEX TO VEDIC LITERATURE

# A CULTURAL INDEX TO VEDIC LITERATURE

*Edited by*
N.N. BHATTACHARYYA

*UGC Project undertaken by School of Vedic Studies,*
*Rabindra Bharati University*

MANOHAR
2007

First published 2007



ISBN 81-7304-732-4

*Published by*

Ajay Kumar Jain for
Manohar Publishers & Distributors
4753/23 Ansari Road, Daryaganj
New Delhi 110 002

*Typeset at*

Digigrafics
New Delhi 110 049

*Printed at*

Lordson Publishers Pvt. Ltd.
Delhi 110 007

# Contents

# Foreword

I am happy to see that *A Cultural Index to Vedic Literature* is going to be published. The *Index* gives, in brief, information relating to such topics as the social life, political and economic conditions, material culture, religion, mythology, etc., in the Vedic age. An attempt has been made to present data relating to the material and spiritual, physical and metaphysical contents, recorded here under relevant keywords which are arranged alphabetically.

The UGC visiting team, headed by Prof. S.D. Joshi, which recommended the establishment of the School of Vedic Studies in Rabindra Bharati University, suggested that the project of preparing a cultural index of Vedic literature should be undertaken by the School. Accordingly, the members of the School of Vedic Studies engaged themselves in compiling such a work under the directorship of Prof. Samiran Chandra Chakrabarti. Data was collected from the original Vedic texts mainly by the project assistants of the School; besides, I and Dr Pradyot Kumar Datta of the School of Vedic Studies and Dr Karunasindhu Das and Dr Taraknath Adhikari of the Dept. of Sanskrit also contributed to the collection of data. There were four posts of project assistants at any given time, and the following scholars worked in these posts from time to time: Dipankar Mukhopadhyay (1990-1), Pranati Ghoshal (1990-3), Suparna Gupta (1990-3), Soma Basu (1990-2), Silpi Das (1991-2), Ashok Kumar Mahato (1993-4), Dr Rita Bhowmik (1993-4), Bratati Goswami (1993-7), Sarbani Bhattacharya (1993-7), Jayanti Bhattacharya (1994-6), Parboty Chakraborty (1994-5), Ranjana Ganguli (1996-7), and Rapti Deb (1996-7). The service rendered by them is greatly appreciated.

It was considered desirable that the data thus collected be evaluated, arranged and edited in its historical perspective. An opportunity presented itself when the late Dr Narendra Nath Bhattacharyya of the Dept. of Ancient Indian History and Culture, Calcutta University, joined the School of Vedic Studies as an Extension Lecturer in 1996. Dr Bhattacharyya was a reputed scholar, adept in both Sanskrit and History, with a good number of publications relating to ancient Indian history and culture to his credit. He was entrusted with the task of editing the data for the *Cultural Index,* and he devoted much time and energy to the work. The structure, treatment and method had all been designed by the editor. He was assisted by the project assistants at every stage.

In the past Dr N.N. Bhattacharyya was associated with us in various ways and the present work will remain as a token of his association with and interest in the programmes of the School of Vedic Studies. I deeply regret that he did not live to see the publication. We are grateful to him for the ungrudging service he rendered in bringing about the publication of the *Index*. Since he was not able to read the proofs of his book it is possible that some errors which could have been avoided had he been able to do so still remain. In the absence of the editor, the proofs were corrected by Dr G.S. Mukherji and Dr Soma Basu to whom I am very grateful.

I take this opportunity to express my thanks to all those who contributed to the preparation of the *Cultural Index* in general and to Manohar Publishers & Distributors in particular for undertaking publication of this *Index*.

*Professor (Director)*
*School of Vedic Studies*
*20 September 2006*

NABANARAYAN BANDYOPADHYAY

# Preface

The project of compiling *A Cultural Index to Vedic Literature* was taken up in the mid-1990s by the School of Vedic Studies, Rabindra Bharati University. In 1993 I was a Visiting Fellow there. At the behest of Professor Samiran Chandra Chakrabarti, Director, SVS, I agreed to take charge of the project, which was completed in 1997, thanks to the valuable services rendered by the Director and academic staff of the SVS, the teachers of the Sanskrit department and the project assistants.

The title of the project is self-explanatory. It endeavours to present a conspectus of what is known as the Vedic age in Indian history by collecting from various texts relevant data pertaining to all aspects of Vedic thought and culture, analysing and interpreting them in a historical perspective and arranging them under more than 1,000 topics in alphabetical order. It serves as a supplement to the celebrated *Vedic Index* (2 vols., London, 1912) by Macdonell and Keith. The latter is a descriptive terminological glossary of Vedic antiquities, and as such can be used successfully only by those who have, to a certain extent, a comprehension of Vedic terms. The present volume contains subjectwise entries which are expected to be of greater usefulness to the readers.

This does not, however, mean that terms representing names and subjects have been ignored. Abridged renderings have been given here from the *Vedic Index* itself, because for many entries it is impossible to add anything more to what has already been collected, classified and interpreted by Macdonell and Keith. In the present volume royal and priestly lineages as well as personal names of kings, chiefs, sages and individuals, which form a considerable part of the *Vedic Index*, have been omitted. Geographical and tribal proper names, and those of some of the Upaniṣadic thinkers whose views have relevance to the growth of subsequent Indian philosophical speculations, have been retained and expanded with useful details. In fact, entries on religion and philosophy as also on ethical, aesthetic and other higher aspects of life have been given greater prominence in the present volume since the authors of the *Vedic Index* confined themselves to those aspects of religious activity that were inseparably connected with the social and political life of the age, such as priestly function, festivals, rituals of royal consecration and so forth.

As far as the entries pertaining to material culture, social institutions, economic conditions, and allied subjects are concerned, the diverse interpretations of the earlier scholars have been retained in certain interesting cases but in other cases these have been replaced by modern views. Numerous valuable works on various Vedic subjects have been published in recent years, from which much has been drawn in the present volume, especially when the topic is of scientific or technical nature or has intricate philosophical implications. The sources have been acknowledged at the end of each such entry.

A sincere attempt has been made to afford the reader a harmonious and well-thought-out picture of Vedic civilization. I am fully aware of the magnitude of the task and my own limitations in this regard. I am grateful for the cooperation of all my colleagues at the School of Vedic Studies: Sri Nabanarayan Bandyopadhyay, Dr Pradyot Datta, Dr Tarak Nath Adhikari and Dr Krishnakali Bhattacharya, all teachers of the Department of Sanskrit, Rabindra Bharati University; the project assistants Dr Soma Basu, Dr Rita Bhowmik, Sri Ashok Mahato, Ms Pranati Ghoshal, Ms Bratati Mukherjee, Ms Sarbani Bhattacharya, Ms Rapti Deb, Ms Ranjana Ganguli, Ms Silpi Das, Ms Suparna Gupta; and the attendent of the SVS Library, Mrs Sipra Dey. It is also a matter of great satisfaction that my esteemed friend Sri Ramesh Jain of Manohar Publishers and Distributors has come forward and taken up the task of bringing out this volume.

NARENDRA NATH BHATTACHARYYA

*Joraghat*
*Chinsurah 712101*
*W. Bengal*

# Abbreviations

Secondary works are mentioned at the end of each entry after the names of their authors or editors. Thus, Macdonell 124 suggests A.A. Macdonell, *Vedic Mythology*, Strassburg 1898, p. 124. When an author has more than one book the date of publication is given after the name of the author, e.g. Bhattacharyya 1990, 213. In the case of contributing authors, their initials are given and the citation follows. For example, word *in* is put between the name of the contributor and the editor or the initials of the Reference Works, e.g. B.K. Ghosh in Majumdar 222-8 or V.M. Apte in *CHI* I. 234-63.

| | | |
|---|---|---|
| *AĀ* | : | *Aitareya Āraṇyaka* |
| *AB* | : | *Aitareya Brāhmaṇa* |
| *ĀGS* | : | *Āśvalāyana Gṛhyasūtra* |
| *ĀpDS* | : | *Āpastamba Dharmasūtra* |
| *ĀpŚS* | : | *Āpastamba Śrautasūtra* |
| *ĀŚG* | : | *Ānandāśrama Saṃskṛta Granthāvali* |
| *ĀŚS* | : | *Āsvalāyana Śrautasūtra* |
| *AU* | : | *Aitareya Upaniṣad* |
| *AV* | : | *Atharvaveda* |
| *BDS* | : | *Baudhayāna/Bodhāyana Dharmasūtra* |
| *BGS* | : | *Baudhāyana/Bodhāyana Gṛhyasūtra* |
| *BhGS* | : | *Bhāradvāja Gṛhyasūtra* |
| *BŚS* | : | *Baudhāyana Śrautasūtra* |
| *BU* | : | *Bṛhadāraṇyaka Upaniṣad* |
| *CHI* | : | *Cultural Heritage of India* |
| *CU* | : | *Chāndogya Upaniṣad* |
| *DŚS* | : | *Drāhyāyana Śrautasūtra* |
| *ERE* | : | *The Encyclopaedia of Religion and Ethics* |
| *GB* | : | *Gopatha Brāhmaṇa* |
| *GDS* | : | *Gautama Dharmasūtra* |
| *GGS* | : | *Gobhila Gṛhyasūtra* |
| *HGS* | : | *Hiraṇyakeśi (= Satyāsāḍha) Gṛhyasūtra* |
| *HIL* | : | *History of Indian Literature* |
| *HOS* | : | *Harvard Oriental Series* |
| *HŚS* | : | *Hiraṇyakeśi (= Satyāsāḍha) Śrautasūtra* |
| *ĪU* | : | *Īśa Upaniṣad* |
| *Jaimini* | : | *Pūrvamīmāṃsā Sūtra of Jaimini* |
| *JAOS* | : | *Journal of American Oriental Society* |
| *JB* | : | *Jaiminīya Brāhmaṇa* |
| *JRAS* | : | *Journal of the Royal Asiatic Society* |
| *JUB* | : | *Jaiminīya Upaniṣad Brāhmaṇa* |
| *KauSū* | : | *Kauśika Sūtra* |
| *KauU* | : | *Kauṣītaki Upaniṣad* |
| *KB* | : | *Kauṣitaki Brāhmaṇa* |
| *KenU* | : | *Kenopaniṣad* |
| *KhaDs* | : | *Khādira Dharmasūtra* |

| | | |
|---|---|---|
| *KKS* | : | *Kapiṣṭhala-Kaṭha Saṃhitā* |
| *KhaGs* | : | *Khādira Gṛhyasūtra* |
| *KS* | : | *Kāṭhaka Saṃhitā* |
| *KŚS* | : | *Kātyāyana Śrautasūtra* |
| *KU* | : | *Kaṭha Upaniṣad* |
| *LŚS* | : | *Lāṭyāyana Śrautasūtra* |
| *MaitU* | : | *Maitrāyanī Upaniṣad* |
| *ManuS* | : | *Manusaṃhitā* |
| *MaU* | : | *Māṇḍukyopaniṣad* |
| *MDS* | : | *Mānava Dharma Sūtra* |
| *MGS* | : | *Mānava Gṛhyasūtra* |
| *MIS* | : | *Medieval Indian Sculpture in the British Museum* |
| *MS* | : | *Maitrāyaṇī Saṃhitā* |
| *MU* | : | *Muṇḍaka Upaniṣad* |
| *Nir* | : | *Nirukta* |
| *PB* | : | *Pañcaviṃśa Brāhmaṇa* |
| *PGS* | : | *Pāraskara Gṛhya Sūtra* |
| *PU* | : | *Praśna Upaniṣad* |
| *RV* | : | *Ṛgveda Saṃhitā* |
| *RVBr* | : | *Ṛgveda Brāhmaṇas* (by A.B. Keith) |
| *ŚāṅkhĀ* | : | *Śāṅkhāyana Āraṇyaka* |
| *ŚāṅkhBr* | : | *Śāṅkhāyana Brāhmaṇa* |
| *ṢaḍB* | : | *Ṣaḍviṃśa Brāhmaṇa* |
| *ŚB* | : | *Śatapatha Brāhmaṇa (Mādhyandina)* |
| *SBE* | : | *Sacred Books of the East* |
| *ŚGS* | : | *Śāṅkhāyana Gṛhyasūtra* |
| *ŚŚS* | : | *Śāṅkhāyana Śrautasūtra* |
| *SV* | : | *Sāmaveda Saṃhitā* |
| *ŚvU, Śvet* | : | *Śvetāśvatara Upaniṣad* |
| *TA* | : | *Taittirīya Āraṇyaka* |
| *TB* | : | *Taittirīya Brāhmaṇa* |
| *TS* | : | *Taittirīya Saṃhitā* |
| *TU* | : | *Taittirīya Upaniṣad* |
| *VDS* | : | *Vāsiṣṭha Dharma Sūtra* |
| *ViṣṇuDS* | : | *Viṣṇu Dharma Sūtra* |
| *VL* | : | *Vedic Literature* (= HIL, ed. J. Gonda, Vol. 1, fasc. 1) |
| *VM* | : | *Vedic Mythology* |
| *VS* | : | *Vājasaneyī Saṃhitā* |
| *YV* | : | *Yajurveda Saṃhitā* |
| *YS* | : | *Yogasūtra* |

# A

**Abbies:** See **Education**.

**Abdication:** Relinquishing the crown formally or by default, a few instances of which are found in the Vedic texts. Devāpi (*RV* 10.98) abdicated the throne in favour of his brother. According to the *Nirukta* (2.10) Devāpi was the elder Kuru prince but his younger brother Śantanu became king. There was a prolonged drought in the kingdom and Devāpi acted as the priest of the king and brought rain by performing a sacrifice. The *Bṛhaddevatā* (8.148 ff) tells the same story but adds that the reason for Devāpi's abdication was his skin disease. King Duṣṭaritu Pauṃsāyana, a king of the Sṛñjayas had to abdicate for his misrule (*ŚB* 12.9.3.1 ff). Though in the age of the later Saṃhitās and Brāhmaṇas kings were invested with divinity and there was a tendency towards royal absolutism, yet royal power was insecure (*aparuddha*) since there are references to kings being expelled from their realms and their efforts to recover their sovereignty (*AV* 3.4.3; *KS* 28.1; *TS* 2.3.1; *MS* 2.2.1; *PB* 12.12.6; *ŚB* 12.9.3.3). See **Deposition, Kingship**.

**Abduction:** Taking a woman away by force or fraud, or sometimes with her consent. It has been a regular feature of patriarchal societies all over the world through the ages, and the Vedic India was no exception. In the epics and Purāṇas, and also in the vast mass of Sanskrit and Prākṛt literature, we have numerous instances of forcible abductions but the Vedic references of such cases are, however, few and far between. The *Ṛgveda* (1.112.19; 1.116.1; 1.117.20; 10.39.7; 10.65.12) contains a few references to Vimada who carried off Purumitra's daughter (Kāmadyū according to Sāyaṇa) against her father's will, but probably with her own consent. In fact marriages by capture, which later came to be known as the *rākṣasa* form of marriage, must have been a regular feature of the Vedic society. The *Āśvalāyana Gṛhya Sūtra* and most of the Dharma Sūtras have given recognition to this form of marriage in which a girl was abducted, with or without her consent, and often after a fight with her relatives. In special cases, especially among the nobles, capture of the girl by force for the purpose of marriage was regarded as a feat of chivalric achievement. The *Baudhāyana Dharma Sūtra* (4.1.15-16) clearly states that 'if a damsel has been abducted by force and has not been wedded according to sacred texts, she is to be treated like a maiden and may be lawfully married to another man'. See **Marriage**.

**Abilities:** The psychic properties of the individual which regulate his behaviour and underpin his actions. In the Vedic tradition these originate from the vital breath or *prāṇa* which is born from the Self, and covers the Self like a shadow, as though an 'ethric double'. This sheath activates the body and mind. As *apāna* it governs the process of generation, as *samāna* it controls the mind, as *udāna* it leads the doer towards good action and as *vyāna* it moves in the innumerable arteries of the body issuing out from the heart (*PU* 3.6). The ordinary sense cognition forms the essential background of sense-perception (*BU* 1.5.3) and its clearness and accuracy depend in some way upon the healthy organic condition of the body (*CU* 6.7), to maintain which certain purificatory disciplines are prescribed. Each sense-perception and each act initiated by the mind on the basis of the sense perception presuppose the existence and the direct awareness of the Self as the Subject or agent of perception (*KenU* 1.2.2). In the first chapter of the *Bṛhadāraṇyaka Upaniṣad* it is categorically stated that man is able to see and hear not with his eye or ear, but with his mind which is the base of everything—desire, will, doubt, belief, disbelief, memory, obliviousness, shame, reflection, fear—all these are veritably the mind. This is an exaltation of the fact of mental understanding over the mere physiological processes of perception.

**Abiogenesis:** See **Cosmogony**.

**Ablution:** Ceremonial washing. The final purificatory bath in *agniṣṭoma* and other sacrifices is known as *avabhṛtha* in which a handful of *kuśa* grass is thrown into water, *mahīya-ṛk* uttered to Varuṇa, *avabhṛtha-sāman* is chanted and the sacrificial utensils are thrown into water (*TB* 1.4.1; *TS* 1.3.14.4; *VS* 8.27). Apart from this, bathing was required on certain occasions. Ritual ablution was a feature of the domestic (*gṛhya*) sacrifices. The rites of coronation included a sprinkling ceremony and the consecration water (*abhiṣecanīyā āpaḥ*) was made up of seventeen kinds of liquids including water from the river Sarasvati, seawater, water from a whirlpool, a pond, a well and dew (*ŚB* 5.2.3.9 ff).

**Abortion:** In the *Atharvaveda* various remedies are suggested for preventing miscarriage or abortion. To prevent the premature birth of a child Kauśika and Sāyaṇa prescribe that the string of a bow be tied on the body of the pregnant woman. Clay from a field mixed with the water should also be given to her and the woman is exhorted to bear the foetus up to delivery just as the earth supports the embryos of beings, plants and mountains. It seems that the pregnant woman was symbolically treated, so that there would not be miscarriage. An amulet of white and yellow mustard, imbued with magical values, is tied on the body of the pregnant woman to prevent the evil spirits attacking and harassing her. These evil spirits cause abortion or the birth of a dead child (*AV* 8.6.9), or pain in her hips (*AV* 8.6.13). They like to devour the embryo of the pregnant woman (*AV* 8.6.23), or they enter the embryo and cause the child to die before or soon after birth (*AV* 8.6.18). The *bheṣaja* for such trouble is to keep the white and yellow mustard seeds in the knot of her garment or *nīvi* (*AV*. 8.6.20). The mustard prevents problems like still birth, labour pain and barrenness (*AV* 8.6.26). The *Atharvaveda* (2.25.3) refers to the demons called Kaṇvas, who eat foetus (*garbhāda*). The plant *pṛśniparṇī* (*hermonitis cordifolia*) is the wonderful divine remedy against the vile tricks of the Kaṇvas, in particular causing abortion. The priest employs it to cut off the heads of the evil brood (*AV* 2.25.1-5). Shende 22-3.

**Absolute:** Term denoting the eternal, infinite, unconditional, perfect and unchanging subject, that is complete in itself, is not dependent on anything else and contains within itself everything that exists. In the Vedic tradition this Absolute is denoted by the terms *brahman* (q.v.), the cosmic principle, and *ātman*, the psychical principle, the identity of which is expressed by the dictum *tat tvam asi* (thou art that). This identity is very tersely explained by Deussen (*PU* 39): 'The *brahman*, the power which presents itself to us materialized in all existing things, which creates, sustains, preserves and receives back into itself again all worlds, this eternal, infinite, divine power is identical with the *ātman*, with which, after stripping off everything external, we discover in ourselves as our real most essential being, our individual self, the soul.' The *Chāndogya Upaniṣad* (3.14) says: 'This my *ātman* in my inmost heart is smaller than a grain of rice, or a barley-corn, or a mustard seed, or a millet grain. . . . This my *ātman* in my inmost heart is greater than the earth, greater than the heavens, greater than all spheres. In him are all actions, all wishes, all smells, all tastes; he holds this all enclosed within himself; he speaks not, he troubles about nothing; this my *ātman* in my inmost heart is this *brahman*. With him, when I depart out of this life, shall I be united. For him to whom this knowledge has come, for him indeed there exist no doubts. Thus spake Śāṇḍilya, yeo Śāṇḍilya' (Winternitz I.250). The *brahman* or the Absolute is described in the *Bṛhadāraṇyaka Upaniṣad* (3.8.8) in negative terms: 'Neither gross, nor minute, neither short nor long; without blood and without fat; without a shadow, not filled by the wind, and not a vacuity; free from attachment; tasteless and odourless; eyeless, earless, speechless, mindless, without heart and without breath and without mouth; measureless and without an inside and outside.' For more details see *ātman* and *brahman*. See also **Acosmism, Akṣara.**

**Absolutism:** See **Kingship, Sovereignty.**

**Abstinence:** The Ṛgvedic peoples were in favour of worldly enjoyments, though abstinence from adultery, witchcraft, gambling, drinking, sensuality and self-deception was encouraged. A fairly detailed description of the *upanayana* and the taboos observed by the *brahmacārins* are found in the *Śatapatha Brāhmaṇa* (11.3.3.1-7) and their essential features are treated at length in the *Gṛhyasūtras*. The numerous vows and observances obligatory for the *brahmacārin* entailed the most rigorous discipline for a prescribed period. Even at the householder stage abstinence from gross sensual pleasure and performance of five *mahāyajñas* (daily duties) were demanded. For details see **Ethics**.

**Abstract Gods:** Two classes of deities whose nature is founded on abstraction are found in the *Ṛgveda*. The class consisting of the direct personifications of abstract notions such as 'desire' is rare, occurring only in the late hymns of the *Ṛgveda*. The other class comprises deities whose names primarily either denote an agent, such as Dhātṛ (creator), or designate some attribute, such as Prajāpati (Lord of creatures). This class judged by the evolution of the mythological creation of the Veda, does not represent direct abstractions but appears in each case to be derived from an epithet, applied to one or more deities, and illustrates a particular aspect of activity. Such epithets gradually become detached and finally attained an independent position. Thus Rohita (the Red One whose female form is Rohiṇī), originally an epithet of the Sun, figures in the *Atharvaveda* as a separate deity in the capacity of a creator. Manyu (wrath), a personification suggested chiefly by the fierce anger of Indra, is invoked in two hymns of the *Ṛgveda* (10.83-84). He is of irresistable might and self-existent. He glows like fire. One short hymn of the *Ṛgveda* (10.151) is devoted to the praise of Śraddhā (faith) who must be invoked morning, noon, and night. Through faith, fire is kindled, oblations offered and wealth is obtained. In the Brāhmaṇas Śraddhā is the daughter of the sun (*ŚB* 12.7.3.11). Anumati (favour of the gods) occurs twice as a personification in the *Ṛgveda*. She is beseeched to be gracious to her worshippers (10.167.3). In the *AV* and *VS* she becomes a goddess of love and presides over propagation. The latter ritually connects her with the moon, representing the day before the full moon. Aramati (devotion, piety) is occasionally personified in the *Ṛgveda*. The name has a counterpart in the Avestic Aramaiti, a genius of earth as well as wisdom. *Sūnṛtā* (bounty) appears to be personified as a goddess two or three times in the *Ṛgveda* (10.40.3; 10.141.2). *Asunīti* (spirit-life) is personified in two passages of the *Ṛgveda* (10.59.5-6), being beseeched to prolong life and grant strength and nourishment. Nirṛti (decease, dissolution) appears about twelve times in the *Ṛgveda* as a personification presiding over death. Other personifications appear for the first time in the later

Vedas, Kāma (desire) is deified in the *Atharvaveda* (9.2; 19, 52). He is not, as in post-Vedic literature, a god of love, but a deity who fulfils all desires. The arrows with which he pierces hearts are referred to in the *Atharvaveda* (3.25.1). He is described as first to be born (*AV* 9, 2.19). The origin of the conception can most probably be traced to the Kāma which is called the 'first seed of mind' in a cosmogonic hymn of the *Ṛgveda* (10.129.4). Kāla (time) is personified as a cosmogonic force in the *Atharvaveda* (19.53.54), and Skambha (support), an abstraction postulated by the speculation of the *Atharvaveda* to uphold the universe created by Prajāpati, comes to be praised as the all-God (*AV* 10, 8.2). Prāṇa (breath) is also deified and identified with Prajāpati (*AV* 11, 4.12). Other personified abstractions of a like nature are to be found in the *Atharvaveda*. Śrī as a personification of beauty or fortune first appears in the *Śatapatha Brāhmaṇa* (11, 4, 3, 3, 1). Macdonell, 1898, 115, 119-20.

**Accidentalism:** The doctrine of accidental origination, mentioned in *Śvetāśvatara Upaniṣad* (1.1), according to which there can be no such thing as cause at all or that every event is absolutely fortuitous. This is known as *yadṛcchāvāda*. In contrast naturalism (*svabhāvavāda*) claims that though the supernatural cause is clearly illegitimate, the concept of the natural cause is not so. The author of the *Śvetāśvatara Upaniṣad* clearly differentiates between naturalism and accidentalism. Later commentators also maintain this difference. Śaṅkara, for example, says: 'By *svabhāva* is meant the power invariably belonging to the natural objects, as for instance the radiation of heat by fire. By *yadṛcchā* is meant purely fortuitous origin.' The Jain logician Guṇaratna also holds that *yadṛcchāvādins* do not recognise cause-effect relation among objects. For details see **Naturalism**.

**Acosmism:** The acosmic view of Reality is known as *niṣprapañca*. *Brahman*, the term by which the Ultimate Reality is known in the Upaniṣads, is the ground of the manifestation of the universe according to the *saprapañca* or cosmic view but, according to the *niṣprapañca*, it is the basis of the illusory appearance of the world. In the terminology of the later Vedānta, the universe is a *pariṇāma* (transformation) of *brahman* according to the *saprapañca* view whereas the *niṣprapañca* view holds it to be a *vivarta* (transfiguration) thereof. The cosmic view of Reality is that the Real is the one substance out of which the many modes constituting the world have come forth and that *Brahman* is *saguṇa* (the bearer of attributes). The acosmic view, on the other hand, regards the Absolute as the distinctionless substrate whereon somehow the illusory world-show appears and that *brahman per se* is *nirguṇa* (attributeless) (*BU* 2.4; *CU* 8.11; *PU* 4). T.M.P. Mahadevan in *Cultural Heritage of India*, I, 169.

**Acrobat:** See **Amusement**.

**Acting, Actor:** See **Amusement**.

**Action, Doctrine of:** See **Karma**.

**Aditi:** The word *aditi* is primarily a noun meaning 'non-binding', 'bondlessness', as distinguished from *diti*, 'binding', derived from the root *da* to bind). Hence, as a goddess, Aditi is invoked to release her worshipper from bondage. Roth had understood the word to mean inviolability, imperishableness; and, when personified as a goddess, to denote eternity. Her sons, the Ādityas, were the sons of eternity, and the solar and luminous gods Varuṇa, Mitra, Aryaman, Bhaga, etc., were pre-eminently the eternal deities as light was regarded as the immaterial and eternal principle. Aditi, eternity, or the eternal, is the element which sustains, and is sustained by, the Ādityas. In the Vedas this conception had not been carried to a definite personification, though the beginnings of such are there. The eternal and inviolable principle in which the Ādityas live, and which constitutes their essence, is the celestial light. Müller comments: 'Aditi, an ancient god or goddess, is in reality the earliest name invented to express the infinite; not the infinite as the result of a long process of abstract reasoning but the visible Infinite, visible by the naked eye, the endless expanse, beyond the earth, beyond the sky.' She is mentioned about 80 times in the *Ṛgveda* though she is not the subject of any separate hymn. The concept of her motherhood is found in such expressions as *dyaur-aditiḥ, aditeḥ-putrāḥ*, etc. The *Nighaṇṭu* (5.5) gives Aditi as a synonym of *pṛthivī* (earth), *vāc* (speech), *go* (cow) and *dyāvāpṛthivī* (heaven and earth). According to V.M. Apte (in Majumdar 371) 'Aditi is unmistakably connected with light in the *Ṛgveda*. Varuṇa, the Āditya, is connected prominently and almost exclusively with Ṛta; so is Aditi. This Ṛta has for its physical basis the belt of the Zodiac. Now the Devas, the lights of heaven, seemed to the ancients to recover their freedom from the clutches of darkness and to restart on their bright career from a fixed point in the east lying on the belt of the zodiac or the Ṛta. This point in all probability, was Aditi. No wonder, the luminaries suddenly emerging thus into freedom and light (emerging in other words into life itself) from this fixed point (Aditi) received the epithet "sons of Aditi".' (*RV* 1.166.2, 2.27.7, 4.12.4, 5.82.6, 7, 87.7, 7.93.7, 10.64.5; *AV* 6.120.2, 15.6.7, 15.18.7; *ŚB* 2.2.1.19; 5.3.1.4, 8.2.1.10, 11.1.3.3; *TS*. 1.2.3.1).

**Ādityas:** The Ādityas are several times described as *aditeḥ putrāḥ* (sons of Aditi). Six Ādityas are enumerated once (*RV* 2.27.1), the number being stated as seven and even eight in the later books of the *Ṛgveda*. Among the Ādityas, Varuṇa, Mitra and Aryaman are Indo-Iranian in origin, while Bhaga, Dakṣa, and Aṃśa seem to be deified abstractions. The sun is probably the seventh Āditya, and Mārtaṇḍa the eighth, whom Aditi casts off and brings back (*RV* 10.72.8, 9), is very likely the setting sun (*AV* 13.2.9; 13.2.37; *TB* 1.1.9.1; *ŚB* 3.5.1.13, 12.2.2.9).

**Administration:** The members of a tribal unit in the Ṛgvedic age were the *viśaḥ* (q.v.), below which came the *grāma* or village (q.v.), the basic administrative unit. The tribe itself was known as *jana* (q.v.). The *grāma* was made up of clusters of houses of several branches of one family (*kula*). The part played by the *kula* in the administrative organisation is indicated by the description of a *kulapā* (*RV* 10.179.2-3) (guardian of the family) forming the entourage of a *vrājapati* or *grāmaṇī* and fighting under his banner. The *grāmaṇī* exercised both civil and military functions. The *senānī* whose military authority in times of war is undeniable, probably had civil functions in times of peace. *Rājan* was the term for a tribal chief in the early Ṛgvedic age though later this term came to denote the king or monarch. The *purohita* (priest) was also an important functionary. We also hear of *dūtas* (messengers) who were undoubtedly the principal means of communication among different tribal principalities. In the *RV* we also come across terms which in later times were undoubtedly applied to the non-monarchical constitutions. Thus we have references to the *gaṇa* with the *gaṇapati* or *jyeṣṭha* (elder) at its head. The last probably corresponds to the *jetthaka* of the Pāli texts. It is not impossible that even in this early period there was the seed of a republican state of the type we find in the early Buddhist times. Moreover, in the Ṛgvedic age the popular assemblies known as the Sabhā, Samiti and Vidatha (q.v.) exerted a great influence on administration. The chief, who was generally the natural leader of the tribe, or an elected leader or one who had inherited the post, seems to have performed his administrative functions in accord with the wishes of the people expressed in such councils or assemblies. In the post-Ṛgvedic period, when kingship had become a recognized institution, we come across a large body of royal officials. Besides the four officials mentioned—*grāmaṇī, senānī, purohita,* we come across *bhāgadugha* (collector of taxes); *sūta* (charioteer and reciter); *saṃgrahitṛ* (the treasurer); *akṣāvāpa* (superintendent of dicing); *kṣattr* (chamberlain), *govikartana* (who maintained cattle wealth); *pālāgala* (the courier); *sthapati* (the judge or area-master); and so forth (*RV* 1.44.10; 114.1; 2.12.7; 4.50.8; 6.8.4; 10.124.8; 173.6; *AV* 4.36.7-8; 6.40.2; 22.1.3; *VS* 3.45-46; *TS* 1.8.9.1 ff; *TB* 1.7.3.1 ff; *ŚB* 5.3.1.1 ff; *MS* 2.6.5; 4.3.8; *KS* 15.4; *PB* 19.1.4). For the maintenance of the machinery of administration which protected the people in war and peace, the king had the right to receive contributions and local service from his subjects. Though originally these may have been voluntary, they soon assumed the form of a tribute (*bali*), a kind of taxation as in the reference to the 'share of village, horses and kine' in the *Atharvaveda* (4.22.2). A tendency towards centralization, with increased power and responsibility vested on the king, was already apparent in the age of the later Saṃhitās and Brāhmaṇas. The grand ceremonies of royal consecration suggest this and also the evidence of the Dharmasūtras which record the appointment of men of the first three castes who were pure and truthful over villages and towns for the protection of the people. These officials were to appoint subordinates possessing the same qualities. We also come across a general statement that the king was entitled to a sixth part of the income of his subjects. (*ĀpDS* 2.10.26.4; *BDS* 1.10.18.1; *VDS* 1.42; *GDS* 10.24-35). See **Kingship, Polity, Popular Assemblies, Republics, Royal Officials, Sovereignty, Taxation**.

**Adolescence:** The problems of adolescence have not been dealt with in the Vedic texts, though the duties of the *brahmacārins*, who were mostly adolescents, have been enunciated. It appears that the custom of *upanayana* was an adaptation of the tribal puberty rites as many ingredients of the latter were physically present in the former. The rites of first menstruation of girls, ceremonial defloration, and other forms of puberty rites are found in the Sūtra literature. The attitude towards individuals between childhood and maturity can be gleaned from the taboos, instructions on keeping off evil spiritis, education and studenthood, and religious initiations. For details see **Education, Marriage** and **Upanayana**.

**Adoption:** In the Vedic age, in the event of the failure to bear natural children, adoption was possible. It was also resorted to when natural children existed but when it was desired to secure the presence in the family of a person of specially high qualifications, as in Viśvāmitra's adoption of Śunaḥśepha (*AB* 7.17). It is not clear that adoption from one caste into another was possible, but there is evidence that Viśvāmitra, a Kṣatriya, adopted a Brāhmaṇa. Adoption was not always in high favour; a hymn of the Vasiṣṭha book of the *Ṛgveda* (7.4.7-8) condemns the practice. It was also possible for a father who had a daughter but no sons to appoint her to bear a son for him. The practice is referred to in an obscure verse of the *Ṛgveda* (3.31.1) as interpreted by Yāska (3.5). It is possible that the difficulty of a brotherless maiden finding a husband may have been due in part to the likelihood of her father desiring to make her a Putrikā, the later technical name for a daughter whose son was to belong to her father's family.

**Adultery:** Adultery was generally regarded among Vedic peoples as a serious offence against the husband by the wife or the reverse. We find in the legal literature of India traces of the rule that an adulterer is to be punished if caught in the act. In some legal texts, however, it was regarded as a minor offence and some material may be adduced indicating an indifference to such matters in Vedic times. Generally in a patriarchal society, which is revealed in the Vedic texts, any connexion with another man's wife was regarded as immoral even though in certain religious rites such a connexion was otherwise allowed. In the ritual of the Varuṇa-praghāsas (*MS* 1.10.11; *ŚB* 2.5.2.20), for example, the wife has to name her lover or lovers, the ritual seems originally to have been a solemn means of the attainment of the fruit of sacrifice. Yājñavalkya's famous saying (*ŚB* 1.3.1.21) that no one cares whether a wife is unchaste (*paraḥ-puṃsā*) or not may, however, be a mistranslation, since the expression *paraḥ-puṃsā* may also mean 'removed from the male persons'. In some Vedic passages (*MS* 1.4.11) the origin of different sages has been traced to uncertain descent. Nonetheless the woman's position was lowered by the prevalence of polygamy and other patriarchal practices. Stories about Ahalyā and Indra are not compatible with the patriarchal standard. The *Yajurveda* (*TS* 7.4.19.2-3; *VS* 23.30, 31) refers to relations between Ārya men and Śūdra women. A spell is found in the *Bṛhadāraṇyaka Upaniṣad* (6.4.11) to expiate the sin of establishing relations with the wife of a Śrotriya. In the Dharmasūtras, a student is forbidden to mix with his teacher's wife. Unless there were illicit relations such taboos would not have been imposed. Macdonell and Keith, I. 396-7.

**Aerial Creatures:** See **Birds**.

**Aerial Gods:** See **Atmospheric gods**.

**Aesthetics:** A systematic study of this branch of philosophy for the Vedic as well as the post-Vedic period is yet a desideratum. As far as the Vedic poetry is concerned, the various terms used in it to express the idea of the beautiful, in the several shades and phases in which it made its appeal, are *kalyāṇa*, *cāru*, *citra*, *peśas*, *bhadra*, *bhandiṣṭha*, *raṇva*, *surūpa*, *lakṣmī*, *vapus*, *valgu*, *vāma*, *śubha*, *śrī*, *śreyas*, *sudṛś*, *svādu*, etc. A careful consideration of several passages where these words are used show that the words express splendour or brilliance, opulence, outstanding energy especially for doing good, and the possession of some hidden or mystic qualities calculated to please and to subdue. The Vedic poets delight in describing Dawn; but they speak more of her rays, of her chariot and horses, of her gifts, of her power to stir and set to work, and of the general effect of her appearance. These suggest that they thought 'handsome is what handsome does.' Going below the pomp and glitter of the surface, they are attracted by the utilitarian significance of a thing. That is what they want to discover and describe. Later, Śrī becomes the goddess of wealth and plenty, *kalyāṇa* and *lakṣaṇa* acquire astrological significances, and *vapus* an appearance involving some *māyā* or magic. Speaking generally, the purely aesthetic connotation of the expressions is tinged by ethico-theological considerations based upon the thesis of *karma* and rebirth, as indicated by the later-day maxim: *yatrākṛtis tatra guṇa vasanti*. It is easy to imagine that the ratiocination of the Brāhmaṇas left no scope for the development of aesthetics. There was an inherent incompatibility between the two. Consequently, the idea of the beautiful becomes invaded, on the one hand, by gross materialism, so that the most expensive or the most elaborate became synonymous with the most beautiful; and on the other, by a craving for the weird and the magical, so that a thing became beautiful because it was not what was everyday life normal or because it was the result of some hidden forces at work. Such a change of feeling could very well have taken place under the influence of the ideas dominating the late Vedic period, though the only actual evidence adducible is the *Śrīsūkta*, which is a relatively late *pariśiṣṭa* of the *RV* (known however to the *Bṛhaddevatā*). Belvalkar and Ranade 20-2.

**Aetiology:** Assignment of a cause, or the philosophy of causation. The term is generally used to denote the science of causes of disease. From the *AV* one can say that although the treatment of diseases was primitive and magical consisting of the use of herbs in combination with spells and water, the knowledge of pathology was anything but elementary. The *AV* enumerates quite a large variety of diseases and the demons which are supposed to cause them. Nevertheless, the *AV* describes in detail the symptoms of diseases especially in regard to consumption, scrofula, dysentery, boils, swellings, convulsions, ulcers, rheumatism, headache, jaundice, cramps, leprosy, etc. See **Medical Science**.

**Affection:** The relation between parents and children was generally of warm affection. The wedding hymn of the *Ṛgveda* (10.85) indicates that the newly married wife rules over her brothers-in-law and entertains a feeling of respect for her husband's parents. The oft-quoted hymn of the *Atharvaveda* (3.30) for securing concord reads: 'Like in heart, of like intent non-hostile do I make you; one another you should love as the cow loves her new-born calf. May the son do the father's will and be of one mind with his mother. May wife to husband honeyed words and peaceful always speak. May not brother his brother hate, nor sister her own sister; in full accord with duty same, should they speak words gently. Same be your drink and common your food, to the same yoke together I bound you. Worship Agni together in harmony like spokes round the nave of a wheel.' Trans. B.K. Ghosh in Majumdar 415-16.

**Affinity:** That the Vedic tribes maintained their linguistic and cultural affinity amongst themselves is proved by their disparaging remarks about other peoples whom they called *anāryas, dāsas, dasyus, paṇis, asuras,* etc. The term *sajāta* (born together) is found once in the *Ṛgveda* (1.109.1), and very often later (*AV* 1.9.3; 2.6.4; 3.3.6; 6.5.2; 6.73.1; 11.1.6-7; *TS* 2.1.3.2; *MS* 2.1.8; *VS*

5.23.10.29, 27.5). The word clearly means a 'relative', or kin. Kinship terminologies are clearly described in the Vedic texts (see **Family**). The *sajātas* also relate to identity or caste (*varṇa*), tribe (*gaṇa, vrāta, samūha,* etc.) or clan (*gotra*) or occupational groups. In the Sūtra period we come across *sapiṇḍa* (those related within six degrees) and *sakulya* (remote) relations.

**Āgama:** One of the two great categories of the Hindu tradition which evolved from Hindu religious ideas and philosophy, practices and rituals the other being *nigama*. *Āgama* indicates what may be described as the Tāntric and Purāṇic domain of religion and ritual which includes *yoga* as a special form of mystico-religious ideology and practice. The origin of the *āgama* tradition is to be traced in the *Atharvaveda* which contains ample materials serving as the substrata of Tantrism. *Nigama* stands for the Vedic world of ideas, centring round what has been called the Vedic *karmakāṇḍa*, the practical religion of Vedic inspiration in which the *homa* or fire-sacrifice to the gods of the Vedic world is noteworthy. Though Āgamic religion and rituals are influenced by the *nigamic* or Vedic, it is a world apart. Later Pāśupata, Pāñcarātra and Śākta-Tāntric texts as well as those of Kashmir and Āgamānta Śaivism, Śaiva Siddhānta and Vīraśaivism belong to the Āgama tradition.

**Ages:** See **Yuga**.

**Agnāyī:** Wife of Agni, a minor goddess in the *Ṛgveda* alluded to infrequently unlike Pṛthivī, Aditi and Uṣas. For example: 'Indrāṇī, Varuṇānī and Agnāyī hither I invite, for weal, to drink the soma juice' (*RV* 1.22.12), and, 'May the dames, wives of gods, enjoy our presents, Aśvinī, Agnāyī and Indrānī' (*RV* 5.46.8). No distinct functions are assigned to her. Her insignificance forms a striking contrast to the prominent place later assumed by the spouses of Rudra and Viṣṇu.

**Agnates:** The word *sajāta*—found in the *Ṛgveda* (1.109.1), *Atharvaveda* (1.9.3; 1.19.3; 2.6.4; 3.3.6; 6.5.2; 6.73.1; 11.1.6-7), *Taittirīya Saṃhitā* (2.1.3.2; 2.2.1.2; 2.6.9.7), *Maitrāyaṇī Saṃhitā* (2.1.8), *Kāṭhaka Saṃhitā* (11.12-13, 12.1), *Vājsaneyī Saṃhitā* (5.23, 10.29, 27.5)—means blood relation in a specific sense, though the term also had wider significance. The more specific word is *jñāti* (*RV* 7.55.5; *AV* 12.5.44; *TB* 1.6.5.2; *ŚB* 1.6.4.3) which means blood relation on the father's side. Another term is *sabandhu* (*RV* 3.1.10, 5.47.5, 8.20.21; *AV* 6.15.2, 8.2.26, 15.8.2-3). In the Sūtra literature mention is made of *sapiṇḍa* (near agnates) and *sakulya* (distant agnates).

**Agni:** The personification of fire in the *Ṛgveda*, who is second in importance only to Indra. The anthropomorphism of the physical appearance of Agni is naturally very slight. He is butter-backed, flame-haired, and eats the oblations with his tongue (*RV* 1.14.7, 3.1.18; 5.4.3; 8.61.18; *VS* 17.79). Wood or *ghee* is his food, and melted butter his beverage, though he is also invited to drink Soma with other gods. He is nourished three times a day. Although he is invoked to partake to the sacrificial offerings himself, he is more prominently the mouth by which the gods eat the sacrifice (*RV* 2.7.6; 3.21.5; 5.11.3; 10.69.2; *AV* 1.7.2). His splendour is naturally his most prominent quality. He shines by day and night. He is called 'smoke-bannered' (*dhūma-ketu*) and is said to support the sky with his smoke (*RV* 2.10.2; 6.10.3; 7.15.10; 8.43.4; 10.45.4). He is a charioteer of the sacrifice and brings the gods in his golden lightning car. He is said to be the son of heaven (Dyaus) and also of heaven and earth. Indra, with whom he is more closely associated than with any other god, is called his twin brother. He is produced daily from the two kindling-sticks (*araṇis*), which are called his parents or mothers, and therefore he is ever young though ancient (*RV* 2.12.3; 4.15.6; 6.49.2; 7.99.4; 8.91.17; 10.1.2; 2.7; 46.9; 91.6; *AV* 1.33.1; etc.). The three-fold nature of Agni is a favourite topic with the Ṛgvedic poets. Agni's origin in the aerial waters is often referred to (*RV* 3.1.12-13; 8.91.5; 10.8.1; *AV* 3.21.7-7; 8.1.11; 39.8; 13.1.50). As the son of Waters (Apāṃ napāt) he became a separate deity. He is also said to be born in the highest heaven and was brought down from heaven by Mātariśvan, the Indian Prometheus (*RV* 1.68.2; 3.23.3; 6.48.5; 8.43.13; 10.4.1-2; 115.1; *AV* 3.21.1, 7; 8.1.11). This is his third origin. He is the earliest representative of the famous Indian trinity, and yet sometimes he is called *dvi-janman* (having two births) from the point of view of a two-fold division of the universe into heaven and earth. His connection with domestic life is a special feature. He is the only *gṛhapati* (master of the house), the *atithi* (guest), and a kinsman of men (*RV* 1.95.3; 3.26.7; 10.88.10; *AV* 12.1.20; 13.3.21; 18.4.11). He is the *dūta* (messenger). As the central figure of the sacrifice, he is called variously *ṛtvij, vipra, purohita, adhvaryu* and *brahman* and is thus the divine counterpart of the earthly priesthood. He is pre-eminently 'omniscient' or 'one who knows all created beings' (*jātavedas*). The funeral hymn (*RV* 10.14) refers to the *havya-vāhana* form of Agni, that burns the dead body on the funeral pyre (*RV* 1.26.3; 75.1; 4.6.4-5; 9.3; 15.1-3; 5.8.2; 7.15.1-2; 8.60.1; *VS* 1.17; 18.51; *TS* 2.5.8.6; *AV* 5.30.4; *TB* 3.7.12.3.-4; *ŚB* 2.3.1.5; etc.).

**Agnosticism:** By agnosticism is meant the line of thinking according to which nothing is known, or can be known, of the existence or nature of God or of anything beyond material phenomena. The earliest reference to this agnosticism is found in the celebrated *Nāsadīya* hymn of the *Ṛgveda* (10.129) in which it is stated that no one on earth is able to say what was the origin of the world and whether it had any creator or not. Even its ruler in the highest heaven may not know the whole thing. In a verse (*RV* 10.31.7) we come across the question: what was the wood and what was the tree out of which they fashioned heaven and earth? The most important part of the *Kena Upaniṣad*,—the part on which the fame of this Upaniṣad deservedly rests—starts, however, with a psychological inquiry as to what must be the main spring of the five psychical functions that we are aware of: thinking, breathing, speech, vision and audition. Why is it that the mind is able to think? Who regulates the vital breath? How is it that the mouth, the eye, and the ear enable us respectively to speak, see and hear? Do the sense-organs enjoy complete autonomy, or is there an entity which controls them all, and which inspires them with the power that each of them possesses? The denial of *ātman's* ability and power of doing or suffering anything and the insistence upon the inexorable character of the law of *karma* (*BU* 3.13, and elsewhere) are both jointly capable of a one-sided development leaning towards passive fatalism. The belief in the impermanence and mutability of things (*MU* 1.3-4, *KU* 1.1.26) and the doctrine of the unknowability of the Real may have conceivably accentuated the move towards philosophical agnosticism. Belvalkar and Ranade 177, 404. See **Atheism**.

**Agriculture:** The Ṛgvedic tribes were predominantly pastoral as is indicated by the fact that the expressions for ploughing occur mainly in the first and tenth books of the *Ṛgveda*, the later portions of the text, and only rarely in other parts. The Aśvins are spoken of as concerned with the sowing of grain by means of the plough (*RV* 1.117.21). Pṛthi Vaiṇya is credited (in *AV* 8.10.24) with the origin of ploughing. In later Saṃhitās (*AV* 2.4.5; 8.2.19; 8.10.24; 10.6.12; 12.2.27; *TS* 7.1.11.1; *MS* 1.2.2, 3.6.8; *VS* 4.10, 9.22, 14.19, 14.21) and Brāhmaṇas (*ŚB* 7.2.2.7; 8.6.2.2; *TB* 2.1.2.5, etc.), however, there are repeated references to ploughing. Sītā appears as the presiding deity of agriculture in an agricultural hymn (*RV* 4.57). The word *kṛṣi* meant for agriculture comes from the root *kṛṣ*, to plough (*RV* 1.23.15, 1.176.2). The term for plougher is *kināsa* though *kārṣivaṇa* is also found (*AV* 6.116.1). The importance attached to agriculture is attested to by the advice to the gambler to take up farming (*RV* 10.34.13). In the *Pañcaviṃśa Brāhmaṇa* (17.1) the Vrātyas are described as not cultivating the soil. Agricultural land was called *urvarā* or *kṣetra*. Manure (*śakan, karīṣa*) was used. Names of various agricultural implements (q.v.) are given. The operations of agriculture are neatly summed up in the *Śatapatha Brāhmaṇa* (1.6.1.3) as ploughing, sowing, reaping and threshing. Ripe grain was cut with a sickle (*dātra, sṛṇi*), bound into bundles (*parṣa*), and threshed on the floor of the granary (*khala*). The grain was cleaned either by a sieve (*titau*) or a winnowing fan (*śūrpa*). The winnower was called *dhānyakṛt* (*RV* 10.94.13) and the grain was measured in a vessel called *urdara* (*RV* 2.14.11). Among the agricultural product references are made to rice (*vrīhi*), barley (*yava, upavāka*), beans (*mudga, māsa*), seasamum (*tila*), and other cereals (*aṇu, khalva, godhūma, nīvāra, priyaṅgu, masūra, śyāmāka*). Production of cucumber (*urvārūka*) and jujube (*karkandu, kuvala, badara*) was well known. According to *Taittirīya Saṃhitā* (7.2.10.2) barley was sown in winter and ripened in summer, rice was sown in the beginning of rains and ripened in autumn, and beans, etc., were sown at the time of the summer rain and ripened in winter. There were two harvests a year (*TS* 5.1.7.3). Winter crops ripened in March-April (*KB* 19.3). Spells to prevent moles and insects which destroy the young shoots, and excessive rain or drought which damage the crops are given in the *Atharvaveda* (6.50.142, 7.11). See **Arable Land, Corns, Grains**.

**Agricultural Animals:** The general term for cattle used in agricultural pursuits is *go*. In the Vedic texts there are references to various kinds of bullocks and oxen used for ploughing or for drawing wagons (*anaḍvāḥ*) in which case they were, it seems, usually castrated (*AV* 3.92; 6.138.2; *TS* 1.8.1). The terms for bulls occurring frequently in the *Ṛgveda* are Usra, Usrika and Usriya (Fem. Usrā, Usriyā) (*RV* 6.12.4; 8.75.8; 9.58.2; 9.74.3; *AV* 12.3.37; *VS* 35.2, 3). Among other terms we come across Ṛṣabha (*RV* 6.16.47; 6.28.8; 10.91.14; *AV* 3.4.6, 3.23.4; *TS* 2.1.3.4; *VS* 21.22; *PB* 13.5.18); Maryaka (*RV* 5.2.5); Mahā Ṛṣava (great bull, *AV* 4.15.1); Vaṃsaga (*RV* 1.7.8; 1.55.1; 1.58.4; 5.36.1; *AV* 18.3.36) and Vṛṣabha (*RV* 1.94.10; 1.107.3; 6.46.4; 7.101.1). There are also references to drought-ox (*anaḍvāḥ*, *RV* 10.69.10; 10.85.10, *AV* 3.11.5; 4.11.1; *AB* 1.14; *SB* 2.1.4.17) and great-ox *mahokṣa* (*ŚB* 3.4.1.2). The term *vāha* is also found (*RV* 4.57.4, 8; *AV* 6.102.1) apparently denoting an ox for drawing the plough. 'The plough was drawn by oxen, teams of six, eight oxen even twelve being employed' (*RV* 8.6.48; 10.101.4; *AV* 6.91.1; *KS* 15.2). Ritual application for yoking a plough is found in Brāhmaṇa literature (ŚB 7.2.2.6). See **Agriculture, Animals, Cattle**.

**Agricultural Implements:** *Lāṅgala* is the regular word for plough (*RV* 4.57.4) and in the later Saṃhitās (*AV* 2.8.4; *TS* 6.6.74). It is variously described as *pavīravat* or *pavīravam* or lance-pointed (*AV* 3.17.3; *TS* 4.2.5.6; *KS* 16.11; *MS* 2.7.12; *VS* 12.71), *suśīman*, or well-lying, and having *tsaru*, a well-smoothed handle. Another term for plough was *sīra* (*RV* 4.57.8; 10.101.3-4; *AV* 6.30.1; 6.91.1; 8.9.16; *VS* 18.7; *MS* 2.11.4; *TB* 1.7.1.2) which was large and heavy, as is shown by the fact that six (*AV* 6.91.1, 8.9.16; *TS* 5.2.5.2; *KS* 15.2, 20.3; *ŚB* 7.2.2.6, 13.8.2.6) or eight (*AV* 6.91.1) or twelve (*TS* 1.8.7.1, 5.2.5.2; *KS* 15.2; *MS* 2.6.2) or even twenty-four (*KS* 15.2) oxen were used to drag it. The word *sīla* in the sense of a plough is found in *Kapiṣṭhala Saṃhitā* (28.8). The terms for ploughshare are *phāla* (*RV* 4.57.8, 10.117.7; *KS* 19.1; *AV* 3.17.5; *MS* 2.7.12) and *stega* (*RV* 10.31.9). The ox was guided by the *aṣṭrā* or goad of the ploughman (*RV* 4.57.4, 10.102.8).

Other terms for goad are *tottra* (*ŚB* 12.4.1.10) and *toda* (*RV* 4.16.11). *Titau* is found once (*RV* 10.71.2) denoting a 'sieve' or perhaps 'winnowing fan' which was used for cleaning corn. Shovel or spade (*khanitra*) for digging is mentioned in the *Ṛgveda* (1.179.6) and cutter or sickle is denoted by the term *dātra* (8.78.10). Cows with sickle-shaped marks on their ears are mentioned (*MS* 4.2.9). The term *sṛṇi* was also used to denoted a sickle (*RV* 1.58.4; 10.101.3; *ŚB* 7.2.2.5).

**Agricultural Rituals:** The sophisticated forms of Vedic *yajñas* have some philosophical significance but their incipient forms do not differ very much from magical beliefs and practices. Although the early Vedic economy was predominantly pastoral, the Vedic tribes later began to depend on agriculture and based some of their ancient rituals upon fertility magic. While most of the Vedic goddesses are connected with vegetation and fertility, the typical goddess of agriculture is Sītā (*RV* 4.57; *AV* 3.17). See **Agricultural Spirits**. With their initiation into the agricultural way of life the Vedic tribes adopted numerous rituals designed to secure the fertility of the fields. Some of these were sexual in character. There are numerous passages in which sexual union is identified with sacrifice (*ŚB* 1.9.2.7; 6.3.1.28; 6.4.3.7; 6.6.2.8). The conception of productive pairs (*ŚB* 2.4.4.21, 2.5.1.11.5, 5.1.3.19, etc.) and fruitful semen (*ŚB* 1.7.2.14, 1.9.2.7, 2.3.1.32, etc.) occur in many passages. In the *Vājasaneyī Saṃhitā* (23.22-31) we come across a passage which clearly shows that sexual union was employed to promote agricultural production. The *Vāmadevya-Sāman* (*CU* 2.13) also supports this and so do other Upaniṣadic passages (*CU* 5.18.1-12; *BU* 6.2.13, 6.4.6-7). The Vājapeya sacrifice (q.v.) is a sophisticated form of agricultural ritual employed as a productive technique to obtain food (*vāja*) and drink (peya).

**Agricultural Spirits:** *Kṣetrasya pati*, Lord of the field, is invoked (*RV* 7.35.10) to grant cattle and horses, to fill heaven and earth, the plants and the waters with sweetness, and to bestow prosperity. The Gṛhya ritual prescribes offerings to him when the field is ploughed. Similarly the *Ṛgveda* (4.56.6) contains an invocation of Sītā, the furrow, to grant rich blessing and crops. This goddess has greater prominence in the Sūtras which deal with the operations of agriculture. She appears as the wife of Indra which may be due to the fact that he is once called Urvarāpati, 'lord of the ploughed field' (*RV* 7.21.3), and her existence is manifested in the four special deities—Sītā, Āsā, Aradā and Anaghā—who are to be worshipped at the furrow sacrifice, the sowing of the crop, the reaping, the threshing floor sacrifice, and putting the crop into the barn. Beside the offering to Sītā in another Sūtra we have the offering to three other deities—Yajā, Samā and Bhūti—who are less concrete. Offering to the guardians of the furrow elevated the character of Sītā. She is called Sāvitrī in the *Taittirīya Brāhmaṇa* and she becomes the heroine of the *Rāmāyaṇa*, the model of wifely truth and chastity, preserving nonetheless some traces of her connexion with the furrow and the fruitful earth. The ploughed field is also a goddess in the Sūtra literature and is described as having a garland of threshing floors. Keith, 1989, I, 186-7.

**Ahi Budhnya:** Ahi Budhnya, the serpent of the deep, is closely associated with the gods Aja Ekapād, Apām Napāt, the Ocean, and Savitṛ. His name is found among the spirits of the atmosphere, and in the *Naighaṇṭuka* (5.4) he is assigned to the middle or aerial region. The only definite traits ascribed to him are that he is born of the waters and is seated in space. Yāska (*Nirukta* 10.44) holds that Ahi Budhnya is connected with the ocean of the air and not to the earthly waters. His malevolence is hinted at by the fact that he is implored not to give his worshippers over to evil (*RV* 7.34.17; 5.41.16; *VS* 5.33; *AB* 3.36; *TB* 1.1.10.3).

**Air:** While the *Ṛgveda* postulates water as the primordial element the concept of five material elements was elaborated in the later Saṃhitās and Brāhmaṇas. For example, it is stated that Prajāpati created the three worlds: the earth, the atmosphere and the sky (*AB* 5.32). From these were born Agni or fire, Vāyu or air, and the Ādityas respectively. It is, however, in the Upaniṣads that we have practically for the first time the doctrine of the five elements in its fullest form. In the fourth Prapāṭhaka of the *Chāndogya Upaniṣad* we come across Raikva's doctrine of the air as the primary substance. Raikva preached to Jānaśruti Pautrāyana an Anaximenean doctrine about Air being the be-all and the end-all of things, the source from which things originate and the haven to which they return. The air is to be understood either as air in the macrocosm or as breath in the microcosm. In either case, it is what inspires man as well as the cosmos. Air, verily, is the ultimate absorbent. When a fire goes out, it goes into the *air*. When the sun sets, it goes into the *air* and when the moon sets it too goes into the *air*. When water dries up, it goes into the *air*. *Air*, indeed, absorbs them all. This happens with regard to the divinities. Now, with reference to the self: *breath*, indeed, is the absorbent. When one sleeps, speech just goes into *breath*; sight goes into *breath*; hearing goes into *breath*; the mind goes into *breath*, for *breath*, indeed, absorbs all this. These two, verily, are the two absorbents, air among the gods, *breath* among others (*CU* 4.3.1-4). Radhakrishnan 404-5; Belvalkar and Ranade 221.

**Aja:** A tribe mentioned, along with the Yakṣus and the Śigrus, in one verse of the *Ṛgveda* (7.18.19) as having been defeated by the Tṛtsus under Sudās. They were probably non-Vedic tribes of the Gaṅgā-Yamunā Doab region who fought against Sudās under the leadership of the king Bheda.

**Aja Ekapād:** Aja Ekapād, 'the one-footed goat', a deity,

is mentioned five times with Ahi Budhnya, and once by himself. The deities with whom he is mentioned are the ocean, the stream, the aerial space, the thundering flood, and all the gods. His aerial connection seems clear despite the preference for the celestial region evinced by the *Naighaṇṭuka* (5.6). In later literature he appears as making firm the two worlds (*AV* 13.1.6) and as born in the east (*TB* 3.1.2.8), and in the domestic ritual he is once joined with Ahi Budhnya. In another tradition he is a form of Agni or Sun.

**Akṣara:** The imperishable one, same as *brahman* (q.v.). The *Bṛhadāraṇyaka Upaniṣad* (3.8.9-11) says the following about the *akṣara*: "Verily, at the command of that Imeprishable (*etasya vā akṣarasya praśāsane*), O Gārgī, the sun and the moon stand in their respective positions. At the command of that Imperishable, O Gārgī, heaven and earth stand in their respective positions. At the command of that Imperishable, O Gārgī, what are called moments, hours, days and nights, half-months, months, seasons, years stand in their respective positions. At the command of that Imeprishable, O Gārgī, some rivers flow to the east from the white (snowy) mountains, others to the west in whatever direction each flows. By the command of that Imperishable, O Gārgī, men praise those who give, the gods (are desirous of) the sacrificer and the fathers are desirous of the *darvī* offering. Whosoever, O Gārgī, in this world, without knowing this Imperishable performs sacrifices, worships, performs austerities for a thousand years, his work will have an end; whosoever, O Gārgī, without knowing this Imperishable departs from this world, is pitiable. But, O Gārgī, he who knowing the Imperishable departs from this world is a Brāhmaṇa (a knower of *brahman*). Verily, that Imperishable, O Gārgī, is unseen but is the seer, is unheard but is the thinker, unknown but is the knower. There is no other seer but this, there is no other hearer but this, there is no other thinker but this, there is no other knower but this. By this Imperishable, O Gārgī, is space woven like warp and woof." Radhakrishnan 232-3.

**Alina:** Name of a people mentioned once only in the *Ṛgveda* (7.18.7). They were defeated by Sudās, together with the Pakthas, Bhalānas, Śivas and Viṣāṇins, with whom they are mentioned. They lived in the north-west of Kafiristan.

**Altar:** Altar was an essential requirement of sacrifices. An altar had five layers, the first, third and fifth being arranged in the same pattern and the second and fourth being of a different pattern. Altars had several forms such as that of a *droṇa* (trough), a chariot-wheel, a *śyena* (hawk), *kaṅka* (heron), *suparṇa* (eagle), etc. (*TS* 5.4.11). The altars required bricks of several shapes—triangular, oblong, square, etc. They were not to be placed one upon the other as one chose but were to be arranged in a particular way. A sound knowledge of geometry and mason-craft was required. The bricks had different names to distinguish them. Every brick was placed after repeating a *mantra* (*VS* 12.53; *TS* 4.2.4.4; *ŚB* 11.8.18, etc.). Each layer consisted of only 200 bricks, 1000 for all five, but for big altars as many as 10800 bricks were required. The time required for piling also varied. On each row of bricks a thick layer of mud was put after touching a dark or bay horse (*VS* 18.73; *TS* 1.5.11.1).

**Altruism:** See **Ethics**.

**Āmbaṣṭhya:** Āmbaṣṭhya is mentioned in the *Aitareya Brāhmaṇa* (8.21) as a king, whose priest for the Rājasūya, or royal inauguration, was Nārada. Presumably the name is local, meaning 'king of the Ambaṣṭhas'. The Ambaṣṭhas were originally a tribe of the Punjab region who were mentioned by Alexander's historians. Later they dispersed in different directions having undertaken different occupations. The law-givers incorporated them as a hybrid caste in the varṇa system by declaring that they sprang from the union of a Brāhmaṇa male and a Vaiśya female.

**Amphibians:** Among the amphibians the Vedic texts refer to frogs (*maṇḍūka—RV* 7.103.1; 10.166.5; *AV* 7.112.2; *TS* 5.4.4.3, 5.7.11.1; *KS* 13.1, 27.7; *MS* 3.14.2; *VS* 24.36; and *māṇḍūkī—RV* 10.16.14; *AV* 18.3.60; *VS* 17.6; *TS* 4.2.1.12; *KS* 17.17; *MS* 2.10.1). The famous frog hymn (*RV* 7.103) compares the recital of the texts by the students to croaking frogs. Some ritual significance has been attributed to frogs (*RV* 10.16.14). Among other amphibians the Vedic texts refer to ducks, swans, crocodiles and various reptiles. *Balākā* or crane is also found (*TS* 5.5.16.1), (*MS* 3.14.3.14), (*VS* 24.22-23) and *haṃsa* (swan) is frequently mentioned (*RV* 1.65.3, 1.163.10, 2.34.5, 3.8.9, etc., *AV* 6.12.1, etc.). *Kakuṭha* (*MS* 3.14.13) and *kakkaṭa* (*TS* 2.5.15.1; *VS*, 24.32) denote crab while *makara* (*TS* 5.5.13.1; *MS* 3.14.16; *VS* 24.35) and *nakra* (*TS* 5.5.13.1; *MS* 3.14.2; *VS* 24.35) are amphibian crocodiles. *Godhā*, which also means an amphibian reptile, occurs in some passages of the *Yajurveda Saṃhitā*.

**Amulets:** See **Charms**. In Vedic texts various amulets are mentioned, often made out of some herbs and tied on the wrist of the patients. An amulet prepared out of *varaṇa* (*crataeva roxburgii*) tree is described to be all-healing (*viśva-bheṣaja*, *AV* 10.3.5). The same source refers to other amulets those made of reed-stalk (*muñja* 1.2.4), meant for curing diseases for example *jangida* plant (19.34.9 f), etc. For a person frightened unnecessarily, an amulet of reed consecrated with a verse (*AV* 1.28) is found (*Kau.Sū.* 26.27). For patients of *kṣetriya* (hereditary) disease, amulets of *arjuna* (*terminalia arjuna*), mustard plants, *saḍaṃ puṣpa*, etc., were also used. For a person suffering from urine-retention an amulet of *haritakī* (*terminalia chebula*) was provided (*Kau.Sū* 25.10). The *Kauśika Sūtra* refers to many such amulets given to diseased persons and also to those possessed by demons and other evil spirits. Thite 110-11.

**Amusements:** Among public entertainers we have references to Sailuṣa (actor, *VS* 30.6; *TB* 3.4.2.1), Vaṃśanartin (acrobat, *VS* 30.21; *TB* 3.4.17.1), Vīṇāvāda and Vīṇāghātin (lute-player *VS* 30.20; *TB* 3.9.14.1; *ŚB* 13.1.5.1; 4.2.8.11), *Āḍambarāghāta* (drum-beater *VS* 30.19; *ŚB* 14.4.8.1). The references to actors suggest dramatical performances. The dialogue-hymns of the *Ṛgveda* were evidently meant for mimering and acting in connection with the rituals. They reflect a tradition of the existence of the public stage. Music (q.v.) both vocal and instrumental was well known. The lute a string-instrument, the flute, a wind-instrument and the drum were well known in the Ṛgvedic age. Numerous references to chariots (q.v.) prove that chariot racing was a favourite sport and a source of entertainment as was hunting. The importance of racing as a sport is attested to by its use in numerous similies and metaphors. How deeply racing, especially chariot-racing had entered into the popular scheme of entertainment is seen from its ritual transformation into a ceremony making it an essential part of royal sacrifices. Gambling (q.v.) was immensely popular (cf. *RV* 10.34) and the terms used in connection with this game are *akṣa, kitava, grābha, glaha, div, dyūta, śeṣaṇa, śvaghnin, saṃrudh* and *samlikhita*. The same holds good gambling which became part of the Agnyādheya and the Rājasūya ceremonies. The dancing of maidens is mentioned. Probably men also danced as is implied in a simile in the *Ṛgveda* (10.76.6). The concept of dancing gods (q.v.) like Indra, Maruts, Aśvins, etc. (*RV* 2.22.4; 6.63.5; 8.20.22; 24.9-22; 24.9.12; 92.2) and dancing nymphs (q.v.) in the company of gods (*AV* 4.37.1 ff; 7.12.2, etc.) shows the popularity of dancing as a form of entertainment. The *Sāmaveda* is a standing monument to the wonderful skill and originality of the ancients in the science of vocal music. In post-Ṛgvedic literature various classes of instrumental musicians are referred to. Among the musical instruments we have references to *āghāti* (cymbal), *āḍambara* (drum), *karkari* (lute) and also *kandavīṇā, gargara, godhā, talava, tunava* (flute), *dundubhi* (drum), *nāḍi* (reed-flute), *piṅgā, bākurā, bhūmidundhuvi* (earth-drum), *lambara* and *vanaspati* (drum), *vāṇa* (harp), *vāṇī* (lyre), *vāṇīci, vādana* (plectrum), *vāditā, vīṇā*, etc.). There is a theory that a precursor of the later classical drama existed in the period of the later Saṃhitās and Brāhmaṇas. This view is supported by the supposed reference to the Naṭa-sūtras by Pāṇini.

**Anarchy:** Regarding the origin of kingship Manu (7.3) says that if the world is without a king it is disturbed everywhere by fear. Thus the Lord created the king for the protection of all. Kauṭilya (1.4) says 'But when the law of punishment is kept in abeyance, it gives rise to such disorders as implied in the proverb of fishes, for in the absence of a magistrate the strong will swallow the weak, but under his protection the weak resist the strong.' The earliest trace of this idea is to be found in the *Śatapatha Brāhmaṇa* (11.1.6.29), that 'whenever there is a drought then the stronger seizes the weaker for the waters are the law'.

**Anatomy:** The interest of the Vedic Indians seems early to have been attracted to the consideration of questions connected with the anatomy of the body. Thus a hymn (*AV* 10.2) enumerates many parts of the body with accuracy and an orderly arrangement. It mentions the heels (*pārṣṇi*), the flesh (*māṃsa*) the ankle-bones (*gulphau*), the fingers (*aṅguliḥ*), the apertures (*kha*) the two metatarsi (*uchalkau*), the tarsus (*pratiṣṭhā*), two knee-caps (*aṣṭhīvantau*), the two legs (*jaṅghe*), the two knee-joints (*jānunoḥ sandhi*). Then come the two knees (*jānu*) the four sides (*catustava*), pliant (*sithira*), trunk (*kabandha*), the hips (*śroṇi*) and the two thighs (*ūrū*) and the props of the frame (*kusindha*). Next come the breast-bone (*uras*), the cervical cartilages (*grīvāh*), the two breast pieces (*stanau*) the two shoulder-blades (*kaphoḍau*), the neck-bones (*skandhau*), and the backbone (*pṛṣṭiḥ*), the collar bones (*aṃsau*), the arms (*bāhū*), the seven apertures in the head (*sapta khani śīrṣāṇi*), the ears (*karṇau*), the nostrils (*nāsike*), the eyes (*cakṣūnī*), the mouth (*mukha*), the jaws (*hanu*), the tongue (*jihvā*), the brain (*mastiṣka*) the forehead (*lalāṭa*), the facial bone (*kākaṭikā*), the cranium (*kapāla*), and the structure of the jaws (*cityā kanvoḥ*). The number of bones in the human body is given as 360 (*ŚB* 10.5.4.12; 12.3.2.3-4). There are several enumerations of the parts of the body (*VS* 19.81-93; *MS* 3.11.9; *KS* 38.3; *TB* 2.6.4) which are hair (*lomāni*), skin (*tvac*), flesh (*māṃsa*), bone (*asthi*), marrow (*majjan*), liver (*yakṛt*), kidneys (*matasne*), gall (*pitta*), entrails (*antrāṇi*), bowels (*gudaḥ*), spleen (*plīhan*), navel (*nābhi*), belly (*udara*), rectum (*vaniṣṭhu*), womb (*yoni*), penis (*plāsi*), face (*mukha*), head (*śiras*), tongue (*jihvā*), mouth (*āsan*), rump (*pāyu*), leech (*vāla*), eye (*cakṣus*), eyelashes (*pakṣmāni*), eyebrows (*utāni*), nose (*nas*), ears (*karṇau*), brows (*bhrū*), waist (*upastha*), etc. Macdonell and Keith II, 358-62.

**Ancestor Worship:** In Vedic belief departed ancestors were thought to survive in the land of the blessed and were deemed to be anxious to assist their living descendants. The Fathers (*pitṛ*) generally are referred to in the *Ṛgveda* and later literature as invoked to confer boons. Men pray to them, as to the gods, for success, for the defeat of enemies, for the gift of rain, for the bestowal of eloquence, or for abundance of food. Even in battle Fathers are invoked as warriors (*RV* 6.75.9). Abode of the Fathers is known as *pitṛ-loka* which is a place of happiness ruled by Yama where a man is supposed to go after death (*RV* 9.113.7-11). The energy of the Fathers had a special purpose the production of offspring, in which their special interest was that the rites for the dead could be kept up by the device of continuing the family. That is why Agastya was persuaded by his ancestors to marry and procreate children. In the overwhelming majority of cases the person inkoved is not an individual but the whole body of Fathers as such. Occasionally an individual ancestor might be invoked, like Kaṇva or Kakṣivant, or a specific group such as the Vasiṣṭhas (*RV* 10.15.8; *AV* 18.3.15). Men, too, occasionally appeared among the gods with divine attributes, such as Kutsa who was invoked along with Indra (*RV* 5.31.9). In the *Atharvaveda* (4.1.22, 4.1.43-44) there is mention of blessings of the ancestors showered upon the newly wed bride, sons, grandsons, etc. The soul leaves the body at death and follows the path of the Fathers (*pitṛyāna*) to go to the place where there is eternal light, and is endowed with lustre like that of the gods (*AV* 11.1.37). Some of the Ṛgvedic *mantras* recited in the rituals speak of the funeral fire as conducting the departed one directly to the *pitṛs* or Fathers, but the later (*Sūtra*) ritual texts lay down that it is only after the *sapiṇḍīkaraṇa* (a *śrāddha*) that the departed person is admitted to the world of the Fathers. Besides the regular offerings which were prescribed for the Fathers, there were others which were to be performed on special occasions such as the birth of a son, a marriage or at the naming ceremony of a child. In the Śrauta ritual a leading place in the cult of the ancestors was taken by the *piṇḍapitṛyajña* which was to be offered after midday on the day of new moon. Details of such rituals connected with ancestor worship are found in the Śrauta and Gṛhya texts.

**Andhra:** People mentioned with the Puṇḍras, Śabaras, Pulindas and Mutibas (*AB* 7.18). The Andhras belonged to the central and eastern Deccan.

**Aṅga:** The name occurs only once in the *Atharvaveda* (5.22.14) in connection with the Gandhārīs, Mujavants and Māgadhas as distinct peoples. They appear also in the *Gopatha Brāhmaṇa* (2.9) in the compound name Aṅga-magadhāḥ. The land of the Aṅgas has been located around the modern Bhagalpur region on the banks of the rivers Sone and the Ganges. Aṅga is regarded as one of the sixteen *mahājanapadas* in the Buddhist literature.

**Animals:** Since the early Vedic tribes were predominantly pastoral the cow was their chief source of wealth. Various types of cows are described in Vedic literature. See **Cattle**. Among other domesticated animals, horses were known as *akra* (*RV* 1.143.7, 1.189.7, 3.1.12, 4.6.3, 10.72.2), *aśva* (*RV* 1.83.1, 4.32.17, 5.4.11, 8.78.2, etc.; *AV* 5.17.15, etc.), *āśu* (*RV* 2.16.3, etc.; *AV* 2.14.6, etc.; *TS* 1.8.10; *ŚB* 5.3.3.3), *marya* (*RV* 7.56.16, 8.43, 25), *rājāśva* (*AV* 6.102.2) and *rohita* (*RV* 1.94.10, 1.139.9, 2.10.2, 3.6.6; *TS* 1.6.4.3; *PB* 14.3.12). the terms for goat are *aja* (*RV* 1.162.2, 10.16.14; *AV* 9.5.1; *VS* 21.9), *chaga* (*TS* 5.6.22.1), *chāga* (*RV* 1.162.3; *VS* 19.89, 21.40-41; *ŚB* 3.3.3.4, 5.1.3.14; *MS* 3.11.2), *basta* (*RV* 1.161.13; *TS* 2.3.7.4; *KS* 17.2; *VS* 14.9, etc.), *mahāja* (*ŚB* 3.4.1.2) etc. Elephants were called *ibha* (*RV* 1.84.17, 4.4.1, etc.), *gaja*, *nāga* (*ŚB* 11.2.7.12), *vāraṇa* (*RV* 8.33.8, 10.40.4), *śukladant* (*AB* 8.23), and *hastin* (*RV* 1.67.7, 4.16.14; *AV* 12.1.25, etc.). Other was known as *udra* (*TS* 5.5.20.1; *MS* 3.14.18; *VS* 24.37) while jackal was known as *ula* (*AV* 12.1.49; *TS* 5.5.21.1, *MS* 3.13.12; *VS* 24.32), *lapāśa* (*RV* 10.28.4; *TS* 5.5.21.1; *MS* 3.14.17), and *sṛgāla* (*ŚB* 12.5.2.5). Various kinds of deer were known as *hariṇa* (*RV* 1.163.1, 5.78.2; *AV* 6.67.3, etc.), *pṛṣata*, *pṛṣati*, (*TS* 5.5.11.1, etc.), *nyaṅku* (*TS* 5.5.17.1; *MS* 3.14.19, etc.), *kuluṅga* (*TS* 5.5.11.1, etc.), *eṇī* (*AV* 5.14.11, etc.), *eta* (*RV* 1.165.2, etc.), and *ṛṣya* (*RV* 8.4.10; *AV* 4.4.5, etc.). *Uṣṭi*, *uṣṭra* (*RV* 1.138.2, 8.5.37, etc.) and *dhurma* (*TS* 1.8.21) stood for camel; *ṛkṣa* (*RV* 5.56.3; *MS* 3.14.17; *VS* 24.36) for bear; *eḍaka* (*ŚB* 12.4.1.4), *petva* (*AV* 4.4.8, 5.18.2; *TS* 5.5.22.1) *meṣa* and *meṣī* (*RV* 1.43.6, 1.116.16, 8.2.40, 20.27.17; *AV* 6.49.2; *VS* 3.59; 49.2; *TS* 7.4.12.1, etc.) for ram and ewe, *kapi* (*RV* 10.86.5; *AV* 3.9.4, 4.32.11, 6.49.1), *kiṃpuruṣa* (*AB* 2.8; *ŚB* 1.2.3.9, 7.5.2.32; *VS* 30.16; *TB* 3.4.12.1) *puruṣa-mṛga* (*TS* 5.5.15.1; *MS* 3.14.16; *VS* 34.35), *puruṣa-hastin* (*VS* 24.29; *MS* 5.5.11.1; *MS* 3.14.11; *VS* 24.30, etc.) for ape, *kaśyapa* (*AV* 4.20.6; *MS* 3.14.18; *VS* 24.37, etc.) and *kūrma* (*AV* 9.4.16; *TS* 2.6.3.3, 5.2.8.4; *MS* 3.153; *VS* 24.34) for tortoise, *kurkura* (*AV* 7.95.2), *mācala* (*JB* 2.440), *śvan* (*RV* 1.161.13, 1.182.4, 2.39.4; *AV* 4.20.7, 6.37.3, etc.) and *sārameya* (*RV* 7.55.2) for dog, *khaṅga* or *khaḍga* (*MS* 3.14.21; *VS* 24.40) for rhinoceros, *khara* (*AA* 3.2.4; *ŚB* 5.1.2.15, 14.1.2.17), *gardhava* (*RV* 3.53.23; *AB* 4.9; *TS* 5.1.5.5, etc.) and *rāsabha* (*RV* 1.34.9, 1.116.2, 4.162.21, 3.53.5, 7.85.7, etc.) for ass, *godhā* (*TS* 5.5.15.1; *VS* 24-35; *PB* 9.2.14), *nakra* (*TS* 5.5.13.1; *MS* 3.14.2; *VS* 24, 35) and *makara* (*TS* 5.5.13.1; *MS* 3.14.16; *VS* 24-35) for crocodile; *jahakā* (*TS* 5.5.18.3; *MS* 3.14.17; *VS* 24.36) for pole-cat, *tarakṣu* (*RV* 10.73.2, 10.95.15; *AB* 7.28; *TS* 6.2.7.5) for hyena, *durvarāha* (*ŚB* 12.4.1.4) and *śūkara* (*RV* 2.27.2, 5.14.1, etc.) for wild boar, *dvīpin* (*AV* 4.8.7, 6.38.2, 19.49.4; *MS* 2.1.9) for panther or leopard, *nakula* (*AV* 6.139.5) for ichneumon, *pāṅktra* (*MS* 3.14.7; *VS* 24.36) for field rat, *maṇḍūka*, *maṇḍūkī* (*RV* 7.103.1, 10.166.5; *AV* 7.112.2, etc.) for frog, *mayūra* (*RV* 3.35.1, 8.1.25, etc.) for peacock, *mahiṣa*, *mahiṣī* (*RV* 8.58.15, 9.92.9, 10.103.4; *VS* 24.28, etc.) for buffalo; *mūs*, *muṣika* (*RV* 1.105.8; *MS* 3.14.17; *VS* 24.36) for mouse, *vaḍavā* (*TS* 7.1.1.2; *TB* 1.8.6.3; *ŚB* 6.5.2.18) for mare, *varāha* (*RV* 1.42.2, 1.105.7, etc.) for wolf, *vṛṣadaṃśa* (*TS* 5.5.21.1, etc.) and *śitpuṭā* (*TS* 5.5.17.1) for cat, *śalyaka* (*VS* 25.35) for porcupine, *śaśa* (*RV* 10.28.2; *VS* 23.56, etc.) for hare, *śuśuka* (*AV* 6.14.3) for dolphin, and *siṃha* (*RV* 1.64.8, 1.95.5, 8.2.11, etc.) for lion. See also **Birds, Insects, Reptiles** and **Worms**.

**Animal Husbandry:** Vedic literature is replete with references to domesticated animals, particularly the cow or ox (*go*). In Vedic India the cow was a major source and measure of wealth and one of the standards of exchange. Large herds of cattle were common. Cow's milk (*kṣīra*) was processed into clarified butter (*ghṛta*) or curd (*dadhi*) and was an important ingredient of daily diet as well as Vedic sacrifice. The *Taittirīya Saṃhitā* (7.5.3.1) mentions that cows were milked thrice daily: morning, forenoon and evening. The first milking provided considerable milk, the later two milkings less. The flesh (*māṃsa*) of both cows and bulls was sometimes eaten. Oxen or bullocks were used for ploughing and drawing carts and wagons. The *RV* (1.62.9) notes that the cattle were red (*rohita*), light (*śukra*), dappled (*pṛṣni*) or black (*kṛṣṇa*) in colour. Ownership of cattle was indicated by markings made on the cattle's ears. The herds were tended by a herdsman (*gopa, gopāla*) while in the fields. As members of a pastoral society, Vedic Indians were particularly interested in animal life and in the taming, training and breeding of livestock. Special attention was given to the cow, bull, goat, sheep and horse. Stallions were sometimes gelded, while only mares were used in driving war chariots. Dogs were used for guarding houses and for hunting. Sheep and goats were kept for their wool and flesh. Leather prepared from slaughtered animals was used for various purposes such as slings, bow strings, chariot traces, reins and whips. Many passages in Vedic literature show the importance of the proper tending and feeding of cattle. According to the *Aitareya Brāhmaṇa* (3.18) among the Bharatas the herds are *saṃgavini* (wandering) during the day and at evening they return to the *goṣṭha* (cattle-shed). The times of *saṃgava*, when the cows used to graze freely on the pasture land, was called *svasara* (*RV* 2.2.2, 2.34.8, 5, 6.62.2, 8, 88.1, 9.94.2). The time cows went to their pasture in the morning is often referred to in the *Ṛgveda* (1.25.16, 10.97-8, etc.). When the cows were out feeding they were separated from the calves which were, however, allowed to join them at the *saṃgava* (*RV* 2.2.2, 8.88.1; *TB* 2.1.1.3), and sometimes in the evenings (*RV* 2.2.2). While grazing the cattle were under the care of a herdsman known as *gopa* or *gopāla* who was armed with a goad (*RV* 10.60.3). But they were liable to all sorts of dangers, such as getting lost, falling into pits, breaking limbs, and being stolen. The marking of the ear of cattle was repeatedly adopted, no doubt to indicate their ownership. The term *gopati*, 'Lord of cows' which is freely used in the *Ṛgveda* (1.101.4, 4.24.1, 6.45.21, 7.18.4; *AV* 3.14.6, etc.) to denote any lord or master, was a natural usage considering that cattle formed the main form of wealth. The Ṛgvedic tribes were prone to stealing or appropriating cattle. The term *gaviṣṭi* (desire for cows) denotes in several passages (*RV* 1.91.23, 3.47.4, 5.63.5, 6.31.3, 6.47.20, 6.59.7, 8.24.9.76.2; *AV* 4.24.5) conflict or battle evidently with reference to cattle raids. The term *gavya* (*RV* 7.18.7) was similarly used. Important tribes as such as the Bharatas were called 'the horde desiring cows' (*gavyan grāmaḥ*) (*RV* 3.33.11). The lowing of cows was compared with songs. Oxen were regularly used and were usually castrated (*AV* 3.9.2; 6.138.2; *TS* 1.8.9.1). Though in the Vedic literature there is no direct allusion to veterinary science, yet some Atharvanic charms indicate that cattle diseases were treated by applying herbs and magic formulae.

**Animal Worship:** Animals figure in the entourage of the gods. The goddess Saramā, who in dog shape finds the cows for Indra, has been regarded as a wind-spirit. The horses of the gods are transferred from the human to the divine sphere. In other cases there lies beneath the animal as companion of the god a trace of the god himself. The eagle brings the Soma down to Indra, but already in the *Ṛgveda* there is a variant form of the myth which indicates that the Soma was obtained by Indra in the form of an eagle (*RV* 10.99.8; Bloomfield, *JAOS*. xvi. 8). If we interpret the myth as the descent of the thunder storm and the rain amid lightning to earth, it becomes tempting to assume that the eagle was none other than the god Indra himself. Pūṣan, again, has a team of goats, but we find that in the *Ṛgveda* he is a knower of paths, and at the horse sacrifice a goat is killed to precede the horse, as it seems, to the world of death (*RV* 1.162.2-4). A goat too is slaughtered at the ceremony of the burning of the dead (*RV* 10.16.4). Hence it is a conjecture not without plausibility that the goat was a form of Pūṣan. The Aśvins, again, are horsemen as their name denotes, but they are never described as actual horses. According to an old tradition (*RV* 10.17.2 as rendered by Sāyaṇa with Yāska, *Nirukta* 12.10) their mother is a mare, and it is a legitimate hypothesis that once they were conceived in the form of a horse as well as in human shape. Likewise in the Avesta, we learn of Verethraghna flying to Zoroaster in the form of the bird Varaghna. But in these cases theriomorphism must be sharply distinguished from those of the birds of omen, which are styled as messengers of the Fathers or of Yama (*RV* 2.42.2; 10.165; *AV* 6.27-9; 11.2.2.11; *TA* 4.28; *Kaus.* 129). The birds themselves were quasi-deities in their own right before they were reduced to the rank of messengers. However, if the evidence of Vedic literature be taken as a whole, it will be seen that instead of direct animal worship, in Vedic religion animals are worwhipped symbolically. See **Totems.** Keith, I. 62-3.

**Animatism:** Animatism means a belief in the wonder-working power of an inanimate object. When a craftsman salutes his tools of work, such a belief of its wonder-working power remains latent in his mind. In the *Ṛgveda* and other Vedic texts sacrificial materials are often considered as deities, as also bows and arrows or chariots. Alongside the concrete figures of the great nature gods with their extended spheres of action, there stand deities with definitely limited functions. Of such deities we have good examples in the *kṣetrasyapati* and Vāstoṣpati, who appear in the *Ṛgveda* itself. They are respectively the spirit who dwells in the field and the protective spirit who has his abode in the house. More concrete still are such cases as Sītā, the furrow, and Urvarā, the field. The personification of furrow later crystallized in the *Rāmāyaṇa* in the concept of Sītā as predominantly a mortal woman, wife of Rāma, and daughter of Janaka. Traces, indeed, remain of her former divinity for the legend tells that hers was no normal birth—she sprang to life from the furrow when her father was ploughing. And, at the end, when she determines to prove conclusively to Rāma and his court that her chastity had not been defiled at the hands of Rāvaṇa during her enforced stay in the palace of her captor, her prayer to the goddess Earth is answered by the appearance of the deity who takes her into her bosom. Not essentially different from these instances are the prayers addressed, and the reverence paid, by the warrior to his weapons, the chariot, the arrow, and the drum, or by the ploughman to the ploughshare, and by the gambler to his dice.

**Animism:** Animism means the attribution of a living soul to plants, inanimate objects and natural phenomena. It also denotes the belief in a supernatural power that organizes and animates the material universe. In a wide sense the term animism is employed to cover all cases of belief in spirits. The basic concept of animism rests upon two aspects of primitive thought. In order to differentiate between life and death they had the concept of a life-principle or soul. The second aspect is concerned with the phantoms which appear in dreams and visions. This led to a subsequent concept of a subtle body (*sūkṣma-deha*). When both the concepts were combined we have a third principle which may be designated as the ghost-soul. In primitive belief everything in nature was supposed to have this ghost-soul or evil spirits. The practice of casting out evil spirit is undoubtedly older than that of propitiating good spirits. For example, even in the present times, during the *śrāddha* ceremony, one class of priests are engaged to carry priests performing the task of the welfare of the dead, for the next world. In the Vedic texts we come across evil beings such as the Ṛbhus, Apsarasas, Gandharvas, Asuras, Rākṣasas, Piśācas and so forth. The relation between the two species of divinities, the gods of nature, especially the lesser deities, and the spirits must have been very close. The animistic conception also prevails in the Vedic idea that the soul is capable of separation from the body, even during unconsciousness, and of continued existence after death. Thus in a whole hymn of the *Ṛgveda* (10.58) the soul of one who is lying, apparently dead, is besought to return from the distance. The Vedic conception of an animistic soul (*RV* 1.11.16; 1.140.8; 10.15.1) is the *asu*, breath, or the energizing principle in man, the life principle. In the Upaniṣads four kinds of soul are mentioned—Vaiśvānara, Taijasa, Prajñā and Turīya. A dream approach to the concept of soul is found in the Yama-Naciketas conversations found in the *Kaṭha Upaniṣad*. What is it that keeps itself awake in man when the bodily tenement seems to have gone to rest in the state of sleep? What is it that creates form after or for the satisfaction of desires in that dream state (2.2.8)? These are purely animistic queries. This is another approach to the problem of soul. 'That by means of which a person is able to discriminate between the nature of dream and the nature of wakefulness—what is that entity that breathes within man (2.1.4)?' The state of dream is only a miniature form of the state of death. In either case, the man seems to sleep; while in the first the forms of experience may probably be remembered, but in the second, what time it may take the human soul to come back (if ever) to its mortal coil, and what 'dreams' it may experience in that state, one cannot even imagine. With the ancients the dream problem was eschatological. The concept of soul has many dimensions in Vedic literature (see **Ātman, Eschatology**). Its elementary form, the ghost-soul, which is fundamental in animistic beliefs, may be traced to the hymns connected with the dead. The deities occurring in those hymns obviously represent certain features which reveal their primitive animistic ingredients.

**Anthropomorphism:** Anthropomorphism means the attribution of a human form or personality to a god, animal or thing. In the Ṛgvedic pantheon anthropomorphism plays an important role. According to the degree and extent of anthropomorphism, the deities of the *Ṛgveda* may be classified as transparent, translucent and opaque. Among the celestial gods Dyaus belongs to the transparent category, being a personification of the sky. Mitra, Sūrya, Savitṛ, etc., are solar deities whose associated natural phenomena are very clear. In the case of Uṣas, the goddess of dawn, the personification is slight, the poet never losing sight of the beautiful physical phenomenon behind the deity. Among the atmospheric gods the Maruts, Parjanya, Vāyu, Vāta are personifications of wind and storm with the least degree of anthropomorphism. This also holds good in the case of Āpaḥ, the waters, the personification being only incipient. Among the terrestrial gods Agni is the personification of the sacrificial fire, Pṛthivī, the personification of earth who is closely associated with Dyaus and Soma who is himself the personification of the *soma*-plant, the juice of which was ever present to the Ṛgvedic poets, the anthropomorphism is less developed. Among the deities in whose case the degree of anthropomorphism is greater (though the physical background may be traced somehow) we may refer to

Varuṇa who falls within the translucent category. It appears that he has something to do with the sky because his partner Mitra is the sun who is regarded as his eyes. He is also connected with the seasons and waters. Pūṣan is the god with a very vague personality, the anthropomorphic details being very few. The only prominent anthropomorphic trait found in Viṣṇu is that he is basically a sun-god. Then comes the god Indra, who has become a concrete personality, but his original physical character and his association with thunderstorms and rain may be discerned. Among the deities whose natural background has sunk into oblivion mention may be made of the Aśvins, Trita Āptya, Apāṃ Napāt, Mātariśvan, Ahi Budhnya, Rudra, Aja Ekapād, Bṛhaspati, etc. They belong to the opaque category and the process of their anthropomorphism is complete. Among the deities who do not fall into these three categories, mention may be made of Aditi whose name means 'non-binding', 'bondlessness', 'infinite', etc. The children of Aditi are known as Ādityas, among whom occur Varuṇa, Indra, Viṣṇu, Mitra, Aryaman, Bhaga, Dakṣa, Aṃśa, etc. Sacrificial utensils too were often deified, as were some abstract principles like Śraddhā, Manyu, etc. Diti is the exact converse of Aditi. In later Vedic texts, however, many nature-gods of the *Ṛgveda* went out of vogue and in their place we come across more concrete cosmic personalities.

**Annals:** The term *ākhyāna* (cf. the Śunaḥśepa-ākhyāna of *AB* 7.18) refers to the events of the past narrated by the Hotṛ priest during any Rājasūya sacrifice. The series of stories used at the Aśvamedha (*ŚB* 13.4.3.2 ff) during the year while the sacrificial horse was allowed to wander at its will is called the cyclic narrative or *pariplāva-ākhyāna* in which also past events were ratified by expressions like 'such battles he fought, such wars he won', etc. The word *ākhyāyikā* occurs in *Taittirīya Āraṇyaka* (1.6.3). The telling itself was known as *vyākhyāna* and the teller was known as *ākhyāna-vid* (*AB* 3.25; *ŚB* 3.6.2.7). The relation of *itihāsa* and *purāṇa* and *ākhyāna* is uncertain. The two former terms refer to a great body of mythology and legendary history available to the Vedic poets, roughly classed as a fifth Veda. Separate *ākhyānas* (with ramifications like *anvākhyānas* or supplementary narratives and *anuvyākhyānas* or explanations) could exist outside the cycle of *itihāsa-purāṇa* and could also be a part of it. Besides all these the Vedic texts in themselves often partly serve the purpose of annals because in them the priestly and royal lineages as well as important events are recorded.

**Anu:** A tribe mentioned with the Yadus, Turvaśas, Druhyus and Purus (*RV* 1.108.8), with the Druhyus (*RV* 7.18.14) and with the Turvaśas, Yadus, and Druhyus (8.10.5). Their mention in a passage of the *Ṛgveda* (8.74.15, compared with 7.18.14) shows that they dwelt on the Paruṣṇī, i.e., Ravi or Irāvatī in the Punjab.

**Apācya:** A tribe in the western region mentioned in *Aitareya Brāhmaṇa* (8.14) in connection with the *Nicyas*.

**Āpaḥ:** As regards *Āpaḥ* (the waters), the personification is only incipient. They are mothers, wives, and goddesses who bestow boons. They are celestial as well as terrestrial. The celestial waters were probably looked upon as an ether-like medium on which the luminaries made their fixed journeys along the Zodiac (*Ṛta*). They could be blocked by Vṛtra in which case rise and movements of these luminaries, were prevented thus causing long darkness. *Āpaḥ* or the waters, are invoked as *āpo* (*Avesta*, *RV* 1, 23.17-22; 6.47.3; 7.49. 1-4; 10, 9.2; 10. 17.10; 10.30.1-15; 10.91.6; *AV* 1.33.1; cf. *Nirukta* 9, 26).

**Apāṃ Napāt:** The deity Apāṃ Napāt, 'child of the waters', is more distinguished than Trita Āptya (q.v.) by being the subject of an entire hymn in the *Ṛgveda* where his name occurs some thirty times in all. He is essentially connected with the waters, his relation being envisaged in diverse ways. Three divine females desire to give him food. He sucks the milk of the first mothers and, at the same time, as a bull impregnates them. He shines without fuel in the waters. Clothed in lightning he mounts upright on the wave-lap of the shining waters; around him the soft golden-coloured water moves. He comes from a golden womb. In the hymn addressed to him he is directly identified with the god Agni but elsewhere, though associated with Agni, he is distinct from him. In the ritual he is connected with the waters; when the priests go for the waters required for sacrifice, it is to Apāṃ Napāt that they address their prayers, and they offer him butter in order to procure suitable waters. Offerings are made to him when the sacrificial victim perishes in water, or when the *Kārīrīṣṭi*, a rain spell, is performed. *RV* 1.70.3; 2.31.6; 2.35.3-5; 3.1.13; 6.48.5; 6.50.13; 10.20.7; 10.30.3-4; 10.45.1-3. Keith I, 135.

**Apes:** Apes, and their various kinds, are mentioned in the Vedic texts as *kapi, kiṃpuruṣa, puruṣa-mṛga, puruṣa hastin, māyu* and *markaṭa*. *Kapi* is another name for *luśa khārgali* (*KS* 30.2), but the name appears rather to be *luśākapi*. *Kiṃpuruṣa* (literally 'What sort of man?' according to Pānini 'ugly man') appears in the Brāhmaṇas (*AB* 2.8; *ŚB* 1.2.3.9, 7.5.2.32) to designate the 'ape' which is seen as a imitation of man. Possibly the same sense is used in some other passages (*VS* 30.16 and *TB* 3.4.12.11). *Puruṣa mṛga*, the 'man wild-beast' (*TS* 5.5.15.1; *MS* 3.14.16; *VS* 24.35) probably means the ape. The word *puruṣa* by itself in two passages of the *Atharvaveda* (6.38.4, 19.39.4) refers to the ape and its cry (*māyu*). *Puruṣa hastin* (the man with a hand) (found in *VS* 24.29 and *MS* 3.14.8) must be the 'ape'. *Māyu* occurs in the list of victims at the horse sacrifice (*TS* 5.5.12.1 and *VS* 24.31). The commentator on the former explains the word as meaning either an 'ape' (*kiṃpuruṣa*) or a 'forest peacock' (*araṇya-mayūra*). The former sense is supported by other passages (*VS* 8.47 and *TS* 4.2.10.1) where the *māyu*, being a substitute for the man, must be an ape. This sense also suits the word where it occurs in the other passage of the Brāhmaṇas (*ŚB* 7.5.2.22). *Markaṭa*, 'ape', is enumerated in the list of victims at the horse sacrifice in three places—(*TS* 5.5.11.1; *MS* 3.14.11 and *VS* 24.30). It is classified in the same Saṃhitās (*TS* 6.4.5.7; *MS* 4.5.7) with man and the elephant as 'taking hold by the hand' (*hastādāna*) instead of taking hold by the mouth (*mukhādāna*). The animal is mentioned several times elsewhere also (*AĀ* 3.2.4; *JB* 1.184; *TS* 3.11.32).

**Aphrodisiacs:** Not much is known about the existing aphrodisiacs used in the Vedic age. That the hair were kept combed is attested by Ṛgvedic evidence. The use of the word *opaśa* (*RV* 10.85.8; *AV* 6.138.1-2; *PB* 4.1.1, etc.) indicates that plaits were worn by women in dressing the hair. Garlands were often worn (cf. *RV* 4.38.6; 5.53.4; 10.184.3). The *Taittirīya Brāhmaṇa* (2.3.10.2) mentions an article called *sthāgāra*, probably an ornament made of a fragrant substance. Collyrium (*añjana*), an eye-salve, and other salves for anointing the body were used.

**Apiculture:** The frequent occurrence of the term *madhu* (*RV* 4.45.4, 7.32.2, 8.4.8; *AV* 9.1.17-19; *TS* 7.5.10.1; *MS* 4.9.7, etc.) in connection with beverage and the taboos against it (*ŚB* 11.5.4.18; *JUB* 1.55.2) show that the use of honey was well known. It appears that honey was collected from natural beehives and that a science of apiculture was yet to develop. *Āraṅgara* is one of the names of the bee found in the *Ṛgveda* (10.106.10). *Saraḥ* or *saragha* is another kind of bee (*RV* 1.112.21; *TS* 5.3.12.12; *ŚB* 13.3.1.4). *Bhṛṅga* is the name of a species of bee, later specified as large and black (*AV* 9.2.22; *MS* 3.14.8 and *VS* 24.28).

**Apotheosis:** Apotheosis is the elevation of man to a divine status. Most of the Ṛgvedic deities are personifications of natural phenomena. In some cases, however, we come across the elevation of a human being into ranks of the divine. Indra might conceivably have been originally a tribal leader, raised to the rank of the king of the gods for his war-like activities. More probably he was not a mortal man but a natural phenomena solidified in the conceptual form of a human warrior. His case is not like that of human Kṛṣṇa identified with Viṣṇu or the human Gautama Buddha conceived of as the *nirmāṇa-kāya* or worldly body of the all-pervading and eternally existing Buddha. In the Vedic texts we come across deifications of the spirits of the forests, trees, pasture, mountains and even household articles. Various implements, animals, constellations, sacrificial utensils, altars, etc., have also been deified. However, clear references to direct apotheosis are not found. Among a few such deities in whose case the process of apotheosis holds good, the name of Bṛhaspati comes first. The *Ṛgveda* devotes eleven hymns to him and mentions him, under that name or as Brahmanaspati, about 170 times. Bṛhaspati is in particular the divine priest; he is not only the Purohita, but also the *brahman*, and the brāhmaṇas constantly play on his position as the *brahman* priest or the *brahman*, the holy power, of the gods. He is the Lord of prayer, the generator of prayer, which he communicated to men. Hence in the later texts he is Lord of speech, Vācaspati, a name which is commonly found in post-Vedic literature. The case of the Aṅgirases is of special interest. Agni is also called the chief among them. Indra is also described as a host of the Aṅgirases and in his feat of the overthrow of Vala the Aṅgirases play a great part through their singing and prayers. They are repeatedly called Fathers by the poets; they are associated with Manu, the Atharvans, the Bhṛgus and Yama (*RV* 10.14.3-6). They also appear with the Ādityas, Ṛudras, and Vasus. Soma is offered to them, they are invoked (*RV* 9.62.9; 3.5.3.7; 10.62) and they are praised as sacrificers who attained Agni and won immortality by sacrifice. The Atharvans are mentioned in the *Ṛgveda* thrice only in the plural, and eleven times in the singular. The essential feature of Atharvan is that he produces Agni, and becomes the messenger of Vivasvant. He practised devotion along with Manu and Dadhyañc, and was helped by Indra. According to the *Atharvaveda* (18.3.54; 5.11; 7.104; 11.6.13), Atharvan brought to Indra a cup of Soma, received from Varuṇa a mystic cow, and dwelt in heaven. The Atharvans as a family appear with the Aṅgirases, Navagvas, and Bhṛgus and live in heaven, destroying goblins. In some passages the word simply means priest as when Atharvans receive cows from Avatha as gifts (*RV* 6.47.24) and a Bṛhaddivā Atharvan (*RV* 10.120.9) seems to have been a real poet. The essential legend concerning him is that with the head of a horse he demanded from the Aśvins the mead (*RV* 1.84.13-14; 1.116.12, 1.117.22, 1.119.9). Further, Indra is said to have found in *saryaṇāvant* the head of the horse hidden in the mountains, and to have slain ninety-nine Vṛtras with the bones of Dadhyañc. The Bhṛgus occur but twenty-three times in all in the *Ṛgveda*, and despite the fact that they are grouped with the Atharvans and as Fathers they show certain distinctions of character from the Aṅgirases. In the Brāhmaṇa literature the father of Bhṛgu is Varuṇa (*AB* 3.34.1; *PB* 18.9.1; *JB* 1.42; 2.202), while Aṅgirases is connected with Agni. In the ritual there are clear references to real Bhārgavas and to their practices as at the fire-piling and the mode of dividing the offerings.

**Apprentice:** Education in Vedic India—whether priestly, military or technical—was based on a very close teacher-student relationship. The student had to learn the practical aspects of their trade by staying as an apprentice in the house of their teacher. The Vedic term for the apprentice is *antevāsin* which literally means 'dwelling near' (*ŚB* 5.1.5.17; *BU* 6.3.7; *CU* 3.11.5, 4.10.1; *TU* 1.3.3, 1.11.1, etc.).

**Arable Land:** The general term for field is *kṣetra* which has been referred to in the Vedic texts as cultivable land (*RV* 10.33.6; 3.31.15; 5.62.70; *AV* 4.18.5; 5.31.4; 10.1.18; 11.1.22; *TS* 2.2.1.2; *CU* 7.24.2). A piece of ploughed land is also known as *urvarā* (*RV* 1.127.6; 4.41.6; 5.33.4; 6.25.4; 10.30.3; 10.142.3; *AV* 10.6.33; 10.10.8; 14.2.14), which is of two types—fertile (*apanasvati*) and waste field (*ārtanā*), (*RV* 1.127.6). Carefully measured off agricultural plots are also mentioned in the *Ṛgveda* (*kṣetram iva kimamuḥ*, *RV* 1.110.5). In the later Saṃhitās cultivable lands have been described both in general and in special senses (*MS* 5.2.3; 5.45.9; 6.47.20; *AV* 2.29.3; 14.2.7; *ŚB* 1.4.1.15-16). According to the *Ṛgveda* arable lands were often a bone of contention as is indicated by the terms like *urvarājit, urvarasa* and *kṣetrasa* (*RV* 2.21.1; 4.38.1; 6.20.1). Trāsadasyu acquired land with Indra's help (*RV* 7.19.3). Apālā's prayer to Indra for fertility of her father's field (*RV* 8.91.5) implies that personal ownership of land was not improbable. Since the fields were supposed to be measured according to the *Ṛgveda*, it is likely that individual ownership of land for cultivation was in vogue. There is no explicit mention of communal cultivation though common cattle and wealth are frequently referred to. In the *Śatapatha Brāhmaṇa* the giving of land as a fee to priests is mentioned. Indications to separate land holdings are available (*RV* 1.110.5; 2.15.3; 3.38.2; 10.2, 10, 33, 6; *AV* 4.18.5) and clear references to measurement of land are found (*RV* 1.110.5; 2.15.3; 3.38, 2; *AV* 6.132.2). Dispute about land or with neighbours is indicated (*TS* 2.2.1). The position of the king with regard to the land is somewhat obscure in the Vedic texts. In the *Atharvaveda* (4.22.2), there is a faint reflection of the king's power to donate land. Whether the king was the actual owner of the land or he enjoyed a symbolic ownership is a question which is not possible to answer at the present state of our knowledge. In the *Jaiminīya Brāhmaṇa* (92.41) it is said that there are three kinds of owners—namely that of heaven, that of the Lokas and that of field of agriculture. Elsewhere the phrases *devānāṃ kṣetrapati* and *manuṣaya kṣetrapati* occur (*TB* 1.84) and it is also stated there (2.41) that Pṛthu Vainya was the first to learn ploughing for agriculture.

**Archery:** See **Army, Weapons**.

**Architecture:** See **Art, Houses**.

**Aristocracy:** See **Nobility**.

**Arithmatic:** The term *rāśi* occurs as one of the sciences in the *Chāndogya Upaniṣad* (7.1.2, 7.1.4). It is explained by Śaṅkara as *gaṇita*, science of numbers, and stands for Arithmetic.

**Ārjikiyā:** Name of a river—upper Indus or Vitastā (the Jhelum) mentioned in the *Ṛgveda* (8.7.29; 8.64.11; 9.65.23; 9.113.2).

**Arms:** See **Weapons**.

**Army:** The *senānī*, or *senāpati*, the commander, held an important position. He was one of the *ratnins*, or king-makers, to whose house the king went first to offer the first oblation in the jewel-offering ceremony. The several kinds of guards that accompanied the sacrificial horse speak of the different kinds of soldiers. A hundred royal princes clad in armour, a hundred warriors armed with swords, a hundred sons of heralds and headmen of villages bearing quivers filled with arrows, a hundred sons of attendants and charioteers bearing staves and a hundred horses used to accompany the sacrificial horse (*ŚB* 13.4.2.5). Six thousand armed warriors protected the sacrificial horse of a particular king (*ŚB* 13.5.4.16). A good army was called *svanīka*. The soldiers were marched in various arranged formations while on a campaign. According to the *Aitareya Brāhmaṇa* (3.14.1) Agni, while fighting with the demons, arranged his army in three rows putting one commander-in-charge of every row or battalion. Thus equipped he defeated the Asuras. The vanguard of the army should always be terrible so as to strike terror in the opponents. A leader of a good army is called *susena* and the conqueror of an army is styled *senājit* (*ŚB* 8.6.1.20). A Rājanya, or man of military class, was expected to be heroic, skilled in archery, certain in his mark, and a mighty car-fighter (*ŚB* 13.1.9.2). In the *śatarudrīya* hymn of the *Vājasaneyī Saṃhitā* we come across various types of soldiers whose protector was Rudra. The god Rudra is termed *senānī* and *senāpati* (commander-in-chief), he is *āśu-senāḥ* and *āśu-rathaḥ* (*VS* 16.34) i.e., his army marches with great speed and his chariot runs at a breakneck speed. The diverse types of soldiers were but the various manifestations of god Rudra. The thirty-fifth verse of the hymn concerned describes Rudra as crowned with a helmet (*vilmin*) and having an amulet (*kavacin*), a mail and defensive armour (*varmin*), and he fought riding on an elephant (*varuthin*). The same hymn also pays homage to his army, the skilled drummer (*dundubhya*) and the players of war band. The army consisted of infantry, cavalry, chariots and elephants; different types of helmets, coats of mail, armour, armoured cars, well-protected elephants, with fortified strong chambers on their back are mentioned in the Vedic texts. A king whose army was famous attained the appellation of *śruta-sena*. Besides fighters there were also musicians and drummers in every army squadron to encourage the soldiers by rousing their military mettle by playing warlike tunes to spur them on to action. See **Fort, War, War Ethics, Warrior Class, Weapons**.

**Arts:** The term 'arts' is multidimensional and includes various forms of crafts, way of living, aspects of human behaviour, aesthetic audio-visuals, music, drama, literature and various cultural refinements, besides architecture, sculpture and painting. The elaborate terminology of buildings, their parts and materials as well as of masonry—such as *āgāra, avasatha, gaya, gṛha, duroṇa, duryoṇa, nivesana, pastyā, śālā, harma* (different forms of houses), *dhanadhāni* (treasure house), *prācīnavaṃśa* (hall), *prāsāda* (palace), *āṣṭrī* (fireplace), *upamit* and *stambha* (pillar), *chandas* (roof), *durya* (door-post), *dvāra* (door), *dvārapidhāna* (door-fastner), etc.—found in the Vedic texts point to the architectural activities of the period. No specimen of Vedic architecture, however, has been found. It appears that temples for worship were unknown though altars (q.v.) were erected for ritual purposes routinely which required an excellent geometrical knowledge. The anthropomorphic description of deities suggests that the science of iconology was known but no specimen of Vedic sculptural art has hitherto been found. Music, both vocal and instrumental, dance and dramatic performances were known. These topics are dealt with elsewhere in this volume.

**Artisans:** See **Crafts, Occupations**.

**Asceticism:** In the *Bṛhadāraṇyaka Upaniṣad* (4.2.22) the knower of the *ātman* is contrasted with those who (1) study, or (2) sacrifice and give alms, or (3) are anchorites and, in another place (3.8.10), with those who sacrifice and make benefactions, and those who practice asceticism. Asceticism plays a similar part in the pursuit of knowledge as the practice of sacrifice. The *Upaniṣad* (3.8.10; 4.4.22) is not inclined towards it, recognizing in it, as in sacrifice, at most a way to the lower bliss of the world of the Fathers. The *Chāndogya Upaniṣad* (2.23) substitutes the faith of the forest dweller for penance. The *Taittirīya Upaniṣad* (1.3 and 9), on the other hand, places value on Vedic study and asceticism, and even insists on the supreme value of the latter. The *Mahānārāyaṇa* (21.2) sets renunciation, *nyāsa*, etc., above asceticism. In later texts (*KU* 33; *PU* 1.10; *MU* 1.2.11) the value of asceticism for obtaining the knowledge of *brahman* is recognized as imperative and sometimes insisted upon. Though asceticism was regarded as belonging to the fourth stage of life in this period, in reality there were many persons who became wandering ascetics (*parivrājaka*) after concluding their studies to learn more from the facts of life. Some travelled to distant lands in search of opponents because to defeat them in an intellectual debate was a point of honour with most students. The presence of royal patrons of learning like Janaka or Ajātaśatru of Kāśi, afforded opportunities for such a display of learning by the learned of the land, and no doubt served as a great inspiration and encouragement to these wandering seekers. Every settlement (*samiti*) had its council of elders (*pariṣad*) as well as the specific Vedic schools (*caraṇas*), whose duty it was to award decisions on points of dispute and to do whatever was considered necessary to maintain the rank and the reputation of the settlement and the district in matters of secular as well as sacerdotal learning. The keen zest for learning is in evidence all through the period. It goes without saying that in such an intellectually sensitive atmosphere there was ample scope for all sorts of bickerings, jealousies, and even open quarrels not only in matters ritualistic but also in matters metaphysical or transcendental. The narrative background of most of the Upaniṣadic *vidyās* amply testifies to this pugnacious spirit. Furthermore, there is evidence to suppose that the philosophical speculations of the Upaniṣadic period were very largely influenced by a set of wandering ascetics and teachers following their own quaint and mystic practices of which we hear more in the post-Upaniṣadic period. The Upaniṣadic impulse to give up all worldly ties and take to a life of homeless wanderings can be satisfactorily explained only by postulating an extraneous influence of this nature. Belvalkar and Ranade 400-01.

**Āśrama Theory:** The theory of four *āśramas* or stages of life is not found in the Saṃhitās and Brāhmaṇas. Even the earlier Upaniṣads do not refer to it. The earliest mention of some kind of distinct stages of life, each stage having its own characteristics, is found in the *Śvetāśvatara Upaniṣad* (6.21) and *Muṇḍaka Upaniṣad* (4.3). In one passage of the *Chāndogya Upaniṣad* (8.5) reference is made only to the Brahmacārin and householder, to whom, as a reward for study, the procreation of children, the practice of *yoga*, abstention from injury to living creatures, and sacrifices, freedom from transmigration are promised. In another place (*CU* 2.23.1) three states are contemplated, but not as consecutive. The brahmacārin may either become a householder or become an anchorite, or remain in his teacher's house all his life. Similarly, a reference (*CU* 5.10) is made to the death of the anchorite in the forest, or the sacrifice in the village. In contrast with all three (*CU* 2.23.1) is the man who stands fast in *Brahman* (*brahmasaṃsthā*). This position of superiority to, and distinction from, the Āśramas later became a fourth Āśrama, the Gṛhastha, or householder (*JBU* 4 cf. *MU* 1, 7), who was in the second stage, being required to pass not only into the stage of *Vānaprastha* but also that of the *Sannyāsin* (*Bhikṣu, Parivrājaka*). The first stage, that of the *Brahmacārin*, was still obligatory, but was no longer allowed to remain a permanent one as was originally possible. The four stages of life *Brahmacarya, Gārhastha, Vānaprastha* and *Sannyāsa* are however directly mentioned in the Dharmasūtras (*ĀpDS* 2.1.21; *GDS* 2.2; *VDS* 7.1-2; *BDS* 2.6.17). As stated in the *Manusaṃhitā* (4.1) the first part of a man's life is Brahmacarya in which he learns at his teacher's house. After he has finished his studies, in the second part of his life he marries and becomes a hosueholder and discharges his debts to his ancestors by begetting sons and to the gods by performing *yajñas* (5.169). When he becomes sufficiently older he retires to the forest (6.1-2) where he spends the third part of his life. The rest of his life he lives as an ascetic (6.33). The fact that *āśrama* is not mentioned in the Saṃhitās or Brāhmaṇas does not however mean that the stages of life were unknown at that period. The concept may be attributed to tribal heritage when the transition from one stage of life to another was ceremoniously adopted through the *rites de passage*. The word *āśrama* is derived from *śram* 'to exert', 'to labour' and etymologically means 'a stage in which one exerts oneself'. Macdonell and Keith, I, 68-9, Bhattacharyya 1990, 25.

**Assault:** See **Criminal Law**.

**Assessor:** The term *sabhācara* (*VS* 30.6; *TB* 3.4.2.1) describes who is dedicated to *dharma*, order or justice. He would, therefore, be a member of the *sabhā* as a law-court, perhaps as one of those who sit to decide cases. Likewise *sabhāsad* (*AV* 3.29.1, 7.12.2, 19.55.6; *KS* 8.7; *MS* 1.6.11; *TB* 1.2.1.26; *AB* 8.21) is probably a technical description of the assessors who decided legal cases in the assembly. There were some kinds of assessment in regard to holdings or properties for the purpose of revenue collection, a task accomplished by officials such as *samgrahitṛ, bhāgadugha, grāmaṇi*, etc.

**Astronomy:** In the Vedic age astronomy came to be regarded as a separate science called *nakṣatra-vidyā* (the science of stars). An astronomer was called a *nakṣatra-darśa* (star-observer) or *gaṇaka* (calculator). According to the *Ṛgveda* (1.115.1, 2.40.4, etc.), the universe comprises *pṛthivī* (earth), *antarīkṣa* (sky, literally meaning 'the region below the stars'), and *div* or *dyaus* (heaven). The earth was considered to be spherical in shape (1.33.8) and suspended freely in the air (4.53.3). The *Śatapatha Brāhmaṇa* describes it expressly as *parimaṇḍala* (globe or sphere). There is evidence in the *Ṛgveda* of the knowledge of the rotation and annual revolution of the earth. It was known that these motions are caused by the sun. According to the *Ṛgveda* (6.58.1), the sun alone is the maker of day and night, twilight, month, and year, and also the cause of the seasons (1.95.3). The *Aitareya Brāhmaṇa* (3.44) states that the sun never sets or rises, the setting or rising of the sun are but changes of its course. Macdonell and Keith refer to the view of Ludwig that the *Ṛgveda* mentions the inclinations of the ecliptic with the equator (1,110.2) and the axis of the earth (10.86.4). The course of the sun is divided into two halves, the *uttarāyana* when the sun apparently goes northwards and the *dakṣiṇāyana* when it goes southwards. Tilak says that according to the *Śatapatha Brāhmaṇa* (2.1.3.1-3) the *uttarāyana* begins from the vernal equinox. But it is clear from the *KB* (19.3) that those periods used to begin respectively from the winter and summer solstices. The ecliptic is divided into twelve parts—the signs of the Zodiac which corresponded to the twelve months of the year, the sun moving through the consecutive signs during the successive months.The *Ṛgveda* (9.71.9) says that the moon shines by the borrowed light of the sun. The phases of the moon and their relation to the sun were fully understood. The *Ṛgveda* mentions thirty-four ribs of the horse (1.162.18) and thirty-four lights (10.55.3). Ludwig and Zimmer think that these refer to the sun, the moon, five planets and twenty-seven *nakṣatras* (stars) but Macdonell and Keith do not support this view. The *Taittirīya Saṃhitā* (2.3.5.1-3) and *Kāṭhaka Saṃhitā* (9.3) state that the moon is wedded to the *nakṣatras*. Later, when Abhijit became the pole-star it was counted as the twenty-eighth *nakṣatra*. In the course of time Abhijit ceased to be the pole-star and the number again came to twenty-seven. The ecliptic was divided into twenty-seven or twenty-eight parts corresponding to the *nakṣatras*, each of which the moon traverses daily during its monthly course. It appears from a passage in the *Taittirīya Brāhmaṇa* (1.5.2.1) that Vedic astronomers ascertained the motion of the sun by observing it with the naked eye. Observations of several solar eclipses are mentioned in the *Ṛgveda* including a passage which states that Atri observed a total eclipse of the sun (5.40.9). His descendants were particularly conversant with the calculation of eclipses (*AV* 13.2.4, 12.36; *ŚB* 4.4.21). In the *Atharvaveda* (19.9.10) the eclipse of the sun is stated to be caused by Rāhu, the demon. At the time of the *Ṛgveda* the cause of the solar eclipse was understood as the occultation of the sun by the moon. Lunar eclipses are also mentioned. In the Vedic Saṃhitās the seasons in a year are generally stated to be five—*vasanta* (spring), *grīṣma* (summer), *varṣā* (rains), *śarat* (autumn) and *hemanta-śiśira* (winter). Sometimes *hemanta* and *śiśira* are counted separately so that the number of seasons in a year becomes six. Vedic Indians counted the beginning of a season by the sun entering a particular asterism. After a long interval of time it was observed that the same season began with the sun entering a different asterism. Thus they discovered the falling back of the seasons with the position of the sun among the asterisms. *Vasanta* was considered the first of the seasons as well as the beginning of the year (*TB* 1.1.2.6-7; 3.10.4.1). The *Taittirīya Saṃhitā* (6.1.5.1) and *Aitareya Brāhmaṇa* (1.7) speak of Aditi the presiding deity of the Punarvasu *nakṣatra* receiving the boon that all sacrifices would begin and end with her. This clearly refers to the position of the vernal equinox in the asterism Punarvasu. There is also evidence to show that the vernal equinox was once in the asterism Mṛgaśirā from whence, in course of time, it receded to Kṛttikā. Thus knowledge of the precession of the equinox existed in the Saṃhitās and Brāhmaṇas. Some scholars maintain that Vedic Indians also knew of the equation of time. It is to be noted in this connection that the word *jyotiṣa* is not mentioned in the Vedic texts in the sense of astronomy. No astronomical text is mentioned in the Saṃhitās and Brāhmaṇas.

**Asuras:** Iranian Aryans were originally designated as Asuras. The undivided Indo-Iranians must have passed a long time in their central Asian common home, for here grew a specific Indo-Iranian culture and religion that may be partially reconstructed by comparing the Veda with the *Avesta*. In the earliest days the Aryans of India must have been connected with the Aryans of Iran, either as friends or as foes, but "actual historical contact cannot be ascertained with any degree of probability. The two peoples turned their backs upon each other as it were and developed their distinctive civilizations apparently without the least mutual influence, although in language, culture and religion their similarity in the earliest period was little short of identity. Geographical barriers are no doubt to some extent responsible for this apparent mutual oblivion, as also the fact that from the Indo-Iranian common home the pre-Indians and the pre-Iranians expanded in two almost opposite directions. All this, however, cannot explain the complete cessation of cultural contact between Iran and India even as early as the Ṛgvedic age. Incompatibility of some sort between the earliest Aryans of India and Iran has to be assumed to explain this camouflaged indifference. Seeds of such incompatibility which later developed into mutual hostility can be clearly seen already in the oldest Aryan religion and cult of these two countries. The primitive Indo-European religion recognized only nature-gods (sky, sun, wind, etc.) and a fire-cult. But already the undivided Indo-Iranians knew a Soma-cult beside the older fire-cult, and abstract deities, beside the older nature-gods. Indo-Iranian society had therefore ceased to be culturally homogeneous even before the forefathers of the Indian and Iranian Aryans parted company, and it is hardly to be doubted that their parting was more the effect than the cause of the cultural contrast revealed in religion. The old Indo-European term *deivo* (the same as the Indo-Iranian *daiva*) was apparently considered inappropriate for the new abstract and ethical deities, and a new term, Asura, perhaps borrowed from a higher civilization, came to be used as their designation. Varuṇa was the chief of these ethical deities just as Indra was the chief of the older nature-gods. The antagonism between the worshippers of the new gods and the old must have been one of the main causes of the estrangement and subsequent cecession of those Aryans who later conquered India, but their antagonism was not confined to the field of religion alone. In India we meet with the curious situation that in the oldest period all the great gods received the title *asura* as a decorative epithet, though later it came to be used exclusively as a term of abuse. In some passages in the Brāhmaṇas the Asuras have been represented as superior to the Devas in the arts of civilized life, and both in Vedic and Purāṇic tradition they are regarded as the elder brothers of the gods. All things considered, it seems difficult to deny that along with the great horde of Daiva-worshipping Aryans, a culturally superior strong minority of Asura-worshippers, too came to India whose cult and religion slighty different from were that of the former and who were for that reason ceaselessly cursed and condemned by the Vedic Aryans, more out of jealousy, it would seem, than out of contempt. For if the Vedic Aryans intentionally suppressed all reminiscences of the Indo-Iranian original move as suggested above, would they not also have suppressed the memory of the Asura-worshippers in the same way if they could? But this they could not, because some Asura-worshippers were physically present among them. After a period of conflict and adaptation there was peace which proved successful to the extent that even the foremost of the Daiva-gods, namely Indra, not only came to be regarded as an Asura in the oldest parts of the *Ṛgveda*, but was also credited with possessing *māyā*, which was a special property of the Asuras and probably signified 'magical power'. It is hardly an accident that in Hindu mythology the architect of the gods is an Asura whose name is Maya; the rude Daiva-worshippers apparently regarded the superior arts and crafts of their rivals as achieved by magic. In spite of the Daiva-bias of the Indians and the Asura-bias of the Iranians their culture and religion continued to be essentially the same till the advent of Zarathustra in Iran. A large number of common cult-words such as haoma (*soma*), zaotar (*hota*), athravan (*atharvan*), manthra (*mantra*), yazata (*yajata*), yasna (*yajña*), azuiti (*āhuti*), etc., and also the whole sacrificial cult, leave no doubt that Vedic and Avestan ritual are of one and same origin. The ceremony of *upanayana* is practically the same in the Veda and the Avesta, and in both the conventional number of gods is the same, namely thirty-three. Both in the Veda and the *Avesta* the picture of the gods is primarily that of an heroic Aryan warrior riding in a chariot drawn by powerful steeds. Like the Vedic gods those of the *Avesta* too hold up the sky to prevent it falling down, and image-worship is equally unknown in the *Avesta* and the Veda. Varuṇa, like his Avestan opposite number Ahura, assisted by Mitra (Avestan Mithra), is the supreme guardian of moral law and the conception of cosmic order is represented in both by the same abstract deity, the Vedic Ṛta = Avestan Asa (qq.v). In the Indo-Iranian epoch there were two different gods, Indra and Vṛtrahan (*vṛtra* = resistance, *vṛtrahan* = resistance-breaker). Indra was nothing but a concrete personalization of mere physical prowess, known in the legends of most primitive civilizations, but he was too Daivic to suit the taste of the stern reformer Zarathustra who did not hesitate to send him to Hades. But the lord Resistance-breaker, i.e., Vṛtraghna, whose function it was to break the resistance put up by evil, continued his glorious career within the Iranian pantheon. Indra and Vṛtrahan were united in the same person only later in the Vedic age. In short, Vedic Indra was the Indo-Iranian Indra (mentioned at Boghazköi) plus Vṛtrahan, whereas Avestan Indra is the Indo-Iranian Indra minus Vṛtrahan. The Nāsatyas who in the Boghazköi inscription are mentioned side by side with Indra and Varuṇa also appear in the *Avesta*, though as a demon-like Indra, and even the minor Vedic god Apāṃ Napāt is represented in the *Avesta* by a god of the same name. To the Vedic Gandharva corresponds the Avestan Gandarewa, and the Vedic Kṛsaṇu the Avestan Keresani. In the Veda, Yama, the son of Vivasvat, is the ruler of the dead, in the *Avesta*, Yima, the son of Vivanhant, is the ruler of paradise. Examples can be multiplied to show that in spite of the Zarathustrian reform, the Iranian religion continued to be much the same as before". B.K. Ghosh in Majumdar 222-7.

**Aśvala:** The ritualistic queries of Aśvala occur thus in the *Bṛhadāraṇyaka Upaniṣad* (3.1): "All this that exists is pervaded by death, is subject to the changes of day and night, and the bright half and the dark half of the month. How could the sacrificer, the Yajamāna, be saved from sharing the fate of all these things? Moreover', asked Aśvala, 'the interval between the earth and the sky is supportless, and so it hangs unpropped at both its ends: how can the Yajamāna ascend through this intermundia?" To all these questions the answer which Yājñavalkya gave was that it was sacrifice alone which would enable the Yajamāna to free himself from the trammels of death, to remain uninfluenced by the dualities of day and night, of the bright and dark half of the month, and to ascend by the ladder of righteousness through the unpropped intermune region. Belvalkar and Ranade 193.

**Aśvamedha:** See **Royal Ceremonies**.

**Aśvins:** From the point of view of the number of hymns addressed to them and also otherwise, the twin-deities, known as the Aśvins, are the most important after Indra, Agni, and Soma. They are not transparent deities but their connection with light is well established. Except in two or three passages, they are assumed everywhere as inseparable. Their paths are said to be golden, Dasra (wondrous) and Nāstaya are their most peculiar and frequent epithets. They are the two husbands or Sūryā whom they carry in their car. They are above all divinities of succour, the deliverers and rescuers, *par excellence*, from distress. They are divine physicians credited in several legends with miraculous cures. The physical basis of the cures has been a puzzle from the days of Yāska till today (*RV* 1.122.3; 1.117.6; 1.117.9; 1.118.4, 1.157.1, 1.180.10, 2.39, 4.36, 4.45, 3-4, 5.73.4, 5.75.3; 5.78.4; 6.62.5; 6.53.1, 5. 7.70.3; 7.73.4; 8.9.17; 8.35.7-9; 10.24.4; 10.61.4; *AV* 3.22.4; *ŚB* 4.1.5.16; *TS* 7.2.7.2).

**Aśvinī:** Excepting Pṛthivī, Aditi, and Uṣas, most of the other goddesses mentioned in the *Ṛgveda* are of very little importance. Agnāyī, Varuṇānī, Aśvinī, and Rudra respectively are only alluded to in a few passages. Aśvinī, along with other wife-goddesses, is invoked to enjoy the presents of the sacrifices. She is described as a matron (*RV* 5.46.8) but no distinct function is assigned to her.

**Atharvan:** Atharvan occurs fourteen times in the *Ṛgveda*, thrice in the plural. The term is also found several times in the *Atharvaveda*. The Iranian equivalent of the term is Athravan which means magician or priest. Atharvan did originally denote a class of magician-cum-priest, but later the term acquired a mystic significance. In the singular form Atharvan is a divine magician or priest who produced Agni through friction (6.15.7; 6.16.13). Agni thus produced by Atharvan became the messenger of Vivasvat (10.21.5). The Atharvan priest established (order) by sacrifices, while the Bhṛgus showed themselves as gods thanks to their skill (10.92.10). By sacrifices Atharvan first extended the paths; then the sun was produced (*RV* 1.83.5). In the plural the Atharvans are enumerated as fathers along with the Aṅgirases, Navagvas, and Bhṛgus (*RV* 10.14.6). They dwell in heaven and are called gods (*AV* 11.6.13). They destroy goblins with a magical herb (*AV* 4.37.7). In a few passages of the *Ṛgveda* the word *atharvan* appears to have the appellative meaning of 'priest'. Thus it is an attribute of Bṛhaddivā, the composer of a hymn (*RV* 10.120.9; cf. 10.120.8). In this sense it seems to be an epithet of Agni, when a seer is described as pouring the libation on the Atharvan (*RV* 8.9.7). The word also means priest when it is said that the Atharvans mix Soma (*RV* 9.4.2) or that they receive a hundred cows from a patron (*RV* 6.47.24). They are mentioned as a class of Pitṛs (q.v.) in the *Ṛgveda* (10.14.6). The term also denotes magic rituals and their performers. It should be noted that the *Atharvaveda* was originally known as *Atharvāṅgirasaḥ*, that is *atharvan* (holy magic bringing happiness) and *aṅgirasa* (hostile or black magic).

**Atheism:** In the Vedic consciousness of the earlier stage all sorts of assorted objects appeared to have aroused great wonder. Everybody and everything that helped the Vedic people to survive in the world appeared to the Vedic poets to have been grand and glorious. Everybody and everything that threatened their survival were either to be brought under control by magical spells or simply placated with extravagant praises. In this sense all sorts of persons and objects appeared to them as deities, the so-called Vedic *devas*. It is futile to search in this early conception of the *deva* any idea of god of later times. These *devas* were often crassly human heroes (*RV* 1.129.2; 3.54.17; 4.2.5), looting food and cattle from the aliens and sharing these among their own tribesmen. They sat with their tribesmen in councils and assemblies and were addressed in fond terms as friends and the best of friends (*RV* 1.26.3; 1.63.4; 1.100.4; 3.31.8; 3.39.5; 3.43.4). Often the *devas* were simply natural phenomena like fire, water and storm. Others were the hill (*parvata*, *RV* 6.49.14), the herb (*oṣadhi*, *RV*. 10.97, cf. *AV* 6.136.1), the tree (*vanaspati*, *RV* 7.34.23, 10.64.8), the forests (*araṇyānī*, *RV* 10.146), and weapons (*āyudha*, *RV* 6.75) like the bow and the arrow. Sometimes, again, these *devas* were simple embodiments of elemental desires, like the 'protection against abortion' (*RV* 10.162), 'the protection against consumptive diseases' and the 'protection against nightmares' (*RV* 10.164). Still the root of atheism is to be sought in the Vedas. 'The beginnings of Indian atheism', Garbe says, 'can be traced back in the Vedic period. In the *Ṛgveda*, the national god Indra is derided in several passages (4.24.10; 10.119) and we read (2.22.5; 8.133.3) of people who absolutely denied his existence even in these early days. We have here the first traces of that native atheism which is so far from indulging in any philosophical reflection that it simply refuses to believe what it cannot visualise and which, in a later period, was known as the dis-belief of the Lokāyata system; that is to say, of crass materialism'(*ERE* II.185). The evidence cited by Garbe, of people doubting or disbelieving in the very existence of Indra, is interesting and has some bearing on our understanding of the origin of Indian atheism. Take the passage, 'O men, that terrible deity about whom people ask, "Where is he?" and about whom people say, "He exists not", have faith in him, who, as punisher, destroys the enemy's wealth for he is "Indra" ' (*RV* 2.12.5). Similarly, another passage states, 'O warriors if it is true that Indra exists, then sing your truthful praises addressing Indra. (The seer called) Nema says 'There is nobody called Indra. Who has seen him? Whose praise art thou going to sing?' (*RV* 8.100.3). These are no doubt references to the people of the Vedic age who doubted and even denied the very existence of Indra. The oldest hymns of the *Ṛgveda* disclose a primitive stage of beliefs. These are productions of simple men who believed that each of the great provinces of nature was animated by its own deity. They had not then risen to the clear idea of one supreme creator. In the pluralistic stage a number of gods like Varuṇa, Agni, Viśvakarman, etc., were looked upon as authors of the universe. It is only when we go to the monotheistic level that the question arises whether god created the world out of his own nature without any pre-existing matter. The idea of a creation of the world by an omnipotent god out of pre-existing matter is reflected in the conception of Hiraṇyagarbha who is said to have arisen in the beginning from the waters pervading the universe and fashioned the world from the shapeless chaos which was all that existed. But how did it happen that the chaos produced Hiraṇyagarbha? Who was the author of the primeval waters? These questions are not answered in the *Ṛgveda*. The 'One' of the Nāsadīya hymn is also a subsequent creation, because in the said hymn it is clearly stated that in the beginning all this was a sea without light; the germ lay covered by the husk and that 'One' was born by the power of heat or fervour. The same idea of pre-existing matter occurs in another hymn (*RV* 10.82.5-6) wherein it is stated that the waters of the sea contained the primordial germ. This germ was the world-egg floating on the primeval waters of chaos, the principle of the universe. From it arose Viśvakarman, the first-born of the universe, the creator and maker of the world. By the conception of *asat*, the non-existent from which the existent is said to have been manifested, the Ṛgvedic poets probably understood a positive condition of creation, a background. We can, therefore, safely come to the conclusion that in the monotheistic level of the *Ṛgveda* the idea of an omnipotent god creating the world out of his own nature without any pre-existing substance is practically absent though occasionally we come across passages indicating the nucleus of such a conception.

**Ātman:** See **Absolute**. The Self, the inner reality, which in the form of pure consciousness is manifested in every being. As infinite and consicous reality this Self or Soul of a man (*jīvātmā*), according to the Upaniṣads, is identical with the Self or Soul of all beings (*sarvabhūtātmā*) and therefore with *brahman* which is the all-pervasive reality (*paramātmā*) underlying all things (*BU* 1.4.1; 1.4.10; 2.5.19; 4.6.5; *AU* 1.1; *MU* 2.2.11; *CU* 3.14.1, 6.2.1, 7.25.2, etc.) The body, the senses, the mind, the intellect and the like are merely sheaths (*koṣas*). In the famous dictum of identity *tat tvam asi*, *tat* meaning 'that' stands for *brahman*, and through it the universe and *tvam* meaning 'thou', for *ātman* or the individual self. The word *ātman* was used in the *Ṛgveda* to denote, on the one hand, the ultimate essence of the universe and, on the other, the vital breath in man. Later, in the Upaniṣads, we see that the word *brahman* is generally used in the former sense, while the *ātman* is reserved to denote the inmost essence in man, and the Upaniṣads are emphatic in their declaration that the two are the same. In this connection we may refer to a passage of the *Śatapatha Brāhmaṇa* (10.6.2.1-11) declaring the identity in essence of the self within and the self without. The cosmogonic conception of *ātman*, like that of *brahman*, had to pass through many stages of thought. For example, in the *Kaṭha Upaniṣad* (4.6) *ātman* is spoken of as born before heat and even the waters. In the

*Chāndogya Upaniṣad* (5.11-18), the sky, the sun, the wind, space and the waters are equated respectively with the head, the eyes, the breath, the body and the bladder of *ātman*. The *Bṛhadāraṇyaka Upaniṣad* (1.4.7) and the *Maitrī* (6.7, 7.7) identify *ātman* with all the gods and powers. In the next stage *ātman* is conceived as the unitary world-soul, the immanent reality of all things (*ŚvU.* 1.15, 4.2-7). A narrower characterization is also met with, (e.g. in the *BU* 1.4), in which it is stated that *ātman* was possessed by a feeling of loneliness and then by self-bifurcation he created his female partner in order to procreate other beings. Under such diverse processes *ātman* gradually stepped towards becoming the ultimate basis of the manifold world and of the individual. According to a passage of the *Praśna Upaniṣad* (4.7-9), 'As birds resort to a tree for a resting-place, even so, O friend, it is the supreme soul (*ātman*) that everythign here resorts.' Before the final identification, the two terms *ātman* and *brahman* were hovering near each other as designations of the ultimate world-ground. After the identification is made the two became interchangeable terms. See **Brahman**.

**Atmospheric Gods:** See **Indra, Trita Āptya, Apāṃ Napāt, Mātarisvan, Ahi Budhnya, Aja Ekapād, Rudra,** the **Maruts, Vāyu-Vāta, Parjanya, Āpaḥ**.

**Atonement:** See **Penance**.

**Attachment:** See **Desire**.

**Attendants:** *Saciva* means 'companion', 'attendant', later a common word for the comrade of a king, his minister, or it is used to designate the Maruts (as found in the *AB* 3.20). *Anucara* (*VS* 30.13; *TB* 3.4.7.1) signifies attendant and its faminine gender (*ŚB* 13.5.4.27) is also found, though infrequently, where slave girls are meant. *Paricara* (*ŚB* 4.3.5.9), *paricaraṇa* (*Ṣaḍ B.* 6.11), and *paricaritṛ* (*CU* 7.8.1) convey the same meaning. Attendant of the door-keeper (*VS* 3, 11, 30.73), or that of the charioteer (*TB* 3.4.9.1), is included in the list of sacrificial victims (*VS* 30.11, 30.73; *TB* 3.4.9.1). *Saṃśravyitṛ* (*KauU* 2.1) designates the attendant who announces visitors.

**Austerity:** The method of the pursuit of the highest truth and of its direct realization on the basis of ascetic austerities and concentrated contemplation (*tapas*) is found in the *Ṛgveda* (10.109.4) which mentions seven *ṛsis* absorbed in *tapas* and of the power of *tapas* in raising the lowest to the highest. In post-Ṛgvedic literature and in later religious systems the performance of austerity was given greater importance.

**Avocations:** See **Occupations**.

**Awl:** Awl or gimlet is indicated by the word *ārā* (*RV* 6.53.8) to denote the weapon of Pūṣan. It is used for piercing leather. The term *vāśī* denotes the weapon of the Maruts (*RV* 1.37.2, 1.88.3, 5.53.4) also called Tvaṣṭṛ (*RV* 8.29.3). It is a carpenter's knife in the *Atharvaveda* (10.6.3).

**Axe:** The axe, called *paraśu* (*RV* 1.27.3; 7.104.21; 10.28.8; 10.53.9) or *kuliśa* (*RV* 3.2.1; 1.32.5) served both as a wood-cutting implement and a weapon of war. *Svadhiti* is a cutting instrument, axe or knife, used to dissect the body of the sacrificial horse (*RV* 1.162.9, 1.62.18, 1.162.20). It is found in the sense of an 'axe' used to cut wood (*RV* 2.39.7, 3.2.10, 8.6.11, 5.7.8, 7.3.9, 8.102.19, 10.89.7). An axe was sharpened by a whetstone (*kṣṇotra*), mentioned in one passage (*RV* 2.39.7). *Svadhiti* denotes a copper knife used to mark the ears of the cattle (*AV* 6.141.2), or a carpenter's knife (*AV* 9.46, 12.3.33), or an 'axe' (*TS* 6.3.3.2) and *VS* 5.4.3).

**Axle:** A spindle upon which a wheel rotates is mentioned as *akṣa* (*RV* 1.30.14, 1.116.9, 3.53.17, 6.24.3, 10.89.8). It was apparently fastened to the body of the chariot (*kośa*) by straps (*akṣā-naḥ*). The heating of the axle was known (*RV* 10.53.7). The part of the axle round which the nave of the wheel revolved was called *āṇī* or pin.

# B

**Bacillus:** Sometimes diseases are supposed to be caused by worms (*kṛmi*). In the *Atharvaveda*, hymns 2.31 and 32 are known as 'worm-destroying (*kṛmināśana*)' hymns, intended to be used in a magico-religious rites. It is stated (*AV* 2.31.1) that he crushes the worms like *khalva* grains with the millstone of Indra. Worms are classified into two classes—the seen and unseen, and are named as the *algaṇḍus*, the *śakunas*, the *avaskara* and the *vyadhvara* (*AV* 2.31.2 and 3.31.4). Some worms are described to be in the entrails, the others in the head and in the ribs of the body. Formulas (*vācas*) are used to draw out, grind and destroy the worms. Worms are described as being of all forms. In *Kauśika Sūtra* (27.14-29) it is prescribed that the hymn from the *Atharvaveda* (2.31) may be used in a magico-religious rite for killing the red worms. The worms are considered to be semi-demons and as such are regarded as a mysterious rather than a physical phenomenon.

**Bāhīka:** Mentioned in the *Śatapatha Brāhmaṇa* (1.7.3.8) as the people of the West, in contrast to the Prācyas or easterners. They are said to have called Agni by the name of Bhava. They probably lived in the Punjab region. In later literature they were associated with the Ārattas and Sindhu-Sauvīras.

**Bālhīka, Bāhlīka:** Bālhīka is the name of a people in the *Atharvaveda* (5.22.5, 5.7.9) in which the fever (*takman*) is called upon to go to the Mujavants, the Mahāvṛṣas, and the Bālhīkas. The Mujavants are quite certainly a northern tribe, and though the passage may contain a pun, on *Bāhalīka* or *Bālhīka* as suggesting 'outsider' (from *bahis*, 'without'), the name might have been chosen from a northern tribe. They could have also been an Iranian tribe after which the Balkh region was named. This is attested to by the evidence of later texts and inscriptions which suggest that they were the inhabitants of Bactria or the Balkh region and had political and cultural relations with the people of India.

**Bandhutā Concept:** In the Brāhmaṇa literature the realm of deities headed by Prajāpati is a kingdom with a graduated order of power and precedence, each member of the pantheon being assigned a definite function and a specified paraphernalia of number, metre, psalm, season, hour, place, priest, consort, oblations, gifts, cups and companions. Indra, for instance, is associated with the number 11, the metre *triṣṭubh*, the season *grīṣma* (summer), the midday oblation, and so forth with Indrāṇī for his wife and Agni, Soma, Varuṇa, Pūṣan, Bṛhaspati, Brahmanaspati, Parvata, Kutsa, Viṣṇu and Vāyu as his companions (*bandhus*). And wherever the number 11 or the metre *triṣṭubh* and the rest appear, the power of Indra is believed to be present there (*AB* 2.25; *TS* 5.4.9; *MS* 1.8.4) through diverse causes or circumstances. The Brāhmaṇa texts show clear indications of a belief in the presence of some subtle, secret, and mystic bond. The bond is subtle because *parokṣapriyā hi devāḥ*: the gods love what is hidden. It is often interpreted in terms of a fancy-etymology (*TB* 1.3-6.1 ff), a myth invested ad-hoc (cf. *ŚB* 2.1.1.5), some obvious similarity or correspondence in the nature of the things (cf. *ŚB* 13.2.10.5), a cosmogonic narrative (cf. *PB* 6.1.6) and the current tradition and practice, possibly with roots in hoary antiquity. The Brāhmaṇa texts identify Indra with his *bandhus* severally and collectively. For the word *bandhu*, the texts use, more or less synonymously, the words *rūpa, tanu* and *nāma*. In the *Aitareya Brāhmaṇa* (7.24) it is said that the Kṣatriya when concentrated has Agni for his deity, the *Gāyatrī* for his metre, the *Trivṛt* for his *ṣṭoma* and the Brāhmaṇa as his *bandhu* or inner essence. Similarly, in the *Kaṭhaka Saṃhitā* (8.4) Agni, Vāyu, Vāk, and Bṛhaspati are brought in connection with each other through sacrifice as their *bandhu*. A direct identification of a thing with its *bandhu, rūpa* (real essence) or *bibhūti* (inner manifestation) was therefore inevitable. Other words sometimes used to denote the *bandhutā* concept are *pratimā* (image), *ātman* (soul), *manas* (mind), *nidāna* (root cause), *vīrya* (vigour), etc. Belvalkar and Ranade, 61-5.

**Banner:** Banners are alluded to as borne in battle in the *Ṛgveda* (10.103.11) and where men bearing ensigns meet in battle, etc. (7.83.2). Such standards were known as *dhvaja*.

**Barāsī:** A garment (*KS* 15.4; *PB* 18.9.16; 21.3.4) of some kind used by the Neṣṭṛ in the Dāsapeya. It is stated as *kṣaumī* in the *Lāṭyāyana Śrauta Sūtra* (9.2.15: *barāsī neṣṭuriti kṣaumī syāt*). Sāyaṇa interprets this garment as a bark-garment which is inferior to cloth. In another place he takes it as untattered raiment.

**Barb:** *Apāṣṭha, śṛṅga,* are the two words used in the sense of 'barb' in the Vedas. *Apāstha* occurs twice (*AV* 4.6.5; 5.18.7) denoting the barb of an arrow and once (*AV* 5.18.7) the word *śatāpāṣṭhām*, in the sense of hundred-barbed, is found. The term *śṛṅga* is used to denote the horn of animals. Thus the barb of the arrow is called its horns (*AV* 4.6.5).

**Barbarians:** See **Dāsa, Dasyu, Mleccha, Paṇi, Rākṣasa, Asura**.

**Barber:** The word *nāpita*, 'barber', is mentioned (*ŚB* 3.1.2.2). But the older word is *vaptṛ* (*RV* 10.142.4) a derivative of *vap*, 'shave'(*RV* 10.142.4; *AV* 6.68). *Nāpita* is mentioned elsewhere too (*KSS* 7.2.8.13 and *AGS* 1.17.16).

**Bark-Garment:** Bark of a tree (*valka*), (alluded to in the *TS* 2.5.3.5) and (*TB* 1.4.7.6) which was seemingly worn as raiment. It is termed as *valkala* in later literature.

**Barley:** *Yava* is a common word used in the *Ṛgveda* (1.23.15; 1.66.3; 1.117.21; 1.135.8; 2.5.6; 2.14.11; 5.85.3; 7.3.4; 8.2.3; 8.22.6; 8.63.9; 8.79.10) to designate any grain. It specifically denotes 'barley' in the *Atharvaveda* (2.8.3; 6.30.1; 6.50.1; 6.50.2; 6.91.1; 6.140.2; 9.6.14; 20.7.3) and onwards (*MS* 4.3.2; *KS* 25.10; 26.5; *TS* 6.2.10.3; 6.4.10.5, 7.2.10.2, *VS* 5.26, 23.30.31; *TB* 1.8.4.1; *ŚB* 2.5.2.1; 3.6.6.9-10; *CU* 3.14.3). It is indicated that the cultivation of barley in the age of the *Ṛgveda* was uncertain. The *Śatapatha Brāhmaṇa* mentions that it grows with rains (1.1.4.20). Elsewhere it is noted that its harvesting season is usually after the spring (*KB* 4.13) and the summer (*TS* 7.2.10.2), and that gazelles eat sprouts of barley (*VS* 23.30; 23.31). The *Jaiminīya Brāhmaṇa* refers to the Ādityas allocating the sacrifice by means of *yava* grains (2.117) and as a well loaded (cart) laden with barley or with beans (1.335) besides being used during the performing of sacrifice (2.41). Another commentator has used the terms *upavāka* and *yava* to designate barley (*VS* 19.22). Since both *upavāka* and *yava* are mentioned along with *kuvala*, *badara* and *karkandhu* (*ŚB* 12.9.1.5) so *upavāka* may differ from *yava*. *Indra-yava*, which was another class of barley, occurs in two texts (*VS* 19.22; 19.10; 21.30 and *ŚB* 12.7.1.3; 12.7.2.9; 12.9.1.5).

**Barley Gruel:** The term *yavāgū* means 'barley-gruel' (*TS* 6.2.5.2; *KS* 11.2; *TS* 2.8.9; *KB* 4.13). But the term is also employed to denote some other kinds of grain (*TS* 5.4.3.2).

**Barn:** The term for barn, in which corn was heaped or stored is *urdara* (*RV* 2.4.11): *adhvaryavo vo divyasva vasvo vaḥ pārthivasya kṣamyasya rājā. tamurdaraṃ na pṛṇatā vaverendraṃ somebhiṣṭadapo vo astu.*

**Barter System:** Although some form of coinage was known to the Vedic Indians, it was principally the exchange or barter system that characterized the sale and purchase of various commodities. The *Atharvaveda* refers to two specific terms by which the barter system was clearly indicated. These terms are *pro-paṇa* and *prati-paṇa*. *Paṇa* with *prati-paṇa* is found in a hymn (*AV* 3.15.4-6) denoting the process of bargaining and selling. The root *paṇ* from which the word is derived, is employed in the later Saṃhitās and Brāhmaṇas (*VS* 8.55; *ŚB* 3.3.3.1; *AB* 1.27; *TS* 6.1.10.1) while *paṇana* (in the *ŚB* 3.3.2.19) denotes 'trafficking'. The word *prati-paṇa* (found in the *AV* 3.15.4) denotes 'barter' or 'exchange'. The *pra-paṇa* (in the *AV* 12.15.4-5) denotes the same, balanced by *prati-paṇa*.

**Basket-Maker:** The word *bidala-kārī* means basket-maker. A female splitter of bamboos (*VS* 30.8; *TB* 3.4.5.1) was regarded as one of the sacrifical victims at the Puruṣamedha (q.v.).

**Bean:** A sort of bean is termed as *māṣa* (in *AV* 6.140.2, 12.2.53; *MS* 1.4.10; 4.3.2; *KS* 12.7; 32.7, *TS* 5.1.8.1, 7.2.10.2, *VS* 18.12, *ŚB* 1.1.1.10 and *BU* 6.3.13). It was harvested in winter (*TS* 7.2.10.2). This corn is listed in *Bṛhadāraṇyaka Upaniṣad* as a cultivated variety of grain. Its flour was used as oblation (*AV* 12.2.53). *Kulmāṣa* (*CU* 1.10.2, 1.10.7) had bean interpreted by some commentators. Some texts mention a taboo on this bean (*MS* 1.4.10 and *KS* 32.7). *Garmut* is a name of a wild bean (*TS* 2.4.4. 1-2). It is used also in adjectival form (*gārmut*, *MS* 2.2.4) to denote prepared with *garmut*.

**Bed:** *Talpa* is the regular term for bed or couch from the earlier texts (*RV* 7.55.8; *AV* 5.17.12; 14.2.31; 4.2.41) and later (*TS* 6.2.6.4; *TB* 2.2-53; *PB* 23.4.2, 25.1.10). One made of *udumbara* wood is specifically mentioned (*TB* 1.2.6.5). The violation of the bed of a Guru, or teacher, is already mentioned in the *Chāndogya Upaniṣad* (5.10.9) while the adjective *talpya*, 'born in the nuptial couch' denotes 'legitimate' in the *Śatapatha Brāhmaṇa* (13.1.6.2).

**Bench:** *Proṣṭha*, denoting perhaps a 'bench', is found in the *Ṛgveda* (7.55.8) in the adjective *proṣṭhasava*, 'lying on a bench', and also uncompounded (in the *TB* 2.7.17.1). In the first passage it is distinguished from *talpa* and *vahya*, but there is not sufficient evidence to show what was the exact difference. Macdonell and Keith, II, 54.

**Besprinkling Ceremony:** The most essential part of the Rājasūya (q.v.) was the Abhiṣeka or besprinkling. It began with offerings to the deities Savitā Satyaprasava, Agni Gṛhapati, Soma Vanaspati, Bṛhaspati Vāk, Indra Jyeṣṭha, Rudra Paśupati, Mitra Satya and Varuṇa Dharmapati. The consecration water (*abhiṣecanīya āpaḥ*) was made up of seventeen kinds of liquid including the water from the river Sarasvatī, sea-water, and water from a whirlpool, a pond, a well and dew. The sprinkling was performed by a Brāhmaṇa priest, kinsman or brother of the king-elect, a friendly Rājanya and a Vaiśya. See **Royal Ceremonies**.

**Beverages:** Of the beverages of the Vedic Indians Soma juice was the most important (*RV* 9.12.7). The plant was brought from some mountains especially Maujavanta (*RV* 1.93.6; 3.48.2; 5.36.2; 5.43.4; 5.85.2). The process of extracting the juice is described in detail. The stalks were crushed between two stones (*RV* 1.83.6). They were sometimes pounded in a mortar with a pestle (*RV* 1.28.4; 1.28.6). The plant was washed in water before crushing (*RV* 9.6.6; cf. 9.16.2). In order that it may yield copious juice, water was sprinkled on the stalks (*RV* 9.7.6; *AV* 9.6.16). It was pounded with both hands (*RV* 9.7.2, 5). Women sang songs when they squeezed the juice of the plant with their fingers (*RV* 9.66.8). Soma juice was pressed in very large quantities (*RV* 3.46.4) and was then strained to remove the impurities (*RV* 9.12.5). It was stored in jars or wooden tubs and was either brown, ruddy or tawny (*kalaśeṣu*, i.e. vessels, *RV* 9.12.5; *droṇa*, i.e. wooden tubs, *RV* 9.15.7; 9.33.2; *babhru*, i.e. brown *RV* 9.33.2; 9.63.4; 9.63.6; *hari*, i.e. tawny *RV* 9.3.9; *aruṇa*, i.e. ruddy *RV* 9.40.2; 9.45.3). It was mixed with curds, clarified butter or milk to improve its taste (*RV* 9.23.3; 9.101.12; 9.82.2; 9.61.13; 9.46.4; 9.64.28; 8.2.3). Other preparations with which it was mixed were *karambha, dhānāḥ, apūpa*, pakti, *saktu*, water and honey (*RV* 8.91.2; 3.5.27; 6.29.4; 5.27.5; 9.74.9; 9.67.32). According to Vedic descriptions Soma juice was sweet and delicious in taste (*RV* 6.47.1). It was believed that it inspired confidence, courage, faith and self-truth and bestowed powers of eloquence and immortality (*RV* 6.47.3; 9.96.5; 8.49.12). It was called pure, purifying (*RV* 9.24.7), and the most heavenly nectar (*RV* 9.110.8). A strong mixture of Soma juice, called *pañcadaśa* is also mentioned (*RV* 10.27.2). Another beverage of the Vedic period was *surā* (intoxicating liquor) which was prepared from barley or wild paddy after distillation (*RV* 8.2.12; 1.116.7; 10.131.4; 10.131.5; 7.86.6; 8.21.14; *MS* 1.2.6; 2.4. 2.4.21; *TS* 1.3.3.3; *ŚB* 12.7.3.8; 1.6.3.2; *CU* 5.10.9). But while the use of Soma juice was highly commended that of *surā* was condemned. Drinking *surā* gave rise to brawls in the assembly (*RV* 8.2.12; *TB* 3.3. 2-3). Its popularity in the later Vedic period is, however, evident since it is mentioned as a reward for the performance of sacrifices (*AV* 4.34.6). The praise of *surā* in the *Aitareya Brāhmaṇa* and the placing of the *surā* vessel in the hands of a king (*AB* 37.4) lead us to conclude that the kṣatriyas were generally in the habit of drinking *surā*. But the evil effects of drinking were known. It was regarded as one of the seven sins forbidden by the Vedas (*RV* 10.5.6) and was classed with anger, senselessness and gambling (*RV* 8.86.6). Realizing its evil effects the Brāhmaṇas avoided drinking it (*KS* 13.2) and good kings, like Aśvapati, proudly declared that there were no drunkards in their kingdoms (*CU* 5.11.5). Another common intoxicating drink was *pariśruta* (*VS* 19.15; 20.59; 21.29; *MS* 3.11.2; *AV* 3.127; 20.127.9; *ŚB* 5.1.2.14). It was prepared either from flowers or by fermenting certain grasses (*AV* 20.127.8-9), while *kīlāla* was a sweet drink prepared from cereals (*AV* 4.11.10; 6.69.1; 10.6.25; 12.1.59; *TB* 2.6; 2.12; 2.13; *MS* 2.7.12; 3.11.3.4). The preparation of another drink, *māsara*, is also described in various texts (*MS* 3.11.2.9; *VS* 19.14.82, 20.68; *TB* 2.6.11.4; *KŚS* 19.1.20.21). It was prepared with a mixture of a mess of rice and some spices (including *śyāmāka* and barley) which was allowed to ferment for three days. The beverage was purified with the help of a filter. Water is described as nectar (*amṛta*) and a remedy (*bheṣaja*) (*RV* 10.101.7; *KB* 12.1; *TB* 1.7.6.3; *BU* 7.10.1). The main sources of water were rivers, wells, springs. Rain water was also used for drinking (*AV* 19.2.1-5; *ŚB* 5.3.4.22). For milk and its various preparations see **Dairy Products**.

**Bhakti:** The concept of *bhakti*, or devotion, was not entirely unknown in Vedic times. The germ of this doctrine is found particularly in connection with the god Varuṇa. Most of the deities in the age of the later Saṃhitās and Brāhmaṇas were subordinated to Yajña, or ritual, the latter being regarded as the highest cosmic principle. In contrast to them stands out the figure of the terrific Rudra whose worship was probably outside the all-embracing net of Yajña rituals. The same remark applies with some modifications to the case of god Viṣṇu. In the cults of Rudra-Śiva and Viṣṇu was the earliest beginning of that doctrine of *bhakti*, or single-minded devotion to a specific object of worship, which is in evidence, in no small measure, in the later Upaniṣads and, in particular, the Epics. The word 'bhakti' implies a passionate yearning of the soul, tormented by the woes and worries of worldly life (saṃsāra), to fly beyond the present and seek rest and solace in rapt contemplation and communion with some Power above. It is impossible to read some of the soul-stirring Vedic hymns to Varuṇa, Savitṛ, and Uṣas, and not feel therein the presence of true *bhakti*, however inadequate may have been its philosophical background. The merit of *bhakti* as a popular, philosophical religion consists in just this that it needs no metaphysical preparation in its devotees. Whether this *bhakti* in its earliest stages had started as hero-worship, as a sort of a deification of the spirit of some great ancestor or tribal chieftain, may very well be debated. The Upaniṣadic passage that has a bearing on the question is the Śāṇḍilya-Vidyā (*CU* 3.14; cf. *ŚB* 10.6.3.2.), where the yearning of the individual to attain the Absolute finds the most philosophically passionate expression besides other passages (like *KU* 1.2.20; 1.2.22; *ŚvetU* 1.3.6; *CU* 5.11.-24). At *BU* 3.7 there is a glorious description of the in-dwelling Lord or Antaryāmin; *BU* 3.8 is an equally famous description of the Immutable Lord or Akṣara who gives the Law to the universe; and at *KU* 2.2.12; *BU* 4.4.22; and *ŚvetU* 5 and 6, is the most pronounced expression of theism and devotionalism that we get in any Upaniṣadic passage. We have the two famous middle *adhyāyas*, 3 and 4 of the *Śvetāśvatara* where the Lord is described as 'The all-creating, omniform guardian of the universe, beyond whom there is nothing higher or subtler; the one immutable and beneficient Puruṣa who dwells within the hearts of all beings and controls their activities also dispensing up to them rewards and punishments according to their *karman*; and the unconcerned seer and master of Nature (*pradhāna*) and of individual souls (*kṣetrajña*), who has sent forth the Vedas, being endowed with supreme cosmogonic power, and yet, in reality, action-less and absolute and perfect. His saving grace somehow leading the believing devotees to rectitude, sinlessness and salvation.' Belvalkar and Ranade, 78-79, 404-11.

**Bhalānas:** Bhalānas, plural, is the name (*RV* 7.18.7) of one of the five tribes—Pakthas, Bhalānases, Alinas, Viṣāṇins, and Śivas—who are mentioned as ranged on the side of the enemies of Sudās in the battle of the ten kings (Dāśarājña). Their original home seems to be the Afghan border. Macdonell and Keith, II.99.

**Bharata:** Name of a people of great importance in the *Ṛgveda* and in the later literature. In the *Ṛgveda* they appear prominently in third and seventh Maṇḍalas in connexion with Sudās and the Tṛtsus (3.53.9; 12.24, 33, 11.12, 7.8.4, 33.6), while in the sixth Maṇḍala they are associated with Divodāsa (6.16.4.5). In one passage (7.8.4) the Bharatas are, like the Tṛtsus, enemies of the Purus. They appear to be the kinsmen of the Tṛtsus. The Bharatas occupied the region watered by the Sarasvatī, Āpayā and Dṛṣadvatī. The geographical position of the Bharatas is clearly shown by the fact that the Bharata kings won victories over the Kāśīs and made offerings on the Yamunā and the Gaṅgā (*ŚB* 13.5.4.11, 21). In the post-Ṛgvedic period they coalesced with their erstwhile enemies, the Purus, to form the Kuru people of later times. In the later literature the Bharatas appear as especially famous. As a King Bharata Dauhṣanti is mentioned as a sacrificer of the Aśvamedha, the horse sacrifice, (*ŚB* 13.5.4) and Śatānīka Satrājita, another Bharata who offered that sacrifice. The *Aitareya Brāhmaṇa* (8.23) mentions Bharata Dauhṣanti as receiving the kingly coronation from Dīrghatamas Māmateya and Śatānīka as being consecrated by Somaśuṣman Vājaratnāyana, a priest whose name is of much later origin. Moreover, in the formula of the king's proclamation for the people, the variants recorded (*TS* 1.8.10.2; *TB* 1.7.4.2; *VS* 1.3.3; *KS* 15.7; *MS* 2.6.7) include Kuravaḥ, Pañcālāḥ, Kuru-Pañcālāḥ and Bharatāḥ; and the *Mahābhārata* consistently recognizes the royal family of the Kurus as a Bharata family. It is therefore extremely probable that the Bharatas in the times of the Brāhmaṇas were merging in the Kuru-Pañcāla people. The ritual practices of the Bharatas are repeatedly mentioned (*PB* 14.4.13, 15.5.24; *AB* 2.25, 3.18; *ŚB* 5.4.4.1 and *TĀ* 1.17.2). Already (in the *RV* 2.7.1, 5, 4.25.4, 6.16.19; *TS* 2.5.9; *ŚB* 1.4.2.2) there is mention made of Agni Bharata ('of the Bharatas'). In the Āprī hymns (*RV* 1.22.10, 1.142.9, 2.1.11, 3.4.8, etc.) there occurs a goddess Bhāratī, the personified divine protective power of the Bharatas : her association in the hymns with Sarasvatī reflects the connexion of the Bharatas with the Sarasvatī in the *Ṛgveda* (3.23.4). Again, (in the *ŚB* 1.4.2.2), Agni is referred to as *brāhmaṇa Bharata*, 'priest of the Bharatas', and is invited to dispose of the offering *Manuṣvat Bharatavat*, 'like Manu', 'like Bharata' (1.5.1.7). Macdonell and Keith II. 94-7.

**Bhāratī:** Frequently invited to the sacrifices along with several other goddesses. 'Let Hotrā pure, sit among gods, amid the Maruts Bhāratī, Ilā, Sarasvatī, Mahī, rest on the grass adorable' (*RV* 1.142.9). 'You, I address, Sarasvatī, and Bhāratī and Ilā all : urge ye us on the glorious fame' (*RV* 1.188.8). 'May Bhāratī with all her sisters, Ilā accordant with the gods, with mortal Agni, Sarasvatī with all her kindered rivers, come to this grass' (*RV* 3.4.8). 'This, Pavamāna's sacrifice, shall the three beauteous goddesses Sarasvatī and Bhāratī and Ilā, mightly ones, attend' (*RV* 9.5.8). 'Let Bhāratī come quickly to our worship, and Ilā showing like a human being. So let Sarasvatī and both her fellows, deft goddesses, on this fair grass be seated' (*RV* 10.110.8). Muir, 339.

**Bhṛgu:** A name occurs twenty-one times in the *Ṛgveda* Mātariśvan brought Agni as a treasure to Bhṛgu (1.60.1) or kindled the hidden Agni for the Bhṛgus (3.5.10). Mātariśvan and the gods fashioned Agni for Manu, while the Bhṛgus with might produced him (10.46.9). The Bhṛgus found Agni lurking in the waters (10.46.2); worshipping him in the waters, they placed him in the abodes of Āyu or men (2.4.2). Sacrificers speak of them together with the Aṅgirases and Atharvans, as their Soma-loving fathers (10.14.6) and invoke Agni as the Bhṛgus (*bhṛguvat*), the Aṅgirases, and Manu did (8.43.13). The Bhṛgus are invoked to drink Soma with all the thirty-three gods, the Maruts, the Waters, the Aśvins, Uṣas, and Sūrya (8.35.3). They are compared with the sun and said to have gained all their desires (8.3.16). In the later Vedic literature Bhṛgu occurs as the name of a seer representing a tribe (*AV* 5.19.1; *AB* 2.20.7). He arises as a spark from Prajāpati's seed and being adopted by Vāruṇi (*AB* 3.34.1; cf. *PB* 1.9.1) is expressly called a son of Varuṇa (*ŚB* 11.6.1.1).

**Bhujyu:** Son of Tugra who is repeatedly mentioned in the *Ṛgveda* as having been saved from drowning in the deep sea by the Aśvins (*RV* 1.112.6.20; 1.116.3; 1.117.14; 1.119.4; 6.62.6; 7.68.7; 7.69.7; 10.40.7; 10.65.12; 10.143.5).

**Bhujyu Lāhyāyanī:** Name of a teacher who was a contemporary of Yājñavalkya. The psychical queries of Bhujyu occur in *Bṛhadāraṇyaka Upaniṣad* (3.3). He told Yājñavalkya that once, while he was touring, he had gone to the house of one Patañcala Kāpya, and found that his daughter was possessed by a Gandharva. Bhujyu asked this Gandharva a very peculiar question : 'Where had the Pārikṣitas gone after their mortal existence?' This question was sufficient to test the omniscience of the Gandharva. 'I ask you the same question', said Bhujyu to Yājñavalkya. 'Can you tell me where the Pārīkṣitas had gone?' The answer which Yājñavalkya gave was that the Pārikṣītas had gone to the place where all the Aśvamedha sacrificers went.

**Bīja:** In the Vedas *bīja* has been used in three different senses. Firstly, as the seed of corn, the main sustainer of life, which serves a healthy prolongation of it. In the above sense it is nothing but food (*anna*). But in another sense it is semen (*retas*) signifying the fertilizing fluid of a male animal or the female germ capable of developing into a new individual when fertilized by male sperm. In the third sense it signifies the primary cause (*kāraṇa*) or every effect (*kārya*). In the Upaniṣads and the *Bhagavadgītā* the idea of *bīja* as germ, semen, and cause is emphasized. The concept of *bīja* has passed through different levels of ideas. The basic idea of *bīja* as the seed of corn was known to the Vedic peoples. The Maruts are invoked to bestow seed of corns (*RV* 5.53.13). *Bīja* (in *AV* 3.14.4) is desired in the form of semen capable of producing valiant sons. In the Vedas *bīja* has both a physical and symbolical meaning. To the Vedic seers the sacrificial altar, oblation, and Soma have symbolical significance. Soma is considered to represent semen, because it is liquid and consists of living energy : *iyaṃ vediḥ para antaḥ*, etc. (*RV* 1.164.35). 'This altar (*vedi*) is the farthest limit of *vāk*. This *yajña* is the centre of the universe. Soma is the profile seed of the fecunding Horse. Brahmā priest is the highest heaven of *vāk*' (Tr. Griffith). Coming back to the physical meaning, the husband enters the wife in the shape of the seed. 'The seed which is placed in her (wife), she develops to a being and sets it forth' (*AB* 7.13.10 Tr. Martin Haug). The *Aitareya Āraṇyaka* (2.5.1) extract shows how *bīja* or *retas* are formed and developed in the body. 'In man he is from the first as a germ. The seed is strength gathered from all the limbs and he thus bears a self in his self. When he connects the seed to the woman, then he causes it to be born.' (Tr. A.B. Keith). Vatsyayan I. 117.20.

**Bindu:** *Bindu* literally mens a drop, or a point. In (*AV* 19.30.5) it is a detached particle, drop, globule, dot, spot, a pearl, a symbol representing the *anusvara*, a coloured mark made on the forehead between the eyebrows, and so forth. In drama, it is the sudden development of a secondary incident which like a drop of water expands and furnishes an important element. In the Veda *bindu* is related to *indu*, the drop, spark and also the moon. The Vedic synonym for *bindu* is *drapsa*. It also figuratively means *śukra*, semen, according to the *Nirukta* (5.14). In the *Ṛgveda* (9.69.2) the word *drapsa* has been used in the meaning of a drop of *Soma* juice, or of *pavamāna soma* rich in sweet juice. *Drapsa* or *indu*, meaning the moon, is well known. (cf. *RV* 7.87.1). In the *Atharvaveda* the word *bindu* occurs meaning drop of water. It is described as all refreshing and golden coming with the roaring of Parjanya (*AV* 19.30.5). *Bindu* as the moon, located on the summit of the head, which in later Tantric and Buddhist tradition has been given much importance, may have been hinted at (*AV* 10.10.19) when it is said to have been produced from the head of Brahmā. In support of the above view it may be stated that *bindu* as the absolute is the moon which melts in the summit of the head and flows through the body and finally pervades the whole body with bliss. The image of *bindu* as the moon is very significant, for some scholars are of the opinion that *bindu* has its origin in *indu*, the moon. *Ātman,* the self or more precisely self-consciousness, is the essence of existence, the nectar (*amṛta*), which shines like a drop of water on the lotus leaf (*MU* 3.2. Tr. R.E. Hume). Vatsyayan II.1-2. 5-6.

**Biology:** See **Botany, Physiology and Zoology**.

**Biped:** *Dvipad* denotes a man as two-footed as opposed to quadrupeds (*RV* 1.49.3; 3.62.14; 8.27.12; 10.97.20; 10.117.8; *AV* 2.34.1; 10.1.24; *VS* 8.30; 14.8; 9.31; 13.17; etc.).

**Birds:** Among the birds the Vedic texts specify four species as aquatic—*Ali*, *Plava*, *Madgu* and *Haṃsa*. The Apsarases in the legend of Purūravas and Urvaśī appear to him like Ātis, probably swans (*RV* 10.95.9; cf. *ŚB* 10.95.9; cf. *ŚB* 11.5.1.4). Birds also appear in the list of animals in the horse sacrifice (*TS* 5.5.13.1; *MS* 3.14.18; *VS* 24.34). Mahīdhara renders them as Ādi (*turdus ginginianus*), and Sāyaṇa quotes a view, according to which the Āti was the Cāsa, or blue jay (*coracias indica*). Plava is the name of an aquatic bird mentioned in the list of victims at the horse sacrifice in the *Yajurveda Saṃhitā* (*TS* 5.5.20.1; *MS* 3.14.15; *VS* 24.34) by which perhaps the 'pelican' is meant. Madgu 'diver' (from the root *majj*, 'diver'), is the name of some aquatic bird which is included in the list of the *Yajurveda Saṃhitās* (*TS* 5.5.20.1; *MS* 3.14.3; *VS* 24.22.34) and is occasionally mentioned elsewhere (*CU* 4.8.1.2). Haṃsa in the *Ṛgveda* (1.65.5, 1.63.10, 2.34.5, 3.8.9) and later (*AV* 6.12.1) denotes the 'gander'. These birds are described as dark in colour on the back (*nīlapṛṣtha*) (*RV* 7.59.7), they fly in troops (*RV* 3.8.9), swim in the water (*uda-prut*) (*RV* 1.6.5.5; 3.45.4), make loud noises (*RV* 3.53.10), and are wakeful at night (*AV* 6.12.1). The *haṃsa* is credited with the power of separating Soma from water (and later milk from water) in the *Yajurveda Saṃhitās* (*KS* 38.1; *MS* 3.11.6; *VS* 19.74; *TB* 2.6.1). It is also mentioned as one of the victims at the horse sacrifice. Among the carnivorous birds we have *Gṛdhra*, *Balāka*, *Syena*, *Saghan*, *Suparṇa*, etc. *Gṛdhra*, the vulture, is often mentioned (*RV* 1.118.4, 2.39.1, 7.104.22, 10.123.8) and in later texts (*AV* 7.951, 11.2.3, 11.9.9, 11.9.10, 11.8.24; *TS* 4.4.7.1, 5.5.20.1; *MS* 4.9.19; *TA* 4.29). The swiftness of its flight (*RV* 2.39.1) and its habit of devouring carrion are especially noticed (*AV* 11.10.8.24; *MS* 4.19.19). More generally the word is used to designate any bird of prey, the eagle (*śyena*) being classed at the chief of the *Gṛdhras* (*RV* 9.96.6). *Balākā* (crane) is mentioned in the list of victims at the horse sacrifice in the *Yajurveda Saṃhitās* (*TS* 5.5.16.1; *MS* 3.14.3.14; *VS* 24.22.23). In the *Ṛgveda* (1.32.14, 1.33.2, 1.118.11, 1.165.2) *Śyena* is the name of a strong bird of prey, most probably the eagle; later (*AV* 3.3.4, 7.41.2, 11.9.9), as in post-Vedic Sanskrit, it seems to mean the falcon or hawk. It is the swiftest of birds (*TS* 2.4.7) and a source of terror for smaller birds (*RV* 2.42.2; *AV* 5.21.6). It is the strongest of birds (*KS* 37.14), and even attacks herds (*RV* 4.38.5). It watches (*nṛ-cakṣas*) over men (*AV* 7.41.2), a reference, no doubt, to its lofty flight in the air. It brings Soma from heaven. *Saghan* is the name of a bird, perhaps eagle or vulture, in the *Ṛgveda* (1.164.20; 2.42.2; 4.26.4; 8.100.8; 9.48.3) and later (*AV* 1.24.1, 2.27.2; 2.30.3; 4.6.3; *TS* 7.5.8.5). In the passages in which it appears as an eater of carrion (*MS* 4.9.10; *TS* 4.29) must be the vulture. The *Jaiminīya Brāhmaṇa* (2.438) mentions an eagle which separates milk from water like the *Kruñc*. In the *Ṛgveda* (10.144.4) the *Suparṇa* is said to be the child of the *Śyena*, but is distinguished from the latter in another passage (*RV* 2.42.2). The *Atharvaveda* alludes to its cry (2.30.3) and describes it as living in the hills (5.4.2). Among other birds we have *Aliklava*, *Ulūka*, *Kapiñjala*, *Kapota*, *Kruñc*, *Khargalā*, *Cakravāka*, *Cāṣa*, *Darvidā*, *Dātyauha*, *Dārvāghāta*, *Dhvāṅkṣa*, *Pakṣin*, *Patatrin*, *Pārāvata*, *Pika*, *Bhāsa*, *Mahāsuparṇa*, *Ropaṇākā*, *Laba*, *Varttikā*, *Vi*, *Śakuna*, *Śakuni*, *Śakunta*, *Śakuntaka*, *Sakuntikā*, *Śakunti*, *Haridrava*, etc. *Aliklava* is a kind of carrion bird (*AV* 11.2.2; 11.9.9). Ulūka is the common word for owl from the *Ṛgveda* (10.165.4) onwards. The bird was noted for its cry (*RV* 10.165.4) and was deemed the harbinger of ill fortune (*nairṛta*)—(*AV* 6.19.2; *TS* 5.5.18.1; *VS* 24.38). Owls were offered at the horse sacrifice to the forest trees (*VS* 24.23; *MS* 3.14.4), no doubt because they roosted there. *Kapiñjala*, the name of the *francoline partridge* or hazelcock, is found in all the *Yajurveda Saṃhitās* (*TS* 2.5.1.1; 5.3.16.1; *MS* 3.14.1; *KS* 12.10; *VS* 24.20.38) and occasionally later (*ŚB* 1.6.3.3; 5.5.4.4; 13.5.1.13; *JB* 1.154.2). *Kapota* is the name of a bird, probably the pigeon (its sense in the later language), occurring from the *Ṛgveda* onwards (*RV* 1.30.4; *AV* 20.135.13; *MS* 3.14.4; *VS* 24.23.30); it is associated in some passages (*RV* 10.165.1-5; *AV* 6.29.2) with the owl (*Ulūka*) as a messenger of *nirṛti* (dissolution, misfortune). This aspect of the pigeon as a bird of evil omen is probably based on an ancient belief which is also found beyond the confines of India. *Kalaviṅka*, a name of the sparrow, is found in the *Yajurveda Saṃhitās* (*TS* 2.5.1.2; *MS* 3.14.1; *KS* 12.10; *VS* 24.20.31) and occasionally later (*ŚB* 1.6.3.4; 5.5.4.5; *JB* 2.154.3). *Kikidīvi* denotes perhaps the blue jay (*RV* 10.97.13). According to the commentator, it means 'partridge' (*tittiri*) in the (*TS* 5.6.22.1). *Kukkuṭa*, cock, occurs in the *VS* (1.16) only. *Kutaru*, according to the commentator Mahīdhara (*VS* 24.23), is synonymous with *Kukkuṭa*, cock. The word is found only in the *Yajurveda Saṃhitās* (*TS* 5.5.17.1; *MS* 1.1.6; 3.14.4; 3.14.20; 4.1.6; *VS* 24.23.39). *Kuṣītaka* denotes, according to the commentary on the one passage of the *TS* (5.5.13.1) in which it is found, the sea-crow (*samudrakāka*). *Kṛkavāku*, the cock, named in the *Atharvaveda* (5.31.2) with sheep, goats and other domesticated animals, was presumably tamed (*TS* 5.5.18.1). In the list of victims at the horse sacrifice (*TS* 5.5.18.1; *MS* 3.14.15; *VS* 24.35), it appears as dedicated to Savitṛ. Yāska (*Nirukta* 12.3) explains this by the fact that it declares the time of day (*kālānuvāda*). The commentator Mahīdhara explains the name by *Tāmra-cūḍa*, re-crested. It is of course onomatopoeic (calling *kṛka*). *Kruñc*, as the name of a mountain-bird, occurs only in the latest Vedic literature (*TA* 1.31.1). *Khargalā* is an owl or other nocturnal bird mentioned in one passage of the *Ṛgveda* (7.104.17). *Cakravāka* is the name, apparently derived from the nature of its cry, of a species of gander (*anascasarca*), the modern *chakua* as it is called in Hindi, or Brahmany duck in English. It is mentioned in the *Ṛgveda* (2.39.3) and in the list of victims at the Aśvamedha, or horse sacrifice, (*MS* 3.14.3.13; *VS* 24.22; 24.32; 25.8) while in the *AV* (14.2.64) it already appears as a symbol of conjugal fidelity, its characteristic in the classical literature. *Cāṣa*, the blue woodpecker (*coracies indica*) is mentioned in the *Ṛgveda* (10.97.13), as well as in the list of victims at the Aśvamedha or horse sacrifice (*MS* 3.14.4; 3.15.9; *VS* 24.23; 25.7), as are *Darvidā*, the woodpecker, (*TS* 5.5.13.1; *MS* 3.14.15; *VS* 24.3); *Dātyauhā*—the word is clearly a variant of *dātyūha*, which occurs in the epics and law books—a gallinule, (*TS* 5.5.17.1; *MS* 3.14.6; *VS* 24.25; 24.39); and *Dārvāghāta*, the woodpecker, (*TS* 5.5.15.1; *MS* 3.14.15; *VS* 3.14.16; *VS* 24.35). *Dhvāṅkṣa*, crow, is mentioned twice in the *Atharvaveda* (11.9.9; 12.48) and once in the Sūtras (*KŚS* 25.6.9). Possibly the same bird is meant by words *Dhuṅkṣā* and *Dhūṅkṣnā*. *Pakṣin* in the *Ṛgveda* (1.48.5; 1.182.5; 10.127.5) and later (*AV* 4.34.4; 11.5.21; 12.1.51; 13.2.33; *KS* 34.8; *AB* 4.23; *BU* 2.5.18) denotes a winged creature, more particularly a bird, while *Patatrin* denotes a flying creature generally in the *Atharvaveda* (3.3.3) or specifically a bird (8.7.24; 10.10.14; 14.2.44). *Pārāvata* occurs in several passages of the *Ṛgveda*. In most places (*RV* 5.62.11; 8.100.6; *AV* 20.135.14) it means coming from a distance but in two passages (*RV* 8.34.18; *PB* 9.4.11) it is regarded as the proper name of a people on the Yamunā. The mention of the Sarasvatī in connection with the *Pārāvatas* in the *Ṛgveda* accords generally with their position on the Yamunā. But *Pārāvata* as the name of a people is clearly suggestive of a totemic name associated with some kinds of pigeons. *Pīka*, the Indian Cuckoo, is mentioned in the list of victims at the Aśvamedha (*TS*

5.5.15.1; *MS* 3.14.20; *VS* 24.39). *Mahāsuparṇa* (*ŚB* 12.2.3.7) denotes a great bird or large eagle. *Ropanaka* is the name of a bird (*RV* 1.50.12); *AV* 1.22.4; *TB* 3.7.6.22) possibly meaning the thrush but Keśava, the commentator on the *Kauśika Sūtra* is inclined to understand the word to mean a sort of wood (26.20). *Laba*, quail (*perdix chinensis*) is one of the victims at the Aśvamedha. *Varttikā* a quail, is mentioned in the *Ṛgveda* (1.112.18; 1.116.4; 1.117.16; 1.118.3; 10.39.13) as having been saved by the Aśvins from the jaws of a wolf. It is also included in the list of victims at the Aśvamedha (*TS* 5.5.11.1; *VS* 24.20; 24.30; *MS* 3.14.1). *Vi* in the *Ṛgveda* (2.29.5; 2.38.7; 6.64.6) and sometimes later (*PB* 5.6.15) denotes any kind of bird. *Śakuna* is mentioned frequently (*RV* 4.26.6; 9.85.11; 9.86.13; 9.107.20; 9.112.2; 10.68.7; 10.106.3; 10.123.6; 10.165.2 and later in *AV* 12.1.51; 12.3.13; 20.127.4; *TS* 3.2.62; *VS* 18.5.3), usually denoting a large bird (*AV* 11.2.24) or a bird which gives omens (*KB* 7.4; *MU* 6.34). *Śakuni* is the same as *Śakuna*, but with a much clearer reference to divination. It was smaller than the *Śyena* or *Suparṇa* (*RV* 2.42.2), gave signs (*RV* 2.42.1; 2.43.3) and foretold ill-luck (*AV* 10.3.6). When it is mentioned (*TS* 5.5.19.1; *VS* 24.40; *MS* 3.14.21) in the list of sacrificial victims at the Aśvamedha, a special species must be meant. Later the falcon is so called, but the raven may be intended; the commentator of the *Taittirītya Saṃhitā* thinks that it is the crow. It is mentioned several times elsewhere (*AV* 2.25.2; 7.64.1; 11.9.9; *KS* 25.7; *AB* 2.15.12; 4.7.3; *ŚB* 14.1.1.31; *CU* 6.8.2). *Śakunta* is a name for 'bird' in the *Atharvaveda* (11.6.8). *Śakuntaka* (*RV* 2.43; *VS* 23.23), *Śakuntikā* (*RV* 1.191.1; *VS* 23.22) are diminutives, meaning 'little bird' in the Saṃhitās. Śakunti is found in the *Ṛgveda* (2.42.3; 2.43.1) denoting a 'bird' of omen. *Harīdrava* is the name of the yellow bird in the *Ṛgveda* (1.50.12; 8.15.7), perhaps the yellow water-wagtail (Sāyaṇa on *RV* 1.50.12; *TB* 3.7.6.2). Among the unidentified birds we have *alaja, kakara, kaṅka, kālakā, kuvaya, kaulīka, goṣādī, ciccika, dhuṅkṣā, dhūṅkṣṇā, pāruṣṇa, pippakā, pulikā, puṣkarasāda, paiṅgarāja, raghat, lopā, vayas, vāyasa*, (crow), *vikakara, vidīgaya, śayāṇḍaka, sāri, śārya, śuśulūka, sicāpū, haṃsasāci*, etc. *Alaja* designates some kind of bird—one of the victims in the Aśvamedha (*TS* 5.4.11.1, 5.20.1; *MS* 3.14.18; *KS* 16.4; *VS* 24.34). *Kakara* occurs in the *Yajurveda Saṃhitās* (*MS* 3.14.1; *VS* 20.24). It probably denotes some 'sort of bird', as rendered by the commentator Mahīdhara. *Kaṅka* is the name of a bird, usually taken to mean 'heron', but at any rate in some passages, rather denoting some bird of prey. It first appears in the *Yajurveda Saṃhitās* (*TS* 5.4.11.1; *VS* 24.31; *MS* 3.14.12; *SV* 2.9.3, 6.1). *Kalaka* is the name of one of the victims at the horse sacrifice (*TS* 5.5.15.1; *MS* 3.14.16; *VS* 24.35) variously identified with a bird or a chameleon. *Kulika* is the name of a bird mentioned in the list of victims at the horse sacrifice in the *Vājasaneyī Saṃhitā* (24.24). The *Maitrāyaṇī Saṃhitā* (3.14.5) has *Pulika* instead. *Pulika* seems to designate some kind of bird in the *Maitrāyaṇī Saṃhitā* (3.14.5). The name appears in the form of *Kulika* in the *Vājasaneyī Saṃhitā* (24.24). *Kuvaya* is the name of some species of bird (*TS* 5.5.17; *VS* 24.29), occurring in the list of victims at the Aśvamedha. The form in the *Maitrāyaṇī Saṃhitā* (3.14.18) is *Kuvaya*. *Kaulika*, like *Kulika*, is the name of some sort of bird in the list of victims at the Aśvamedha (*VS* 24.24; *MS* 3.14.5). *Goṣādī* ('sitting on a cow') is the name of a bird in the list of victims at the Aśvamedha. *Ciccika* is a bird mentioned with the equally unknown *Vṛṣarava* in one hymn of the *Ṛgveda* (10.146.2). It may perhaps be compared with the *Citaka* mentioned by Darila in his commentary on the *Kauśika Sūtra* (24.20). *Dhuṅkṣā* is the name of some sort of bird in the list of victims at the Aśvamedha (*MS* 3.14.12; *VS* 24.31). *Dhuṅkṣṇā* is the form in the *Taittirīya Saṃhitā* (5.5.19.1). It is glossed as 'white crow' (*śveta-kākī*) *Paruṣṇā*, occurring in the list of victims at the Aśvamedha (*MS* 3.14.4; *VS* 24.24) appears to mean some kind of bird. *Pippaka* is mentioned in the list of victims at the Aśvamedha (*TS* 5.5.19.1; *MS* 3.14.2; *VS* 24.40). *Putikā* seems to designate some kind of bird in the *Maitrāyaṇī Saṃhitā* (3.14.5). The name appears in the form of *Kulika* in the *Vājasaneyī Saṃhitā* (24.24). *Puṣkara sāda* 'sitting on the lotus', is the name of an animal in the list of victims at the Aśvamedha (*TS* 5.5.14.1; *MS* 3.14.12; *VS* 24.31). It can be a 'bird' or perhaps according to the commentator on the *Taittirīya Saṃhitā*, a 'bee'. *Paiṅga rāja* is the name of one of the victims at the Aśvamedha (*TS* 5.5.13.1; *MS* 3.14.16; *VS* 24.34). That a bird is meant is certain, but what particular kind is quite unknown. *Raghat* occurs once in the plural in the *Atharvaveda* (8.7.24), where the Paippalāda recension reads *Vaghataḥ*. *Lopā* is mentioned in the list of victims at the Aśvamedha (*TS* 5.5.18.11), where Sāyaṇa explains it as a king of bird, perhaps the carrion crow (*śmaśānaśakum*). *Vayas* denotes in the *Atharvaveda* (12.3.1) and later (*KS* 11.2; *TB* 3.12.5.9; *ŚB* 3.1.2.21, 3.3.3. etc.) the 'age' of animals or men. *Vāyasa* in the *Ṛgveda* (1.164.32) and later (*Nirukta* 4.17) denotes a 'large bird'. The sense of 'crow' occurs in the *Ṣaḍviṃśa Brāhmaṇa* (6.8) only. *Vikakara* is the name of some bird, a victim of the Aśvamedha (*VS* 24.20; *ĀŚS* 20.14.5). *Vidīgava* is the name of an animal in the *Taittirīya Saṃhitā* (5.6.22.1) and the *Taittirīya Brāhmaṇa* (29.9.3; *ĀŚS* 20.22.13). The commentary on the former takes it as a kind of cock (*kukkuṭa-viśeṣa*), that on the latter as a white heron (*śveta-baka*). *Śavaṇḍaka* is found in the *Taittirīya Saṃhitā* (5.5.14.1) as the name of an animal which in the *Maitrāyaṇī Saṃhitā* (3.14.14) and *Vājasaneyī Saṃhitā* (24.33) is written as *Sayaṇḍaka*. The commentator on the *Taittirīya Saṃhitā* equates the word with *Kṛkalāsa*, 'chameleon'. *Sāri* occurs in the list of victims at the Aśvamedha (*TS* 5.5.12.1; *MS* 3.14.14; *VS* 24.33). It seems clear since it is described as 'of human speech' (*puruṣa-vāc*), that it was some kind of bird, possibly the later *Sārikā* ('starling') *Sārisaka* is an utterly obscure expression found in one passage of the *Atharvaveda* (3.14.5). Its identity is unknown. Macdonell and Keith, I. 38, 130, 132, 152, 172; II. 193, 196-97, 200, 233, 240, 243, 261, 287, 294, 297, 356, 373-74, 401-02, 451, 498, 521, 537.

**Birth Ceremonies:** As is natural the domestic ritual devotes much space to the minute description of large number of rites, mainly magical in essence which accompany the child from even before birth to its death. In the third or fourth month or even later after pregnancy takes place the rite for quickening a male child, Puṃsavana, the essence of which consists in the placing in the nostril of the wife by her husband of a Nyagrodha shoot, which is pounded, either by a young girl, or a student or a wife who is keeping a vow, or a Brahmabandhu, a term which is perhaps best taken as a Brāhmaṇa by birth only, not by learning. A further rite is that to prevent an abortion, or more generally to secure the safety of the embryo, which is accomplished by offering a cooked mess, and rubbing butter on the limbs of the wife. The ceremony of the parting of the hair is performed once only during the pregnancy, and is not repeated: it is celebrated in the fourth month or later. The wife sits west of the fire, her husband puts round her neck an *udumbara* branch with an even number of unripe fruits; he parts her hair from the front backwards with *darbha* grass, *virātara* ('very male') wood, a full spindle, and a porcupine's quill; he also makes her look at the mess of rice, sesame, and *ghee*, and asks her to see in it offspring. Some authorities allow two lute players to sing in the occasion. One special Gāthā is prescribed which should end with the name of the stream on which the people dwell, and one or two such verses have been preserved to us. Other authorities provide for Brāhmaṇa women siting beside her, and uttering phrases indicating that she is to be the mother of living children. Old Brāhmaṇa women are said also to be the authorities for the acts to be done in these cases. The wife should keep silence after the rite until the stars appear, when she should touch a calf, say the *vyāhṛtis, bhuḥ bhuvaḥ, svar*, and then speak. There are also ceremonies for the actual birth: the place is anointed against Rākṣasas : The priest loosens all the knots in the house, as in ceremony all doors and locks are opened; water and the *turvāntī* plant are placed before the mother. If the child dies in birth, special rites are ordered. When the child is born alive, a fire is lit in the house to warm utensils and be used for the child, which is by throwing into the fire gains of corn and hemp, with formulae to drive away demons of various kinds. For ten days the offering of sesame and rice grains is prescribed. On the twelfth day the special fire disappears, the old household fire comes out into use, the purification of the wife and child having been performed. Keith, II. 366-7.

**Blyxa Octandra:** *Avaka* is an aquatic plant (Blyxa octandra) frequently referred to in the *Atharvaveda* as well as in the later Saṃhitās. (*TS* 4.6.1.1; 5.4.2.1; 5.4.4.3; *VS* 17.4; 25.1; *MS* 2.10) and Brāhmaṇas (*ŚB* 7.5.1.11; 8.3.2.5; 9.1.2.201; 9.1.2.22; 13.8.3.13). The Gandharvas are said to eat it (*AV* 4.37.8). Its later name is *śaivāla*, and it is identical with the *śīpāla*). Śīpāla is found once in the *Atharvaveda* (6.12.3), where it may mean either a pool abounding in *śīpāla* plants or the proper name of a river or lake. Macdonell and Keith I. 39.

**Blanket:** The word *kambala* is referred to in the *Atharvaveda* (14.2.66.67) denoting a 'blanket' or 'woollen coverlet'.

**Boat:** The word *nau* is denoted to the meaning of ship or boat (*AV* 2.36.5; 5.19.8; *TS* 5.3.10.1; *VS* 10.19; *AB* 4.13; 6.6; *ŚB* 1.8.1.4; *JB* 1.332, 1.166). Another word *sutarmānau* is mentioned in the *Aitareya Brāhmaṇa* (1.3.1). *Sairāvati* is the word which means a particular kind of vessel wherewith one can cross the sea is found in the *Aitareya Brāhmaṇa* (6.29.1), and in the *Jaiminīya Brāhmaṇa* (2.421; 3.269) it is mentioned that the father and son crossing the stream by means of boat. *Plava* signifies boat in the *Ṛgveda* (1.182.5), *Atharvaveda* (12.2.48), *Taittirītya Saṃhitā* (5.3.10.2, 7.3.5.2), the *Jaiminīya Brāhmaṇa* (2.422) and *Pañcaviṃśa Brāhmaṇa* (11.10.16). In the *Śatapatha Brāhmaṇa* (1.8.1) and the *Jaiminīya Brāhmaṇa* (1.165) there is a mythological story of great flood where mention of strong vessel is met with. This was used to keep Manu afloat in that vessel which sailed over the mighty waters of the illimitable fathomless deep ocean. The daily sacrifice known as Agnihotra is compared to a ship (*ŚB* 2.3.3.15). There is a reference to a golden boat in the *Jaiminīya Brāhmaṇa* (1.29). To reach the abode of Prajāpati the golden boat helps the worshippers who offered *svadhā* to gods. It is metaphorically explained. *Nāvāja* designates ship-propeller in the *Śatapatha Brāhmaṇa* (2.3.3.5).

**Body:** In the *Ṛgveda śarīra* is used for body in general. *Vapus* is used more frequently and Sāyaṇa has explained this word as *prakāśātmaka rūpa* (lustrous form) (cf. *RV* 1.102.2) or as just form (cf. *RV* 1.1.8). The word *deha* has not been directly used; its derivative *dehya* occurs twice (*RV* 6.47.2; 7.6.5). Besides other synonyms *aṅga* is used five times for a part of the body or of *yajña* (cf. Sāyaṇa on 10.109.5). *Tanu* is used eight times and is sometimes interpreted by Sāyaṇa as body (cf. *RV* 4.10.6) *Tanukṛt* (*RV* 1.31.9) is interpretated as the maker of the body. *Tanu* is also used for denoting limbs of the body. Apart from the general meaning of *śarīra*, viz., body and sometimes its parts in plural number (cf. *RV* 6.25.4; 10.16.3 for the latter) in the context of divine entities like Indra, Savitṛ, Agni, Vāyu, etc., the *Ṛgveda* (10.136.3) contains reference to *śarīra* as a material entity. The 'golden hand' of Savitṛ and numerous similar allusions ascribe 'divinity of the body' and divine manifestations such as Indra, Savitṛ, Vāyu, etc. Thus the *Ṛgveda* uses the word *śarīra* in general, *vapus* with the association of lustre and beauty of the body, *varṣman* in the sense of accumulation or aggregation and strength, *aṅga* for parts and *tanu* both for parts and the whole. The *Śatapatha Brāhmaṇa* speaks of *śarīra* as the repository of 'everything'. 'The *śarīra* is known as such because everything (mind, speech, vital force organs, etc.) rests in it.' (*ŚB* 6.1.1.4). The Upaniṣads generally use the word *śarīra* for the body; the *śarīra* is associated with mortality and the *ātman* is sometimes described as *aśarīra* (*CU* 8.12.1). The mortal or transient nature of *śarīra* is described: *bhasmāntaṃ śarīram* (*IU* 17). The earthly nature of the body is spoken of as *asya puruṣasya*, etc., in the *Bṛhadāraṇyaka Upaniṣad* 3.2.13. The speech of the dead man returns to the fire, his breath (returns) to air, his eyes to the sun, his mind to the moon, his ears to the directions (of space) and his body to the earth. . . . The body rests in *prāṇa* and the *prāṇas* are seated in the body (*TU* 3.7). *Śarīra* has been said to be *yajña*. "He desired : 'Let me sacrifice further with a greater sacrifice. He tortured himself. He practised austerity, glory and vigor went forth. The glory and vigor, verily, are the vital breaths. So when the vital breaths departed, his body began to swell. His mind, indeed, was in his body.' (*BU* 1.2.6) (Tr. Hume). The most famous metaphor for the body is that of the chariot (*ratha*) in *KU* 1.3.5. That the body is a 'veil' or 'envelope' of the soul, the *ātman*, the intelligent principle which acquires manifestation through the body, is the purport of the following passage. 'Not female nor yet male is it/Nor yet is this neutre (eunuch)/Whatever body he takes to himself./ With that he becomes connected.' (Tr. Hume, *ŚvU* 5.10). Vatsyayan I, 74-7.

**Booty:** *Udāja* is the word used in the *Maitrāyaṇī Saṃhitā* (1.10.16; 4.3) to denote the share of the booty of war taken by the king after a victory (*saṃgrāmaṇ jitvā*). This sense also suits *niraja*, the variant of both being found in the *Kāṭhaka* (28.3) and the *Kapiṣṭhala Saṃhitās* (44.3).

**Botany:** The Vedic literature contains a large number of terms used to describe plants and their parts, including their external features and internal structures. In numerous passages of the Vedic texts the structure and features of a tree have been compared to those of a human body which presupposes a rudimentary conception of plant anatomy. The Vedic people had also some knowledge of plant physiology as they were aware of the phenomenon of storage of energy in the body of plants, of the role played by light in the absorption of food by plants and of the nourishment of the plants drawn from manure (*karīṣa, śakṛt*). The idea of plant-pathology is found in the *Atharvaveda* (6.50) and Sāyaṇa's commentary on it gives a long list of the abnormal states in plants caused by extraneous factors. That the biological evolution was preceded by a geological and cosmic evolution is amply attested by such Upaniṣadic passages (*CU* 1.12; *BU* 6.4.1; *TU* 2.1; cf. *RV* 10.97.1) which state that from cosmic substrate were produced in succession ether, air, fire, water, earth and plants. In post-Vedic literature the science of botany was called Vṛkṣāyurveda, the knowledge of life of trees. See **Herbs**, **Plants**, **Trees**.

**Bow:** *Apaskamba, Apāṣṭha, Ārtni, Godhā, Jyā, Jyākā, Tisṛdhanvan, Dhanus, Dhanvan, Niṣaṅgathi, Paruṣa, Parṇa, Parṇadhi, Piṅgā, Pyukṣṇa, Bāṇa, Bāṇavant, Bunda, Śara, Śaravyā, Śaru, Śaryă Śāri, Śṛṅga, Sāyaka,* etc., are Vedic terms associated with the bow, its name, parts and functioning. The main weapon in the Vedic literature is the bow and arrow. Every knight of note is a distinguished archer, and the best bowmen invariably decided the fate of an armed engagement. The best beloved of a warrior's possession is bow or *dhanus* (*RV* 8.72.4, 8.77.11, 9.99.1, 10.125.6; *AV* 4.4.6, 5.18.8, 7.50.9; *VS* 16.10; *PB* 7.5.6; *AB* 7.14; *ŚB* 1.5.4.6, 5.3.1.11). The *Atharvaveda* (4.6.4) describes the curved shape of the bow as *vakra*. The bow-string (*jyā*) *RV* (4.27.3.; 6.75.3, 10.51.6; *AV* 1.1.3, 5.13.6; 7.42.1; *VS* 16.9, 29.51) was kept relaxed and strung up only when needed for shooting (*RV* 10.166.3; *AV* 6.42.1; *VS* 16.22) mentions the string of the bow, the playing of the arrow (*pratidhā*), the bending of the bow (*ā-yam*) and the shooting (*as*) of the shaft. As the string was drawn back to the ear, discharged from the ear, the arrow was called *karṇayoni* (*RV* 2.24.8), having the ear as its points of origin. The manufacture of bows was regular profession, as evidenced by the mention of the *dhanuskāra* (*VS* 30.7) and *dhanus-kṛt* (*VS* 16.46). *Jyākāras* (*VS* 30.7) specialised in the craft of making strings. The commonest word denoting arrow is *iṣu* (*RV* 2.24.8, 8.7.4; *AV* 1.13.4; *VS* 16.3; *Nirukta* 9.18), the other synonyms being *śaryă, śārī* and *bāṇa*. The *Ṛgveda* (6.75.15) mentions arrows with poisoned heads of horn which were distinct from other metal-headed arrow (*ayomukham*). There is mention of poisoned arrows in the *AV* (4.6, 5.18.8, 5.18.15) and the *Atharvaveda* (4.6.7, 4.6.8) indicated vegetation as the source of poison. The arrows were feathered in order to balance them in their flight (*RV* 6.75.11, 18.18.14; *AV* 5.25.1). The *Atharvaveda* specifies the parts of the arrow as the shaft (*śalya*), feather-socket (*praṇadhi*), the point (*śṛṅga*) the neck of the point to which the shaft is fixed (*kulmala*) and *apaṣkamba* and *apaṣṭha* are of dubious meaning (*AV* 4.6, cf. *AV* 3.25.2; *MS* 3.8.12). The *Aitareya Brāhmaṇa* (1.25) mentions an arrow's point (*anīka, śalya, tejana*) and feathers (*parṇāni*). *Śalya* and *tejana* here stand for the upper and lower parts of the shaft. The *Śatapatha Brāhmaṇa* (6.5.2.10) gives the length of an arrow as five spans or three feet which suggests a composite bow. The mention of *iṣu-kṛt* in *Vājasaneyī Saṃhitā* (16.46. cf. *RV* 1.184.3) and *iṣu-kāra* in *Vājasaneyī Saṃhitā* 30.7; *Taittirīya Brāhmaṇa* 3.4.3.1 shows that arrow-making had become a distinct profession early in the Vedic period. The word *jyā-kāra* means bow-maker. It denotes the maker of bowstrings (*VS* 30.7; *TB* 3.4.3.1) as one of the sacrificial victims of the human sacrifice. *Piṅgā* in the *Ṛgveda* (3.6.99) has the sense of bowstring according to Sāyaṇa. *Jyā, jyāka* is the regular word for 'bowstring' in the *RV* and later. *Jyāka* means 'bowstring' with a contemptuous sense in the *Ṛgveda* (10.133.1) and in the simple sense in the *Atharvaveda* (1.2.2). Some scholars think bowstring as barb which is again synonymous to words like *apāṣtha, śṛṅga*. The bowstring consisted of a thong of ox-hide. Macdonell and Keith, I. 25 ff, II 27ff.

**Brahman:** It is the all-pervasive reality in Indian religio-philosophical tradition. In the earlier Vedic texts the word *brahman* is used in various senses like prayer, priest, hymns, chants and ritual formulae, and also as the essence of cosmic phenomena which was identified with various deities including the older concept of Puruṣa (q.v.). *Atharvaveda* 4.6.1-2, *Taittirīya Saṃhitā* 7.3.1.4; *Taittirīya Brāhmaṇa* 2.2.1.4, 2.8.9.6 ff., *Śatapatha Brāhmaṇa* 2.1.4.10 ff, 3,1,4,15, etc. In the Upaniṣads, with the general enlargement and universalizing of the concept of *brahman*, not only everything in the universe is identified with it, but also it is correlated with the finite ego, the essence of the organic and mental functions of the human person, in other words with the individual self or soul (*ātman, BU* 1.2, 1.4; *MU* 6.17; *CU* 3.18; *AU* 1, etc.). In reply to Gārgī's question (*BU* 3.6) Yājñavalkya says, that this world is woven, warf and woof, on water; water on wind; wind on atmosphere; atmosphere on the world of the Gandharvas; the world of the Gandharvas on the sun; the sun on the moon; the moon on the stars; the stars on the world of Indra; the world of Indra on the world of Prajāpati; and the world of Prajāpati on the world of *brahman*. A passage of the same text (5.5.1), however, makes *brahman* an emanation from the primeval waters : 'In the beginning this world was just water. That water emitted the real, that is, *brahman,*' but elsewhere in the *Bṛhadāraṇyaka Upaniṣad, brahman* is described as self-existent (*svayambhū*). In the *Muṇḍaka Upaniṣad* (1.1.8) it is stated that by austerity *brahman* becomes built up from which food is produced : from food life-breath, mind, truth and the worlds. In the concluding portion of the *Aitareya Brāhmaṇa brahman* is said to be the wind into which the five divinities of lightning, rain, moon, sun and fire are merged in death, and out of which they later emerge in life. In the *Bṛhadāraṇyaka Upaniṣad* (5.12), *brahman* is identified with food and life. The *Chāndogya Upaniṣad* (3.18) states that *brahman* has four quarters, speech, breath, eye and ear and identifies it with earth, water, air, fire, space and other objects (4.11-13). Elsewhere in the same Upaniṣad (7.2.ff) *brahman* is identified with the elements like earth, water, fire air and space and also with the abstract principles like speech, mind, conception, thought, meditation, understanding, strength, memory and others. In the *Taittirīya Upaniṣad* (3.1-7) *brahman* is progressively conceived in terms of food, austerity, life, mind, understanding and bliss. In the *Aitareya Upaniṣad* (5.3), *brahman* is identified with Indra. Prajāpati and all the gods as well as with the five gross elements (*mahābhūtāni*), namely earth, wind, space, water and fire. In the *Kauṣītaki Upaniṣad* (2.1-3) *brahman* is identified with *prāṇa* or breathing-spirit. From all these it appears that the non-dualist character of *brahman* was formed through a process of evolution. In a legend of the *Bṛhadāraṇyaka Upaniṣad* (3.9.1-9) we find that Yājñavalkya was pressed by Śākalya to state the real number of the gods. Unwillingly he reduced, in seven steps, the popular number of 3306 gods to one, and that one was *brahman*. The well-known myth of the *Kena Upaniṣad* (4.1-6) speaks of *brahman* as the true source of the energy by means of which the fire burns, the wind blows and Indra performs his vaunted exploits. With this enhancement of the power and position of *brahman*, need was also felt for a universal, instead of a particular world-ground embracing all phenomena as parts of it. According to the *Taittirīya Upaniṣad* (2.6), having created the world *brahman* entered into it. The *Chāndogya Upaniṣad* (6.3) speaks of the originally existent, after it had procreated heat, water and food, entered and animated them. The *Bṛhadāraṇyaka Upaniṣad* (1.4.7) says : 'He entered here, even to the gingernail-tips, as a razor would be hidden in razor case, or fire in a fire-holder.' See **Absolute, Akṣara, Ātman**.

**Brahman:** *Brahman* is found in many passages in the *Ṛgveda* and later in the sense of 'priest' (*RV* 1.10.1, 1.33.9; 1.101.5; 1.108.7; 1.158.6; 2.39.1; 4.50.8 4.50.9, 4.58.2; 5.29,3; 5.31.4; 5.32.12; 5.40.8; 7.7.5; 7.42.1; 8.7.20; 8.17.2; 8.31.1; 8.32.16; 8.33.19; 8.45.39; 9.96.6; 10.28.11; 10.141.3. In not a few cases the priesthood as a profession is clearly alluded to, nor is there any reason to doubt that in all cases the word has the technical sense of a member of the priesthood (*RV* 1.108.7; 4.50.8; 4.50.9; 8.7.20; 8.64.7; 9.112.1; 10.85.29).

**Brāhmaṇas:** The Brāhmaṇas and three other castes find mention for the first time in the Puruṣasūkta (*RV* 10.90). The word 'brāhmaṇa' is infrequent in the *Ṛgveda* and it denotes various callings and qualifications (1.108.7; 4.50.8; 8.7.20; 8.45.39; 8.53.7; 8.81.30; 9.112; 10.85.29). In specific cases the term 'Brāhmaṇa' is used in the *Ṛgveda* (1.80.1; 1.164.34; 2.2-6; 6.33.11; 8.16.7;

10.71.11) in the sense of a priest or one praising the gods. The authors (2.81) of the *Vedic Index* remark: 'it seems certain that in the *Ṛgveda* this Brāhmaṇa or Brahmin is already a separate caste differing from the warrior and agricultural castes.' The supremacy of the Brāhmaṇa is reflected distinctly in the *Atharvaveda* (5.3.2; 6.13.1; 6.44.2; 19.62.1) and the *Taittirīya Saṃhitā* (1.7.3.1). The *Atharvaveda* (5.17.19) mentions the harming consequences of robbing the Brāhmmaṇas of their cows. The *Taittirīya Saṃhitā* (2.6.2.5) refers to the dependence of the ruling class on the priestly power testifying the superior position of the Brāhmaṇas. The *Pañcaviṃśa Brāhmaṇa* (11.1.2. *brahman hi pūrvaṃ kṣattrāt*) and the *Aitareya Brāhmaṇa* (33.4 *bhūyān vai brāhmaṇaḥ kṣattriyāditi Varuṇa uvāca*) also express the same thing. In the *Aitareya Brāhmaṇa* (7.29.2) a Brāhmaṇa is noted as the recipient of gifts (*ādāyi*), drinker of the offering (*āpāri*) and *āvasāyi* meaning dwelling everywhere and *yathākāma-prāpya* i.e., moving at pleasure. The *Śatapatha Brāhmaṇa* (11.5.7.1) mentions four characteristics of a brāhmaṇa : purity of descent, befitting conduct, glory and making people perfect by teaching and his four privileges, honour (*arcā*), gift (*dāna*), freedom from oppression (*ajyeyatā*) and freedom from being killed (*avddhyatā*). Elsewhere the *Śatapatha Brāhmaṇa* (5.4.6.9) mentions four *varṇas* and refers to a Brāhmaṇa as *bhagavant* (*ŚB* 14.6.1.2). The *Kāṭhaka Saṃhitā* (19.12) also states that he is provided with good food and entertainment wherever he goes. Brāhmaṇas were mainly teachers of the society, specially they were the torch of spiritual knowledge, as evidenced by the *KB* (4.18). The king was the ruler of three castes but not of the Brāhmaṇas. In the coronation ceremony the priest (*VS* 10.18) announces to the people : 'This man is your king. O ye people, Soma is the king of us, Brāhmaṇas.' When a king gives all his land and everything on it to the priest the gift excludes the property of a Brāhmaṇa, as noted in the *Śatapatha Brāhmaṇa* (13.5.4.29). Elsewhere (*ŚB* 2.5.11.9) it speaks of the special privilege of a Brāhmaṇa in a law-court : 'if a Brāhmaṇa and non-Brāhmaṇa have a litigation, one should support the Brāhmaṇa. The position of the Brāhmaṇa in the society was highly enhanced, as evidenced by the *Śatapatha Brāhmaṇa* (2.6.10.2). One should not revile a Brāhmaṇa or strike him, nor draw blood from him. Elsewhere (*ŚB* 13.3.5.3) it declares that the murder of a Brāhmaṇa was the most serious offence. The Brāhmaṇas aimed at efficiency in priesthood and sacred knowledge. The *Taittirīya Saṃhitā* (7.5.18.1) and *Vājasaneyī Saṃhitā* (12.22) extol the spiritual glory of the Brāhmaṇas. The *Śatapatha Brāhmaṇa* (8.2.6.10) also speaks highly of spiritual lustre and elsewhere (*ŚB* 2.1.3.6) it enjoins that 'whosoever desires to be endowed with holy lustre (*brahmavarcase*), let him set up his fires in spring, for the spring is the priesthood and he will certainly become endowed with holy lustre.' Chakraborty 1986, 10.

**Brahma-Yajña:** One's own daily study of the Veda (*ŚB* 11.5.6.3-18). *Taittirīya Āraṇyaka* (2.10-13) refers to the place, position, purification and other necessary preliminaries before sitting down to study (*svādhyāya*) cf. *ĀGS* 2.2.2-3.3.4. The *Śāṅkhāyana Gṛhyasūtra* 1.4. prescribes several hymns and verses of the *Ṛgveda* for reciting in the *brahmayajña*. It was to be performed once either after morning *homa* or after midday offering or after Vaiśvadeva.

**Braid:** Wearing of hair in braid or plait (*kaparda*) was a practice of both the sexes. A young lady being four-plaited (*catuṣkapardā*) is narrated in the *Ṛgveda* (10.114.3). In the *Vājasaneyī Saṃhitā* (11.56) the epithet of the goddess Sinīvālī is found as 'wearer of fair braids' (*su-kapardā*). Rudra is described as 'wearer of braid' (*kapardin*) in the *Ṛgveda* (1.114.1, 5) and *Vājasaneyī Saṃhitā* (16.10, 29, 43, 48, 59) refers to it as Pūṣan's epithet. The Vasiṣṭhas wore their braids in the right side and so they were called *dakṣiṇatas kaparda* (*RV* 7.33.1).

**Breath:** In some Vedic texts *prāṇa*, the cosmic life-breath is thought to be the Lord of beings (Prajāpati) by whose blessings bounty and other essentials of human life are fulfilled. *Prāṇa*, the life-breath or the vital energy, is the giver of all that we see with our eyes, the words we speak, and the bounty we enjoy. Everything becomes possible on account of the rhythmic play of *prāṇa*. The name of *prāṇa* is bestowed on Mātariśvan and on wind. It is the nectar of existence. (*AV* 9.1.2) *Prāṇa* is eulogized in the *Atharvaveda* 11.4.1. *Prāṇa* being Prajāpati invested with the attributes of Parjanya. *Prāṇa* is associated with the sun as the life of the universe. (*Mait U* 6-8). Blessings are sought from *prāṇa* (*AV* 11.4.26). In the *Chāndogya Upaniṣad* (1.3.3) *prāṇa* has been defined thus : *yad vai prāṇ iti sa prāṇāḥ*. In the Upaniṣads *prāṇa* has been used in two senses : (1) *prāṇ neva prāṇo nāma bhavati* (*BU* 1.4.7). When breathing, he becomes breath (*prāṇa*) by name. (2) *prāṇo asmi prajñ'tma . . . prāṇaṃ evamṛtaṃ* (*KU* 3.2). 'I am the breathing spirit, the intelligential self . . . / The breathing spirit, indeed, is mortality' (Tr. R.F. Hume). In the narrow sense *prāṇa* denotes one of the vital airs, of which five are usually enumerated. It is *prāṇa* which moves and winks (*prāṇaṃ nimiṣaca, MU* 2.2.1). *Prāṇa* is to be meditated upon as the sacred fire thus : *prāṇo vai vāyuḥ*, etc. (*Mait. U.* 6.33); the *prāṇa* breath, the *vyāna* breath, the *apāna* breath, the *samāna* breath, the *udāna* breath. 'This whole world, whatever there is, was created from the moves in Life' (*KU* 2.6. Tr. Hume). *Prāṇa* and *apāna* are only the marks of life functions. See **Prāṇa**, Vatsyayan I. 97-104.

**Breath Infusion:** According to the doctrine of ancient Indian medicine the 'breaths go away' from a person and therefore he is diseased. Further, by mystically putting breaths in his body, it is hoped that the patient will be cured. Thus in *Maitrāyaṇī Saṃhitā* (2.5.1) it is said, 'His breath has gone away who is diseased' (*prāṇo hi vā etasyāpakrānto'thaitasyānayati*', cf. *Kāṭhaka Saṃhitā* (30.3) : *prāṇena vā eṣa vyṛddhyate yasyāmayati*. 'He lacks in breath who is ill', also *Pañcaviṃśa Brāhmaṇa* (16.13.2): *prāṇenvaiva vyṛd-dhyate ya āmayāvī*). In the *Atharvaveda* (7.53.2 ff) the physician says to the patient, 'Let thy breath and expiration be here allies; thy expiration, breath, let them come again. . . . Let not the breath leave this man; let not expiration, leaving him now go away. . . . Enter ye in, O breath and expiration as two draft oxen a stall. . . . We impel hither thy breath; I impel away thy disease (*yakṣma*); Let Agni here, desirable one, assign us life time from all sides.' Similarly in the *Atharvaveda* (8.1.1) we read, 'Let thy breath's expiration rest here.' Thite, 62.

**Bṛhaspati:** Bṛhaspati, also called Brahmanaspati (lord of prayer), has but few physical features, and these are the usual ones ascribed to all other gods. Like Agni, he is both a domestic priest and a brāhmaṇa priest and the generator of all prayers. He is identified with as well as distinguished from Agni. Being often invoked with Indra (some of whose epithets like *maghavan* and *vajrin* he shares), he is drawn into the Indra myth of the release of the cows. Thus, he has no homogeneous character, combining in himself, as he does, martial as well as priestly elements. As the divine brāhmaṇa priest, he seems to have been the prototype of Brahman, the chief of the later Hindu triad. Bṛhaspati is very interesting from the point of view of the later religious and philosophical developments of India (*RV* 1.40.5, 1.190.1, 2.1.3, 2.24.9, 3.62.4, 7, 4.50, 4.5.6, 5.43.12, 6.16.30, 6.73.3, 7.97.5, 6, 7, 10.72.2, 10.112.9; *AV* 5.18.8, 9; *MS* 1.9.2; *VS* 1.9.2; *VS* 20.11; *TS* 6.4.10; *AB* 8.26.4; *ŚB* 4.1.2.4).

**Bridal Garment:** A garment, named *Vadhūya* was worn by the bride at the time when marriage ceremony takes place and afterwards given to a Brāhmaṇa, referred to in the marriage hymn of the *Ṛgveda* (10.35.34) and the *Atharvaveda* (14.2.41; 14.2.42). Bride's dress (*vadhvaḥ vastra*) appears in the *Atharvaveda* (14.2.41).

**Bucket:** The term *kośa*, which denotes bucket, is mentioned in the *Ṛgveda* (1.130.2; 3.32.15; 4.17.6). It was used to lift water from a well or Soma from a big container, as opposed to the *kalasa* (*RV* 9.75.3; *AV* 18.4.30), which is used in the sacrifices.

**Bundle:** *Pālada* occurs twice in one hymn of the *Atharvaveda* (9.3.5.17), which seems to mean bundles of straw or reeds used to thatch the house and render the sides wind and weather proof.

**Butter:** See under **Dairy Products**.

# C

**Cake:** *Apūpa* is the general word from the *Ṛgveda* (3.52.7) onwards for a cake, which might be mixed with ghee (*ghṛtavant, RV* 10.45.9), or be made of rice (*vrīhi*), or barley (*yava—ŚB* 4.2.5.19; *vrīhi*—2.2.3.12). In the *Chāndogya Upaniṣad* (3.1.1) the term is interpreted differently. The term *pakti* denotes a cooked object, probably a kind of cake, in the Saṃhitās (*RV* 6.29.4; *Vājasaneyī Saṃhitā* 21.59). *Puroḍāśa* is also a form of cake. The term *kapāla* denotes an earthenware utensil, used as a cooking pot, especially for preparing cakes or *puroḍāśa*. Regarded as one of the ten sacrificial implements, it is referred to in the *Taittirīya Saṃhitā* (1.6.8.3).

**Cakra:** *Cakra*, disc or wheel, is an important symbol serving manifold conceptual purposes. The entirety of the universe has been conceived as a cosmic wheel, *viśvacakra* or the wheel of Brahma. In the sense of the wheel of existence (*bhavacakra*), it refers to the law of nature as ever moving and rotating, implying a cyclical view of changes. The *saṃsāracakra* is also of the same meaning. In its microcosmic meaning, it denotes the human body or the individual soul (*cakrapuruṣa*). In the Vedas *cakra* represents the wheel of time wherein, among its three hundred and sixty spokes, there are twelve fellies and three naves. The solar chariot is sometimes described as one-wheeled (*ekacakra*), symbolizing the disc of the sun. The *cakra* represents Viṣṇu, the all-pervading Divine, striding over three regions: fire, lightning and sun (*RV* 1.22.17). The disc of the sun revolves in the upper sky, unwastingly like a wheel. It has all the characteristics of the chariot-wheel with a felly (*sanemi*) and car poles (*RV* 1.164.14). Sometimes the disc of the sun is referred to as a chariot or a chariot-wheel but more so as a wheel with all its common characteristics, viz., hub and felly (*nābhi* and *nemi*). The car which moves on a single wheel represents the sun itself and the rays, which have seven naves, draw it as one. Yāska has given the etymological derivation of *cakra* as: *cakram caratervā krāmatirvā* (*Nir.* 4.27). The sun's disc (*cakra*) representing time has been referred to in a good number of Vedic verses (cf. *RV* 1.164.48). Owing to its luminosity and radiance, the chariot (*ratha*) of the sun is viewed as golden (*RV* 8.5.29). *Cakra* does not only mean the sun's disc that floods the whole region with light and life, but it also serves as the weapon in the form of a discus. In a hymn of the *Atharvaveda* (10.2.31) the sun has been compared with the human body. In another hymn of the *Atharvaveda* we find that *cakra* is the symbol of time (*AV* 10.53.2). Vatsyayan 2.47, 50-4.

**Calotropis Gignatea:** *Arka*, as the name of the three *calotropis gignatea* is found in one obscure passage of the *Atharvaveda* (6.72.1). It is often referred to in the *Śatapatha Brāhmaṇa* (9.1.1.4; 9.1.1.9) and its leaf is known as *arka-parṇa* or *arka-palāśa*, (1.2.3.12; 13).

**Canary Seed:** A cultivated millet (*panicum frumentaceum*) is referred to as *śyāmāka* in the Vedic literature (*AV* 19.50.4; 20.135; 12; *MS* 2.11.4; *TS* 1.8.1.2; 4.7.4.2; *VS* 18.12; *JB* 2.267; *ŚB* 10.6.32; 12.7.1.9; *CU* 3.14.3). Associated with the spring (*KS* 10.2), its seeds are very light and usually scattered by the wind (*AV* 19.50.4) and pigeons feed on it (*AV* 20.135.12). Max Müller interprets it as 'canary seed' (SBE. 1.48).

**Cantons:** Zimmer, who was one of the earliest to study the social and political order of the Vedic peoples, regarded the *viś* as a unit of military organization and identified it with the *gau* (Pagus), or Canton, into which the Teutonic peoples were divided according to Tacitus. According to him, the division of the Vedic peoples was not merely geographical but a military one. The organized *viśaḥ* or the people, fought against their enemies under the leadership of the *viśpati*, who acted as the commander of that section of the tribal host. Zimmer quotes a large number of passages to prove the above point. Thus, according to him, *Ṛgveda* 2.26.3 clearly refers to this character of the *vis*, which is contrasted with *jana, janma* and *putra*, while the next passage cited clearly speaks of the fighting *viśaḥ* (*RV* 4.24.4). Again, the *Ṛgveda* 19.84.4 describes the host as divided in *viśaḥ*. To these, cited by Zimmer, we may add the evidence of another passage which, though it does not confirm the fighting nature of the *viś*, describes Maruts' army as having been divided into *vrāta, gaṇa* and *śardha*. Many scholars have attempted to refute Zimmer's view. Macdonell and Keith have gone deeper into the question and, having discussed the interpretation of the passages cited, have come to the conclusion that the rendering *gau* has little foundation (6.2.307) in relation to *viś*. Now, in regard to the real character of the *viśaḥ* it is difficult to pronounce any clear opinion. But, while differences must exist in regard to the acceptance of Zimmer's theory of the threefold division of the people into *jana, viś* and *grāma*, it will be difficult to deny that in those days the *viś* was a unit of military organization. The passage (*RV* 5.43.1) about the Maruts throws more light on the point. Of the three divisions, the word *vrāta* retained its old meaning of a collective entity (*samūha*) for a long time. This is clear from Sanskrit lexicons and commentaries on Pāṇini, which equate *gaṇa* with *vrāta* meaning *samūha* or group. It is not improbable that, owing to the constant tribal enmity, each settlement had to be on its guard or to send a quota of soldiers to the tribal host.

**Caraṇa:** Various schools of the Veda. *Caraṇa* also indicates a body of people who, though pledged to the reading and study of a particular *śākhā* or branch, had a wider curriculum which included other texts as well. Bhattacharyya 1990, 45.

**Carnivores:** Various carnivores and their characteristics are referred to in the Vedic literature. *Siṃha* denotes the lion in the *Ṛgveda* (1.64.8; 1.95.5; 3.2.11; 3.9.4; 3.26.5; 4.16.14) and later (*AV* 4.36.6; 5.20.1; 5.10.2; 5.21.6; 8.7.15; *TS* 5.5.21.1; *KS* 12.10; *MS* 2.1.9; *KU* 1.2). The roaring (*nād*) of the lion is often alluded to and is called thundering (*stanatha*) (*RV* 5.83.3; *AV* 5.21.6). He wanders about (*ku-cara*) and lives in the hills (*giri-ṣṭha*) (*RV* 1.154.2; 10.160.2). It is clearly the dreaded wild beast that kills animals (*mṛgo bhīma upahatnuḥ*, *RV* 2.33.11), to which Rudra is compared. When Agni, who has entered the waters, is compared to a lion (*RV* 3.9.4), the reference may be to the latter's habit of springing on animals at their watering holes. That a jackal should defeat the lion is spoken of as a marvel (10.28.4). The lion, being dangerous to men (*RV* 1.174.3), was trapped (*RV* 10.28.10), kept in waiting for an ambush (*RV* 5.74.4) or chased by a hunting band (*RV* 5.15.3; 15.1.31). Dogs were terrified of lions (*AV* 5.36.6). The lioness (*siṃhī*) was also famous for her courage. The aid given by Indra to Sudās against the vast host of his enemies is compared to the defeat of a lioness by a ram (*petva*) (*RV* 7.18.17). The gaping jaws of the lioness when attacking men are alluded to in the *Aitareya Brāhmaṇa* (6.35.1). The lioness is also mentioned in the *Yajurveda* and the *Brāhmaṇa* (*TS* 1.2.12.2; 6.2.7.1; *VS* 5.10; *ŚB* 3.5.1.21; *MS* 3.8.5). *Dvipin* or panther or leopard is mentioned in the *Atharvaveda* (4.8.7; 6.38.2; 19.49.4) and the *Maitrāyaṇī Saṃhitā* (2.1.9). *Ṛkṣa*, bear, is found only once in the *Ṛgveda* (5.56.3) and seldom later (*MS* 3.14.17; *VS* 24.36; *JB* 1.184). Evidently, the animal was scarce in the regions occupied by the Vedic Indians. No more frequent (*RV* 1.24.10; *ŚB* 2.1.2.4; *TA* 1.11.1) is the use of the word in the plural to denote the seven bears, later called the seven *Ṛsis*, the constellation of the Great Bear. *Durvarāha* probably denotes a wild boar, and is mentioned in the *ŚB* (12.4.1.4) and the *JUB* (1.51.4). *Sūkara*, wild boar, has the appearance of being an onomatopoeic word (making the sound *sū*); it is more probably a very old word going back to the Indo-European period, and cognate with the Latin *su-culus* (little pig), being transformed in sense by popular etymology. It occurs in the *Ṛgveda* (7.55.4) and later (*AV* 2.27.2; 5.14.1; *MS* 3.14.21; *VS* 24.40; *CU* 5.10.2). It appears once in the *Atharvaveda* accompanied by *mṛga* (*AV* 12.1.48), the combined words apparently meaning wild hog, as opposed to *varāha*, boar. *Varāha* is found in the *Ṛgveda* (1.61.7; 8.77.10; 9.97.7; 10.28.4) and later (*AV* 8.7.23; 12.1.48; *KS* 8.2; *MS* 3.14.19). The god Rudra is described as the boar of heaven (*RV* 1.114.5; *TS* 6.2.4.2; 7.1.5.1). The use of dogs to hunt the boar is once alluded to (*RV* 10.86.4). The variant form of the word *varāhu*, is not used except metaphorically of divinities (*RV* 1.88.5; 1.121.11; *TĀ* 1.9.4). *Tarakṣu*, the hyaena, is mentioned in the list of victims at the horse sacrifice in the *Yajurveda* (*TS* 5.5.19.1; *MS* 3.14.21; *VS* 24.40). Sālāvṛka is found twice in the *Ṛgveda* (10.73.2; 10.95.15), apparently denoting the hyaena or wild dog. This sense also seems appropriate in the later narrative of the destruction of the Yatis by Indra (*TS* 6.2.7.5; *AB* 7.28.1; *KU* 3.1), who is said to have handed them over to the *sālāvṛkas*. *Sālāvṛkeya* (*PB* 8.1.4; 13.4.16; 14.11.28; 18.1.9; 19.4.7; *JB* 1.185; *KS* 8.5; 11.10; 25.6; 36.7; *KU* 3.1; *AV* 2.27.5) is a variant form of the same word, meaning literally descendant of a *sālāvṛka*; the *feminine* is *sālāvṛkī*, (*TS* 6.2.7.5; *MS* 3.8.3). *Ula* is the name of some unknown wild animal, perhaps, the jackal. It is mentioned in the *Atharvaveda* (12.1.49) and later Saṃhitās (*TS* 5.5.12.1; *MS* 3.13.12; 3.14.2; *VS* 24.31). Lopāśa, probably a jackal or fox, is mentioned in the *Ṛgveda* (10.28.4) and is included in the list of victims at the Aśvamedha in the *Yajurveda Saṃhitās* (*TS* 5.5.21.1; *MS* 3.14.17; *VS* 24.36). *Vṛka*, wolf, is mentioned frequently in the *Ṛgveda* (1.42.2; 1.105.7; 1.116.14; 2.29.6; 6.51.14; 7.38.7) and also later (*AV* 7.95.2; 12.1.49; *KS* 12.10; *MS* 3.14.4; *VS* 4.34; 19.10; 19.92). It was an enemy of sheep (*RV* 8.34.3) and of calves (*AV* 12.4.7), being dangerous even to men (*RV* 1.105.11; 1.105.18; 2.29.6). Its colour is stated to be reddish (*aruṇa*) (*RV* 1.105.18). The 'she-wolf' *vṛkī* is also mentioned several times in the *Ṛgveda* (1.116.16, 1.117.17; 1.185.4; 6.51.6; 10.127.6). *Kurkura* is the name for the dog in the *Atharvaveda* (7.95.2). *Śvan* in the *Ṛgveda* (1.161.13; 1.182-4; 2.39.4) and later (*AV* 6.37.3; 11.2.2; *PB* 8.8.22) is the word for dog, the feminine being *śūnū* (*AV* 4.20.7; *ŚB* 6.5.2.19). The dog was a tame animal (*RV* 2.19.4) and used to guard the house from thieves and other intruders (*RV* 7.55.5). It was also employed in hunting the boar (*varāhaya RV* 10.86.4), but was no match for the lion (*AV* 4.236.6). To eat dog's flesh was the last resort to despair and hunger (*RV* 4.18.3). The remains of the feast were given to the dog (*AV* 6.37.312; 9.14.16). A hundred dogs are mentioned as a gift in the *Dānastuti* (q.v.) in a Vālakhilya hymn (*RV* 8.55.3). Being unclean (*JB* 1.5.1.4; *ŚB* 12.4.1.4), dog is regarded as unfit for sacrifice and was, in fact, to be driven away from one (*RV* 9.101.1). Saramā figures in legend as Indra's faithful dog (*RV* 1.62.3, 1.72.3), searching for the cows. Rudra is the lord of dogs (*śvapati* in the *Yajurveda*, *VS* 16.28; *KS* 17.13; *MS* 2.9.5; The 'dog-keeper' (*svāmin*) is mentioned in the list of sacrificial victims at the

Puruṣamedha (human sacrifice) in the same Saṃhitā (*VS* 16.27; 30.7; *TB* 3.4.3.1). The four-eyed (*catur-akṣa*) dogs of certain texts (*RV* 10.14.10; 10.14.11; *AV* 18.2.11; 18.2.12; *TĀ* 6.3.1; *TB* 3.8.4.1; *ŚB* 13.1.2.9) are, of course, mythological. *Sārameya*, descendant of Saramā, Indra's mythical dog, is applied to a god on earth in the *Ṛgveda* (7.55.2), as also to the dogs of Yama (*RV* 10.14.10).

**Carpenter:** *Takṣan* (*RV* 9.112.1; *AV* 10.6.3; *MS* 2.9.5; *KS* 12.10.18.13; *VS* 16.27, 30.6; *TB* 3.4.2.1; *ŚB* 1.1.3.12; 3.6.4.4) denotes carpenter, manufacturer of all types of wood work like chariots and wagons, sometimes even carved, finer works (*RV* 1.161.9, 3.60.2, 10.86.8). Axe (*kuliśa*, *RV* 3.2.1; *paraśu*, *KS* 12.10) was used as a working tool. Tvaṣṭṛ is mentioned in the *Atharvaveda* (12.3.33) as the presiding deity of carpenters, who was identified with Viśvakarman. In the *Ṛgveda*, the fashioning of the world has been compared with the carpenter's art and skill.

**Cart:** In the Vedic age the cart, drawn by oxen or steeds, was the most important vehicle for carrying loads and other forms of transportables. Chariots were made for easy and comfortable travelling or for racing or for war but carts and their bigger forms, the wagons were most frequently used. The word *śakaṭa* is mentioned in the *Chāndogya Upaniṣad* (4.1.8) to designate 'cart'. It is also used in the *Ṛgveda* (10.146.3) and *Jaiminīya Brāhmaṇa* (1.264) in the same sense. Another word *anas*, mentioned in the *Ṛgveda* (4.30.10; 10.85.10; 10. 86.18; *ŚB* 1.1.2.5; *CU* 7.15.1), means draft wagon. *Anaḍvāha* is another word which is used to denote wagon. The wagon was usually drawn by oxen, as in wedding processions (*RV* 10.85.11). *Vipatha* used to denote a rough vehicle, which was meant for bad tracks (*AV* 15.2.1). Indra is described as being seated in a cart (*RV* 1.121.7). Another reference of the bridal wagon is found in the *Ṛgveda* (10.85.10), where the bridal wagon of Sūryā had a carving. Oxen i.e., *anaḍ-vāḥ* were utilised for drawing carts (*anas*) (*RV* 3.53.18; 10.59.10; 10.85.10; *AV* 3.11.5, 4.11.1), and *ŚB* (2.1.4.17). According to *Kātyāyana Śrautasūtra* (15.15) they were normally castrated, but not regularly. Athough rare, female draft beasts were also employed for this purpose (*AV* 4.11; *ŚB* 5.2.4.11; 5.2.4.13).

**Caste:** The caste system, which has characterized the social fabric of India through the ages, may be seen as interelated and self-contained units grouped in a hierarchy of varying status. All over the world, there is a four-fold social division comprising the intellectual class, the ruling class, the trading class and the working class. These four classes are known in India as the four *varṇas* comprising respectively the Brāhmaṇas, the Kṣatriyas, the Vaiśyas and the Śūdras. The earliest theoretical indication of this division is found in *Ṛgveda* 10.90.12. Being mainly normative, this division does not explain the structural formation and the functional role of the caste system. In fact, there are thousands of castes and the law-givers, throughout the ages, have tried to bring them into the pale of an idealized four-fold system by adopting various methods. The caste system has several characteristics. First, every caste has a caste profession. Second, every caste is endogamous i.e., a man belonging to a particular caste does not marry a woman of a different caste. Third, every caste is autonomous and is guided by its own social laws and customs. Fourth, every caste has a specific status, high or low, in the social hierarchy, with exclusive rights and privileges of its own. It should also be remembered that the highest caste is not always the dominant one. It is, and it has been, the castes of the middle rank which are the most powerful and influential. Fifth, the number of castes is ever-increasing. At every period of history one comes across the emergence of new castes, and this process is ongoing. There cannot be any encroachment into exclusive areas of other castes. For instance, a barber canot switch his occupation and become a washerman. Change of occupation is, however, permitted so far as the higher castes are concerned, e.g. Brāhmaṇas or Kṣatriyas can take up the occupations of the Vaiśyas and the Śūdras, the argument being that not all Brāhmaṇas are born learned enough to teach the Vedas and perform religious rites and not all Kṣatriyas are born strong enough to become administrators or warriors. But when a Brāhmaṇa or a Kṣatriya takes up a lower occupation, his social position is lowered to the rank of the Śūdras although he retains his caste identity. The caste system originated and evolved under diverse historical conditions, one of which was the process of incomplete detribalization. The *pañca-kṛṣṭi* of the *Ṛgveda*, has been explained by Yāska as the five classes of men; it included the four *varṇas* while the *Niṣādas* were the fifth. *Ni* means 'down', and *sad* means 'to settle'. Of the eight peoples associated with the Niṣādas, as we find in the Rudrādhyāya of the *Yajurveda*, the Vrātas, Puñjiṣṭhas, Śvanis and Mṛgāyus were hunters while the Takṣan, Rathakāras, Kulālas and Karmāras left the tribal fold and settled in Vedic society as members of the lower castes having undertaken the occupations of carpenter, chariot-maker, potter and blacksmith respectively. The working of such a social process of detribalization, by which specific castes are formed on the basis of certain occupations in the bigger Hindu social hierarchy, can be seen in India even today. The commentator Mahīdhara explains the word Niṣāda as it occurs in the *Vājasaneyī Saṃhitā*, as denoting a Bhilla or Bhil. The Buddhist Jātakas describe them as hunters and foresters. The Purāṇas mention the Kirātas, Bhillas, Nahālakas, Bhrāmaras and Pulindas as descendants of the Niṣādas and describe them as black, low-statured, short-armed, having high cheek bones, a flattened nose, red eyes and copper-coloured hair-characteristics, still conspicuous among many hill tribes of present-day India. There has been no dearth of scholarly works on the caste system. Early writers on this subject—such as Senart, Risley, Nesfield, Ibbetson and others—who were influenced on the one hand by the values of the Western civilization and on the other by the evolutionist approach of the nineteenth century, tried to explain this multiple-cum-crystallized system on the basis of a single standard or principle. As a result, their conclusions became mostly subjective. While modern writers like Louis Dumont have criticized the earlier approaches as one-sided and based on preconceived notions, they in their turn have introduced a kind of complex and highly sophisticated, sociological terminology in the name of objective analysis. Their concept must have some relevance in a limited scale or local extent but they are not sufficiently capable of comprehending and explaining such a vast and complicated social phenomenon. Moreover, since the caste system is still a living institution, with a profound influence on public life, scholars working in this field sometimes, owing to secret machinations, knowingly or unknowingly, become victims of abstruse political purposes. In fact, even in the British period the caste system has been efficiently utilized for political interests. Hutton himself has admitted that many researches on the caste system were politically motivated; that, in every census, political considerations had the leading role and the British arbitrarily created numerous subcastes with the professed aim of dissociating them from the main current of Hindu society. In many cases, studies on the caste system have been influenced by the personal views and prejudices of the scholars. Sherring, Maine and Fick describe this artificial invention of the crafty Brāhmaṇas as the most disastrous and blighting of all human institutions; the most baneful, hard-hearted and cruel social system for damning the human race. On the other hand, Dubois, Low, Townsend, Hutton and some other experts hold that it is the main cause of the fundamental stability and contentment in Indian social life. It provides every man with place, career, occupation companionship, club, trade-union, benefit of society and a sense of community with others; it is a form of socialism which, through ages, protected the Hindu society from anarchy and from the worst evils of industrial and competitive life. Various such views may be quoted, but eulogy or condemnation is not the right way of approach. The existence of the caste system is not dependent on how one views it. So long as the diverse historical processes under which this sytem has come into existence and the various social, economic, political and cultural forces by which it has been sustained—in other words, the objective conditions on which it survives—do not become defunct or inefficacious, it will continue to exist. There are certain features of which one should take note. The system has never remained fixed; every now and then, new castes and subcastes have come into existence and their mutual relations have been readjusted. What is most interesting is that internally the system is essentially flexible, always subject to change; but externally it is rigid; the changes cannot transgress the given limit. The designs change, but the frame does not. According to the ancient Indian sociologists, the caste system is applicable to all forms of society, where numerous races meet and mingle. It is possible to synthesize them in a greater society by placing them in four basic castes. If different groups of persons work according to their capacity and skill in diverse walks of life, and if the society guarantees that the persons concerned and their descendants, following their traditional occupations, will not die of starvation, the society thus formed by mutual cooperation of each social group naturally becomes more powerful. Apart from this cooperation, another assurance given to masses it was that of absolute cultural freedom. Every group was allowed to follow their traditional social practices, cults and rituals, law and customs. See **Brāhmaṇas**, **Detribalization**, **Kṣatriyas**, **Mixed castes**, **Occupations**, **Śūdras**, **Vaiśyas**, **Varṇa**.

**Categories:** The seventh *prapāṭhaka* of the *Chāndogya Upaniṣad* contains a conversation between Nārada and Sanatkumāra in which physical, psychological and metaphysical categories are described. Sanatkumāra begins, however, in the peculiar fashion, familiar to students of Upaniṣadic philosophy, of piling categories over categories so as to constitute a philosophical sortie. He begins by telling Nārada that all the learning he (Nārada) had hitherto acquired was merely a 'Name'; that, whoever meditated upon the 'Name' of *brahman* would himself reach as far the name itself extends, but no farther. Sanatkumāra then proceeds to say that speech is better than Name, and that *manas* is better than speech; that *saṃkalpa* is better than *manas*, and that *citta* is better than *saṃkalpa*; that *dhyāna* is better than *citta*, while *vijñāna* is superior even to *dhyāna*. So far, a number of psychological categories have been strung together for us, even though to us the meanings of the words cannot be definitely ascertained. Curiously enough, Sanatkumāra holds that power is superior to knowledge. He is not merely content to say that physical power is superior to knowledge, but that food is superior to power as well as is the cause of it; that water is superior to food, as it is also its cause. Superior to water is fire, and superior to fire is *ākāśa* as their respective causes. From the 13th section onwards he says, once more, that Memory is stronger than *ākāśa*; that Hope is stronger than Memory; and that finally *prāṇa* or the vital principle, which is a psychologico-metaphysical category, is superior to the barely psychological category of Hope. As in other places, so even here, the vital breath is magnified beyond all measure. 'In it are all beings centered, as in the nave are centered the spokes of a wheel'. Verily, the vital breath is itself the father and the mother, the brother and the sister, the preceptor and the Brahmin Belvalkar and Ranade, 231-3.

**Cattle:** The Vedic Indians were primarily pastoral; the stress laid by the poets on the possession of cows is almost hyperbolic. The term for sacrificial fee, *dakṣiṇā* is explained as referring originally to a cow placed on the right hand side of the singer for his reward. The singers delight in comparing their songs to Indra with the lowing of cows to their calves. At night and in the heat of day, cows seem to have been kept in the fold; for the rest of the day, they were allowed to wander at will, being milked thrice. Bulls and oxen on the other hand regularly served for ploughing and drawing carts, a purpose for which horses were not much used. Second to cattle came horses, which the Indians required both for drawing chariots during battle and for the horse-race, which was among their favourite sports. Other domesticated animals were sheep, goats, asses, and dogs, the last being used for hunting, for guarding and tracking cattle and for keeping watch at night. The economic utility of cattle was great. Sale appears to have regularly consisted in barter in the *Ṛgveda* (4.24.10). Ten cows were regarded as a possible price for an image of Indra to be used as fetish. Cattle constituted the chief form of wealth and the only original *dakṣiṇā* (sacrificial fees). The word *dakṣiṇā* in fact is an adjective meaning 'right' or 'valuable', with an ellipse of *go* (cow), because the sacrificial fee was a cow placed 'on the right side' of the singer to be rewarded. Similarly one of the words for 'fight' was *gaviṣṭi,* 'a search for cows' (*RV* 1.91.23; 3.47.4; 5.63.5; 6.47.20). The name of *aghnyā* ('not to be killed'), applied several times to the cow. There are even special terms like *sva-sara* for the time of the grazing of the cows in the morning, and *saṃ-gava*, for the time when the grazing cows are driven home together for the milking. The *Ṛgveda* is aware of the dangers to which the grazing cows were liable, such as being lost, falling into pits, breaking limbs, and being stolen. The ears of cattle were probably marked to indicate ownership. See **Animal Husbandry**, **Domestic Animals**, **Pastoral Economy**.

**Causation:** There was practically no systematic theory of causation in the Upaniṣads. Śaṅkara, the later exponent of Vedānta philosophy, always tried to show that the Upaniṣads looked upon the cause as mere ground for change which though unchanged in itself, in reality had only an appearance of suffering change. This he did on the strength of a series of examples in the *Chāndogya Upaniṣad* (6.1) in which the material cause, e.g. the clay, is spoken of as the only reality in all its transformations as the pot, jug or plate. It is said that although there is diversity of appearance, in that one is called plate, the other pot, and yet another jug, these are only empty diversities. Thus, when different objects of nature have been spoken of in one place as the product of the combination of the three elements of fire, water and earth, the effect signifies a real change produced by their compounding. This is, in germ, the *pariṇāma* theory of causation advocated by the Sāṅkhya school (*CU* 6.2.4). Dasgupta, 52-3.

**Cavalry:** Cavalry played a very important part in warfare, being especially indispensable in situations requiring quickness of movement as the horses were fast-moving animals. Cavalry as an organized force may be traced to the post-Vedic period but not earlier. We have references to horses (*RV* 1.22.6; 1.22.7-8; 6.46.13-14) and war chariots drawn by horses (*RV* 1.3.1, etc.) and in the *Atharvaveda* (4.21.4) we hear of dust-raising horsemen but we have no indication that the cavalry as a disciplined force existed in the days of the *Ṛgveda*. For details see **Warfare**.

**Cedi:** Name of a people who, with their king Kasu, the Caidya, are mentioned only in a Dānastuti ('Praise of Gifts'). Occurring at the end of one hymn of the *Ṛgveda* (8.5.37-39), where their generosity is celebrated as unsurpassed. They feature later in the epic with the Matsyas, and lived in Bundelkhand region. In Vedic times they were probably situated in much the same locality. Macdonell and Keith I, 263.

**Celestial Gods:** The oldest among the gods of heaven, going back to the Indo-European period, and identical with the Greek Zeus, is Dyaus, a personification of the sky, which, however, did not advance beyond the idea of paternity. He is called a ruddy bull bellowing downwards, a poetic description, probably, of the colour of lightning, the fertilizing power of rain and the thunder of heaven. Dyaus is generally paired with Pṛthivī, the earth, in the compound Dyāvāpṛthivī, the Universal Parents, who are celebrated in six hymns. The comparatively small number of hymns addressed to Varuṇa hardly does justice to his importance in the *Ṛgveda*. The personification has so far advanced that his physical basis remains obscure. It has been suggested that the word Varuṇa is probably the same as the Greek word Ouranos (sky), though phonetic difficulties make the identification uncertain. Varuṇa is the upholder of the physical and moral order symbolized in *ṛta*, with which he is more intimately connected than any other god. He is a king and a universal monarch, whose golden abode in heaven is lofty and firm, and has a thousand columns and doors. He wears glistening garments and has spies whom none can deceive. He is predominantly called the Asura, who rules by means of his *māyā*. By this power he sends forth dawns and makes the sun (who is also described as his eye) traverse the sky. He supports heaven, earth and air.

He, with Mitra, is most frequently invoked as a bestower of rain. He regulates the seasons. Neither god nor mortal may violate his ordinances. Varuṇa's special connection with the waters is unmistakable. He is their regulator and causes the rivers to flow. He is above all the *dhṛtavrata*, the upholder of ordinances such as the fixed paths of the luminaries across the sky. He stands out preeminently as the moral governor among all the deities. The fetters (*pāśas*) with which he binds sinners are characteristic of him in this capacity. Every hymn to Varuṇa consists of a prayer for forgiveness for sins. The physical basis of the idea of Varuṇa may be uncertain but it is generally believed to be the encompassing sky. This original conception, it is supposed, goes back at least to the Indo-Iranian period since Ahura Mazdah (the wise spirit) of the *Avesta* agrees with the Asura Varuṇa in character, though not in name. Mitra is so closely associated with Varuṇa that only one hymn (*RV* 3.59) is directly addressed to him and his individual character cannot be definitely established. His distinctly peculiar epithet is *yātayai-jana*, the 'bestirrer of the people', because he marshals people into activity as the great Āditya. Mitra is a sun-god, the guardian of faithfulness in the *Avesta* and Ṛgvedic evidence points to Mitra as a solar deity in the aspect of a benevolent power of nature as suggested by the name Mitra which originally meant 'an ally'. Sūrya is the most concrete of the solar deities, the name (which designates the orb of the Sun as well as the god) showing that his character as a luminary was always present in the minds of the poets. As the all-seeing god, he is often called the eye of Mitra, Varuṇa, Agni, and other gods. The dawns produce Sūrya and he is to be the son of the goddess Aditi and of Dyaus. Savitṛ is preeminently a golden deity. His eyes, arms, hands and tongue are golden; so are his car and its pole. He diffuses golden splendour. In the famous Gāyatrī stanza (*RV* 3.62.10), which has remained the sacred morning prayer of the Hindus for more than two thousand years, he is invoked to confer his splendour on, and stimulate the thoughts of, the worshipper. Pūṣan is a god with a very vague personality, the anthropomorphic details being very few. He has a beard and braided hair. His chariot is drawn by goats and he carries a golden spear, an awl, and a goad. His favourite food is *karambha* ('gruel'). He is connected with marriage in the wedding hymn (*RV* 10.85). He acts as the envoy of Sūrya with his golden aerial ships, and as a charioteer drives downward the golden wheel of the sun. The only prominent anthropomorphic trait, nay, the main characteristic of the nature of Viṣṇu—a minor deity in the *Ṛgveda* is his three steps which give him the exclusive epithets *uru-gāya* ('wide-going') and *uru-krama* ('wide-stepping'). Two of his steps are visible but the third or highest is invisible, far beyond the flight of birds, and is like an eye fixed in heaven, shining brightly down. The word Aditi is primarily a noun meaning 'non-binding' 'boundlessness' as opposed to Diti, 'binding', derived from the root *da* 'to bind'. Hence as a goddess, Aditi is naturally invoked to release her worshipper from bondage. The Ādityas are described as *Aditeḥ-putrāḥ* ('sons of Aditi') several times. Diti is the exactly opposite point on the path of the Zodiac in the west, where the lights went out. It is not necessary to suppose that the name of Diti as a goddess was merely an antithesis of Aditi, formed from the latter to express a positive sense, as, *sura,* 'god', was later (by false etymology) evolved from *asura* 'demon'. Six Ādityas are enumerated once (2.27.1), the number being seven and even eight in the last books of the *Ṛgveda*. Among the Ādityas, Varuṇa, Mitra, and Aryaman are Indo-Iranian in origin, while Bhaga, Dakṣa, and Aṃśa seem to be deified abstractions. The sun is probably the seventh Āditya, and Mārtaṇḍa the eighth, whom Aditi casts off and brings back (10.72.8;9), is very likely the setting sun. In the case of Uṣas, the goddess of Dawn, the personification is slight, with the poet never losing sight of the beautiful physical phenomena behind the deity. Gaily attired, like a dancer with a garment of light, she rises in the east and exhibits her graces. She is ever youthful, being born again and again, though ancient. Her association with the sun is naturally very close. He is her lover, but as she precedes him she is also said to be his mother. She is the night's sister and is also associated with Agni. From the number of hymns addressed to them and, even otherwise, the twin deities, known as the Aśvins, are the most important after Indra, Agni, and Soma. They are notional deities, their connection with light being well established. Except in two or three passages, they are usually assumed inseparable. Their paths are said to be golden. *Dasra* (wondrous) and *nāsatya* are their most peculiar and frequent epithets. They are the two husbands of Sūryā, whom they carry in their car. They are above all succouring divinities, the deliverers from distress and rescuers *par excellence.* They are divine physicians with several legends of miraculous cures to their credit. From the days of Yāska, their physical basis remains a puzzle to date. See **Dyaus**, **Varuṇa**, **Mitra**, **Sūrya**, **Savitṛ**, **Pūṣan**, **Viṣṇu**, **Vivasvat**, **Ādityas**, **Uṣas**, **Aśvins**, Majumdar, 367-72.

**Cereals:** As now, cereals formed the most important part of Indian food, among whch barley occupied the most important place in the Vedic Age (*RV* 1.23.15; 1.117.21; 1.135.8; 2.5.6; 2.14.11; 3.42.7, 5.85.3, 9.68.4; *VS* 18.12; *TS* 4.7.4; 6.4.10; *KS* 15.5; *MS* 3.10.2; 4.3.2; *AV* 2.8.3; 6.30.1; 6.50.1; 6.91.1; 6.141.2; 8.7.20; 9.1.22; 9.6; 12.1.42). In the *Atharvaveda* it is called one of the two immortal sons of heaven, the other being rice (*AV* 12.142; 8.7.20). It was ground and formed into cakes (*RV* 3.28.1; 3.41.3; 3.52.2; 4.32.16; 6.3.7; *MS* 3.10.2), which were dipped into ghee before eating (*AV* 10.9.25). Sweets cakes (*apūpa*) of barley flour were also prepared. Parched barley (*dhānāḥ*. *RV* 19.21.22; *KS* 11.2; *TS* 6.5.11.4; 3.1.10.2; *AV* 18.3.69 *TB* 1.5.11.2; *ŚB* 4.4.3.9; 13.2.1.4) was eaten either with *soma* juice (*RV* 3.35.7) or ground into a meal, which was mixed with *curda*, clarified butter, *soma* juice, water (*Śaktu RV* 10.71.2; *VS* 19.21; *TS* 6.4.10.6; *KS* 15.7; *ŚB* 1.6.3.16, 9.1.1.8; 12.9.11.5) or milk (10.86.15). A gruel was also prepared with barley (*yavagū, TS* 6.2.5.2; *KS* 11.2; *TA* 2.88; *KU* 4.13). Sometimes a mess of barley was cooked in water or milk (*RV* 8.69.14; 8.77.10). In all the Saṃhitās, except the *Ṛgveda* (*VS* 18.12; 19.22.89; 21.29; *ŚB* 12.7.1.2; 12.7.2.9), we find it is used in preparing groats (*ŚB* 12.9.1.5) but it may also have been used as a substitute for barley. We find no definite mention of rice in the *Ṛgveda* but it is referred to frequently in the post-Ṛgvedic literature (*TB* 1.8.10; *KS* 15.5; *AV* 6.140.2; 7.7.20; 9.6.14; *ŚB* 5.5.5.9; *BU* 6.3.22; *CU* 3.14.3). The *Yajurveda* mentions five varieties of it (*kṛṣṇavrīhi, TS* 1.8.10; 3.1.5.9; *KS* 10.6; *śuklavrīhi* (*KS* 11.5; *TS* 1.8.10; *JB* 1.43; *CU* 5.10.6) *aśuddānya, TS* 1.8.10; *ŚB* 5.3.3.2) of which the best was *mahāvrīhi* (*TS* 1.8.10; *AB* 8.16). A mess (*odana*) was prepared with rice cooked in water (*AV* 4.14.7; 4.11.3; *BU* 6.4.16) or milk (*kṣīraudana, AV* 13.2.20; *ŚB* 2.5.3.4; 11.5.7.5; *BU* 4.13). Rice was also eaten with curds (*dadhyodana, BU* 6.4.15), sesamum (*tilaudana, BU* 6.4.17), ghee (*ghṛtaudana Śaṅkh A* 12.8) *mudga* beans (*mudgaudana, Śaṅkh A* 12.8) and meat (*māṃsaudana, Śaṅkh A*. 12.8; *ŚB* 11.5.7.5; *BU* 6.4.18). Parched rice could also be eaten (*parivāpa, TS* 3.1.10.1; 6.5.11.4; 7.2.10.4; *KS* 34.11; *VS* 19.21.22, *AB* 2.24; *TB* 1.5.11.4) *tājāḥ, MS* 3.11.2; *TB* 2.6.4; 3.8.14.4; *VS* 19.13.81; 19.21.42; *ŚB* 12.8.2.7) or prepared into a drink after boiling it (*AV* 5.5.1). The well-known preparation *civḍā* had come into use and was known as *pṛthuka* (*TB* 3.8.14.3). It was prepared as now, by moistening rice grains with water, slightly parching and then flattening them with a pestle. We also find the mention of a preparation of rice, milk and sesamum called *kṛsara* (*AV* 5.5; *Ṣaḍ B*. 5.2; *MS* 2.6.6; *KS* 10.1; 15.6; *TS* 1.8.9.3; *AV* 10.9.26; 11.1.18; 12.3.18; 12.3.30; *AB* 1.1; *ŚB* 1.1.4.3; 2.5.3.4; 5.2.3.2; 6.6.1.8; *TB* 2.8.14.3; *CU* 3.14.3). The excavation of Maheshwara and Navdatoli have shown that people in this region were using wheat, rice, *masūra, māsa, arahar, gram, pea* and *kulatha* as early as about 1200 BC, while rice was a common food grain in the Madhyadeśa about 800 BC, as rice husk was parched in mud plaster at Hastinapur. *Godhuma* or wheat, is frequently referred to in the plural in the *Yajurveda* (*MS* 1.2.8; *VS* 18.12; 19.22; 19.89; 21.29) and *Brāhmaṇas* (*ŚB* 12.7.1.2; 12.7.2.9; *BU* 6.3.22), and is expressly distinguished from 'rice' (*vrīhi*) or 'barley' (*yava*), *TB* (1.3.7.2). 'Groats (*śaktavaḥ*) made of this grain are also mentioned (*ŚB* 12.5.1.5). The word occurs in the singular in the *Śatapatha Brāhmaṇa* (5.2.1.6). Some inferior varieties of cereals were also used (*priyāṅgu, VS*. 18.12; *TS* 4.7.4; *KS* 10.11; *BU* 6.3.13; *anu VS* 18.12; *śvāmāka VS* 18.12; *TS* 1.8.10; 2.3.2; 4.7.4; *MS* 2.6.6; 2.11.4; *KS* 10.2; 15.5; *ŚB* 10.6.3.2; 12.7.1.9; *KB* 4.12; *nīvāra, VS* 18.12; *KS* 12.4; 15.5; *MS* 2.6.6; 2.4.10; *TS* 1.8.10; 4.7.4; *ŚB* 5.1.4.14, 5.3.3.5; *TB* 1.3.6.7; *gavīdbukā TB* 5.4.3.2; *MS* 2.6.5; 4.3.8; *VS* 1.7.3.6; *ŚB* 14.1.2.29, 2.4.11.13; 9.1.1.8; *āmba* or *nāmba, TS* 1.8.10.1; *KS* 15.5; *MS* 2.6.6; *ŚB* 5.3.3.8; *upavāka*). These were used in preparing groats and gruel (*MS* 3.11.2; *VS* 19.22.90; *ŚB* 22.7.1.3; 22.7.2.9.)

**Chance:** In the *Śvetāśvatara Upaniṣad* (1.2), *yadṛcchā* or chance has been mentioned as the first principle since what happens by Necessity (*niyati*), happens as if by predetermination. Whether this predetermination is personal or impersonal, it does not concern us much to merit a discussion here. But that things happen as if by predetermination or fate, as destiny is a familiar doctrine even outside the pale of Indian thought. On the other hand, chance occurs when one cannot adequately account for the cause of an event. In the case of necessity we could, at least, assign a reason in predestination; in the case of chance it is not possible to assign any reason at all. This is most excellently illustrated in accidents, with which everybody is familiar. As to whether we can assign any reason for this accident itself; in other words, whether accident itself may, with a deeper knowledge of facts, be accounted for rationally cannot be ascertained. It is evident that, at the time of the *Śvetāśvatara*, chance was so severed from the doctrine of Necessity (*niyati*) that it formed a different principle altogether. See **First Principles**.

**Chanting:** The *Sāmaveda* consists of two parts: the *ārcika* or the verse collection and the *uttarārcika*, the 'second verse collection'. Most of these verses are composed in *gāyatrī* metre or in *pragātha* stanzas, which are made up of *gāyatrī* and *jagatī* lines. There is no doubt that, from the beginning, the stanzas and songs composed in these metres were intended for singing. The purpose of both parts is to teach melody, which is always the essential element. The scholar, who wished to be trained as an *udgātṛ*-priest in the schools of the *Sāmaveda* had to first learn the melodies. The word *sāman*, although frequently used for the designation of the text that had been either made or destined for singing, means originally only 'tune' or 'melody'. The *ārcika* is nothing but a collection of five hundred and eighty-five *yonis* or single stanzas, which are sung to about double the number of different tunes. The *uttarārcika*, the second part of the *Sāmaveda*, consists of four hundred chants, mostly of three stanzas each, in which the *stotras* which are sung at the chief sacrifices are found. When singing, the priests emphasize these various notes through movement of hands and fingers. The number of known melodies must have been very large, and even at that very early period every melody had a special name.

**Chariot:** The Ṛgvedic chariot *ratha* is a two-wheeled vehicle. The car of the Aśvins is said to have been built by the *Ṛbhus*, which had a threefold construction (*RV* 1.14.2.1.3.4.9, 1.47.2; 1.118.1-2; 1.157.5; 7.71.4; 10.41.1). *Kośa*, denoting the box of the chariot, and possibly made of wicker work or leather on a light wooden frame, is fixed on a wooden axle termed *akṣa*, made of *araṭu* wood (*RV* 8.46.27). The *Ṛgveda* 8.5.29 mentions *akṣa* made of gold as *hiraṇyaya* without denoting a metal axle. It is fastened by straps of cowhide. On each side, the wheels are fixed to the ends of the axle and secured by linchpins on their outer faces. But there is uncertainty whether *āṇi* stands for the lynchpin or the end of the axle. The metal tyres are fixed to the wheel besides *pradhi*, *ara* and *nābhya*, denoting felly spokes respectively in the *Ṛgveda* 1.32.15; 5.13.6; 7.20.14; 8.77.3; 10.78.4; *Kāṭhaka Saṃhitā* 10.4 etc. *Pavi* means the rim of wheel in the *Ṛgveda* 1.180.1. The rim and the felly together are called *nemi*. The hole in the nave is termed *kha*. There are some specified numbers of spokes in a wheel. The Vedic chariot wheel seems to have four to eight spokes. The felly of the wheel might have been occasionally a single piece bent into a circular shape in the *Ṛgveda* 7.32.20. A wheel thus made must have required more than four spokes. A central pole projected forwards from the bottom of the chariot passed its end through a hole as *kha* in the yoke in the *Ṛgveda* 7.91.7 (*tardman* in *AV* 14.1.40). This pole rose at an angle with the chariot floor usually in a curve, but perhaps sometimes also in a straight line. A stout pin, as *sanyā* or bolt, is provided through the chariot pole against which the yoke is tied with leather straps as found in the *Ṛgveda* 3.6.6; 5.56.4; 10.60.8. The yoke, *yuga* is laid across the necks of the horses on either side of the pole. The words *raśmi* and *raśanā* seem to denote the traces though they also signify the reins fastened to the bit as *śiprā* in the horse's mouth in *Ṛgveda* 1.163.2; 4.1.9; 8.7.8, etc. *Śiprā* in the *Ṛgveda* 1.101.10 fastened to a bar of wood, i.e. *vāni* in the *Ṛgveda* 1.119.5 presumably signifies the two bars of wood to which the traces were fastened at right angles to the pole. *Praṣṭi* in the *Ṛgveda* 1.39.6 and 8.7.28 may mean a third horse. But two horses were usually yoked to a chariot. *Daśābhīśu* occurs in the *Ṛgveda* 10.94.7 as the ten bridles seemingly pointing to five horses yoked to a chariot. The practice of yoking horses and asses in chariots during war is mentioned in the *Ṛgveda* 1.116.2. A single horse was sometimes yoked to a chariot (*RV* 10.101.11; 10.131.3). The *RV* (4.16.20, 10.39.14) refer to the Bhṛgus as chariot makers. The *Ṛgveda* associates them with the legend of the acquisition of fire by the human race. *Rathakāra* appears as a functional caste as early as the *Atharvaveda* 3.5.6. The warrior called *savyeṣṭha* in *Taittirīya Saṃhitā* 1.7.9.1 had a charioteer, referred to as *savyeṣṭha sārathi*. *Savyaṣṭhṛ* in the *Atharvaveda* 8.8.23 stood on the left or sat on a seat called *garta* or *vandhura*. In the *Ṛgveda* 10.53.7 a chariot with eight seats is mentioned, though the Aśvins' chariot having three seats and supports in the *Ṛgveda* 1.34.9; 7.71.4 might have secured the rider's balance when the vehicle was at full speed (*RV* 1.34.2). The bow and arrow in the *Ṛgveda* 1.6.75 (*AB* 7.19.2) were the all-important weapons of the warrior. The necessary quivers containing arrows and spears must have been tied to the box of the chariot. The *sārathi*, as a driver of the chariot, stands on the right to guide his horses. He is aptly called *sthātṛ*, provided he has no seat (*RV* 6.75.6). The *Vājasaneyī Saṃhitā* 3.36 mentions the inviolable chariot of Agni. The Yajus texts pray for the *mahāratha*, a great car-fighter in the ritual of the Aśvamedha (*TS* 7.5.18.1; *VS* 22.22). The terms *rathagṛtsa*, skilled in chariot fight, *rathaujas*, mighty in fight (from chariot) and *rathecitra*, glorious in chariot, occur in the *Taittirīya Saṃhitā* 4.4.3.1 as epithets of the chieftain and commander. The charioteer wore a turban, an ornament called *niṣka*, garland *sraj* on the upper part of his body. The *Vājasaneyī Saṃhitā* 30.11 mentions *anukṣattṛ* who according to Sāyaṇa on *TB* 3.4.91, is the charioteer's attendant. *Pariṣkaṇḍa* in *Vājasaneyī Saṃhitā* 30.13 speaks of two forerunners as *puraḥsara*, or two footmen beside a chariot. The chariot of the Vrātya is called *vipatha* drawn by two beasts guided with a goad termed *pratoda* in the *Atharvaveda* 15.2.1 and *Pañcaviṃśa Brāhmaṇa* 17.1.14. A covered chariot is elsewhere alluded to in the *Taittirīya Saṃhitā* 3.5.11.1. Such a chariot would have little use in war. There are references to the spokes of the wheel in the *Pañcaviṃśa Brāhmaṇa* 7.7.13; *Chāndogya Upaniṣad* 7.15.1. The *Śatapatha Brāhmaṇa* 12.5.1.5 mentions two smashed chariots that are to be united into one. The chieftain and commander are described as *rathaprota*, fixed on a chariot, and *asamaratha*, possessing a matchless chariot respectively in the *Śatapatha Brāhmaṇa* 8.6.1.18. The charioteer figures as one of the *ratnins* in the *Pañcaviṃśa Brāhmaṇa* 19.1.4. The charioteers claimed one-fourth of the booty when the Bharatas sacked the property of the Satvants (*AB* 2.25). The *Chāndogya Upaniṣad* 5.13.2 refers to a mule-car laden with slaves and jewels, having presumably formed the prize of victory. The wheels of the battle-chariot rolled fast and far in the wake of an army's progress, but they would operate effectively only on a vast plain before them, and would serve little practical purpose in an inhospitable terrain. Chariot racing continued as a popular sport and formed an important part of the Vājapeya ritual.

**Charioteer:** *Ratha-gṛtsa* in the *Vājasaneyī Saṃhitā* (15.15) and the *Aitareya Brāhmaṇa* (3.48.9) denotes a 'skilled charioteer' (cf. *TS* 4.4.3.1; *MS* 2.8.10; *KS* 17.9). Other terms for a charioteer are *rathin* and *rathī* (*Rathin RV* 1.122.8; 5.83.3; 6.47.38; 8.4.9; 10.40.5; *Rathī* 1.25.3; 2.39.2; 3.3.6; 5.87.8; 7.39.1, etc. *Rathin*, *AV* 4.34.4; 7.63.1; 7.77.1; 11.12.24; *TS* 5.2.2.3; *VS* 16.26; *ŚB* 8.7.3.7; etc. *Rathī*, *TS* 4.7.15.3). These terms denote one who goes in a chariot, an expression which includes both the driver and the warrior who accompanied him (6.2.204, 206). See **Sūta**.

**Chariot-maker:** The term *rathakāra*, 'chariot-maker', is mentioned in the *Atharvaveda* (3.5.6) as one of those who are to be subject to the king, seeming to stand as an example of the industrial population. He is also referred to in the *Yajurveda* (*KS* 17.13; *MS* 2.9.5; *VS* 16.17; 30.6), and in the *Brāhmaṇas* (*TB* 1.1.4.8, 3.4.3.1; *ŚB* 13.4.2.17). In all these passages, as well as probably in the *Atharvaveda* also, the *rathakāra* already forms a caste. The later system regards the *rathakāra* as the offspring of a Māhiṣya (the son of a Kṣatriya husband and a Śūdra wife), but it is unreasonable to suppose that such an origin is historically accurate. The *rathakāras* must rather be deemed to have been a functional caste. Macdonell and Keith 2, 203-04.

**Chariot-warrior:** The warrior in the chariot is designated as *asthātṛ* or car-fighter in the *Ṛgveda* 6.47.26. He seems to be the same as *rathin* or *ratheṣṭha*.

**Charms:** Generally, the magical charms of the *Atharvaveda* could be used for good and bad purposes. Especially in matters pertaining to love, human nature is inscrutable. The frustrations in love affairs, jealousy and personal ambitions display various shades of the aspirations of men and women. The *Atharvaveda* 6.13.8 mentions a charm that could turn a man into a eunuch. The woman urges the plant to turn the man into eunuch, who wears matted or plated hair and a hood (*kurīra*). He is thus castrated (*vadhri*) and becomes a eunuch (*klīva*). In another rite for making the male organ stout, an amulet of *arka* is used. By means of its magical power, the male organ (*śipa*) is made to agree limb to limb with that of a woman (*AV* 6.72.1). The male organ (*śipa*) is expected to be as large as that of *tāvādara* (a deer), inflated by wind, like that of *parasvat* (a deer), an elephant, donkey (*gardhava*) or vigorous horse (*AV* 6.72.2-3). A woman who desires that her rival should be ruined, may employ a charm using the *Atharvaveda* (7.114) and *Kauśika* (36.39) for achieving her purpose. In another hymn (1.14), the imprecations of a woman against her rival are more vigorous. She withdraws the *bhaga* (the peculiar lustre of the body, Sāyaṇa), like a garland from a tree. In the same way, a woman who desires that her rival should not have male child employs hymn 7.34 as a charm. According to *Kauśika* (30.33), the hymn is an appeal to Agni to drive off the rivals, born and unborn. It uses the word *sapatna* (7.34.1), which might be the reason for its employment against rivals, *sapatnī* by *Kauśika*. Hymn (*AV*) 7.35 is used if a woman intends that her rival should not have any child at all. The practitioner of the rite desires that the rival should not have any male child (7.34). The *Atharvaveda* 6.18 and 7.45 mention the interesting instance of a jealous husband, who is unsure of his wife's love for him. A magical rite performed by a priest, extinguishes for the woman, the fire of jealousy, the heat of his heart (6.18.1). Sometimes in an undesirable love affair between a man and a woman, a charm (*AV* 4.33) is used to prevent it. Agni, in this case, is offered oblation for securing good field, *kṣetra* (4.33.1-2). All sin and hatred are removed (4.33.7). Apart from being used to further personal ends, the *Atharvaveda* charms also had a positive influence on the relations between men and women. Unlucky marks on a woman's face and body are considered handicaps and the Atharvanic priest (*nirlakṣmyam*) may be used to remove an ugly spot on forehead; auspicious signs are produced and all unlucky, demonic marks are removed away to Arāti (a demon 1.18.1). All the evil signs are driven away by the gods (1.18.2). Similarly, fierceness in a woman, her body, hair and look are driven away by the charm uttered by the priests (*vācāpanhanma*, *AV* 1.18.3). There are a number of charms for securing matrimonial happiness. Even outside the marriage hymn (14.1-2), there are many spells regarding matrimonial happiness. By means of an offering called *bhūtahavi*, the offering of ghee and barley, a husband is expected to prosper and grow superior to his wife by his power (6.78.1). The *Atharvaveda* holds that inexhaustible wealth makes a couple happy (6.78.2). In another case when a man's wife runs away with her paramour, the *Atharvaveda* 6.77 prescribes a charm for her return (*Kauśika* 36.5.9). A rope is tied to a cross beam and to the middle post of the house. Also, a foot of the bed is tied to the *upala* plant. Sesame grains are offered in fire. In this symbolical ritual, the rope and foot of the bed suggest that she should come home and sleep on it. Hymn 6.77 describes how the heaven and earth, the mountains and, indeed, the whole world have stood firm, hence the husband contends that he shall take his wife to stay steadfast in his house (6.77.1). He urges the fire to restore his wife to him with his hundred and thousand ways of returning. See **Magic**, Shende 64-73.

**Chemistry:** In the *Ṛgveda* there is a mention of gold, silver, copper and bronze. Gold was used for ornaments like anklets and rings. Metal vessels, tools, and armour were made mainly of bronze. All this affords evidence of the knowledge of metallurgy. We also find a reference to the tanning of hides (infra). Dyeing garments with certain natural vegetable colours and the preparation of fermented drinks from Soma juice, barley grain and milk (curd) are also mentioned in the same text. The *Yajurveda* speaks of lead and tin among other metals. Gold, according to the *Atharvaveda*

(19.26), was regarded as an effective agent for prolongation of life. Lead was looked upon as an antidote to spells of sorcery. Thus, it may be inferred that several chemical processes were utilized. The process of smelting inevitably led to a crude understanding of the chemical process of combustion. There are many references in the Vedic literature to show that people were familiar with the process of tanning (*RV* 8.5.38) and the use of leather in making slings, strings, reins and whips (*RV* 1.121.9; 6.46.14; 47.26, 53; 9, 75.11). Since there is a mention of pottery as an art, there must have been earthenwares and wooden vessels. The art of dyeing their garments red, purple and brown was also known to the Vedic Indians. In the *Atharvaveda*, there is a separate class of hymns classified under the heading *āyuṣyāni*, for the prolongation of life and preservation of youth and health. The Atharvanic alchemical notion of *āyuṣyāni* later transformed into *rasāyana*. Besides, there were specialized craftsmen in different metals who knew how to process raw metals with the help of various kinds of alloys. See **Medical Science**, **Metals**, **Occupations**.

**Chick-pea:** *Khalva* is a species of grain or leguminous plant, stated in *Vājasaneyī Saṃhitā* (18.12) and *Bṛhadāraṇyaka Upaniṣad* (*Kānva* 6.3.13, *Madhyandina* 6.3.22). It is often identical to *phaselus raditus*. Mahīdhara and Śaṅkara gloss it by *caṇaka* (chick-pea), and *nispaya* respectively.

**Citron:** *Jāmbira*, 'hollow of the knee', occurs once in the *Maitrāyaṇī Saṃhitā* (3.15.3). The word also occurs in the form of *Jāmbila* in the *Kāṭhaka Saṃhitā* (5.13.1) and *Vājasaneyī Saṃhitā* (25.3). Mahīdhara, in his commentary on the latter text, interprets the word as 'knee-pan', which he says is so named because of its resemblance to the citron *jāmbīra*. The later Mahāyāna Buddhist deity Jambhala, with his emblem citron, might have received his appellation from the Vedic term *jāmbila* or *jāmbira*.

**Civil Procedure:** As regards civil law, our knowledge is mainly confined to the ownership of land, succession, and partition of property. Individual property or individual ownership of land for the purposes of cultivation was recognized. This individual tenure of land turned out to be (in actual practice and fact, if not in legal theory) tenure by a family, rather than by an individual. It is in this context that 'the conquests of fields', so often referred to in the Saṃhitās, must be understood. Communal property in the sense of 'ownership by a community' or that a family should live together, with undivided shares in the land. With settlement and peaceful occupation of the country, inheritance of landed property must have been in force even earlier than the age of the Sūtras, which state them clearly for the first time. In this age, the word *dāya* had already come to mean 'inheritance', of 'a father's property', which was to be divided among his sons either during his lifetime or after his death. In a legal sense, the property of the family was the property of the head of the house, usually the father. The *Taittirīya Saṃhitā* (3.1.4) has the famous episode of Manu's division of property among his sons. Nābhānediṣtha was excluded from the inheritance, but as compensation was taught how to appease the Aṅgirasas and secure cows from them. An important aspect of this account is that the property divided was movable property and not land, which was considered the foundation of wealth. This was so because, while cattle could be and was used individually, land could not be freely disposed of. In the *Aitareya Brāhmaṇa* version of the story, the sons are said to have made the division, leaving only Nābhānediṣtha in the care of their aged father. Does this suggest that the sons were legally owners with their father? The evidence however seems to be in favour of the rule of *patria protestas*. The sons, when grown up, might claim the property and induce the father to divide it, but this cannot amount to the doctrine that every child on birth had a legal share in the property. The legend of Śunaḥśepa points to the developed *patria protestas* of the father. As regards the division, preference was given to the elder son if it took place after the death of the father; during his lifetime, preference was usually given to the elder son but not rarely to another (*PB* 16.4.4). There is not much information available regarding the legal relations of husband and wife after marriage. The husband, in all probability, had no right on the wife's dowry and earnings. The *Śatapatha Brāhmaṇa* (4.4.2.13), however, says that women own neither themselves nor an inheritance. As regards civil procedure, voluntary arbitration appears to be the earliest form of judicial procedure, in which the plaintiff (*praśnin*), the defendant (*abhi-praśnin*) and the arbitrator or judge (*praśna-vivāka*) figured, as the three appear in the list of victims at the Puruṣamedha in the *Vājasaneyī Saṃhitā* (30.10). It is uncertain whether assessors were called in. The *jñātṛ* is very probably a technical legal term for a witness in civil transactions. Ordeals were but rarely used for deciding civil disputes. Their use as evidence in civil law, however, is proved by the case of Vatsa who demonstrated his parity of descent by walking through fire without sustaining any burn. The oath, though not mentioned as an independent instrument of evidence, must have formed part of the ordeal declaration when there was an occasion for it. Majumdar, 438-40.

**Civil and Criminal Law:** Theft, burglary, highway robbery and cheating (chiefly) and gambling are among the crimes recorded, with cattle-lifting at night being a very frequent one. Marriage of brother with sister was looked upon as incest. Tying the criminal to a stake was a common form of punishment. The epithet *śatadāya*, i.e., 'one the price of whose blood was one hundred' (coins) shows that the system of *wergeld* (*vairadeya*) or blood-money was probably in force. Whereas death was one of the punishments for theft in later times, it was not so in the Ṛgvedic age. The aim seems rather to have been the satisfaction of the person wronged. Our knowledge of civil law is as scanty as it is of criminal law. As we have seen, land seems not to have been an article of commerce. Movable property could change hands by gift or by sale, the latter taking the form of barter. The *Ṛgveda* records that, in the opinion of one poet not ten cows were an adequate price for an image of Indra, which was undoubtedly to be used as a fetish. The haggling of the market is once clearly referred to. The standard of value seems to have been the cow, and no coin appears to have been known, though the origin of currency may be seen in the frequent references to *niṣkas* as gifts. The *niṣka* most probably was an ornament in the shape of a necklace of gold or silver (*RV* 5.19.3 *niṣkagrīva niṣkeṇa subarṇena alaṃkṛtagrīvāḥ*). At a later date the name was transferred to a gold coin. Property doubtless passed by inheritence and could be acquired originally by a man's own efforts in creaction or discovery. Dowry and the price of the bride played a considerable part in early Vedic economy, as is seen by the stress laid upon both in the Saṃhitās. The only form of contract about which we know anything was the loan *ṛna*. The Vedic Indian was an inveterate gambler, and for that, among other causes, he seems always to have been ready to incur debt. The rate of interest is unknown, althouth a reference to payments of an eight or a sixteenth may allude either to interest or instalments of principal. At any rate, the debtor might as a result be reduced to slavery, as we learn from an interesting hymn (*RV* 10.34). In it, an unsuccessful dicer recites his fatal fascination for the dice and his consequent ruin and enslavement with its results for his family. Of civil procedure, we know only so much as may be inferred from a single word, *madhyamaśī*. This may denote one who intervenes between two parties as an arbitrator, though it has also been used as a reference to the king as being surrounded by his retainers in his camp. As regards the criminal cases in the post-Ṛgvedic period, serious crimes like killing an embryo, the murder of a Brāhmaṇa, and the murder of a man occur in lists of sins together with minor defects, much as the possession of bad nails. Other more serious crimes mentioned are stealing gold and drinking the *surā*, while treachery to the king is recognized as a capital offence. In the case of theft, in the *Chāndogya Upaniṣad*, we find the axe ordeal applied, apparently under the direction of the king; as a part of criminal procedure, however, this remains the only known case of an ordeal in Vedic literature. We also have very little information regarding civil law. The use of an ordeal in this connection is attested only by the case of Vatsa, who proved his purity of descent by walking unharmed through fire. Presumably, civil cases may have been decided by the king with assessors, but this view rests only on the analogy of another peoples and on the later practice in India itself. We know for certain that a Brāhmaṇa had preference in his law cases. But whether because it was a moral duty of the witnesses to bear testimony in his favour, or for the judges to give judgement for him, cannot be decided from the passage of the *Taittirīya Saṃhitā* which records the preference. Majumdar 360-1, 439-40, 493-6; Rapson, 87-8, 119-20.

**Clarified Butter:** An important article of food in the life of the Vedic Indians. Clarified butter was consumed directly as an edible substance and was also used to cook various delicacies. It was *ghṛta* (popularly known as *ghee*), or clarified butter, which was offered to gods during sacrifices. Agni is called Havyavāhana because he is not only sustained by *havya* or clarified butter but also carries it to the deity to whom it is offered. It is also known as *ājya*. *Ghee* was sometimes prescribed as magico-religious medicines; for it was considered to be a power substance. It is praised many times as being identical to life (*āyur vai ghṛtam*: *TS* 2.3.2.3; cf. *MS* 2.3.5; *KS* 11.8; 21.7). It was used as an apotropic substance when mixed with certain herbs. Ghee prepared with mixing *vacā* (Acorus Colomus) in it was prescribed for destroying evil spirits (causes of diseases). Similarly, the *ghee* prepared along with *Brāhmī*, *siddhārthaka* (white mustards), *khuṣṭha* (costus spuiosus), *saindhava*-stone-salt, *sārivā* (hemidesmus indicus or ichonocarpus frutesceons), *vacā* and *pippali* (piper longum) was called Abhaya (fearless).

**Clothing:** See **Dress**.

**Collector:** The term *bhāgadugha*, 'dealer out of portions', 'distributor', was an appellation of one of the king's 'jewels' (*ratnin*) in the *Yajurveda Saṃhitās* (*TS* 1.8.9.2; *KS* 15.4; *MS* 2.6.5; 4.3.8; *VS* 30.13) and *Brāhmaṇas* (*TB* 1.7.3.5; 2.4.8.1; *ŚB* 1.1.2.17; 5.3.1.9). What his functions exactly were is uncertain. Sāyaṇa in some places (*ŚB* 5.3.1.9) interprets the term as 'tax-collector'. It may also mean (*ŚB* 1.1.2.17) a 'carver', thus making this functionary either a revenue officer or a mere court official.

**Collective Ownership:** Although private property and individual ownership became a regular feature in the socio-economic life of the Ṛgvedic age, there are relics of a more primitive pre-class society and of collective life in the *Ṛgveda*. In the *Ṛgveda* (7.76.5) a clear picture of primitive communism is found: 'Being united with the *common cattle* they become of one mind; they strive together, as it were; nor do they injure the rituals of the gods: nor injuring each other they move with health.' Here are a few other examples of collective ownership along with a significant reference to the past: 'As in the past he (Agni) generated the *common wealth* for the living beings' (*RV* 3.2.12). 'Let the *common cow* be moving swiftly' (*RV* 6.26.1). 'We invoke Indra, the custodian of *common wealth* and the giver of wealth for protection' (*RV* 8.99.8). 'O Agni, your brilliance comes to us and you brought the cows of *Ṛta* equally to us' (*RV* 1.141.1). Such examples can be multiplied to show that the *Ṛgveda,* during the long period of its composition, witnessed the transition from pre-class to class society and that it actually contains the relics of ancient collectivity and equality. The concluding verses of the *Ṛgveda* are really significant. The poet is lamenting lost life, trying to restore the bliss of equality and unity once enjoyed by the Vedic peoples of the earlier age. See **Distribution**.

**Collyrium:** The term *añjana* is found in the *Atharvaveda* (9.6.11) with the sense of collyrium.

**Comets:** The term *dhūmaketu* (*AV* 19.9.10) occurs as an epithet of death. Literally the word means 'smoke bannered'. The term seems to denote more correctly the comets, which in primitive belief, were associated with omens and portents.

**Commanding Officers:** The *senānī* is considered as a general appointed by a king in the *Ṛgveda* 7.20.5; 9.96.1; 10.84.2; *Kāṭhaka Saṃhitā* 17.11; *Maitrāyaṇī Saṃhitā* 2.9.4; *Taittirīya Saṃhitā* 4.5.2.1. *Vājasaneyī Saṃhitā* 15.15; 16.17; *Śatapatha Brāhmaṇa* 8.6.1.21. He seems to act as the officer of the king in the battlefield and to have led trivial expeditions. The office of the *senānī* indicates the stability of the Vedic military organization. The standing armed force of the king must have been organized and commanded by the *senānī*, besides the contingents led by the *grāmaṇī*. The *Sāmāvidhāna Brāhmaṇa* 3.6.1.10 tells that in battle he commands the front where the chiefs stood. The *Aitareya Brāhmaṇa* 8.23.10 calls him the *senāpati*, commander of the army: The *senānī* is one of the king's *ratnins* in *Kāṭhaka Saṃhitā* 15.4; *Maitrāyaṇī Saṃhitā* 2.6.5; 4.3.8; *Taittirīya Saṃhitā* 1.8.9.1 *Taittirīya Brāhmaṇa* 1.7.3.4; *Śatapatha Brāhmaṇa* 5.3.1.1.

**Common Women:** In one passage of the *Ṛgveda* (1.167.4) *sādhāraṇī* i.e., common women seems to refer to courtesans. In the *Ṛgveda* (1.126.5), the *viśyā iva vrā anasvantaḥ* seems best translated by Geldner's '*die auf karren wie die clandirnen fahrend...*' for *viśyāḥ* is feminine plural. The later word veśyā for prostitute, from the same root as viśyā, presumably denotes the woman who dwelt in a house common to all men. See **Hetairai, Prostitution, Women**.

**Concentration:** The *Kaṭha Upaniṣad* (6.10.11) defines *yoga* as firm control of the senses. So the *yogin* is *apramatta*, undistracted. The *Muṇḍaka Upaniṣad* refers to Ṣaḍaṅga-yoga as comprising *āsana* (posture), *prāṇāyāma* (restraint of breath), *pratyāhāra* (withdrawal of the senses), *dhyāna* (meditation), *dhāraṇā* (concentration), *samādhi* (absorption) in 6.18. The process of *yoga* is further described in the said Upaniṣad (6.19-29). Yoga (joining) is defined as oneness of mind and the senses. See **Yoga**.

**Consciousness:** The third chapter of the *Kaṭha Upaniṣad* contains the dialogue between Indra and Pratardana, which advances the doctrine of *prajñātman* and which is suggestive of various types of consciousness. (i) Indra first identifies himself with truth and tells Pratardana that to know him would be most beneficial to man. (ii) Indra then identifies himself with *prāṇa* and asks Pratardana to meditate on him as life and as immortality. All *prāṇas* are really one; otherwise, neither perception nor action would be possible. (iii) Indra then tells Pratardana that *prāṇa* is *prajñā*, and that they both live together in the body and depart together. (iv) Indra further emphasizes the significance of consciousness and tells Pratardana that without consciousness no thought occurs and, therefore, no knowledge is possible. (v) Indra then asks Pratardana to try to find out not what speech is, but the speaker; not what smell is, but the smeller; not what sound is, but the hearer; not what food is but the eater; not what actions are but the doer. (vi) Finally, Indra goes on to identify this *prāṇa* with the conscious self or *prajñātman*. This self is full of bliss and is imperishable. In the *Praśnopaniṣad* (4.1-11), the question of Sauryāyaṇī Gāryya asks Pippalāda to instruct him about what happens in the conditions of sleep and dream, as opposed to that of wakefulness. He is told that in such a state the senses become inactive but consciousness remains. There are three points to be noticed in the analysis of dream-consciousness. In dreams, man experiences not merely what has already come in a wakeful state, but he also experiences what he may not have experienced. In the earlier Upaniṣads reference has been made, no doubt, to the distinction between the waking state and dream, and in the *Chāndogya Upaniṣad* there is evidently a recognition of a fourth state mentioned in the dialogue between Indra and Prajāpati (8.5-7); nor is the reference to the fourth state wanting in the *Maitrāyanī Upaniṣad* as in 6.19 or 7.11; but it is only in the *Māṇḍūkyopaniṣad*, for the first time, that we find a systematic enumeration of the different states of consciousness, and it is only there that the *turīya* or the fourth is directly contrasted with the other three. It is the fourth dimension of psychology. See **Epistemology**. Belvalkar and Ranade, 276-7, 293-5, 323-4.

**Consecration:** See **Royal Ceremonies**.

**Cooking:** The term *pakva*, 'cooked' is used as meaning 'cooked food' (*RV* 6.63.9; *AV* 6.119.2; 12.3.55; *ŚB* 1.5.1.26; 2.6.1.7), or 'cooked milk' (*RV* 1.62.9; 2.40.2; 3.30.14; 6.44.24). The word is also used in connection with 'baked' bricks (*ŚB* 6.1.2.22, 7.2.1.7). The term *pacata*, like *pakti*, denotes 'cooked food' in the *Ṛgveda* (1.61.7, 10.116.8) and later (*VS* 21.60, 23.13, *KB* 8.21). The word Paktṛ means the man who cooks food (*AV*

10.9.7, 11, 25; 11.1.17; 12.3.17; *ŚB* 3.3.4.17). There were cooks and servers of food (*AV* 9.6.5; 1, 3.17; *ŚB* 1.2.2.14). Many implements and utensils were used in cooking. Some of these were made of clay, wood and stone while others were made of metals. Leather vessels were used for storing liquids. Some of the common cooking implements were a cooking pot (*sthālī*), a ladle (*sruva*) and a spoon (*darvī*). Cups (*śarāva*) were used for measuring food stuffs and a grindstone and a mortar were regarded as very important. Vessels of copper, iron and stone were in common use besides earthenware. Sometimes gold vessels and those made of wood were also used. Potsherds (*kapāla*) were used for baking cakes. The omentum of a victim was grilled in a vessel (*vapāśrapaṇi*) and meat was roasted on spits (*hṛdayaśūla*). An earthen utensil was used only once but if it had to be reused, it was burnt afresh. Metallic utensils were cleaned with ashes and the wooden ones by scraping. Om Prakash 27, 111-12.

**Constellations:** Constellation denotes one of the various groups into which ancient observers divided the stars. Almost 90 separate groups are now recognized. The stars in any particular constellation are not necessarily associated with one another, but merely happen to lie in the same part of the sky as seen from the earth. The stars are denoted by the word *nakṣatra* and are mentioned singly, in groups and in connection with the sun and the moon (*RV* 1.50.2; 5.59.13; 7.86.1; 10.64.8; 68.11; 85.13; 111.7; *AV* 6.10.3; 128.3; 15.6.2; 5.24-10; *VS* 22.29; 23.43; 30.21; 39.2; *TS* 1.8.13.3; 3.4-5.1; 1.2.2.2; 2.6.2.6; *KS* 35.15; 37.12; *PB* 10.1-1; *TĀ* 4.10, 12, etc.) The *Taittirīya Saṃhitā* (4.4.10.1-3) and *Kāṭhaka Saṃhitā* (39.13) expressly mention 27 *nakṣatras* or stars. Later on when Abhijit (*MS* 2.13.20) became the pole star, it was counted as the 28th *nakṣatra*. In the course of time Abhijit ceased to be the pole star and the number again came down to 27. Among these 27 stars, Kṛttikās are unquestionably the Pleiades, a cluster of stars in the constellation, Taurus. The names of the seven stars forming this constellation, and given in *Taittirīya Saṃhitā* (4.4.5.1); *Kāṭhaka Saṃhitā* (11.4) and *Taittirīya Brāhmaṇa* (3.1.4.1), include three *abhrayanti*, 'forming clouds', *meghayanti* 'making cloudy', *varṣayanti*, 'causing rain', which clearly refer to the rainy Pleiades. The words *kṛttikā* possibly means 'web', from the root *kṛt* 'spin', Rohinī, ruddy, is the name of the conspicuously reddish star, a Tauri or Aldebanran, and denotes the group of the Hyades, a groups of stars in Taurus near the Pleiades. Mṛgaśīrṣa or Mṛgaśiras, also called Invakā or Invagā, seems to be the faint stars near the Orionis. They are called Andhakā, 'blind' in the Śāntikalpa of the *Atharvaveda*, probably because of their dimness. Ārdrā, 'moist' is the name of the brilliant star, an Orionis. But the names by which it is styled, in the plural as Ārdrās in the *Śāṅkhāyana Gṛhya Sūtra* (1.26) and the *nakṣatrakalpa* (10) point to a constellation of two or more stars. Punarvasu, 'the two that give wealth again', denotes the two stars, A and B Geminorum, on the heads of Castor and Pollux. Tiṣya or Puṣya includes the somewhat faint group of stars in the body of the Cancer, the fourth sign of the Zodiac, Aśreṣās or Aśleṣās denotes stars of the Hydrae group. Maghās, the 'bounties', are associated with Leonis. Phalgunī, Phalgunyau, Phalgū, Phalgunīs, Phalgunyas, is really a double constellation, divided into *pūrva*, 'former', and *uttara*, both belonging to the Leonis, 'hand', is made up of the five conspicuous stars in Corvus, a number which the word itself suggests. Citrā, 'bright' is the beautiful star, a Virginis, Svāti or Niṣṭyā is later clearly the brilliant star Arcturus, its place in the north being assured by the notice in the *Śāntikalpa* (3) where it is said to be 'ever traversing the northern way' (*nityam uttara-mārgagam*). Viśākha is the couple of stars, Librae. This mansion is later called Rādhā according to the *Amarakośa*. But probably Rādhā is merely an invention due to the name of the next *nakṣatra*. Anurādhā, wrongly conceived as meaning 'that which is after or follows Rādhā'. Anurādhas or Anurādhā 'propitious', in the group of Scorpionis. Vicṛtau, 'the two releasers', denotes primarily two stars at the extremity of the tail of the Scorpion. Āṣāḍhās 'unconquered', distinguished as Pūrvas, 'former', and Uttaras, 'latter', are really two constellations of which the former is composed of Sagittari stars. Abhijit is the brilliant star Lyrae with its two companions, Śroṇā, 'lame', or Śravaṇa, 'ear' denotes the bright star Aquilae Sravistnas 'most famous' or later Dhaniṣṭhas 'most wealthy' is a star in the Dolphin in harmony with the Manazil and Sieou. Śatabhiṣaj or Śatabhiṣa, 'having a hundred physicians', seems to be Aquarii, with the others around it vaguely conceived as numbering a hundred. Proṣṭha-pādas 'feet of a stool', or later Bhādra-padas (*Śāntikalpa* 5, etc.) 'auspicious feet', is a double asterism forming a square belonging to the Pegsai and Andromedae. Revatī, 'wealth', denotes a large numebr of stars (later 32), of which Piscium is close upon the ecliptic where it is crossed by the equator. Aśva-Yajau, 'the two horse-harnessers', denotes the star Arietis. Aśvinyau and Aśvinī are later names. Apabharaṇīs, Bharaṇīs, or Bharaṇyas, 'the bearers' is the name of the small triangle in the northern part of the Ram known as Muṣca of the Arietis group.

**Contract:** See **Law of Contract**.

**Copper:** It is difficult to determine the sense of the word *ayas* used in the *Ṛgveda* (1.57.3; 1.163.9; 4.2.17; 6.3.5). The epithets of Agni as *ayodaṃṣṭra*, with teeth of *ayas* (*RV* 1.88.5, 10.87.2), referring to the colour of his flames, and the description of the car-seat of Mitra and Varuṇa as *aysothūṇa* (*RV* 5.62.8) with pillar of *ayas* lead us to assume that it meant more bronze than iron.

*Ayas* is noted in *Vājasaneyī Saṃhitā* (18.13) in the list of six metals beside *śyāma* and *loha*. If *śyāma* is taken in the sense of black and *loha* in that of red metal, i.e. as iron and copper respectively, *ayas* may be better explained as 'bronze'. *Lohāyasa* in *ŚB* (5.4.1.1), lit. red metal is either copper or an alloy of copper and some other metal. *Lohitāyasa* in *Maitrāyaṇī Saṃhitā* (2.11.5) and *Kāṭhaka Saṃhitā* (18.10) also seem to mean copper.

**Cord:** The term *raśanā* is mentioned in the *Ṛgveda* (1.162.8) and means fastening of a horse. The term is also used to denote rope in general (*RV* 2.28.5; *AV*.8.78.1; 10.9.2; *VS* 21.46; 22.2; 28.33; *TS* 6.6.4.3; *ŚB* 3.6.3.10). Another term *son-nahana* is also mentioned in the *Taittirīya Saṃhitā* (1.1.2.2; *ŚB* 1.3.3.6, 2.6.1.15), which means rope or cord used for binding sacrificial grass.

**Corn:** See under **Grains**. The general term for grain is *śasya*. The Vedic texts refer to *kulmāṣa* (beans), *garmut* (wild bean), *godhūma* (wheat), *taṇḍula* (rice grains), *tirya, tila* (sesamum) *dhāna* (grains of corn), *dhānya* (grain), *piṇḍa* (flour ball), *pūlpa* or *pūlya* (shrivelled grain), *plāśuka* (fast growing rice), *yava* (barley), *vrīhi* (rice), *śāli* (rice), *śaktu* (groats), *śasya* (corn) and so forth. Various methods of cultivations, ploughing, use of manure, irrigation, reaping, winnowing, storing, etc., are described in the Vedic texts. The Vedic Indians were keen in the preservation of their harvest and were cautious about the elements which damage their production. See **Agriculture**.

**Corngrinder:** The *Ṛgveda* 9.112.3 refers to a term *upala-prakṣiṇī* which denotes the occupation of a woman, as opposed to her son who is a poet (*kāru*) and to that of her husband who is a physician (*bhiṣaj*). Yāska (*Nirukta* 6.3) renders the word as 'maker of groats' (*śaktukārikā*). The word may also be explained as the operation of grinding corn. *Upala* means a mortar in which the corn was placed and then beaten with a pestle.

**Coronation Hymn:** In the *Ṛgveda* there is evidence that popular choice and support were vital to the king, and various hymns, passages or similies point to this. Thus, in the *Ṛgveda* (10.124.8), we hear of the similie like 'subjects choosing a king', *tārhaṃ viśo na rājānaṃ vṛṇānā bībhatsuvo apa vṛtrādatiṣṭan*. The celebrated coronation hymn of the *Ṛgveda* (10.173) speaks of the acceptance of the king by the *viśaḥ*. The same occurs in the *Atharvaveda* with some modifications (*AV* 6.87.88). The priest thus addresses the king-elect; 'Come unto our midst, remain steadfast and immovable, (May) the people all like (welcome) you and may you not fall from your position. Be ye steadfast here and may ye not come down. Remain here as firm as Indra and uphold the *rāṣtra* (or the state). Indra held it fast with his offering of *havis*, for it, Soma and Brahmanaspati have said the same. Firm the heaven, firm the earth, firm the universe, firm the mountains so firm be also this kind of men (*viśāṃ*). Let the state held by you be firm through king Varuṇa, the Deva Bṛhaspati. Indra and Agni. Steadfast in your position, you win over Soma by oblations of butter. Let Indra make you the sole gatherer of the tribute from your people.' The last verse in the Atharvavedic hymn means: 'Vanquish you firmly and without fail your enemies, let them be crushed under your feet. All the quarters unanimously welcome you and for firmness, the Assembly (*samiti*) appoint you.' See **Royal Ceremonies**.

**Cosmography:** The *Ṛgveda* indicates the earth by various words such as *mahī*, *pṛthivī* or *ūrvī* (the broad), *uttāna* (the extended), and *apārā* (the boundless). The universe is conceived as consisting of two or three units, i.e. of either the earth and the sky (heaven), or the earth, the air (the atmosphere) and the sky. Often each of these constituents was regarded as having three parts or layers, so that they were either six units or three earths and three heavens or nine units of three earths, three atmospheres and three skies (cf. Macdonell). The highest of the three earths was believed to have been inhabited by men just as the third or highest heaven was occupied by the gods, the fathers and Soma (*RV* 1.34.8; *AV* 6.21.1). The conception of three earths and of the highest earth is based on the belief about the existence of a nether world. The *YV* (*VS* 17.67; cf. *AV* 4.14.3) speaks of the earth, air, heaven and the world of light i.e., the vault of the sky. The earth and the sky were sometimes conceived as circular, like the wheels at the two ends of the axle representing the intervening space (*RV* 10.89.4), while the hemispherical vault of the sky led to the conception of the two great bowls turned towards each other (*RV* 6.55.20). Both the descriptions point to the belief about the circular shape of the surface of the earth; but the second, apparently, refers to the globular conception of the universe, consisting two halves, viz., the earth and the sky. This reminds us of the later idea of the Brahmāṇḍa or the cosmic egg (q.v.). The distance between the earth and the sky is given in the *Aitareya Brāhmaṇa* (2.17.8; cf. *AV* 10.8.18) as 1000 days journey for a horse, while the *Pañcaviṃśa Brāhmaṇa* (16.8.6, 21.1.9) considers that altitude (is as high as) 1000 cows standing one upon another.

**Cosmic Egg:** See **Hiraṇyagarbha**.

**Cosmogony:** The problem of the origin and nature of the world-stuff is a philosophical one, and is not neglected by the Ṛgvedic poets. *Ṛgveda* 10.190 tells us that from heat (*tapas*) were produced *ṛta* and *satya*; then might, the ocean, and *samvatsara* (year) were produced in succession. The *Ṛgveda* (10.72.2) says that *sat* was produced from *asat*. From the mythological point of view, each one of the gods in turn is said to be the creator of the universe, which is sometimes looked upon as the finished product of the carpenter's and joiner's skill. For example, *Ṛgveda* 10.31.7 asks 'What was the wood, which the tree, out of which they fashioned heaven and earth' *Ṛgveda* 10.121 takes up the problems of creation on a monotheistic level and tells us that Hiraṇyagarbha arose from the great waters, pervading the universe, and thus created the world out of eternally pre-existing matter. But *Ṛgveda* 10.129, the well-known Nāsadīya hymn, describes creation from the highest monistic level. In the beginning, there was no 'non-existent', because this creation arose therefrom, nor the 'existent', because its usual manifestations, the firmament or the heaven beyond it, were not then. The one breathed by itself, breathless, and there was nothing beyond it. There was no death then; how could there be anything immortal then? There was no light which could give us distinction of night or day. This suggests the highest philosophical truth and therefore the Absolute cannot be characterized because there is no characterizing categories. *Tapas* is the warming up of being into existence, whereby the primary antithesis in the Absolute is implied of namely the opposition of ego and non-ego. The hymn further tells us that Desire (*kāma*), the germ of the mind betraying self-consciousness, is the bond binding the existent to the non-existent. The doubt expressed at the end, whether anyone knows the truth about creation, is a beautiful expression of the ignorance of the wise. This hymn rises to the breathtaking heights of monism and leaves behind the dualistic metaphysics of the hymn to Viśvakarman (10.82). In it, we are told that the waters contained the primordial germ, the floating world-egg from which arises Viśvakarman, the first-born of the universe—the creator-maker of the world. The Nāsadīya hymn, in the terminology of modern philosophy, makes nature and spirit both aspects of the One, the Absolute, which is neither the self nor the non-self. There are hymns of a philosophical import in the *Atharvaveda*, although they are inspired more by practical considerations than by a longing for the Ultimate Reality. The hymns definitely imply a high level of metaphysical thought. There is some exaggeration in Winternitz's opinion that in these hymns there is more of the mystery-mongering so characteristic of a magician than the search for truth that distinguishes a philosopher; and, that they do not represent even a transitional stage between the creative thought of the philosophical hymns of the *Ṛgveda and the philosophy of the Upaniṣads.* The idea of a supreme god like Prajāpati, as the creator and preserver of the universe, and that of an impersonal creative principle (which for the two chief doctrines of the Upaniṣads), and some technical terms such as *brahman, tapas, asat,* are met within the *Atharvaveda*. The conception of Rudra-Śiva in the *Atharvaveda* certainly represents a transitional stage between the conception of Rudra in the *Ṛgveda* and the systematic philosophy of Śaivism in the *Śvetāśvatara Upaniṣad*. Original and otherwise, profound philosophical ideas do crop up now and then in the *Atharvaveda*. *Kāla* or time, as the first cause of all existence (*AV* 19.53.5.6), is a truly philosophical notion, but around it are woven metaphors that give a mystic turn to the great idea (19.53). Similarly *prāṇa* (breath) and *kāma* (passion) are described as First Causes in *AV* 11.4 and 9.2 respectively. The Rohita hymns (*AV* 13.1-4) contain a sublime glorification of the 'Red One' (the genius of the sun) as a cosmogonic power. Along with this are found mystical fancies such as the exaltation of the sun as a primeval principle under the guise of a *brahmacārin*, and the glorification of the Ox, the Bull, the Cow, and the Vrātya, each being alternately looked upon as the highest being, in (11.5; 4.11; 9.4; 10.10; 15) respectively. The *Atharvaveda* (10.2) is but an imitation of the philosophical hymn (10.121) of the *Ṛgveda* and tastes of the realization of *brahman* in man, from the physical aspect. The *Atharvaveda* (11.8) suggests the idea of *brahman* as the First Cause of all existence and of the oneness of man with the world-soul. *Prāṇa* plays an important part in the psychology and metaphysics of the Upaniṣads. *Prāṇa* is breath of life, life, or life-principle. In the singular, *prāṇa* is a frequent appellation of the *ātman*. A favourite theme with the Upaniṣads is a description of this *prāṇa*, which is identical with the intelli_ .nt self, and of its relations to the *prāṇas* (plural), i.e. the organs of the soul (breath, speech, sight, hearing and the organ of thinking). The reciprocal action between these organs of the soul and the corresponding five forces of nature—wind, fire, the sun, the quarters of heaven and the moon—are also often touched upon. See **Ātman, Brahman, Hiraṇyagarbha, Prajāpati, Prāṇa, Puruṣa, Viśvakarman.**

**Cosmology:** The universe, the stage on which the actions of the gods are enacted, is regarded by Vedic poets as divided into the three domains of earth, air or atmosphere and heaven. The sky, when regarded as the whole space above the earth, forms with the latter the entire universe, consisting of the upper and the nether world. The vault (nāka) of the sky is regarded as the limit dividing the visible upper world from the third or invisible world of heaven, which is the abode of light and the dwelling place of the gods. Heaven, air and earth form the favourite triad of the *Ṛgveda*, constantly spoken of explicitly or implicity (8.10.6; 8.90.6 and c.). The solar phenomena, which appear to take place on the vault of the sky, referred to heaven while those of lightning, rain and wind belong to the atmosphere. But when heaven designates the whole space above the earth, both classes of phenomena are spoken of as taking place there. In a passage of the *Atharvaveda* (4.14.3; cf. *VS* 17.67), the 'vault of the sky' comes between the triad of earth, air, heaven and the world of light, which thus forms a fourth division. Each of the three worlds is also subdivided. Thus three earths, three atmospheres, three heavens are sometimes mentioned, or when the universe is looked upon as consisting of two halves, we hear of six worlds or spaces (*rajāṃsī*). This subdivision probably arose from the loose use of the word *pṛthivī* 'earth' (*RV* 1.108.9;10; 7.104.11) in the dual two denotes the three worlds (just as the dual *pitarau* 'two fathers' regularly denotes 'father and mother'). The earth is variously called *bhūmi, kṣam, gmā* the great (*mahī*) the broad (*pṛthivī* or *urvī*), the extended (*uttāna*), the boundless (*apārā*), or the place here (*idam*) as contrasted with the upper sphere (1.22.17.154.1.3). The conception of the earth being a disc surrounded by an ocean does not appear in the Saṃhitās. But it was naturally regarded as circular, being compared with a wheel (10.89.4) and expressly called circular (*parimaṇḍala*) in the *Śatapatha Brāhmaṇa*. The four parts of the compass are already mentioned in the *Ṛgveda* in an adverbial form (7.72.5; 10.36.14; 10.42.11) and in the *Atharvaveda* as substantives (*AV* 15.2.1 ff.). Hence four quarters (*pradiśaḥ*) are spoken of (10.19.8), with the term also used as being synonymous with the whole earth (1.164.42), which is described as four pointed (10.58.3). Five points are occasionally mentioned (9.86.29; *AV* 3.24.3; 3.24.6), while that in the middle (10.42.11) where the speaker is, denotes the fifth. The *Atharvaveda* also refers to a sixth (the zenith being added) and even a seventh point. The same points may be meant by the seven regions (*diśaḥ*) and the seven places (*dhāma*) of the earth, spoken of in the *Ṛgveda* (9.114.3; 1.22.16). Heaven in the *div* is also commonly termed *vyoman*, sky or pervaded with light, the luminous space, *rocana* (with or without *divaḥ*). Designations of the dividing firmament, besides the vault, are the summit (*sānu*), surface (*viṣṭap*) and ridge (*pṛṣṭha*), as well as the compound expression ridge of the vault (1.125 5 cf. 3.2.12) and summit of the vault (8.92.2). Even a third ridge in the luminous space of heaven is mentioned (9.86.27). When three heavens are distinguished, they are very often called the three luminous spaces: (*trīrocanā*), a highest (*uttama*), a middle, and a lowest being specified (5.60.6). The highest is also termed *uttara*, and *pārya* (4.26.6; 6.40.5). In this third or highest heaven (very often *parame rocane* or *vyomani*) the gods, the fathers and Soma are regarded as abiding. Heaven and earth are coupled as a dual conception, called by the terms *rodasī, kṣonī, dyāvā-pṛthivī* and others, and spoken of as the two halves (2.27.15). The combination with the semi-spherical sky causes the notion of the earth's shape to be modified, when the two are called 'the two great bowls' (*camvā*) turned towards each other (5.55.20). Once they are compared to the wheels at the two ends of an axle (10.8-9.4). The *Ṛgveda* makes no reference to the supposed distance between heaven and earth, except in such a vague phrase as 'nor even the birds can soar to the abode of Viṣṇu' (1.155.5). But the *Atharvaveda* (10.81.8) says that the two wings of the yellow bird (the sun) flying to heaven are 1000 days journey apart. A similar notion is found in the *Aitareya Brāhmaṇa*, where it is remarked (2.17) that '1000 days' journey for a horse, the heavenly world is distant here. Another *Brāhmaṇa* states that the heavenly world is as far from this world as 1000 cows standing on each other (*PB* 16.8.6; 21.1.9). The air or intermediate space (*antarikṣa*) is hardly susceptible of personification. As the region of mists and cloud, it is also called *rajas*, which is described as watery (1.124.5; cp. 5.85.2) and is sometimes thought of as dark. When it is spoken of as 'black' (1.35.2; 1.4.9; 8.43.6), the triple subdivision is referred to as the three spaces of *rajāṃsī* (4.53.5; 5.69.1). The highest is then spoken of as *uttama* (9.22.5) *parama* (3.30.2) or *tṛtīya*, the third (9.74.60; 10.45.3; 10.123.8), where the waters and Soma are and the celestial Agni is produced. The two lower spaces are within the range of our perception, but the third belongs to Viṣṇu (7.99, cf. 1.155.5). The latter seems to be the 'mysterious' space once referred to elsewhere (10.105.7). The twofold subdivision of the atmosphere is more common. Then the lower (*upara*) or terrestrial (*pārthiva*) is contrasted with the heavenly (*divyam* or *divaḥ*) space (1.62.5; 4.53.3). The uppermost stratum, being contiguous with heaven (*div*) in the twofold as well as the triple division, seems often to be loosely employed as synonymous with heaven in the strict sense. In regard to such matters, it would not be reasonable to expect absolute definitions or consistency in statements of different poets or even the same poet. The air being above the earth in the threefold division of the universe, its subdivisions, whether two or three, would naturally have been regarded as above it also; and one verse, at least (1.81.5, cf. 1.90.7) clearly shows that the terrestrial space is in this position. Three passages of the *Ṛgveda* (6.9.1; 5.81.4, 7.80.1), however, have been thought to lend themselves to the view that the lower atmosphere was conceived as under the earth, to account for the course of the sun during the night. But the luminary shines upwards at night, while it turns round so as to shine downwards in the daytime. That the light which the sun's steeds draw is sometimes bright and sometimes dark (*RV* 1.115.5), or that the *rajas* which accompanies the sun to the east is different from the light with which he rises (*RV* 10.37.3). There being no direct reference to the sun passing below the earth, the balance of probabilities seems to favour the view that the luminary was supposed to return east, the way it came, becoming entirely darkened during the return journey. As to what becomes of the stars during the daytime, a doubt is expressed (*RV* 1.24.10), but no conjecture is made. The atmosphere is often called a sea (*samudra*), as the abode of celestial waters. It is also assimilated to be earth inasmuch as it has mountains (*RV* 1.32.2), etc., and seven streams, which flow there (*RV* 1.32.12), etc. Owing to the obvious resemblance, the term mountain (*parvata*) very often in the *Ṛgveda* refers to clouds, the figurative sense being generally clear enough. Further, the word 'rock' (*adri*) is regularly used in a mythological sense for 'cloud' as enclosing the cows released by Indra and other gods. The rain clouds as containing the waters, as dripping, moving and roaring are peculiarly liable to theriomorphism as cows whose milk is rain. The cosmic order or law prevailing in nature is recognized under the name of *ṛta* (properly the 'course of things'), which is considered to be under the guardianship of the highest gods. The same word also designates 'order' in the moral world as truth and 'right', and in the religious world as sacrifice or 'rite'. Macdonell 8-11.

**Costus Speciosus:** *Kuṣṭha* is the name of a plant (*costus speciosus* or *arabicus*) which is prominent in the *Atharvaveda* (5.4; 6.102; 19.139). It grew especially on the mountains along with the Soma on the high peaks of the Himālayas (*himavant*), where the eagles rest, and was thence brought to men (5.4.1; 5.4.2; 5.4.8; 19.39.1). Like Soma, it is said to have grown in the third heaven under the famous *aśvattha* tree, where the gods were wont to assemble, and thence it was brought in a golden ship (*RV* 5.4.3-6; 6.75.1; 6.75.2; 19.39.6-8). As a remedy, it held the highest place among herbs, being called by the auspicious name *nagha-māra* and *naghāriṣa*, and styled the offspring of Jīvala and Jīvalā, the 'lively' ones (*RV* 5.4.1; 19.39.4). It cured headache (*śirsāmaya*), diseases of the eyes, bodily affliction (*RV* 5.4.10), but especially fever. Hence it is called 'fever-destroyer' (*takma-nāśana*) and it also cured consumption (*yakṣmā*). From its general properties it also was named 'all-healing' panacea (*viśva-bheṣaja*) (*RV* 19.39.9). Its aromatic qualities were apparently known, as it is classed with 'salve' (*añjana*) and 'nard' (*nalada*) (*RV* 6.102.3). Macdonell and Keith I. 175.

**Council:** *Saṃgati* in one passage of the *Ṛgveda* (10.141.4) seems to have the sense of *samiti*, 'assembly of the people'. Another term (*saṃgrāma*) denotes primarily the 'assembly', either in peace (*AV* 12.1.56) or in war (*AV* 4.24.7) when it seems an 'armed band'. Its normal sense in the *Atharvaveda* (5.21.7; 11.9.26) and later *TB* (2.1.3.1) is war or battle council.

**Cosmo-physiology:** Speculations about cosmo-physiology relate to the humoral theory of Āyurveda, which propound that wind (*vāyu*), bile (*pitta*) and phlegm (*kapha*) are the three basic elements activating, sustaining and maintaining the life-principle. The origin of this theory may be traced to the three world components, viz., air, fire and water, which similarly sustain, maintain, and motivate the world. Such ideas are foreshadowed in the Vedic texts. Though the basic approach of the *Atharvaveda* is magical, certain abstractions relating to *prāṇa* or vital breath and the like are found therein. The cosmic element of *vāyu* or *vāta* (air) is considered the motor *par excellence*, which activates the entire universe. Its physiological manifestation is the vital breath or *prāṇa* which, according to Āyurveda, regulates all functions of life (*Suśruta-Saṃhitā*, 1.14.4; *Caraka-Saṃhitā* 1.18.49). *Pitta*, which maintains the thermal balance of the body, is a manifestation of the cosmic principle of Agni (fire) in living organisms (*Caraka-Saṃhitā*, 1.12.11; 1.21.9; *Suśruta-Saṃhitā*, 1.21.10). The cosmo-physiological aspect of Agni is suggested by the Vedic epithet Vaiśvānara and the Avestan expression *Vahufrayan*, both meaning 'the fire of digestion' present in all animate bodies. The Āyurvedic notion of fire (*tejas*) in the body is nothing but an extended idea of the concept of Vaiśvānara. The term, meaning that which results from water, corresponds to the cosmic primordial water (*āp*). This primordial element was viewed as 'mother', as a vivifying liquid of nectar. Some other epithets show it as the fluid matrix from which the birth of living organisms was possible. Its physiological element *kapha* in the human body is also credited with the same properties. Both *āp* and *kapha* signify the fluid-matrix in which all the operations of life are possible.

**Couch:** In the *Ṛgveda* (7.55.8) and *Atharvaveda* (4.5.3, 4.20.3; 14.2.30) *vaḥya* denotes a 'couch' or 'bed' of a comfortable kind used by women. *Sāyaṇa* in the *Atharvaveda* (3.25.1; 5.29.8) and later (*ŚB* 11.5, 1.2, 11.5.7.4) denotes a 'couch', *śirṣaṇya* in the *Brāhmaṇas* (*AB* 8.5; 8.12; 8.17; *KU* 1.5; *SŚS* 17.2.8) denotes the 'head of a couch' (*āsandī*).

**Courier:** One of the *ratnins* or king-makers who had a significant part to play in the Rājasūya. The designation of this official is *pālāgala*. This term occurs in the *Śatapatha Brāhmaṇa* (5.3.1.11), apparently in the sense of 'messenger' or 'bearer of news'.

**Court-dicer:** Among the *ratnins* or king-makers, as described in the *Śatapatha Brāhmaṇa* (5.2.3.9 ff), we come across *akṣāvāpa*, that is, the court-dicer or the 'keeper of dice'. This post appears to resemble the one which was held by Kaṅka (Yudhiṣṭhira) in the court of the Matsya king Virāṭa. But *akṣāvāpa* was not merely a royal companion in the play of dice. In fact, apart from a mere game for amusement, dice had a ritual significance. In the Rājasūya the king had to take part in a ritual dicing. Dice were employed for distribution of wealth in the *sabhā* or assembly hall, in which the dicer had an important part to play. So, it appears that the court-dicer was an important functionary in the Rājasūya.

**Cover:** In the *Śatapatha Brāhmaṇa* (5.3.1.11), the 'covering' for a bow (*dhanus*), presumably made of skin, is denoted by the word *pyukṣṇa*.

**Cow Product Therapy:** Among the bovine-products, butter, ghee, curds, butter-milk, cow dung and bovine urine were used for medicinal purposes, especially in treating worms, wind, file, phlegm, fistula, bleeding, wounds, etc. (*Kau Sū* 15.11; 26.14; 28.14; 29.22 ff). Against swellings or tumor, cow urine was used, consecrated with the *Atharvaveda* (6.57). The use of cow dung for leprosy was widely current (*Kau Sū.* 26.22). Thite 123-4.

**Cramming:** The frog-hymn (*RV* 7.103) gives us a glimpse of the educational system of the Ṛgvedic age. The fifth verse gives a picture of the earliest Vedic school by drawing a comparison between the croaking of the frog to a chorus of voices, wherein a teacher's recitation of the Vedas, section by section (*parvan*), is repeated after him by his pupils. The first verse of the hymn suggests, through a simile, that this concerted school-recitation sprang into life suddenly, at a stated time, because frogs raised their rain-inspired voices at the opening of the monsoon, after lying low for the rest of the year. Evidently, the entire instruction was verbal.

**Creeper:** *Vratatī* in the *Ṛgveda* (8.40.6) and later (*TB* 1.5.1.3) denotes a 'creeping plant'.

**Crimes:** The crimes enumerated in the Vedic literature are of varying degrees. Besides real crimes, we find that a minor bodily defect like the possession of bad nails and discoloured teeth was looked upon as crime (cf. the list in *MS* 4.1.9; *KS* 31.7; *TB* 3.2.8.11). Marrying a younger daughter when her elder sister was still unmarried was coupled with, though not equated with, murder. The *Chāndogya Upaniṣad* (5.11.5) mentions that Aśvapati's list of sinners includes a drinker of intoxicating liquor, a thief, and one who does not maintain a sacrificial fire. The *Taittirīya Saṃhitā* (4.5.10.2) states that a slayer of an embryo is a criminal. The *Maitrāyaṇī Saṃhitā* (4.1.9) and *Kāṭhaka Saṃhitā* (27.9) refer to the same. *Vīrahatyā* is one of the crimes, referred to in the *Taittirīya Āraṇyaka* (10.10); The *Taittirīya Saṃhitā* (1.5.2.1 and 2.2.5.5) and the *Vājasaneyī Saṃhitā* (30.5) mention the slaying of a man. *Virahā* is found in other Vedic texts, like *Kāṭhaka Saṃhitā* (31.7), *Maitrāyaṇī Saṃhitā* (4.1.9) and *Pañcaviṃśa Brāhmaṇa* (12.6.8). The slaying of a Brāhmaṇa is referred to in the *Taittirīya Saṃhitā* (2.5.1.2), where Indra is called a Brāhmana-slayer for his smiting off three heads of Viśvarūpa, son of Tvaṣṭṛ. The *Taittirīya Saṃhitā* (10.38) declares that the slaying of a Brāhmaṇa is a worst murder, though the *Śatapatha Brāhmaṇa* (13.3.1.1) states that the sin of murdering a Brāhmaṇa may be expiated only by the performance of an Aśvamedha. The *Ṛgveda* (5.4.6) refers to thieves binding a wayfarer with ropes in a forest. Yāska (3.14) refers to this *ṛc* and to the thieves. Burglary, highway robbery, cheating at gambling and cattle-lifting are heard of in the *Ṛgveda*. Another *ṛc* (10.5.6) states that the wise have prescribed seven acts of crimes and that one who commits any one of these is a sinner. Sāyaṇa enumerates seven lapses as crimes: drinking, dicing, craving for enjoying woman, hunting, physical striking, abuse by harsh or ugly words and other way of vitiating life. Yāksa (*Nir.* 6.27) also refers to this *ṛc* and mentions seven crimes like stealing, violating the bed of the preceptor, slaying of the Brāhmaṇa, slaying of the embryo, drinking, repeated performance of sinful acts and telling a lie. He comments that one indulging in even one of these crimes becomes sinner. The expressions for the general concept of crimes in the Vedic literature are *agha aṃhu, āgas, enas, pāpa, pāpman, kalmāṣa, kilviṣa, doṣa, hiṃsā, pātaka*, etc.

**Curative Waters:** In Vedic texts, water is considered to be a powerful curing substance and is sometimes deified and praised as being medicinal. Thus, in the *Ṛgveda* (1.23.19) it is said that there is ambrosia (*amṛtam*) and remedy (*bheṣaja*) (cf. *AV* 1.6.2). Further, the poet says, in waters there are all the remedies, *viśvāni bheṣaja* (*RV* 1.23.20; 10.9.6; *AV* 1.6.2). Elsewhere it is said that waters are remedial, and disease-expelling (*AV* 3.7.5; cf. 6.91.3). In the *Atharvaveda* (19.2.3), the waters are treated in similar terms. In the *Brāhmaṇa* texts, waters are described as peace (*śānti*) and remedy (*bheṣaja*) (*AB* 7.5; *KB* 3.6, 7, 8, 9; *GB* 2.1.25; *ŚB* 1.2.2.11; 1.7.4.9; 1.7.4.17; 1.9.3.2; 1.9.3.4; 2.6.2.18; 3.3.1.7; cf. *TA* 1.26.5). In the *Atharvaveda* (6.24.1 ff) the heavenly waters are sought to remedy heat-burn. Immortality may also be obtained from the healing waters (*AV* 11.6.23). In the *Atharvaveda* (8.7.3) the waters are said to have made the dreadful disease *yakṣma* disappear. In the *Ṛgveda* (1.23.22), waters are requested to carry away all the evil in the form of unfaithfulness or giving curse or of disorderliness (cf. *RV* 1.9.8; *AV* 7.89.3). In the *Atharvaveda* (19.40.3), waters are requested to prolong life. Many more references can be cited to show how, in the Vedic age, water was supposed to be a curing substance and as such was deified, praised and requested to cure and prolong life.

**Curds:** See **Dairy Products**.

**Currency:** The exchange of commodities or the principle of barter seems to have been in vogue, but cow had already come to be regarded as a unit of value (*RV* 4.24.10). But it was not the only unit of exchange. Gold and silver coins were also in use. The *niṣka* are originally a gold neck-ornaments. A number of square or round gold pieces were strung together into a necklace, which was worn both by men and women. The isolated pieces of fixed weight and standard, were afterwards used as coins. According to Macdonell and Keith, *niṣka* originally denoted 'a gold ornament worn on the neck' (*RV* 2.33.10; 8.47.15) as is shown by the epithet *niṣka-grīva* (*RV* 5.19.3), 'having a gold ornament on the neck'. As early as the *Ṛgveda* (1.126.2) traces are seen of the use of *niṣkas* as a sort of currency, for a singer celebrates the receipt of a hundred *niṣkas* and a hundred steeds; he could hardly require the *niṣkas* merely for personal adornment. Later, the use of *niṣkas* as currency is quite clear (*AV* 10.127.3; *ŚB* 11.4.1.10, 11.4.18; *GB* 1.3.6). A *Ṛṣi* praises king Bibhindu for giving him forty thousand coins on one occasion, and eight thousand on another (*RV* 8.2.41). Manā was the name of another gold coin. This was probably taken by the Paṇis to Western Asia, where it was known as Minā. The word Manā occurs in the following verse of the *Ṛgveda* (8.78.2): 'O Indra, bring us jewels, cattle, horses and *manās* of gold' (*saca manā hiraṇyayā*). This word is derivable from the Sanskrit root *man*, to measure, or *man* to prize or value, and the coin must have been of a fixed and recognized weight or standard. There must also have been some sort of impression on it, authorized and approved by the king, to make it pass as genuine current coin. Very probably the impression was that of a cow or bull, the original unit of exchange or barter, and the coin itself represented, as it still does, the price of a cow or bull (*kāñcana mūlyam*), when a live one could not be given or presented to a Brāhmaṇa or priest. There were also silver coins, and a *niṣka* of silver is mentioned in the *Pañcaviṃśa Brāhmaṇa* (17.1.14). Probably silver coins called *ravis* were also in vogue in *Ṛgveda* times (*RV* 5.33.6). In view of what has been said above, it appears that some form of coinage was in vogue in the Vedic period. It should be pointed out in this connection that the lowest unit of the weight of coins, as also other forms of measurement, was known as *kṛṣṇala*, which denotes the berry of the *abrus precatorius*, used as a weight according to the later authorities, one *māṣa* (bean) being equated to four *kṛṣṇalas*. In the sense of a weight it occurs in the *Taittirīya Saṃhitā* (2.3.2) and other Saṃhitās (*MS* 2.2.2; *KS* 11.4) and later (*TB* 1.3.6.7).

**Cymbal:** Cymbal is a musical instrument consisting of a concave brass or bronze plate, struck with another or with a stick etc., to make a ringing sound. The Vedic word for this instrument is *āghāṭa* or *āghāṭi*. It is referred to in the *Ṛgveda* (10.146.2) and the *Atharvaveda* (4.37.4).

# D

**Dairy Products:** Milk (*kṣīra*), also called *go* or *payas* played a large part in the economy of the Vedic Indians (*RV* 1.109.3; 167.7; 8.2.9; 9.67.32; 10.87.16; *AV* 2.26.4; 5.19.5; 8.3.15; 10.9.12; *TS* 3.4.8.7; etc.). It was either drunk fresh (*RV* 1.62.9; 180.3; 3.30.4), or made into butter or curds (*RV* 6.48.18; *TS* 2.5.3.5) or was cooked with grain to make a mess (*RV* 8.77.10; *AV* 13.2.20). The popularity of milk in the later Vedic age is testified by the fact that the cow is called a blessing (*vara*) (*TB* 3.12.5.7). Fresh milk (*TS* 2.5.3.3; *KS* 17.6; *AV* 9.4.4; *ŚB* 3.3.3.2; *PB* 9.5.5; 18.4.2; *TB* 2.7.2), boiled milk (*ŚB* 3.2.2.10; 6.3.3.2) and cream of boiled milk (*śara*, *ŚB* 3.3.3.2) were in common use. Goat's milk was also used (*TB* 4.1.6.1, 5.1.7.4; *ŚB* 14.1.2.13). There were some people who lived on milk alone (*payavrata*) (*ŚB* 9.5.1.1; *KB* 8.9). It was curdled by mixing it with a little sour milk, pieces of creeper called *pūtikā*, bark of *palāśa* tree or *kuvala* (jujube). The curds prepared by mixing *kuvala* were not regarded as pure (*ātañcana*) (*TS* 2.5.3.5). Curds were widely used (*AV* 3.12.7; 4.34.6; *TS* 2.5.3.4; *KS* 34.3; *PB* 18.5.12; *ŚB* 14.1.2.12; *JB* 2.348) and were sometimes mixed with *soma* juice and barley meal (*RV* 1.127.2; 5.51.7; 7.32.4). The term *payasyā* in the later *Saṃhitās* and *Brāhmaṇas* (*TS* 2.3.13.2; *TB* 1.5.11.2; *AB* 2.22; 2.24; *ŚB* 2.4.4.10) denotes curds and was said to consist of a mixture of sour milk and hot or cold fresh milk. The process of churning with a churning stick was known (*RV* 1.28.4; cf. *BU* 6.3.13). The mixture of curds and minute globules of butter, when the latter have not been removed, was called *pṛṣadājya* (*ŚB* 3.1.3.8, *RV* 10.90.8; *TS* 3.2.6.2). We find a mention of *dadhanvat* which was probably cheese with two varieties, one with pores and the other without (*RV* 6.48.18). A preparation of curds with boiled milk was very popular. The solid part of this preparation was called *āmikṣā* (*TS* 2.5.5.4; 3.3.9.2; 6.2.5.3; *MS* 2.1.9; *VS* 19.21.23; *AV* 10.9.13; *ŚB* 1.8.1.7; 1.8.1.9; 3.3.3.2; *TA* 2.88; *JU* 2.438; *CU* 8.8.5; *KS* 19.7) while the liquid part was called *vājina* (*TS* 1.6.3.10; *VS* 19.21.23; *ŚB* 2.4.4.21; 3.3.3.2; 9.5.5.7). Butter was heated before use with a view to clarifying it (*RV* 1.134.6; 2.10.4; 4.10.6; 4.58.8; 5.12.1). The term *phāṇṭa* in the *Śatapatha Brāhmaṇa* (3.1.3.8) is said to denote the first particles of butter produced by churning. It was creamy butter, which was mixed with *soma* juice (*RV* 10.29.6) and used in frying *apūpas* (*RV* 10.45.9) and for dipping cakes (*AV* 10.9.25). It was also used in making offerings to gods and manes. While solidified clarified butter was used by adults, fresh butter was used by children (*AB* 1.3). Om Prakash 65-9.

**Dakṣiṇāgni:** Sacrificial fire, also known as *anvāhār-vapācana* because rice was cooked on it, with which the *piṇḍa-pitṛyajña* offerings to ancestors were performed on the day of the new moon. Śabara on Jaimini 12.2.3; *Taittirīya Brāhmaṇa* 1.1.10. The fire was lighted to the south-east of the Gārhapatya on a semi-circular mound. The fire, with which *dakṣiṇāgni* was established, could be brought from the house of a person belonging to any caste, provided he was prosperous. It could also be brought from the *gārhapatya* fire, or it could be produced by attrition. *ĀŚS.* 1.2.1; *BGS* 2.17. Bhattacharya 1990, 47.

**Dancing Gods:** Indra has been thought of in the *Ṛgveda* as (*RV* 1.130.7) one who also made others to dance and delight (*RV.* 2.22.4; 8.24.9; 8.24.12; 8.92.2). *Nṛtuḥ* equals *nartayitā* in one of his epithets (*RV* 8.92.3). His close associates, the Maruts and the Aśvins, are also dancers. As the leaders of a troupe of dancers (*RV* 5.52.12; 8.20.22) the Maruts are extolled. Dancing and singing are also attributed to Aśvins, who dance in association with Sūrya (*RV* 6.63.5). Dancing was one of the accomplishments of these gods.

**Dancing Nymphs:** The concept of nymphs is closely related to the dancing gods. They are consorts of the Gandharvas (*RV* 10.123.5, 7.33.9, 7.33.12, 7.10.95; 10.132.6) but do not belong to the category of gods; they are the semi deities. By the time of the *Atharvaveda*, they became Indra's favourite dancers. Descriptions of the Apasaras as dancing with the Gandharvas are found in abundance *AV* (4.37.1; 4.37.4; 4.37.5). Being the presiding deities of the dice, prayers were offered to them for success at it and for averting ill-luck. Men and women sang and danced even amidst the disease and pestilence they feared. They gathered in the assembly house (*AV* 7.12.2), *sabhā*, which was the meeting place for social entertainment including music and dance. The hymn addressed to the Earth (*AV* 12.1.1, 12.1.41) presents picture of joyous life, where the mortals sing and dance. Dancing Gandharvas and the Apsarases help us visualize the picture of a society where dancing and music were regarded as an integral part of everyday life, whether in joy or in sorrow, as a profession or as an important communal activity.

**Darśa-pūrṇamāsa:** Yajña (q.v.) performed at the time of the new-moon and full-moon: *darśa* means *amāvasyā* or new-moon and *pūrṇamāsa* means full-moon. The *ĀpŚS* 3.14.11-13 describes *darśapūrṇamāsa* as a sacrifice, which is to be performed throughout a person's life. It is regarded as the archetype of all other Iṣṭis (q.v.), the *yajña* in which the performer employs four priests. It begins with *anvārambhaṇīye-ṣṭi* when the sacrificer resolves to perform it and employs the priests. It is followed by *śākhāharaṇa* (bringing of fresh branches of *palāśa* or *śamī* tree by the Adhvaryu), *barhirāharaṇa* (bringing bundles of *kuśa* grass), *idhmāharaṇa* (bringing fuel sticks), *sāyamdoha* (milking the cows in the evening), *brahmāvaraṇa* (choosing the brāhmaṇa or priest), *praṇitāpranayana* (filling up vessels with sacred water), *nirvāpa* (taking out handfuls of grains or a portion of other sacrificial materials), *prokṣaṇa* (sprinkling water on sacrificial material), the *haviṣkṛt* call (invocation of Mother Earth as the Corn Mother, followed by pulverizing the grains of rice and baking, *puroḍāśa* (cake on potsherds), *patnīsannahana* (girding up the sacrificer's wife, cf., wife's role in Aśvamedha, q.v.), *barhirāstaraṇa* (strewing the *vedī* or altar with *kuśa* grass), recital of *sāmidhenī* verses (*RV* verses 3.27.1 ff) and *prayaramantras* (invocation of fire), making two *āghāras* (pouring of *ājya* or clarified butter in a continuous stream), *hotṛvaraṇa* (selection of the *hotṛ*, q.v. priest), five *prayāja* offerings (addressed to five sacrificial articles, each symbolizing a deity), offerings to Agni-Sviṣṭakṛt, cutting off a portion of cake called *prāśitra* for Brahmā, *iḍopahvānam* (invocation of the Mother Goddess Iḍā by the Hotṛ), cutting off portions of the *puroḍāśa* or sacrificial cake and eating by the sacrificer and the four priests, cooking of a mess of boiled rice called *anvāharya* as fee for the four priests, recitation of the *sūktavāka* (formally addressed to Agni) by the Hotṛ, throwing the *prastara* (first handful of *kuśa* grass that is cut) by Adhvaryu into fire, *śaṃyuvāka* (offering made to the wives of the gods), and concluding rituals desiring prosperity, happiness, and fulfilment of human desires. It appears that *darśa-pūrṇamāsa* was originally a simple agricultural rite which later assumed sophisticated garb. For details see *Taittirīya Saṃhitā* 1.1.1-13, 1.6-7, 2.5-6; *ĀŚS* 1.1.4.1, 1.13.10; *ĀpŚS* 1-4; *KŚS*. 2-4; *BŚS*. 1. Bhattacharyya 1990, 50-1.

**Dāsa:** *Dāsa*, like Dasyu, sometimes denotes enemies of demoniac character in the *Ṛgveda* but in many passages (cf. *RV*. 5.34.6; 6.22.10; 6.33.3; 6.60.6; 7.83.1; 10.38.3; 10.69.6; 10.83.1; *AV* 5.11.3) the word refers to human foes of the Aryans. The Dāsas are described as having forts (*puraḥ*) and their clans (*viśaḥ*) are mentioned in the *Ṛgveda* (2.2.4; 4.28.4; 6.25.2). It is possible that the forts, which are called 'autumnal' (*śaradīḥ*), may be mythical, but there was some historical basis of it. The *dāsa* colour (*varṇa*) is probably an allusion to the black skin of the indigenous tribes, which is also directly mentioned. They are called *anās*, 'noseless' and *mṛdhra-vāc*, 'of hostile speech' (*RV* 5.29.10) and are probably called phallus-worshippers (*śiśnadevaḥ*, 'whose deity is a phallus') (cf. *RV*. 7.21.5; 10.99.3). It is significant that constant reference is made to the differences in religion between Ārya and Dāsa or Dasyu (*RV*. 1.33.4-5; 4.16.9; 5.7.10; 5.42.9; 6.14.3; 8.70.10; 10.22.7-8). The wealth of the Dāsas was no doubt considerable (*RV* 1.176.4; 4.30.13; 8.40.6; 10.69.5; *AV* 6.90.2) and in terms of being civilized, there is no reason to suppose they were inferior to the invaders (*RV*. 2.12.11; 4.30.14; 6.25.5). Leading Dāsas were Ilībiśa, Cumuri and Dhuni, Pipru, Varcin, Sambara.

**Dāśarājña:** The territory known to Vedic settlers was divided into a number of tribal principalities ruled normally by chiefs. The Dāśarājña, or the battle of the ten chiefs, is an important historical event alluded to in various hymns of the *Ṛgveda*. As many important tribes and personalities figured in this famous battle, it is worthwhile discussing the conflict. Sudās was a Bharata chief of the Tṛtsu family which had settled in the country and later came to be known as Brahmāvarta. At first Viśvāmitra, a scion of the Kuśika family of the Bharatas, was the priest of Sudās and led him to victorious campaigns on the Vipāś and Śutudri. Viśvāmitra, however, was later dismissed by Sudās, who appointed Vasiṣṭha as his priest, probably on account of the superior Brahmanical knowledge of the Vasiṣṭhas. Thereupon, a long and bitter rivalry ensued between the two priests and, in revenge, Viśvāmitra led a tribal confederacy of ten chiefs against the Bharatas. The federation consisted of the five well-known tribes, Puru, Yadu, Turvaśa, Anu and Druhyu, along with five of little note, viz., Alina, Paktha, Bhalānas, Śiva and Viṣānin. In the bloody and decisive struggle on the Pāruṣṇī, the Bharatas emerged victorious, utterly routing the confederacy. The Anu and Druhyu chiefs were drowned, while Purukutsa of the Purus met his death. There was another battle that Sudās had to fight, in which the three non-Aryan tribes, Ajas, Śigrus and Yakṣus had united under the chief Bheda; but these new assailants also met with the same fate and were defeated, being slaughtered on the Jumna. Majumdar 249.

**Dasyu:** The word is originally of doubtful meaning in the many passages of the *Ṛgveda* later to be applied clearly to denote a superhuman enemy in 1.100.18; 2.13.9 etc. In several passages human foes, specially the aborigines, are designated as Dāsas or Dasyus. In *Ṛgveda* 1.103.3; 1.117.21; 2.11.18; 3.34.9; 7.5.6; 10.49.3, Dasyu is regarded as opposer of the Aryans, being defeated with the aid of the gods, and sometimes by people (*RV* 5.70.3; 10.83.6). The Dasyu is called *a-karman* to mean riteless in the *Ṛgveda* 10.22.8, *a-devayu*, 'indifferent to the gods' in 8.70.11; *a-brahman*, 'without devotion' in 4.16.9, *ayajvan* 'not sacrificing' in 8.70.11; *ayajyu* in 7.6.3; *avrata*, 'lawless' in 1.51.8, 6.14.3, 9.41.2, *anyavrata* 'following strange ordinance' in 8.70.11, *devapeyu* 'reviling the gods' in the *Atharvaveda* (12.1.37). Dasyus are devoid of rites, addicted to strange vows, god hating and so forth, being diffrentiated from the Aryans in terms of religion. They were also compared with the **Dāsa**—though being distinct from them in not having their own clans or Viśaḥ. As an epithet of Indra, the terms 'dasyu-hantā', in the *Ṛgveda* (1.51.5, 1.103.4; 10.95.7; 10.99.7; 10.105.11) and *dasyuhan* in *RV* (1.100.12; 6.45.24; 8.76.11; 8.77.3, 10.47.4) etc., are used in the sense of a slaughter of the Dasyus without any correspondence to Dāsa. The term Dasyu also denotes a province, corresponding to the substitute word as Iranian Dañhu. Its original meaning was enemy, as in a developed sense of the terms hostile country, conquered country, province and so on, found in the Iranian word retaining the significance of enemy. The meaning of human enemy may also be traced to the strife of gods and demons. Another attempt is connected with the contrast of different words i.e., *dasyu, dañhu, deva* and *daeva* as a result of the diverse religious views separately suggested both in two speeches—Indian and Iranian. So, originally, this word might have meant a land ravaged as a result of invasion and, also, hostile human foe. Individual Dasyus like Cumuri, Śambara, etc., as hostile people were usually called by a cognate name of Dāsa, appearing in Vedic literature and derived from the same root as 'das' meaning 'lay waste', 'suffer', 'want', 'waste away'. In the *Aitareya Brāhmaṇa* (7.18) the descendants of Viśvāmitra are called Dasyus i.e., *dasyūnāṃ bhūyeṣṭhāḥ*, Macdonell and Keith I, 347-8.

**Day:** The term *ahan* denotes 'day', (*RV* 4.16.19, 8.26.3). Night is also termed the dark (*kṛṣṇa*), as opposed to the light (*arjuna*) day (*RV* 6.9.1). *aho-rātra* (*RV* 10.190.2; *AV* 13.3.8; *VS* 23.41) is a regular term for 'day and night combined'. The day itself is variously divided. In the *Atharvaveda* (9.6.46), a division into 'the rising sun' (*udayan sūryaḥ*), 'the coming together of the cows' (*saṃ-gava*), 'midday' (*mādhyan-dina*), 'afternoon' (*aparāhṇa*), and 'sunset' (*astaṃyan*) is found. In the *Taittirīya Brāhmaṇa* (1.5.3.1, 4.9.2), the same series appears with 'early' (*prātar*) and 'evening' (*sāyāhna*) substituted for the first and last members, while a shorter list gives *prātar, saṃgava, sāyam*. In the *Maitrāyaṇī Saṃhitā* (4.2.11), there is the series 'dawn' (*uṣas*), *saṃgava, madhyaṃdina* and *aparāhṇa*. The morning is also, according to Zimmer, called *api-śarvara* (*RV* 3.9.7), as the time when the dark is just past. It is named *svasara* (*ṚV* 2.34.8, 9.94.2), as the time when the cows are feeding, before the first milking at the *saṃgava*, or when the birds are wakening (*RV* 2.19.2, 2.34.5). It is also called *pra-pitva* (*RV* 7.41.4, 8.1.29), according to Zimmer. But Geldner points out that the term refers to the late midday, which also is called *api-śarvara* as bordering on the coming night, being the time when day is hastening to its close, as in a race (cf. *mama prapitve apiśarvare*, *Ṛgveda* 8.1.29 on which Sāyaṇa comments upon as *apiśarvare-śarvariṃ rātriṃ apigataḥ kālaḥ apiśarvare*. From another point of view, evening is called *abhi-pitva* (*RV.* 1.126.3, 4.34.5), the time when all come to rest. Or again, morning and evening are denoted as the dawning of the sun (*udita-sūryasya*) or its setting (*ni-mruc*). The midday is regularly *madhyaṃ ahnām* (*RV* 7.41.4), *madhye* (*RV* 8.27.20), or *mādhyaṃdina. Saṃgava* (cf. *RV* 5.76.3) is the forenoon, between the early morning (*prātar*) and midday (*mādhyandina*). The divisions of time less than the day are seldom precisely given. In the *Śatapatha Brāhmaṇa* (12.3.2.5) however, a day and night make up 30 *muhūrtas*; 1 *muhūrta* = *kṣipra*; 1 *kṣipra* = 15 *etarhi*; 1 *etarhi* = 15 *idāni*, 1 *idāni* = 15 *breathing*: 1 *spiration* = 1 twinkling (*nimeṣa*), etc. In the *Śāṅ Ā* (7.20) the series is *dhvaṃsayo, nimeṣaḥ, kāṣṭhāḥ, kalāḥ, kṣaṇā, muhūrta, ahorātraḥ*. A thirtyfold division of day as well as of night is seen in one passage of the *Ṛgveda* (1.123.8) by Zimmer, who compares the Babylonian sixtyfold division of the day and night. But the expression used—thirty *yojanas*—is too vague and obscure. The longer divisions of time are regularly 'half month' (*ardha-māsa*), 'month' (*māsa*), season (*ṛtu*) and 'year' (*saṃvatsara*), which often (*TS.* 7.1.15; *MS* 3.12.7; *VS* 22.28; *Śāṅkh Ā* 7.20; *BU* 3.8.9) occur in this sequence after *ahorātrāṇi* ('days and nights').

**Dead, Disposal of:** The funeral hymns of the *Ṛgveda*, seem to have been composed especially for ritual purposes. As cremation and burial were both in vogue, we have both burial and cremation hymns. But the character of the respective hymns shows that burial was the earlier custom. During burial of a warrior the bow was placed in his hand but the priest eventually took away (*RV* 10.18.9). The martial spirit of the Vedic people finds expression in this ritual. Twice in the *Ṛgveda*, man has been called *mṛtyubandhu* 'regarding death as relation'. The idea, that the dead in heaven are nourished by the piety of the relatives on earth, is found in the *Atharvaveda* which refers to the burial of seed-corn with the dead. These corns would become wishes and nourish him in heaven. A gentler but more sophisticated spirit is revealed in the cremation hymn (*RV* 10.16), where Agni is addressed as Jātavedas and requested not to burn him, not to scorch him either, not to tear asunder his skin or body, but to send him to the Fathers. The poet wishes the eye of the dead to go to the sun, the breath to the wind, to heaven or to earth or to the waters or to the plants. Here, the idea is incipient that after death the body merges into the four or five basic elements like earth, water, fire, air or space. The idea of retribution is far short of the idea or life after death occurs faintly in the *Atharvaveda* and it clearly appears for the first time in the Upaniṣads. See **Death**.

**Death:** The Vedic notion of the life after death was the outcome of a prolonged process, which eventually assumed a concrete conceptualization in the Upaniṣadic age. That the soul does not perish with the body, that there is something of man that survives the dissolution of his physical envelope, is at the base of all funeral observances and gift in honour of the manes. The human body is a conglomeration of various elements, and we find accordingly a late Vedic passage thus addressing the dead (10.16.3): 'Let thy eye go unto the sun and unto the wind the breath (*ātman*), Repair unto the Heaven or unto the Earth in accordance with the law; or go unto the water if that be beneficial to thee (or) stand firm with (thy) limbs within the plants.' But the inner soul apparently is something distinct from these. The Vedic expression for it (cf. *RV* 1.113; 16.140.8; 10.15.1, etc.) is either the *asu* breath or the energizing principle in man; in other passages it is the *manas*, mind or the thinking and feeling principle in him, which is located, according to the *Ṛgveda* (8.100.5; cf. 10.50), within his heart and that this inner self of man, after death has some kind of a body, is apparent from a passage like *Ṛgveda* 10.16.5: 'May he be united with his body, O Jātavedas', compare also the *Śatapatha Brāhmaṇa* 12.3.2.5 f. After death, the soul of the good or pious man went to the realm of the Blessed where Yama, or Yama and Varuṇa, ruled as kings. A tolerably full picture of this realm is to be found in the *Ṛgveda* 9.113.7 ff., 'wherein is everlasting lustre, wherein the sun; in that eternal undecaying world . . . where Vaivasvata (Yama) is king, wherein is the Heaven's enclosed space (shrine); where are these vigorous waters . . . where is wandering as one lists in the third sphere of the inmost Heaven; where the worlds are full of light . . . where are eager wishes and strong desires, wherein is the seat of the Radiant one; where is food and full delight . . . wherein are joys and transport and happiness and felicity and where the longing of desire are fulfilled—there make me immortal.' Elsewhere, (*RV* 1.154) we read of Viṣṇu's realm where are 'fleet and many-horned kine and where is a spring of unfailing myth', and of Varuṇa's brilliant and hundred illumined houses (7.88.5). This realm of pious dead is said to be 'in the highest heaven', or 'in the midst of heaven by the side of the ruddy morn (*RV* 10.14.8, 10.15.7), etc. 'It is a region where all imperfections of the world are at an end and where one lives in the companionship of the gods, drinking celestial drink with them' (either Soma or *ghṛta* or honey—*RV* 10.154.1) and listening to heavenly songs. This is, of course, the lot of the righteous dead who in heaven regularly receive food offerings bestowed by their successors and who have themselves performed *iṣṭapūrtas* (benevolent gifts and pious adorations) with the fruit of which they become united after death. The Vedic Aryans have not preserved for us an equally detailed picture of hell, or the realm of the unblessed sinners. This is probably because these people were a hopeful and cheerful race, who did not relish depicting the gruesome colours and horrors of hell. They called upon the gods to burn, to smash and annihilate the impious enemies; they no longer cared to inquire after their subsequent fate. The later doctrine of the impermanence of heavenly joys—*kṣīṇe puṇye martyalokaṃ viśanti*: when merit is exhausted they enter the world of mortals—was not yet formulated; so that the pious worshipper once admitted to the Realm and the Blessed, remained there forever. Belvalkar and Ranade, II, 25-7.

**Debt:** Śapha means one-eighth amount of interest in the *Ṛgveda* and the *Atharvaveda* one-eighth and one-half of one-eighth amount of interest is ascertainable as *śapha*, but one-sixteenth as *kalā* in repayment of interests. In the *Atharvaveda* (6.119.1), borrowing without the intention of repaying the debt, is mentioned. Presumably, the interest would be paid in kind. How far a debt had a heritable interest or obligation is not precisely known. The *Kauśika Sūtra* (46.36.40) regards three hymns of the *Atharvaveda* (6.117-119) as applicable to the occasion of the payment of a debt after the creditor's demise. For the payment of a debt by a relative, the evidence is even less clear.

**Defendant:** *Abhi-praśnin* means defendant in the Vedic texts. This term occurs after *praśnin* and is followed by *praśnavivāka* in the list of victims for the Puruṣamedha as given in the *Taittirīya Brāhmaṇa* (3.4.6.1) and the *Vājasaneyī Saṃhitā* (30.10). The commentators, Sāyaṇa and Mahīdhara, see in it merely a reference to an iquisitive man. But the term appears to have been a legal reference of some sort, perhaps indicating the defendant as opposed to plaintiff and judge.

**Deified Conditions:** Conditions or various conceptual phenomena or abstract principles are often deified in the Vedas. Of deified entities, special interest attaches to Aramati, 'devotion', who is also described as the great one. Another spirit who may with propriety be referred to the Indo-Iranian period is Puraṃdhi, whose name occurs some nine times in the *Ṛgveda*; she is usually mentioned along with Bhaga, who is himself a representative of this class of gods, but who has become an Āditya, twice or thrice with Pūṣan and Savitṛ, and once with Agni and Viṣṇu. A goddess Dhīṣaṇā, who is mentioned about a dozen times in the *Ṛgveda*, may also be a goddess of abundance or the impulsion; Anumati, 'favour of the gods' is twice personified in the *Ṛgveda* (10.59.6; 167.3) and is besought to be propitious and to grant long life. In the *Yajurveda* and in the *Atharvaveda* she appears as a goddess who presides over propagation and favours love and in the Sūtras she is clearly understood as connected with the moon. Sunṛtā (*RV* 1.40.3; 10.140.2), 'bounty', is personified here and there in the *Ṛgveda*, while, on the contrary, the spirit of niggardliness, Arāti (*AV* 5.7), 'avarice', is represented as a demon in the *Atharvaveda*. Asunīti (10.59.5. 6) 'spirit leading', is besought in the *Ṛgveda* in one hymn to grant long life. Most of these abstractions are clearly rather thin and feeble, and some at least seem more poetic than living realities. This is not, however, the case with the goddess Nirṛti, dissolution, or misfortune, who is found in the *Ṛgveda* (Macdonell, 120) as a personification presiding over death. The *Maitrāyaṇī Saṃhitā* (3.6.3) connects with her specifically dice, women, and sleep as the three most evil things. Another deity who is of importance in the popular thought, but who appears very late in the literature, is the goddess Śrī, first definitely recorded in literature in the *Śatapatha Brāhmaṇa* (10.4.3.1). Śrī appears in the Sūtra literature, where we find it as the offering to the all-gods and is prescribed to make offerings at the end of the bed to Śrī, at the foot to Bhadrakālī, and in the privy to Sarvānnabhuti. Keith 211.12.

**Demonology:** Through the *Yajurveda* and the *Atharvaveda*, and all the subsequent Vedic literature, the enemies of the gods are called Asuras. This connection, however, can only be traced in the later texts, where it is mentioned occasionally. In the singular, the term is found but three times certainly: Varcin (*RV* 7.99.5), Pipru (*RV* 10.138.3), and the wolfish Asura (*RV* 2.30.4); a fourth case is very doubtful and may instead refer to Varuṇa (*RV* 10.124). In the plural form, there are at most eight cases, predominantly in the tenth book; in them the gods, as a body, appear opposed to the Asuras as in the later texts, or as Indra scattering them (*RV* 8.96.9; 8.97.1; 10.157.4; 10.53.4; 10.82.5; 10.124.5 etc.). The term Asura is applied also to Namuci, and to Svarbhānu, while Indra, Agni and the Sun are called slayers of Asuras. In comparison with the Asuras, Paṇis are unimportant demons, who play no great part in the literature after the *Ṛgveda*. They are the demons who withhold the cows, or rather the *ghee* in the cow, from Indra or his allies, Agni, Bṛhaspati, the Aṅgirasas or Soma, and are overthrown by him. The word normally has a plural form, but a single Paṇi repeated four times represents the group. The Dāsas or Dasyus are also made into enemies of the gods, though, like the Paṇis, their primitive function was undoubtedly different; in their case, it was probably that of indigenous tribes, who opposed the Aryan advance. That in many cases historic men might be implied, when Dāsas are overthrown, is true; but gods of the defeated people might also be denoted, and in more general terms powers of the air opposed to the gods: Dasyus seek to scale heaven (*RV* 8.14.14; 1.33.7), while Indra vanquishes them from birth (*RV* 1.51.6; 8.77.1-3); he wins the sun and waters after defeating them (*RV* 1.100.18; 10.73.5); a Dāsa is husband of the water (*RV* 1.32.11), and the Dāsas have autumnal forts, doubtless in the air. Of the individual names of the demons, Vṛtra ranks first; he is a serpent with power over lightning, mist, hail, and thunder, when he fights with Indra; he bears the name Dānava as well since he is the offspring of Danu. His abode is hidden in the waters, but also stays on summit or lofty heights, which suggest the waters of the air. By name, he encompasses the waters rather than hold it back by concealing it; the cloud mountain is, therefore, said to be within his belly. He has ninety-nine forts, which Indra shatters as he slays him. From the single Vṛtra the Vedic conception has often produced many Vṛtras, and we also find that the name, in plural, has been used to mean foes. It may be that the use in plural is not simply a direct generalization of Vṛtra as a demon. The *Brāhmaṇas*, which tell many tales about Vṛtra, make him out to be the moon, swallowed at new-moon by Indra as the sun. Vala is a pale figure compared to Vṛtra; he is mentioned in the myth of the Paṇis. Bṛhaspati or Indra takes away the cows which he had in his forts, his fences are burst by Indra or his hole is opened. Arbuda appears seven times as a beast whose head Indra struck off: he seems to be cognate to Vṛtra with whom or Ahi he is mentioned (*RV* 2.11.20; 2.14.4; 1.51.6; 8.3.19; 8.32.2; 10.67.12 of the snake priest Arbuda Kādraveya, *ŚB* 13.4.3.9). Svarbhānu (*RV* 5.60; Rāhu occurs in *AV* 19.9.10; a late passage), the Asura, is more interesting; he is clearly the demon who eclipses the sun, and who has to be overthrown by Atri or the Atris, and by Indra. Though he is mentioned several times in the *Brāhmaṇas*, his place in post-Vedic mythology is regularly taken by Rāhu. The *Atharvaveda* also knows of Grahas who affect the moon. Urana who had ninety-nine arms, is mentioned once (*RV* 2.14.4). But we hear a good deal of Viśvarūpa, the three-headed son of Tvaṣṭṛ, slain by Trita and by Indra for the sake of his cows, and who in the later Saṃhitās (*TS* 2.5.1.1) appears as the Purohita of the gods, though akin to the Asuras. Keith 230, 234-5.

**Demonometry:** The term *bhūta-vidyā* is one of the sciences enumerated in the *Chāndogya Upaniṣad* (7.1.2). It seems to mean the 'science' of creatures that trouble men, and of the means of warding them off.

**Dentistry:** *Dant, danta,* tooth, is frequently mentioned in the *Ṛgveda* (7.55.2; 10.68.6; *AV* 5.2.3.3; 29.4; 6.56.3 etc.). The more usual form is *danta* (*RV* 4.6.8; 6.75.11; *AV* 4.3.6 etc.). Cleansing (*dhay*) the teeth was an ordinary act, especially in preparation for a sacrifice and accompanied bathing, shaving of the hair and beard (*keśa-śmaśru*) and the cutting of the nails (*MS* 3.6.2). A hymn of the *Atharvaveda* (6.140) celebrates the appearance of the first two teeth of a child, though its exact interpretation is doubtful. In the *Aitareya Brāhmaṇa* (6.14) there is a reference to a child's first teeth falling out. The word seems in the *Ṛgveda* (4.6.8) once to denote an elephant's tusk. Whether dentistry was practised is doubtful. The occurrence in the *Aitareya Āraṇyaka* (2.1.5) of *hiraṇaya-dant*, gold-toothed, as the name of a man, is perhaps significant especially as it is certain that the sealing the cavity in teeth with gold was known in Rome as early as the legislation of the Twelve Tables. Macdonell and Keith, I. 339.

**Deposit:** The Vedic literature refers little to any law of deposit. The *atharvaveda* (19.48.1) refers to things within the box. The term *aparidānam* (*ŚB* 2.4.1.11) means deposit or trust of an article to somebody else, i.e. gift for a fixed period to be returned in future. Another term *nidhi* is met with in the *Ṛgveda* (1.183.4; 7.67.7) in the sense of place of deposit or deposit or store and then treasure (*RV* 2.24.6; 8.29.6; 10.68.6, *AV* 10.7.23). The *Śatapatha Brāhmaṇa* (1.1.1) shows how a contract was sanctified with a ceremonial practice.

**Deposition:** In both the *Saṃhitā* and *Brāhmaṇa* texts, cases of dethronement and expulsion of kings from their kingdom can be found. The *Śatapatha Brāhmaṇa* (12.9.3.1) records the case of king Duṣṭaritu Pauṃsāyana who inherited the kingdom, which came down to him through ten generations (*dasa puruṣam rājyan*), but was expelled for misdemeanour and maltreatment of subjects. The *Śatapatha Brāhmaṇa* (12.9.3.1) also describes the expulsion of *Revottaras rātava cākra sthapati* by the Sṛñjayas. Here the king is expelled along with his *sthapati* or special officer. A special ceremony called Rādyajña, has been referred to in the *Pañcaviṃśa Brāhmaṇa* (19.7.1 to 19.7.4), by which a deposed king may get back his kingdom or a ruling king may win back the loyalty of the subjects. The *Atharvaveda* (3.3.5) gives the description of 'a king who, expelled from his kingdom, is living in another country; later on he was recalled and reinstated. An element of democracy can be easily traced in this deposition and recalling of kings. This goes to prove that though kingship was hereditary in character, the voice of the people acted as a healthy check on the monarch and that subjects could depose a king who maltreated the people and had the privilege to recall and reinstall him.'

**Desert:** *Dhanvan*, desert, is repeatedly mentioned in the *Ṛgveda* (2.38.7; 3.45.1; 4.17.41.1). Death from thirst in the desert was not rare (*AB* 2.19), and the value of a spring in the desert was fully appreciated (*RV* 10.4.1. cf. 6.34.4; 19.2.2). The great desert to east of the Sindhu (Indus) and the Śutudri (Sutlej) is possibly referred to in one hymn of the *Ṛgveda* (10.86.20). The term *maru* (*TA* 5.1.1) also refers to desert.

**Desire:** In the *Ṛgveda* (10.129) *kāma* is said to have been the first movement that arose in the one. It is mentioned as a great cosmogonic force in the *Atharvaveda* (9.2). The conception of sexual dualism as a creative process in terms of procreative process has given much importance to the *kāma* doctrine, and in this connection we frequently come across such terms as *jan*, *sṛj* (procreation), *garbha* (womb), *retas* (semen), etc. In subsequent Indian tradition, *kāma* came to be looked upon as one of the *trivargas*, or three aims of life, the other two being *dharma* and *artha*.

**Despotism:** The kingship extolled in Brāhmaṇic songs and ritual is not merely a 'Patriarchal Presidency'. The monarch is not merely a chief noble, the first among equals, 'President of Council of Peers'. In a famous Atharvanic laud *rājā* of the Kurus, is extolled as a *deva* who surpassed mere mortals (*martyas*). The consecrated king is the lord of all beings. He is called *viśvasya bhūtasya adhipati*, and is further described as the devourer of the people—*viśāmattā* (*AB* 8.17). *rājā ta ekaṃ mukhaṃ tena mukhena viśo'tsi* (*KU* 2.6). He is surrounded by armed kinsman and retainers (*AB* 3.48). He can 'banish a Brāhmaṇa at will, mulet and overpower a Vaiśya at will, and exact labour from or slay a Śūdra at will' (*AB* 7.29). Further, he claims the power of giving his kingdom away to anybody he liked. Raychaudhuri, 153-4.

**Destiny:** See **Chance**, **First Principles**.

**Detribalization:** The caste system originated and evolved under diverse historical conditions, one of which was the process of incomplete detribalization. The working of such a social process of detribalization, by which specific castes are formed on the basis of selected or given occupations in the bigger Hindu social hierarchy, can be seen in India even today. In some cases the tribes disintegrated owing to the change in the mode of production, which eventually resulted in the growth of a new society based on a broader social platform. In other cases it was due to pressure from outside. Being dissociated from their environment, they became occupational groups at the first stage and then became transformed into castes of varying status under the bigger fold of Hindu society, according to the importance of their profession and service. But this detribalization did not work in one direction. Many tribes, unable to subsist in their traditional environment, came to villages and towns and settled in bigger localities on the basis of different occupations and eventually became part of the larger Hindu society. The problem of the law-makers of ancient India was to incorporate various such detribalized castes into the framework of the imaginary but idealized fourfold social order or *varṇa* system and to explain and rationalize their existence in the prescribed set up. They tried to solve this problem by inventing the theory of *varṇasaṅkara* or 'mixed caste', according to which the origin of each functioning caste was attributed to uneven hypergamic or hypogamic marriage. The transformation of the well-known regional tribes like the Āndharas, Ābhiras, Āvyantyas, Drāviḍas, Licchavis, Khasas, Oḍras, Puṇḍras, Niṣādas, Bhojas, Māgadhas, Vaidehikas, etc., into occupational castes may thus be explained similarly. In most cases the tribal background of the castes is amply transparent. Castes like the

Kaukkuṭa, Kaivarta, Kṣatṛ, Pulkasa, Meda, Āhiṇḍika, Kārāvara, etc., are described as being descended from the Niṣādas, the well-known general name of the primitive hunting tribes. Likewise, ancient tribes like the Ambaṣṭhas, Āndhras, Veṇas, Sātvatas, Bhojas, Māgadhas have been describes as the ancestors, either in the paternal or the maternal line, of many a known caste. In certain cases the very names of the castes indicate their tribal affiliation. It is only in the professional names of the castes like *Ayaskāra* (heater of metal), *Aśvika* (dealer in horse), *Gopa* (milkman), *Carmakāra* (leather-worker), *Karmakāra* (blacksmith), *Kulāla* (potter), *Modaka* (confectioner), *Takṣan* (carpenter), *Tantuvāya* (weaver), *Naṭa*, *Nartaka* (public entertainer), *Nāpita* (barber), *Tailika* (oilman), *Dhīvara* (fisherman), *Buruḍa* (bamboo-worker), *Bhiṣak* (physician), *Rajaka* (washerman), etc., that the tribal identity recedes into the background. What is suggested here is that in India, especially among the backward communities, the demarcation line between the tribal and the caste system is not very clear because the latter, in reality, is the consequence of detribalization, a process which is not yet complete. Tribal elements still exist in the structural set up and functional role of the caste system, as also in institutions like village communities, customary laws, folk religions, and oral traditions, etc. Bhattacharyya 1988, 35, 38-40.

**Devayāna:** The way of the gods, literally. The conception of Devayāna marks the second stage in the conceptualization regarding the fate of the departed ones. Originally heaven and hell were conceived respectively as the abodes of the pious and the sinners. Later the former category was bifurcated into the ways of the Gods and Fathers (Pitṛyāna). The followers of this line believed that by practising faith (*śraddhā*), truthfulness (*satya*) and austerities (*tapasyā*) an individual would go to the path of the gods and never return to the world. *Chāndogya Upaniṣad* 5.10.1, 6.2.16, *Bṛhadāraṇyaka Upaniṣad* 6.2.15; Bhattacharyya, 1990, 52.

**Devayajña:** Offering fuel-sticks to fire with *svāhā* uttered after the name of the deities in the dative case. *ĀpDS* 1.3.14.1; *BDS* 2.6.4. It is almost the same as *homa*.

**Devotion:** See **Bhakti**.

**Diarrhoea:** *Āsrāva* (discharge) denotes a disease, thrice referred to in the *Atharvaveda* (1.2.4; 2.3.2; 6.44.2), the precise nature of which is uncertain. The scholiast (*AV* 1.2.4; cf. 2.3.2) in one place interprets it as painful urination (*mutrātisāra*), while Lanman suggests diabetes. Bloomfield takes it to be diarrhoea and Zimmer argues that as the remedy is called 'wound healer' (*arus-srāṇa*), the sense is 'the flux from unhealed wounds'. Whitney renders it 'flux', and questions Bloomfields's rendering. Ludwig translates it vaguely as 'sickness' and 'cold'. Macdonell and Keith, I. 74.

**Die/Dice:** The term *akṣa* occurs frequently, from the *Ṛgveda* onwards, both in the singular and plural, meaning 'die' and 'dice'. Dicing, along with horse-racing, was one of the main amusements of the Vedic Indians. Despite frequent mention of the game in the literature, however, there is considerable difficulty in obtaining any clear picture of the mode in which it was played. The term for dicing is *sam-rudh* (*AV* 7.50.5). The terms *div* (*RV* 10.27.17; *AV* 7.50.9, 7.109.5) and *dyuta* (*AV* 12.3.46) also designate the game of dice. See **Gambling**.

**Dietery Treatment:** Food in general is regarded as a substance generating energy and some kinds of food are considered to have curing capacities. Therefore, food is prescribed as a curing substance in the magico-religious medicine of ancient India. Thus, in a rite against dementia the physician gives cooked rice (*bhakta*) to the patient for eating, after having consecrated it with the *Atharvaveda* 5.7. (*Kau Sū* 28.12). Against the diseases caused by curses of others, he gives some food in which powder of *khalatula*-leaf is mixed and which is consecrated with the *Atharvaveda* 5.16 (*Kau Sū* 29.16). In a rite for curing the *kṣetriya*-disease, cooked rice consecrated with the *Atharvaveda* 3.7 is given to the patient (*Kau Sū* 27.31). To the woman suffering from puerperal disease, churned food (i.e. water and flour mixed and churned) and consecrated with *Atharvaveda* 5.6. was to be given (*Kau Sū*. 28.16). When somebody is diseased due to being possessed by some evil spirits, the physician makes the patient eat rice-pap cooked in milk, on the fire of bird-nest. Before giving it to the patient, he pours the remnants of the offering performed with the *Atharvaveda* 6.2.2 on it and consecrates it with the same stanza (*Kau Sū*. 29.17). In order to fecundate a sterile woman, he prescribes *kṛsara*, i.e. pap of rice and sesame. In the rite for curing fever, the physician makes the patient drink slime of roasted (black-rice) corns (*lāja*), after having recited the *Atharvaveda* 5.22. On it (*Kau Sū*. 29.18). Thite, 125-6.

**Dīkṣaṇīya-iṣṭi:** A form of *iṣṭi* required in the Agniṣṭoma (q.v.), the rules of which are laid down in *ĀpŚS*. 10.4.9; *KŚS* 7.2.31-32, 7.3.23; *Jaimini* 5.3.29.31, 7.1.3-10, 11.4.48-49, etc. After performing this *iṣṭi*, with rites resembling those followed for the process of the birth of a new baby, a person becomes *dīkṣita* or initiated as if he receives a new life.

**Dinner Etiquette:** Early Vedic texts give us some idea about dinner etiquette. From a simile in the *Ṛgveda* we learn that the Vedic Indians ate their meals in a sitting posture (*RV* 6.30.3). Men avoided eating with their wives (*ŚB* 10.5.2.9) and women, generally, did not eat their food in the presence of male memebrs (*ŚB* 1.9.2.12). Moderation in food is advised from very early times. It is said that if a person ate only twice a day he would be so wise and intelligent that his sayings would never fail (*ŚB* 2.4.2.6; *TB* 2.4.2.6). People observed a fast whenever they performed some sacrifice (*AB* 7.11; cf. *ŚB* 2.1.4.1). Students were expected to go out to beg for food as it was supposed that the practice created a sense of humility in them (*GB* 1.2.1-8). We also find the beginnings of some taboos in the Saṃhitās. The use of exudation of trees (*niryāsa*) was forbidden on account of their red colour (*TS* 2.5.1.3). *Māsa* (pulse) was forbidden probably because it was considered exotic.

**Disc:** See **Cakra**.

**Discourse:** *Brahmodya* is a theological discourse consisting chiefly in the enumeration of negative qualities (*aguṇa*). Therefore, it may have to be taken in a sense of *nirguṇa* as unqualifiedness, unconditionedness, etc. The term *vākovākya* (*CU* 7.1.2, 7.1.4, 7.2.1) denotes the art of disputation, according to Śaṅkara.

**Discus:** The *cakra* or discus was weapon used in war, and hurled against an adversary with sure effect (*RV* 8.96.9). It was one of the weapons of Indra, and of the gods of later Purāṇic lore. The discuss was sharp-edged and rapidly turned on the point of the digit finger of the right hand, before being hurled against an enemy. The use of this weapon required great practice and skill and it, at once, cut down that limb against which it was aimed.

**Disease:** See **Diarrhoea, Dysentery, Eye-disease, Fever, Hoemorrhoids, Headache, Heart disease, Jaundice, Lameness, Leper, Painful Urination, Physician, Rheumatism, Sura-sickness, Swellings, Tumours, Ulcers.** See **Medical Science**.

**Dish:** The word *sthālī* is used to denote a dish which is mentioned in the *Jaiminīya Brāhmaṇa* (1.53), *Taittirīya Brāhmaṇa* (1.1.4.4-5; 1.6.7.1) *Kāṭhaka Saṃhitā* (32.7), *Aitareya Brāhmaṇa* (7.12), and *Śatapatha Brāhmaṇa* (2.1.4.6).

**Disposal of the Dead:** The ritual texts recognize only cremation, which therefore must be adjudged as the normal mode of disposing of the dead in the Vedic period. The only burial rites, which the texts describe, pertain to the bones of the cremated dead, which are interred with ceremony, and the burial of children under two years of age. The hair and nails of the dead person are shaved and pared and the dead body is washed, anointed, garlanded, and clothed in a new garment. It is then borne by men or taken in a cart drawn by cows to the *śmaśāna* (crematorium) and placed on the funeral pyre in the midst of three fires, produced from the three sacred fires, if the deceased as an *āhitāgni* had maintained them. The wife of the deceased is then made to lie down on the pyre by the side of the dead and if the deceased was a Kṣatriya, his bow is placed in his hand. Her brother-in-law or some other representative of the husband then makes her rise from the pyre with the Ṛgvedic stanza 10.18.8 and the bow is either taken off, with the next stanza, or, according to the Gṛhya Sūtras, is bent, broken, and thrown into the pyre. That the ritual does not contemplate the burning of the widow is certain; her lying on the pyre and her subsequent recall to life are only symbolical of her immolation. If the deceased was an *āhitāgni*, such of his sacrificial utensil as are made of stone, copper, or earthenware are taken by the son, the rest being burnt with the corpse in the *śālāgni*. A goat, mentioned as a share of the funeral fire even in the *Ṛgveda*, and a cow are sacrificed; the omentum, and other parts of the cow are placed on the various parts of the dead body and burned with it. According to the Gṛhya ritual, it is when the dead body is being burned that the dead is addressed with the Ṛgvedic verses 10.14.7 ff., 10.16.1-6; 10.17.3-6; 10.18.10-13, etc., exhorting him 'to go forth by those ancient paths whereon the Fathers of old have gone, to meet the two kings, Yama and Varuṇa, and gather himself to the Fathers, to leave all blemish behind, to run past the four-eyed bridleless dogs—the two sons of Saramā, etc. If the deceased was not an *āhitāgni* the body is burned silently. After the burning, the mourners (chiefly *sapiṇḍas* up to the seventh degree) return, never once looking back, bathe and offer libations of water. On the threshold of the house, they sip water and touch purifying and auspicious things like water, fire, cow dung, etc., and then enter it. The place of the burning is cooled by spinkling over it a mixture of milk and water and reciting the Ṛgvedic verses (10.16.13 ff). On the third day, but usually on the tenth day, the gathering of the bones takes place. The urn containing the bones is deposited in a pit, the deceased being addressed with the verse: 'Approach, Mother Earth', etc. (*RV* 10.18.10). Only the *Śatapatha Brāhmaṇa* and the allied *Kātyāyana Śrauta Sūtra* mention the ceremony of the erection of a memorial to the dead, a long time after death. The buried bones are exhumed at night and re-buried next morning in a secluded spot away from the village and a mound erected over them. The mourners return, after placing a barrier between the living and the dead (in the memorial mound). The *Ṛgveda* (10.18.3-4) refers to a stone as such a barrier. *Cultural Heritage of India*, I, 260-1.

**Distance:** Like all nations of the world the primary unit of measuring distance, according to the Vedic Indians, was footsteps. The lowest measure of distance was *aṅguli* or finger-breadth (*ŚB* 10.2.1.2) and the highest was *yojana*. The question of measurement of distance especially arose owing to the measurement of the land for agriculture or for pasturing of cattle in which sense the terms *gavyūti* (*RV* 1.25.16, 3.62.16; 5.66.3, 7.77.4) and *gavya* (*AB* 4.28) are found in the Vedic texts. Later the word *gavyūti* used to denote the sense of a measure of distance as found in the *Pañcaviṃśa Brāhmaṇa* (16.13.12). Another term for distance is *traipāda*, which denotes a measure of distance, 'three-quarters' of a *yojana*, in the *Pañcaviṃśa Brāhmaṇa* (16.33), *ŚŚS* (14.41.12), where half a *yojana* is termed *gavyūti* and a quarter *krośa*. The term *aratni* denotes the measure equal to 24 *aṅgulas* or 'finger-breadths' (*ŚB* 10.2.1.3). The word *krośa* denotes as a measure in terms of a distance covered by 'a shout' or the range of the voice (*PB* 16.13); also this word denotes 'about two miles'; more exactly 1.8 miles. The term *yojana* denotes a distance of four *krośas* or about nine miles (*RV* 1.23.8, 2.13.3, 10.78.7, 86.20, etc.; *AV* 4.26.1; *MS* 2.9.9, 3.84; *TB* 2.4.2.7 etc.). The *yojana* was sometimes calculated as *krośas* or 18 miles.

**Distress:** Disease is sometimes considered as distress (*aṃhas*) and the efforts for curing are connected with freeing the patient from distress. Thus in *Kāṭhaka Saṃhitā* (10.9) we read 'caught by distress is he who is diseased' (*aṃhasā va eṣa gṛhito ya amayavī*). Therefore, an offering to Indra Amhomuc (one who releases from distress) is to be offered so that he will make the patient free from distress (*KS* 10.9). Many times prayers are made to gods to free the devotees from distress. Thus in the *Ṛgveda* (8.67.7) it is said, 'For one who is sinless (sin = cause of disease), who has not committed a sin, for him, have freedom from distress, O Ādityas' (*RV*. 8.18.5). Ādityas are described as those who know how to remove distress. Similarly, in the *Ṛgveda* (8.18.6) Aditi is requested to protect the devotees from distress. In the *Ṛgveda* (10.97.15) herbs are requested to deliver the devotees from distress. Mitra and Varuṇa are described as those who lead the devotees across distress. In the *Atharvaveda* (19.44.8) waters, along with Varuṇa, are requested to free the devotees from distress and in the *Atharvaveda* (11.6.1 ff) also many gods are requested to do the same. Thite 218-9.

**Distribution:** In the *Ṛgveda* (1.55.7; 1.180.5; 8.46.26; 8.60.8; 8.99.4) the word *dāna* has often been used in the sense of distribution. It is derived from *dā*, meaning to derive. Later the word came to denote 'making gift' when the society lost its ancient tribal equality. The Ṛgvedic passages also refer to *dāna* or distribution as a designation of the sacrificial feast in which the gods were invoked. In the history of the ancient system of distribution, oldest of all was the distribution of food. Then came the distribution of chattels and inanimate movable objects acquired by warfare, and the last, the division of land for purposes of agriculture. According to *Nighaṇṭu* words like *brahman*, etc., have originally meant food and material wealth at the same time, thus referring to a period when the distinction between the idea of food and that of material wealth did not develop. In the *Ṛgveda* (3.49.4) Indra is described as the divider of shares (*bhāga*) of food (*vāja*), and as such regarded as the mightiest among the gods. But the most significant reference to the division of food along with a distinct mention of common meal is found in the *Ṛgveda*. 'Having superiors, intentful, be ye not divided, accomplishing together, moving on with joint labour, come hither, likeminded. Your drinking (be) the same, in common your share of food; in the same harness do I join you together, worship ye Agni united, like spokes about a nave' (*RV* 3.30.5-6). Evidently, these passages refer to a period of primitive communism when collective labour and common meal determined human relationships. By the distribution of wealth in the form of cattle, etc., and subsequently that of chattels and inanimate movables acquired by warfare, the second stage was reached. This type of wealth is indicated in the *Ṛgveda* by the term *vārya*, which has been interpreted by Sāyaṇa as wealth in the form of cattle (*gavādi dhanānām*) and also as 'wealth in the form of crops' (*vrīhiyavādinām*). Although wealth in the form of cattle or crops indicate an advanced, i.e. clear divided state of social development, the word for wealth still concealed within itself the old communistic conception. In its derivative meaning, *vārya* is that (coming from the root *vṛ*) which is by nature divisible. Likewise the word *bhāga* stood at the same time for 'wealth' and 'share', thus indicating that there was originally no wealth that was not shared out. Division of wealth looted from the aliens occurs frequently in the *Ṛgveda* (1.20.8; 1.73.5; 1.102.4; 1.103.6; 1.112.1; 1.135.2-3; 1.162.3; 1.183.4; 2.10.6; 2.19.5; 2.23.2; 2.24.14; 3.28.4; 3.30.18; 5.42.5; 5.86.5; 6.22.4; 7.56.21; 8.36.1-6; 8.26.8; 8.96.21; 10.51.2; 10.114.3; etc.) and in many such verses the ancient law of division is stressed. The division of land is practically absent in the *Ṛgveda* because, as we have said many times, the early Vedic peoples were predominantly pastoral. They were more interested in counting wealth in terms of cattle, and their attention to agriculture was drawn only at a later period.

**Diti:** The name of Diti is a goddess occurs only three times in the *Ṛgveda* in connection with Aditi, Mitra and Varuṇa. *Diti* is the exactly opposite point on the path of the zodiac in the west, where the lights go out. It will not be necessary on this theory to suppose that the name of *diti* as a goddess was merely an antithesis to that of *aditi*, formed from the latter to express a positive sense, as *sura* 'god', was later (by false etymology) evolved from *asura* 'demon' (*RV* 4.2.11; 5.62.8; 7.15.2; *AV* 7.7.1; 15.18.4; 16.6.7; *VS* 18.22). In later tradition Diti was the mother of the Asuras or Daityas.

**Divination:** The principle of divination is in large measure directly due to the doctrine of mimetic knowledge; if the use of a representation of things can produce them, it is also legitimate, if less easy, to deduce the future of events from the behaviour of things, which are supposed to be an imitation of the events. Varied are the means such as: the fire of the sacrifice and the victim of the sacrifice suited to give knowledge by their magic connection with the gods as well as religious conceptions: more clearly connected with the activity of divine powers in Vedic belief is the drawing of omens from the flight and the movements of animals, which are clearly connected with gods or spirits of the dead or demons. When a ceremony is performed to win for a maiden a husband, the side from which crows first appear is that from which her wooer will come (*KB* 34.24). The movement of the cow at a particular moment in the Soma sacrifice shows the fortune of the sacrificer (*ŚB* 4.5.8.11). The owl is invoked to fly round the village and give signs for the future; it is a bird which flies to the dwelling of the gods, and the *Ṛgveda* already knows birds of omen (*HGS* 1.17.3). The hyena's howl is uttered either of its own will, or on the prompting of other powers (*HGS* 1.17.1). The character of the bride can be judged by her choice of balls of earth taken from various places (*GGS* 2.1.3 ff); the sex of the future child believed to be by the fact whether the member of the body of the prospective mother, which a Brāhmaṇa boy touches accidentally has a masculine or feminine name. Keith, 390-1.

**Divine Craftsman:** See **Viśvakarman**.

**Divine Honours:** The highest fate of man was accordingly by an admission into the realm of the blessed to the companionship of the gods. Yama himself is believed to have been the first mortal to exercise the privilege of dying; and, the younger Vedic poetry speaks of many more deified ancestors like Manu, Nahuṣa, the Aṅgirasas, etc. Once admitted into the rank of the gods, they could be worshipped like other gods; and, they also possessed the power of influencing the good or evil. Hence, we find passionate appeals to the Manes to help their sons and grandsons on earth and not to injure them in any way. And just as we have a large mass of myths and legends regarding the assistance rendered by gods like Indra, Varuṇa or Aśvins to their pious devotees, we can conclude that in the late Vedic period there were in popular vogue a number of stories regarding the communion or specific occasion between the living and the dead. Compare in this connection the story of king Uccaissravas Kaupāyeya narrated in the *Jaiminīya Upaniṣad Brāhmaṇa* 3.29 f. The belief in ghosts and possession by spirits or Gandharvas is clearly presupposed in the *Brāhmaṇas*; and, its beginnings can be traced to the late Vedic texts. Belvalkar and Ranade, 27-8.

**Divine Implements:** There is no essential distinction between the worship of natural objects conceived as living and the worship of objects made by human hands. It is obvious, however, that the worship of such objects tends to be restricted in effect and importance. This is borne out by the evidence of the *Ṛgveda* where we find two implements of the ploughman, *suna* and *sīra* which may be the ploughshare and the plough, are invoked as deities, and that in the *Śatapatha Brāhmaṇa* a cake is assigned to them in the sacrifice. The warrior invokes them to drive away the demons and the danger; in the *Atharvaveda* (V.20) a whole hymn is devoted to the praise of the implements. The priest naturally is more prominent in the *Ṛgveda*, where the sacrificial post is deified perhaps as a remnant of tree worship. It is called divine, and is asked to allow the sacrifice to go to the gods, but the sacrificial grass (*RV* 2.3.4; 10.70.4) and the divine doors (*RV* 1.142.6) are celebrated. The pressing stones have three hymns (*RV* 10.76.94.175) given to them; they are unageing, immortal, and more powerful than the heaven itself. They are compared to steeds or bulls, their sound in the pressing reaches the sky. They bestow wealth and offspring, driving away the demons. The wheel and pestle (*RV* 1.28.5.6), so the carts (*RV* 10.13) are also deified and the *Atharvaveda* adds to the category various ladles and invents a great deity in the remnant of the sacrifice, the *ucchiṣṭa*. It is possible to draw a distinction between the cases of the deities of the plougher and the warrior, and those of the priest. In their case the presence of the deity at the sacrifice is treated with so much reverence, while in the former cases the reverence is not due to anything save the essentially valuable character of the objects, and the mystic powers which are deemed by man to live among them. It is particularly easy to understand how the arrow or even the plough can be regarded as animate; the worship of the priestly implements would thus be rather more fetishistic in origin than real and direct worhip of the implements for themselves the question. Keith, 188-9.

**Divine Punishment:** Punishment was considered by the Ṛgvedic Indians as inflicted in the form of disease, poverty or suffering on earth in this very life, and not any frightful suffering after death. Yet occasionally, and in some late passages of the *Ṛgveda*, we find a new feature of the realm of the unblessed described in sure accents. Thus, in the *Ṛgveda* 7.104 we read 'burn, slay and pierce and hurl down into bottomless darkness and let them boil like a caldron of flames. Punish them with your deadly thunderbolt with your scorching darts. Give them over to the Dragon; consign them to the lap of Nirṛti; sweep them away with all their offspring. Let them sink without a sound underneath the weight of the three worlds. The punishment in Hell, one might imagine, was just as unending as the reward in Heaven; and both were frankly and unmitigatedly sensuous. As to the belief in metempsychosis, its traces are very rare even in the earlier Vedas.' Belvalkar and Ranade, 27.

**Division:** The term *parus* means first a 'limb' or 'member' of the body (*RV* 1.162.18, 10.97.12; *AV* 1.12.3; etc.) and is then applied metaphorically to the division of the sacrifice (*RV* 10.53.1; *TB* 1.6.9.1) or of the year (*TS* 2.5.61). Another term for division is *parvan*, which denotes the knots of the reed or the joints of a plant (*AV* 12.3.31; *TS* 1.1.2.1; *ŚB* 6.3.1.31), and more generally a part of limb of the body (*RV* 1.61.2,

4.19.2, 8.48.5, 10.89.8; *AV* 1.11.1, 2.9.1, 6.14.1, 11.8.12, 12.5.71; *AB* 3.31; *ŚB* 1.6.3.35; 3.4.4.2; 6.1.2.31; 10.4.5.2). It also designates a period of time, probably with reference to the breaks in the month at new and full moon (*RV* 1.94.4; *VS* 13.4; *ŚB* 1.6.3.35, 6.2.2.34; *KŚS* 5.2.13; 8.8.46; 24.4.30; *SŚS* 14.5.6; *ĀŚS* 9.2.3, etc.).

**Divisions of India:** The later Vedic literature refers to the three broad divisions—Brahmāvarta or Āryāvarta, Madhyadeśa and Dakṣiṇāpatha. There is also a fivefold division with the enumeration of the residents therein, which we come across for the first time in the *Aitareya Brāhmaṇa* (8.14), though it has, in a way, been anticipated by the *Atharvaveda* (19.17.1.9). The *Aitareya Brāhmaṇa* divides the whole country into five parts, viz., (1) Dhruvā Madhyamā Pratiṣṭhādiś or Madhyadeśa or middle country, (2) Prācīdiś or the eastern quarter, (3) Dakṣiṇādiś or the southern quarter, (4) Pratīcīdiś or the western quarter, and (5) Udīcīdiś or the northern quarter. The extent and limits of these divisions cannot be defined with any degree of certainty.

**Dolichos Uniflorus:** *Khalakula* is the name of a kind of pulse (Dolichos Uniflorus) found in *Bṛhadāraṇyaka Upaniṣad* (Kānva 6.3.13; Mādhyandina 6.3.12), which is explained as *kulattha* by Śaṅkara.

**Domestic Animals:** *Ass*: The term *khara* is mentioned in the Vedic texts to denote ass. It is mentinoed in the *Aitareya Āraṇyaka* (3.2.4), where a team of asses is alluded to. Probably the passages in the *Śatapatha Brāhmaṇa* (5.1.2.15; 14.1.2.17; 14.2.2.30), where the word is used to denote an earth mound on which the sacrificial vessels were placed, presuppose the sense of ass, the mound being shaped in this form. The word *gardabha* was also used to denote ass. It is referred to in the *Ṛgveda* (3.53.23), *Atharvaveda* (5.31.3), *Aitareya Brāhmaṇa* (3.34) and *Śatapatha Brāhmaṇa* (4.5.1.9, 12.7.1.5). The ass as inferior to the horse was referred to in the *Taittirīya Saṃhitā* (5.1.2.1.2). It was also the best bearer of burdens among animals and is also referred to in the *Taittirīya Saṃhitā* (5.1.5.5). The feminine form of *gardabha* is *gardabhī*, which is mentioned in the *Atharvaveda* (10.1.14) and *Bṛhadāraṇyaka Upaniṣad* (1.4.8). The word *rāṣabha* also means ass. It is referred to in the *Ṛgveda* (1.34.9, 1.116.2, 1.62.21, 3.53.5, 8.85.7), *Taittirīya Saṃhitā* (5.1.5.7), *Kauśitaki Brāhmaṇa* (18.1) and *Śatapatha Brāhmaṇa* (6.1.1.11, 6.3.1.23, 6.3.2.3, 6.4.4.3).

*Buffalo:* The word *mahiṣa* means buffalo. It is referred to in the *Ṛgveda* (6.8.4; 9.92.6; 9.96.6; 10.123.4). Its femine form is *mahiṣī* (*KS* 23.6; *MS* 3.8.5; *Ṣaḍ.B.* 5.7.11). The importance of *mahiṣī*, the she-buffalo, was emphasized so much that the term was employed even to denote the royal queen. The word *sṛjaya* also means black buffalo. It is also referred to in the *Taittirīya Saṃhitā* (5.5.14.1), *Maitrāyaṇī Saṃhitā* (93.14.14) and *Vājasaneyī Saṃhitā* (24.2.3).

*Calf:* The term *atṛṇāda* denotes a 'newborn calf' that has not starty eating grass (*BU* 1.5.2). The terms *vatsatara, vatsa-tari* denote a young calf (*TS* 1.8.17.1; 1.8.18.1; *VS* 24.5; *KS* 24.2; *AB* 1.27.2, etc.). *Trivatsa* denotes a 'three-year-old' calf (*VS* 14.10; 18.26; 28.27; *PB* 16.13, 18.9, 21.14, etc.). *Dharuṇa* is a term which denotes a 'suckling calf' (*VS* 8.51). Another term for calf is *vatsa* (*RV* 3.33.3; 4.18.10; *AV* 4.18.2; 12.4.7; *TS* 6.4.11.4). The above references are made to the use of a calf to induce the cow to give milk (*TS* 2.3.6.2; *JUB* 2.13.3) and to the separation of the cows from the calves at certain times (*RV* 5.30.10; 8.88.1; 8.6.1; 8.8.8; 8.9.1; 8.11.7 etc.). The term *tṛyavi* designates a calf eighteen months old. The etymological meaning is apparently having a three-sheep 'period'—that is, having periods of six months thrice, just as the adjective *pañcavi* means 'having five periods of six months' or 'thirty months old' (*RV* 3.55.14; *KS* 17.2, 18.12, etc.). The term *tṛyavi* occurs in the *Vājasaneyī Saṃhitā* 14.10, 18.26, etc.

*Camel:* Both *uṣṭi* and *uṣṭra* are words for camel, of which the former is quite rare (*RV* 10.106.2; *TS* 5.6.21.1; *KS* 15.2). Roth and Aufrecht hold that in the *Ṛgveda* (1.138.2; 8.5.37; *AV* 20.127.2; 20.132.13; *VS* 13.50) and the *Brāhmaṇas* (*ŚB* 1.2.3.9; *AB* 2.8), the sense is 'humped bull' or 'buffalo' but the former thinks that in the *Vājasaneyī Saṃhitā* (24.28) the sense is doubtful and 'camel' may be meant. The animal was used as a beast of burden, yoked in fours (*AV* 20.127.2). The term *dhūmpra* was also used for camel (*TS* 1.8.21.1).

*Cow:* The term *go* is used to denote cow (*RV* 1.83.1, 1.135.8; 2.23.18). Another term *ukṣaṇaḥ* is found in the *Ṛgveda* (1.168.2; cf. *AV.* 3.11.8; *VS* 21.20); *gāvo dhenavaḥ* (*RV* 1.173.1; 6.45.28; 10.95.6; *VS* 21.19 etc. cf. *JB* 1.38). The terms *prātardoha*, *saṃgava* and *sāyaṃdoha* (*TS* 7.5.3.1) denoted the cows that were milked thrice a day; i.e. early in the morning, at noon and in the evening. Another term for *go* is used to denote *svasara* (*RV* 2.2.2; 2.34.8; 5.62.2, 8.88.1, 9.94.2) and *svadhiti* (*RV* 8.5.37; *PB* 17.14.2; *AB* 8.21; 8.23; *ŚB* 13.5.4.8). Cows were used for various purposes (*ŚB* 5.2.4.13). The term *abhivānya-vatsā* means cow with a calf which has to be won over (*AB* 7.2; *TB* 1.6.8.4). Other terms are *gṛṣṭi*, which means young cow (*RV* 4.18.10; *AV* 2.13.3; 8.9.24, 19.24.5) *karkī* (*AV* 4.38.6; 4.38.7), *dughā* (*RV* 8.50.3; 10.67.10; *VS* 28.16; 28.39) *vāśita* (*AV* 5.20.2; *KS* 13.4; *TB* 1.1.9.9; *AB* 6.18.10; 6.21.14), which denotes a cow desiring the bull, *vaśā* (*RV* 2.7.5; 6.63.9; 10.91.14; *AV* 4.24.4, 10.10.2; 12.4.1; *TS* 2.1.4.4, 2.1.4.5, 3.4.2.2; *KS* 13.4; *TB* 1.2.5.2, etc.) *rohinī*, red cow (*RV* 8.93.13, 8.101.13; *JB* 3.20; *AV* 13.1.22; *TS* 6.1.6.2; *ŚB* 2.1.2.6, 4.5.8.2), *dhenu*, milch cow, (*RV* 1.32.9, *saha-vatsā*, 'with her calf', 1.34.4, 2.2.2, 2.34.8; *AV* 5.17.18, 7.104.1; *TS* 2.6.2-3; *MS* 4.4.8; *VS* 18.27; *ŚB* 2.2.1.21), etc. *Dhenu* mostly means female cows (*AV* 3.23.4; *PB* 25.10.23). *Dhenuṣṭarī* is a cow or barren cow, which also denotes that which has ceased to give milk (*KS* 13.6; *MS* 2.5.4). *Dhenu* is found in the

*Ṛgveda* (3.34.4), which is used in the senses of lips (*RV* 1.101.10.3.1.9), speech (*RV* 4.58.6, 1.55.4, 1.141.1, 8.32.22, 10.104.3, 10.104.10), cow (*RV* 5.62.2), Vāyu's cow of plenty (*RV* 1.2.3), beloved (*RV* 5.30.9) and streams (*RV* 7.21.3, 3.34.3). *Starī* and *Sūtavaśā* occur in the *Ṛgveda* (1.101.3; 1.116.2; 1.117.20; cf. *TS* 2.1.5.4; 6.1.3.6, *KS* 37.5; *TB* 2.7.4.1) *Pṛṣni* is that cow (*JB* 2.255) which is to be looked upon as *Śrī* because it brings prosperity to the society. See **Cattle**.

*Dog:* The word *kurkura* means dog. It is referred to in the *Atharvaveda* (7.95.2). The word *macala* also denotes dog in *Jaiminīya Brāhmaṇa* (2.440). The word *śvan* also means dog in the *Ṛgveda* (1.161.13; 1.82.4; 2.39.4) *Atharvaveda* (6.37.3; 11.2.2) *Pañcaviṃśa Brāhmaṇa* (3.8.22). Its feminine form is *śunī*. It is also referred to in the *Atharvaveda* (4.20.7) and *Śatapatha Brāhmaṇa* (6.5.2.19). In the *Ṛgveda* (2.39.4) the dog is used as a domestic animal and also to guard the house from thieves and other intruders (7.55.5). It was employed in hunting the boar (*RV* 10.86.4). Being unclean, the dog is regarded as unfit for sacrifice (*JB* 1.51.4 and *ŚB* 12.4.1.4) and is driven away from the place of sacrifice (*RV* 9.101.1). To eat dog's flesh was a last resort of despair and hunger (*RV* 4.18.3). The bones of the feast were given to the dog in the *Ṛgveda* (6.37.3).

*Goat: Aja* is the ordinary name for goat in the *Ṛgveda* (1.162.2; 10.16.4; *AV* 9.5.1; *VS* 21.9, 23.56 etc.). The goat is also called *basta, chāga, chāgala*. Goats and sheep (*ajāvayaḥ*) are very frequently mentioned together (*RV* 10.90.10; *AV* 8.7.25; *VS* 3.43). The female goat is spoken of as producing two or three young ones (*TS* 6.5.10.1), and goat's milk is well known (*TS* 4.1.6.1, 5.1.7.4). The goat is representative of Pūṣan and plays an important part in the ritual of burial (*RV* 10.16.4). The occupation of a goatherd (*ajapāla*) was a recognized one, being distinguished from that of a cowherd and of a shepherd (*VS* 30.11; *TB* 3.4.9.1). Another term *basta* for 'goat' is found in (*RV* 1.161.13; *TS* 2.3.7.4, 5.3.1.3; 5.7.10.1; *KS* 17.2; *TB* 1.3.7.7). The term *mahāja* denotes the biggest pieces of goat (*ŚB* 3.4.1.2).

*Horse:* The horse being used for hunting, drawing the chariot in the battle and racing was a very important animal to the Vedic Indians. There were many terms to denote the horse. The term *akra* (*RV* 1.143.7; 3.1.12; 4.6.3; 10.77.2) denotes a horse, with *aśva* being the commonest in Vedic literature. The horse is also called 'the runner' (*atya, sapti*), 'the swift' (*arvant*), 'the strong', for pulling (*vājin*) and 'the speeding' (*haya*). A white horse with black ears is mentioned in the *Atharvaveda* (5.17.15) as of special value. Horses were highly prized (*RV* 1.83.1; 4.32.17; 5.4.11; 8.78.2, etc.), and were not rare. Horses from the Indus were of special value (*BU* 6.2.13; *SĀ* 9.7). The term *haya* is found once in the *Vājasaneyī Saṃhitā* (22.19) in the sense of horse. *Dāna* is in three passages of the *Ṛgveda* (5.27.5; 7.18.23; 8.46.24) to designate a chariot horse. The term *āśu* the 'swift', is frequently used without *aśva* to denote the chariot-steed in the *Ṛgveda* (2.16.3, 31; 2, 38.3; *AV* 2.14.6; 4.27.1; 13.2.3; *TS* 1.8.10; *ŚB* 5.3.3.3) onwards. *Pūrva-vah* is a term applied to the horse (*aśva*) in the *Taittirīya Brāhmaṇa* (1.1.5.6) and elsewhere (*ŚB* 2.1.4.17; *KS* 13.3). It may either refer to a horse fastened in front as a 'leader' or may merely mean 'drawing (a chariot) for the first time', as understood by the commentator of the *Taittirīya Brāhmaṇa*. The term *pṛṣṭya* in the *Atharvaveda* (6.102.2) denotes the side horse (mare). The term *praṣṭi*, like *pṛṣṭya*, denotes a 'side horse', which, however, possibly did not necessarily mean a horse running beside the yoke-horses, but may also have meant a third horse yoked in front as a leader. This seems to be indicated by the reference in the *Ṛgveda* (1.39.6; 8.27.8) to the *praṣṭi*—here applied to the Maruts. The term *mahāsuhaya* denotes 'great or high-spirited horse', as the description in the *Bṛhadāraṇyaka Upaniṣad* (6.2.13; *CU* 5.1.12) of the steed from the Indus (*saindhava*) which tears away the peg of its hobble (*padbisaśaṅkhu*). The term *rohita* denotes a 'red horse' (*RV* 1.94.10; 2.10.2, 3.6.6; *TS* 1.6.4.3; *PB* 14.3.12, etc.) There were many superstitions about each and every animal and naturally about horses too. Thus, a horse with all four feet and the central part of the mouth being white is considered to be a good omen. On the other hand, a horse with black feet and with the remaining body white is of ill omen. Activities of a horse have a significance of prognosis. Thus if a horse cries loudly in early morning, it suggests that there will be an invasion. Sometimes the horse, (like cow) is considered to be a place of residence of gods. Thus, its head is Brahmā, the eye the Sun, the forehead, the Moon, the nose, the Nirṛti, etc. Similarly, mythical origin of horses is narrated. Thus, the horse came into existence out of the swollen eye of Prajāpati (*ŚB* 13.3.1.1) or out the tears of Brahmadeva or of Agni. In this way, horse is not merely an animal but a magico-religious phenomenon. It is therefore quite in keeping with the magico-religious nature of the horse, that medicine is applicable to it. Thus, in connection with the horse-sacrifice (Aśvamedha), certain ritual is prescribed if the horse, which is to be sacrificed, falls ill after the preliminary rites had started. Before the horse is killed, it is, as a part of ritual, let loose for one year. During that period, if it is caught by fever called *upatapāt*, one should offer a sacrificial cake to Agni, pap to Soma, and a sacrificial cake to Savitṛ (*TB* 3.91.17.1-2). Similarly, if the horse suffers from any skin disease, one should offer a pap to Pūṣan, a pap to Rudra and a sacrificial cake to Vaiśvānara (*TB* 3.9.17.2 f). If the horse suffers from an eye disease, an offering is to be made to the sun (*ŚB* 13.3.8.4). The magico-religious connection of the sun and eye is well known (cf. *RV* 10.90.13). 'From the eye (of the primordial man-victim) the Sun was born.' When there is an epidemic among horses or when they are suffering from a very dangerous disease, a worship of Viṣṇu, Śrī and some other deities including the primordial horse, viz., Uccaiśśravas, is to be performed.

*Mare:* The word *vaḍavā* means mare. It is referred to in *Taittirīya Saṃhitā* (7.1.1.2), *Taittirīya Brāhmaṇa* (1.8.6.3, 3.8.22.3) and *Śatapatha Brāhmaṇa* (6.5.2.19). The masculine form is *vaḍava* (*TS* 2.1.8.3). The mare is also termed *aśvā, atyā, arvatī*. They were used for drawing chariots (*RV* 1.126.3; 7; 18; 22; 7.69.1) and carts (*ŚB* 5.5.4.35). No mention is made of riding them in battle, but they were used for other purpose (*RV* 5.61.1, 5.61.2, 5.61.3). the word *aśva-sāda* is referred to in *Vājasaneyī Saṃhitā* (30.13).

*Ox:* Vāha is referred to in the *Ṛgveda* (4.57. 4; 4.57.8) and the *Atharvaveda* (6.102.1), apparently meaning ox, used for drawing the plough. A great castrated ox (*mahānirasta*) is regarded as sacrificial fee (*dakṣiṇā*) in the house of Sūta at the royal consecration (Rājasūya), stated in *Maitrāyaṇī Saṃhitā* (2.6.5), *Kāṭhaka Saṃhitā* (15.4) and *Taittirīya Saṃhitā* (1.8.9.1). *Gaura* is a species of ox stated with *gavaya* (*RV* 1.16.5; 4.21.8; 4.58.2; 5.78.2; 7.96.6; 7.98.1; *MS* 3.14.10; *VS* 24.28; *AB* 3.34). Wild (*āraṇya*) *gauras* are mentioned in *Vājasaneyī Saṃhitā* (13.48). In the *Ṛgveda* (1.84.10, 4.12.6, 9.12.3), *gauris* are also found. *Gaura-mṛga* (*VS* 24.32; *AV* 2.8) dentoes 'the *gaura* wild beast'. The term *gavaya* means another species of ox (*RV* 4.21.8; *MS* 3.14.10; *KS* 16.17; *VS* 24.28) and is referred to with *gaura* and *mahiṣa*. It is also stated as being wild (*MS* 2.7.17; *KS* 16.17; *TS* 4.2.10.3; *VS* 13.49). *Paṣṭhavāh* (*TS* 4.3.5.2; *VS* 14.9, 17.27, 24.13) is a term for a four-year-old ox, as interpreted by commentators. *Turyavāh* (*MS* 3.11.11, 3.13.17; *TS* 4.3.3.2; *VS* 14.10, 18.26) also denotes 'a four-year-old' ox. Draught ox is often referred to as *anaḍvāh* and *vahni* (*TB* 1.8.2.5).

*Ram:* The Vedic word for ram is *eḍaka* (*ŚB* 2.5.2.15, 12.4.1-4; *JB* 1.51.4). Other, more popular words are *petya* and *meṣa* (*AV* 4.4.8; 5.19.2). *Petya* is mentioned as overcoming the horse, a miracle, that has a parallel in the *Ṛgveda* (7.18, 17), where the *petya* overcomes the lioness. The animal is also found in the list of victims at the *Aśvamedha* sacrifice (*TS* 5.5.22.1; 6.2.8.4; *VS* 29.58-59; *TB* 1.3.5.3), etc. *Meṣa* is used to denote ram (*RV* 1.43.6; 116, 16; 8.2.40; 10.27.17; *AV* 6.49.2; *VS* 3.59; 19.90; 24.30; *TS* 7.4.12.1; *ŚB* 3.3.4.18), while *meṣī* means sheep (*RV* 1.43.6; *VS* 3.59; 24.1; *TB* 1.6.4.4). Both the words are used to denote wool (*RV* 8.86.11) of the sheep, especially as employed for the soma filter. A wild (*āraṇya*) ram is found in the *Vājasaneyī Saṃhitā* (24.30).

**Door:** Being used from the *Ṛgveda* (1.13.6) onwards, i.e. the *Atharvaveda* (6.3.22; 14.1.63; *VS* (30.10); *Śatapatha Brāhmaṇa* (11.1.1.2; 14.3.1.13), the two terms as *dvār* and *dvāra* denote the door of a house. In the *Atharvaveda* (10.8.43) *navadvāra* is traced as having nine openings of the body. The term *dvāra-pidhāna* expresses a door-fastener in the *Śatapatha Brāhmaṇa* (11.1.1.1), and the *Lāṭyāyana Śrauta Sūtra* (1.3.1; 2.3.9) denotes *dvārabāhu* expressed as door-posts. In a metaphorical sense, *dvārapa* is only found in the *Aitareya Brāhmaṇa* (1.30) meaning the door-keeper, wherein Viṣṇu is termed the door-keeper of gods in order to protect them from evils (*CU* 3.13.6). Often, the head of the family was so-called. The word *dur* means door. It is used several times in the *Ṛgveda* (1.68.10; 1.1113.4; 1.121.4; 1.188.5; 2.2.7) to denote 'door', both literally and metaphorically. The form *dvāra* is referred to in the *Śatapatha Brāhmaṇa* (1.6.1.19; 4.3.5.9; 4.6.7.9; 11.4.4.2). The framework of the door of a house is denoted by the term *ātā*, which is found in the *Ṛgveda* (1.56.5, 1.113.14, 3.43.4, 9.5.5). It also mentions its plural form *ātāiḥ* in the same sense. The term also occurs in the *Vājasaneyī Saṃhitā* (29.5).

**Dowry:** We have very little information about the legal relations of wife and husband after marriage, in respect to property or belongings. It may be assumed that the husband did not normally appropriate the wife's dowry, as well as her earnings, if any. The rise of the recognition of a women's property as their own (*strī-dhana*), is only found in later Dharmaśāstras. The *Brāhmaṇa* literature does not encourage proprietary rights of woman. They own neither themselves nor an inheritance, says the *Śatapatha Brāhmaṇa* (4.4.2.13; cf. *MS* 4.64; *TS* 6.5.8.2; *Nirukta* 3.4). The sale of a daughter was not unknown (*MS* 1.10.11; *KS* 36.5; *TS* 2.3.4.1; *TB* 1.1.2.4), but a certain amount of discredit seems to have been attached to it (*RV* 1.109.2). Dowries were not infrequently given, especially when damsels suffered from bodily defects (*RV* 6.28.5; 10.27.12; *AV* 5.17.12).

**Dream Portents:** The meaning of dreams was an interesting part of Vedic magic and is dealt with in various passages, including an *Atharvan Pariśiṣṭa*. The *Ṛgveda* already regards as ominous the making of a garland or neckband in a dream. Ten dreams which presupposed death are recorded in the *Aitareya Āraṇyaka*: when a black man with black teeth kills him, when a boar kills him, when a wild cat springs on him, when one eats and then spits out gold, when one drinks honey and eats lotus roots, when one goes to a village with asses or bears, or when one drives south a black cow with a black calf, wearing a garland of nard. If one has a dream one should wash one's mouth. Keith, 191-2.

**Dress:** The dress (*vasana* or *vastra*) consisted of two garments according to the strictly Ṛgvedic evidence, namely the *vāsas* (or 'lower garment' in a narrow sense) and the *adhivāsa* (an 'overgarment' or an 'upper-garment'), though in the days of the later Saṃhitās, the *nīvi* (or under-garment) came to be used in addition. The Maruts wear deer-skins, and a *muni* (10.136.2) is clad in skins or soiled garments. The *atka* (a 'garment') appears to be described as woven and well-fitting, though the real meaning of the word is doubtful. Woollen clothing was in vogue. A sort of mantle or clock (*drāpi*) is often mentioned. A kind of embroidered garment (*peśas*) seems to have been used by female dancers (*RV* 1.92.4.5; 2.3.6, etc.). A special garment was worn by the bride at the marriage ceremony; it was later given to a Brāhmaṇa and is called *radhuya*. The Maruts are described as wearing mantles adorned with gold. There was a general fashion for dressing well as may be inferred from words like *suvāsas* (well-clad) and *suvasana*, and there were garments of different colours too. There is no clear evidence of any differentiation between male and female dress. *Ūrṇa-Sūtra* (woollen thread) is repeatedly mentioned in the later Saṃhitās and Brāhmaṇas, but *ūrṇa* denoted not merely sheep's wool but probably goat's hair also. Clothes were generally woven of sheep's wool. The fondness of the Vedic people for ornamental or embroidered garments was as keen as in later periods. The dress in this period seems to have consisted of three garments—an under-garment (*nīvi*), a garment proper (*vāsas*), and an over-garment (*adhi-vāsas*), like a mantle or cloak. The *Śatapatha Brāhmaṇa* describes the set of sacrificial garments as consisting of a silk under-garment (*tārpya*), a garment of undyed wool, an over-garment and a turban (*uṣṇīṣa*). The turban was worn by men as well as by women. A royal headgear or turban was worn at the Rājasūya and Vājapeya ceremonies by the king. The turban of the Vrātya is referred to. *Upānaha* or sandal was made of boar-skins. The combination of *daṇḍopānaha* is mentioned, i.e. (staff and sandals) in the *Kauṣītaki Brāhmaṇa*. Skins were used as clothing. The frequent use of the variant terms for warp and weft shows the great development of the art of weaving garments. The *praghāta* or closely woven ends of a cloth to which the trimming, fringe, or border of a garment (*daśā*) is attached, is mentioned. The *Sāṅkhāyana Āraṇyaka* (11.4) refers to a garment of saffron. But uncoloured woollen garments are also mentioned. From the way the sacred thread was worn outside, it can be inferred that the over-garment which passed over the left shoulder and under the right arm. The *Śatapatha Brāhmaṇa* (11.5.1.1) has an interesting legend to explain why man alone wears clothes.

**Drink:** The drink *pariśrut* is first mentioned in the *Atharvaveda* (3.12.7; 20.127.9). It was distinct from both *surā* and *soma* (*ŚB* 5.1.2.14; 5.5.4.10; 11.5.5.13; 12.7.1.7) but was intoxicating. According to Mahīdhara (*VS* 2.34), the liquor was made from flowers (*puṣpa*). Zimmer thinks that it was the family drink, and this is supported by the fact that in the *Atharvaveda* it occurs twice as a household beverage (*VS* 19.15, 20.59, 21.29; *MS* 3.11.2). Hillebrandt is of the opinion that it was very much the same as *surā*. *Somarasa*, the *soma* juice was the most popular drink in the Ṛgvedic age and was mainly had in connection with sacrifice. *Surā* or ordinary wine was also used at Vājapeya sacrifice. The term *pāna* 'drink', occurs in the *Śatapatha Brāhmaṇa* (13.4.2.7) and the Upaniṣads (*BU* 4.1.43; *CU* 8.2.7). The term *pānta* occurs several times in the *Ṛgveda* (1.122.1, 8.92.1, 9.65.28, 10.88.1), apparently (*Nirukta* 7.25), meaning 'drink'. See **Beverage**.

**Druhyu:** Druhyu is the name of a people mentioned several times in the *Ṛgveda*. In one passage (*RV* 1.108.8) it occurs in the plural, with the Yadus, Turvaśas, Anus and Purus, suggesting that these are the famous five peoples of the *Ṛgveda*. Again, the Druhyu king shares in the defeat of his allies by Sudās, and appears to have perished in the waters (7.18). In a second passage, Druhyu, Anu, Turvasa and Yadu are all mentioned in the singular (8.10.5), while in another Puru and Druhyu occur (6.46.8). From the tribal grouping it is probable that the Druhyus were a north-western people, and the later tradition of the epic connects Gandhāra with the Druhyus. (Macdonell and Keith, I. 385) See **Tribes**.

**Drum:** The term *vanaspati* primarily means tree (*RV* 1.166.5; 3.34.10; 5.7.4; 5.41.8; *AV* 11.6.1, 11.9.24) though in some passages, it indicates a wooden drum (*VS* 9.12; *AV* 12.3.15). *Lambara* is a type of drum (*BU* 5.12.1). The term *dundubhi* denotes a musical instrument which is used during war. Drums were to be beaten at the sacrificial rites, i.e. at Mahāvrata. *Dundubhi* apparently denotes a kind of drum used both in war as well as in peace (*RV* 1.28.5; 6.47.29; 6.47.31; *AV* 5.20.1, 5.21.7, 5.31.7, 6.38.4, 12.1.41; *TB* 1.3.62.2; *ŚB* 5.1.5.6; *VS* 16.35). A special type of drum, i.e. earth-drum, was made by digging a hole in the ground and covering with a hide. It was used at *mahāvrata* rite (*KS* 34.5; *SA* 29.45; *TB* 3.4.13.1; *BU* 2.4.6), which was performed at winter solstice to drive away the influences hostile to the return of the sun. A drummer is enumerated as a sacrificial victim at the human sacrifice. The term *āḍambara* denotes a sort of drum (*VS* 30.19).

**Dwelling:** Dwelling is mentioned by the term *āvasatha* (*AV* 9.6.5; *TB* 1.1.10.6, 3.7.4.6). The precise sense of this term appears to be a place for the reception of guests, especially Brāhmaṇas and others on the occasion of feasts and sacrifices. The *Śatapatha Brāhmaṇa* (12.4.4.6) uses the said term in the more general sense of house or abode. Details of *āvasatha* in the latter sense are given in the Sūtras (*ĀSS* 5.9.3). *Duryoṇa* occurs in the *Ṛgveda* 1.174.7; 5.29.10; 8.6.10; 9.3.1; 14.1.63 and later, i.e. *Taittirīya Brāhmaṇa* 1.2.3.1; *Śatapatha Brāhmaṇa* 3.1.1.6, etc., in the sense of a house, including a stall for cattle, a shed for corn, etc. The householder is called *śālāpati* as a lord of the house in the *Atharvaveda* 9.3.12. *Niveśana* means dwelling in the *Ṛgveda* 4.19.9; 7.19.5. At a later stage it is sometimes contrasted with *gṛha* as a resting place for animals. *Veśman* appears in the *Ṛgveda* 10.107.10; 10.146.3; the *Atharvaveda* 5.17.13; 9.6.30; *Aitareya Brāhmaṇa* 8.24.6 to denote a house. The *oka* is alluded to in the *Ṛgveda* 1.132.5; 8.25.17; 9.86.45 to designate a house, compared with a term *okas* in the *Ṛgveda* 1.66.2; 2.19.1; *Maitrāyaṇī Saṃhitā* 2.5.3 also suggesting the same meaning. *Dama* is found frequently in the *Ṛgveda* 1.1.8; 2.1.2 and *Vājasaneyī Saṃhitā* 8.24, signifying house. *Gaya* as a sense of house is a common word in the *Ṛgveda* 1.74.2; 5.10.3; 6.2.8, etc., and sometimes occurring onwards, i.e. the *Atharvaveda* 6.3.3; 6.84.1; *Vājasaneyī Saṃhitā* 27.3. Its sense includes the inmates as well as their belongings. It is equivalent to a household having a family unit entitled to its worthy of it and living in the Ṛgvedic age as a fairly large dwelling. *Harmya* denotes a house without meaning a palace as a unity. Such a sense appears to have been implied in the *Ṛgveda* (7.55.6). The term *pariṣṭha* is fairly near to *proṣṭha*, likely to have denoted the outer *verandah* of a house (*RV* 10.97.10). The terms *duroṇa, parimit, gaya, durya, duryā, dur, āgāra, śālā, dama* and *duroṇa*, have already been referred to (*RV* 10.107.10; 1.74.2; 5.10.3; 6.2.8; 7.1.11; 1.68.5; 1.113.4; 2.2.7; *AV* 5.17.13; 9.6.30; 6.3.3; 5.31.5; 6.10.6; 7.3; 8.6.10; 9.3.1; 14.1.63; *AB* 8.24.6; *ŚB* 1.3.2.14; 3.1.1.6; *Kau.U* 2.15). In the *Śatapatha Brāhmaṇa* 1.3.2.14 a single house called *ekaveśman* of a king is contrasted with the numerous dwellings of the people. The term *agniśālā* denotes a three or four-roomed house (*RV* 7.55.8). The term *duroṇa* denotes home literally and metaphorically (*RV* 3.1.18; 3.25.5; 4.13.1; 5.76.4; *AV* 7.17.3; *VS* 33.72). The term *vasati* denotes a house, generally abode (*RV* 1.31.15; 5.2.6; *VS* 18.15; *TB* 2.3.5.4; 3.7.3.3). The term *mahāśālā* was applied for an expression of a great house (*CU* 5.11.1). The term *upamit* denotes a designation of some part of the house (*RV* 1.59.1; 4.5.1; *AV* 9.3.1). In the *Ṛgveda* it means an upright pillar. The word *pratimit* is meant as a characteristic item, a support, of the house in the *Atharvaveda*.

**Dyaus:** The oldest among the gods of heaven, going back to the Indo-European period, and identical with the Greek Zeus, is Dyaus, a personification of the sky, a personification which, however, did not advance beyond the idea of paternity. He is called a ruddy bull bellowing downwards, a poetic description, probably, of the colour of lightning, the fertilizing power of rain and the thunder of heaven. The image of the beautiful star-studded sky of the night is obviously called up when Dyaus is once compared with a black steed, bedecked with pearls. He is generally paired with Pṛthivī, the earth, in the compound Dyāvāpṛthivī, the Universal Parents, who are celebrated in six hymns. *Ṛgveda* 1.90.7; 4.1.10; 4.17.4; 4.72.3; 5.36.5; 5.58.6; 6.72.3; 8.20.17; 10.68.11.

**Dysentery:** Dysentery is mentioned in the *Atharvaveda* (9.8.9) as one of the fatal diseases and the term used to denote it is *apvā*. The term may also stand for diarrhoea. The *Atharvaveda* (1.2.4; 2.3.2; 6.44.2) refers to *āsrava*, which means 'flux' or discharge and as such it may be taken as diarrhoea. *Apyā* affecting the stomach (*AV* 9.8.9), is invoked to confound the enemy (*RV* 10.103.12; *AV* 3.2.5; *SV* 2.12.11; *VS* 17.44). Weber considers that it is diarrhoea accompanied with fever. This view is supported by Bloomfield, and was apparently that of Yāska. *Visūcikā* is the name of a disease mentioned in the *Vājasaneyī Saṃhitā* (19.10; *MS* 3.11.7; *KS* 37.18; *TB* 2.6.1.5; *ŚB* 12.7.3.2) as a result of over-indulgence of Soma drinking. It seems clearly to be 'dysentery', or 'sporadic cholera'. The term apparently means 'causing evacuations in both directions'.

# E

**Ear-ring:** *Karṇa-śobhana* denotes an ornament for the ear in the *Ṛgveda* (8.78.3). Some deity is called 'gold-eared' in another passage of the *Ṛgveda* (1.122.14).

**Earth-drum:** *Bhūmi-dundubhi* means earth-drum. Actually a pit covered with a hide was beaten at Mahāvrata rite. This has been called earth-drum. (*TS* 7.5.9.3; *PB* 5.5.19; *KS* 34.5).

**Economic Inequality:** The concept of private ownership of land grew among the Indians in the later Vedic period. Trade and commerce flourished and wealth began to be accumulated in the hands of a few, leading to economic inequality. The rise of landed aristocracy of some intermediaries between the king and the peasants, is attested to by the *Taittirīya Saṃhitā* (2.1.1.2), which refers to a person craving for a village (*grāmakāma*), whom gods granted special privileges of making folks dependent on him and of enabling him to grasp the mind of his equals (*TS* 2.1.3.2). The *Ṛgveda* (1.55.4; 5.39.4) mentions *mahākulas* and *maghavans*, i.e. rich people. The verse (10.107) of the *Ṛgveda* is a clear evidence of the munificence of rich patrons, highly praising the sacrificial fees (*dakṣiṇā*). The chiefs of men or gods are depicted as living in palaces called *harmya* (*RV* 1.21.1; 1.166.4; 9.71.4; 10.73.10). The rich had plenty of gold and jewellery and even in the Ṛgvedic age they had the tendency to hoard their valuables under the ground, so is referred to in the *Ṛgveda* (8.29.6). Social inequality prevailed as we find a mention of people involved in debt on account of gambling (*RV* 10.34.10). Debtors were sometimes bound to posts by their creditors (*RV* 10.34.4). A verse of the *Ṛgveda* (8.47.17) indicates that the rate of interest was one-fourth (*śapha*) and one-sixteenth (*kalā*). Another verse of the *Ṛgveda* (2.28.9) shows how the persons involved in debt passed their days in anxiety, as not to be conscious of dawns, i.e. the light of the day. Such was the severity of life, full of tortures of the persons in debt. From this evidence of the *Atharvaveda* (6.118.1-2) we may assume that the people were frequently in debt due to gambling and sometimes tried to avoid payment though, of course, such non-payment was regarded as a sin involving evils in the next life. In the *Ṛgveda* (10.42.10) we learn of a prayer to Indra, asking to be rid of evil thoughts born of poverty and subdue hunger by acquiring cattle and possessing wealth. A verse of the *Ṛgveda* (10.117.3) speaks of Bhoja, a giver who gave food to the poor and emanciated men begging for food. The next verse (10.117.4) denounces one for not offering food to the begger. Again in the next verse (*RV* 10.117.5) the seer advises a rich man to give and satisfy the person who begs something of him. Chakravarti 220-2.

**Economic Life: See Agriculture, Barter System, Cattle, Implements, Metals, Transport. Also see Collective Ownership, Contract, Currency, Debt, Deposit, Distribution, Economic inequality, Engineering, Food gathering economy, Forms of wealth, Gift, Gold standard, Guilds, Individual ownership, Industries, Inheritance, Iron, Land tenures, Leather Industry, Low profession, Merchant, Migration, Moneylending, Price, Roads, Royal ownership, Sea-borne trade, Ship-building, Slave-labour, Specialization, Taxation, Textile Industry, Trade and Commerce, Trade routes, Treasure, Urbanism, Usury, Utensils (household), Village Economy, Weaving, Weights and Measures.**

**Edible Millet:** *Pākadūrvā*, in a verse of the *Ṛgveda* (10.16.13), along with *kiyāmbu* and *vyalkaśā* plants is said to have produced a kind of edible millet. In the *Atharvaveda* (18.3.6) the word is read as *śāṇḍadūrvā*. *Pākadūrvā* is probably, as Sāyaṇa understands it, *paripākvadūrvā*, 'ripe or edible millet'. *Śāṇḍadūrvā* is explained by the commentator in various ways, as millet 'having egg-shaped roots' (i.e. *sāṇḍa* not *śāṇḍa*), or as 'having long joints', with the additional remark that it was called *bṛhaddūrvā*, 'large millet'. In the *Taittirīya Āraṇyaka*, on the other hand, the commentary explains *pākadūrvā* as small millet.

**Education:** *Abbeys:* Though institutionalized bodies of monks and nuns governed by an abbot or abbess were very much in vogue in the subsequent Buddhist period, the vast mass of Vedic literature does not have any positive evidence in regard to their existence. Of course, there were hermitages (*āśramas*) manned by students of sacred lore and headed by spiritual leaders (Ṛṣis) holding certain episcopal rights, often dynastically. Lists of such teachers holding hermitages are found in the *Śatapatha Brāhmaṇa* (10.6.5.9), *Bṛhadāraṇyaka Upaniṣad* (6.3.14) and *Śāṅkhāyana Āraṇyaka* (15.1). Unlike the abbeys, these hermitages were not controlled by any central authority. Each of them, as it appears, was meant for imparting knowledge of a particular Vedic *śākhā* or school. The *Sāmaveda Sūtras* refer to *Brāhmaṇacaraṇas* (schools) and as many as fifteen *caraṇas* of the Vājasaneyins are known. Pupils were given free board and lodging and in return the pupils served the teacher and gave him fees (*gurudakṣiṇā*). That the education in these hermitages was not merely literary, but also included physical and moral training, is seen from the hard, daily routine of the pupils and the code of moral conduct prescribed for them. The elaborate Buddhist and Jain monastic systems must have their roots in Vedic tradition historically, but the data found are not sufficient to outline the process of their development.

*Brahmacarya:* The *Atharvaveda* (11.7) refers to a *brahmacārin*, who is a Vedic student gathering sacred fuel for fire-worship and bringing alms, begged from door to door, to the teacher. The very first verse may be cited as a sample. 'The *brahmacārin* incessantly covering (world by his glory) roams in the two worlds; the gods have the same thoughts (of grace and favour) about him; he fills his teacher by his austerities'. Verse 3 says, 'The teacher leading (the boy) near him makes the *brahmacārin*, like unto a foetus' (here the word *upanayamānaḥ* appears). Verse 4 states that the heaven and earth are the *samidh* (the fuel stick) of the *brahmacārin* and that the *brahmacārin* by his *mekhalā* (girdle), by his *samidh* and by his life of hard work fills the world with austerities. Verse 6 tells us that the *brahmacārin* wears the skin of a black antelope and has a long beard; verse 13 says that the *brahmacārin* offers *samidh* into fire (or if fire is not available) to the sun, to the moon, to the wind or into waters. This hymn thus brings out most of the characteristic features of the *brahmacārin* and of *upanayana* (viz., deerskin, *mekhalā*, offering of *samidh*, begging and a life of hard work and restraint). From the reference to the beard and from the words 'this man' (*ayaṃ puruṣaḥ*) occurring in the *Atharvaveda* (8.1.1) and elsewhere, it appears probably that *upanayana* was performed rather later in those ancient days than in the days of the Sūtras. The *Śatapatha Brāhmaṇa* (11.5.4.1-17) contains many and almost complete details about the life of *brahmacārins*, which bear a very close similarity to those taught in the *Gṛhya Sūtras*. A brief summary is set out below. The boy says, 'I have come unto *brahmacarya*' and 'Let me be a *brahmacārin*'. Then the teacher asks him, 'What is your name?' The teacher then takes him near (*upanayati*) and holds the boy's hand with the words, 'You are the *brahmacārin* of Indra; Agni is your teacher, I am your teacher, N.N.' SBE vol. 44 Part V, P. 86 (addressing the boy by his name). Then he consigns the boy to (the care of) the elements and instructs him 'Drink water, do work (in the teacher's house), put a fuel stick (on the fire), do not sleep (by day).' He repeats the Sāvitrī (*mantra* sacred to Savitṛ). Formerly, it was repeated a year after the boy came as a *brahmacārin*, then at the end of six months, 24 days, 12 days, 3 days; but one should repeat to the brāhmaṇa boy the verse at once (on the very day of upanayana); the teacher repeats it to him first each *pada* separately, then the half and the whole. Being a *brahmacārin* one should not drink honey (*ŚB* 11.5.4.18). *Brahmacarya*, in reality, means period of studenthood. *Brahmacārin* means an inquisitive student who, after his upanayana (q.v.), resorted to a teacher for learning and stayed with him for a period of no less than twelve years. After completing his studies he ordinarily got married and had a settled domestic life. It is the first stage of *āśrama* (q.v.), the others being *gārhasthya* (q.v.), *vānaprastha* (q.v.) and *sannyāsa* (q.v.). A longer period of *brahmacarya* was not unknown. A student who remained with his teacher till his death was known as *naiṣṭhika brahmacārin*, or perpetual student. The student had to serve the teacher by tending his cattle, begging for food and looking after his sacred fires. He was expected to abstain from certain activities; he should not look at the sun and avoid honey, flesh, perfumes, garlands, sleeping by day, rubbing oil on the body, putting collyrium in the eyes, travelling in a cart, wearing shoes and holding an umbrella, love-affairs, anger, covetousness, infatuation, worthless and proud discussion, laying on musical instruments, luxurious baths with hot water, making the teeth attractively clean, an ecstatic state of mind, dancing, singing, gazing at women or touching young women, gambling, serving a low person, injury to animals, obscene talk, drinking wine and so on. Not only was he expected to avoid gazing at a woman or touching her, but if he suffered from night emissions he was required to bathe, worship the sun and make penance with specific *mantras*. Further, he should not assist his teacher's wives in their toilet and bath, nor wash their feet, nor shampoo them. A student who is full twenty years old shall not honour the young wife of a teacher by clasping her feet. After finishing the entire course of study, the student should return to his own house. This was done after performing a rite called *samāvartana* (q.v.). A ceremonial bath was the main feature of the rite and that is why a student who had completed his course of study and taken the ceremonial bath was known as a *snātaka* (q.v.). *ŚGS* 2.11-12, 4.8. *HGS* 1.9-13, *BDS* 1.2.37; 2.2.45; *DŚS* 6.1, 7.11, *ĀpDS* 1.1.2.26-32; 1.1.4.29; *GDS* 1.2.37.

*Ceremonies:* Some of the ritualistic details of the educational ceremonies of *upākarma* and *utsarjana* are worth noting for their educational bearings. The term *upākarma* is part of the full expression *chandasāṃ upākarma*, meaning for study and conservation of Vedic texts. The ceremony is also known as *śravaṇa* as it began in Śrāvaṇa month by keeping people out of work after the sowing or harvesting was over. It is celebrated by the teacher uttering the *sāvitrī mantra* before his assembled pupils.

*Controversies:* The Vedic term for academic controversies is *vākovākya*, which is found in *Śatapatha Brāhmaṇa* (4.6.9.20; 11.5.6.8; *CU* 7.1.2.4). It is explained by Śaṅkara as the art of disputation. Disputations on spiritual matters were known as *brahmodya*.

*Female Education:* Women were eligible for the discipline of *brahmacarya*. The *Ṛgveda* (5.7.9) refers

Education

to young maidens completing their education as *brahmacāriṇīs*. Thereafter, they gained husbands and merged like rivers in ocean of life. The *Ṛgveda* (3.55.16) mentions young unmarried and learned girls getting married to learned bridegrooms. The *Vājasaneyī Saṃhitā* (8.1) similarly states that a daughter should be married to a learned one likewise after the completion of her *brahmacarya*. The *Atharvaveda* (11.6) refers to maidens qualified by their *brahmacarya*, a disciplined life of studentship. Female scholars were often known. According to the available evidence, women were found to share in the intellectual interests referred to in the *Bṛhadāraṇyaka Upaniṣad* (3.4.1, 4.5.1). In the *Aitareya Upaniṣad* (2.1), women were permitted to participate in philosophical discussions. The glaring example is Gārgī Vācaknavī. In the *Bṛhadāraṇyaka Upaniṣad* (6.4.17) there is a mention of an interesting ritual for prayer on the birth of a learned lady, *paṇḍita*. The *Kauṣitakī Brāhmaṇa* (7.6) tells of an Aryan lady, Pathyasvātī, proceeding to the north for study and obtaining the title of Vāk as Sarasvatī for her learning. In the *Maitrāyaṇī Saṃhitā* (3.7.3); *Taittirīya Saṃhitā* (6.1.6.5), *Śatapatha Brāhmaṇa* (3.2.4.3-6) women were taught some of the fine arts like dancing and singing, which were regarded as accomplishments.

*Graduation:* At a stage of holding degrees in ancient India, we find hints of some graduate students, viz., *snātaka, vidyāsnātaka, vratasnātaka, vidyā-vratasnātaka* and *samāvṛtta*. A student designated *snātaka*, having completed a course of study, is referred to in the *Śatapatha Brāhmaṇa* (11.3.3.7; 12.1.1.10). A disciple performing the *samāvartana* occasion after having finished the study of the Veda, but before observing his vows, is termed *vidyāsnātaka* in *Gobhila* (3.3.21.3) and *Pāraskara* (2.5.3.32-35) Gṛhya Sūtras. A pupil attending the convocation after his vows are observed, but before finishing the study of the Veda, is designated in the said Gṛhya Sūtras as *vratasnātaka*. Performing the *samāvartana* both, after having finished such vows and study, a disciple is called *vidyāvratasnātaka*, mentioned also in those Gṛhya Sūtras. A special feature of some categories such as *vidyāsnātaka* and *vratasnātaka* is to be equal to each other in regard to the Vedic study and observation of vows.

*Holidays:* From very early times Vedic studies were stopped on various grounds. The *Taittirīya Āraṇyaka* (11.15) has a very important statement on this subject. It is stated that at *brahmayajña* there are two cases in which the study of the Veda ceases, namely, when the man himself is impure or when the place is impure. The *ĀpDS* (1.4.12.3) quotes the *Vājasaneyī Brāhmaṇa* (the *Śatapatha*) to the effect that Vedic study is *brahmayajña*; when it thunders, when lightning flashes, when a thunderbolt strikes, when the wind blows, these are its *vaṣaṭkāras*; during such occurrences Vedic study is fruitless. The *Aitareya Āraṇyaka* (5.3.3) notes that if there be unseasonal rain, one should take a break from the Vedic studies for three nights. The subject of *anadhyāya* is discussed in the Gṛhya and Dharmasūtras and in almost all Smṛtis which lay down more elaborate rules regarding the cessation of Vedic studies.

*Inauguration:* The Vedic term of studies commenced with the *upākarman* ceremony, which was performed some time during the bright fortnight of the month of Śrāvaṇa (July-August) when the herbs appear, or during the rainy season. The Vedic study then went on for four and a half months or five and a half months or six months, at the end of which came the *utsarga* (discharge) ceremony which formally closed the first term in the month of Pauṣa or Māgha. After this there is a break for five or six months from studying. This appears to be the long vacation of the ancient university. Or, according to the Dharmasūtras, the Vedas may be studied during the bright fortnight and the Vedāṅgas during the dark one. This almost year-long recitation was subject to numerous interruptions (*anadhyāyas*) or 'no-lesson' intervals, which came about on special occasions such as births and deaths, portents, miracles, lightning, thunder, rains or eclipses, and normal occasions such as the 14th and 15th days of the two fortnights, and last days of the seasons, etc. The large number of these interruptions is not surprising as the ancients held that it was better to have no recitation at all, rather than have an error creep into it and, by way of repetition, become an integral part of the Veda itself. The preservation of the Vedic literature by a meticulously correct and scientific method of recitation, down to the minutest part of it, viz., the syllable, was their chief concern, because in the beginning, Vedic texts were not available in a written form and even later were not available in a written form. Impure places were to be avoided for the recitation. Personal purity and good health were also essential conditions for study. After the completion of the whole course came the ceremony of *samāvartana* after which the student was called a *snātaka*, or one whose studentship is considered terminated with a ceremonial bath. Thereafter, he could either get married and set-up a household or, in exceptional cases, remain celibate, to manage and support his family from which he was so long absent.

*Initiation:* The term *upanayana* is used literally, denoting the introduction of the pupil. It means 'the leading of the student to the teacher' by his father or any other relation anticipated, as that sense is in the *Śatapatha Brāhmaṇa* (11.5.3.13). The *brahmacārin* starts on his academic career by taking on the *savitṛ vrata* as a part of the *upanayana*. The study of the Vedas is supposed to have been due to Savitṛ in the *Śatapatha Brāhmaṇa* (11.5.4.6) involving certain observances maintained by the students. These observations had to be performed before learing the different Vedic texts. For details see **Upanayana**.

*Knowledge:* In the *Atharvaveda* (6.116.1; 11.7.10) and later (*TS* 2.1.2.8; 5.1.7.2; *AB* 8.23.8, 9), etc., the word *vidyā* denotes knowledge. There were many branches of learning during the Vedic period, besides the usual study or the Vedic Saṃhitās, such as *viṣavidyā, nakṣatravidyā, brahmavidyā, bhūtavidyā*, etc. The three Vedas are termed by *trayī-vidyā*, the three-fold knowledge as early as the *Taittirīya Brāhmaṇa* (3.10.11.5) and the *Śatapatha Brāhmaṇa* (5.5.5.6). In the *Śatapatha Brāhmaṇa* (11.5.6.8) and *Bṛhadāraṇyaka Upaniṣad* (2.4.10; 5.4.11), it occurs in the lists of subjects of study. Knowledge of the Absolute is regarded as the *summum bonum* of the attainment of knowledge. The term *brahmavidyā* is the name of one of the sciences enumerated in the *Chāndogya Upaniṣad* (7.1.2). It is also mentioned elsewhere (*BU* 1.4.20). A type of knowledge of divine beings (*devajānavidyā*) among the branches of sciences is enumerated in the *Śatapatha Brāhmaṇa* (10.5.2.20; 13.4.3.10) and the *Chāndogya Upaniṣad* (7.1.2; 7.1.4; 2.2.1; 7.7.1). In the *Chāndogya Upaniṣad* (7.1.2; 7.1.4) *devavidyā* appears, according to Śaṅkara, to denote *Nirukta* or exegetics, but explained by Raṅgarāmānuja as the science of the worship of gods as *devatopāsanāprakāra vidyā*. Knowledge of snakes is science enumerated in the *Śatapatha Brāhmaṇa* among the various branches of learning. This knowledge treated as *sarpavidyāvedaḥ* is laid down in the *Śatapatha Brāhmaṇa* (13.4.3.9). In the *Chāndogya Upaniṣad* (7.1.2; 7.1.4; 7.2.1; 7.4.1; 7.7.1) it has been recognized as *sarpadevajānavidyā*. Its sections being called *parvan*, are referred to as subjects of studies. In the *Gopatha Brāhmaṇa* (1.1.10) it has one form termed by *sarpaveda*.

*Lifelong Student:* Although normally the tenure of studenthood or *brahmacarya* was of twelve years, there were some students who preferred to take up lifelong *brahmacarya* and stay with the teachers forever. These students were known as *naiṣṭhikas*.

*Moral Training:* Moral training formed the very pivot and the backbone of the educational system, and development of character was the one ideal that dominated it. The numerous vows and observances obligatory on the pupil (*brahmacārin*) after the *upanayana*, which was a kind of initiation by the *guru* (teacher) into a new spiritual life, entailed on him the most rigorous discipline for a prescribed period. During this time, he was to live religiously as a student in the house of his teacher. His daily routine include begging alms, collecting fuel, looking after the sacrificial fires, tending his teacher's house, learning, and practising austerities. The maintenance of chastity was obligatory on the part of the *brahmacārin*. Thus, the ancient universities were residential, and a more perfect tutorial system was followed than is possible in any modern university, the pupil being under the observation of the *guru* for all the twenty-four hours. The daily begging of alms, on which the student lived, was for the inculcation of 'plain living and high thinking', and had probably little or nothing to do with the financial status of the pupil or of the teacher with whom he resided. Attention may be drawn in this connection to some interesting practical and thoroughly human aspects in the educational system of this age, as reflected in the *Taittirīya Upaniṣad* (1.11). After the admonition, 'Let the *ācārya*, the parents, etc., be your gods', comes the frank admission that the preceptors, as human beings, may have their weaknesses, but it is not their weaknesses but their good points that have to be copied by the pupils. A very practical streak is revealed in the advice to the pupil to continue the family-line by marrying and begetting children, to attend to *kuśala* or well-being (in a worldly sense), to make gifts and practise charity, for fear (*bhaya*) of public opinion or out of shame (*hriya*), if not out of the generosity of the heart.

*Physical Training:* That physical training was an integral part of the educational scheme is clear from the unmistakable trend of the numerous prayers for the grant of vigour and strength that form part of the *upanayana* ceremonial. The begging of alms, morning and evening, the gathering of fuel-sticks, and the manual labour involved in the worship and tending of the fire made for sufficient hard work or exercise for the student. The recitation of the Vedic texts was a strenuous vocal exercise. But the *prāṇāyāma* or lengthening of life span by the control of breath, which formed part of the daily *sandhyā* (morning, noon and evening prayers) adoration, was not only an ideal exercise for the lungs but also one that penetrated all parts of the body as any careful student of Yogic exercises can testify. Lastly, it must be noted that the *daṇḍa-pradāna* (handing the staff to the initiated boy) was a regular ceremony, and the staff was certainly an excellent weapon for self-defence.

*Pupil:* The term for pupil was *antevāsin*, or who resided in the house of the teacher. The admission into studenthood required several rituals. *Upanayana* is a term which means the initiation of a student entering a new life. The youth is initiated by the teacher. In the *Atharvaveda* (11.5.3) this ritual is mentioned. Here all the characteristics, i.e. wearing of an antelope skin, collection of fuel, etc., are found. The student lives in the house of his teacher which was known by the terms of *Ācārya-kula* which is why the student was known as *vāsin* and also *antevāsin*. Introduced to it by the teacher, the pupil entered *brahmacarya* and lived with the teacher. After entering studentship, a pupil is designated *upeta*, which is referred to in the *ŚSS* (4.8.1) and *PGS* (3.10.10). In the *Śatapatha Brāhmaṇa* (5.1.5.17), *Bṛhadāraṇyaka Upaniṣad* (6.3.7), *Chāndogya Upaniṣad*

(3.2.5), etc., all the characteristics are summed up including details of initiation into a new life, wearing of an antelope skin, collecting of fuel, begging after kindling the sacrificial fire, the preservation of secrecy and so forth (cf. *AĀ* 3.2.6; *AS* 8.11). Facts about instruction in certain rites and doctrines with the use of the standard terminology of the Preceptor-pupil relationship are preserved in the Upaniṣads. After completion of the course of study the student became *snātaka* and returned to his house (*ŚB* 11.3.3.7, 12.1.1). A student taking the ceremonial bath after completing studenthood was literally called *snātaka*. Later on after graduation this served as a diploma.

*Self-Reciting: Svādhyāya* means one's recitations of the Veda to oneself. The Vedas had been orally handed down for so many centuries, even after having been taken down in writing and publication of the printed editions. But the oral edition has been preserved in an unbroken succession of teachers. Various *śākhās* and *sampradāyas*, i.e. Vedic Schools, had also undertaken the task of transmitting the heritage with unparalleled accuracy. More stress is laid down on study of the sacred texts than performing specific ritual acts in the *Kāṭhaka Saṃhitā* (37.7); *Pañcaviṃśa Brāhmaṇa* (23.7.3) and *Taittirīya Brāhmaṇa* (2.7.1.1) for preserving spiritual knowledge. Indeed, the importance is repeatedly insisted upon (*ŚB* 1.7.2.3; 11.3.4.3-6, 11.5.7.10) by the use of the term *svādhyāya*. The *Śatapatha Brāhmaṇa* (11.5.6.3) regards it as a form of sacrifice to the *brahman*. The *Taittirīya Āraṇyaka* (2.9-15) regards *svādhyāya* as *brahmayajña* and lays down certain direction as to the exact place and time of study.

*Subjects of study:* Upaniṣads contain several lists of subjects of study, and these give us a good idea of the wide range of knowledge in those days. One such list mentions not only Veda, Itihāsa, Purāṇa and spiritual knowledge, but also grammar, mathematics (*rāśi*), chronology (*nidhi*), dialectics (*vākovākya*), ethics, astronomy, military science, science of snakes, and knowledge of portents (*daiva*). There are a few more branches of knowledge mentioned in this list, such as *pitrya* (science relating to the manes), *devavidyā* (etymological interpretation of divine names or knowledge of gods), *bhūta-vidya* (demonology or science of elements), *devajānavidyā* (dancing and music or mythology) whose exact scope or nature cannot be defined. It is extremely unfortunate that we have no texts preserved regarding many of these subjects. But the list shows how a very comprehensive view of education was developed at the close of the Vedic age. It also demonstrates that the six subjects comprised in the Vedāṅga, formed only a small portion of the curriculum of study, and not the whole of it, as is popularly believed.

*Teacher:* The pivot of the whole educational system of ancient India was the teacher, variously called *ācārya, guru, upādhyāya*. That instruction was oral is established by the *Ṛgveda* 7.10.3.5, which likens the croaking of frogs to the learning process wherein 'when one of these frogs follows another in making noise just as a learner repeats the words of the teacher'. In the beginning the father alone may have taught his son. The story narrated in the *Bṛhadāraṇyaka Upaniṣad* (5.2.1) and the story of Śvetaketu Āruṇeya, whose father taught him everything he knew (*BU* 6.2.1, 6.2.4), illustrate this. But even from very ancient times the practice of sending (*CU* 5.3.1) boys to learn from an *ācārya* had become usual. The *Chāndogya Upaniṣad* itself says in one passage (6.1) that, for twelve years, Śvetaketu Āruṇeya's father placed him as a student with a teacher. The same Upaniṣad (3.11.5) says that the father should impart the *madhuvidyā* to his eldest son or to a worthy pupil only. As the boy stayed with the teacher in the latter's house, and all instruction was oral, the teacher's position assumed the greatest importance. Satyakāma Jābāla (*CU* 6.14.2, 3.11.3; *KU* 2.9; *MU* 1.2.3) says to the teacher (*CU* 4.9.3), 'I have heard from persons like your revered self that knowledge, when learnt from *ācārya*, reaches the highest excellence.' The *Śvetāśvatara Upaniṣad* (6.23) places the *guru* almost on a level with god and showers the highest devotion on him.

*Vedic Schools:* The existence of Vedic schools in post-Ṛgvedic age, even before the establishment of *Sūtra-caraṇas*, in clear evidence that even in early times, centres of Vedic learning presided over by celebrated Vedic teachers were well known. The *Sāmadeva Sūtras* refer to *Brāhmaṇa-caraṇas* (Schools) and as many as fifteen *caraṇas* of the Vājasaneyins are known, including the Kāṇva and Mādhyandina ones that have survived. The only Saṃhitā-*caraṇas* known are those of the Bāskalas and Sākalas for the *Ṛgveda*. The separate *Saṃhitā* and *Brāhmaṇa-caraṇas* originated owing to a difference in the texts of the Saṃhitās and *Brāhmaṇas* respectively. Whatever we might think of Maxmüller's theory of the origin of Saṃhitā and *Brāhmaṇa-caraṇas*, it is important to note that numerous Vedic schools existed all over the country. The example of the assembly of the learned in the court of Janaka shows that debates (philosophical and literary) were often held under royal auspices.

**Ekāha:** One-day sacrifice, also known as *aikāhika*, the typical example of which is *agniṣṭoma*. Some sacrifices are classified as those that are finished in one day (and so called *ekāha*), those that are performed for more than one but not more than twelve days (and so called *ahīna*), and those that extend beyond twelve days (and are called *sattra*). *Jaimini* 10.6.60-61. Among the important *ekāhas* are sacrifices like Viśvajit, Gosava, Sarvasvāra, Bṛhaspatisāra, Śyena, Udbid, Vrātyaṣtoma, etc. Bhattacharyya 1990, 159.

**Election:** The necessity of a ruler is forcibly emphasized in several works. The *Aitareya Brāhmaṇa* (1.14) says that the gods thought they were worsted because they had no king. Therefore, they elected one by consent. The *Ṛgveda* 10.173, which corresponds to the *Atharvaveda* 6.87 and 8.8.1-2, has been taken as an election hymn by some writers (e.g. Jayaswal in *Hindu Polity*, p. 7). But one is constrained to say that it is probably nothing of the kind. The only words that may lend some colour to the theory of election are, 'Let all the people desire thee' (as king) in the *Ṛgveda* (10.173.1), but those words may apply as a benediction even in the case of one who is already a king. In the *Atharvaveda* (3.4.2) there is a reference to the election of a king by the people. 'The people (*viśaḥ*) chose thee to govern the kingdom, these quarters, the five goddesses (chose thee).' In the *Atharvaveda* (3.5.6 and 7) also there is a faint allusion to the election of a king of nobles, king-makers, sūtas and headmen of villages, by the makers of chariots, and the skilled workers in metals. These 'king-makers' are called *ratnins* in other Vedic texts. In connection with the twelve offerings in the Rājasūya, called *ratnināṃ havīṃṣi*, the *Taittirīya Brāhmaṇa* (1.7.3) states that the *ratnins* give the (*rāṣṭra*) kingdom (to the king). So, it appears that the conception was that the king got the kingdom from nobles, high functionaries and the common people. But whatever we might think of the election of kings as a means of popular control over them, there is no doubt that the people continued to play an important part in politics. Thus, particular stress is laid on the necessity of concord between the king and his electors in a passage in the *Atharvaveda* (3.4) which, by the way, is a clear testimony of the prevalence of the system of election of the kings. Besides, it is held by some scholars that an essential part of the coronation ceremony was a solemn oath taken by the king that if he opposed the people, he might lose all the merit he had accumulated in his life. But it is doubtful whether the question here is of opposing (lit. oppressing) the people or the priest by whom the oath was administered. The popular control in the affairs of states was exercised, as in the Ṛgvedic period, through the two popular assemblies, *sabhā* and *samiti*. These are also referred to in the later *Saṃhitās* and *Brāhmaṇas* in terms which indicate an effective exercise of authority not only in the general administration but also over the person of the king. Thus, we find a fervent prayer put in the mouth of the king: 'May the *samiti* and the *sabhā*, the two daughters of Prajāpati, concurrently aid me' (*ŚB* 4.1.4.1-6; cf. 7.12). It is significant to note that this passage describes the popular assemblies as issues of the same Prajāpati, from whom the king, according to the theory of this divinity, derives all his power and authority. Thus, both monarchy and the popular assemblies are placed on the same footing as divine institutions according to the *Śatapatha Brāhmaṇa*. Other passages (*AV* 6.88.3; 7.12) in the literature of this period also indicate that the king took particular care to be in the good grace of the assemblies and that the loss of their favour and support was regarded as a dire calamity for him. Kane III, 20, 28-9.

**Elements:** In the famous creation hymn of the *Ṛgveda* (10.129), the question is raised whether the fathomless waters existed before the formation of the world and the answer is given in affirmative. The conception of the cosmic ocean recurs in other mythologies as well, notably in some Greek cosmogonies and in the Egyptian and Babylonian legends of creation. Among the Greeks a number of cosmogonies were devised, the prime component of the universe being the ocean according to Homer; water and earth, according to Hironymus and Hellanicus; water and slime, according to Athenagoras; and, water, according to Thales (Gomperz, T., *Greek Thinkers*, I, London, 1901, 56 ff). The ancient Egyptians believed that in the beginning the world was a waste of water called Nu or Nun, and it was the abode of the great father (Erman, A., *Handbook of Egyptian Religion*, London, 1907, 26 ff). In Babylonian mythology, both Apsu and Tiamat were forms of water. The former represented the orderly framework of nature, the water of the annual inundation which irrigated the Babylonian plain. The latter represented the destructive and anarchic aspect and was mythologically pictured as a dragon who was slain by Merodach or Marduc. In later Babylonian mythology an attempt was made to reconcile the antagonism between the two conceptions of this watery element by making Apsu and Tiamat complementary principles (Sayce, A.H., *Religion of Ancient Egypt and Babylonia*, II, London, 1902). It should be pointed out in this connection that Taimāta or Tiamat, the water-dragon whom the Babylonian Indra vanquishes, actually figures in the *Atharvaveda* under that very name (*AV* 5.13.3). The conception of water-dragon is not, however, absent in the *Ṛgveda*. Oldenberg regards the Apāṃ Napāt as originally a distinct god—a water-dragon—who later got identified with Agni because of the latter's relation to the cloud-water in the form of lightning. In the *Aitareya Brāhmaṇa* (5.32) it is stated that Prajāpati created the three worlds: the earth, the atmosphere and the sky. From these worlds three luminaries were born: Agni was born from the earth, Vāyu from the atmosphere and Āditya from the sky. In the Nāsadīya hymn (10.129.1), the question is raised whether the fathomless waters existed before the formation of the world. Waters are said to have given birth to Agni (10.2.7; 10.91.6; cf. 3.3.3; 3.9.4). Savitṛ is sometimes called *apām napāt*, son of waters (10.149.2), and the epithet is more commonly applied to Agni. Waters are also connected with Aditi (10.63.2), and in another passage (1.185.1), they are said to know the birth place of heaven and earth. Instead of the five elements of later philosophy, the *Ṛgveda* postulates only water as the primordial element or matter from which others gradually evolved. The *Aitareya Brāhmaṇa* (5.32) says: Prajāpati desired, 'May I be multiplied, may I be propagated.' He practised *tapas*, as a result of which he created the three worlds—the earth, the atmosphere and the sky. He brooded over these worlds, and so three luminaries were born—Agni from the earth, Vāyu from the atmosphere and Āditya from the sky. In the *Taittirīya Brāhmaṇa* (2.2.9) we find that the non-existing entity desired to have a form and began to practise *tapas* as a result of which smoke was produced. Then fire, flames and rays were produced in succession. All these again produced vapours which were condensed like a cloud. That burst open the urinary bladder of Prajāpati which produced the ocean. Then Prajāpati wept and his hot tears fell into the waters and became solid earth. In the *Bṛhadāraṇyaka Upaniṣad* (3.6.1) we find that Gārgī opens a discussion with the philosopher Yājñavalkya by asking for an explanation of the popular theory that, 'All this world is woven, warp and woof, on water.' In another passage, in the same text (5.5.1), it is categorically stated that in the beginning the world was just water. Likewise, the *Chāndogya Upaniṣad* (7.70.1) states, 'It is just water solidified that in this earth, that in the atmosphere, that in the sky, that in the gods and men, beasts and birds grass and trees, animals together with worms, flies and ants; all these are just water solidified.' In the *Kaṭha Upaniṣad* (4.6), the following is stated: 'He who was born of old from *tapas* was born of old from the waters.' The *Aitareya Upaniṣad* comments that right from the waters he drew forth and shaped a person. Similarly, in the *Kauṣītaki Upaniṣad* (1.7), the world of *Brahmaṇ* is said to be the waters. Other elements like earth, air, fire, space, etc., are also frequently mentioned in different texts (cf. *AU.* 5.3, *MU.* 3.2, *ŚU.* 1.1-3, etc.). It is said in *Chāndogya Upaniṣad* (1.9.1) that, 'Verily, all things here arise out of space. In the *Bṛhadāraṇyaka Upaniṣad* (3.8.7) the following is stated: 'That is above the sky, that which is beneath the earth, that which is between the two, sky and earth, that which people call the past and the present and the future—across space alone is that woven, warp and woof'. Bhattacharyya 1971, 2 ff. See **Earth**, **Water**, **Fire**, **Air**, **Space**.

**Elephants:** The use of elephants was always confined to the kings and their nobility. The elephant in the *Ṛgveda* (1.64.7; 4.16.14; 4.4.1; 8.33.8) is mentioned as *mṛga, hastin, ibha* and *vāraṇa*. The *Ṛgveda* (10.40.4) describes hunters following wild elephants, possibly to capture them. The *Ṛgveda* (4.4.1) addresses Agni as a king attended by his followers on his elephant (*ibha*). Sāyaṇa and other Western scholars take *ibha* to signify an elephant, which is its usual meaning in Sanskrit literature. From the context it can be seen that elephants, as a royal mount in the Vedic literature, were used in the field of battle (*RV* 10.106.7), A very obscure passage seems to speak of two mad elephants bending their forequarters and smiting the foe, which proves the use of elephants in war. In the *Ṛgveda* (8.45.5) if the word *apsaḥ*, as explained by Sāyaṇa, is taken to mean a *darśanīyagajaḥ*, we may probably get reference to the use of the elephant for decorative purpose also. The *Sāmāvidhāna Brāhmaṇa* (3.6.11) mentions elephants among the four divisions of the army. The *Adbhuta Brāhmaṇa* uses the word *gaja* for the elephant. It was already used in warfare in the time of Ktesias. The Buddhist and the epic tradition of the fighting elephants must have owed something to earlier antiquity. The absence of direct and more explicit references to the use of elephants in war in the later Vedic literature is doubtless due to the character of that literature; there was not much room in the *Brāhmaṇas* and the Upaniṣads for discussing the arms or the dispositions of the battle. The *Yajurveda Saṃhitās* refer to the elephant-keeper *hastipa* as representing a regular profession (*VS.* 30.11; *TB* 3.4.9.1).

**Emancipation:** See **Liberation**.

**Emblica Offcinalis:** This plant is called *āmalaka* or *āmalakā* in the Vedic texts (cf. *JUB* 1.38.6).

**Embroidery:** Embroidery has always been a traditional occupation taken up mainly by the females. In the Vedic texts we come across a term *peśaskarī* which denotes a female embroiderer (*VS* 30.9; *TB* 3.4.4.1) as *peśas*, is an embroidered garment (*RV.* 2.3.6; 4.36.7; 7.34.11; 7.42.1; *VS.* 19.82, 19.89, 20.41; *AB* 3.10) for a female dancer (*RV* 1.92.4-5). Making of such dresses thus existed as a regular female occupation. They are enumerated in the list of victims at the *puruṣamedha* (*VS* 30.9; *TB* 3.4.4.1). But the term *peśaskarī* may have other significance as well. Thus *peśaskarī* is considered by Mahīdhara as the wife of a worker on gold in *Taittirīya Brāhmaṇa* (3.3.4.5). *Suvarṇaṃ hiraṇyam peśalam.* Needles, referred to in the *Ṛgveda* (7.18.17), indicate the use of stitched garments. Chakraborty, 222.

**Embryology:** The *Atharvaveda* gives a long list of charms which cover the whole field from conception to birth and nourishment of the child. The *strīkarmāṇi* of the *Atharvaveda* have charms and spells for all stages of embryonic development.

**Emperor:** *Samrāj* in the *Ṛgveda* (3.55.7; 3.56.5; 6.27.8; 8.19.32) and *Vājasaneyī Saṃhitā* (5.32; 13.35; 20.5) means 'superior ruler', 'sovereign' as expressing a greater degree of power than king (*rājan*). In the *Śatapatha Brāhmaṇa* (5.1.1, 13), in accordance with its theory of Vājapeya and Rājasūya, the *samrāj* is asserted to be a higher authority than a king, and to have become one by the sacrifice of the Vājapeya. There is, however, no trace of the use of the word as 'emperor' in the sense of an 'overlord of kings', probably because political conditions furnished no example of such a status as, for instance, was attained in the third century BC by Aśoka. At the same time, *samrāj* denotes an important king like Janaka of Videha (*ŚB* 11.3.2.1; 11.3.2.6; 11.2.2.3; *BU* 4.1.1; 4.3.1). It is applied in the *Aitareya Brāhmaṇa* (8.14) as the title of the eastern kings. Macdonell and Keith, II. 433.

**Endogamy:** See **Exogamy**.

**Engineering:** Engineering in the Vedic age should be viewed in terms of the construction of houses, making of chariots, pottery, carpentry, smithy and so forth. *Gṛha* or *dama* is used to denote a house. The sides of the house were called *pakṣa* and the door *dvāra*, while the door with its framework was termed *ātā*. From passages in the *Atharvaveda* (3.12; 9.3), Zimmer has suggested the following possible method of construction. On a good site, four pillars (*upamit*) were set up against which beams were propped as supports (*pratimit*). The pillars were then joined on top by cross beams (*parimit*). Bamboo (*vaṃśa*) was used as ribbing over a ridge called *visuvant*. Finally, the ribs were covered with a kind of thatching. The walls were set up with grass tied in bundles (*palada*), which were bound together. Some terms like *sadas* (sitting room) and *patnīnāṃ sadana* (wives' room) suggest that the dwellings were compartmented. The chariot (*ratha*) was an important piece of military equipment from the beginning of the Vedic age. It generally had two wheels (*cakra*), each consisting of rim (*nemi*), felly (*pradhi*), nave (*nabhya*) and spokes (*ara*), connected by a non-revolving axle (*akṣa*), the end of which (*ani*) fit into the nave holes (*kha*). Solid wheels were also sometimes used. The body of the chariot (*kośa*) was attached to the axle and was possibly constructed with wicker work or leather stretched over a light wooden frame. A seat for the warrior was provided. From the axle a pole (*iṣā*) ran perpendicular to the front of the chariot where it was joined to a yoke (*yuga*), which was secured to the necks of the horses. The chariot also consisted of other minor auxilliary parts. Mention of such words as *kulya* (canal) and *khanitrimā āpa* (water obtained by digging) in the *Ṛgveda* (3.45.3 and 7.49.2 respectively) suggests that some kind of irrigation system which utilized well-water was in existence. *Karmāra*, the 'smith', is mentioned several times in the Vedic Saṃhitās (*RV* 10.72.2; *AV* 3.5.6; *KS* 17.13; *MS*. 2.9.5; *VS* 16.27; 30.7; cf. *karmāra RV* 9.112.2; *TB* 3.4.3.1). in the *Atharvaveda* (3.5.6) smiths appear with fisherman (*dhīvānaḥ*) and chariot-builders (*rathakāraḥ*), all being classified as clever workers (*manīṣiṇaḥ*). Little is known of the smith's methods of work and of his tools. No doubt he smelted (*dhmā*) the ore in the fire; hence he is called *dhmātṛ*, the 'smelter' (*RV*. 5.9.5). He made metal vessels (*gharma ayasmaya*) (*RV*. 5.30.15) to be put on the fire; even the Soma cup could occasionally be made of hammered metal (*ayo-hata*) (*RV*. 9.1.2). *Takṣan* 'carpenter' is mentioned in the *Ṛgveda* (9.112.1) and often later (*AV*. 10.6.3; *KS* 12.10; 18.13; *MS* 2.9.5; *VS* 16.27; 30.6; *TB* 3.4.2.1; *ŚB* 1.1.3.12; 3.6.4.4). He was employed to do all sorts of work in wood, such as making chariots (*ratha*) and wagons (*anas*). Carved work of a finer type also seems to have fallen to his lot (*RV* 10.86.5; *AV* 19.49.8; cf. *RV* 1.161.9; 3.60.2). The axe (*kuliśa*, *RV*. 3.2.1; *paraśu*, *KS* 12.10) is mentioned as one of his tools, and perhaps the *bhurij*, a word however, is of uncertain meaning.

**Entourage:** Of the entourage of the king and his servants, the *senānī*, leader of the army, who appears in a few hymns, may have been a general appointed by the king to lead an expedition. The *grāmaṇī* probably led a minor portion of the host in war and was identical with the *vrājapati*. Far more important, in the estimation at least of the composers of the hymns, was the *purohita* or domestic priest. The Vedic *purohita* was the forerunner of the brāhmaṇa statesmen who, from time to time in India, have shown conspicuous ability in the management of affairs; and, there is no reason to doubt that a Viśvāmitra or a Vasiṣṭha was a most important element of the government of the early Vedic realm. It is clear, too from the hymns which are attributed to the families of these sages, that the *purohita* accompanied the king to battle, and seconded his efforts for victory by prayers and spells. In return for his faithful service, the rewards of the *purohita* were doubtless large; the *dānastūtis* of the *Ṛgveda* tell of the generous gifts of patrons to the poets, and we may safely assume that the largest donations were those of kings to the *purohitas*. At the royal consecration the entourage of the king played an important part. The list of *ratnins*, 'jewels', given by the *Taittirīya* texts, consists of the brāhmaṇa, i.e. the *purohita*, the *rājanya*, the *mahiṣī*, the first wife of the four allowed to the king by customs, the *vāvātā*, 'favourite wife', the *parivṛkti* 'discarded wife', the *sūta* 'charioteer', the *senānī* 'commander of the army', the *grāmaṇī* 'village headman', the *kṣattṛ*, 'chamberlain', the *saṃgrahitṛ*, 'treasurer', the *bhāgadugha*, 'collector of taxes' or 'divider of food', and the *akṣāvāpa*, 'superintendent of dicing' or 'thrower of dice'. The *Śatapatha Brāhmaṇa* also has the huntsman and the courier, while the *Maitrāyaṇī Saṃhitā* adds the *takṣan*, carpenter and *rathakāra*, chariot-maker. In an older list of eight *vīras*, heroes, given in the *Pañcaviṃśa Brāhmaṇa* are found the brother, son, *purohita*, *mahiṣī*, *sūta*, *grāmaṇī*, *kṣattṛ* and *samgrahitṛ*. In the interpretation of the names of several of these officers, we are faced with the doubt whether we are to recognize in them merely courtiers or public functionaries. According to native tradition, the *sūta* is the charioteer, but it seems much more probable that he was at once a herald and a minstrel. In one passage that is attributed to him, the inviolability of this conclusion is clearly pointed. The *grāmaṇī* has already been met with as a military official in the period of the *Ṛgveda*. Propably at this time a *grāmaṇī* was both, for civil and military purposes at the head of each village. It may be conjectured that he owed his position to the kings, while the *grāmaṇī par excellence* presided over the city or village where the royal court was situated. It is also far from unlikely, despite the silence of the texts, that the civil functions of the *grāmaṇī* were more important, for the post is emphatically declared, at several places, to represent the summit of the ambition of the vaiśya. If later analogy is to help us, we may conjecture that the *grāmaṇī* formed the channel through which the royal control was exercised and the royal dues received. Rapson 85-6, 116-17.

**Epicentre:** See **Nāvi**.

**Epistemology:** The word denotes the theory of knowledge with regard to its methods and validation. In the early Vedic texts, there are certain indications of epistemology but its details have not come to us till the beginning of the traditional sixfold philosophies of India. The *Ṛgveda* postulates the validity of empirical knowledge, while in the later *Saṃhitās* and *Brāhmaṇas* we come across various speculations regarding cosmology and metaphysics, with particular reference to the concept of sacrifice as the basic source of the understanding in relation to various world-views. It is, however, in the Upaniṣads that we come across the beginning of a regular science of epistemology. The conception of 'knowledge' or 'cognition' has evolved out of 'the knowledge of some secret doctrine or other sacrificial science', which has been insisted upon in the *Brāhmaṇas* and *Āraṇyakas*. The longing for this true knowledge, leading to the disregard of all pleasures, finds poetical expression in the legend of Naciketas in one of the most remarkable and beautiful *Upaniṣads*, the *Kāṭhaka*. But in the *Maitrāyaṇī Upaniṣad* (1.2-4), one of the latest, it lends to an utter contempt of the world and that pessimistic trait of thought, which recurs so often in the Buddhist as well as later Indian literature. The fact is that although basically the old Upaniṣads are not pessimistic, describing as they do *Brahman* and *ātman* as *ānandamaya* (consisting of 'joy'), belief in the unreality of the world must ultimately lend to contempt for it. Thus, we find in the *Upaniṣads* vigorous and creative philosophical thought clothed in the language of poetry. No wonder they make a powerful appeal to the heart and the head. The thinkers seek the truth earnestly and so their thoughts become a fervent expression of the ever unsatisfied human yearning for knowledge. All the philosophical systems and religions of India, heretical or orthodox, have sprung from the *Upaniṣads*. The theological-philosophical systems of Śaṅkara. Rāmānuja and others are founded on the *Vedānta Sūtras* of Bādarāyaṇa which, in their turn, are reared on the doctrines of the *Upaniṣads*. Reference has already been made to the profound influence of the *Upaniṣads* on human thought outside India. We may now represent a few fundamental tenets of the *Upaniṣads* in the form of propositions in the manner of Deussen. (1) The *ātman* is the knowing subject and as such can never become an object for us and is, therefore, itself unknowable. It can only be defined negatively. When later Vedānta defined it as 'being thought and bliss' (*sat-cid-ānanda*) on the basis of the frequent references to these separate elements scattered in the older *Upaniṣads*, it was nothing but a negative characterization because 'being' is rather a not-being in an empirical sense, thought is the negation of all objective being, and bliss is the negation of all suffering. (2) As the *ātman* is the metaphysical unity expressing itself in all empirical plurality—a unity found only in our consciousness—it is the sole reality. To know the *ātman* is, therefore, to know everything. There is really no plurality; there can be no becoming; 'change' is a mere name. (3) The pantheism of the Upaniṣads is but a compromise between the two opposite points of view—the metaphysical one, which does not recognize any reality outside of the *ātman*, i.e. consciousness, and the empirical one according to which a manifold universe exists external to us. The *ātman* being the Universe, remains the sole reality although the universe is real. But what distinguishes Upaniṣadic pantheism from that of Europe is the subtle distinction made by the Upaniṣads when they state that the universe is in god, but never that the universe is god. God (or *ātman*) is transcedent as well as immanent. (4) Thus, when it is stated that the universe is the *ātman*, the identity remains very obscure. This obscurity was sought to be removed by borrowing the well-known empirical category of causality and representing that the *ātman* is the chronologically antecedent cause and the universe is its effect, its creation. Majumdar 501-2; Belvalkar and Ranade, 277, 369, 437-9.

**Epithets:** *Kṣatra*, in the general sense of 'dominion', 'rule', 'power' as exercised by gods and men, occurs frequently from the *Ṛgveda* (4.17.1; 5.62.6; *AV* 3.5.2; 5.18.4; *TS* 2.4.7.2; *TB* 2.4.6.12; *VS* 27.7) onwards. The word is also found in the concrete sense of 'rulers' in the *Ṛgveda* (1.157.2; 8.35.17) and later (*AV* 4.22.2; *VS* 10.17; *TB* 2.7.6.3); however, nowhere in the *Ṛgveda* does it mean what it regularly denotes in the later *Saṃhitās* (*AV* 2.15.4; 9.7.9; 12.5.8; 15.10.5; *TS* 1.6.1.2, 2.2.11.2; *VS* 5.27; 14.24; 18.38), the ruling class as opposed to the priests (*brāhmaṇa*), the subject people (*viś. vaiśya*), and the servile class (*śūdra*). A *kṣatrapati* is mentioned several times (*TS* 1.8.14.2; *VS* 10.17, *TB* 1.7.8.5; *ŚB* 5.4.2.2) as an equivalent of 'king'. The term *kṣapāvan*, denotes 'protector of the earth'. It is an epithet of a king (3.55.17), or denotes a king (1.70.5, 7.10.5, 8.71.2, 10.29.1) in the *Ṛgveda*. The word is significant as showing the function of the king as the protector of the tribal territory. The term *mahārāja* denotes a 'great king'. It is frequently referred to in the *Brāhmaṇas* (*AB* 7.34.9; *KS* 5.5; *ŚB* 1.6.4.21, 2.5.4.9; *BU* 2.1.19; *MU* 2.1). It seems to mean no more than a king, or rather perhaps a reigning and powerful king, as opposed to a mere prince, who would be called *rājan*.

**Eroticism:** See **Kāma**.

**Eschatology:** In the *Śatapatha Brāhmaṇa* it is said that those who do not perform rites with correct knowledge are born again and suffer death again. In a hymn of the *Ṛgveda* (10.58), the soul (*manas*) of a man, apparently unconscious, is invited to come back to him from the trees, herbs, the sky, the sun, etc. In many of the hymns there is also the belief in the existence of another world, where the highest material joys are attained as a result of the performance of the sacrifices and also in a hell of darkness underneath, where the evil-doers are punished. In the *Śatapatha Brāhmaṇa* we find that the dead pass between two fires, which burn evil-doers but let the good go by; (*ŚB* 1.9.3.1). It is also said that everyone is born again after death, is weighed in a balance and receives reward or punishment according to good or bad deads. It is easy to see that scattered ideas like these, with regard to the destiny of the soul of man, according to the sacrifice that he performs or other good or bad deeds form the first rudiments of the later doctrine of metempsychosis. The idea that man enjoys or suffers, either in another world or by being born in this world, according to his good or bad deeds, is the first beginning of the moral ideas. These ideas, of the possibilities of a necessary connection of the enjoyments and sorrows of a man with his good and bad deeds, when combined with the notion of an inviolable law or order, which was gradually growing with the conception or *ṛta*, and the unalterable law, which produces the effects of sacrificial works, led to the law of *karma* and the doctrine of transmigration. The description of heaven in the *Ṛgveda* is only elaborated in the other *Saṃhitās* and *Brāhmaṇas*. The essentials are the same. The *Atharvaveda* tells us how the head man is conducted upwards by the Maruts, with gentle breezes fanning him until he recovers his complete body and meets the Fathers who reside in the company of Yama. The idea that the dead in heaven are nourished by the piety of the relatives on earth is also found in the *Atharvaveda*. Such nourishment may either be buried with the dead, so that the grains of corn and sesame may turn into wish-cows in heaven, or the nourishment may be conveyed through subsequent offerings. This is indeed the germ of the later *śrāddha* idea. The *Ṛgveda* conception of *nirṛti* as a place of darkness has been developed by the *Atharvaveda* into a *naraka-loka* (hell), which is the abode of female goblins, and a place of utter darkness. The *Śatapatha Brāhmaṇa*, the *Jaiminīya Brāhmaṇa* and *Kauṣītaki Brāhmaṇa* add their own touches to this horried picture of hell. The two paths, one of the *devas* and the other of the *pitrs*, are naturally mentioned, as they have been already foreshadowed in the *Ṛgveda*. The theory of metempsychosis does not appear to have been very clearly formulated in the *Saṃhitās* and *Brāhmaṇas*, though the doctrine that the agony of death is to be endured not only once but repeatedly, as one may die repeated deaths in the next world, prepares us for the very important part that the theory plays in the Upaniṣads where the conception of repeated deaths is merely transferred from the next world to the present. The idea of reward and punishment, after death, in exact correspondence to the good and bad deeds of a person in this life, has gained a firm hold in this period. The attainment of immortality and the company of the gods in the heaven—a highly ennobled form of earthly life perpetuated in the surroundings of bliss—is the deeply cherished aim of, and incentive to, the practice of piety and good works in this life. That man is the architect of his own fate becomes a perfect truth according to this theory. And the highest merit of philosophical thought in this period is the development of the doctrine that reward and punishment are not eternal. This is but a logical development. How can the limited good or evil that men can do in the brief span of a single life on earth bring endless pleasure or pain in the next world? Hence follows the theory that penance and atonement can purify, and absolve, the soul of guilt and decrease the period of suffering. The Brāhmaṇa doctrine, that whatever food a man consumes in this world in return consumes him in the next world (*ŚB* 12.9.1.1), is but the transfer from the physical to the moral plane of the law that action and reaction are equal and opposite. Similarly, the enjoyment of the rewards, which is in exact measure to the good deeds performed, must sometime come to an end. Thus, there is the prospect of rebirth again for both the pious and the wicked. So arises the wonderful conception of a beginningless and endless circuit of birth and death; the so-called *saṃsāra* or 'bondage of life and death' culminating in the unique conception of ultimate happiness which is much higher than that of a life in heaven. It is a conception of freedom from *saṃsāra*, which is the true *mokṣa* (release) or absolution. Belvelkar and Ranade 25-6, Majumdar 449-50.

**Ethics:** Throughout the course of Indian ideological speculations, ethics have never been completely divorced from religion; the relations between man and man generally form a side issue of the larger problem of the relation between man and god. In the Vedic times, for instance, we find that if one wanted to be happy and desired that his rival should be miserable, all he had to do was to prove by words and deeds, that he himself was a pious worshipper who never missed his daily oblations to the gods, whereas the other fellow was a niggardly person who knew not sacrifice; and then Indra and Varuṇa were expected to do the needful. With the Vedic people, therefore, virtue was knowledge; knowledge as to the time, form, and prescription attending an offering for the gods; while vice was ignorance in these respects, with the elaboration of the teachnical part of the sacrifice and the growth of the special class of experts who made a monopoly of the art, this intellectualistic trend of the moral doctrine would have reached an undesirable extreme and rendered virtue a byword for finesse and fusiness over little things, but for two elements of safety, one original to the system and the other borrowed from without. We have ample evidence in the earliest parts of the Veda to prove that the several hymns to gods were not all estranged from true poetry and moral fervour. It does the Vedic poet great wrong to think of him as always a greedy beggar, trafficking with the gods for the goods of the world. At times he rose above the earth and conceived of the godhead with piety and almost the spirituality of a mystic. This latent religious feeling, we have reasons to suppose, gained a new base of life by the fusion of the Vedic and non-Vedic cultures, which we have been considering here from different standpoints. We have already seen that it exhibited a tendency towards magic, divination, and propitiation of a number of small, local, often malignant spirits and totems. Such a primitive faith is universally swayed by large feelings and emotions, gross but sincere and unsophisticated. These emotions refuse to be crowded out or permanently suppressed by elaborations in ceremonials, by priestly formularies and high sounding philosophies. The *Ṛgveda* 7.86.6 and 88.5-6 clearly show that the consciousness of sin (*anṛta*, *āgas*, *enas*) was recognized. Sin resulted from the violation of *ṛta* or 'order' in the moral sphere (i.e. of 'truth' and 'right') as well as in the religious one (i.e. of sacrifice or rite), or of the commands of god. In the unalterable law of good or bad effects, flowing from good and bad conduct, are to be found the first germs of the law of *karman* (that most outstanding characteristic of Indian thought)—binding on gods and mortals alike. Offering prayers and performing rites, in short, living in perfect harmony with the will of gods—this was the ideal moral life according to the *Ṛgveda*. Man owes some duties to his fellow-beings (10.117). The *Ṛgveda* 5.85.7 tells us that an offence against a friend, neighbour, or comrade, or even a stranger, is a sin (*āgas*). Adultery, witchcraft, gambling, drinking, senselessness and self-deception are ranked as deviations from the moral life. The view therefore, that the so-called uncertainty of the fate of evil after death is a vagueness characteristic of the comparative indifference to mortals, and that if gods are extolled as true it is not an assertion of ascertained truth, iṣ wrong. That life is a duty and responsibility is the central ethical teaching of the Brāhmaṇas. Man is born with certain *ṛṇas* or debts which he must discharge in his life. He has a debt to pay to the lower creatures. And he discharges these debts, if he worships the gods, studies the Veda, performs funeral ceremonies, is hospitable to guests, and offers oblations to the *bhūtas*. Thus, there is no lack of high moral sense and noble sentiments. Selflessness must characterize all our actions. The Brāhmaṇas have a remarkable sacrifice, the Sarvamedha, wherein everything is to be sacrificed to attain the freedom of the spirit. Prayer and good works constitute godliness, which is the first requisite of a good life. Truthfulness is utterance and action is the foundation of moral life. There are hints in the Brāhmaṇas that excessive ritualism was bringing on a reaction. For example, knowledge rather than sacrificial gifts or asceticism, is valued in the *Śatapatha Brāhmaṇa* (10.5.4.16), although asceticism is also held up as a great ideal elsewhere (*TB* 3.12.3). The theory that confession, implying repentance, somewhat mitigates the guilt is seen in the *Śatapatha Brāhmaṇa*. Inner purity was insisted on, as much as external purity. Truth, performance of *dharma* (duty), respect for parents, love of fellow-beings, and abstinence from theft, adultery, and murder were the *sine qua non* of a good life. The ethical doctrine of *karman*, connected with the doctrine of transmigration, is beautifully developed in the *Bṛhadāraṇyaka Upaniṣad*. With pointed examples the doctrine is thus set forth: '. . . Just as an embroidress undoes a small portion of a piece of embroidery, and out of it creates a different, quite new and more beautiful design, so man, when he has stripped off his body and has rid himself of non-knowledge, creates for himself a different, quite new and more beautiful form, that of the spirit of an ancestor or of a Gandharva, of a *Brahman* or of a Prajāpati, of a god or of a man, or that of that some other being. . . . As he has acted as he has lived, so he becomes; he who has done good, is born again as a good one, he who has done evil, is born again as an evil one. He becomes good through good action, bad through bad action.' Therefore it is said, 'Man here is formed entirely out of his desire, and according to his desire in his resolve and according to the performance of the action in his destiny.' *Bṛhadāraṇyaka Upaniṣad* 4.4. Tr. by Winternitz (I, 259). The ethical basis of the Upaniṣadic doctrine as expressed in the simile, 'As water does not stick to the leaf of a lotus-flower, so evil action does not stick to him who knows this (that the self is *Brahman*)' (*CU* 4.14.3) is not to be construed to mean that knower was given all laxity. Rather, the simile shows that the knower was regarded as inherently incapable of evil actions. Belvalkar and Ranade 19-20, Majumdar, 185-6, 449, 474-5.

**Etymology:** *Nirukta* is represented according to tradition, by a single work, the *Nirukta* of Yāska, which itself states, 'without this (science) there can be no understanding of the (Vedic) *mantras* (1.15). However, it is a commentary on an older list of Vedic words, called the *Nighaṇṭu* or the *Naighaṇṭuka*, to each of which one of the more illustrative Vedic passages ought to be understood as attached. Yāska himself mentions many earlier Niruktakāras. The *Brāhmaṇas*, *Āraṇyakas*, and *Upaniṣads* offer as many as about 600 etymologized words, through proper etymologies, synonymous expression, explanation of one Vedic word by another and brief annotations of whole verses and hymns. This etymologizing is sometimes done by implication as in *tvaṣṭā, takṣat, vayram* (*ṚV* 10.61.6). Yāska's borrowing from this earlier material is quite evident, though he probably was the first to formulate general principles of etymology. The desire to glorify the sacrifice often dictated the necessity of explaining through a derivation, some who brought into relation with a myth or legend, the various names of the sacrifice, the materials employed in it, and the priests, gods, and hostile demons associated with it. Curiously, some of the myths and legends do give the clue to the right derivation of the words, and must have been especially designated to make the etymological process less dry for the ritual-minded priests for whom they were primarily intended. The *Taittirīya Saṃhitā* and *Maitrāyaṇī Saṃhitā* contain the largest number etymologized of the Ṛgvedic words. Among the *Brāhmaṇas*, the *Śatapatha Brāhmaṇa* and the *Aitareya Brāhmaṇa*, and among the *Āraṇyakas*, the *Aitareya* are notable in this respect. Among the Upaniṣads, only the *Bṛhadāraṇyaka Upaniṣad* and *Chāndogya Upaniṣad* occasionally take to etymologizing on the basis of etymological principles formulated by Yāska and accepted by modern scholars. These etymologies may be classified thus: (1) Etymologies rendered probable both by the phonetic and semantic history of the word. This principle stresses the value of both sound and sense. (2) Those based primarily on the semantic evolution of a word. Some of the etymological equations exhibit a semantic change, often based on similarities and giving rise to metaphor and transference of which the latter assumes diverse forms or tendencies. Etymological equations based on the semantic identification of phonetically similar words (e.g. *aṅgāra = aṅgiras; puriṣaya = puruṣa;* etc.) illustrates a tendency inherent in folk etymology, whereby association by sound may affect the meaning, just as association by sense may bring about changes in the form of words. When two words have the same form, the meaning of the unfamiliar one is assimilated with that of the familiar word. If they don't have an identical but a similar form, the less known word assimilates itself phonetically to the better known word. The grouping of words according to their phonemes plays a great part in folk-etymology. The mind seeks to establish relations between the external form of words which are sometimes inversions in terms of their meaning and contrary to common sense. Anecdotal etymologies, which form an important part of folk-etymology, are copious in *Brāhmaṇa* literature. Thus, the etymologies of *agni, aśva, udumbara, vidyut, pṛthivī*, etc., are connected with the legend of Prajāpati; those of *āṣāḍhā, aparājitā*, etc., with the legend of the *deva-asura* contest; and, those of *puṣkara* and *śakvarī* with the Indra-Vṛtra fight in the *Śatapatha Brāhmaṇa, Taittirīya Brāhmaṇa, Aitareya Brāhmaṇa, Kauṣitaki Brāhmaṇa*, and other *Brāhmaṇas*. The agreeably susprising feature of these attempts at etymologizing is that some of them do give a clue to the right derivation, as for example *pṛthivī* from $\sqrt{prath}$, *śakvarī* from $\sqrt{sak}$ and *āṣāḍha* from $\sqrt{sah}$, *Cultural Heritage of India*, I. 275-7.

**Eulogies:** In the *Ṛgveda* (1.31.13, 2.12.6, 5.52.12) there is a reference to *kīri* or songs of praise meant for accomplished persons. In the *Ṛgveda* (1.127.7, 6.67.10) kīsta means a praiser or poet.

**Eunuch:** They are treated as a class neither śūdras nor brāhmaṇas, and are regarded as sacred to Prajāpati in the *Śatapatha Brāhmaṇa* (13.6.2.12).

**Evening:** The term *doṣā* denoting 'evening', is frequently referred to from the *Ṛgveda* (1.34.3, 2.8.3, 4.2.8, 5.5.6, 6.5.2) onwards (*AV* 6.1.1; *Nirukta* 4.17), usually in contrast with *uṣas* 'dawn'. In the *Chāndogya Upaniṣad* (6.13.1) the word is contrasted with *prātar* 'early'. Another word for evening is *sāya* (*TB*. 1.5.3.3; *KB* 2.8; *ŚB* 7.3.2.18) which is found in the *Ṛgveda* and later, usually appearing in the adverbial form *sāyam* (*RV* 5.77.2; 10.146.4; *AV* 3.12.3; 4.11.12; 8.6.10) 'in the evening'.

**Evil Speaking:** Evil speaking (*kuyavāc*) appears in one passage of the *Ṛgveda* (1.17.4.7) to denote a demon slain by Indra, who is personified by the barbarian opponents opposed to the Aryans. The term is applied to the Dasyus. The *Ṛgveda* (5.29.10; 5.32.8) has an expression as *mṛdhra-vāc*, 'speaking insultingly'. Sāyaṇa refers to evil-speaking, or abusive expressions or insulting somebody as *kutsitaṃ śabdāyantaṃ* and *imṛbhābhibhūtam*.

**Excellence in Speech:** In the *Atharvaveda* (8.10.5-7) there is a reference to *vāk* on incantation for acquiring extraordinary charm of speech and manner. It deals with a restrictive incantation, a charm against an opponent in debate, referred to in the *Atharvaveda* (2.27). During the Ṛgvedic period the Indo-Aryan folks valuing soft, sweet and courtly speech had invented some rituals to achieve charms in speech. Success in assembly and triumph in debate, were greeted with joy by the friends of equal mind. Social prestige through intelligent speech is vouchsafed in the *Ṛgveda* (10.71.10). At the later Vedic age an Indo-Aryan society had even invented a prescription for procuring a son not only attending the assembly or conference, but also having naturally cultured speech as *suśrūṣita vāk* by learning in the lores, clearly noted in the *Bṛhadāraṇyaka Upaniṣad* (6.4.17,18).

**Exegesis:** We find the earliest interpreation of the Vedic *mantras* in the Brāhmaṇas; but the word rising from the depths (*ninyā vacāṃsi*, *RV* 4.3.16), as the *mantras* are called by the Vedas themselves, have not been adequately handled by the Brahmanical expositions. The Brāhmaṇas were not concerned with giving systematically an esoteric interpretation of the Saṃhitās. Technically, they can be regarded as *karma mīmāṃsā* and not as *brahma mīmāṃsā*, that is to say, authoritative dissertation on ritual practice and not on spiritual knowledge. The connection of the Vedic *mantras* with rituals is very deep. The chief aim of the *Brāhmaṇas* is to give a clear and connected account of the rituals, with occasional exegetical comments, where it is assumed that the listeners are already perfectly familiar with the atmosphere in which these rituals arose. Every detail of a ritual has to be accompanied by a *mantra*; and so the *Brāhmaṇas* have quoted extensively from the Saṃhitās and, in many cases, may have paraphrased the *mantras* without attempting any kind of esoteric interpretation. Perhaps, this was thought unnecessary, and was supposed to belong rather to the *adhyātma* than to the *adhiyajña* point of view with which the *Brāhmaṇas* were more directly concerned (in commenting upon *RV* 10.71.5). Yāska remarks: 'It speaks of the meaning as being the flower and the fruit of the words. Exoterically, knowledge of the rituals and of the gods are respectively the flower and the fruit; but esoterically, the knowledge of the gods and of the self are the flower and the fruit of the word (*Nirukta*, 1.20). Nothing could express more clearly the double relation that the *mantras* bear to *jñāna* and *karma*). So it was enough for them to explain incidentally the connection of the *mantras* with the rites and stop there. Though the *mantras* were evidently composed in a ritualistic atmosphere, it cannot be claimed that each and every *mantra* of the Saṃhitās always has a necessary reference to some rite. Of course, the ritualists of later days have insisted upon the dogma that 'the sole import of the *mantras* lies in an urge to ritualistic action alone', and have tried to connect with a rite. But, naturally, this could not be done with a *tour de force*, as in many cases the import of the *mantras* had no direct reference to the rites to which they were applied. In the recital of the *śāstras*, or the laudatory hymns, the Brahmanical injunction can govern the act of recitation alone but, obviously, it cannot prevent the inspired thought from diving deep into the esoteric meaning (*upaniṣad, rahasyam*) of the word; and surely it cannot be its intention to do so (the *RV* repeatedly draws attention to the esoteric meaning of the *mantras*: cf. 1.164.39; 4.3.16; 8.100.10; 10.71.3; 10.71.4; 10.71.5; 10.114.8; 10.125.7; etc.). The *Nirukta* insists upon a thorough knowledge of the secret of the Vedas (1.18). The *Gopatha Brāhmaṇa*, while fully defining the scope of the Vedas speak expressly of their *rahasyam* (1.2.10). *Cultural Heritage of India* I, 313.

**Existence:** The famous *nāsadīya* hymn (10.121) begins with the statement that there was once a time when there was neither non-entity nor entity. The idea is also reflected in another verse (10.72.2) in which it is stated that, in the earliest age of the gods, the existent sprang from the non-existent. In the second part of the first verse of the hymn under discussion, it is said that in the beginning there was neither the atmosphere nor the sky above. Though regarded as the eternally existing parents of the universe, we have seen that, in many places of the *Ṛgveda*, heaven and earth are spoken of as being created by themselves. In the third part, the question is raised whether the fathomless waters enveloped all before the formation of the world, and in the third verse of the said hymn the answer is given in the affirmative. We have already come across the conception of primordial waters enveloping the universe and gods like Hiraṇyagarbha, Viśvakarman and others issuing therein. In the second and third verses of the *nāsadīya* hymn it is said that there was neither death nor deathlessness, nor the distinction of day and night. Darkness was then covered up by darkness; everything was undistinguished and fluid. That self-sustained one, existing in void and wrapped in nothingness, breathed calmly and was developed by the power of *tapas*. In another hymn (1.164.6) we are confronted with a similar question: what was that one in the form of the unborn which supported these six worlds? However, in the fourth verse of the *nāsadīya* hymn we are told that this one, which was developed by the power of *tapas* or inherent heat, was seized by *kāma* or desire, the first germ of mind, the earliest link between non-entity and entity. In the fifth verse, the poet goes on to speak of the impregnating powers and mighty forces of receptive capacities and active energies, but in the next two verses the poet confesses to himself inability to declare how the universe was produced. The gods themselves came into existence at a later stage of creation. No one on earth is therefore able to say what the origin of the world was, and whether it had any creator. Even its ruler in the highest heaven may not know the whole thing. The *Nāsadīya-Sūkta* of the *Ṛgveda* (10.121) is repeated in the *TB* (2.3.9.3 ff). The ideas of entity and non-entity are frequently met with in the later Saṃhitās and the *Brāhmaṇas*. In the *Atharvaveda* (10.7.10) it is said that both entity and non-entity exist within the god Skambha. Another verse of the same text (17.1.19) says: Entity is founded on non-entity; what has become is founded on entity. In a passage of the *Śatapatha Brāhmaṇa* (10.5.3.1) it is stated that in the beginning this universe was neither existent nor non-existent. There was then only mind which wished to become manifested. It practised fervour and then created voice; voice created breath; breath created eye; eye created ear; ear created ritual; and, ritual created fire. In the later texts like the *Taittirīya Āraṇyaka* (1.11.1), the development of existence from non-existence is ascribed to seven *ṛṣis* like Agastya, etc. The term *tapas* of the *nāsadīya* hymn occurs abundantly in post-Ṛgvedic literature in the sense of fervour. In the *Śatapatha Brāhmaṇa* (11.5.8.1) Prajāpati, who is described as being the universe, is said to have desired to propagate himself and to have practised *tapas*, and in the same text (13.7.1.1), the self-existent *Brahman* himself is similarly related to have practised *tapas*. In the *Taittirīya Brāhmaṇa* (3.12.3.1) we came across the following statement: Let us worship the first born god by whom the universe is encompassed, the self-existent *Brahman*, who is the highest *tapas*. He is at the same time father, mother and son. *Tapas* was produced as the first object. In the *Atharvaveda* (17.1.24), however, *tapas* means the heat of the sun. There it is also connected with Agni (7.61) and also with *karman* (11.8.2). In another cosmogonic text of the *Taittirīya Brāhmaṇa* (2.2.9.1 ff) it is stated that the universe was originally non-existent and from that condition existence was produced. The non-existent (*asat*) became fervent and from that fervour smoke, fire and light were generated in succession. In the tenth verse of the said passage it is stated that from the non-existent mind was created, from mind Prajāpati and from Prajāpati all beings. In the *Ṛgveda* the term *brahman* is used in the sense of prayer. In the *Taittirīya Saṃhitā* (7.3.1.4) the term *brahman* is also used in the sense of prayer, but here a difference is made. It is stated that the hymns, the chants and the ritual-formulae all are finite while the constituents of *Brahman* are infinite. This *Brahman* is no doubt a ritual entity which is proved by other references to be found in the *Taittirīya Brāhmaṇa* (2.2.1.4) and the *Śatapatha Brāhmaṇa* (2.1.4.10 ff, 3.1.4.15). In the *Atharvaveda* (9.6.1-2) we come across an attempt to identify *Brahman* with something of the *puruṣa* type, while in the *Brāhmaṇas* like the *Śatapatha Brāhmaṇa* (7.4.1.14, 7.5, 3.7, 14.1.3.3), *Brahman* is more frequently identified with the fire, and particularly with the sun. In the same text it is also stated that there is nothing earlier and nothing higher than *Brahman* (10.3.5.11) that sustains the heaven and the earth (8.4.1.3). In other passages *Brahman* is declared to be the same as Prajāpati (13.6.2.8; cf. 11.2.3.1 ff). Another passage of the same *Brāhmaṇa* (13.7.1.1) relates that having found the mere practice of *tapas* fruitless, *Brahman* made an offering of itself into the beings, and of beings into itself. The *Taittirīya Brāhmaṇa* (13.7.1.1) speaks of *Brahman* as being the material cause of the universe, the wood and the tree out of which the world was fashioned. Elsewhere in the same text (3.12.9), it is categorically stated that *Brahman* has created and fashioned the whole world. Thus we find that already in the age of the *Brāhmaṇa* literature *Brahman* is spoken of as the enlivening principle and so even sometimes placed above Prajāpati, the world creator. The final stage in the philosophical apotheosis of *Brahman* is, however, its identification with the *ātman* or with the soul within. Bhattacharyya, 1972, 21 ff.

**Exogamy:** It is difficult to say with certainty within what limits marriage was allowed. The dialogue of Yama and Yamī in the *Ṛgveda* (10.10) seems clearly to point to a prohibition of the marriage of brother and sister. In the *Gobhila Gṛhya Sūtra* (3.4.5) and the *Dharma Sūtras* (*ĀDS* w.t. 15.16, etc.) are found prohibitions against marriage in the *gotra* (family) or within certain degrees on the mother's and father's side, but in the *Śatapatha Brāhmaṇa* (1.8.3.6) marriage is allowed in the third of fourth degrees. According to Harisvāmin (on *ŚB* loc.cit) marriage is allowed in the second degree of relationship among the Saurāṣṭras, while the Dākṣiṇātyas allowed marriage with the daughter of the mother's brother. The prohibition of marriage within the *gotra* was not strictly followed in all cases though naturally marriages outside the *gotra* were frequent. Similarly someness of caste was also not essential to marriage, as hypergamy was permitted even by the Dharma Sūtras, so that a brāhmaṇa could marry wives of any lower caste, a kṣatriya wives of the two lower castes as well as of his own caste and a *vaiśya* a *śūdra* wife apart from one belonging to his own caste. Instances of such intermarriages are common in the epic, and are viewed as normal in the *Bṛhaddevatā*. Chakraborty 1981, 277-8.

**Explanations:** Explanatory writings are referred to in the *Bṛhadāraṇyaka Upaniṣad* (2.4.10; 4.1.4.2, 5.11) as *anuvyākhyāna*. Śaṅkara interprets it as 'explanation of the *mantras*'. As the term in the plural follows Sūtras, this interpretation is reasonable. Some scholars however, equate the word with *anvākhyāna* 'supplementary narrative'.

**Eye Disease:** *Alaji* is the name of a disease of the eye in the *Atharvaveda* (9.8.20). The term *alaji* denotes a discharge at the junction of the cornea and the sclerotica. *Dūṣīkā*, 'rheum of the eyes', is mentioned as a disease in the *Atharvaveda* (16.6.8) and later (*KS* 34.12; 25.9; *ŚB* 3.1.3.10), *viśara* is the name of another disease, perhaps 'tearing pains' of the eye in the *Atharvaveda* (2.4.2).

**Eyeliner:** A salve or eye-liner or collyrium is referred to as *añjana* in the *Atharvaveda* (4.9, 6.102.3, 9.6.11, 9.19.44) which came from mount Trikakubh and was used to anoint the eyes. This ointment is declared potent to remove jaundice and other diseases (*AV* 19.44.1 ff).

# F

**Family:** The term *kula* denotes a family. It is an undivided word occurring in the Vedas after the period of the Saṃhitās. In the *Śatapatha Brāhmaṇa* (1.1.2.22, 2.1.4.4; 2.4.1.14; 11.5.3.11; 11.8.1.3; 13.4.2.17; *BU* 1.5.32; *CU* 3.13.6, etc.) this word denotes the 'home' or 'house' of the family and by metronym the family itself, as connected with home. Its use clearly points out a system of individual families undoubtedly consisting of several members under the headship of the father or the eldest brother (in absence of father) owing to dwelling in one undivided family. Being distinct from *gotra* it seems to mean family in a narrower sense of the members still living in one undivided family. The term *vaṃśa* represented spiritual as well as filial succession (according to Pāṇini as *saṃkhyā vaṃśyena*) interpreted so that *vaṃśo dvidhā vidyayā janmanā ca* (2.1.19). In the Vedic age, the idea of family or the lineage was conveyed by the word *kula*. In the Ṛgvedic period the word *kula* being not figurative in denoting the home or the family is also conjunct with the word *kulapā*, protector of the house side by side with the term *vrājapati*, the leader or chief of the settlement so found in the *Ṛgveda* (10.119.2). The heads of households or lineages were in some way subordinate to the leader or chief of the whole settlement, comprising many households or lineages as is suggested from the instance of Indra being attended by the Maruts treated by *vrājapati* also associated with the *kulapās*.

**Family Head:** Leaving the question of blood relationship open, we must regard the village as comprising a number of families or *kulas*. These were under the control of the *kulapās* or family heads, either exercising the autocratic right of a *pater familias* or acting as the manager of a coparcenary family group. Zimmer regards them as having been vested with the almost autocratic powers as was residing in Roman *pater familias*. Against this view there is clear evidence that in India, the family-head, whether the father of children or the agentic group, had little of the powers of a Roman father and that in localities where the joint-family existed, the members were invested with rights of equal ownership or of enjoyment. There is another word to denote a village, e.g. *vṛjana*, in which sense it is taken by Roth and other Vedic scholars. Sāyaṇa, in some places, makes it mean *saṃgrāma* or battle. Bandyopadhyaya 28.

**Family Relations:** *Brother*: Bhrātṛ is the common designation of 'brother' from the *Ṛgveda* (1.264.1, 4.3.13, 5.34.4) onwards. It is also applied to a relation or close friend generally, but here the persons concerned are, it should be noted, in the *Ṛgveda* (1.161.1; 1.170.2; 3.53.5; 4.1.2; 6.51.5; 8.43.16) deities, who are brothers of one another or of the worshipper. Thus, in the early literature, the word has not really lost its precise sense. The derivation from the root *bhṛ*, 'support', is probably correct, designating the brother as the support of his sister. This harmonizes with the fact that in Vedic literature the brother plays the part of protector of his sister when bereft of her father, and that maidens deprived of their brothers (*abhrātṛ*) meet an evil fate (*RV* 1.124.7; 4.5.5; *AV* 1.11.1). The gradation of the relations in the home is shown by the order in the *Chāndogya Upaniṣad* (7.15.2), where father, mother, brother and sister are successively mentioned. Strife between brothers is occasionally referred to (*AV* 3.30.2; *ŚB* 4.1.5.3).

*Brother-in-law:* Devṛ denotes wife's brother-in-law as well as husband's brother in the *Ṛgveda* (10.85.46). He is included with the sisters of the husband in a sense, with the wife's brother having no occurrence corresponding to *Devṛ*. The wife of the husband as well as elder brother rules over the family in the *Ṛgveda* (10.85.45). At the same time the wife is to be devoted to her husband in the *Ṛgveda* (10.85.44) and also friendly to him in the *Atharvaveda* (14.2.18). In the case of the husband's death, the so-called *devṛ* performs the duty of begetting a son in the *Ṛgveda* (10.40.2) by marrying the widow, constituting the later Indian system known as *niyoga*.

*Child:* In the *Upaniṣads* (*CU* 5.1.11, 5.24.5; *KU* 2.6) *bāla* denotes 'boy', young child. According to the *St. Petersburg Dictionary, bāla* is the stage of childhood extending up to the 16th year. Other Vedic terms for children are *tānva, naḥ, putra, putrikā, pantra sunu*, etc., which, of course, transgress the limit of childhood in many cases.

*Cousin:* In the *Atharvaveda* (5.22.12, 10.3.9) the term *bhrātṛvya* is related to brother and sister having an expression of relationship. Such a sense denotes a cousin and also enemy (*AV* 2.18.1; 8.10.18; 8.10.33; 10.9.1) and in the *Saṃhitās* (*KS* 10.7; 27.8; *TS* 3.5.9.2; *VS* 1.17; *AB* 3.7; *PB* 12.13.2; *ŚB* 1.1.1.2, etc.). In an undivided family the relations of cousins would easily develop into rivalry and enmity. As such, its original meaning must be treated as 'nephew', which denotes 'brother's son'. In the *Kāṭhaka Saṃhitā* (27.8) we have the story of a falsehood to a *bhrātṛvya*. In the *Atharvaveda* (2.18.1; 10.9.1); *Taittirīya Saṃhitā* (1.3.2.1), etc., various spells aiming at destroying one's rivals have been contained, among whom the cousin was also counted. In an analogical sense the word *pitṛvya* denotes brother of a father.

*Couple:* The word *dampatī* denotes the couple in the *Ṛgveda* (1.127.8; 2.39.2; 5.22.4; 8.69.16). It is more often used in the dual to designate 'the master and the mistress'. An expression may legitimately be deemed to show the high status of women at the time of the *Ṛgveda*. The term *dampatī* in the sense of husband and wife is found in the *Ṛgveda* (5.3.2; 8.31.5; 10.10.5) and the *Atharvaveda* (6.123.3; 12.3.14).

*Co-wife:* The word *sapatnī* occurs in the *Ṛgveda* in the sense of 'co-wife' (3.1.10, 3.6.4); in the first and the last Maṇḍalas, it means co-wife as a 'rival' (1.105.8; 10.145.1-5). In post-Vedic Sanskrit the word becomes a synonym for 'rival'. The *Ṛgveda* (10.86.13) as an epithet *su-snuṣā* in the latter sense.

*Daughter:* The term *duhitṛ* denotes daughter in the *Ṛgveda* (8.101.15; 10.17.1; 10.40.5; 10.61.5; 10.61.7) and the later *Saṃhitas*. (*AV* 2.14.2; 6.100.3; 7.12.1; 10.1.25; *ŚB* 1.7.4.1, 1.8.1.8). The word appears to have been derived from the root *duh*, meant to milk in a sense of maiden nourishing a child as a milker of the primitive family. The term *putrikā* in the later literature (*MDS* 9.127; *GDS* 28.20; *VDS* 17.17) has the technical sense of the daughter of a man without sons, whom he gives in marriage on the express terms that her son shall perform funeral rites for him, and be counted as belonging to his line. The custom as well as the name is recognized by Yāska in the *Nirukta* (3.5) and traced to the *Ṛgveda* (1.124.7). Such daughters serving as sons to their fathers were also known as *dāyāda* and *putrikā*.

*Daughter-in-law:* The term for daughter-in-law is *snuṣā*. The term means daughter-in-law, primarily in relation to father-in-law and mother-in-law. The word appears in the *Ṛgveda* (10.86.13) in the epithet *su-snuṣā*, 'having a good daughter-in-law'. The word also appears in the later *Saṃhitās* and *Brāhmaṇas* in connection with daughter-in-law's respect for her father-in-law (*AV* 8.6.24; *AB* 3.22.7; *TB* 2.4.6.12). Often violation of this respect was caused by spirituous liquor (*MS* 2.4.2; *KS* 12.12).

*Elder Sister's Husband:* Denoted by the term *dīdhiṣupati* (*KS* 31.7).

*Father:* Pitṛ, common from the *Ṛgveda* onwards, denotes 'father' not so much as the 'begetter' (*janitṛ*—*RV* 4.17.12), but rather as the protector of the child, this being probably also the etymological sense of the word. The father in the *Ṛgveda* (4.17.17, 8.86.4) stands for all that is good and kind. Hence, Agni is compared with a father (*RV* 10.7.3), while Indra is even dearer than a father (*RV* 7.32.19, 8.1.6). The father carries his son in his arms (*RV* 1.38.1), and places him on his lap (*RV* 5.43.7), while the child pulls his garment to attract attention (*RV* 3.53.2). In later years the son depends on his father for help in trouble (*RV* 10.48.1), and greets him with joy (*RV* 7.103.3). It is difficult to ascertain precisely how far the son was subject to parental control, and how long such control continued. Reference is made in the *Ṛgveda* (2.29.5) to a father's chastising his son for gambling, and Ṛjrāsva is said to have been blinded by his father (*RV* 1.116.16; *AB* 7.12-18; *ŚB* 5.3.3.3). From the latter statement Zimmer infers the existence of a developed *patria potestas*, but to lay stress on this isolated and semi-mythical incident would be unwise. If there is no proof that a father legally controlled his son's wedding, and not much that he controlled his daughter's (*JUB* 3.12.2), the fact is in itself not improbable. There is again no evidence to show whether a son, when grown up, normally continued to stay with his father, his wife becoming a member of the father's household, or whether he set up a house of his own; probably the custom varied. Nor do we know whether the son was granted a special plot of land on marriage or otherwise; or, whether he only came into such property, after his father's death. But any excessive estimate of the father's powers over a son who was no longer a minor and naturally under his control, must be qualified by the fact that in his old age the sons might divide their father's property (*RV* 1.70.10; *AB* 5.14; *JB* 3.156), or he might divide it amongst them (*TS* 3.1.9.4-6) and that when the father-in-law became aged he fell under the control of his son's wife (*RV* 10.85.46). There are also obscure traces that in old age a father might be exposed, though there is no reason to suppose that this was usual in Vedic India (*RV* 8.51.2; *AV* 18.2.34). Normally the son was bound to give his father full obedience (*RV* 1.68.5). The later *sūtras* show in detail the acts of courtesy which he owed his father, and they allow him to eat the remnants of his father's food (*ĀpDS* 1.1.4.11). On the other hand, the father is expected to be kind. The story of Śunaḥśepa in the *Aitareya Brāhmaṇa* (7.12; *ŚŚS* 15.17) emphasizes the horror which the father's heartless treatment of his son was viewed. The Upaniṣads (*KU* 2.15; *BU* 1.5.25) insist on the spiritual succession from father to son. The kissing of a son was frequent and usually a token of affection, even in mature years. On the failure of natural children, adoption was possible. It was even resorted to when natural children existed, when it was desired to secure the presence in the family of a person of specially high qualifications, as in Viśvāmitra's adoption of Śunaḥśepa (*AB* 7.17). It is not clear whether adoption from one caste into another was possible, for there is no good evidence that Viśvāmitra was, as Weber holds, a kṣatriya who adopted a brāhmaṇa. Adoption was also not always in high favour and it may be accidental or not that a hymn of the Vasiṣṭha book of the *Ṛgveda* (7.4.7) condemns the usage. It was also possible for the father who had a daughter, but no sons, to appoint her to bear a son for him. At any rate the practice appears to be referred to in an obscure verse of the *Ṛgveda* (3.31.1) as interpreted by Yāska. Moreover, it is possible that the difficulty of a brotherless maiden finding a husband may have been due in part to the possibility of her father desiring to make her a Putrikā, the later technical name for a daughter whose son is to belong to her father's family. There can be no doubt that in a family the father took precedence over the mother (*ŚB* 2.5.1.18). There is no trace of family as a land-owning corporation. The duo form *pitarau* regularly means 'father and mother', 'parents' (*RV* 1.20.4; 2.17.7; 7.67.1). Macdonell and Keith I, 526-9.

*Father-in-law: Śvasura* denotes father-in-law of the wife (*RV* 10.28.1; 10.85, 46; 10.95.4; *AV* 8.6.24; 14.2.26). The daughter-in-law (*snuṣā*) in the normal case when the father-in-law was the head of the family to which her husband belonged in fact as well as in age, was bound to pay him all respect (*RV* 10.95.4; *AV* 8.6.24; *MS* 2.4.2; *KS* 12.12; *AB* 3.22.7). When the old man had ceased to exercise control, she became mistress (*samrājñī*) over him and his wife (*RV* 10.85.46). In the plural (*RV* 10.95.12; *AV* 14.2.27) the word denotes the 'parents-in-law'.

*Grand-daughter:* From the masculine term *napāt* we find *naptrī* in a faminine sense denoting the grand-daughter. The sense of great-grandson is accurately conveyed as early as the *Ṛgveda* (8.17.13) by *praṇapāt* used beside *napāt* expressing a grandson. *Naptrī* a faminine form of the word *napāt* is found in post-Ṛgvedic literature. There is also another masculine word *naptṛ* which is transformed into the *naptrī* in a faminine sense, being practically limited to the Saṃhitās (*RV* 1.50.9; 8.2.24; 9.9.1; 9.14.5; 9.69.3; *AV* 1.28.4; 2.14.1; 7.82.6). Sāyaṇa says in the *Ṛgveda* (9.69.3) the word *naptṛ* has a sense of sons. Yāska also explains in the *Nirukta* (3.4) such a term in the *Ṛgveda* (3.31.1) denoting the grandson as being produced from a daughter as *naptāramupāgamaddauhitraṃ pautram*.

*Grandfather: Tatāmaha*, grandfather, is found in the *Atharvaveda* (5.24.17; 8.4.76). Another term *pitāmaha* (grandfather), beside *tatāmaha*, denotes in the *Atharvaveda* (5.5.1; 9.5.30; 11.1.19: 18.4.35, cf. *TS* 1.8.5.1; 7.2.7.3; *VS* 19.36; *ŚB* 5.5.5.4) the paternal grandfather, apparently as a father in a higher sense. The great-grandfather is *prapitāmaha* and *pratatāmaha* (*AV* 18.4.75). It is significant that there are no corresponding Vedic words for maternal grandparents, and that the words used in the later language such as *mātāmaha*, are imitations of the terms for paternal relations. The grandmother (*pitāmahī*) is not mentioned in the extant Vedic literature.

*Grandson: Napāt*, 'grandson' in Vedic literature apparently has both the wider sense of descendant and the narrower one of grandson in the Saṃhitās (*RV* 10.10.1; 6.20.11; *VS* 21.61; *KS* 22.2). In the Brāhmaṇas the word seems hardly to have the sense of 'descendant' at all, while it denotes not only grandson, but also great-grandson in the sequence sons, grandsons, great-grandsons (*AB* 7.10.3). The *Aitareya Brāhmaṇa* (32.10) mentions the term *naptṛ* as a great-grandson. *Pautrāyaṇa* is also found in the *Chāndogya Upaniṣad* (4.1.1) in the sense of a great-grandson with reference to Jānaśruti Pautrāyana. Hence the Vedic family may be taken to have been a working unit of four generations. Grandson is also expressed by *pautra* in the *Atharvaveda* and later (*AV* 9.5.30; 11.7.16; *AB* 7.10.3; *TB* 2.1.8.3). While the sense of great-grandson is accurately conveyed as early as the *Ṛgveda* (8.17-3) by *pra-napāt*, used beside *napāt*, 'grandson', *naptrī*, the feminine, is practically limited to the Saṃhitās (*RV* 3.31). Another term *naḥ* has been taken to mean grandsons.

*Husband:* The general term for husband is *pati* in the Vedic texts. Here we come across husbands in relation to other members of the family such as *agre didhiṣupati* (husband of a younger sister), *dampatī* (couple) and *pati*, the generic husband who protects the wife. Another term for husband is *bhartṛ*. *Bhartṛ*, besides having the literal sense of 'bearer', means 'supporter' or 'master' in the older literature (*AV* 11.7.15; 18.2.30; *ŚB* 2.3.4.7). In one passage of the *Ṛgveda* (5.58.7) 'husband' is certainly the most natural sense of *bhartṛ*, but, even then, parents are often (*AV* 5.5.2) denoted by the same term. In the *Kāṭhaka Saṃhitā* (31.7) *didhiṣupati* denotes husband of the elder sister. *Didhiṣu* may also denote a wooer. Traditionally, the term of *didhiṣu* means an elder sister in a case of marriage of the younger sister before her. The word *nanandṛ* occurs only once in the *Ṛgveda* (10.85.46), where it denotes, according to Sāyaṇa, the 'husband's sister', over whom the wife is to rule. This interpretation is confirmed by the fact that the same position is ascribed to the husband's sister—no doubt while unmarried and living in her brother's care—by the *Aitareya Brāhmaṇa* (3.22).

*Husband's Sister:* See **Husband** Known as *nanandṛ* in the *Ṛgveda* (10.95.46). The term denotes, according to Sāyaṇa, 'husband's sister' over whom the wife is to rule. Husband's unmarried sister living with her brother and brother's wife is mentioned in *Aitareya Brāhmaṇa* 3.22.

*Maternal Uncle:* Little is heard of maternal uncle in the Vedic period. *Māturbhrātā* occurs once in the *Maitrāyaṇī Saṃhitā* (1.6.12) as the designation of maternal uncle, who bears the name of *mātula* (*ĀGS* 1-24.4, etc.) in the Sūtra period.

*Mother: Mātṛ* is the regular word for 'mother' from the *Ṛgveda* onwards (1.24.1, 7.101.3, etc.; *VS* 13.21; *AB* 2.6, etc.), being a formation probably developed under the influence of an onomatopoetic word *mā*, used like *ambā* (*MS* 1.12.20; *TS* 7.4.19; *VS* 23.18; *TB* 3.9.6.3) and *nanā* (*RV* 9.112.3). The latter, which finds parallel with *tāta* or father, is found in *Ṛgveda* (9.112.3). The dual term *mātarā* is used for parents as also are *pitara* and *mātarā-pitaro* (*RV* 3.33.3, 7.2.5; *VS* 19.19) and *mātā-pitaraḥ* (*TS* 1.3.10.1; 6.3.11.3), mentioned in connection with the sale of Śunaḥśepha for adoption by Viśvāmitra in the *Aitareya Brāhmaṇa* (7.18 ff).

*Mother-in-law: Śvaśrū* denotes mother-in-law of the husband (*RV* 10.85, 46; *AV* 14.2.26) as well as of the wife (*RV* 10.34.3). She, as also her husband, if he became unable to manage the family (*RV* 10.85, 46), fell under the daughter-in-law's sway, but otherwise was entitled to regards (*AV* 14.2.26). A gambler in the *Ṛgveda* (10.34.3) complains of having lost the favour of his wife's mother as one of the misfortunes brought upon him by dicing.

*Sister:* The term *bhaginī* means sister literally, appearing as a fortunate one having a brother in the *Ṛgveda* (3.31.2). Yāska and Sāyaṇa also refer to the term *bhaginī* in the *Nirukta* (3.6) and the commentary of the said passage respectively to denote sister. *Svasṛ* is the regular word from the *Ṛgveda* onwards (*RV* 2.32.6.55.4; 8.101.15; 10.108.9) for sister. Like the word *bhrātṛ*, the term sister can be applied to persons or things not precisely so related. For example, in the *Ṛgveda* the fingers and the seasons are sisters, and night is dawn's sister, for whom, as the elder, she makes way (*RV* 1.124.8; 1.62.10). The Paṇis offer to adopt Saramā as their sister (*RV* 10.108.9), but this use is not applied any more than in the case of *bhrātṛ* to ordinary human beings. The sister stood in a close relation to her brothers. If the father was dead or feeble, the sister was dependent on her brother and on his wife, as it appears from the *Ṛgveda* (10.85.46) and the *Aitareya Brāhmaṇa* (3.37.5). Moreover, maidens without brothers were apt to find marriage difficult, and to degenerate into hetairai (*AV* 1.17.1, *Nirukta* 3.5). A sonless father was anxious to make his daughters *putrikās*, in order that they themselves, instead of the husbands, should count the daughters' sons as their own. *Svasrīya* occurs in the sense of sister's son in *Taittirīya Saṃhitā* (2.5.1.1) and *Maitrāyaṇī Saṃhitā* (2.4.1).

*Son, Son-in-law: Sūnu* is a common word for son in the *Ṛgveda* (1.26.3; 2.38.5; 6.52.9) and the *Atharvaveda* (6.1.2; 7.22; 12.3.33). The use of this word in the *Ṛgveda* (1.1.9 etc.) is found predominantly in relation to the father, but rarely in the connection to the mother (cf. *RV* 5.42.2). *Putra* is however, the usual name for son from the *Ṛgveda* onwards (*RV* 2.29.5; 5.47.6; 6.9.2 etc.; *AV* 3.30.2). The term *putra* (*RV* 8.69.8; *AB* 5.14; 6.33; *ŚB* 11.6.1.2; *PB* 13.3.21 etc.) was often used as an affectionate form of addressing a younger man, not merely a son proper. Reference is frequently made to the desire for a son (*RV* 10.183.1; *AV* 6.81.3; 11.1.1; *TS* 6.5.6.1; 7.1.8.1; *TB* 1.1.9.1). *Jāmātṛ* is the term for a son-in-law in the *Ṛgveda* (8.2.20). The word *vijāmātṛ* also occurs (*RV* 1.109.2) denoting an 'unsatisfactory son-in-law'. Friendly relation between son-in-law and father-in-law is referred to in the *Ṛgveda* (10.28.1). See **Kinship**.

*Wife:* The most common expression for wife, *bhāryā*, does not occur in all the Saṃhitās. It appears in the *Aitareya Brāhmaṇa* (7.9) in the sense of a family member who is to be maintained. In the *Bṛhadāraṇyaka Upaniṣad* (3.4.1; 4.5.1) the term clearly means wife. Husband and wife were together known as *dampatī* while the remarried wife was *punarbhū*. Wife's brother was known as *śyāla* (*RV* 1.109.2).

**Farming:** There are numerous references in the Vedic texts which show that peoples in those days were very much interested in agriculture. The cultivation of the soil was no doubt known in the Ṛgvedic age, as is indicated by the identity of the expressions *yavaṃ kṛṣ* and *śasya* in the *Ṛgveda*, with *yao karesh* and *hahya* in the *Avesta*. Referring to the ploughing in the seed and to the grain which resulted. *Kṛṣ* or its derivative occurs in the *Ṛgveda* and post-Ṛgvedic texts (1.23.15; 1.176.2; 4.57.4, 8.20.19; 8.22.6; 10.34.13; *AV* 2.4.5, 8.2.19, etc.; *MS* 1.2.2, 3.6.8; *VS* 4.10, 9.22, 14.10-21 etc.; *ŚB* 7.2.2.7). Later Saṃhitās and Brāhmaṇas make frequent reference to ploughing. As per the *Pañcaviṃśa Brāhmaṇa* 17.1, the Vrātyas outside the pale of Vedic culture, are described as not cultivating the soil. Deities are invoked in connection with farming. Indra is appealed to stay on guard in the tilled field (*RV* 1.74.3). *Kṣetrasya pati* or *kṣetrapati*, the lord of the fields is praised for successful farming (*RV* 4.57.1-3). *Śuna, sīra* and *sītā*—all personifications of some agricultural operations—are implored for success (*RV* 4.57.8, 10.101.3). Also, Indra and Pūṣan are evidently connected with field and seed and Parjanya, rain god, eulogized. Indra is at least once called *urvarapati*, 'lord of plough-land'. Besides Agni, who makes the fields prosper (*RV* 8.31.14), Indra is viewed as deeply concerned in procuring and/or protecting the fields. Sacrifice is figuratively spoken of as ploughing, sowing and reaping (*RV* 10.101.3-6). A similar observation is found in the *Śatapatha Brāhmaṇa* (7.2.2.4). See **Agriculture**.

**Feather-holder:** In the *Atharvaveda* (4.6.5), the part of the shaft in which the feather of the arrow is fastened is called *parṇadhi*. The term *parṇa* in the *Ṛgveda* (1.116.15; 1.182.7; 1.183.1; 4.27.4) denotes the 'wing' of a bird. It also means the 'feather' in an arrow in a late passage of the *Ṛgveda* (10.18.14) and more often later (*AV* 5.25.1; *KS* 25.1; *AB* 1.25, 3.26).

**Females:** See **Women**.

**Female Dancer:** Description of the ever-ancient and ever-young Uṣas, as a dancer, appears again and again in the *Ṛgveda* (1.48.5; 1.123.2). Like a dancer, she adorns herself with rich ornaments (*RV* 1.92.4). Decked by her mother she displays her charms to her lover and brings forth treasures, breaking the gates of darkness. Perhaps dancing existed as a recognized vocation for girls. That is why we find the professional dancer Uṣas displaying her charms by unveiling herself with boldness and frankness. The description of her dress is very suggestive. The description of the group-dance of gods (*RV* 10.72.7) leads us to believe that dancing was a popular pastime and that it was performed collectively in circles.

**Female Principle:** The conception of *yoni* (female organ, female womb), as the first principle, reminds us of a very primitive cosmogonical belief according to which the world has born of a female principle. The root of the conception should not be sought in literature and philosophy but in cults and rituals. There are reasons to believe that the Sāṅkhya conception of *prakṛti* in its earlier stages, had a close bearing on the cults and ideas centering round the *yoni* or the female organ of generation. In fact, the primitive concept of *prakṛti* had nothing to do with the serious metaphysical questions. In the earliest phases of man's social existence, his thought was conditioned by the urge to promote the propagation of his race and the production of crops. Peoples of the past instinctively projected their own experiences to the objects around them and thus associated various ideas in order to constitute a practical philosophy of life, making unconscious use of the only principle available to them, viz., the principle of analogy. Thus, they came to the conclusion that natural productivity, should be viewed in terms of human productivity, and earth mother in terms of human mother. In the *Ṛgveda* Mother Earth or Pṛthivī is so closely associated with Dyaus that generally they are celebrated conjointly, Dyaus being never lauded alone in any hymn, while Pṛthivī alone is invoked in only one short hymn of the *Ṛgveda* (5.84). The *Atharvaveda* contains a bigger hymn (12.1) on Mother Earth, which is known as Bhūmi-sūkta. The personification is so slight that the attributes are mainly those of the physical earth. Both, the *Ṛgveda* and the later Saṃhitās and Brāhmaṇas do not exclusively mention *prakṛti*, which in later Sāṅkhya philosophy is not only the primordial matter but the germinal principle of creation. In spite of numerous references to sex rites and the concept of generation in terms of sexual dualism, the Brāhmaṇa literature does not bring the concept of *prakṛti* in connection with sacrifices in which sexual acts or their imitations were necessary ingredients. The goddess who is associated with Vājapeya sacrifice is Aditi. It is only in the Upaniṣads that we come across the concept of *prakṛti* in connection with *puruṣa*. In the *Śvetāśvatara*, the Sāṅkhya is mentioned by name, and the expression *svabhāva* mentioned therein (6.1) evidently means *prakṛti*. The explicit reference to the *gūṇas* in the *Maitrī* (3.5, 5.2) is also suggestive. *Prakṛti* is mentioned as the female principle in the *Kaṭha* (4.7). In the *Śvetāśvatara* (1.9, 4.5) she is described as unborn and having three constituent qualities—*sattva, rajas* and *tamas*; she is also equated with *māyā* or illusion (4.9-10). In the *Maitrī* (3.2), five subtle elements (*tanmātra*) and five gross elements (*bhūta*), are mentioned in conection with *prakṛti* possessed of three *guṇas*. In another passage of the same work (6.10), she is described as the undifferentiated matter while a third passage (6.30) describes how the process of differentiation in *prakṛti* takes place. As is known to all the term *pradhāna* is sometimes used instead of *prakṛti*. In the *Śvetāśvatara* (1.10; 6.10; 6.16) *pradhāna* is identified with *prakṛti*. Here *pradhāna* is the primordial matter as well as the female principle. We have already referred to a passage of *Śvetāśvatara* (4.10) in which the *prakṛti* of the Sāṅkhya is identified with the *māyā* of the Vedānta.

**Ferryman:** The word *sambin* designates ferryman (*RV* 10.42.7; *AV* 9.2.6).

**Festival:** *Samana* is a word of somewhat doubtful sense in the *Ṛgveda*. Roth renders it either battle (*RV* 6.75.3.5; 9.96.9; 10.143.4; *AV* 6.92.2; *VS* 9.9) or festival (*RV* 2.16.7; 6.60.2; 7.2.5; 8.12.9; 9.97.47; 10.55.5; 86.10; *AV* 2.36.1). Pischel thinks that it was a general popular festivity, to which women went to enjoy themselves (*RV* 1.124.8; 4.58; 6.75.4; 7.2.5; 10.86.10; 168.2), poets to win fame (*RV* 2.16.7; 9.97.47), bowmen to gain prizes at archery (*RV* 6.75.3.5), horses to run races (*RV* 9.96.9; *AV* 6.92.2), and which lasted until morning (*RV* 1.48.6) or until a conflagration, caused by the fires kept burning all night, scattered the cerebrators (*RV* 10.69.11). Young women (*RV* 2.36.1), even elderly women (*RV* 7.2.5) went there to find a husband and courtesans to make profit from the occasion (*RV* 4.58.8).

**Fetishism:** Fetish is an inanimate object worshipped by the ancient people for its supposed inherent magical power or as being inhabited by a spirit. Often, fetish is something used for abnormal stimulation or for attracting sexual design. Sometimes it is a thing that evokes irrational devotion or respect. In many cases the purely temporary nature of the divine character of the fetish is quite obvious. Thus, in the household ritual, during the nights after marriage in which the newly wedded pair are bidden to observe chastity, a staff clad in a garment and made fragrant is placed between them. This is traditionally asserted to be the Gandharva Viśvāvasu. The tradition is confirmed by the fact that the ritual prescribes for the taking away of the staff a formula addressed to that spirit. Another fetish is the wheel, which represents the sun. In the Vājapeya sacrifice, a wheel-shaped cake of grain is placed on the top of the post, to which the animal victim is tied; the sacrificer mounts the ladder, saying to his wife, 'Come, let us two mount to the sun.' He then mounts and seizes the wheel saying, 'We have attained the sun, O gods.' At the Mahāvrata festival of the winter solstice, an Aryan and a *śūdra* strove over a white round skin, which is stated to be a symbol of the sun; the Aryan conquers the sun and strikes down the *śūdra* with the skin. Animals too, later at least, served as living fetishes; of this the instances, though not numerous, are singularily clear. At the Śākamedha sacrifice, in an offering to Indra, a bull was invoked; when it bellowed, the offering was made. The meaning is made plain beyond doubt not only by the fact that Indra is elsewhere called a bull, but also because in the *Atharvaveda* a bull is addressed thus: 'Men call the Indra.' Besides, Verethraghna, the Avestan parallel to Indra, has a bull form. Moreover, in the Brāhmaṇa (*ŚB* 2.5.3.18) Indra is invoked to come and slay Vṛtra and the following of the bull clearly establishes the fact that god has come to receive the proferred sacrifice with satisfaction. Another sacrifice, recorded for us only in the Gṛhya ritual, the Śūlagava, shows us water and food offered to a bull, a cow, and a calf, the two former of which are each placed in a hut; when they have touched the offerings, the latter are offered to Rudra, his consort and the victorious one. The horse plays a considerable part in this capacity, especially in connection with the sun, which is compared to, and described as, a white horse, and fire. At the Ṣoḍaśin form of the Soma sacrifice, when the chant at sunset is being performed, not only is gold held in the hands of the priests, but a horse, either white or black, is to be present, (*TS* 6.6.11.6) clearly to represent the sun; and, in the case of the colour being black, to represent the setting of the sun. In the piling of the fire, the bricks of the fire altar are put in place in the presence of the horse which is made to breathe over them. Thus, Agni is superintending, in person, the making of his own altar. Even more striking is the participation of the horse in the act of selection of clay for the making of the fire pan. The horse, along with a goat and an ass, is taken to the place where clay is to be found. The place where the horse sets its foot down is chosen as the precise spot from which clay is to be used. The horse appears also as representative of Agni in the ceremony of kindling the fire from the firesticks (*ĀpŚS* 5.10.10; 14.17; *KŚS* 4.8.25.26; 9.13.ff). During its performance, a horse, preferably white but, if not, then red with black knees, looks on to encourage the advent of the flame; when the fire is kindled a horse precedes it eastwards, and in its footsteps the fire is deposited. The goat however, is not merely connected with Agni. As we have seen above, it is at least probable that the goat was used in the horse sacrifice and in the burial rite as a fetish of Pūṣan, the lord of the ways. The cow also could serve as a fetish, and in the ritual be hailed as Iḍā and Aditi. In the *Yajur Veda* the cow which is given in payment for the Soma is addressed as Aditi. These are scanty enough remains of fetishism, and we cannot assert that, even such as they are, as proof of a wider extension of the concept at an earlier period. The fire ritual, which is richest in them, is precisely that part of the religion of the Veda which is most completely sacerdotalized. The use of the horse and the goat may not, in the slightest degree, be original elements of the ritual, but may have been deliberately introduced by the priests who were the most devoted admirers of symbolism. They not only found symbolism in every conceivable rite, but were quite capable of inventing the rite to contain the symbol. Keith I. 67-70.

**Fever:** *Takman* was the name of the fever imagined as a demon in the *Atharvaveda* (5.22). Fever was called the king of diseases on account of its frequency and violence. Numerous charms were addressed in a hymn to *takman*. A variety of symptoms of the ailment are given in the *Atharvaveda*.

**Field:** The use of the word *kṣetra*, 'field' in the *Ṛgveda* points clearly to the existence of separate fields (*RV* 10.33.6; cf. 3.31.15; 5-62, 62, 7), carefully measured off (*RV* 10.110, 5). In some passages, however, the meaning is less definite, indicating cultivated land generally (*RV* 1.100.18; 18; 9.85, 4; 91.6). In the *Atharvaveda* (4.18.5; 5.31.4; 10.1, 18, 11.1, 22; *TS* 2.2.1, 2; *CU* 7.24.2) and later, the sense of a separate field is clearly marked, though the more general use is also found (*AV* 2.29.3; 14.2, 7; *ŚB* 1.4, 1, 15-16). The deity Kṣetrasya Pati (*RV* 4.37, 1, 2; 7.35, 10; 10, 66, 13; *AV* 2.8.5), 'lord of the field' should probably be understood as the god presiding over each field, just as Vāstospati presides over each dwelling. *Khila* (*AV* 7.115, 4; *ŚB* 8.3.4.1) and *khilya* (*RV* 6.28.2; 10.142, 3) also appear to have the same meaning. According to Roth, these terms denote the wasteland lying between cultivated fields; but he admits that this sense does not suit the passage of the *Ṛgveda*, in which it is said that god places the worshipper on unbroken *khilya*. *Urvara* is with *kṣetra* the regular expression, from the *Ṛgveda* (1.127, 6; 4.4.6; 5.33.4; 6.25, 4; 10.30, 3; 142.3) onwards, denoting a piece of ploughland. Fertile fields (*RV* 1.127, 6) are spoken of as well as waste fields. See **Agriculture**.

**Firearms:** The Turkish word *top* and the Persian *tupang* or *tufang* are derived from the Sanskrit *dhupa*. It means a rocket. In the *Ṛgveda* there is evidence to show that Agni is praised for vanquishing an enemy. The *Atharvaveda* 1.16.4 shows the employment of firearms with lead shots. The *Aitareya Brāhmaṇa* 1.4.8 describes an arrow with fire at its tip. The term *sūrmī* in the *Ṛgveda* 1.5, considered in the light of its use as the death penalty for criminal offenders, must have been of the nature of a hollow tube.

**Fire-place:** *Āṣṭrī* in *Ṛgveda* (10.165.3) is the word that seems to denote a fire-place. The term *agniśālā* designates part of the sacrificial apparatus (*VS* 19.18), which is applied in the *Atharvaveda* (9.3.7) to describe a part of an ordinary house, presumably the central hall where the fire-place was kept. *Dhṛṣṭi* found in *Śatapatha Brāhmaṇa* (14.3.1.22), *Taittirīya Āraṇyaka* (5.9.8) and *KŚS* (26.2.10) seems to denote fire-tongs.

**Fire Ranger:** The *Vājasaneyī Saṃhitā* (30.16) and *Taittirīya Brāhmaṇa* (3.4.11.1) refer to the word *dāvapa*, which means watchers should guard against conflagration in the forest.

**Fire-therapy:** *Taittirīya Brāhmaṇa* (1.96) says that a person who is suffering from a lingering disease is caught by Agni and Varuṇa (*TS* 2.10.4.5). A dead man is supposed to belong to Agni (*agneyaḥ pramitaḥ*: *KS* 11.5). In *Maitrāyaṇī Saṃhitā* (3.2.1) Agni is connected with curing of diseases. Thus, he is requested, 'Come, Agni, bringing milk and make me unite with power.' (*RV* 1.23.23; 10.161.1) Agni is expected to repell the evil beings (causes of disease). Also see *Taittirīya Brāhmaṇa* (1.4.10.1). Thite, 222-3.

**First Born:** In the *Ṛgveda* there can be no doubt as to who is the real first man. It is Manu or Manus. He is essentially the first of sacrificers, and the establisher of sacrifice, though he appears with other old sacrificers, such as Aṅgiras, Bhṛgu, Atharvan, Dadhyañc, Atri, and Kāṇva. The gods, Mātariśvan, or Kāvya Uśana, are said to have given Agni to Manu (*RV* 1.36, 10; 1.128.2; 8.23-17). In the Brāhmaṇas he constantly appears as connected with the sacrifice, and the dictum is laid down that, whatever Manu said, was the law beneficial like medicine, a fact which accounts in part for the tradition which makes him the great legal authority of India. Of the legends of Manu the most important is that of the deluge, of which he is warned by a fish. He escapes through the agency of the fish, which carries his ship about until it rests on a mountain peak, in post-Vedic mythology called *naubandhana* (*ŚB* 1.8.1.1-10). This fish in the epic becomes Brahman, and in the Purāṇas the full legend of the Avatāra of Viṣṇu is recounted. Thereafter, Manu with his daughter Iḍā, the personification of the sacrificial food, produces the human race. The legend may be alluded to in a very late book of the *Atharvaveda* (19.39.8). Another story connects him with the law of the division of property. Nābhānediṣtha was deprived by his brothers of share in the patrimonial heritage, which they divided amongst themselves when he was keeping his period of studentship. Manu, however, enables the young man to console by obtaining, in place of his share, a boon from the Ātityas, after he has appeased Rudra, who appears on the place of sacrifice, to claim all the cattle left by the sacrificers as a fee for Nābhānediṣtha (*AB* 5.14). It seems that Manu was already in the *Ṛgveda* considered to be the son of Vivasvant whose name he actually bears in one case (*RV* 8.52.1). In the later texts he is quite regularly called son of Vivasvant (*AV* 8.10.24; *ŚB* 13.4.3.3). He is accordingly a brother of Yama, or a duplication of that personage, but Manu unlike Yama is concerned with the living. Hence, in the *ŚB* (13.4.3.3-5) the difficulty is reconciled by making Manu the ruler of men, Yama of the dead. Keith, 228-9.

**First Cause:** See **Ātman, Brahman, Cosmogony, Existence, god, Īśvara, Kāla, Kāma, Prajāpati, Prāṇa, Puruṣa, First Principle.**

**First Principle:** The first chapter of the *Śvetāśvatara Upaniṣad* opens with the usual enquiry into the nature of the First Principle. It involves various views on the point held by the current schools of philosophy. It includes time (*kāla*), inherent nature (*svabhāva*), necessity (*niyati*), chance (*yadṛcchā*), the elements (*bhūtāni*), the womb (*yoni*) and the person (*puruṣa*) separately as the first principle of creation. In addition, there is, of course, the conception of Brahman solidified into that of *īśvara*. In the *Atharvaveda*, *kāla* or time as the first cause of all existence (19.53, 5, 6) is a truly philosophical notion, and round it are woven metaphors that give a mystic turn to the great idea (19.53). The entire passage reads as follows: 'Time drives as a horse with seven reins, thousand-eyed, unaging, possessing much seed. Him the inspired poets mount. His wheels are all beings. He brought the beings together, and duly encompasses them. Being the father, he became the son of them all. Then, verily, there is no other brilliance that is higher. Time generated the yonder sky, these earths. What is and what is to be stood out sent forth by Time. Time created the earth; in Time burns the sun; in Time are all existent, Kaśyapa springs from Time, so also the fervour, *tapas*. From Time came into being the waters; from Time (came) the *Brahman*, fervour, the quarters. By Time the sun rises; in time he goes to rest again. Time generated of old what is, and what is to be. From Time the *ṛcs* came into being; the *yajus* also was born from Time. Time set in motion the sacrifice. Having conquered all the worlds by *Brahman*, this Time moves on as the Highest God.' According to the traditional interpretation, *svabhāvavāda* maintains that the effects are self-existent and are produced neither by different things as causes nor by themselves, inasmuch as no cause can be discovered for the filaments of the lotus or the eye-like marks on the peacock's tail. The *svabhāva* theory is brought out in the *Mahābhārata* (12.229.2 ff) endorsing sentiments like, 'Through nature (*svabhāva*) they are impelled to activity, and in the same manner they desist therefrom; all these beings as well as non-beings. Human endeavour exists not.' In Aśvaghoṣa's *Buddhacarita* we have reference to the Svabhāvavādins who hold that all things arise from inherent properties—both good and evil . . . and since all this the world thus arises spontaneously, therefore also all effort of ours in vain. . . . That the nature of the embryo in the womb is produced as composed of hands, feet, belly, back and head and that is also united with the soul—the wise declare that all this comes of itself spontaneously. 'Who causes the sharpness of the horn? Of the various natures of beasts and birds? All this has arisen spontaneously; there is no acting from desire, how can there be such a thing as will?' The *yadṛcchā* or chance theory is popularly illustrated by the familiar *kākatālīya* maxim: the crow had no idea that its perch would cause the palm-branch to break, and the palm-branch had no idea that it would be broken by the crow's perch; but it all happened by pure chance. Guṇaratna distinguishes *svabhāva* and *yadṛcchā* stating that by the former is meant the transformation of objects by themselves, because of their inherent nature. Clay is transformed into pot and not into cloth because of its inherent nature (*svabhāva*). *Yadṛcchā*, (chance) on the other hand, is the occurrence of an object without any previous plan. Here is no room for cause-effect relation. It is simply the doctrine of accidentalism. *Svabhāvavāda* and *Yadṛcchāvāda* are therefore vitally opposed to each other, but both the doctrines are at one in rejecting the idea that nature reveals a supernatural power working behind it. The doctrine of *niyati*, though it is sometimes translated as necessity, actually means a predetermination, and apart from the *Śvetāśvatara*, we have no direct reference of a 'doctrine of destiny' in the Vedic literature. The doctrine of *niyati* was popular among the *Ājīvikas*, the sect which was introduced by Gośāla Maṅkhaliputta, a contemporary of the Buddha. The doctrine of elements may be traced to the *Ṛgveda* which mentions the waters as the primary element. The doctrine of five elements, namely earth, water, fire, air, and space is foreshadowed in the *Aitareya Brāhmaṇa* (5.32). In the Upaniṣads (*BU* 5.5.1) it is stated that, in the beginning of the world there was just water which being solidified became earth. In the *Aitareya Upaniṣad* (5.3); *Muṇḍakopaniṣad* (3.2); *Chāndogya Upaniṣad* (1.9.1) and *Bṛhadāraṇyaka Upaniṣad* (3.8.7) we come across the doctrine of five elements. This elemental cosmology was accepted as the world-ground by later philosophers such as Ajita Keśakambalin and also by the Lokāyatas or Cārvākas. The conception of *yoni* or the female womb later developed into that of *prakṛti*. In fact, the *Suśruta Saṃhitā* which refers to the same First Principles, as is done by the *Śvetāśvatara*, substitutes *prakṛti* for *yoni*. The primitive empirical and analogical belief in the equation of earth and woman, of natural and human fertility, forming the infrastructure of numerous agricultural rites, revealing the mode of securing the material means of subsistence, invariably connects the mystery of nature with that of the human body, from which it transpires that the birth of the universe is the result of the same or similar process as the birth of the human beings. In primitive Tantric cosmogony woman as the mother of the race was considered essentially to be the life producer. Her organs and attributes had been the life-given symbols *par excellence*. The concept of *yoni*, i.e. female organ or female womb, as the first principle found its best theoretical expression in the Sāṅkhya concept of *prakṛti* or *pradhāna*, the material as well as the female principle of creation, the substratum of the earlier Tantras. *Puruṣa* as the first principle appears in the later Vedic Saṃhitās and Upaniṣads. The origin of this concept is to be found in the *Puruṣa-sūkta* of the *Ṛgveda* (10.90) in which we come across the elevation of the sacrifice into a world-principle. There are two other hymns besides the said hymn in which the deity is represented as either the agent, the object, or the subject of sacrifice (10.81.5, 10.130.2-3). It is not very easy to find out the precise idea which is expressed in the *Puruṣa-sūkta*. It was written at a period when the ceremonial sacrifice had become largely developed and when a mystical meaning was attached to the various materials and instruments of the ritual. The *puruṣa* is described as having a thousand heads, a thousand eyes and a thousand feet and is equated with the universe. This is, in all probability, a secondary development of the original conception. Then we are told that all the regions sprang from this *puruṣa*, who became diffused everywhere among things animate and inanimate. Then we have the myth of reciprocal generation of *virāj* from *puruṣa* and again of *puruṣa* from *virāj*. In the second part of the *puruṣa-sūkta* it is stated that the gods offered up this *puruṣa* as the victim for a sacrifice. His body was divided in many parts. The brāhmaṇa was his mouth, the rājanya his arms, the vaiśya his thighs and the śūdra his feet. The moon was produced from his soul; the sun from his eye; Indra and Agni from his mouth; Vāyu from his breath; atmosphere from his navel; sky from his head; earth from his feet; and the four quarters from his ear. The conception of *puruṣa* has an interesting history. From the symbolic sacrificial principle, *puruṣa* was conceptually developed into a kind of creator god and was variously called Prajāpati, Viśvakarman, Brahmanaspati and eventually *Brahman*. The term *puruṣa* mentioned in the *Śvetāśvatara Upaniṣad*, however, presupposed the *puruṣa* of the Sāṅkhya philosophy denoting the male principle of creation, though the conception of *prakṛti* as the female principle was substituted by the term *yoni*. Finally, *Brahman* (q.v.) is mentioned as the First Principle. The search for the nature of this deity began in the Upaniṣads. Many visible objects of nature such as the sun or the wind on one land and the various psychological functions in man were tried, but none could render satisfaction to the great ideal inherent in it. There is the *ātman* not in man alone but in all objects of the universe, the sun, the moon, the world; and *Brahman* is this *ātman*, and therefore there is no plurality at all. As from clay all that is made of clay is known, as from an ingot of black iron all that is made of black iron is known, so from this *ātman* the *Brahman* is known. The essence of man and the essence of the universe are one and it is *Brahman*. From *Brahman* it has come forth and to it will it return. He has himself created it out of himself and then entered into it as its inner controller (*antaryāmin*). Here is thus a glaring dualistic trait of the world of matter and *Brahman* as its controller. In other places, however, we find it asserted most emphatically that these are but names and forms, and when *Brahman* is known everything else is known. It is on account of *Brahman* that the fire burns and the wind blows. It is the active principle in the entire universe, and yet the most passive and unmoved. The world is its body, yet it is the soul within. It creates all, wills all, smells all, tastes all, pervades all, silent and unaffected (*CU* 3.14.4). Again, the growth of the doctrine that *Brahman* is the 'inner controller' in all the parts and forces of nature and of mankind as the *ātman* thereof, and that all the effects of the universe are the result of his commands which no one can outstep, gave rise to a theistic current of thought in which *Brahman* is held as standing aloof as God and controlling the world. It is by his ordaining, it is said, that sun and the moon are held together, and the sky and earth stand held together (*BU* 3.8.1). God and soul are distinguished again in the famous verse of *Śvetāśvatara* (4.6).

Two bright-feathered bosom friends
Felt around one and same tree;
One of them tastes the sweet berries,
The other without eating merely gazes down.

**Fish:** The general Vedic term for fish is *matsya*. It is mentioned only once in the *Ṛgveda* (10.68.8), but frequently later (*AV* 11.2.25; *MS* 3.9.5; 3.14.2; *VS* 24.21; 34; *TS* 26.6.1; *ŚB* 1.8.1.1). *Mahāmatsya*, a great fish, is mentioned in the *Bṛhadāraṇyaka Upaniṣad* (4.3.18). *Karvara*, a word found in one passage of the *Atharvaveda* (10.4.19), seems to mean some kind of fish caught by a fisherman (*pauñjiṣṭha*). *Kulikaya* or *kulipaya* is the form in the *Taittirīya Saṃhitā* (5.5.13.1). The latter is found also in the *Vājasaneyī Saṃhitā* (24.21, 35) and *purikaya* in the *Atharvaveda* (11.2.25), variants probably due to the faulty tradition of an unfamiliar name. *Jasa* is the name of some aquatic animal or fish in the *Atharvaveda* (11.2.25) and the *Taittirīya Saṃhitā* (5.5.13.1). The commentary on the latter text explains it as *makara*, probably meaning dolphin. The word also occurs in the *Gopatha Brāhmaṇa* (2.2.5). *Rajasa* occurs once in the *Atharvaveda* (10.2.25), apparently as the name of a kind of fish. Roth, however, understood it as an adjective meaning impure. *Śakula* in the later Saṃhitās (*AV* 20.136.1; *VS* 23.28), denotes an unknown species of fish.

**Fisherman:** *Parṇaka, ānda, mārgāra, pauñjiṣṭha* and *kaivarta* or *kevarta* are fishermen who are mentioned as enlisted victims of the human sacrifice (*VS* 30.16; *TB* 3.4.12.1; *AV* 10.4). *Bainda, maināla* and *dhaivara* catch fish with the help of a net (*VS* 30.16; *TB* 4.1.2, 3.4.12.1). *Śauṣkala* and *dāsa* also are fishermen who catch fish by means of a fish-hook (*VS* 30.16; *TB* 3.4.12.1). According to the *St. Petersburg Dictionary*, *śauṣkala* is a man who lives on dried fish or flesh. Sāyaṇa thinks of *parṇaka* as one who catches fish by putting a thick fence round the water.

**Five Peoples:** The early Vedic populace was known by terms like *pañcajanāḥ pañcakṛṣṭi* and so forth, the number five being conventional in India. In a general sense, these terms denote people in their entirety. The term *pañcajanāḥ*, the 'five peoples' are mentioned under various names in Vedic literature (*AB* 3.31, 4.27; *TS* 1.6.1.2; *KS* 5.5, 32.6; *BU* 4.2.9). But who is meant by the five is very uncertain. The *Aitareya Brāhmaṇa* (3.11) explains the five to be gods, men, Gandharvas and *apsarases*, snakes and the Fathers. Aupamanyava (*Nirukta*, 3.8) held that the four castes (*varṇa*) and the Niṣādas made up the five. Sāyaṇa (*RV* 1.7.9) is of the same opinion. Yāska (*Nirukta* 3.8) thinks that the five are the Gandharvas, Fathers, gods, Asuras, and Rāksaṣas. None of these explanations can be regarded as probable. Roth and Geldner think it refers its all the peoples of the earth; just as there are four quarters (*diś*), there are peoples at the four quarters (N.E.S.W.), with the Aryan folk in the middle. Zimmer opposes this view on the ground that the inclusion of all peoples in one expression is not in harmony with the distinction so often made between 'peoples' (*RV* 8.9.2; 8.70.11; 10.28.8) that the Soma is referred to as being among the five tribes that are mentioned (*RV* 9.65.23), that the five tribes are mentioned as on the Sarasvatī (*RV* 6.61.12) and, that Indra is *pāñcajanya* (*RV* 5.32.11; 9.66, 20), 'belonging to the five peoples'. He concludes that Aryans alone are meant, and in particular the five tribes of the Anus, Druhyus, Yadus, Turvaśas and Purus, who are all mentioned together in one or perhaps two hymns of the *Ṛgveda* (1.108.8) and four of whom occur in another hymn (*RV* 8.10.5). In the *Śatapatha Brāhmaṇa* (13.5.4.14) and the *Aitareya Brāhmaṇa* (8.23) the five peoples are opposed to the Bharatas, and in the former work seven peoples are alluded to. The use of the word *pañcakṛṣṭayaḥ*, to denote five great tribes, clearly shows that, besides pastoralism, agriculture had long become their chief occupation. Macdonell and Keith, I, 466-9.

**Flags:** In the *Ṛgveda* (7.85.2; 10.103.11) to denote flags or banners various expressions like *dhavaja, akra* (1.143.7), *ketu* (*RV* 1.27.12), *bṛhatketu* (*RV* 5.8.2), *sahasraketu* (*RV* 1.119.1) were used. Flag was a symbol and an emblem counted among the insignia of ancient Vedic kings.

**Flies:** See under **Insects**.

**Flour:** The term *piṣṭa* (pounded), which may denote 'flour' is mentioned in the Brāhmaṇas (*AB* 2.9; *ŚB* 1.1.4.3, 6.5.1.6). In the *Atharvaveda* (12.2.53) a reference is made to pounded beans (*māsaḥ*).

**Flower:** *Puṣpa* in the *Atharvaveda* (8.7.12; 10.8.34) and later (*VS* 22.28; *PB* 8.4.1; 15.3.23; *TS* 5.4.4.2; *CU* 3.1.2; *BU* 6.4.1) generally denotes a flower.

**Flute:** The term *tūṇava* is the name of a wooden musical instrument, which probably denotes flute (*TS* 1.4.1; *MS* 3.6.8; *KS* 23.4, 34.5; *PB* 6.5.13; *TB* 3.4.13.1). The term *tūṇava-dhma* means a flute-blower (*VS* 30.19-20; *TB* 3.4.13.1) because *tūṇava* indicates a flute. *Nāḍi* means a musical instrument, a 'reed flute' in the *Ṛgveda* (10.135.7) as well as the *Kāṭhaka Saṃhitā* (23.4, 24.5), where in one passage it is mentioned along with the *tūṇava*.

**Folk:** The term for folks or people is *viśaḥ*. The god Agni is the leader and protector of settlers (*viśām gopa*) and the epithet *viśpati* as lord of settlers, is mainly connected with him. Again sacrificers in general are spoken of as *viśaḥ* folk people, of Manu, the father of man (*RV* 4.37).

**Food:** In the list of foods, there are various items which are either grains or products of grain. They are mainly as follows: (1) Parched grains (a) *dhāna*, (b) *parivapa*, (c) *lāja*, (d) *pṛthuka*; (2) Flour meal/groats—(a) *piṣṭa*; (b) *śaktu*; (3) Porridge-*karambha*; (4) Gruel-*yavagu*, *Dhāna*: It appears frequently from *Ṛgveda* onwards (*VS* 19.21; 19.22; *TB* 1.5.11.2) and indicater both fried rice and fried barley. Its frequent occurrence indicates its popularity. As per *Ṛgveda* (3.52.1; 4.24.7; 8.91.2) these parched grains were used to prepare *karambha*. Sometimes they are used as *soma*-admixture also. *Parivāpa*: It appears in late Vedic literature (*KS* 34.11; *TS* 3.1.10.1; 6.5.11.4; 7.2.10.4; *VS* 19.21, 19.22; *AB* 1.5.11.2) and specifically denotes fried grain of rice. As per *Taittirīya Brāhmaṇa*, it was a usual offering to Devī Bhāratī in the Jyotiṣṭoma ritual (*bhārati parivāpena TB* 1.5.11.2). *Lāja*: It is referred to in *Yajurveda Saṃhitā* and Brāhmaṇas (*MS* 3.11.2; *VS* 19.13, 19.81, 21.42; *TB* 2.6.4; *ŚB* 12.9.1.2. 13.2.1.5) and denotes another form of fried or parched rice. Sāyaṇa clarifies its nature *lāja vrīhiprabhāvaḥ puṣpavad vikaśitaḥ* (Sā on *TB* 1.8.15). Probably it was used to prepare the famous drink *māsara* (*saspa tokma lāja nagnabucurnaiḥ saṃsargo māsaram*, Mahīdhara on *VS* 19.14). *Pṛthuka*: It is another type of parched grain. Most probably it is flattened parched rice which Sāyaṇa calls *cipitaka* (*pṛthukas cipitakaḥ*, Sā on *TB* 3.8.14). It was used as an offering of Rudra in the *anna-homa* rite. *Piṣṭa*: It appears in late Vedic literature (*AB* 2, 9; *ŚB* 1.1.4.3, 1.2.1.2) and denotes the flour-meal of any grain. *Atharvaveda* (12.2.53) explains it as pounded beans. Probably it was used to prepare cakes or gruels. *Śaktu*: It is sort of ground meal, more precisely barely meal (*KS* 15.2; *TS* 6.4.10.6; *VS* 19.21-22; 9.1.1.8). *ŚB* (5.5.4.22) refers to the flour dried fruits like *karkandhu*, *kuvala*, *badara*, etc., in the Sautrāmaṇi ritual. However, *Ṛgveda* (10.72.2) refers to this word once only to mean a sort of grain, before it is winnowed by a sieve (*titau*). *Karambha*: In the list of dishes, prepared with grains, *karambha* is a sort of porridge (*TS* 3.1.10.2; 6.5.11.4) made of unhusked, parched and kneaded barley (*VS* 19.22; *ŚB* 2.5.2.14; 4.2.4.18) or sesame (*AV* 4.7.3). Occasionally it was prepared with the powder of fried grains and curdled milk or ghee. As per *Taittirīya Brāhmaṇa* (1.5.11.3) it is the sacrificial portion of Pūṣan. *Yavāgu*: as regards gruel, we can mention *yavagu* (*MS* 1.10.1; *KS* 11.2; *TS* 5.4.3.2, 6.2.5.2; *TS* 2.8.8), which may be a sort of liquor, made of other kinds of grain. According to the *Taittirīya Āraṇyaka* (2.8.8) it was prescribed for the kṣatriya sacrificer on the day of their initiation. Green vegetables and fruits were also consumed. Meat formed an important part of the diet. The flesh of ox, sheep and goat, deer and occasionally of horse, was normally eaten. Eating of beef was in vogue with some restriction. Generally it was the flesh of the ox rather than of the cow that was eaten. Barren cows (*vaśās*) were also slaughtered for the purpose of food. The flesh of the cow was eaten especially during the sacrifices.

**Food Gathering Economy:** The Ṛgvedic economy was mainly pastoral, though in the later period of the *Ṛgveda* stock-raising was supplemented by agriculture. But like modern conditions, even in the Vedic period there was a process of uneven development. There were at least a few tribes that depended on food-gathering in the forms of collecting roots and fruits, hunting as well as catching fish. A few of these tribes were later incorporated within the caste system and were given lower ranks in the social hierarchy. Among such tribes mention may be made of the *mṛgāya* (*AV* 10.1.26; *VS* 16.27, 30.7; *TB* 1.5.1.1, 3.4.3.1; *PB* 14.9.12), who made their livelihood by fishing or by hunting. The word *mṛgayā* also finds place in the *Ṛgveda* (10.40.4). Among other hunting tribes, mention is also found of *kaivarta* or *kevarta, pauñjiṣṭha, dāsa, maināla, bainda* and *ānda* (*VS* 30.16), who were also fish-catchers. For the purpose of hunting bow and arrow and spear were sometimes employed (*RV* 2.4.2.2) but the usual practice was the use of the normal instruments of capture, namely nets and pitfalls. The net was known as *pāśa* (*RV* 3.45.1), *midha* (*RV* 9.83.4, 10.73.11), *jāla* (*AV* 10.1.30), which was fastened on pegs (*AV* 8.8.5). Pits were used for catching antelopes and were called *ṛṣyāda*, 'antelope-catching'. Apparently, the boar were captured in a chase, with the help of dogs (*RV* 10.86.4). Large games were also caught by the use of net and pitfalls. The modes of catching fish are little known, for the only evidence available are the explanations of the various names mentioned in the *Yajurveda*. Sāyaṇa (*TB* 3.4.12.1) says that *dhaivara* is one who takes fish by netting a tank on either side; *dāsa* and *śauṣkala* do so by means of a fish-hook (*baḍisa*); *bainda*, *kaivarta* and *maināla* by means of a net (*jāla*); *mārgāra* catches fish in the water with his hands; *ānda* by putting in pegs at a ford (apparently by building a sort of dam); *parṇaka* by putting a poisoned leaf on the water. But none of these explanations can claim much authenticity.

**Foot-soldier:** Foot-soldiers are mentioned in *Atharvaveda* 7.62.1 where Agni is said to conquer the most powerful opponents, as a combatant on a chariot overcomes men fighting on foot. *Satpati, rathiva, pathin*, etc., are terms associated with infantry. In *Atharvaveda* (7.62.1) *patti* is used to designate the foot-soldier in war as opposed to *rathin*, charioteer, the latter defeating the former. *Vājasaneyī Saṃhitā* (16.19) in the *Śatarudriya* mentions *patti* as one of the epithets of Rudra as *pattināṃ patti*, lord of footmen.

**Forenoon:** *Purvāhṇa* is the term which denotes 'the earlier (part of the) day', forenoon. It is a common designation of time from the *Ṛgveda* (10.34.11) onwards (*AB* 7.20; *ŚB* 1.6.3.12, 3.4.4.2; *CU* 5.11.7; *Nirukta* 8.9). When the cows were out feeding they were separated from the calves, which were, however, allowed to join them at the *saṃgava* (*RV* 86.3), *Taittirīya Brāhmaṇa* 2.1.1.3; *Chāndogya Upaniṣad* 2.9.4; *JUB* 1.12.4; *ĀŚS* 3.12.2. The term *saṃgava* denotes the time when the grazing cows are driven together for milking. In the division of the day, the word denotes the period before midday, 'forenoon'. It is found in the *Ṛgveda* (5.76.3) and often later (*AV* 9.6.46; *MS* 4.2.11; *TB* 1.4.9.2; *ŚB* 2.2.3.9; *CU* 2.9.4; *JUB* 1.12.4).

**Forest Fire:** Forest fire (*dāva*) is mentioned in the *Atharvaveda* (7.45.2) and the *Śatapatha Brāhmaṇa* (11.2.7.32). In the latter works such fires are referred to as occurring in spring. According to Sieg, a hymn of the *Ṛgveda* (10.14.2) describes a forest fire. Watchers were employed to guard against surprise from such conflagrations (*dāva-pā*) *Vājasaneyī Saṃhitā* (30.16; *TB* 3.4.11.1).

**Forest-guardian:** *Vana-pā* 'forest-guardian' is included in the list of victims at the Puruṣamedha in the *Vājasaneyī Saṃhitā* 30.19; *Taittirīya Brāhmaṇa* 3.4.11.1. Another terms for forest-guardian is *dāvapā*.

**Fort:** *Pur* appears frequently in the *Ṛgveda* (1.53.7; 1.58.8; 1.131.4; 1.166.8; 3.15.4; 4.27.1) and later. (*TB* 1.7.7.5; *AB* 1.23; 2.11; *ŚB* 3.4.4.3; 4.3.3.25; 9.1.1.2-3; *CU* 8.5.3), meaning 'rampart', 'fort', or 'stronghold'. Such fortifications must have been occasionally of considerable size, as one is called 'broad' (*pṛthvī*) and 'wide' (*urvī—RV* 1.189.2). Elsewhere (*RV* 4.30.20) a fort 'made of stone' (*aśmanmayī*) is mentioned. Sometimes strongholds 'of iron' (*āyasi*) are referred to (*RV* 1.58.8; 2.20.8; 4.27.1; 7.3.7; 7.15.4; 7.95.1; 10.101.8), but these are probably only metaphorical. A fort 'full of kine' (*gomati*) is mentioned (*AV* 8.6.23), showing that strongholds were used to hold cattle, 'Autumnal' (*śāradi*) forts are named, apparently as belonging to the *Dāsas*; this may refer to the forts in that season being occupied against Aryan attacks or against inundations caused by overflowing rivers. Forts 'with a hundred walls' (*śatabhuji*) are spoken of (*RV* 1.166.8; 7.15.14). *Durga*, 'hard to approach', occurs in the *Ṛgveda* as a neuter substantive only, sometimes in the sense of 'fort', 'stronghold' (*RV* 5.34.7; 7.25.2).

**Fortune:** *Śrī* is the term for fortune dwelling in all good and auspicious things. It signifies social distinction to fame and food by material prosperity. In the *Śatapatha Brāhmaṇa* (10.4.1.40) it is intended to be explained as such commented upon by Sāyaṇa: *varṇatrayāt-makātvamupajīvya karmanaḥ śrīyasonnadalakṣaṇaṃ phalaṃ*. But in the text there is no reference to favour any such grouping of the distinctive objects of aspiration associated with the three classes of men generally in the *Aitareya Āraṇyaka* (1.4.2.10). Perhaps it means both *yaśas*, i.e. fame and *anna*, i.e. food, in an intellectual and material point of view. In the *Ṛgveda* (7.41) *bhaga* is continually played down as good fortune. Generally it means wealth as well as property of a family. *Prabha* (*RV* 10.42.9, *AV* 4.38.3) denotes 'winning throw' at dice, which is also a symbol of fortune.

**Fried Grains:** The term *parivāpa* in the later Saṃhitās (*TS* 3.1.10.1; 6.5.11.4; 7.2.10.4; *KS* 34.11; *VS* 19.21.22) and Brāhmaṇas (*AB* 2.24; *JB* 1.5.11.2, etc.) denotes 'fried grains of rice'.

**Friendship:** Mitra denotes 'friend' in the *Ṛgveda* (1.58.1; 67.1.75.4; 156.1; 170.5; 2.4.1.3 etc.), and later *Atharvaveda* (5.19.15; 11.9.2; *KS* 27.4; *TA* 10.80; *TS* 6.4.8.1; *TS* 1.7.8.7; *AB* 6.20.17; *ŚB* 4.1.4.8). According to the *Taittirīya Saṃhitā* (6.2.9.2) a wife is a man's friend and in the *Śatapatha Brāhmaṇa* (1.5.3.17) the value of a friend is insisted upon. Treachery to a friend is reprobated (*TB* 1.7.1.7).

**Fresh Butter:** *Navanīta*, 'fresh butter', is mentioned frequently in the later Saṃhitās (*TS* 2.3.10.1; 6.1.1.5; *KS* 11.7; *MS* 2.3.4) and the Brāhmaṇas (*ŚB* 5.3.2.6; *JUB* 3.5.3). According to the *Aitareya Brāhmaṇa* (1.3) this is the kind of butter which is fit for anointing an embryo (*garbha*), while the gods receive *ājya*, men fragrant ghee (*ghṛta*), and the fathers *āyuta*. Elsewhere (*TS* 2.3.10.1), it is contrasted with *ghṛta* and *sarpis*.

**Fruit:** Flowering and fruit bearing plants are mentioned in the *Ṛgveda* (6.49.14; 7.34.23; 7.35.23; 7.34.57; 10.97.1; *AV* 19.31). It is also obvious that fruits were a valuable part of the diet (*RV* 10.95.5; 10.97.16; 10.146.5) but we come across specific names only in the later Saṃhitās and the Brāhmaṇas. Three varieties of jujube (*ŚB* 5.5.4.22; 12.9.1.5), *badara* (a large sized jujube) *Kāṭhaka Saṃhitā* 20.20; *Maitrāyaṇī Saṃhitā* 3.11.2; *Vājasaneyī Saṃhitā* 19.22.90; 21.30; *Taittirīya Brāhmaṇa* 1.8.5.1; *Śatapatha Brāhmaṇa* 5.4.10; 12.7.1.3; *Jaiminīya Brāhmaṇa* 2.156.5; *kuvala* (an average sized jujube) *Maitrāyaṇī Saṃhitā* 3.11.2; *Vājasaneyī Saṃhitā* 19.22.89; 21.29; *Śatapatha Brāhmaṇa* 5.4.10; *Chāndogya Upaniṣad* 7.31; *karkandhu* (a small sized jujube) *Maitrāyaṇī Saṃhitā*

3.11.2; *Kāṭhaka Saṃhitā* 12.10; *Vājasaneyī Saṃhitā* 19.23; 21.32), *bilva* (*aegle marmalos*) *Atharvaveda* 20, 136.13; *Maitrāyaṇī Saṃhitā* 3.9.3; *Aitareya Brāhmaṇa* 2.1; *Śatapatha Brāhmaṇa* 13.4.4.8 and *kharjūra* (*phoenisilvostris*) (*Kāṭhaka Saṃhitā* 11.10; 36.71; *Taittirīya Saṃhitā* 2.4.9.2) are mentioned in the *Yajurveda*. Mango is mentioned for the first time in the *Śatapatha Brāhmaṇa* (14.7.1.41) while *āmalaka* (myrobalan fruit) in the *JUB* (1.38.6).

**Full Moon:** The word *rākā* (*RV* 2.32.4, 5.42.12; *TS* 1.8.8.1, 3.4.9.1-6; *KS* 12.8; *AB* 3.37) means 'full moon day'. It is personified as a goddess. The term *pūrṇa-māsa* denotes the full moon and the festival of that day, occurring frequently in the later Saṃhitās (*TS* 1.6.7.2, 2.2.10.2, 3.4.4.1, 7.4.8.1; *TB* 1.2.1.14, 3.5.7.13; *ŚB* 2. 2.4.8). The term *pūrṇa-māsa*, denoting the 'night of the full moon, is celebrated in the *Atharvaveda* (7.80.1) as sacred, while it is repeatedly mentioned later (*TS* 1.6.9.1, 3.4.9.6; *AB* 7.11; *ŚB* 1.2.2.4).

**Funeral Rites:** See **Disposal of the Dead**.

**Furniture:** Various kinds of houses were constructed in the Vedic age. The houses were not devoid of useful furniture, which consisted mainly of the things required for lying and sitting as well as various kinds of containers. Mats, door-mats and curtains were also used for decorative purposes. Pillows, mattresses and coverlets were also in use. *Upabarhaṇa* denotes a pillow or cushion, especially of a seat, occurring in the *Ṛgveda* (10.85.7), *Atharvaveda* (9.5.28; 12.2.18-20, 15.3.7) and the Brāhmaṇas (*ĀŚS* 8.12; *ŚB* 13.8.4.10; *TB* 1.1.6.10; *KS* 28.4, etc.). The term for seat was *āsandī* (*AV* 14.2.65; 15.3.2; *TS* 7.5.8.5; *VS* 8.58; 19.16; *AB* 8.5, *ŚB* 3.3.4.26; 5.2.1.22). To a certain extent, the *āsandī* looked like a modern chair or bench, the sitting space being called *āsāda*. It was covered with a cushion (*āstaraṇa*), a pillow (*upabarhaṇa*) and a support (*upāśraya*). Long reclining chairs are also mentioned (*AV* 14.2.65). The *Śatapatha Brāhmaṇa* (5.5.4.1) repeatedly describes the *āsandī* in terms which suggest that it was an elaborate seat. *Paryaṅka* is also the name of a seat (*Kau U.* 1.5), which seems to correspond to what is elsewhere called *āsandī* (*AV* 15.3.3). *Prastha*, which perhaps denotes a bench, is found in the *Ṛgveda* (7.55.8) and also in the *Taittirīya Brāhmaṇa* (2.1.17.1). *Vāhya* denotes in the *Ṛgveda* (7.55.8) and the *Atharvaveda* (4.5.3; 20.3; 14.2.30) a couch or bed of a comfortable kind used by women. Sāyaṇa in the *Atharvaveda* (3.25.1, 5.29.8) and the *Śatapatha Brāhmaṇa* (11.5.1.2; 11.5.7.4) denotes a couch and seems to be the same as *vāhya*. *Śīrṣanya* denotes the head of a couch (*AB* 8.5; *Kaus.U.* 1.5; *SŚS* 17.2.5) since it is especially related to *āsandī*. *Talpa* is the regular term for bed or couch (*RV* 7.55.8; *AV* 5.17.12; 14.2.31; *TS* 6.2.6.4; *TB* 2.2.5.3; *PB* 23.4.2; 25.1.10). It should be mentioned in this connection that violation of the *talpa* of *guru* is already mentioned in the *Chāndogya Upaniṣad* (5.10.9) and the adjective 'legitimate' in the *Śatapatha Brāhmaṇa* (13.1.62).

**Furrow:** *Sītā*, furrow; occurs in the *Ṛgveda* (4.57.6-7) and often later (*AV* 11.3.12; *TS* 5.2, 5.4.5, 6.2.5; *KS* 20.3, etc.). The term *kṛtsnam* is used in the *Jaiminīya Brāhmaṇa* (2.303.307) in the sense of field-furrow where during the whole year grains were cultivated. (cf. *PB* 4.101; 4.7.16.10).

# G

**Gambler, Gambling:** *Kitava*, 'the gambler', is frequently referred to in the *Ṛgveda* (2.29.5; 5.85.8; 10.34.7; 10.34.10; 10.34.11; 10.34.13) and later (*AV* 7.50.1; 7.109.3; *VS* 30.8; 18.22; *AB* 2.19). A father is described as chastising his son for gambling (*RV* 2, 29.5). The gambler seems at times to have fallen, along with his family, into servitude, presumably by selling himself to pay his debts (*RV* 10.34). Technical names (*TS* 4.3.3.1 ff; *VS* 30.18) for different sorts of gamblers are given in the *Yajurveda Saṃhitās* are *ādinava-darśa, kalpin adhi-kalpin* and *sabhā-sthānu*. All these are vague though the last (Mahīdhara on *VS* 30.18; Sāyaṇa on *TB* 3.4.16.1) has usually been taken as a satirical name derived from the gambler's addiction to the dicing place (*sabhā*), 'pillar of the dicing hall'. The first literally means 'seeing ill-luck', and may refer to the quickness of the dicer to note an error on the part of his antagonist, or to his eagerness to see the defeat of his rival. The term *svaghnin* (*RV* 1.92.10; 2.12.4; 4.20.3; 8.45.38; 4.16.5) denotes 'gamester' or 'professional gambler'. *Dyūta* means dicing or a play of the dice. Such a game is also mentioned in the *Atharvaveda* (12.3.46) and the Sūtra literature, viz., the *Kātyāyana Śrauta Sūtra* (15.6.2); the *Lāṭyāyana Śrautasūtra* (4.10.23), etc. According to the Pāṇinian system the two words, i.e. *dyuta* and *dyuna* are accepted as a recognized play, simultaneously formed from the same root *div* appearing as a sense of play. The earliest available literary evidence is the Gambler's Hymn in the *Ṛgveda* (10.34). It shows that the game of dice was prevalent during the Vedic period. The 'warning' given by the gambler of the *Ṛgveda* not to play with dice went unheeded, as is clear from references found in the *Yajurveda* (*VS* 10.28) which accommodates gambling in the rituals named Agnyādheya and Rājasūya. Gamblers could not desist from playing even when they lost everything at the stakes. They continued to haunt the gambling hall (*sabhā*) and stood watching the game being played by others. Therefore, they are jocularly called *sabhā-sthānus*, or the pillars of the hall in the *Yajurdeva* (*VS* 30.18). The term *sabhā-sthānus* may be explained also in a different way (see **Sabhā**). Since it was not possible to prevent people from indulging in gambling, it became necessary to regularize the game. In the *Yajurveda* (*TS* 1.8.9) itself there is a reference to a superintendent of gambling (*akṣāvāpa*) to assist the king in controlling gambling. Dicing was a royal sport and there must have been a separate department of dicing in the royal courts even during the time of the *Yajurveda*. The *Atharvaveda* refers to gambling and considers that success could be secured by prayer to Apsarases (*AV* 4.38.1-4). Non-payment of debt incurred in gambling required punishment (*AV* 6.118).

**Gandhāri:** *Gandhāri* is the name of a people in the north-west of India. In the *Ṛgveda* (1.126.7) the good wool of the sheep of the Gandhāris is referred to. The Gandhāris are also mentioned with the Mujavants, Aṅgas, and Magadhas in the *Atharvaveda* (5.22.14). Gandhāris (*HŚS* 17.6; *ĀŚS* 22.6.18) or Gāndhāris (*BŚS* 21.13) are also spoken of in the Śrauta Sūtras. They were settled in Vedic times on the south bank of the Kubhā up to its junction with the Indus. The *Aitareya Brāhmaṇa* (7.34) and *Śatapatha Brāhmaṇa* (8.1.4.10) refer to Nagnajit, king of Gandhāra.

**Gaṇa Deities:** The mythology of the Veda recognized a certain number of more or less definite groups of divine beings, generally associated with some particular god. The largest and most important of these are the Maruts, whose number in the *Ṛgveda* is variously stated to be 21 or 180, who are constantly described as attending Indra in his war-like exploits. The same group under the name of Rudras is occasionally with their father Rudra (7.10.4; 7.35.6). The number of the Rudras, treated as a separate class, in the Brāhmaṇas is stated to be eleven in the *Aitareya Brāhmaṇa* and *Śatapatha Brāhmaṇa*, but is thirty-three in the *Taittirīya Saṃhitā* (1.4.11.1). The smaller group of the Ādityas, whose number in two passages of the *Ṛgveda* is seven or eight and in the Brāhmaṇas becomes twelve, is in the *Ṛgveda* constantly associated either with their mother Aditi (7.10.4 & c) or with their chief Varuṇa (7.35.6 & 9). This group is more definite than that of the Maruts inasmuch as its members have separate names. A third group, the Vasus, frequently mentioned in the *Ṛgveda* is more vague than the two, for they are neither characterized nor is their number mentioned. That they were conceived as specially connected with Indra, is shown by two passages in which Varuṇa or Aditi with the Ādityas, Rudra with Rudras, and Indra with the Vasus, are invoked (7.10.4; 7.35.6). But in later Vedic texts Agni is the leader of the Vasus. They are regarded as eight in number in the *Aitareya Brāhmaṇa* and *Śatapatha Brāhmaṇa*; the three groups of the Ādityas, Rudras and Vasus are invoked together in a few passages of the *Ṛgveda* (2.31.1; 10.66.12; cf. 7.10.4; 7.35.6). The Brāhmaṇas distinguish, as three kinds of gods, the Vasus of earth, the Rudras of air, and the Ādityas of heaven (*ŚB* 1.3.4.12; 4.3.5.1). In the *Chāndogya Upaniṣad* (3.6-10) five groups are mentioned, the Vasus being connected with Agni, the

Rudras with Indra, the Ādityas with Varuṇa, and Maruts with Soma, and the Sādhyas with Brahmā (cf. *RV* 10.9.7; 10.9.16). There is besides the group of the semi-divine Aṅgirases who are chiefly connected with Bṛhaspati and the small one of the three Ṛbhus who are nearly always associated with Indra. Finally, a comprehensive group is formed of the Viśvedevāḥ or all-gods, who occupy an important position in the sacrifice, for at least forty entire hymns of the *Ṛgveda* are devoted to their praise. It is a factitious, sacrificial group meant to represent all the gods so that none is excluded in laudations intended to be addressed to all. But the all gods are sometimes conceived as a narrower group, being invoked with other groups, such as the Vasus and Ādityas (2.3.4). Macdonell 130.

**Gaṅgā:** Gaṅgā, the modern Ganges is mentioned directly in the *Ṛgveda* only once, in the Nadī-stuti or 'Praise of Rivers' (10.75.5). But it is also referred to in the derivative form *gāṅgeyaḥ* as an epithet of Vrukakṣa. The name of this river does not occur in the other Saṃhitās, but appears in the *Śatapatha Brāhmaṇa* (8.5.4.11), where victories of Bhārata Dauḥṣanti on both Gaṅgā and Yamunā are referred to, and in the *Taittirīya Āraṇyaka* (2.20) special honour is assigned to those who dwell between the Gaṅgā and the Yamunā, this being, no doubt, the region in which that text originated.

**Gomatī:** *Gomatī*, 'possessing cows', is mentioned as a river in the Nadī-stuti, or 'Praise of Rivers' in the tenth *Maṇḍala* of the *Ṛgveda* (10.75.6). In that hymn the river flowing into the Indus must be meant, and its identification with Gomal, a western tributary of the Indus, cannot be doubted. Elsewhere in the *Ṛgveda* (8.24.30) the accentuation of Gomatī shows that a river is meant.

**Gandharvas:** With the Apsaras or Apsarases are associated even in the *Ṛgveda*, a male being or beings named Gandharva. In the later Saṃhitās they are spoken of as forming a distinct class by the side of gods, Fathers and Asuras (*AV* 11.5.2; *TS* 7.8.25.2). Their number is fixed as 27 in some Yajus texts and is even said to be 6333 in the *Atharvaveda* (11.5.2). The evidence of the *Ṛgveda* is, moreover, so scanty and vague that no certain conclusion as to its definite original character is attainable. It is worthy of note that the name is found only once in books II to VII, while in book VIII it occurs twice as that of a being hostile to Indra. The word seems sometimes to be only an appellative. In the *Ṛgveda*, Gandharvas seems to be localized in the high region of air or sky. He is a measurer of space (*RV* 10.139.5). He is found in the fathomless space of air (*RV* 8.66.5). He is heavenly (*divya*) and stands erect on the vault of heaven (*RV* 10.123.7). He is the lover on whom the Apsaras smiles (*RV* 10.123.5). His abode is in heaven (*AV* 2.2.1-2) and the blest live with the Gandharvas (*AV* 4.34.3). In several passages Gandharvas is closely connected with some form of celestial light. Thus, he is brought into relation with sun, 'the golden-winged bird', the messenger of Varuṇa (*RV* 10.123.6), with the sunbird (*RV* 10.177.2), with the sun steed (*RV* 1.163.2), with *soma* likened to the sun (*RV* 9.85.12). He is further connected with the 27 stars of the moon's orbit (*VS* 9.7) and in particular with Rohinī (*AV* 13.1.23). He is possibly also associated with the rainbow in one hymn of the *Ṛgveda* (10.123). In the *Vājasaneyī Saṃhitā* (18.38 ff) the Gandharvas are enumerated with Agni, Sun, Moon, and Wind. In post-Vedic literature one of the names of the mirage is 'city of the Gandharvas'. Moreover, in the *Ṛgveda* the Gandharva is often associated (chiefly in the ninth book) with Soma. He guards the place of *Soma* and protects the races of the gods (*RV* 9.83.4), observing all the forms of Soma, he stands on the vault of heaven (*RV* 9.85.12). Together with Parjanya and the daughter of the sun, the Gandharvas cherish Soma (*RV* 9.113.3). Though Gandharva's mouth the gods drink their beverage (*AV* 7.73.3). The *Maitrāyaṇī Saṃhitā* (3.8.10) states that the Gandharvas kept *Soma* for the gods, but allowed it to be stolen. Doubtless owing to this association with Soma, Gandharvas are described as knowing plants (*AV* 4.4.1). *Soma* is further said to have dwelt among the Gandharvas or to have been stolen by the Gandharva Viśvāvasu, but to have been bought from the Gandharvas, as they were fond of females, at the price of the goddess Vāc (*AB* 1.27; *TS* 6.1.6.5; *MS* 3.7.3). 'Gandharvas in the waters' and the 'aqueous nymphs' are alluded to as the parents of Yama and Yamī (*RV* 10.10.4). *Soma* poured in water is called 'the Gandharva of the waters' (*RV* 9.86.36). Gandharvas, connected with the Apsarases, are also said to dwell in the waters in the *Atharvaveda* (2.2.3; 4.37.12). The union of Gandharvas with the water nymphs is typical of marriage. They are, therefore, connected with the wedding ceremony, and the unmarried maiden is said to belong to Gandharvas as well as to Soma and Agni (*RV* 10.85.40-41). There are only two or three references to their physical appearance in the *Ṛgveda*. They are wind-haired (*RV* 3.38.6) and have brilliant weapons (*RV* 10.123.7). The *Atharvaveda* is more definite (especially 4.37.8.6.1 ff). Here they are said to be shaggy and to have half-animal forms, being in many ways antagonistic to men. Elsewhere, however, they are spoken of as handsome (*ŚB* 13.4.3.7-8). The *Ṛgveda* mentions that Gandharvas wears a fragrant (*surabhi*) garment (10.123.7), while in the *Atharvaveda* (12.1.23) the odour (*gandha*) of the earth is said to have given rise to the Gandharvas.

**Gārgī:** The cosmogonical queries of Gārgī occurs in *Bṛhadāraṇyaka Upaniṣad* (3.6). Gārgī, the daughter of Vācaknu seems to have been so well equipped with intellectual abilities as to be able to encounter even the great philosopher Yājñavalkya. Gārgī asked him what it was that sustained water and gave it support; literally, what it was in water which was 'woven like warp and woof'. Yājñavalkya answered that it was air. 'What is the substratum of air?' Gārgī asked, Yājñavalkya replied, 'The intermundia.' 'What is then the substratum of the intermudance region?' 'The Gandharva world.' 'What is the support of this Gandharva world?' 'The world of the Sun'. 'On what does the world of the Sun repose?' 'On the world of moon.' To further successive questioning of Gārgī, Yājñavalkya went on saying that the world of the moon was buttressed up by the world of the stars, the latter by the world of the gods, the latter by the world of Indra, the latter by that of Prajāpati, and the latter by the Brahmaloka. Then, when Gārgī went on to ask what is was that the world of *Brahman* itself hung from, Yājñavalkya stopped her. But later Gārgī again put two questions: 'What is it in which that which is above the heaven and below the earth and in intermundance regions is woven like warp and woof?' Yājñavalkya's answer was that it was Ether or Ākāśa 'What is it?' asked Gārgī finally, 'which gives support to this Ether itself?' Yājñavalkya answered that it was what we might call the Akṣara or the immutable *Brahman*. Yājñavalkya then gave a philosophical discourse on the nature of this immutable *Brahman*, Belvalkar and Ranade 198-9.

**Gārhapatya:** One of the three kinds of fire required in sacrifice. Also known as *prajāhita* (Jaimini 12.1.13) it means the domestic fire which is to be permanently maintained. *Āp.ŚS* 6.2.13. It is kept on a circular mound and set up by attrition. From the *gārhapatya* fire, other fires (*āhavanīya* and *dakṣiṇā*) are kindled for sacrificial purposes. Bhattacharyya 1990, 62.

**Garland:** *Sraj*, 'garland', is mentioned in the *Ṛgveda* (4.38.6; 5.53.4; 8.47.15; 8.56.3) and later (*AV* 1.14.1; *PB* 16.4.1; 18.3.2; 18.7.6; *ŚB* 13.5.4.2) as often worn by men, when anxious to appear handsome, as at a wedding and so on. The Aśvins are described as 'lotus-wreathed' (*puṣkara-sraj*) (*RV* 10.184.3).

**Gāyatrī:** The sacred verse (*RV* 3.62.10) quoted in other Vedas also, is addressed to Savitṛ (the sun) and is interpreted as a prayer and the source and inspirer of everything. Literally it is 'we contemplate that esteemed refulgence of the divine Savitṛ who may inspire our intellects'. It must be recited several times in *saṃdhyā* everyday.

**Generosity:** Rich persons are described by the term as *dhaniṣṭha* in the plural of superlative degree. In the *Ṛgveda* (8.68.10) the term *indrota* is mentioned as a giver of gifts. This word is twice referred to as praise of generosity, i.e. liberality as a giver of gifts. There is in the *Ṛgveda* (8.68.15) a hymn on generosity. A generous patron has the epithet of *maghavat*, benevolent and liberal. A hymn (*RV* 1.10) containing the word *maghavat* refers to Indra as the powerful one in exerting power for distribution of possessions. A wealthy generous patron is praised for *dakṣiṇā*. There are about forty hymns containing praises of generosity known as *dānastuti*. The stanzas express the poets' gratitude for the favour received from their noble patrons' generosity.

**General:** The term *senānī*, 'leader of an army' is the title of the royal 'general'. He is mentioned in the *Ṛgveda* (7.20.5; 9.96.1; 10.84.2), where also (10.34.12) the word is used metaphorically. He is also referred to in the *Śatarudrīya* (*VS* 16.17; *KS* 17.11; *MS* 2.9.4; *TS* 4.5.2.1) as well as elsewhere in the *Yajurveda Saṃhitās* and *Brāhmaṇas* (*VS* 15.15; *KS* 17.9; *MS* 2.8.10; *ŚB* 8.6.1.21). He is one of the *ratnins* of the king (*TB* 1.7.3.4; *MS* 2.6.5, 4.3.8; *KS* 15.4; *ŚB* 5.3.1.1). Presumably, he was appointed by the king, not by the people to command in war, especially to lead little frays in person. In the *Aitareya Brāhmaṇa* (8.23) this official is called *senāpati*.

**Geographical Ideas:** The *Ṛgveda* generally mentions tribes or clans and not geographical areas particularly. But the expressions *saptasindhavaḥ* (q.v.), literally meaning 'the seven rivers', is also used, in one instance at best, as the designation of a definite country, no doubt comprising the valleys of the rivers in question (*RV* 8.24; cf. 1.32.12; 1.34.8). The seven rivers are often taken to be the five Punjab streams (viz. the Jhelam, Chenab, Ravi, Sutlej and Beas) together with the Indus and the Sarasvatī, though some scholars are inclined to substitute, the Sarasvatī by the Kabul or Oxus. There is also a view that no importance need be attached to 'Seven', which was a favourite conventional number both in the *Ṛgveda* and in later works. A hymn of the latest stratum of the *Ṛgveda* (10.136.8) seems to exhibit the knowledge of the eastern and western sea. A division of the country into zones, i.e. one in the central area and the others on its borders in the different directions, developed in later Vedic period. The *Śatapatha Brāhmaṇa* (17.3.8) mentions the Prācyas or the peoples of the eastern country and also the Bāhīkas or the people of the West. The same Brāhmaṇa (11.4.1.1; cf. *GB* 1.36) refers to the Udīcya Brāhmaṇas. The *Aitareya Brāhmaṇa* (8.14) mentions the Madhyamadiś, 'the central or middle region' as well as the regions in the East (*Prācya*), South (*Dakṣiṇa*), the West (*Pratīcya*), and the *North* (*Udīcya*). Among the peoples of the outer zones, mention is made of the Sātvats ruled by kings styled Bhoja in the south (Probably in Vidarbha or Berar region) and of the Uttarakurus and Uttaramadras beyond the Himavat in the north. The geographical name Madhyadeśa is post-Vedic, but the *Aitareya Brāhmaṇa* (8.14) indicates the same name by the expression Dhruvā Madhyamā pratiṣṭhā-diś. In this middle region the Kurus, the Pañcālas (q.v.), the Vasas and the Uśīnaras are mentioned as inhabiting. This middle land seems to have been regarded as bounded in the east by the countries of the Kosalas and the Videhas and in west by the desert (the Maru or Marwar region in Rajasthan). The *Baudhāyana Dharmasūtra* (1.1.2.9 ff) mentions the same middle region as Āryāvarta and defines it as the territory lying to the east of Adarśana, also known as Vinaśana, where the Sarasvatī lost herself in the sands near Kurukṣetra (cf. *JUB* 4.26; *PB* 25.10.6), to the West of Kālakavana (near Allahabad), the south of the Himavat and to the north of the Pāriyātra or Pāripātra (the Western Vindhyas with the Aravalli range). According to a different view quoted in the same work (1.1.2.10), Āryāvarta lay between the Gaṅgā and Yamunā. It is interesting to note that the Āryāvarta of Baudhāyana became famous as Madhyadeśa 'the middle country' in the *Manusmṛti* (2.21).

**Geography:** See **Cosmography, Divisions of India, Geographical Ideas, Mountains, Rivers, Tribes**.

**Ghṛta:** The term *ghṛta*, the modern ghee or 'clarified butter', is repeatedly mentioned in the *Ṛgveda* (1.134.6, 2.10.4; 4.10.6; 5.12.1) and later (*VS* 2.22; *AB* 3.13.5; *ŚB* 1.8.1.7, 9.2.1.1) both as in ordinary use and as a customary form of sacrifice. According to a citation of Sāyaṇa's commentary on the *Aitareya Brāhmaṇa* (1.3), the distinction between *ghṛta* and *sarpis* consisted in the latter being butter fully melted, while the former was butter melted and hardened (*ghanibhūta*). Because the butter was thrown into the fire, Agni is styled 'butter-faced' (*ghṛta-pratīka*) in the *Ṛgveda* (1.143.7, 3.1.18, 5.11.1, 10.21.7), 'butter-backed' (*ghṛta-pṛṣtha*) in the *Ṛgveda* (1.164.1, 5.4.3, 7.2.4), 'propitiated with butter' (*ghṛta-prasatta*) in the *Ṛgveda* (5.15.1), and 'fond of butter' (*ghṛta-prī*) in the *Atharvaveda* (12.1.20, 18.4.41). Water was used to purify the butter; the waters were, therefore, called 'butter-cleansing' (*ghṛta-pū*). In the *Aitareya Brāhmaṇa* it is said that Ājya, Ghṛta, Āyuta, and Navanīta pertain to gods, men, *pitṛs*, and embroys respectively.

**Gift:** The word for gift in the *Ṛgveda* is *dāna*, which is especially desired—in the *dānastutis* (*RV* 1.126) which contain psalms in praise of munificence. The word *dāna* is derived from *dā* meaning division or distribution. Originally, *dāna* or gift was equated with sacrificial feast where the participants were given a share of goods (*RV* 1.48.4; 1.55.7; 1.180.5; 8.46.26, etc.). One of the characteristics of the brahmins is the right to receive the gifts, which is obligated on the other castes to present (*ŚB* 11.5.7.1). The gods are invoked in the *Ṛgveda* to make gifts to the devotees in kine and steeds. The lord of bestowing gifts and distribution was Varuṇa. The term *dānastuti* seems first to occur in the *Bṛhaddevatā* (6.45.92), which are intended to explain the Ṛgvedic hymns relating to the praises of gifts. *Daksiṇā* was an important part of the Vedic ritual, as reflected in the *Ṛgveda* and later Vedic texts referring to gifts to priests performing the sacrifice. Jaimini (6.7-12) refers to the Viśvajit sacrifice which required the sacrificer—the king—after his glorious conquests to give all he had (*viśvajita sarvasvena yajeta*). The gift of Nachiketā to Yama at the Viśvajit is mentioned in the *Kaṭha Upaniṣad* (3.16). The term *sarvasva* meant all properties including even one's own belongings. From another story of the *Śatapatha Brāhmaṇa* (13.7.1. 14-15; cf. *AB* 8.2.1), we learn that Viśvakarman while about to give the Earth as *dakṣiṇā* to Kaśyapa, his priest, was strongly reproached with the stanza: 'No mortal must give me away, thou art foolish, Viśvakarman Bhanvana. . . .' Thus, the gift-law was gradually modified even in the Vedic age. Gifts to gods were offered to fire, who was believed to have been the messenger of all gods. According to Jaimini, however, the *devatā* was not a corporeal being and hence incapable of accepting a gift (see Śabara 9.1.6-9). Hopkins thinks that the gifts of land to priests which seems to be the first sign of land transactions in Brāhmaṇas was an actual gift of land; but it is unlikely.

**Goad:** In the Vedic texts we come across three terms to denote the goad. The first is the *astra* or badge of agriculture (*RV* 4.57.4; 6.53.9; 6.58.2), the second is *tottra* for driving cattle (*ŚB* 12.4.1.10), and the third one is *toda* (*RV* 4.16.11), meaning impeller (*RV* 6.6.6; 12.1.3. See also *TS* 2.8.5.4; *TĀ* 6.6.2 etc.). The *Ṛgveda* (9.112.3) refers to a term *upala-prakṣiṇī*. The word may also be connected with the operation of grinding corn. *Upala* means a mortar in which the corn was placed and then pounded with pestle.

**Goddess:** Goddesses occupy a very subordinate position in Vedic belief and worship. The only one of any importance is Uṣas. Next to her comes Sarasvatī. Pṛthivī, hardly separable from Dyaus, is praised in one short hymn of three stanzas. Rātri, night, is also invoked in one hymn (*RV* 10.127). Like her sister Dawn, she is called the daughter of Heaven. Night probably became a goddess by way of antithesis to Dawn, with whom she is invoked in several verses as a dual divinity. Vāc, personified speech, is celebrated in one hymn (*RV* 10.125), in which she describes herself. A legend about Vāc frequently referred to in the Brāhmaṇas is that of Soma being bought back from the Gandharvas at the price of Vāc transformed into a woman (*AB* 1.27). Puraṃdhi, whose name occurs about nine times in the *Ṛgveda*, is goddess of plenty. Parendī, commonly regarded as identical with Puraṃdhi, is generally considered a goddess of riches and abundance. Another goddess of abundance is Dhīṣanā, mentioned nearly a dozen times in the *Ṛgveda*. Ilā, nourishment, is the personification (mentioned less than a dozen times in the *RV*) of the offering of milk and butter, thus representing plenty derived from the cow. In the *Śatapatha Brāhmaṇa* she is called the daughter of Manu (1.8.1.8; 11.5.3.5) as well as of Mitra-Varuṇa (1.8.1.27; 14.9.4.27; *ASS* 1.7.7). The name of the goddess Bṛhaddivā occurs four times in hymns to the

Viśvedevas. She is called a mother (*RV* 10.64.10) and is mentioned with Ilā (*RV* 2.31.4; 5.41.19), Sarasvatī and Rākā (*RV* 5.42.12). Rākā probably from $\sqrt{r\bar{a}}$ , (to give) is mentioned only twice in the *Ṛgveda* as a rich and bountiful goddess, who is invoked with others (*RV* 2.32.7; 5.42.17). Sinīvālī is referred to in two hymns of the *Ṛgveda* (2.32; 10.184). She is a sister of the gods, broad-hipped, fair-armed, fair-fingered, prolific, a mistress of the family and is implored to grant offspring. She is invoked with Sarasvatī, Rākā is called the wife of Viṣṇu. The later Saṃhitās and the Brāhmaṇas also mention a goddess Kuhu, a personification of the new moon. Rākā and Sinīvālī are in later Vedic texts connected with phases of the moon, the former being the presiding deity of the actual day of full moon, and the latter, of the first day of new moon. Pṛṣṇi, the mother of the Maruts, presumably represents the mottled storm-cloud. Saraṇyū occurs once in the *Ṛgveda* (10.17.2) as the name of Tvaṣṭṛ's daughter, wedded to Vivasvat. The most likely interpretation seems to be that which identifies her with the sun-maiden Sūryā or Uṣas, the Dawn. Goddesses as wives of the great gods similarly play an insignificant part in the Veda. They are altogether without independent characters, simply representing the spouses whom such gods as Indra must have had. Hardly anything about them is mentioned but their names, which are simply formed from those of the gods with the feminine suffix *ānī*. Thus Indrāṇī is simply 'wife of Indra'. Vāruṇī and Agnānī also occur in the *Ṛgveda* but rarely. Rudrāṇī is not found till the Sūtras, but she plays a decidedly more important part in the cult than any of the other goddesses in *-ānī*. The wife of the Aśvins is once in the *Ṛgveda* called A śvinī (Sūryā). The 'wives of the gods' (*devānaṃ patnīḥ*), occasionally mentioned in the *Ṛgveda*, in the Brāhmaṇas have an established place assigned to them in the cult apart from the gods (*ŚB* 1.9.2.11).

**Gold:** *Candra* (*RV* 2.2.4; 3.31.5; *TS* 1.2.7.1; *KS* 2.6; *VS* 4.26; *ŚB* 3.3.3.4) denotes gold in the *Ṛgveda* and other Vedic texts. *Jātarūpa* (*AB* 8.13) is also used in the same sense. *Rajatajātarūpa* (silver and gold) is mentioned in the *Lāṭyāyana Śrautasūtra* (1.6.24) and *Śāṅkhāyana Śrautasūtra* (3.19.9). *Hiraṇya* in the sense of gold is frequently referred to in the *Ṛgveda* and later texts (*RV* 1.42.5; 4.10.6; *AV* 2.36.7; 5.28.6). The extraction of gold from earth (*RV* 1.117.5; *AV* 12.1.6; 12.1.26; 12.1.44) was also known. Washing for gold is also noted in the *Taittirīya Saṃhitā* (6.1.7.1) and *Śatapatha Brāhmaṇa* (2.1.1.5). Gold was also collected from river-beds and that is why the Indus is called *hiraṇmaya* in the *Ṛgveda* (10.75.8). The Sarasvatī is also depicted as *hiraṇyavartanī* (*AV* 6.61.7). *Hiraṇya* means ornaments of gold in the *Ṛgveda* (1.122.2; *VS* 15.50). A golden currency, weights of gold, *astāprud*, is mentioned in the *Kāṭhaka Saṃhitā* (11.1) and *Taittirīya Saṃhitā* (3.4.1.4). A golden *śatamāna* means weight of a hundred *kṛṣṇalas* in the *Śatapatha Brāhmaṇa* (5.5.3.16) and *Taittirīya Saṃhitā* (2.3.11.5). Gold was obtained by smelting from ore as evidenced in the *Śatapatha Brāhmaṇa* (6.1.3.5; 12.4.3.1). Gold was an object of gift as recorded in the *Ṛgveda* (6.47.23), where we learn of the gift of ten lumps of gold (*daśa hiraṇya-piṇḍam*) to a priest by Divodāsa. The *Atharvaveda* (19.26, 1-3) refers to the belief of the people. 'One that dies of old age becomes he who wears it (gold). . . . For lifetime thee, for splendor thee and for force and strength—that with brilliance of gold thou might shine out among the people'. The term *añja* or *añji* in the sense of ornaments is found in the *Ṛgveda* (1.64.4) but the word *alaṃkāra* is mentioned for the first time in the *Śatapatha Brāhmaṇa* (3.4.1.36; 13.8.4.7) and *Chāndogya Upaniṣad* (8.8.5). During marriage gold-ornaments were gifted to the daughter by the father, as for example *niṣka* in the *Ṛgveda* (2.33.10). *Kurīra* in the *Ṛgveda* (10.85.8) means head ornament, and *karṇaśobhana* ear-rings (*RV* 8.78.3). The *Atharvaveda* also mentions *tīritā* (8.6.7). *Parihastā* (6.71.1-2) meaning hand-clap is found in *Kauśikasūtra* (35.11) as an ornament used as an amulet. The *Atharvaveda* refers to *pravarta* (15.2.1 ear-ornament), golden amulets (1.35), *niṣkarīvā* (5.14.3 necklace of *niska*-coins) and *kurira* (6.138.2). The *Vājasaneyī Saṃhitā* mentions goldsmith (30.17), jeweller (30.7) (*maṇikāra*) and golden ornaments (15.50) (*hiraṇyaiḥ*) like *opaśa* (*TS* 4.1.5.3; *MS* 2.7.5). The *Śatapatha Brāhmaṇa* (6.7.1.7) refers to *rukmapāśa*, a golden chain. Golden ornaments were worn on the breast even as early as the *Ṛgveda* (1.166.10 *vakṣaḥsu rukmā*). Indra (*RV* 8.68.3) is said to have worn golden ornaments on his hands. Maruts are also said to have worn golden ornaments like young suitors, sons of wealthy house (*RV* 5.60.4; 8.5.28-29); the Aśvins are invited to 'ascend the car with golden seats'. The *Baudhāyanaśrautasūtra* (6.13) mentions goldsmith and blacksmith separately. The *Sāṅkhāyana Gṛhyasūtra* (1.22.16-17) states that in *sīmantonnayana* the wife is to sing merrily by wearing many gold ornaments. The use of ear-rings is also heard of in *ĀpŚS*. (20.2.5).

**Golden Germ:** See **Hiraṇyagarbha**.

**Goldsmith:** The term *hiraṇyakāra* denotes 'goldsmith' (*VS* 30.17; *TS* 3.4.14.1).

**Gold Standard:** We find reference to definite weights of gold, indicating a gold currency in the later Vedic age. Thus the *Śatapatha Brāhmaṇa* (5.5.5.16) mentions a gift or *dakṣiṇā* consisting of three hundred gold coins. Here *śatamāṇa* or 'measures of hundred' mean weight of a hundred *kṛṣṇalas*. 'Gold weighing hundred grains' (*ŚB* 12.7.2.13), four gold plates weighing hundred grains (*ŚB* 13.4.1.6) are also mentioned.

**Gosava:** A one-day Soma sacrifice consisting of strange practices. The *Taittirīya Brāhmaṇa* 2.7.2 briefly describes it. The *ĀpŚS* 22.12.12-20; 22.13.1-3 says that for a year thereafter the sacrificer should follow *paśuvrata* (act like cattle). Bhattacharyya 1990, 64.

**Gotra:** Exogamous social groups. The term occurs in the Vedic literature denoting various meanings as cloud, mountain, cowstall, herd, etc. In the latter sense it seems to mean the family or clan. In the *Chāndogya Upaniṣad* 4.4.1 it is found to explain the meaning of family. In the latter literature stress is laid on the prohibition of marriage within a 'gotra' (*Gobhila Gṛhya-sūtra* 3.4.4). The origin of the *gotra* concept can be explained in terms of the primitive concepts of totemism and exogemy. Change of 'gotra' was exceptional, such as the case of Śunaḥśepa and Gṛtsamada found in the *Aitareya Brāhmaṇa* 7.13-16.

**Government:** See **Administration, Judicial Administration, Kingship, Officials, Polity, Statecraft**.

**Governor:** *Sthapati* is the designation of a royal official or governor mentioned in the *Atharvaveda* (2.32.4; 5.23.11) and other later Saṃhitās and Brāhmaṇas (*TS* 4.5.2.2; *KS* 17.12; *MS* 2.9.3; *VS* 16.19; *PB* 17.11.6, 17.11.7, 24.18.2; *ŚB* 5.4.4.17). Revottaras-cakra was the *sthapati* of the exiled Duṣṭaritu Pauṃsāyana, a king of the Sṛñjayas, *Śatapatha Brāhmaṇa* (12.8.1.17; 12.9.3.1).

**Grains:** *Dhānya* primarily denotes grain in general (*RV* 6.13.4; *AV* 3.24.2; 3.24.3; 5.29.7, 6.50.1; *KB* 11.8; *JB* 1.19, 2.38, 2.266). *Dhānyarasa* is a grain (*AV* 2.26.5). *Dhānyabīja* (*RV* 5.53.13) is a seed which produces corn. *Dhānya* is a derivative term of *dhāna*. *Khalva* is a sort of grain or leguminous plant. (Mahīdhara *VS* 18.12; *BU* 6.3.13; *MS* 2.11.4). Some kinds of cultivated grain are referred to in the process of ripening (*JB* 2.294) *ṛtabatas saṃ-vatsaraḥ kṛtsnaṃ annādhyaṃ pachati*. *Tokman* denotes green shoots of any grain (*RV* 10.62.8; *KS* 12.11; *VS* 19.13; 19.81; 21.30, 21.43), viz., rice, large rice, seed and barley (*AB* 8.5.8.16). *Śasya* is a common term to mean any corn (*AV* 7.11.1, 8.10.24; *MS* 4.2.2; *TS* 3.4.3.3, 5.1.7.3, 7.5.20.1, etc.). Two harvests a year are recorded (*TS* 5.1.7.3); barley and rice ripened in summer, rice in autumn, beans and sesamum in the winter and the cold seasons (*TS* 7.2.10.2). The performance which accompanied the charm for procuring increase of grain (*AB* 6.79.1-3; *KauSū*. 21.7) consists of placing a stone upon a grain-bag, sprinkling it, laying upon it a handful of grain with each of the three stanzas and so forth. A charm for protection of grain from lightning and heat (*AV* 7.11), viz., *mā no vadhīr vidyutā deva śasyaṃ mota vadhīr raśmibhiḥ sūryasya*. Exorcism of vermin infection on grain in the field is mentioned (*AV* 6.50.1-3). A long line of pestiferous insects is mentioned by Keśava and Sāyaṇa in connection with a hymn of *KauSū*. 51, 17-22. The performer of this spell walked about the grain field hacking a piece of lead with an iron instrument, scattered stones upon the field, tied a hair through the mouth of a *trada* (insect) and bent his head downward into the middle of the field. He made an offering to *Āsā* (region), *Āsāpati* (lord of the regions), to the two Aśvins and to Kṣetrapati.

*Barley:* The specific term for barley in the *Ṛgveda* (1.23.15; 66.3; 117.21; 135.8; 176.2; 2.56; 14.11; 5.85.3; 7.34; 8.2.3; 22.6; 63.9; 78.10) is *yava*, the word also being used to denote corn in general. In the *Atharvaveda* (2.8.3; 6.30.1; 50.1-2; 91.1; 141.2; 142.1-2; 7.7.20; 9.1.22; 6.14; 12.1.42), *Taittirīya Saṃhitā* (6.2.10.3; 6.4.10.5; 7.2.10.2), *Kāṭhaka Saṃhitā* (25.10; 26.5), *Maitrāyaṇī Saṃhitā* (4.3.2), *Vājasaneyī Saṃhitā* (5.26; 18.12; 23.10), *Taittirīya Brāhmaṇa* (1.8.4.1), *Śatapatha Brāhmaṇa* (1.1.4.20; 2.5.2.1; 3.6.1.9-10; 4.2.1.11; 12.7.2.9) and *Chāndogya Upaniṣad* (3.14.3) *Yava* expressly denotes barley. The harvest came after spring (*KB* 4.12-13), in the summer (*TS* 7.2.10.2).

*Beans:* The term for the beans is *kulmāsa* (*CU* 1.10.2.7). These were of numerous varieties. A special brand was known as *garmut* (*TS* 2.4.4.1-2; *KS* 10.11; *MS* 2.2.4).

*Chaff:* Denoted by the word *palāva* in *Atharvaveda* (12.3.19) and *JUB* (1.54.1).

*Corn:* The general term for corn is *śasya* (*AV* 7.11.1; 8.10.24; *TS* 3.4.3.3; 5.1.7.3; 7.5.20.1; *MS* 4.2.2). *Dhāna* also denotes corn (*AV* 1.16.2; 3.35.3; 6.29.4; *AV* 18.3.69; 4.32-34; *VS* 19.21-22) of a special type which was mixed with Soma. A derivative of the former is *dhānya* which, though later became the name of rice, originally stood for corn in general (*RV* 6.13.4; *AV* 3.24.2-4; 5.29.7; 6.50.1). According to *Bṛhadāraṇyaka Upaniṣad* (6.3.22) there are ten cultivated grains beans (*tila-māṣāḥ*), *panicum miliaceum* and *italicum* (*anupriyaṅgavaḥ*) maize and wheat (*godhūmaḥ*), *lentils* (masūrāḥ) and pulses (*khala-kulāḥ*). The horse is called corn-eating (*dhānyāda*, *AB* 8.21; *ŚB* 13.5.4.2). Purification of corns is mentioned in the *Ṛgveda* (10.94.13).

*Lentil: Ervum hirsutum*, is known as *masūra* in *Vājasaneyī Saṃhitā* (18.12). The *Bṛhadāraṇyaka Upaniṣad* (6.3.22) refers to it as one of the ten cultivable grains.

*Millet:* It is mentioned with added suffix of *taṇḍula* in the *Śatapatha Brāhmaṇa* (10.6.3.2) and *Chāndogya Upaniṣad* (3.14.3). Cultivated millets are referred to in later *Saṃhitās* and *Brāhmaṇas* (*TS* 1.8.1.2; 2.3.2.6; 4.7.4.2; *MS* 2.11.4; *VS* 18.12; *KS* 10.2; *ŚB* 12.7. 1.9; *KB* 4.12). The lightness of its seed is alluded to in the *Atharvaveda* (19.50.4), which also says that it is the food of the regions (*AV* 20.135.12).

*Mustard Seed:* Denoted by the word *sarṣapa*, it occurs only a few times in later Vedic texts (*CU* 3.14.3; *ṢaḍBr* 5.2; *SŚS* 4.15.8).

*Pulses:* Among various pulses *Khalakula* (*BU* 6.3.22) is mentioned as a cultivable grain, which Sāyaṇa identifies with *Kulattha* (*dolichos uniflorus*). *Khalva* is another kind pulse mentioned with other grains in the

*Vājasaneyī Saṃhitā* (18.12) and as being crushed with the *dṛṣad* in *Atharvaveda* (2.31-1; 5.23.8; cf. *BU* 6.3.22).

*Rice:* The common term for rice is *taṇḍula* though in a broad sense the word denotes grains in general. The word is not found in the *Ṛgveda*, but in the *Atharvaveda* (10.9.26; 11.1.18; 12.3-18; 29.30) and other *Saṃhitās* (*MS* 2.6.6; *KS* 10.1) and *Brāhmaṇas* (*AB* 1.1; *ŚB* 1.1.4-3; 2.5.3.4; 5.2.3.2; 6.6.1.8) we have numerous references to it. *Śyāmāka-taṇḍula* is mentioned in the *Śatapatha Brāhmaṇa* (10.6.3.2) and *Chāndogya Upaniṣad* (3.14.3). Another variety *apamārga-taṇḍula* is found in the *Śatapatha Brāhmaṇa* (5.2.4.1.5) Husked and unhusked rice is referred to in the *Taittirīya Saṃhitā* (1.8.9.3). The word *dhānya* later came to denote paddy though originally it stood for grains in general. *Nīvāra* is wild paddy , references to which are found in abundance in the later *Saṃhitās* and *Brāhmaṇas* (*KS* 12.4; *MS* 3.4.10; *VS* 18.12; *ŚB* 5.1.4.14; 5.3.3.5; *TB* 1.3.6.7 etc.). *Plāsuka* is found in the *Śatapatha Brāhmaṇa* (5.3.3.2) as an epithet of *Vrīhi* or paddy in the sense of 'shooting up rapidly'. *Vrīhi* is never mentioned in the *Ṛgveda*, but it is frequently alluded to in the *Atharvaveda* (6.140.2; 8.7.20; 9.6.14) and later *Saṃhitās* (*KS* 10.6; 11.5; *MS* 3.10.2; 4.3.2, *VS* 18.12; *AB* 2.8; 8.16; *ŚB* 5.5.5.9). In the *Taittirīya Saṃhitā* (7.2; 10.3) it is said to ripen in autumn. Reference to its cultivation in south-east India is found (*KS* 12.4.5.6; *TB* 1.7.3.4). Black and white rice is contrasted and the distinction of dark, swift-growing (*āśu*) and large (*mahā*) rice is made (*TS* 1.8.10.1; *AV* 11.4.13; *CU* 5.10.6). *Śāli* is a later word for rice.

*Sesamum:* Seed from which edible oil was extracted was known as *tila* in the later *Saṃhitās* and *Brāhmaṇas* (*AV* 2.8.3; 6-140.2. 18.3.69; 4.32; *TS* 7.2.10.2; *MS* 4.3.2; *VS* 18.12, *ŚB* 9.1.1.3). It is often mentioned in connection with *māṣa* or 'kidney bean' (*AV* 6.140.2; *VS* 18.12; *BU* 6.3.22; *CU* 5.10.6). The *Taittirīya Saṃhitā* (7.2.10.2) attributes its production in the cold season. *Hemanta, taila* and *taula* are terms for sesamum oil.

*Wheat:* The word for wheat is *godhūma* which occurs frequently in the later *Saṃhitās* (*MS* 1.2.8; *VS* 18.12; 19.22; 21.28) and *Brāhmaṇas* (*ŚB* 12.7.1.2; 12.7.2.9 cf. *BU* 6.3.22). It is expressly distinguished from rice and barley (*TB* 1.3.7.2). Flour or dust made of this grain is also mentioned (*ŚB* 12.9.1.5).

**Grāma:** See **Village**.

**Grāmaṇī:** See **Village Headman**.

**Grammar:** The *Ṛgveda* celebrates Vāc (personified speech) as a goddess (10.125). Some stanzas of the *Ṛgveda* are capable of being given grammatical explanation. Expressions like *catvāri śṛṅgā* and *sapta-sindhavaḥ* have been interpreted by Patañjali in terms of four parts of speech as seven cases. There are speculations on letters, syllables and words in the Brāhmaṇas as also terms like *akṣara, varṇa* (masculine) and *vibhakti* which Pāṇini has used without definition. In the *Śatapatha Brāhmaṇa* (13.3.1.18) we meet with names for singular and plural. In the *Chāndogya Upaniṣad* we find classification of letters and technical terms such as *svara* (vowels), *sparśa* (consonants) and *women* (sibilants). The next landmark was reached when the Saṃhitā texts were reduced to the *pada-paṭha*, wherein each word is exhibited separately in its individual grammatical form, followed by word signs like *iti* and also by symbols like *avagraha*, etc., to distinguish case terminations, to analyse compounds and to mark out a few special cases of accentuation. Yāska distinguishes a Northern and/or Eastern school of grammarians and mentions nearly twenty predecessors such or Sākaṭāyana, Pārgya and Śākalya. The *semanteme* (root) containing the general meaning of the word and the *morpheme* (inflection or the suffixes or preffixes) which gives difinite form to the general meaning are distinguished. The theory of the verbal origin of nouns stressed by Yāska may be said to be the foundation of the whole system of Pāṇini. Yāska states that there are four kinds of parts of speech—*nāman* (noun), *ākhyāta* (verb), *upasarga* (preposition) and *nipāta* (particle)—terms later used by Pāṇini. The Prātiśākhyas do not refer to grammar, but presuppose a long continued study of grammatical subjects quoting the different opinions of the earlier grammarians. Of the sixty-four grammarians, referred to as the predecessors of Pāṇini, a few must have belonged to the Vedic age. *Cultural Heritage of India* I, 281-3.

**Grāmyavādin:** See **Village Judge**.

**Granary:** In the *Atharvaveda* (2.14.2) there is a word *upānasa* which, according to Sāyaṇa, means, either a 'granary' or a 'wagon full of grain'. The word also occurs in the *Ṛgveda* (10.105.4).

**Great Bear:** Seven *ṛṣis* (*RV* 10.82.2; *AV* 6.40.1; *ŚB* 2.1.2.4, 13.8.1.9) denote the 'Great Bear'.

**Gṛhya Rituals:** The distinction between the three fires of the *Śrauta* cult and the single fire of the householder was recognized as early as the *Ṛgveda*. Certain ceremonies, such as the morning and evening fire service and the new and full moon sacrifices as well as some other cereal and animal sacrifices, are common to both the cults, the difference being one of elaboration only. On the other hand, the personal and family rites belong exclusively to the *gṛhya* (domestic), and the *soma* sacrifice exclusively to the *Śrauta* cult. The occasions for the setting up of the domestic fire for its uninterrupted maintenance were marriage, the death of the head of the family, or the division of the family property. The material is the same as at the *Śrauta* offerings, with the difference that the *soma* is never one of the offerings and that the animal victim is not very common. The daily morning and evening offerings, after sunrise and sunset, are made of barley or rice (cooked or raw) to Sūrya and Prajāpati and to

Agni and Prajāpati, respectively. The five great sacrifices (*pañca-mahāyajñas*) to be performed daily are: (1) The sacrifice to the gods (*deva-yajña*) is made out of the food (prepared for the morning or evening meal) over which some milk, curds or butter is poured, and is offered silently into the fire by the householder with his hands. (2) The sacrifice to the beings (*bhūta-yajña*) consists of oblations (*balis*) placed on the ground, inside the fire-chamber or outside and offered to the four elements (*pṛthivī, āp, vāyu* and *ākāśa*), to Prajāpati, to *Kāma*, and to the all-gods, and, finally, in the dustbin to the demons. (3) The remnants of the *balis,* besprinkled with water, are poured out towards the south to the *pitṛs*, that is the *pitṛyajña*. (4) The *brahmayajña* consists of the *svādhyāya* or daily recitation of Vedic texts. (5) The sacrifice to men (*manuṣyayajña*) is offered when a guest is fed or a beggar is given food, before the householder has his meal. The new and full moon sacrifice are offered very much in the same way as those of the *śrauta* cult, with the difference that, instead of the cakes, the mess of cooked food is prepared in the *sthālīpāka* manner. There are also other periodical *gṛhya* sacrifices: (1) The *Śrāvaṇa* sacrifice to the serpent takes place on the full moon day of the *Śrāvaṇa* month, in the monsoon, when the use of a high couch for sleeping becomes necessary for four months. A *bali* to the divine serpents concludes the ceremony. This performance is repeated every night silently, until (2) the ceremony of *pratyā-varohaṇa* (redescent) or the *āgrahāyanī* festival, which takes place on the full moon of Mārgaśīrṣa, when the temporary use of the high bedstead is given up. The agricultural rites are, in a sense, seasonal or periodical. There are ritual ceremonies formally consecrating the various stages of agricultural operation. (1) The plough is set in motion for the first time under an appropriate *nakṣatra* (Rohiṇī or Jyeṣṭhā). (2) The sacrifice to *Sītā* (the rustic deity of the field-furrow) is offered on the field itself. There are, further, rites at (3) the sowing of the seed; (4) the reaping of the crop; (5) the threshing of the corn; (6) the putting of the grain into the barn; and (7) the partaking of the first fruits of the harvest. The *śūlagava* (spit-ox) sacrifice, so called because an ox is offered to the spit-bearing Rudra, is most important of these. The *bauddhavihāra* in which a lump of boiled rice besprinkled with *ājya* is placed in a basket of *palāśa* leaves, which is kept hanging on a tree for Rudra. 'The *sthālīpāka* offering to Kṣetrapati, represented by a bull, is put in leaves and placed on the beaten track of the cows without a fire. The ceremony of *vṛṣotsarga* (the letting loose of a bull) on the Kārttika full moon to ensure the good breeding of cattle. Some minor rites consisting of the recitation of appropriate formulas to ensure their health and safety'. Among the occasional ceremonies fall the following: (1) Guest-reception—It is an elaboration of the daily *manuṣya-yajña*. There is an authorized list of guests, including a teacher, an officiating priest, a king, a *snātaka* and a marriage-relation. (2) The building of the house—the selection of the site is determined by the quality and condition of the soil, etc. The digging of pits for the posts, the erection of the posts along with a water-plant to prevent fire, and the putting up of the beams and the roof are all stages marked by ritual acts. (3) The *caitya* sacrifice—A *bali* is offered to the *caitya*, which is either a religious shrine or a memorial erected in the memory of a teacher or some other distinguished person. *Cultural Heritage of India*, I 254-7.

**Grinder:** The term *upalaprakṣiṇī* appears in the *Ṛgveda* (9.112.3) and denotes a grinder, the occupation of a woman as opposed to that of her son, who is a poet (*kāru*) and to that of his father who is a physician (*bhiṣaj*). The term, however, has other explanations. Yāska explains *upalaprakṣiṇī* as one who makes groats (*śaktukārikā*). Macdonell and Keith have referred to a number of views on *upalaprakṣiṇī*. Roth, Grassmann and Zimmer connect her to the operation of grinding corn. Pischel considers that *upalaprakṣiṇī* denotes a woman that assisted at the crushing of *soma*. Von Schroeder points out that there is no objection to regarding *upala* as the mortar in which the corn was placed and then pounded with the pestle. He renders the word literally as 'one who fills the (lower) stone (with corn)'. Macdonell and Keith I, 94.

**Group Commander:** *Vrājapati* is found once in the *Ṛgveda* (10.179.2) and also in the *Atharvaveda* (7.72.2). The comrades attend Indra, the *Vrājapati* as *Kulapās*. Zimmer holds the *Vrājapati* refers to the head of the families being subordinate in war to the village headman, called *grāmaṇī*. But Whitney says that the term denotes a chieftain surrounded by the leading men, the family heads, not necessarily merely a village headman. *Vrāja* occurs in the *Atharvaveda*, adverbially in the sense of the troops. According to Sāyaṇa the term *vrāja* is variously used in the Vedic texts. It also means a house worthy to be gone as *vrāja gantavya gṛhaḥ*. In the later period the term *vrājapati* occurs in a sense of leader of the village associated to a large family as a special group. Griffith understands the word as 'Lord of clans'.

**Group Deities:** See **Gaṇa Deities**.

**Gruel:** *Karambha* is the name, from the *Ṛgveda* onwards (*ṚV* 1.187.16; 3.52.7; 6.56.1; 8.102.2; *AV* 6.16.1; *TS* 3.1.10.3, 6.5.11.4, etc.), of porridge made of grain (*yava*), which was unhusked, parched slightly, and kneaded (*ŚB* 2.5.2.14; 4.2.4.18). It was the special sacrificial portion of Pūṣan, no doubt in his capacity of an agricultural deity. *Karambha* was made of barley (*upavāka, VS* 19.22) or the sesame (*tirya. AV* 4.7.3).

**Guard:** The term *pāyu* means guard of protector. It is referred to in the *Ṛgveda* (1.147.3; 2.1.7; 4.2.6; 6.15.8; 8.18.2; 8.60.19; 10.100.9; 4.4.3; 4.4.12).

**Guardian of Law:** The *Śatapatha Brāhmaṇa* (5.3.3.5; 5.3.4.5) calls the king *dhṛta-vrata*, 'upholder of dharma'. In the later Vedic period due to the fusion with the concept of *ṛta*, *dharma* gained a moral content. Law is 'truth' or *dharma* (*ŚB* 6.7.3.11). We learn from the *Aitareya Brāhmaṇa* (8.17) that the king was the 'guardian of law' and from the *Śatapatha Brāhmaṇa* (9.4.1.1) that he was 'sustainer of the realm'. The whole thing implies that the king could not be the maker of law; he was merely the executive head whose function was to maintain law. This idea of law of *dharma* is best expressed in the *Bṛhadāraṇyaka Upaniṣad* (1.4.14): *Brahman* was no strong enough. So he created still further, the most excellent *dharma*. *Dharma* is the force of power. There is nothing higher than *dharma*. Henceforth, even a weak man rules a stronger person with the help of *dharma*, as with the help of a king. This *dharma* is equivalent to truth. In the *Muṇḍakopaniṣad* truth has been conceived as a moral category. The above passage of the *Bṛhadāraṇyaka Upaniṣad* shows also the supremacy of *dharma* over physical or military power connoted by the term *kṣattara*. This concept of superiority of *dharma* to physical force has exerted a great influence on the socio-political life of ancient India, resulting in the rise of social and political institutions, all aimed at the realization of ultimate purpose of law. The divine epithets like *dhṛtavrata* and *dharmakṛt* (*AV* 20.54.2; 20.62.6) show that the earthly kings were guardians of law. The epithet *dharma-dhṛta* (maintainers of duty), applied in the *Atharvaveda* (1.25.1) to gods, express the idea that even the gods observed the everlasting status of natural and moral order.

**Guilandina Bonduc:** *Pūtikā* is the name of a plant often mentioned (*KS* 34.3; *ŚB* 14.1.2.12, cf. 4.5.10.4; *PB* 8.4.1; 9.5.3) as a substitute for the *soma* plant. It is also mentioned in the *Taittirīya Saṃhitā* (2.5.3.5) as a means of making milk curdle, being an alternative to the bark of the *butea frondosa* (*parṇa-valka*). It is usually identified with the *guilandina bonduc*, but Hillebrandt makes it out to be the *basella cordifolia*.

**Guilds:** The Vedic Indians took to joint undertakings at a very early period, as evidenced by the functions of the *Sabhā*, *Samiti*, *Vidatha* and *Gaṇa*. It is indicated in the last hymn of the *Ṛgveda* (10.191.3), which speaks of the spirit of the age when the Indians did whatever they did after due deliberation and mutual agreement in a meeting or association. The joint undertaking of priests in the Vedic sacrificies, like the *Jyotiṣṭoma* and the mode of distribution of sacrificial fees (*dakṣiṇā*), shows how the principle of partnership was already formulated. The words *śreṣṭhin* and *śraiṣṭhya* in Vedic literature indicate the formation of trade guilds even in that early period. But we have little information about the laws of different associations in the Vedic age. Even the earlier Dharmasūtras are silent on the law of joint undertaking. *Viṣṇu Dharma Sūtra* (5.125-6) speaks of criminal combination of traders and provides punishment for those who corner goods and enhance prices of trade-condition. The partner of such association, if found to have sold its goods on his own account, is to be punished with the highest amercement (*uttama-sāhasa*). He also lays down laws for controlling weights, cheating and adulteration of goods. From the above discussion we may infer that secular partnerships had not assumed importance in the early Vedic period and even in the period of the earlier Dhamusūtras, though we find the germs of such combinations or groups as indicated by words like *śreṇi* (*RV* 1.163.10) *vrāta, gaṇa* (*RV* 3.26.6, 5.53.11) and *puga*. The *Gautama Dharmasūtra* (11.21) enjoins that 'cultivators, traders, herdsmen, money lenders and artisans (have authority to lay down rules) for their respective classes'. This shows that in the post-Vedic period these classes of people formed guilds which became powerful enough to extract from the king the privilege of formulating laws for their owns groups.

**Guṅgu:** Guṅgu is a goddess mentioned in the *Ṛgveda* with Sinīvālī, Rākā, Sarasvatī, Indrāṇī and Varuṇānī (*RV* 2.32.8). Sāyaṇa identifies Guṅgu with Kuhū. Guṅgū is the new moon.

# H

**Habitation:** See **Housing, Settlements**.

**Haemorrhoids:** *Arsas* is the name of a disease mentioned in the *Vājasaneyī Saṃhitā* (12.98), with consumption and other ailments. It appears to designate 'haemorrhoids', as in the later medical literature.

**Hair Styles:** Hair or *keśa* of the head is referred to in the *Atharvaveda* (5.19.3; 6.136.3), *Vājasaneyī Saṃhitā* (20.5; 25.3) and *Śatapatha Brāhmaṇa* (2.5.2.48). People had a great consciousness of hair. In the several hymns of the *Atharvaveda* (6.136.6.137) plentiful growth of hair is desired. Cutting and shaving of hair (*vap*) were in vogue (*AV* 8.2.17; *ŚB* 5.5.3.1). Long hair was regarded womanly, as stated in the *Śatapatha Brāhmaṇa* (5.1.2.14). The term *śalalī* denotes the quill of the porcupine, which was used for parting the hair and anointing the eyes as mentioned in the *Kāṭhaka Saṃhitā* (23.1); *Taittirīya Brāhmaṇa* (1.5.6.6). Another term for hairstyles is *stuka*, which means 'a tuft' of hair or wool (*RV* 9.97.17; *AV* 7.74.2; *KS* 25.6 and *ŚB* 3.2.1.13). The word *pulastin* (*KS* 17.15) or *pulasti* (*TS* 4.5.9.1; *VS* 16.43) occurs in the sense of 'wearer of plain hair' as opposed to *kapardin*, 'wearer of braided hair'. Locks were known as *sikhaṇḍa*, parting of hair as *siman* and top-knot as *śikhā*.

**Hair Treatment:** In order to stop hair from falling, herbs of pacificatory (*śānta*: cf. *KauSū* 8.15 f) class, grown trees, in water, and other selected places, are applied (*AV* 6.21). In order to make the hair grow, a paste of heated *śīrṣa* (*vanquiena spinosa*) and nuts of *akṣa* (*bibhītaka bellerica terminalia*), consecrated with *AV* (6.2), and subsequently cooled, is applied on the head. (*KauSū*. 8-9).

**Hall:** The term *prācīṇavaṃśa* denotes a hall that is supported by a beam of the roof facing the east (*ŚB* 3.1.1.6-7; 3.6.1.23; 4.6.8.20; *KS* 22.13).

**Hand-guard:** The battle-hymn of the *Ṛgveda* (6.75) refers to *hastaghna*, to be used by the warrior, or the left arm to avoid the friction of the bow-string. In *Ṛgveda* (6.75.14) the *hastaghna*, or handguard, of the archer is compared to a snake. Lāṭyāyana has *hastatra* and the *Mahābharata hastavāpa* as its equivalent.

**Hand-fighting:** *Muṣṭi-han* (*RV* 5.58.4; 6.26.2; 8.20.20; *AV* 5.22.4) denotes a hand-to-hand fighter, i.e. the ordinary warrior as opposed to the charioteer. It also denotes hand-to-hand fighting between two persons.

**Hariyupiyā:** Mentioned in a hymn of the *Ṛgveda* (6.27.2) as the scene of the defeat of the Vṛcīvants by Abhyāvartin Cayamāna. It may denote either a place or a river, since many battles seem to have been fought on the banks of rivers. Ludwig took it to mean the name of a town on the river Yavyāvatī, which is identified with it in Sāyaṇa's commentary on the passage. Hillebrandt thinks that it is the river Iryab (Hakiab), a tributary of the Kurum (Krumu). Macdonell and Keith II. 499.

**Hastipa:** Elephant keeper (*VS* 30.11; *TS* 3.4.9.1.) See **Occupation**.

**Haviryajña:** A sacrifice in which there is burnt offering but no Soma. There are seven such sacrifices. (1) *Agnyādheya*, wherein burning coals are placed for the generation of the *gārhapatya* and other fires at a particular time and place by a particular person to the accompaniment of certain *mantras*. It comprises the bringing of *araṇis* (two wooden logs), establishment of the fire brought by the Adhvaryu priest by the sacrificer and his wife, the cooking and eating of *brahmaudana*, chanting of *sāmans* by the Brahmā priest and dice-playing by the sacrificer (*TB* 1.1.2-10; 1.2.1; *ĀŚS* 2.1.9 ff; *KŚS* 4.7-10, etc.). (2) Agnihotra kindling, maintenance and worship of fire, in which oblations to Agni and Prajāpati are offered and the daily *homa* is performed by the sacrificer himself (*TS* 1-5.2.1; *KS* 9.2). (3) *Āgrayana* which is the rite of offering the first corn. (4) *Cāturmāsya*, or the seasonal celebration, lasting for a period of four months which begins from the waxing on the eleventh day of the full moon in *Āṣāḍha* (June-July). (5) *Darśapūrṇamāsa*, which is the sacrifice of new moon and full moon days and regarded as the archetype of the sacrifices belonging to the *iṣṭi* category (*TS* 1.1.1-13; 1.6-7; 2.5-6). (6) *Nirūḍhapaśubandha*, which consists of animal sacrifice offered to Agni, Sūrya or Prajāpati (*TS* 1.3.5-11; 6.3-4; *ŚB* 3.6.4 ff; 11.7.1 ff). (7) *Sautrāmaṇi*, in which a bull, a sheep and a goat are dedicated to Indra, Sarasvatī and Aśvins respectively (*VS* 19.21; *TS* 1.8.2; *TB* 1.4.2; 1.8.5-6; 2.6-7; *ŚB* 4.6.2).

**Haviṣkṛt:** Literally, it means 'one who separates the grains from the husks. According to *Taittirīya Brāhmaṇa* 2.2.4, it indicates the formula for calling a person. In the case of a brāhmaṇa it is *ehi* (come hither), for a kṣatriya *āgahi* (approach), for a vaiśya *ādrava* (hasten hither) and for a śūdra *ādhava* (run hither) cf. *Śatapatha Brāhmaṇa* 1. 1.4.12; *ĀpŚS* 1. 19.9-10. According to Sāyaṇa the term means the person who prepares the *havis*, as also the formula used to call him. Jaimini III. 2.59 holds that in certain Vedic passages *haviṣkṛt* indicates an injunction to summon thrice the wife or any other person who separates grains.

**Headache:** *Śīrṣakti* is a common word for 'headache' in the *Atharvaveda* (1.12.3; 9.8.1; 12.2.19; 12.5.23).

*Śirṣāmaya* (*AV* 8.5.3; 8.12.3; 8.17.2; *KU* 1.5; *ŚSS* 18.2.8), 'disease of the head' is mentioned in the *Atharvaveda* (5.4.10; 9.8.1).

**Head of the Family:** *Gṛhapati* is a common term in the *Ṛgveda* (6.53.2) and onward (*AV* 14.1.51; 19.31.13; *ŚB* 4.6.8.5; 8.6.1.11) to mean the householder as master of the house, which is also indicated by another word *gṛhapā* found in the *Vājasaneyī Saṃhitā* (30.11). In the *Ṛgveda* (1.12.6; 6.48.8; *VS* 2.27; 3.39; 9.39; 24.24), etc., *gṛhapati* is repeatedly used as an epithet of Agni. Similarly, the mistress is so-called by *gṛhapatnī* in the *Ṛgveda* (10.85.26; *AV* 3.84.6). The duties of a householder are treated as *gārhapatya* in the *Ṛgveda* (1.15.12; 6.15.19). The term *jaspati* occurs once in the *Ṛgveda* (1.185.8) as a sense of the 'head of the family'. The derivative form is also found from such a word as *jaspatya* in the *Ṛgveda* (5.28.2; 10.85.23), denoting the sense of 'lordship of children'.

**Head Ornament:** *Kumba* is mentioned with *opaśa* and *kurīra* as an ornament of woman's hair in the *Atharvaveda* (6.138.3). *Kurīra*, like *opaśa* and *kumba*, denotes some sort of a female head ornament in the description of the bride's adornment in the wedding hymn of the *Ṛgveda* (10.85.8) and in the *Atharvaveda* (6.138.3). According to the *Yajurveda Saṃhitās* (*TS* 4.1.5.3; *MS* 2.7.5; *VS* 11.5.6), the goddess Sinīvālī is described by the epithets *su-kapardā, su-kurīrā, su-opaśa*, as wearing a beautiful head-dress. According to Geldner, the word *kumba* originally meant 'horn'; but this is uncertain, as this sense is not required in any passage in which the term occurs (*GB* 1.3.21). Macdonell and Keith, I. 163-4.

**Heart Disease:** *Hṛdayāmaya*, 'disease of the heart' is mentioned in the *Atharvaveda* in connection with *yakṣma* (5.30.9) and with *balāsa* (6.14.1; 6.127.3). Zimmer, who thinks that *balāsa* is consumption, connects the name with the later view of the medical *Saṃhitās*, that love is one of the causes of the disease. But it would be more natural to see in it a disease affecting the heart. *Hṛdyota* (*AV* 1.22.1. cf. 6.2.4.1) and *hṛdroga* (*RV* 1.50.11), 'heart disease', are also mentioned. Macdonell and Keith II. 506-7.

**Heaven:** See **Eschatology**. The spirits of the departed ones are supposed to go to some kind of paradise where Yama and the Fathers live in the midst of joy, enjoying various pleasures (*RV* 10.14.8; 88.25; 107.2). *Nāka* denotes the firmament in the *Ṛgveda* (1.60.10; 125.5; 3.2.12; 4.13.5; 7.86.1; 99.2; 8.103.2; 9.73.4, etc.) and the *Atharvaveda* (7.18.1; 18.2.47; 13.1.7; *VS* 15.10; *PB* 18.7.10; *ŚB* 8.5.3.4). It is often used with the epithet highest (*uttama*) in the *Atharvaveda* (4.14.6; *VS* 9.10; 12.63), or third (*tṛtīya*) referring to the threefold division of earth, atmosphere and sky (*div*). The *nāka* is said to be on the third ridge (*pṛṣtha*) above the luminous space (*rocana*) of the sky (*VS* 15.50).

**Hell:** See **Eschatology**. Hell is represented as a place of punishment for the evil doers. This is characterized as low and dark, as a kind of pit (*RV* 9.73.8; 10.152.4). There is, however, no sordid picture of hell and its terrors. According to the *Ṛgveda* (1.164.30) the soul of the dead moves in its own power, the immortal one having a common origin with the mortal one, i.e. the body. He passes into the next world *sarvatanuḥ saṅgaḥ* with whole body and all his members (*AV* 5.6.11; 18.4.64; *ŚB* 5.6.1.1; 9.1.8.6; 12.8.3.31; *TS* 5.3.52; 6.3; 6.6.3; *TB* 3.8.20.5; 10.11.1). In the *Ṛgveda* (2.29.6, 3.26.8; 4.5.5; 25.6; 7.104, 3, 10.17; 10.125.4) there are hints of evil awaiting evil-doers but it is not until the *Atharvaveda* (2.14.3; 5.19.3; 30.11; 8.2.24; 12.4.36; 18.3.3; *VS* 30.5; *ŚB* 11.6.1; *TB* 1.42-44) that a hell of punishment is set out and it is in the *Śatapatha Brāhmaṇa* (6.2.2.27) and *KB* (12.3) that good and evil deeds are said to produce happiness or hell hereafter. But there is no clear hint of the *naraka* of later times in the *Ṛgveda* as the ultimate destination of the wicked. The Vedic poet not being deeply moral, his verses do not convey as would those of a man convinced of sin warnings of future judgement.

**Heman, Hemanta:** Early Winter (*RV* 10.161.4; *AV* 6.55.2; 8.2.22; 12.1.36; *KS* 36.6; *TS* 2.6.1.1; 5.7.2.4; *VS* 13.58; *TB* 1.4.10.10; *ŚB* 1.5.4.5; 10.4.5.2; 11.2.7.32).

**Helmet:** The use of helmet may be evidenced from a few passages of the *Ṛgveda* where the word *śiprā* (*RV* 5.54.11; 8.7.25) seems to signify a helmet. Geldner accepts *śiprā* (*RV* 8.7.25; 5.54.11) as a helmet. Presumably in *ayaḥ-śiprā* (*RV* 4.37.4), *hiraṇya-śiprā* (*RV* 2.34.3), *hari-śiprā* (*RV* 10.96.4) and *hiri śiprā* (*RV* 2.2.5; 6.25.9) we have references to helmets of metal. *Śiprin* in the *Ṛgveda* (1.29.2; 1.81.4; 6.44.14) would denote 'one wearing a helmet'.

**Hemp:** *Bhaṅgā*, 'hemp', is mentioned in the *Atharvaveda* (11.6.15). In the *Ṛgveda* (9.61.13) it is an epithet of *soma*, presumably in the sense of 'intoxicating', which then came to designate 'hemp'. *Śana* denotes a kind of 'hemp', *cannabis sativa* or *crotolavia juncea*. It is mentioned in the *Atharvaveda* (2.4.5) as growing in the forest, and used like the *jaṅgīḍa*, as a remedy against several diseases. It also occurs in the *Śatapatha Brāhmaṇa* (3.2.1.11; 6.6.1.24; 6.6.2.15).

**Henotheism:** In the *Ṛgveda* there is no fixed order of seniority among the gods, as in a pantheon, in the strict sense of the term. Far too many functions, attributes, and offices are held in common by two or more deities. There is a sort of communism or democracy among them, though it is not consistent, and for this, 'the belief in individual gods alternately regarded as the highest' (i.e. Henotheism or Kathenotheism as Max Müller has named it) is responsible. The special deity that the poet happens to be invoking monopolizes, for the time being, all the highest attributes. The god is addressed for the moment as if he were the greatest and even the only god. Almost in the same breath, however, (in the very next stanza or hymn) this mighty god is described as dependent on others. In fact, the joint exercise of various powers, functions, and notable deeds by two or more, or all the gods, is almost a favourite theme in the *Ṛgveda* hymnology. In a thoroughly impartial spirit, the mutual co-operation, interdependence and subordination of the various deities in pairs or larger groups is often described. There is hardly a god in the *Ṛgveda* so insignificant as not to receive homage from others, not excluding the highest. It should, however, be remembered that the divine host of the *Ṛgveda* is not a pantheon (technically speaking) with an acknowledged overlord which accounts for this apparently inconsistent evaluation of divinities in the *Ṛgveda*. It has been urged, for example, that the inconsistency may be due to the partiality of particular *ṛṣi* or Vedic *śākhā* to a particular god. But the force of this argument is considerably weakened by the large number of Ṛgvedic repetition, and (on the whole) their even distribution throughout the text. As Bloomfield observed, 'They mark the entire Mantra literature as, in a sense, epigonal, and they forbid pungent theories about profound differences between the family books, their authors, and their geographical provenience' (*Rigveda Repetitions*, Preface, p. xviii). It has also been contended, as Macdonell (*Vedic Mythology*, p. 16) points out, that Viśvadevas or all-gods, all the deities, even the lesser ones, are praised in succession and that as the great mass of the hymns was composed for the ritual of the offering, which included the worship of almost the entire pantheon, the technical priest could not but know the exact relative position of each god in that ritual. The explanation rests on the assumption that the ritualists of a later age, when sacrificial technique was enormously developed, had to, and could, preserve very scrupulously the mythological values or Ṛgvedic poetry.

**Herbivore:** See under **Cattle**. Among the herbivores the Vedic texts refer to the elephant, horse, goat, camel, rhinoceros, deer, ram, etc., *Ibha* is a word of somewhat doubtful sense and interpretation. It is found only in the Saṃhitās (*TS* 1.2.14.1; *VS* 13.9), and specially in the *Ṛgveda* (1.84.17; 4,4.1; 9.57.3). In the opinion of Pischel and Geldner it denotes elephants. The view is supported by the authority of the commentators Sāyaṇa and Mahīdhara. The *Nirukta* (6.12), too, gives elephant as one of the senses of the word. The derivative word *ibhva* may, thus, be naturally explained as denoting 'great', 'rich', 'mighty', merely 'rich' and so forth. *Gaja*, the common name of the elephant in epics and later Sanskrit, is only found in the late *Adbhuta Brāhmaṇa*. *Nāga* appears once in the *Śatapatha Brāhmaṇa* (11.2.7.12) in the form *mahānāga*, where great snake or great elephant may be meant. In the *Bṛhadāraṇyaka Upaniṣad* (1.3.24) and in a citation found in the *Aitareya Brāhmaṇa* (8.22) the sense of elephant is clearly intended. In the Sūtras the mythic *nāga* already occurs. *Mṛgahastin*, the animal with a hand, is mentioned in two passages of the *Ṛgveda* (1.64.7; 4.16.14), in which the elephant is also meant. Later, the adjective *hastin* alone became the regular name of the animal. The elephant is also denoted in the *Ṛgveda* by the descriptive term *mṛga*, *vāraṇa* (*RV* 8.33.8; 10.40.8), the wild or dangerous animal. The adjective *vāraṇa* similarly became one of the names for elephant in the later language. Pischel's view that the catching of elephants, using tame female elephants, is already alluded to in the *Ṛgveda* (8.2.6; 10.40.8) seems very doubtful. In the *Aitareya Brāhmaṇa* (8.23.3) elephants are described as black, white-toothed, and adorned with gold. *Vāraṇa* in two passages of the *Ṛgveda* (8.3.8, 10.40.8) is taken by Roth as an adjective with *mṛga*, meaning wild beast. But the sense intended must have been elephant, with the usual sense of *vāraṇa* in the *Atharvaveda* (5.14.11) denoting a female elephant. *Śukla-danta* white-tusked is applied as an epithet to *mṛga*, wild beast, in the *Aitareya Brāhmaṇa* (8.23.3). By this term an elephant must be meant. The animal was tamed for its strength (*RV* loc. cit; *AV* 2.22.1; 2.22.3) as well as its virility (*AV* 3.22.6; 6.70.2). It is mentioned with man and monkey as one of the beasts that take hold by the hand (*hastadāna*), as opposed to those that take hold by the mouth (*mukhadāna*) (*TS* 6.4.5.7; *MS* 4.5.7). It was tamed, as the expression *hastipa*, elephant-keeper, shows and tame elephants were used to catch others. But there is no trace of its use in war, though Ktesias, and Megasthenes both record such in their times. *Akra*, in several passages of the *Ṛgveda* (1.143.7; 1.189.7; 3.1.12; 4.6.3; 10.77.2) means, horse. *Aśva* is the commonest word for horse in the Vedic literature. The horse is also called the runner (*ātya*), the swift (*arvant*), the strong, for pulling (*vājin*), the runner (*sapti*), and the speeding (*haya*). The mare is fermed *aśvā, atvā, arvatī, vaḍavā*, etc. Horses of various colour were known, green (*harita, hari*), red (*aruṇa, aruṣa, pisaṅga, rohita*), dark brown (*syāva*), white (*śveta*), etc. A white horse with black ears is mentioned in the *Ṛgveda* as being of special value (*AV* 5.17.15). Horses were highly prized (*AV* 1.83.1; 4.32.17; 5.4.11; 8.78.2), and were not rare, as Roth thought, for as many as four hundred mares are mentioned in one *Dānastuti* 'Praise of Gifts' (*RV* 8.55.3; 5.33.8; 6.47.22; 6.47.23; 6.47.24; 6.63.10; 8.6.47; 8.46.22). They were on occasion ornamented with pearls and gold (*RV* 10.68.11). Owing to their swiftness, mares were preferred for drawing chariots. They were also used for drawing carts, but were not originally so employed (*ŚB* 5.5.4.35). No mention is made of riding in battle, but for other purposes it was not unknown. Horses were often kept in stalls (*RV*

9.86.41; *AV* 6.77.1; 19.55.1) and fed there. But they were also allowed to go out to graze and were then hobbled (*RV* 1.162.14; 1.162.16; *BU* 6.2.13; *CU* 5.1.12; *SA* 9.7). They were watered for getting themselves cooled after racing (*RV* 2.13.5; 2.34.3; *MS* 1.11.6). Their attendants are frequently referred to as *aśvapāla* (*ŚSS* 16.4.5), *aśva-pā* (*VS* 30.11; *TS* 3.4.9.1) and *aśvapati* (*VS* 16.24; *KS* 17.13). Stallions were frequently castrated (*vadhri VS* 8.46.30). Besides reins (*raśmayaḥ*), reference is made to halters (*aśvābhidhānī*), *AV* 4.36.10; 5.14.6; *AB* 6.35; *ŚB* 6.3.1.26; 13.1.2.1) and whips (*aśvajani RV* 5.6.2.7; 6.75.13; *VS* 29.50). Horses from the Indus were of special value (*BU* 6.2.13; *SA* 9.7), as also horses from the Sarasvatī (*RV* 10.75.8). *Pūrvayaḥ* is a term applied to the horse (*aśva*) in the *Taittirīya Brāhmaṇa* (1.1.5.6) and elsewhere (*ŚB* 2.1.4.17; *KS* 13.3). It may either refer to a horse fastened in front as a leader or merely mean drawing for the first time, as understood by the commentator on the *Taittirīya Brāhmaṇa*. *Haya* is found once in the *Vājasaneyī Saṃhitā* (23.19) in the sense of horse. *Mahāsuhaya*, a great (i.e. high-spirited) horse, is how steed from the Indus (*saindhava*), which tears away the peg of its hobble (*padbisa-śaṅkhu*), is described in the *Bṛhadāraṇyaka Upaniṣad* (6.2.13). *Haya* denotes horse in the *Ṛgveda* (5.46.1; 7 7.4.4; and later, *Vājasaneyī Saṃhitā* 7.47; 22.19). In the *Atharvaveda* (6.102.2) Rājāśva (king's horse) merely seems to denote a powerful horse. *Rohita* denotes a red horse in the *Ṛgveda* (1.94.10; 1.134.9; 2.10.2; 3.6.6). *Aja* is the ordinary name for goat in the *Ṛgveda* and later literature. (*RV* 10.16.4; 1.162.2; 1.162.4; *AV* 9.5.1; *VS* 21.9). The goat is also called *basta, chaga* and *chāga*. Goats and sheep (*ajavayaḥ*) are very frequently mentioned together (*RV* 10.90.10; *AV* 8.7.25; *VS* 3.43). The female goat is spoken of as producing two or three kids (*TS* 6.5.10.1) and goat's milk was well-known (*TS* 4.1.6.1; 5.1.7.4). As representative of Pūṣan, the goat plays an important part in the ritual of burial (*RV* 10.16.4). The occupation of a goatherd (*ajapāla*) was a recognized one, being distinguished from that of a cowherd and a shepherd (*VS* 30.11; *TB* 3.4.9.1). *Chāga*, goat, is found in the *Ṛgveda* (1.162.3) and not rarely later (*VS* 19.89; 21.40; 21.41; *ŚB* 3.3.3.4; 5.1.3.14; *MS* 3.11.2). *Basta* denotes the goat in the *Ṛgveda* (1.161.13) and the later literature (*TS* 2.3.74; 5.3.1.3; 5.7.10.1; *KS* 17.2; *VS* 14.9; *TB* 1.3.7.7; *BU* 1.4.9; *AV* 8.6.12; 11.9.22). *Mahāja* a great goat (*aja*) is mentioned in the *Śatapatha Brāhmaṇa* (3.4.1.2). *Uṣṭi, uṣṭra*, both of these words mean camel, of which the former is quite rare (*RV* 10.106.2; *TS* 5.6.21.1; *KS* 15.2). Roth and Aufrecht hold that in the *RV* (1.138.2; 8.5.37; 8.6.48; 8.46.22; 8.46.31), *AV* (20.127.2; 20.132.13), *VS* (13.50) and the *Brāhmaṇas* (*ŚB* 1.2.3.9; *AB* 2.8) the sense of 'humped bull' or 'buffalo' is found. *Dhumra* (*TS* 1.8.21.1) is camel. *Koṅgo* on *khaḍga* (*MS* 3.14.21; *VS* 24.40) seems to be rhinoceros. *Eni* (*AV* 5.14.11; *RS* 5.5.15.1; *MS* 3.4.17; *VS* 24.38) was female antelope, perhaps the female form of *ela* (*RV* 1.165.2; 169.6-7; 5.54.5, 10.77.2) the skin of which is said to be worn by the Maruts (*RV* 1.166.30). *Pisa* (*RV* 1.64.8) is taken by Sāyaṇa to mean a deer (*ruru*, *TS* 5.5.19.1; *VS* 24.27; 24.29; *MS* 3.14.9). *Eḍaka* appears to denote a 'vicious ram' in the *Śatapatha Brāhmaṇa* (12.4.1.4; cf. 2.5.2.15) and the *JB* (1.51.4). *Meṣa* denotes 'ram' in the *Ṛgveda* (1.43.6; 1.116.16; 8.2.40; 10.27.17) and later (*AV* 6.49.2; *VS* 3.5.9; 19.90; 24.30; *TS* 7.4.12.1; *Saḍ.B.* 1.1; *ŚB* 3.3.4.18), while *meṣī* means 'sheep' (*RV* 1.43.6; *VS* 3.5.9; 24.1; *TB* 1.6.4.4). Both words are also used to denote the wool (*meṣa RV* 8.36.11; *meṣī* 9.8.5; 9.86.47; 9.107.11) of the sheep, especially as employed for the *soma* filter. A wild (*āraṇya*) ram is mentioned in the *Vājasaneyī Saṃhitā* (24.30).

**Herbs:** Herbs are sometimes considered to be deities and praised in the *Ṛgveda* (10.97.23); the *soma* is called the best herb. In the *Atharvaveda* (6.91.2) a hair-increasing herb is praised as the most-excellent (*śreṣtha*) of remedies, the best (*variṣtha*) of plants equal to Soma and Varuṇa. The same is said of a herb which is used for the sake of making someone impotent (*AV* 6.138.1). The *kuṣtha*-plant used for removing *takman* (a fever) is addressed as the best (*uttama*) of the herbs, and as the tiger among beasts of prey (*AV* 19.39.4). The herb called *muñja* is said to have 'hundred remedies' pertaining to flux and other diseases (*AV* 2.3.2). An apotropic herb, *apanarga*, is described as the wiper (*apanarga*) and controller (*vasin*) of disease (*AV* 4.17.8), and the mistress of remedies (*AV* 4.17.1). The plant is described as all-healing (*viśvabheṣaja AV* 19.39.5; 8; 9). The *kanva* herb is said to be life (*āyus*)—giving, famous and all-healing (*viśvabheṣaja AV* 6.52.3). The plant named *nitatni* is also eulogized as 'all healing' (*AV* 6.126.3). Homages are also paid to the herbs (*AV* 6.20.2) along with Varuṇa and other dieties. The herbs are supposed to be aware of their own power (*AV* 6.109.21). The herbs are thus supposed to be deities on whose favour the cure of the patient depends. The physician says, 'Propitious to thee (the patient) be the herbs,' (*AV* 8.2.15). 'Propitious to thee, be rice and barley, free from *balāsa* (name of a disease), causing no burning; drive off the *yakṣma*, make these free from distress' (*AV* 8.2.17). Elsewhere it is said, 'the blood-drinking evil being the embryo-eating *kanva*, do thou make disappear, O spotted-leaf . . . remove the life-obstructing *kanvas*. O divine spotted-leaf, burn them like fire'. (*AV* 2.25.3 ff). Herbs are requested for good delivery (*AV* 8.6.9-10) and for other purposes. The *samī* plant is lauded for manifold purposes (*AV* 6.10.3). In the *Atharvaveda* (6.72.1), the *arka* (plant) is similarly lauded. The *nitatni* herb, which one uses for fastening the hair, is said to be 'born of divine one, namely, the earth' (*AV* 6.136.1). Similarly, the *varaṇa* is called a divine forest-tree which wards off the *yakṣma* disease (*AV* 6.85.1). In the *Atharvaveda* (8.7.4) it is said, 'I call for thee (the diseases) the plants that belong to all the gods; formidable, giving life to me.' See also **Medicinal Plants**.

**Herd:** The word *yūtha*, means herd. It is referred to in *Ṛgveda* (1.10.2; 1.81.7, 3.55.17, 4.2.18, 4.38.5, 4.38.5, 5.4.19, 9.71.9). *Atharvaveda* (5.20.3) and *Taittirīya Saṃhitā* (5.7.2.1).

**Herdsman:** The terms *gopa*, *gopāla* and *paśupa* denote herdsman. While grazing, the cattle were under the care of a herdsman (*gopa, gopāla*) armed with a goad, and they were liable to all sorts of dangers, such as being lost, falling into pits, breaking limbs and being stolen (*RV* 1.120.8; 6.54.5; 6.5.4.7). The marking of the ears of cattle was repeatedly adopted, no doubt, to indicate ownership (*RV* 6.28.3; *MS* 4.2.9). The term *paśupa* seems to have meant herdsman. It is referred to in the *Ṛgveda* (1.114.9, 1.114.6; 4.6.4, 10.142.2). Metaphorically the word *paśupa* is applied to Pūṣan.

**Hereditary Kingship:** Kingship in post-Ṛgvedic period was sometimes hereditary, as is indeed shown by several cases where the descent can be traced. Mention may be made in this connection of the Pārikṣitas and the kings of Janaka's line; hereditary kingship is also suggested by the expression *daśapuruṣairājya*—a kingdom of ten generations—occurring in the *Śatapatha Brāhmaṇa* (12.9.31-3). But elective monarchy was not unknown (*AV* 8.12). Sometimes the selection was made by the people and occasionally by the ministers. The choice was ordinarily limited to the members of the royal family only, as is shown by the legend in Yāska (*Nir.* 2.10) of the Kuru brothers Devāpi and Śāntanu.

**Hermionitis Cordifolla:** *Pṛśniparṇi* (having a speckled leaf) is the name of a plant mentioned in a hymn of the *Atharvaveda* (2.57.7), which was used as a protection against evil beings procuring abortion, called *kaṇvas* (presumably a sign of hostility to the *Kaṇva* family). It also appears in the *Śatapatha Brāhmaṇa* (13.8.1.16), being identified with *permionitis cordifolia* by the *St. Petersburg Dictionary*, but in a subsequent contribution Roth suggests that it is the same as a plant later called *lakṣmaṇa*, and regarded as curing barrenness. The scholiast on the *KŚS* (25.7.17) thinks that the *glycine debilis* is meant. Macdonell and Keith II, 18-19.

**Heroic Man:** Heroic man (*vīra*) in the *Ṛgveda* (1.18.4; 1.114.8; 4.29.2; 5.20.4; 5.61.5) and later *Atharvaveda* (2.26.4; 3.5.8), etc., means 'man' as strong and heroic. But, collectively, in the singular this word denoted male offspring as an object of great desire, or *putra* to the Vedic Indians (*RV* 1.1.3; 6.24.10, 6.45.6). But in the *Pañcaviṃśa Brāhmaṇa* (19.1.4) a list of eight-*vīras* of the king is found constituting his supporters and entourage. These eight *vīras* were brother of a king his son, *Purohita*, *Mahiṣī*, *Sūta*, *Grāmaṇī* .*Kṣattṛ* and *Saṃgrahitṛ*.

**Hetairai:** In the *Ṛgveda* (1.134.3; 3.53.8; 8.17.7; *AV* 14.1.36; 20.136.5; *AB* 5.7.8; 15.2; *VS* 30.22; *TB* 3.4.15.1) there are many references to illegitimate love and to the abandonment of the offspring of such unions (*RV* 2.29.1). Even a protege of Indra is often mentioned as the *paravṛkta* or *paravri* (*RV* 2.13.12; 2.15.7; 4.19.9; 4.30.16). The 'son of a maiden' (*kumārī-putra*) is spoken of in the *Vājasaneyī Saṃhitā* (30.6). The terms *puṃścalī* (*AV* 14.1.36, 20.136.5; *AB* 3.27) means harlot and there are other clear references to prostitution. The *Taittirīya Saṃhitā* (7.4.19.2, 7.4.19.3) and *Vājasaneyī Saṃhitā* (23.30.23.31) refer to illicit unions of śūdra and Ārya, both male and female and several types of women whose designation apparently meant 'courtesan' (*atitvari*, *VS* 30.15; *TB* 3.4.11.1), while the 'dyeing woman' (*rajayitrī*) is dedicated to sensuality (*VS* 30.12; *TB* 3.4.7.1). There are many references to hetairai in other passages of the *Ṛgveda*, especially where mention is made of Uṣas, the goddess of Dawn, who in their view is the characteristic Hetaira. At any rate, there is little, doubt that the 'dancer' (*nṛtu*) referred to in one passage of the *Ṛgveda* (1.92.4) was a Hetaira. When women are referred to as going to the *samana*, or 'place of meeting', hetairai are probably meant (*RV* 4.58.8; 6.75.4; 10.168.2). Grave cases of immorality are also alluded to in the *Ṛgveda* (10.162.5). Girls who had lost their natural protectors—father or brother—were likely to be reduced to live by immorality (*RV* 1.124.7; 2.29.1; 4.5.5; *AV* 1.17.1).

**Himavant:** *Himavant* 'snowy' appears as an epithet of mountain in the *Atharvaveda* (12.1.11). There seems no reason to deny that in all the passages the word refers to the mountains now called Himalaya, though it is possible that the name may include mountains not strictly belonging to the Himalayan range (*AV* 4.9.9; 5.4.2, 8; 5.25.7; 6.95.3; 10.121.4; *TB* 5.5.11.1; *VS* 24.30, 25.12; *AB* 8.14).

**Hiraṇyagarbha:** In the field of cosmogonical speculations the concept of the World-Egg, i.e. the universe in the shape of an egg floating on the primordial waters, is current among all mythologies of the world. The idea that life remains latent in egg was quite in accordance with primitive empiricism, and therefore it is not at all difficult to understand why the egg was so significant in ancient cosmogonical and cosmographical speculations. The Egyptians believed that Ra, the god of brightness, first appeared as a shining egg that floated upon the water's breast. He rose from the primordial waters as the sun-egg. The god Ptah also came from the egg which, according to one myth, was produced by the Chaos-goose, and to another, issued from the mouth of Khnumu (cf. Erman, A., *Handbook of Egyptian Religion*, Eng. tr. London, 1907, pp. 26 ff).

According to the Rhapsodist cosmogony of ancient Greece, we also find the idea of the Cosmic-Egg, from which was issued the first Orphic god. Zeller points out that the said idea is directly borrowed by the Greeks from the Phoenicians (*Pre-Socratic Philosophy*, I, London, 1881, pp. 102 ff). But we shall see that exactly the same idea is found in Indian legends. The Ṛgvedic conception of the Golden Germ, or Hiraṇyagarbha, emanating from the primeval waters (10.121) later developed into that of the World-Egg of *Brahman.* Full development of the conception of the World-Egg theory is, however, to be found in the post-Ṛgvedic literature. Hiraṇyagarbha is said to have arisen, in the beginning, from the great water pervading the universe and thus created the world out of the eternally pre-existing matter. The epithet Prajāpati is also applied to him. He is described as the lord of all beings, who upholds heaven and earth, who gives life and breath, whose command even the gods obey, who is the god over all gods, and the one animating principle of their being (*RV* 10.121). It is interesting to note that in another passage of the *Ṛgveda* we are told that the waters contained the primordial germ, the floating egg from which arose Viśvakarman, the creator and maker of the world (10.82). In the Nāsadīya hymn (10.129.1), the question is raised whether the fathomless waters existed before the formation of the world. Waters are said to have given birth to Agni (10.2.7; 10.91.6; cf. 3.1.3; 9.4). Savitṛ is sometimes called *apām napāt*, son of waters (10.149.2), and the eipthet is more commonly a reference to Agni. Water are also connected with Aditi (10.63.2), and in another passage (1.18.1), they are said to know the birthplace of heaven and earth. Instead of the five elements of later philosophy, the *Ṛgveda* postulates only water as the primordial element, or matter from which others gradually evolved. In the *Śatapatha Brāhmaṇa* we have a number of legends on creation. According to one (VI. 1.1.8 ff), Prajāpati wanted to become numerous and, practising fervour, he created at first *Brahman* and then the triple science which became his support. Resting on that support he produced waters and entered them with that triple science. There arose an egg which he touched. He said, 'Let it exist, let is multiply.' Then he created the earth out of the waters. He toiled and practised fervour and thus created foam, clay, saline soil and sand, gravel, rock, ore, gold and plants, and with these he clothed the earth. In another passage of the same text (11.1.6), the waters seem to have believed to be coeval with Prajāpati or to have preceded him. In the beginning this universe was nothing but water. The waters desired, 'How can we be reproduced?' So saying, they toiled and performed austerity, and a Golden Egg came into existence. Being produced, it then became a year, wherefore this golden egg floated about for the period of a year. From it, Prajāpati came into existence. In the *Chāndogya Upaniṣad* (3.19), where the idea of the World-Egg is found, it is stated that in the beginning the world was merely a non-entity, and from this state it became existent. Likewise, Prāṇa of the earlier texts continues to develop as a cosmogonic principle in the Upaniṣads until it becomes identical with *Brahman* (cf. *Kau.Su* 2.1-2). The *Bṛhadāraṇyaka Upaniṣad* (1.4.7) speaks of the formless creator as having entered the body right up to the tips of the nails and assumed therein the name and function of the *prāṇa. Kāla*, or time of the *Atharvaveda*, also occurs as a cosmogonic force in the *Maitrāyaṇi Upaniṣad* (6.14), in which, it is identified with *Brahman*, as well as in the *Śvetāśvtara* (1.2). The conception of Hiraṇyagarbha or Golden Germ, is found mainly in the *Śvetāśvatara* and the *Maitrāyaṇi Upaniṣad*. In the former work (3.4; 4.12), Hiraṇyagarba is described as one created by the Supreme Being, while in the latter (6.8; 7.7) he is made identical with the *ātman* or *Brahman*.

**Historical Narratives:** Itihāsa, as a kind of literature, is repeatedly mentioned along with Purāṇa in the later texts of the Vedic period. The earliest reference to both occurs in the fifteenth book of the *Atharvaveda* (15.6.4 ff). Itihāsa then appears in the *Śatapatha Brāhmaṇa* (13.4.3.12.13) the *Jaiminīya Brāhmaṇa* (1.53), *Bṛhadāraṇyaka Upaniṣad* (2.4.10; 4.1.2; 5.11), *Chāndogya Upaniṣad* (3.4.1.2; 7.1.2.4; 2.1.71.1). In the latter it is expressly declared with Purāṇa to make up the fifth Veda, while the *SSS* (16.2, 21.27) makes the *Itihāsa-Veda* and the *Purāṇa-Veda* appear also in the *Gopatha Brāhmaṇa* (1.10) while the *Śatapatha Brāhmaṇa* (13.4.3.12, 13) identifies the Itihāsa as well as the Purāṇa with the Veda. In one passage Anvākhyāna and Itihāsa are distinguished as different classes of works, but the exact point of distinction is obscure. The former was probably supplementary. The *Taittirīya Āraṇyaka* (2.9) mentions Itihāsas and Purāṇas in the plural. There is nothing to show in the older literature what distinction there was between Itihāsa and Purāṇa. The Itihāsa-Purāṇa was a collection of the old legends of all sorts—heroic, mythological, cosmogonic, genealogical and so forth and this branch of literature was known to Patañjali.

**Holy Mountains:** Here and there, the *Ṛgveda* invokes the mountains with other deities such as Indra, Savitṛ, or with the waters, trees, plants, heaven and earth. They are described as rejoicing in the sacrificial offering. Parvata, the mountain, is once found invoked as a companion of Indra in the dual compound Indraparvata. In the Brāhmaṇas, we hear a good deal of the salve from the mountain Trikakubh, which had wonderful powers. In the late *Hiraṇyakeśi Gṛhya Sūtra* there occurs an obscure phrase which suggests that in applying slave to the eyes, it was thought that the spirit of the mountain entered into the performer of the rite. Keith, 187-8.

**Homa:** Offering made to fire in the name of different deities. It is necessary in numerous ceremonies and rites. To perform *homa* a raised square platform known as *sthaṇḍila* is built. In the middle of this, a line is drawn from north to south, and five straight lines from east to west are drawn from the middle one. The area covered by these six lines is where the fire should be made. To the north of the platform are kept *havis*, *idhma* (fuel) and *barhis* (*kuśa*). The brāhmaṇa sits on the south facing the north, while the sacrificer sits on the west facing the east, i.e. to the priest's left. Offerings are thrown into the fire with *mantras.* If there is no specific directive about the dieties to whom the offerings are to be made, the deities should be Agni, Indra, Prajāpati and Viśva-devas. At the end, there are offerings to Agni Sviṣṭakṛt (*ĀGS.* 1.3; *SGS.* 1.7).

**Honey:** Honey is considered to have a magico-medicinal power-substance. Before they were bound around the neck of a patient, amulets were put in sour milk and honey for three days (*Kau.Su.* 26.15). To a patient suffering from dropsy, the physician gave a drink of half water and half butter-milk mixed with honey. The drink was consecrated with the *Atharvaveda* (6.96).

**Honey Plant:** *Madhugha* or *madhuga*, 'honey-plant', is the name of a sweet herb in the *Atharvaveda* (1.34.4; 6.102.3).

**Honey-whip:** The words *madhukaśā* and *madhoḥ-kaśā* mean honey-whip. These are referred to in the *Ṛgveda* (1.22.3; 1.157.4), *Atharvaveda* (10.7.19; 9.1.5), and *Pañcaviṃśa Brāhmaṇa* (21.10.12). These were used by the Aśvins to impart sweetness to the sacrifice.

**Horse Keeper:** In the *Vājasaneyī Saṃhitā* (30.11) and *Taittirīya Brāhmaṇa* (3.4.9), we come across such terms as *aśvapā* and *aśvapati* or a horsekeeper, *aśva-naya* or a horse leader and *aśvasāda* or a horse rider, which also occur respectively in *Vājasaneyī Saṃhitā* (16.24), *Kāṭhaka Saṃhitā* (17.13) and *Chāndogya Upaniṣad* (6.8.3; 6.8.5).

**Horse Sacrifice:** See **Royal Ceremonies**.

**Hotṛ:** One of the four major priests required to perform a sacrifice. He is the 'invoker' who must praise the gods and invoke them to the sacrifice. It is his duty it is to select the canon for each particular rite of the Soma sacrifice by selecting the verses applicable to it from the hymns of the *Ṛgveda* and to recite them.

**Hotrā:** Hotrā is frequently invited to the sacrifices along with Sarasvatī and several other goddesses. 'Let Hotrā pure, set among gods, amid the Maruts, Bhāratī, Ilā, Sarasvatī, Mahī rest on the grass adorable.' (*RV* 1.140.4).

**Hotwater-therapy:** Sometimes hot water was used for curing certain diseases. It was used in the case of fever (*Kau.Sū.* 26.25). When somebody was bitten by a serpent, the wound was washed with hot water, along with the recital of the *Atharvaveda* (5.13.5), (*Kau.Sū.* 29.8). The process is described in *Kau.Sū* (29.9). In the case of swelling of the neck, sprinkling of hot water consecrated with the *Atharvaveda* (7.74) was required (*Kau.Sū.* 32.10). For the sake of easy delivery, an offering was to be performed with the *Atharvaveda* (1.11.1). Then, the remnants of that offering were poured in hot water, which was sprinkled on the pregnant woman. (*KauSū.* 33.1).

**House:** *Niveśana* appears in the *Ṛgveda* (7.19.5) to denote 'dwelling'. It is also used to mean 'ant-hill', living place of the ants (*RV* 4.19.9). *Bṛhac-chandas* occurs in the *Atharvaveda* (3.12.3) denoting 'broad-roofed', an epithet of 'house' (*śālā*). *Veśman* appears in the *Ṛgveda* (10.107.10; 10.146.3), *Atharvaveda* (5.17.13; 9.6.30) and *Aitareya Brāhmaṇa* (8.24.6) to signify 'house', in which place a man is adjusted. Single house (*eka-veśman*) of the king is discriminated with the abundant dwelling of the people (*ŚB* 1.3.2.14). *Dama* is found several times in the *Ṛgveda* (1.1.8; 1.61.9; 1.75.5; 1.43.4; 2.1.2) and *Vājasaneyī Saṃhitāeī* (8.24) which designates 'house'. *Oka* signifies 'house' in the *Ṛgveda* (1.132:5; 8.25.17; 8.49.3; 9.86.45). *Okas* has the same meaning (*RV* 1.66.2; 2.19.1; *MS* 2.5.3; *AV* 1.2.93). *Duroṇa* designates 'home' both literally and figuratively in the *Ṛgveda* (3.1.18; 3.25.5; 4.13.1; 5.7.6.4). *Atharvaveda* (7.17.3) and *Vājasaneyī Saṃhitā* (33.72). *Harmya* (*RV* 1.21.1; 1.166.4; 9.71.4; 9.71.4; 9.78.3; 10.73.10; *TB* 3.7.6.3) means 'house', including the stabling (*RV* 2.56.16; cf. 10.106.5). It was encompassed by a fence or wall of some kind, expressed in the *Ṛgveda* (7.55.6). House of Yama is found in the *Atharvaveda* (18.4.55). The word *śālā* is used in the *Atharvaveda* (5.31.5; 6.106.3; 8.6.10; 9.3.1,14.1.63), *Taittirīya Saṃhitā* (1.2.3.1) and *Śatapatha Brāhmaṇa* (3.1.1.6), which designates 'house' in the wider sense. It is also found to mean 'stall' for cattle, 'shed for corn', etc. (*AV* 3.12.1, cf. 9.3.1). The head of the household was called *śālā-pati* (*AV* 9.3.12) 'lord of the house', head of the household. According to the *Atharvaveda* (9.4.21) the house was fixed with two sides, four sides, six sides, eight sides and also ten sides. *Duryona* is referred to the *Ṛgveda* (1.174.7: 5.29.10; 5.32.3) to indicate 'house'. *Gṛha* is alluded to in the *Ṛgveda* (2.42.3; 3.5.3.6; 4.49.6; 8.10.1), *Atharvaveda* (1.27.4; 7.83.1), *Vājasaneyī Saṃhitā* (2.32; 4.33), *Aitareya Brāhmaṇa* (2.31; 8.21) and *Śatapatha Brāhmaṇa* (1.1.2.72; 1.6.1.19), where it is meant as 'house'. *Gaya* is alluded to in the *Ṛgveda* (1.7.4.2; 5.10.3; 5.44.7; 6.2.8), *Atharvaveda* (6.3.3; 6.84.1) and *Vājasaneyī Saṃhitā* (27.3) in the sense of 'house'. The word is also similar to 'household', for it takes in the meaning of the inmates as well as their possession. *Āvasatha* referred to in the *Atharvaveda* (9.6.5), *Taittirīya Brāhmaṇa* (1.1.10.6; 3.7.4.6), *Śatapatha Brāhmaṇa* (12.4.4.6), *Chāndogya Upaniṣad* (4.1.1) means abode.

This term reveals the sense of a place where guests, especially brāhmaṇas and others, were accepted during feasts and sacrifices. This place is considered somewhat like a modern *dharmaśālā*, a rest house for pilgrims. This word is used in the more general meaning as 'residing place' in the *Atharvaveda* (3.12). The Vedic people used hut or house as a dwelling whose roof is made of beams (*vaṃśa*) and grass (*tṛṇa*) (*AV* 3.12.5; 9.3.4). The term *palada* (*AV* 9.3.5; 9.3.17) is supposed to be bundles of straw or reeds, used for thatching house and making the sides wind and weather proof. The word *agniśālā* signifies a place for keeping the sacrificial fire in the *Atharvaveda* (9.3.7). It is a part of an ordinary house and may be presumed as the central hall. *Āgāra*, an uncommon word is referred to in the *Kauṣītaki Upaniṣad* (2.15) to mean 'house'. *Āgāra* is mentioned in the *Atharvaveda* (4.36.3) to designate 'chamber' according to Bloomfield (*SBE* 42.35). A hall or shed named *prācīnavaṃśa*, denoting 'having the supporting beam of the roof facing the east', is referred to in the *Śatapatha Brāhmaṇa* (3.1.1.6; 3.1.6.7; 3.6.1.23; 4.6.8.20) and *Kāṭhaka Saṃhitā* (22.13). *Dhanadhānī* means treasure-house in the *Taittirīya Āraṇyaka* (10.67). But Sāyaṇa interprets it as a deity who gives wealth to his devotees. The *Atharvaveda* (9.3.7) mentions a part of the house as women's quarter, termed *patnī-sadana*, on the main building, measuring the site by digging the pits for the posts, setting up the door and putting up the beams and the grass on the roof. Patnīśālā is also mentioned in *Vājasaneyī Saṃhitā* (19.18), *Śatapatha Brāhmaṇa* (4.6.9.8; 10.2.3.1; *AB* 5.22). So far as the parts and ingredients of a house are concerned, we have references to *akṣu* or wickerworks for houses made of mud and straw (*RV* 1.180.5; *AV* 8.8.18; 9.3.18), *agniśālā* (*AV* 9.3.7; *VS* 19.18) and *āṣṭrī* (*RV* 10.165.3) or fire-place, *upamit* (*RV* 1.5.9.1; 4.5.1; *AV* 9.31) *stambha* (*KS* 30.9; 31.1) and *skambha* (*RV* 1.34.2; 4.13.5) or pillar; *chandas* (*AV* 3.22.3) or roof, *dur, dvāra* or door (*RV* 1.13.6; *AV* 8.3.22; 14.1.63; *VS* 30.10; *ŚB* 1.6.1.19; 4.3.5.9; 11.4.4.2), *dvārapidhāna* or door-fastner (*ŚB* 11.1.1.1); *pakṣa* or side-post (*AV* 9.3.4), *parigha* (*ŚB* 11.1.1.1) or bar (*CU* 2.24.6 ff), *parimit* or cross-beam (*AV* 9.31), *palada* or bundle of straw for thatch (*AV* 9.3.5, 17); *pratimit* or support (*AV* 9.3.1), *viṣūvant* or ridge of the roof (*AV* 9.3.8), *sthūṇā* or pillar or post (*RV* 1.59.1; 5.45.2; 62.7; 8.7.14; 9.18.13; *AV* 3.12.6; 14.1.63; *ŚB* 14.1.3.7), etc.

**Household Deities:** The deity of the house and the home is Vāstospati, 'lord of the dwelling', who is invoked in one short hymn of the *Ṛgveda* (7.54.1-3) to bless man and beast, to remove diseases, to make cattle and horses prosper, to afford protection, and to grant a favourable entry. He is elsewhere described as the destroyer of diseases, is identified with Soma, brought into close connection with Tvaṣṭṛ, an artificer, and he is likened to Indra in connection with Soma pressers. In the late tenth book (*RV* 10.61.7) he appears as an observer of ordinances, who was fashioned by the gods. His character is made clearer by the fact that the Gṛhya Sūtras prescribe that offerings are to be made to him upon entering new house. There is no possible ground for supposing that either Pūṣan or Rudra, or Agni, or any other god is designated by the title, though Rudra actually bears the style in one passage (*TS* 3.4.10.3). The god is clearly the god of the house, who when a new house is built, comes and abides in it. In the Sūtras we hear more generally of deities of the house. Keith 188.

**Householder:** Householders are denoted in the term *gṛhapati* in the *Pañcaviṃśa Brāhmaṇa* (25.15.3). A householder, having a big house, is expressed as *mahāśālā* in *Chāndogya Upaniṣad* (5.11.1). In the *Atharvaveda* (9.3.12) the householder is called *śālāpati* to denote the lord of a house. *Gṛhya* denotes the members of the house in the *Śatapatha Brāhmaṇa* (2.5.2.14; 3.4.1.6; 12.4.1.4), etc. He is also equated with family, i.e. *gṛha* in *Śatapatha Brāhmaṇa* (1.7.4.12). *Ayasthūna* was also a term for householder or *gṛhapati*. His proper role in ritual is described in the general term for householders, which is *gṛhastha*.

**Human Sacrifice:** See **Puruṣamedha**.

**Hunter:** *Mṛgayu* (*RV* 10.40.4; *AV* 10.1.26; *VS* 16.27, 30.7; *PB* 14.9.12; *TB* 1.5.11, 3.4.3.1) means hunter. A number of persons who live either by hunting or fishing (viz., *mārgāra, kevarta, pauñjiṣṭha, maināla, bainda, ānda*, etc.) are enlisted as sacrificial victims (*VS* 30.16; *TB* 3.4.12.1). *Pāśin* (*RV* 3.45.1, 9.73.4; *AV* 17.1.8; *AB* 4.10) also denotes the hunter, having a noose. *Kirāta* is another term and the general name of the hunting tribes residing in the mountain cover and living on hunting, as stated in *Atharvaveda* (10.4.14); *Vājasaneyī Saṃhitā* (30.16) and *TB* (3.4.12.1). Birds were caught in nets (*pāśa, nidha, jāla, RV* 3.45.1, 9.83.4, 10.73.11; *AV* 10.1.30). Pits were used for catching big games (*RV* 10.39.8, 10.86.4, 10.51.6, 10.78.1, 5.15.3, 5.74.4).

**Hymns:** In the *Ṛgveda* (1.40.5) and later (*AV* 15.2.1, 19.54.3; *TB* 15.4.1) the term *mantra* means the 'hymn' as the product of the singer's creative thought. In the later Saṃhitās and Brāhmaṇas (*AV* 5.14.23; *Kau.B.* 26.1.5; *ŚB* 1.4.4.6, 11.2.1.6; *Nirukta* 7.1; *CU* 7.1.3) the word is regularly used to denote the poetic and prose utterances of the *Ṛṣis*, including not merely the verse-parts of the Saṃhitās, but also the prose formulae that betray their style and their special and archaic character.

# I

**Ilā:** Ilā is frequently invited to the sacrifices along with Sarasvatī and several other goddesses. Ilā, Sarasvatī and Mahī are three goddesses who bring delight and peace (*RV* 1.13.9). They rest on the grass and are adorable (*RV* 1.142.9). Sarasvatī, Bhāratī and Ilā bestow glorious fame on people (*RV* 1.188.8). Bhāratī with all her sisters, Ilā accordant with the gods, Agni, Sarasvatī and all her kindred rivers, are frequently addressed to bestow grace (*RV* 3.4.8). Ilā, Sarasvatī and Mahī bring wealth, being seated harmless on the Kuśa grass (*RV* 5.5.8). Sarasvatī, Bhāratī and Ilā, attend the *Pavamāna* sacrifice (*RV* 9.5.8). Bhāratī with her companions, Ilā showing like a human being and Sarasvatī with other deft goddesses present themselves before the worshippers (*RV* 10.110.8).

**Illegitimate Lover:** In the *Ṛgveda* (9.32.5) young women are mentioned as wooing their lovers. Their meetings were not always lawful or standardized or in accordance with social norms (*RV* 9.56.3; 10.34.5). An illegitimate lover was often a victim of *Puruṣamedha* (*VS* 30.9; *TB* 3.4.4.1). In the *Bṛhadāraṇyaka Upaniṣad* (6.4.11) Indra appears as the lover of Ahalyā, wife of Gautama. It was a case of illegitimate love, and since a god was involved in such an affair it appears that the practice was fairly common. The Vedic texts also betray incestuous relations between man and woman. The famous dialogue hymn, in which Yama and Yamī are characters, is suggestive of this. Prajāpati's incestuous relation with his daughter should also be taken into account. The ritual of the Varuṇa-Praghāsas (*MS* 1.10.11; *ŚB* 2.5.2.20) demands that the wife should name her previous lover or lovers and such declarations were taken in good humour. All sex-affairs were not necessarily illegitimate. In some sacrifices the union of an Ārya male and śūdra female was compulsory. In case of male-female relations the Vedic texts do not take a rigid moralistic stand.

**Immorality:** See **Amṛta, Amṛtatva**.

**Image Worship:** There is a divergence of opinion among scholars regarding image worship in Vedic India. Max Müller's view is that the religion of the Vedas knows no idol. Wilson holds the same view. Macdonell (*VM* 17-18) observes that, 'The physical appearance of the gods is anthropomorphic, though only in a shadowy manner, for it often represents only aspects of their natural bases figuratively described to illustrate their activities.' But quite an opposite view is expressed by others. Bollensen says that from the common appellation of the gods as *divo naras*, i.e. 'men of the sky', or simply as *naras*, i.e. 'men', and from the epithet *nṛpeśas*, i.e. 'having the form of men', it may be concluded that the Vedic Indians did not merely assign human forms to their gods in imagination, but also represented them in images. The *Ṛgveda* 1.25.12; 2.33.9; 3.4.5; 5.52.15 and a few such passages have been suggested by him in support of his view. S.V. Venkateswara has quoted a number of passages, such as the *Ṛgveda* (1.21.1; 4.58.3; 8.69.12), etc., to prove that the Vedas have an iconography. He has assigned the foremost place to the *Ṛgveda* (4.24.10), which is 'Who will buy my Indra for ten cows?' He holds that the context shows that there were permanent images of Indra made and hired for what was, in all probability, an Indra festival. Venkateswara has also referred to the *Ṛgveda* (1.10.1; 3.53.5-6; 4.17.4; 6.28.6; 7.56.14; 100.6; 8.69.12; 10.184.1; *Atharvaveda* (7.33.1 ff); *Taittirīya Saṃhitā* (1.7.12.1 ff) in support of his thesis. Scholars like Bollensen and Venkateswara have mainly utilized the anthropomorphic descriptions of the Vedic deities. But Keith (1.58) remarks, 'Though it would be wrong to ignore the anthropomorphic character of the gods, the Vedic pantheon has none of the clear-cut figures of the Greeks, and unlike the Greek deities it is seldom difficult to doubt that anthropomorphic forms but faintly veil the phenomena of nature.' B.C. Bhattacharyya in the long introduction to his work on *Indian Images* has also expounded the view in favour of image worship. Bloomfield (*Religion of the Veda* 89) writes, 'The mind of the Vedic poet is the rationalistic mind of the ruminating philosopher, rather than the artistic mind which reproduces the finished product. . . . On a pinch we could imagine a statue of the most material of the Vedic gods, Indra; but it is hard to imagine a statue of the god Varuṇa. As a matter of fact, there is no record of Vedic icons or Vedic temples.' R.P. Chanda (MIS London 1936) remarks that up to the time of Yāska, which synchronizes with the last phase of the Vedic period, the Vedic gods had not been invested with the forms in which they appear in the epics and Purāṇas. J.N. Banerjea, *Development of Hindu Iconography*, Calcutta 1956, 42 ff.

**Imperialism:** Details are lacking, but some of the *Ṛgveda* hymns speak of higher types of sovereign power for which the princes and chiefs fought. Of that we have the word *ekarāja* (*RV* 8.37.3) which meant nothing but a 'sole ruler' dominating over a vast area. Next, we have the word *samrāj* which meant a higher of type of sovereignty than that exercised by the ordinary king. Varuṇa especially is called a *samrāṭ* more than once (*RV 3.55.7; 56.5; 4.17.8; 8.19.32; cf.*

VS 5.32; 13.35, 20.5). In addition to this we have *adhirāja*, which in later literature meant a suzerain ruler of higher authority. It occurs in the *Ṛgveda* (10.128.3) where the speaker claims higher sovereign power: *vasavo rudrā ādityā uparispṛsam maugraṃ yettam-adhirājamakron*. The same expression occurs in the *Atharvaveda* (6.98.1; 9.10.24), *Taittirīya Saṃhitā* (2.4.14.2), *Maitrāyaṇī Saṃhitā* (4.12.3), *Kāṭhaka Saṃhitā* (8.17), etc. For details see **Kingship**.

**Implements:** *Awl:* The term for awl is *vāsī* (*RV* 1.37.2, 88.3; 5.53.4; 8.29.3), which is regarded as a weapon of the Maruts and as held by the god Tvaṣṭṛ. In the *Atharvaveda* (10.6.3) it is mentioned as a tool of carpenters.

*Axe:* Known by the terms *praśas* and *svadhīti*. The former is found in the *Aitareya Brāhmaṇa* (2.6) as an instrument of cutting. *Svadhīti* is more specific in denoting an axe, which was used for dissecting the sacrificial victims (*RV* 1.162.9 ff; 2.39.7; 3.2.10; 5.7.8; 7.3.9; 8.102.19; 10.89.7). In the *Atharvaveda* the term has the same meaning, which also refers to the weapon made of copper (6.141.2; 9.4.6; 12.3.33; 18.2.35). In one place in the *Ṛgveda* (10.92.15) it is referred to as the thunderbolt of Indra, but the later Saṃhitās (*TS* 6.3.3.2; *VS* 2.15) categorically refer to it as axe.

*Basket: Mūta* in the later Saṃhitās and Brāhmaṇas denotes a woven basket. *Mūtaka* means small basket (*KS* 36.14; *TB* 1.6.10.5; *ŚB* 2.6.2.17; *LSS* 8.3.8). The word *pavana* in the *Atharvaveda* (4.34.2; 18.3.11; *Nir* 6.9) denotes either a sieve or a winnowing basket.

*Blade:* In a general way, blade is denoted by the term *kṣura* (*RV* 1.166.10; 8.4.16; 10.28.9) which is described in the *Atharvaveda* (6.68.1-3; 8.2.7) as razor; *kṣurdhāra* (*JUB* 3.13.9) denotes the edge of a razor, like *kṣurasya-dhārā* of the *Bṛhadāraṇyaka Upaniṣad* (3.3.2).

*Bucket:* The word *āhāva* denotes a pail or bucket especially in connection with a well (*avalā*, *RV* 1.34.8; 6.7.2; 10.101.5; 112.6; Nir. 5.26). Another word *udañcana* which is mentioned metaphorically in the *Ṛgveda* (5.44.13), means a bucket in the Brāhmaṇas (*AB* 7.32; *ŚB* 4.3.5.21).

*Cooking Pan:* The regular word for a cooking pot is *ukhā*, usually mentioned in connection with sacrifice from the *Ṛgveda* onwards. It was *mṛnmayī*, i.e. made of clay (*RV* 1.162.13-15; 3.53.22; *AV* 12.3.23; *TS* 4.1.5.4; 5.1.6.3; *VS* 11.59). *Pacana* in the *Ṛgveda* (1.162.6) and the *Śatapatha Brāhmaṇa* (6.5.43.3-4; 14.1.2.21) denotes a vessel for cooking food. *Sthālī* also denotes a cooking pot, usually in the later Saṃhitās and Brāhmaṇas (*RV* 8.6-17; *TS* 6.5.10.5; *VS* 19.27; *AB* 1.11). *Sthālī-pāka*, a dish of rice or barley boiled in milk, is mentioned in the *Bṛhadāraṇyaka Upaniṣad* (6.4-18), *Aitareya Āraṇyaka* (3.2.4) and *Sāṅkhāyana Āraṇyaka* (11.6).

*Cord:* The word for cord or rope is *rasanā*. In the *Ṛgveda* (1.162.8) it has the sense of *rajju* or rope. It refers to various fastenings of a horse (*RV* 1.163.2,5; 4.19; 9.87.1; 10.18.14; 79.7). In later Saṃhitās the more general sense of rope is meant (*AV* 8.78.1; 10.9.2; *VS* 21.46; 22.2; 28.22; *TS* 6.6.4.3; *ŚB* 3.6.3.10). The word *raśmi* is not rarely found in the sense of a rope generally (*RV* 1.28.4; 4.22.8; 8.25.18; *AB* 4.19) but more usually it denotes either the reins or the traces of a chariot (*RV* 8.7.8; 10.130.7; *TS* 1.6.4.3; *VS* 23.14; *TB* 1.2.4.2). *Rajju* in the *Ṛgveda* (1.162.8) and later (*AV* 3.11.8; 6.121.2; *TS* 2.5.1.7; *ŚB* 1.3.1.14; 10.2.3.8; 11-3, 1.1, etc.) denotes rope or cord.

*Crate:* In the *Ṛgveda* (1.161.10; 162.13; 10.86-18) and the *Atharvaveda* (5.17-14) the word *sūnā* apparently means a woven wickerwork basket or crate for holding flesh.

*Fan:* The word *dhavitra* occurring in the *Śatapatha Brāhmaṇa* (14.1.3.30; 14.3.1-21) and *Taittirīya Āraṇyaka* (5.4.33) denotes a fan made of hide or leather, for blowing the sacrificial fire.

*Goad:* There are many terms for goad. In the *Atharvaveda* (15.2.1) and *Pañcaviṃśa Brāhmaṇa* (17.1.14) *pratoda* denotes the 'goad' of the Vrātya. Later the word was regularly used for 'goad' in general. *Aṣṭrā* is the plougher's goad, the badge of agriculture, which is mentioned several times in the *Ṛgveda* (4.57.4; 6.53.9; 6.58.2; 10.102.8). *Tottra*, a goad for driving cattle is mentioned in the *Śatapatha Brāhmaṇa* (12.4.1.10). *Toda* appears once to denote a goad in the *Ṛgveda* (4.16.11) but more often it is an agent noun meaning 'impeller'.

*Handle:* In the *Aitareya Brāhmaṇa* (6.24), *vajra* denotes the handle and *kuḷā* means the 'head' of a hammer. In later Saṃhitās (*TS* 4.2.5.6; *KS* 16.12; *AV* 3.17.3; *MS* 2.7.12) the word *tsaru* means a handle. As a handle of the plough it is also widely mentioned in later Saṃhitās and Brāhmaṇas.

*Kettle:* A pot with a lid (*apidhāna*) and hooks (*aṅka*), by which it could be hung over a fire (*RV* 1.162.13; *AV* 18.4.53), made of iron or bronze (*ŚB* 13.3.4-5), and used for boiling or cooking (*TS* 1.8.10.1; *AB* 1.1; *ŚB* 1.7.4-7; 2.5.3.4) is frequently mentioned in the *Ṛgveda* (1.7.6; 7.104.2; 9.52.3; 10.86.18; 167.4) and later Saṃhitās (*AV* 4.7.4; 9.5.6; 11.1.16; 3.18; 18.4.16; *TS* 1.6.1.2; *KS* 5.6; 32.6; *MS* 1.4-4.9).

*Knife:* Though the word *asi* denotes sword, in the *Ṛgveda* (1.162.20; 10.79.6; 86.18) and *Atharvaveda* (9.3.9; 10.1.20; 11.9.1) it denotes sacrificial knife and a knife used for various purposes, including the slaying of an enemy. *Praśas* in the *Aitareya Brāhmaṇa* (2.6) is also used in the sense of a knife.

*Ladle:* Juhū is the regular name in the *Ṛgveda* (8.44.5; 10.21.3) and *Atharvaveda* (18.4.5-6) for the tongue-shaped ladle in which butter was offered to the gods. In the Brāhmaṇas (*TB* 1.3.10.4; 3.7.4.9; *ŚB* 2.4.2.13) the name for the wooden ladle used for stirring up the oblations is *mekṣaṇa*.

*Leather Container:* A leather bag to hold fluids is mentioned in the *Ṛgveda* (1.191.10; 4.51.1; 5.83.7; 6.48.18; 103.2; 8.5.19; 9.18) and later texts (*AV* 7.18.1; *TS* 1.8.19.1; *VS* 26.18-19; *TB* 1.8.3.4; *PB* 5.10.2) as *dṛti*. In one passage (*RV* 7.89.2) it is called *dhmāta* or inflated. Milk and liquor are mentioned as being kept in bags (*PB* 14.11.26; 16.13.12). *Bhastrā* in the *Śatapatha Brāhmaṇa* (1.1.2.7; 1.6.3.16) also denotes a leather bottle or pouch.

*Mat:* References to mats made of split reeds are found in the *Śatapatha Brāhmaṇa* (3.5.3.9 cf. *ŚŚS* 8.3.24).

*Mortar:* The regular expression for mortar is *ulūkhala*, occurring frequently also in the compound *ulūkhala-muṣala*, 'mortar and pestle' (*RV* 1.28.6; *AV* 9.6.15; 10.9.26; 11.3.5; 12.3.1; *TS* 5.2.8.7; 7.2.1.3; *ŚB* 1.1.1.22; 4.6).

*Needle:* From the Ṛgvedic age to modern times, the term for needle is *sūcī* (*RV* 2.32.4; *AV* 11.10.3; *VS* 23.33; *TB* 3.9.6.4; *AB* 3.18; *ŚB* 13.2.10.2-3; *JUB* 10.10.3).

*Net:* The word for the net for catching animals is *mukṣijā* (*RV* 1.125.2; *Nir* 5.19).

*Peg:* Wooden peg is denoted by the term *śaṅku* (*RV* 1.164.48; *ŚB* 3.5.1.1; 2.2; 6.1.3; 13.8.4.1; *AB* 3.18). The pegs by which a skin is stretched out is referred to in the *Śatapatha Brāhmaṇa* (2.1.1.10).

*Pestle:* The word *muṣala* denotes a pestle in later Saṃhitās (*AV* 10.9.26; 11.3.3; 12.3.13; *TS* 1.6.8.3) and Brāhmaṇas (*ŚB* 12.5.2.7, etc).

*Plough, Ploughshare:* The regular word for plough in the Vedic texts (*RV* 4.57.4; *AV* 2.8.4; *TS* 6.6.7.4; *Nir.* 6.26) is *lāṅgala*. It is described as 'lance pointed' (*pavīravat*), 'well-lying' (*suśīmom*) and having a smooth handle (*tsaru*) in most texts (*AV* 3.17.3; *TS* 5.2.5.6; *KS* 16.11; *MS* 2.7.12; *VS* 12.71). Another term for plough is *sīra* mentioned in the *Ṛgveda* (4.57.8; 10.101.3-4), and later Saṃhitās (*AV* 6.30.1; 91.1; 8-9-16; *VS* 18.7; *MS* 2.11.4; *TB* 1.7.1.2). The ploughshare was known as *phāla* (*RV* 4.57.8; 10.117.7; *KS* 19.1; *AV* 3.17.5; *MS* 2.7.22). Another term for ploughshare is *stega* (*RV* 10.31, 9; *AV* 18.1.39).

*Pot:* Among the various kinds of pots used in the Vedic age *kaṃsa* denoted those made of metals (*AV* 1.10.5; *AB* 8.10; *BU* 6.3.1; *Nir* 8.3; *SĀ* 12.8). *Kalaśa* was a common word for a jar or pitcher which was mostly made of clay, tough metallic jars were not unknown. The wooden Soma tub (*droṇa-kalaśa*) is also mentioned (*RV* 1.117.12; 3.32.15; 4.27.5; *AV* 3.12.7; 9.1.6, 18-4.13; *TS* 1.1.8.1; 4.1.5.4; 5.1.7.2; *VS* 1-22; 11.59). *Kumbha* also denotes a pot which is same as *kalaśa* (*RV* 1.116.7; 117.6; VII. 33.13; *AV* 1.6.4; 3-12.7; *VS* 19.87). See **Vessels**.

*Pounding Stone:* Dṛṣad appears in the *Ṛgveda* (7.104.22; 8.72.4 and 2.31.1; 5.23.8) to denote a stone used to pound grain (cf. *ŚB* 1.1.1.22; 2.6.1.9; *TS* 1.6.8.3; 1.6.9.3).

*Razor:* See **Blade**.

*Rope:* See **Cord**. In the latter Saṃhitās and Brāhmaṇas, *Saṃnahana* denotes a band or rope (*TS* 1.1.2.2; *ŚB* 1.3.3-6; 2.6.1.15). *Rasanā, rajju* and *raśmī* also denote rope.

*Scissors:* The word *bhurij* in some passages (*RV* 8.4.16; *AV* 20.127.4) denotes scissors and in others (*RV* 4.2.14; 9.26.4; 75.5) an apparatus, being of the nature of a carpenter's vice.

*Sickle:* The term for sickle in the *Ṛgveda* (8.78.10; *Nir.* 2.1) is *dātra*. Cows with sickle-marks on their ears are mentioned in *Maitrāyaṇī Saṃhitā* (4.2.9). *Parśu* occurs in some passages of the later Saṃhitās (*AV* 12.3.31; *TS* 3.2.4.1) and also denotes sickle, being apparently a variant of *Paraśu*. Another term for sickle is *sṛṇi* (*RV* 1.58.4; 101.3; 106.5; *Nir.* 5.28).

*Shovel:* Spade or shovel for digging is mentioned in the *Ṛgveda* (1.179.6) as *khanitra*.

*Sieve:* The word *titau* found in the *Ṛgveda* (10.71.2) stands for sieve or perhaps winnowing basket, which was used to separate corn from husks or non-edible times. *Pavana* in the *Atharvaveda* (4.34.2; 18.3.11; cf. *Nir.* 6.9) denotes an implement for purifying grain from husks, etc., and either a sieve or a winnowing basket may be meant.

*Strap:* A thong or strap is denoted by the word *varatrā* (*RV* 4.57.4; *AV* 11.3.10; 20.135.13) which was used to fasten the oxen to the yoke (*RV* 10.60.8). It also denotes a strap which was used in drawing water from the well (*RV* 10.106.5).

*Tongs:* A wooden implement acting like a pair of tongs, used for lifting an iron-pot from fire is described as *śapha* in the *Aitareya Brāhmaṇa* (1.22) and *Śatapatha Brāhmaṇa* (14.2.1.16) Fire-tongs, known as *dhṛṣti* are mentioned in later texts like the *Śatapatha Brāhmaṇa* (14.3.1.22) and *Taittirīya Āraṇyaka* (5.9.8). *Parīśāsa* is the name of an instrument of the nature of tongs, used to lift the sacrificial kettle off the fire (*ŚB* 14.1.3.1; 2.1.16; 2.54; 3.1.20).

*Vessel:* There was several kinds of vessels. Soma vessels were known by the name *amatra* (*RV* 2.14.1; 5.51.4; 6.42.2), *kadru* (*RV* 8.45.26), *cāpya* (*VS* 19.88; *MS* 3.2.9; *KS* 38.3; *ŚB* 12.7.2.13; 9.1.3), *camasa* (*RV* 1.20.6; 110.3; 8.82.7; 10.16.8; 68.8; 96.9; *AV* 7.73.3; 18.3.54; *VS* 18.3; *Nir* 11.2; 12.37), *camu* (*RV* 3.48.5; 8.2.8; 9.20.6 etc.; *ŚB* 13.8.2.1, etc.). Among other kinds of vessels, mention may be made of *kośa* (*RV* 1.130.2; 3.32.15; 4.17.6) *dru* and *droṇa* made of wood (*RV* 1.161.1; 5.86.3; 6.2.8; 8.66.11; 9-93.1; etc.). *pātra* or drinking vessel (*RV* 1.82.4; 110.5; 162.13; 2.37.4; *AV* 4.17.4; 6.142.1; 9.6.17; 12.3.25; *TS* 5.1.62; 6.3.4.1; *VS* 16.62), *pānnejana* (*ŚB* 3.8.2.1; 13.5.2.1), etc.

*Winnowing Fan:* A fan for winnowing grains is mentioned as *paripavana* in *Nir.* (4.9.10).

*Wooden Dish:* Wooden vessel or dish is denoted by the term *pisila* in the *Śatapatha Brāhmaṇa* (2.5.3.6).

**Impotency:** That impotency in man was a great problem for his wife even in the Vedic age is attested by the fact that a woman having an impotent man as a husband is known as *vadhrimati* in the *Ṛgveda* (1.117.24; 6.62.7; 10.39.7; 10.65.12). The Aśvins are generally invoked to bring to the restoration of the virility of the husband.

**Imprecation:** The *Atharvaveda* is full of imprecatory verses. The text was originally known as *Atharvāṅgirasaḥ*. Atharvan is holy magic bringing happiness while Aṅgiras means hostile magic comprising curses against enemies, rivals, evil beings and the like. Imprecatory verses or rites are called *abhicāra*. The purpose of some is defensive but the majority of them are offensive in purpose and directed against human enemies. Evil spirits are first called upon to come out in the open and proclaim their real character, for as soon as they do that, they lose their dangerous power of injuring. The most effective metal against the demons is lead. There are two imprecations (*AV* 8.95.96) directed against the kidneys of an enemy. The purpose of the hymn (*AV* 7.70) is to frustrate the enemy's sacrifice. Most typical of the hymn of this *genre* are perhaps those with refrain 'he who hates us whom we hate' (*AV* 2.19-23). It is interesting to note that in one hymn (*AV* 5.22) *takman* (fever) has been asked to seize the *śūdra* and the *dāsī* or to go away to the Mujavants or 'to the Vāhīkas further beyond'. In the last verse the author says quite maliciously that he is sending *takman* to the Gandhāras, Aṅgas and Magadhas. Though condemned in the religious texts, Brahmanical, Buddhist or Jain, the exorcisms of the *Atharvaveda* were much in demand, and the ritual texts contain numerous exorcism-formulae and descriptions of magic rites by means of which the enemy could be annihilated. See **Magic**.

**Incantations:** Incantation means the uttering of magical formula, spell, charms, etc., of which the Vedic texts are full. But the *Atharvaveda* is specially called a book of incantations. The *mantras* of the *Atharvaveda* were meant for application. 'House and home, field and river, grain and rain, cattle and horses, trading and gambling, journeying and returning, serpents and vermin, furnish the special themes for these prayers and charms.' Thus, the *Atharvaveda* (1.13.1 ff) is a charm to conciliate the goddess of lightning. Protection against fire is likely to be achieved by the means of a special charm (*AV* 3.21.1-2). Abundance of grain is secured by the means of the incantation of the *Atharvaveda* (3.24.4-5). The incantation of sowing seed is expressed in the *Atharvaveda* (6.142.1-3). The *mṛgāra-sūktas* (*AV* 4.23-29) are incantations of averting distress. Least savoury of the magic charms of the *Atharvaveda* are those of witchcraft (*abhicāra*) and the like, which constitute the Aṅgiras part of the Saṃhitā. See **Imprecations**. Along with charms for victory, longevity, cure from fever, etc., we also find charms for winning a maid's heart (*AV* 2.30.1-4). The *Atharvaveda* (7.37.1 ff) is an incantation put in the mouth of a newly married bride, by which her husband is guarded from the touch of any other woman (cf. *AV* 3.25.2). Quite a number of medicinal charms are included in the *Atharvaveda*. The *Kauśika Sūtra* refers to various medicines which are to be given to the patients along with the recital of specific *Atharvaveda* verses. There are several charms against snake bite (cf. *AV* 5.13.1 ff). The *Atharvaveda* (5.20-21) are two most important battle-charms, which were also used directly as battle songs. See **Magic**.

**Incest:** Incest was not unknown as is attested by the dialogue of Yama and Yamī in the *Ṛgveda* (10.10), in which the sister calls her brother to bed. Yama's refusal, however, proves that it was not approved socially. There is also another hymn (*RV* 10.162.5) in which reference to such intercourse appears. Mention is further made in the *Ṛgveda* (10.61.5-7) to the relation between Prajāpati and his daughter which is, however, interpreted mythologically in the Brāhmaṇas (*AB* 3.33; *ŚB* 1.7.4.1). That incest, however, actually did take place is understood from the *Atharvaveda* (8.6.7).

**Individual Ownership:** The Vedic Indians were initially pastoral and were interested in common pasture land (*RV* 1.25.16). Gradually they took to agriculture and craved for possession of land. Cattle rearing and agriculture, both being acceptable occupations, promoted settled life and developed the institution of property. Property was thus initially collective and then individual. The term *sva* means one's possession. The Ṛgvedic peoples defeated their rivals and looted their property, or spoils of war. This is denoted by the term *loptra* in Indo-Aryan language. Terms like *rayi, raya, bhaga, riktha, rekna, paṇa, dhana, apnes* and *magha*, used in the *Ṛgveda* (2.1.12; 2.16.1; 2.38.10; 2.6.2; 6.20.7) indicate the idea of their wealth. In the earliest stratum of the *Ṛgveda*, when the Vedic Indians were mainly pastoral, cow was their property. Gradually *paśu* meaning cattle including horses (*RV* 5.61.5), and even men (*RV* 3.62.14), were accepted as wealth and ultimately *rayi* became the generic term for wealth in kine, steed, metal, grain and herbs. The *Ṛgveda* mentions other moveable property also like gold (2.15.9; 2.33.9; 5.60.4) and copper (*ayas*, 4.21.7; 5.30.15). By immovable property we are to consider land and houses. Land was of four types—pastoral forest, land for houses and arable land. *Dama* and *Sadma* are found in the *Ṛgveda* (2.1.2; 2.8.38; 3.6.3; 3.48.2; 3.55.14; 4.1.18) in the sense of houses which were treated as property. The *Ṛgveda* (10.34.10-11) speaks of a gambler taking shelter in another's house and suffering loss of personal wealth. Elsewhere (*RV*

6.50.3, 6.67.2), we find a prayer to Mitra and Varuṇa for a personal house belonging to one's own. The concept of individual ownership had already made its appearance in the Ṛgvedic age. In the post-Ṛgvedic literature individual ownership is a *fait accompli*.

**Indra:** Indra, the favourite national god of the *Ṛgveda*, has the largest number of hymns. Nearly 250, i.e. about one-fourth of the total number of hymns in the *Ṛgveda*, are addressed to him. He has more myths woven around him and a more developed anthropomorphism on the physical side than any other god. He is not a purely Indian creation and his name is pre-Indian (a demon in the *Avesta*). The cosmic aspect of his nature, as the liberator of the Waters, is older than the martial one. His physical proportions and powers are stupendous, almost cosmic. His arms bear the *vajra*, his exclusive weapon, though he also carries a hook and wields the bow and arrow. He is a car-warrior (*ratheṣṭha*), whose golden car is drawn by two steeds. He is more addicted to Soma, which stimulates him to battle, than any other god, the epithet *somapa* 'Soma-drinker', being characteristic of him. His father is Dyaus according to some passages, Tvaṣṭṛ according to others. Agni is his twin brother, most often conjoined with him as a dual divinity. The Maruts are his principal and constant allies, the epithet *marutvant* applied to him is therefore explained to him. The essential myth, forming the basis of his nature and repeated frequently and with variations, is the Vṛtra myth. Accompanied by the Maruts and exhilarated by Soma, he attacks Vṛtra, often called the Ahi (serpent). He smashes Vṛtra who encompasses the Waters, and so deserves the exclusive epithet *apsu-jit* 'conquering in the Waters'. In this struggle, which is constantly renewed, he also pierces the mountains and releases the pent-up waters, like imprisoned cows. The demons, whom Indra throws down, dwell on the *parvata* or *giri* (mountain or cloud) and an *adri* (rock) is said encompass the Waters. The clouds containing the Waters are figured as fortresses (*pura*) of the aerial demons, described either as autumnal or as made of iron or stone, and as being 90, 99 or 100 in number. He is, therefore, characteristically called the fort-destroyer (*purbhid*) but his exclusive and chief epithet is 'Vṛtra-slayer' (*Vṛtra-han*). The release of the Waters is simultaneous with the winning of light, sun, and dawn. Independently of the Vṛtra fight also, he is said to have found the light, the dawn or the sun, and made a path for the latter. The cows mentioned with the sun and dawn must be understood to be the morning beams. The gaining of Soma is also associated with the winning of the cows and the sun and with the Vṛtra fight. His connection with the thunderstorm is indicated when he is said to have created the lightning of heaven and directed the flow of the waters downwards. The cosmic actions usually attributed to all the gods are attributed to him also. His particular achievement is that he settled the quaking mountains and plains. As the destroyer of demons he is naturally the favourite god of battle, invoked more often than any other god by warriors. He protects the 'Aryan colour' and subjects the blackskins—the Dasyus. He is so generous to his worshippers that *maghavā* 'bountiful' is his almost exclusive epithet. Besides the Vṛtra myth, other minor stories are also related to him, such as 'shattering the car of Uṣas and stopping the steeds of the sun'. Some of the stories have an historical element also, when he is said to have aided Sudās. Indra, with his physical superiority, his excesses in eating and drinking and his cruelty in killing his own father Tvaṣṭṛ, forms a marked contrast to Varuṇa, the upholder of moral order. The true character of Indra can be understood by ascertaining that of Vṛtra, his opponent. The indigenous commentators and a number of scholars look upon Vṛtra as the demon of drought, confining the waters within the clouds. A more reasonable view is that Vṛtra was originally a frost and winter demon, from whose grasp the waters have to be wrenched free every year; that, thunderstorm and rain are not the only natural basis of the Vṛtra myth, and, that the geographical and climatic environments, in the later home of the Vedic Indians, only helped so to revive the original myth as to render very plausible the interpretation of the mythological figure of Indra as the god of the thunderstorm. References to Indra are legion. See Macdonell, 54-66.

**Industries:** The word *śilpa* is mentioned in the sense of industries. Among the craft, toy-making, glass-works, weaving, works of gold and wood have been mentioned in the Vedic texts. *Hiraṇyam* refers to the calling of the goldsmith and *aśvatariratha* means construction of chariots fit to be drawn by she-mules. Chariot-wrights held an important position in the society. They were called *rathakāras* and their representatives used to attend the coronation ceremony of the king. Carpenters (*takṣa*) leather-workers, wine-makers (*surākṛtaḥ*), have been mentioned in the Saṃhitās and Brāhmaṇas. Weaving, knitting, sewing, embroidery were widely practised by the womenfolk. A female embroiderer was called *peśaskārī, peśa* meaning ornamentation or embroidery. Plaiting of mats with the leaves and fibres of *plakṣa* tree was also a profession for the ladies but it was also taken up by men. The *Śatapatha Brāhmaṇa* refers to brick-making (6.2.1.9). It is evident from the *Śatapatha Brāhmaṇa* (6.2.1) that the Indians of that age were expert in the art of brick-making. The bricks were necessary for the construction of colossal sacrificial altars. The references to vessels made of gold, silver, bell-mental, lead, iron, etc., prove the existence of goldsmiths, silversmiths, ironsmiths and workers in lead and bell-metal. Various vessels used in sacrifice and the pestle and mortar were made of stone. Stone-cutting was one of the professions. During the consecration or coronation ceremony the kind had to seek the consent of the representatives of various crafts. The inclusion of two artisan classes, viz., chariot-wright and carpenter in list of king-makers goes to prove the importance attached, and high status assigned, to industry in the Vedic age. The *Śatapatha Brāhmaṇa* also refers to potters (*kulāla*) (11.8.1.1). Women dyers were called *rajayitrī*, women workers in thorns, *kaṇṭakīkārī* and female basket-makers were termed *vidalakārī*. Rope-makers used to prepare rope from the bark of the tree known as *rajjudala* (*ŚB* 13.4.4.5). A very comprehensive list of industries is to be found in the list of victims at the *puruṣamedha*, as given in *Vājasaneyī Saṃhitā* (30) and the *Taittirīya Brāhmaṇa* (3.4). Among such industries, mention may be made of carpenter (*takṣa*), potter (*kulāla*), blacksmith (*karmāra*), jeweller (*maṇikāra*), arrowsmith (*iṣukāra*), bow-maker (*dhanuṣkāra*), maker of the bow-string (*jyākāra*), rope-maker (*rajju-sarja*), cane-worker of basket maker (*vidalakārī*), worker in thorns (*kaṇṭakīkārī*), expert in embroidery (*peśaskārī*), distiller of liquor (*surākāra*), image-maker (*peśita*), expert in preparing unguents and cosmetics (*anjañī-kārī*), scabbard-maker (*koṣa-kārī*), furrier (*ajina-sandha*), tanner (*carmāra*), goldsmith (*hiraṇyakāra*), and so forth. See **Crafts, Implements, Occupations**.

**Inequality:** See **Caste System**.

**Infantry:** See **War**.

**Infinite:** See **Brahman**.

**Inheritance:** Besides collective ownership, since individual ownership was in vogue among the Vedic Indians the question of inheritance and division of property must have been an important feature in the economic life of the time. Although the Vedic texts do not explicitly lay down the rules relating to *Dāyabhāga* or inheritance and partition, they provide some clue to the understanding of the situation. *Dāya* occurs in the *Ṛgveda* (10.114.1) only in the sense of reward of exertion (*śrama*), but later it means inheritance—that is, a father's property which is to be divided among his sons either during his lifetime or after his death. It is clear that the property belonged to the head of the house, usually the father. Other members of the family only had moral claims upon it, which the father could ignore. If his sons were physically stronger than him, however, the father could be coerced. From the references in Vedic literature we are told that partition of property took place during the lifetime of the father, as for example, Manu (*RV* 3.45.4; 10.61; *TS* 3.1.9.4; *AB* 5.14), the primeval man himself, divided his property during his lifetime among his sons. It was not a fair division because one of his sons, Nābhānediṣṭha, was deprived of his share. The *Jaiminīya Brāhmaṇa* (3.156) reports that the sons of Abhipratātin Kākṣaseni divided the property among themselves, while he was alive. In the *Atharvaveda* (3.30.2) there is a prayer for family concord, 'be the son submissive to the father, likeminded with the mother', from which we may infer that sons might have waited for partition even up to their mother's death. The verses 3 and 5 of this hymn may be quoted here: 'Let not brother, not sister; becoming accordant (*samoanch*) of like course speak the words auspiciously (*bhadraya*)' and 'having superior (*jyayasvant*) intentful, be ye not divided, accomplishing together, moving on with joint labour (*sadhura*) come hither speaking what is agreeable one to another; I make you united'. The commentator brings about the significance of the word—*jyayasvant* as *jyeṣtha-kaniṣtha-bhāvena parasparaṃ-anusarants* and hence we may infer that sometimes the younger brothers might have continued to live jointly under the eldest brother, with the latter becoming the head of the family. The elder brother is conceived of a giver of wealth to the younger one in the verse (*RV* 7.32.24) (*jyāyaḥ kanīyasaḥ*). In the *Taittirīya Saṃhitā* (3.1.9.4) Manu is said to have divided his property among his sons. He omitted Nābhānediṣṭha, whom he afterwards taught how to appease the Aṅgirasas, and to procure cows. This is a significant indication that the property he divided was movable property, it was not land (*urvara*). Women were excluded from partition or inheritance, according to the *Śatapatha Brāhmaṇa* (4.4.2.13), though the *Nirukta* (3.4) has a different view which justifies the proprietary rights, of women. Detailed rules of inheritance appear in the later texts (*AB* 7.17; *ŚŚS* 15.27.3; *ŚB* 1.7.2.22, 3.2.1.18) but no clear picture emerges. The heir is called *payada* (*ŚB* 12.4.3.9; *Nirukta* 3.4; *AV* 5.18.6, 14) and receiver (a-da) of inheritance.

**Initiation:** Upanayana (q.v.) in the Vedic age was the initiation into student life. The *Atharvaveda* (11.5.1 ff) has a hymn which gives all the characteristic features of religious studentship. The youth is initiated (*upa-ni*) by the teacher into a new life; he wears an antelope-skin, and lets his hair grow long; he collects fuel and begs, learns, and practises penance. All these characteristics appear in the later literature. The student lived in his teacher's house (*ācāryakulavāsin, antevāsin*). His term of studentship was normally fixed at twelve years (*AB* 5.14; *ŚB* 3.6.2.15; 11.3.3.7; *TB* 3.7.6.3; *CU* 2.23; 4.3.5; 10.2; *BU* 6.3.15; etc.). Apart from studenthood, initiation was required in various walks of life, from the *rites de passage* (*AB* 1.3; *ŚB* 3.3.3.12) to the entry into a religious creed. In the case of Vedic sacrifices the sacrificer must undergo an initiation or *dīkṣā* ceremony, the rules of which were laid down in the Brāhmaṇa literature and the later Śrautasūtras. The king was to be initiated with elaborate rituals (see **Royal Ceremonies**) for the attainment of overlordship and other marks of royal greatness (*ŚB* 5.2.3.9 ff; *TB* 2.7.15-16).

**Insects:** Various kinds of insects are mentioned in the

Vedic literature. A few of them, such as the *alpaśayu* (*AV* 4.36.9), *upakvasa* (*AV* 6.50.2), *ejakta* (*AV* 5.23.7), *prakaṅkata* (*RV* 1.191.7), *pluṣi* (*RV* 1.191.1, *MS* 3.14.8; *VS* 24.29; *BU* 1.3.24), *maguṇḍi* (*AV* 2.14.2) and *sūcikā* (*RV* 1.191.7) have not been properly identified though their characteristics are described. Cochineal insects like *Indragopa* have also been referred to (*BU* 2.3.6) while winged insects are dealt with under the broad category of *pataṅga* (*AV* 6.50.1; *BU* 6.1.19). *Jabhya* and *tarda* (*AV* 6.50.1-2) denote insects destructive to grains. *Pipīla* and *pipīlikā* (*RV* 10.16.6; *AV* 8.567; 20.134.6; *MS* 3.6.7; *PB* 5.6.10; 15.17.8; *BU* 1.4.9) denote ants of various grades. *Upajihvikā, upajikā* and *upadikā* (*RV* 8.102.21; *AV* 2.3.4; 6.100.2; *ŚB* 14.1.1.8; *TB* 1.1.3.4; *TA* 5.1.4) also denote a species of ant. To these ants is attributed in the *Atharvaveda* (6.100.2) the power to bring out curative properties from water. *Araṅgara* (*RV* 1.106.10), *bhṛṅgā* (*AV* 9.2.22; *MS* 3.14.8; *VS* 24.29), *madhukara* (*TS* 1.5.6.5; 4.2.9-6; *TB* 3.10.10.1; *ŚB* 1.6.2.1.2; *CU* 3.1.2; 6.9.1), *saragh, saraghā* (*ŚB* 3.4.3.14; *TB* 3.10.10.1; *PB* 21.4.4) and *saraḥ* (*RV* 1.112.21; *TS* 5.3.12.12; *ŚB* 13.3.1.4) denote various kinds of bees. *Ūrṇanābhi* and its variant readings *ūrṇavābhi* and *urṇāvant* (*TB* 1.1.2.3; *KS* 8.1; *ŚB* 14.5.1.23) are all names of the spider. *Khadyota* (*CU* 6.7.3.5) stands for fireflies, *tṛṇajalāyuka* (*BU* 4.2.4) for caterpillar and *tṛṇaskanda* (*RV* 1.172.3) for grass-hopper. Various kinds of flies are mentioned under such names as *daṃśa* (*CU* 6.9.3; 10.2), *makṣa, makṣā, makṣikā* (*RV* 1.162.9; 4.45.4; 7.32.2; 10.40.6; *AV* 9.1.17; 11.1.2; 9.10; *BU* 3.3.2) and *maśaka* (*AV* 4.36.9; 7.56.3; 11.3.5; *BU* 1.3.24; *CU* 6.9.3; 10.2), which denotes mosquito or liting fly.

**Instruction:** See **Education**.

**Intercalation:** See **Months**.

**Inter-State Relations:** In the early Ṛgvedic period there were various tribal settlements (based on kinship). States in the modern sense, comprising a heterogeneous population, began to make their appearance in the later Ṛgvedic period and the system was fully established in the age of the later Saṃhitās and Brāhmaṇas. So, originally interstate relation meant inter-tribal relation. This relation was characterized by convergences and divergences as happens in the case of all states at all periods of history. The Vedic tribes came into conflict with the indigenous non-Vedic tribes. Descriptions of such conflict are found in the legends of Indra's slaying of the Dāsa chiefs and destruction of their forts. Not only did they fight against the non-Vedic tribes but they fought among themselves as well. The *dāsarājña* is an important historical event of the Ṛgvedic age in which Sudās, chief of the Tṛtsu-Bharatas defeated a federation, consisting of the five well-known tribes, namely, Puru, Yadu, Turvaśa, Anu and Druhyu (q.v), along with five of little ones, viz., Alina, Paktha, Bhalānas, Śiva and Viṣānin. In this battle the Bharatas emerged victorious (*RV* 7.32.2-5; 83.8; *AV* 10.128.12). There was another battle in which the Bharatas, under Sudās, defeated three non-Aryan tribes, the Ajas, Śigrus and Yakṣus, who were united under a chief named Bheda (*RV* 7.18.19). The Bharatas and Tṛtsus merged with each other and also with their erstwhile enemies the Purus, and later came to be known as Kurus. This shows that, along with mutual conflicts, a syncretistic conception also guided the inter-state relations. Connected with the Kurus were the Krivis who moved to the east, across the Yamunā, and came to be known as the Pañcālas. The Kurus along with the Pañcālas, Vasas and Uśīnaras occupied the Madhyadeśa. The Kuru-Pañcālas were the people *par excellence* in the post-Ṛgvedic period, and are referred to as a united nation. The Gangetic divide and the region around it became politically integrated under the Kuru-Pañcālas. In other parts of India also there were tribal conflicts and subsequent amalgamations. The process of this historical transformation cannot be minutely worked out due to the piecemeal nature of evidence at our disposal, but one point which should not be missed in this connection is that most of the older tribes of the *Ṛgveda* sunk into oblivion in the post-Ṛgvedic period. The emergence of the new tribes, or principalities like those of the Matsyas, Śālvas, Ikṣvākus, Kāsis, Kosalas, Videhas, Aṅgas, Vaṅgas, Magadhas, Vidarbhas, Sātvants, Naiṣadhas, Uttarakurus, Uttaramadras, Mujavants, Kekayas, Bāhlīkas, Mahāvṛṣas, Kambojas, etc., is suggestive in this respect. The relation of these peoples with the power-centre of the Madhyadeśa, represented by the Kuru-Pāñcālas, appear to have been anything but friendly. There is the story of the defeat of Dhṛtarāṣṭra, king of the Kāśis, by Śatānīka Satrājita, a Bharata or Kuru king (*ŚB* 13.5.4.9). Similar conflicts characterized the Vedic history, and despite numerous attempts by the rulers of the powerful states, an all-Indian political unity was never achieved in the Vedic age.

**Invasion:** See **War**.

**Iron:** See **Metals**.

# J

**Jana:** *Jana* means an individual. But it is used in the *Ṛgveda* and in later literature in a collective sense, i.e. to denote a people or a tribe. Thus, the 'five tribes' (*pañcajanāḥ* or *janāsaḥ*) are frequently referred to in the *Ṛgveda* (8.6.46; 48); *yādvajana* and *yādvāḥ* mean the Yadu tribe. Thus, *jana* was a tribal and social unit among the Vedic Aryans. The word *rājan* has association with *jana*. The *Ṛgveda* (5.5.4) contains a prayer for providing the *jana* with a chief. The *Ṛgveda* (10.174.5) speaks of the success of a victorious king over enemies and his lordship over the *jana*. The *Ṛgveda* (10.159.6) speaks of the conjuration of the queen ending with the following statement: 'I have displaced rival wives, risen superior to them and thereby I rule over this man and the *jana*.' The king (*rājan*) is described as protector (*gopa*) of the people (*janasya*) in the *Ṛgveda* (3.43.5). Soma is called *gopatin janasya*, 'protector of the people' in the *Ṛgveda* (9.35.5). There are various theories in regard to the relation of the *jana* with *grāma, viś, vṛjana, vrāja, kula, gotra* and *varṇa*. Their convergences and divergences cannot be satisfactorily explained.

**Janapada:** Tribal territories, people, land, the *Aitareya Brāhmaṇa* 8.14; *Śatapatha Brāhmaṇa* 13.4.2.17; *Taittirīya Brāhmaṇa* 2.3.9.9, etc.

**Jaṅgiḍa:** Healing plant (*AV* 2.4; 19.34-35) used as an amulet against such diseases as *takman, balāsa, āśārīka, viśarīka, pṛṣṭyamaya, viṣkandha, saṃskandha, jambha* (q.v) as well as fevers and rheumatic pains. It may be *terminalia arjuneya*.

**Jar:** The word *kumbha* means jar. It is referred to in the *Śatapatha Brāhmaṇa* (1.1.2.7; 1.1.2.8) . The word *pātra* refers to the drinking vessel (*JB* 1.282). *Pātra* is a large wooden jar and *graha* is a small cup, like a saucer. It was made of earth. It was used at *soma savana*. The feminine form, *pātrī* occurs (*AB* 8.17; *ŚB* 1.1.2.8; 2.5.3.6; 2.6.2.7) in the sense of vessel of jar.

**Jāra:** Lover. *Ṛgveda* 1.66.8; 117.18; 134, 3; 152.4; 8.9.1; 9.32.5, *Vājasaneyī Saṃhitā* 30.9; *Taittirīya Brāhmaṇa* 3.4.4.1; *Bṛhadāraṇyaka Upaniṣad* 6.4.11.

**Jāratkārava:** The eschatological queries of Jāratkārava Ārtabhāga occurs in *Bṛhadāraṇyaka Upaniṣad* (3.2). Jāratkārava's question was: 'They say that Death eats up everything; what deity is there, that eats up Death himself?' The answer which Yājñavalkya gave is that the Deity which may be regarded as eating up Death should be called water, which consumes Agni, the Death. This answer is yet on the ritualistic plane. The second question which Jāratkārava asked was: 'Does the vital breath leave a sage when he dies, as it leaves the body of an ordinary man?' Yājñavalkya's answer to it was: 'The vital airs stand pent up within the dying body of the sage, and the body when dead, remains inflated and puffed up'. This perhaps means that when an ordinary man dies his *liṅgaśarīra*, or subtle body, leaves its former tenement, but that of the sage does not. The third question that Jāratkārava asked was: 'What is the condition of the Self when it leaves the human body? Does it thereafter lead an embodied or disembodied existence?' This question Yājñavalkya is shrewd enough not to answer in the presence of the assembly in the court of king Janaka. He takes Jāratkārava by the hand, leads him out of the assembly, and holds some conversation with him there. We are only given to understand that the conversation turned on the topic of *karma*, that a man's action was the determinant of his fate. Meritorious actions would procure for him a meritorious life, while evil deeds would lead him to a very sinful and evil existence. Belvalkar and Ranade 194-5.

**Jātakarma:** A ritual performed after the birth of a child. Early references to this rite are found in *Taittirīya Saṃhitā* 2.2.5.3-4; *Bṛhadāraṇyaka Upaniṣad* 6.4.24-8; *Jaimini* 6.3.38, etc. According to certain Gṛhyasūtras it should be performed before the umbilical cord is cut. *PGS* 1.16; *GGS* 2.7.17. It consists of a *homa* uttering a *mantra* in the child's right ear, giving the child a mother's breast and addressing the mother with *mantras* (*ĀGS* 1.15.1-4; *ŚGS* 1.24.1-12).

**Jātarūpa:** Gold. The *Aitareya Brāhmaṇa* (8.13), *Bṛhadāraṇyaka Upaniṣad* (6.4.25); *Naighaṇṭuka* (1.2; *Lāṭyāyana Śrauta Sūtra* 1.6.24; cf. 8.1.3; *Kāṭhaka Saṃhitā* (10.16; 13.3; *Śāṅkhāyana Śrauta Sūtra* 3.19.9). See **Metals**.

**Jaundice:** *Hariman* in the *Ṛgveda* (1.50.11) and the *Atharvaveda* (1.22.1; 9.8.9; 19.44.2) denotes 'yellowness' as a disease, 'jaundice'.

**Jewel:** Jewels like pearls or precious stones have not separately figured in the Ṛgvedic or even Vedic concept of wealth. But that does not mean that they were not collected or not available. As a matter of fact, the word *maṇi* figuring in the *Ṛgveda* (1.33.8) and quite a number of times in the *Atharvaveda* (1.29.1; 2.4.1-2; 8.5.1) has been taken by Vedicists to denote a 'jewel', whether pearl or diamond or anything else. *Maṇi* is also mentioned in the *Taittirīya Saṃhitā* (7.3.14.1), *Kāṭhaka Saṃhitā* (35.15), *Aitareya Brāhmaṇa* (4.6) as an amulet against all kinds of evil. It is evident that the *maṇi* could be strung on a thread (*sūtra*), which is referred to in the *Pañcaviṃśa Brāhmaṇa* (20.16.6) and elsewhere

(*JUB* 1.18.8; cf. 3.4.13; *JB* 2.248; *ŚB* 12.3.4.2). The *maṇi* was certainly worn round the neck, for in the *Ṛgveda* (1.122.14) occurs the epithet *maṇigrīva,* 'having a jewel on the neck'.

**Jeweller:** The term *maṇi-kāra* seems to have meant jeweller, considered as a sacrificial victim at the *puruṣamedha Vājasaneyī Saṃhitā* (30.7) and *Taittirīya Brāhmaṇa* (3.4.3.1).

**Judges:** In the Rgvedic age, the king was the highest judicial authority as he was in the subsequent periods of Indian history, though no direct passage of the *Ṛgveda* alludes to the sovereign as acting in this capacity. There were assessors (*sabhāsads*) who decided legal cases in the assembly (*AV* 3.29.1; 7.12.2; 19.55.6; *KS* 8.7; *MS* 1.6.11; *TB* 1.2.1.26; *AB* 8-21). *Sabhācara* also denoted a member of the Sabhā functioning as a law court, perhaps as one of those who sit to decide cases. According to the *Śatapatha Brāhmaṇa* (5.4.4.7) the king wields the rod of punishment (*daṇḍa*) but is not subject to it. At any rate, he delegated his judicial jurisdiction to an *adhyakṣa* or royal officer (*KS* 27.4). Petty offences in the village seem to have been left to the *grāmyavādin* or village judge (q.v.) for disposal. In the later Vedic age we find the real beginnings of the civil and criminal law. For the first time, we meet with the theory that a crime is a disturbance of public peace and that the penalty for a crime in the shape of fine must be paid to the kind or to a brāhmaṇa authorized by him. That the king himself personally administered civil and criminal justice is attested by the Dharmasūtras. It was customary for the king to invest the administration of justice to qualified judicial officers, specially *śrotriyas* or brāhmaṇas of high learning. Difficult cases were referred to the *pariṣad* or a specialized assembly (*GDS* 11.19; 12.43; 28.50).

**Judiciary:** The plausibility of the conclusion that the king exercised criminal and civil jurisdiction, assisted by assessors, must rest on analogy and on the later practice in India. The regular word for jurisprudence in the *Ṛgveda* (1.22.18; 164.43; 3.3.1; 17.1; 60.6; 5.26.6; 63.7; 72.2) is *dharma*. The king administered justice with the assistance of the legal advisers, including the Purohita. Judges were also appointed, though there is little data regarding such appointments. But the village judges, the *grāmyavādins* are frequently mentioned. Theft, burglary, highway robbery and cheating are among the crimes recorded, with cattle lifting at night being a very frequent one. Tying the criminal to a stake was a common form of punishment. One word in the *Ṛgveda* shows that the system of wergeld was in force. A man is given the epithet *śatadāya*, which denotes that the price of his blood was a hundred cows. Even in the age of the later Saṃhitās and Brāhmaṇas private vengeance was permitted by allowing *vairadeya* or wergeld, the money or wealth in any form to be paid for killing a man as a compensation to his relatives. For evidence, eye-witnesses were more important than informers. Ordeals were also probably looked upon as valid tests of innocence or guilt. The *Ṛgveda* (3.53.22) is supposed to denote a heated *paraśu*, used as an ordeal while the *Ṛgveda* (1.158.4 ff) refers to Dīrghatamas having been subjected to fire and water ordeals. These are, however, plausible suggestions, though no definite conclusions are possible. In one passage of the *Ṛgveda* there is a probable reference to the employment of trained men to recover stolen cattle. Serious crimes like killing an embryo, the murder of a brāhmaṇa, and the murder of a man occur in the lists of sins. Other, more serious, crimes mentioned are stealing gold and drinking the *surā,* while treachery to the king is recognized as a capital offence. Among civil cases the *Ṛgveda* refers to the recovery of debts (*ṛnaṃ saṃni*). The loan was the only contract known to that period and unpaid debts were punished with a period of servitude to the creditor. The word *dāya* has already come to mean inheritance of 'a father's property which is to be divided among his sons either during his life time or after his death'. The *Taittirīya Saṃhitā* (3.1.9.4) has the famous episode of Manu's division of property among his sons. Laws of partition are referred to in *Pañcaviṃśa Brāhmaṇa* (16.4.4). As regards civil procedure voluntary arbitration appears to be the earlier form of judicial procedure in which the plaintiff (*praśnin*), defendant (*abhipraśnin*) and the arbitrator or judge (*praśnavivāka*) figured. The *jñātṛ* is very probably a technical legal term for a witness in civil transactions. The king may have presided and the tribe or the assessors may have judged. In the case of theft in the *Chāndogya Upaniṣad* (6.16.1-2) we find ordeal applied, but this is the solitary case of an ordeal known in Vedic literature as a part of criminal procedure. In the Sūtras we hear of the king striking a confessed thief with his own hand. The Sūtras fix the wergeld of the kṣatriya at 1000 cows, of the vaiśya at 100 and of the śūdra at 10, with a bull over and above for the king, according to the text of Baudhāyana. This seems to indicate a stage when the royal power had extended sufficiently to secure that the wergeld should be accepted, and that the insult to the royal peace required the appeasement of the king and his reward for his intervention by the gift of a bull. The lower position of women is shown by one text which assign in her case only the same wergeld as for a śūdra. See **Civil and Criminal Laws, Judges, Jurisprudence**.

**Jurisprudence:** See **Civil and Criminal Laws, Law of Contract, Law: Dharma, Law of Gift, Law of Inheritance, Law of Joint Undertaking, Law of Properties, Marriage Oath, Ordeal, Pleading**.

**Jyotiṣṭoma:** Soma sacrifice which generally occupies

Jyotiṣṭoma

five days are: (i) choosing of priests and performance of *madhuparka, dīkṣaṇīyeṣṭi* and *dīkṣā*; (ii) *prāyaṇīyeṣṭi*, i.e. opening *iṣṭi*, purchase of *soma*, *ātitheyeṣṭi* (*iṣṭi* offering hospitality to Soma), *pravargya* and *upasad* or homage twice a day on the second day, (iii) *pravargya* and *upasad* on the third day, (iv) *pravargya, upasad, agnipraṇayana, agnīṣomapraṇayana* and animal sacrifice on the fourth day; and (v) pressing of Soma, offering it and drinking it, *udayanīya* (concluding *iṣṭi*) and *avabhṛtha* (final purificatory bath on the fifth day).

# K

**Kahola:** A philosopher whose metaphysical queries appear in *Bṛhadāraṇyaka Upaniṣad* (3.5). He asked Yājñavalkya how was it possible to realize the great Self immanent in the whole universe. Yājñavalkya's answer was that he who was able to bear the extremes of hunger and thirst, of grief, infatuation, age and death, rise higher than all desires for sons or riches or fame, up to a mendicant's life putting aside all considerations of learning and leading the guiltless life of a child, alone was able to realize this *ātman*, everything else being only an illusion. Belvalkar and Ranade 197.

**Kāla:** Cosmic principle mentioned in the *Ṛgveda* (10.42.9) and the *Atharvaveda* (19.53.1 ff). For details see **Time**.

**Kāma:** The *Atharvaveda* presupposes a good deal of development about Kāma, the desire. The *Atharvaveda* considers Kāma as the personified primordial power, on the same level as *eka, sat, Brahman*, Viśvakarman and Svayambhū (Bloomfield, *SBE* 42, p. 591). The desire and passionate longing (*kāma*) is the first seed of mind (*AV* 19.52.1). From Kāma, the heaven was produced (*AV* 19.52.3), the person having the same heart or mind (i.e. having love or desire to be united (*AV* 19.53.4). Thus, *kāma* in the mind of men and women is considered to be the same as the creative power of the universe. *Kāma* is identified with Agni, to whom offerings are made. The identification is quite appropriate, since he the first god born produces fire or heat in the hearts of the lovers (*AV* 9.2.1.19). The men and women who have fallen in love with each other are the representatives of *Kāma*. Love is the basis of creation. Thus, Kāma is the creator. Kāma produces fever, parching of mouth and other sensations in the body and mind of the lovers. These led the Atharvavedic poets to identify Kāma and Agni. The persons in love appear most attractive to each other. The Atharvavedic poet considers that Kāma has auspicious and graceful forms, when he becomes real and enters men and women (*AV* 9.2.25). Kāma, the love between men and women, makes the love pine for each other and, at the same time, makes them most attractive for each other. Love between men and women leads to the preparation of the race and the poet fancies that the same force of love is behind the creation of the universe too. Thus, love is deified (*AV* 9.2.19.52). Kāma is the highest god (*AV* 92.8). The poet of the *Atharvaveda* (9.2) and (19.52) speaks more on Kāma as the creator. It should also be noted that Eros, the Greek god of love is connected with the creation of the Universe (Plato, *Symposium* 6). The Atharvavedic poet thus realizes that love (*kāma*) is the product of mind and this feeling that enters the human minds and makes the forms of men and women pleasing and graceful, are the real or corporeal forms of Kāma (*AV* 9.2.25). Shende, 48-9.

**Kamboja:** Yāska, in his *Nirukta* (2.2), refers to the speech of the Kambojas as differing from that of the other Āryas. The Kambojas were later settled to the north-west of the Indus, and are known as Kambujiya in the old Persian inscriptions. There was a possible connection of the Madras, or more or probably the Uttara Madras, with the Kambojas, who probably had Iranian as well as Indian affinities. One of their important settlements lay near Kandahar, as the Aramaic version of the Shar-i-Kuna inscription of Aśoka appears to have been meant for them.

**Kāmpila:** In passages of the *Yayurveda Saṃhitā* (*TS* 7.4.19.1; *MS* 3.12.20; *VS* 23.18; *TS* 3.9.6; *ŚB* 13.2.8.3) the epithet *Kāmpila-Vasini* is applied to a woman, perhaps the king's *mahiṣī* or chief wife, whose duty was to sleep beside the slaughtered animal at the horse sacrifice (Aśvamedha). Kampila (Kampilya) is the name of the town in the later literature and the capital of Pāñcāla in Madhyadeśa.

**Kāraskara:** *Kāraskara* is the name of a people mentioned in the *Baudhāyana Śrautasūtra* (20.13.14); cf. *BDS* (1.2.14).

**Karma, Doctrine of:** All the Indian systems agree in believing that each action of an individual leaves behind it some sort of potency which has the power to ordain for him joy or sorrow in the future, depending on whether it is good or bad. When the fruits of the actions are such that they cannot be enjoyed in the present life or in a human life, the individual has to be born again, as a man or any other being, in order to suffer or enjoy them. The Vedic belief that the *mantras*, uttered with the correct accent at the sacrifices, with the proper observance of all ritualistic details, exactly according to the directions and without the slightest error, has something like a magical virtue to produce automatically the desired object immediately or after a lapse of time, was probably the earliest form of the *karma* doctrine. It postulates a semi-conscious belief that, at a distance of time, certain mystical actions can produce certain effects without the ordinary process of the instrumentality of visible agents of ordinary cause and effect. When the sacrifice is performed, the action leaves such an unseen magical virtue, called the *adrṣṭa* (the unseen) or the *apūrva* (not being before), that by it the desired object will be achieved in a mysterious manner, for the *modus operandi* of the *apūrva* is unknown. In the Saṃhitās, there is also this notion that he who commits wicked deeds suffers in another world, whereas he who performs good deeds enjoys the highest material pleasure. These were probably associated with the conception of *ṛta*, the inviolable order of things. Thus, these are probably the elements which built up the *karma* theory, which we find pretty well established but not emphasized in the Upaniṣads, where it is said that depending on good or bad actions men will have good or bad births. If there is a gradation in the *karmas* and *yogas* performed in this life, it is only reasonable to suppose that there is a corresponding gradation in the fruits of enjoyment in the next world; all should not be assigned an equally enduring life of happiness and facility of the world of the blessed. That there is a soul in man and similar spirits in trees, plants, birds, animals, etc., and that they are all capable of remaining dissociated form their outward trappings, is an old prevailing belief of the Vedic period. And, while there were the tribal totems suggesting the habitation of a man's spirit in specific tress or animals, subsequently, with the elaboration of the magico-sacerdotal theory of the innumerable inward correspondences in things, and with the facile identifications like that of the Yajamāna with the *paśu* (beast) or with the *prastata* (grass), it is not very unreasonable to imagine that the doctrine of metempsychosis could not have delayed very long in the coming. Consequently, after it has been made very probable that a doctrine like that of the transmigration of the soul was implicit in the Vedic or, at any rate, in the early Brāhmaṇa speculation, the possibility of its being placed at this period on a distinctive basis by an acquaintance with the customs of some other peoples is not, or need not be, ruled out absolutely. However, the essential Aryan contribution to the full-fledged dogma of transmigration comes, first from their belief in pantheism or panpsychism, which made it possible for the soul to inhabit not some specific totems only, but almost everything in the animate and inanimate creation; and, secondly, from their theory of *karma*, which regulated the soul's wanderings and gave the dogma a moral background. In the Pañcāgnividyā as enumerated in the *Chāndogya Upaniṣad* (i.8 ff), a more developed doctrine of *karma* and its allied features is found. These are: (1) The doctrine of *karma*, or of postmortem rewards and punishments for us good or bad actions in the various stages of evolution of the dogma; (2) The doctrine of metempsychosis, which made it possible for the rewards and punishments being meted out in the world below, except in the case of those elected for eternal reward in the abode of *Brahman* or for an eternal detention either in hell or in an unending succession of lives and deaths, and (3) the eschatological doctrine of the two paths, the successive stages of the soul's ascent or descent being arrived at partly arbitrarily but partly also by a consideration of the physical, physiological, and ritualistic correlates of the facilities in man. In the *Bṛhadāraṇyaka Upaniṣad* (3.2), in reply to Jāratkārava's question on death and other kindred topics what Yājñavalkya said, we are given to understand, the conversation turned on the topic of *karma*: 'That a man's action was the determinant of his fate; that if he did good actions, he would reap good results therefrom, while if he did bad actions, he would have to suffer evil, i.e. meritorious actions would procure for him a happy life, while evil deeds would lead him to a very sinful evil existence.' Our deeds then must be regarded as our angels. For good or evil, they are the shadows that stand by us still. Elsewhere in the same *Upaniṣad* (14.4.1-25) Yājñavalkya says: 'Man's future existence is made for him by his previous acts; as a man has acted and behaved so shall he also be in a future state of existence. He becomes pure by pure deeds, and sinful by sinful deeds. In fact, the actions of man are the guardians of his destiny. As a man desires in his life so does he will, and as he wills, so does he act.' It is in the fitness of things, therefore, that a man should resolve to do good deeds in this life so as to secure for himself a future worthy state of existence. For, when the mortal body lies like a slough, the disembodied spirit flies away taking along with itself the whole stock of its merits and demerits. Dasgupta 71-2, Belvalkar and Ranade 82, 106-7, 195-207.

**Karmakāṇḍa:** A theoretical division of the Vedic texts, it pertains to those portions which apply to some ritual or sacrifice. The Mīmāṃṣakas hold that the main purpose of the Vedas is to denote some *karma* or rite, and therefore all those portions which do not exclusively speak of rituals should be considered redundant or figurative. Bhattacharyya, 1991, 82.

**Karoti:** Karoti is mentioned in the *Śatapatha Brāhmaṇa* (9.5.2.15) as a place, or perhaps a river, where Tura Kāvaseya made a fire-altar, i.e. a seat of the fire-cult *par excellence.*

**Kāśī, Kāsya:** A people who gave their name to a territory. The name Kāśī denotes (in the plural—*ŚB* 13.5.4, 19.21; *AV* 5.22.14) the people of Kāśī (Benares), and Kāsya, the king of Kāśī. The *Śatapatha Brāhmaṇa* (13.5.4.19) tells of Dhṛtarāṣṭra, king of Kāśī, who was defeated by Śatānīka Satrājita, with the result that the Kāśīs, down to the time of the Brāhmaṇa period gave up the kindling of the sacred fire. Satrājita was a Bharata. We also hear of Ajātaśatru as a king of Kāśī (*BU* 2.1.1, 3.8.2; *Kau.U* 4.1), and no doubt Bhadrasena Ajātaśatrava, a contemporary of Uddālaka, was also a king of Kāśī. The Kāśīs and Videhas were closely connected, as was natural in view of their geographical position. The compound name Kāśī-Videha occurs in *Kauṣītakī Upaniṣad*; in the *Bṛhadāraṇyaka Upaniṣad* (3.8.2) Gārgī describes Ajātaśatru as either a Kāśī or a Videha king. The *ŚŚS* (16.29.5) mentions one Purohita as acting for the kings of Kāśī, Kosala, and Videha; and the *BŚS* (21.13) mentions Kāśī and Videha in close proximity. Kosala and Videha were in close connection, and Kosala is found combined in the compound name Kāśī-Kauśalyas of the *Gopatha Brāhmaṇa* (1.2.9). Though Kāśī is a late word, it is quite possible that the town is older, as the river Vāraṇavatī referred to in the *Atharvaveda* (4.7.1) may be connected with the Vārāṇasī (Benares). Macdonell and Keith I. 153-5.

**Kettle:** *Caru* (*RV* 1.7.6; 7.104.2; 9.52.3; 10.86.18; *AV* 4.7.4; 9.5.6; 11.1.16; *MS* 1.4.4, 1.4.9; *KS* 5.6, 32.6; *TS* 1.6.1.2) signifies kettle or pot, having a lid (*apidhāna*) and hooks (*arika*) to hang on fire (*RV* 1.162.13; *AV* 18.4.53), and made of iron or bronze (*ŚB* 13.3.4.5). It was used as offering bowl to Rudra (*ŚB* 13.3.4.5).

**Khāṇḍava:** It is mentioned in the *Taittirīya Āraṇyaka* (5.1.1) as the southern boundary of Kurukṣetra. There seems no reason to doubt its identity with the famous Khāṇḍava forest of the *Mahābhārata*, which lay in the vicinity of Indraprastha. The name also occurs in the *Pañcaviṃśa Brāhmaṇa* (25.3.6).

**Kidney Beans:** *Mudga* designates a cultivated grain named 'kidney bean' (*phaseolus mungo*) in *Maitrāyaṇī Saṃhitā* (2.11.4), *Kāṭhaka Saṃhitā* (18.9) *Taittirīya Saṃhitā* (4.7.4.2) and *Vājasaneyī Saṃhitā* (18.12).

**Kīkaṭa:** The name of these people occurs only in one passage of the *Ṛgveda* where they appear as hostile to the Vedic tribes and as under the leadership of Pramagnanda. Yāska (*Nirukta* 6.32) declares that Kīkaṭa was the name of a non-Aryan country, and later Kīkaṭa is given as a synonym of Magadha. The Kīkaṭas were thus a non-Aryan people living in the country later known as Magadha.

**Kinship:** See **Family**.

**Kingship:** *Absolutism:* From the primary warlord and collector of *bali* or tribute, the Vedic king came to be regarded as a sovereign ruling over the people; the lord of the territory in which the people lived, the sole judge wielding the rod of punishment and the protector of *dharma*. The idea of territorial sovereignty was the result of the final settling down of the tribes, and the giving up of their nomadic habits, of which we find traces in the Vedic literature. Tribal names gave rise to place names and almost all the kingdoms came to have fixed boundaries. In the case of the Kuru country, we have a clear account of its territorial limits. Territorial epithets came to be applied to princes. We have innumerable instances of this in the Vedic literature. A king Prātīpīya of the Kuru family is described as Bālhīka (*ŚB* 12.9.3); a second prince Bhīma is described as Vaidarbha or ruler of the Vidarbha region; two other princes Dhṛtarāṣṭra and Ajātaśatru are designated Kāsya or ruler of the Kāśī kingdom, two princes of Kośala are described as Kauśalya, i.e. Para Atnāra and Hairaṇyanābha. Such local epithets are very common and we find them applied even to ordinary people, to distinguish them from others of the same name. Thus Proti is called Kausāmbeya, Citra is called Gaṅgāyani, Āśvalāyana is called Kausalya, while one more is called Naimiṣya. The importance of this conception of territorial sovereignty is also felt in the coronation ritual. The king is made to ascend the quarters, i.e. the north, south, east and west, symbolic of his supremacy over these regions. Furthermore, the suzerain overlord's ideas of conquest embraced the whole region of the country then known, extending from the hills to the sea. In regard to the newer ideas about the nature of sovereignty, some further light is thrown by the Rājasūya (q.v.) ritual. In the Abhiṣecanīya, the king was made to make offerings to Savitṛ Satyaprasava, Agni Gṛhapati, Soma Vanaspati, Bṛhaspati Vākpati, Rudra Paśupati, Mitra Satya, and Varuṇa Dharmapati, with a view to his investment with their authority and functions. We need not stretch our imagination, but the text as well as the interpretation is so clear that it gives a full import of the ceremonies and their constitutional significance. The priest himself addressed the king thus and prayed 'May Savitṛ quicken thee for ruling, Agni for householders, Soma for trees, Bṛhaspati for speech, Indra for lordship, Rudra for cattle, Mitra for truth and Varuṇa for the lord of the law.' The meaning is apparent; the prince was vested with supreme ruling authority and this comprised the general overlordship of the people, full governing authority, general superintendence over the plants and animals (i.e. agriculture and cattle) and the power of administering the laws as the viceregent of lord Varuṇa, the divine judge *par excellence*. The consummation of investiture was attained by the king-elect's stepping over the tiger skin (symbolic of his greatness and conquest of enemies; cf. the epithet *vyāghrapratīka*), his investment with the wooden sacrificial sword symbolizing regal and legal authority, his identification with Indra and Varuṇa, and the proclamation of his immunity from punishment (*adaṇḍya*), which in those days made him free from jealousy or intrigue of rivals and factions. Bandyopadhyaya, 19-91.

*Coronation:* See **Royal Ceremonies**.

*Caste of:* Normally it was desired that a king should be a *kṣatriya*. This we read in the *Śatapatha Brāhmaṇa* (5.1.12). To the king (*rājan*) doubtlessly belongs the Rājasūya; for by offering the Rājasūya he becomes king, and the brāhamaṇa is unsuited for kingship. *Rājana eva rājasūyam*, etc. A brāhmaṇa king is, however, contemplated in a passage of the *Aitareya Brāhmaṇa* (8.23). We have references to śūdra, āyogava and even non-Aryan kings in other Vedic texts. King Jānaśruti Pautrāyana is branded a śūdra

Kingship

in the *Chāndogya Upaniṣad* (4.2.1). King Marutta Avikṣita is styled Āyogava in the *Śatapatha Brāhmaṇa* (13.5.4.6). In legal codes, Āvogava denotes a member of a mixed caste, a descendant of a śūdra by a vaiśya wife. Niṣāda Sthapatis (kings or chieftains) figure in Sūtras.

*Divinity of:* The germ of the theory of divine right of kings probably goes back to the *Ṛgveda*. In the *Ṛgveda* there is a hymn (4.42) of king Trāsadasyu, son of Purukutsa, who says 'The gods rely on the might of Varuṇa, while I am the lord of the people, (*kratuṃ sacante varuṇasya devā rājāmi kṛṣṭeḥ*, etc.); I am Indra and Varuṇa, I am the wide and the deep Heaven and Earth, I am the son of Aditi'. Here, there is an explicit claim by a king to be identical with the mightiest and greatest gods of the Vedic pantheon. In the *Atharvaveda* (6.87.1-2) it is said about the king 'May all the people long for you, may not the kingdom be lost from your hands, may you stand firm in the world like Indra and may you uphold the kingdom'. In the *Śatapatha Brāhmaṇa* (5.1.5.1; 4), it is said that *rājanya* is a manifestation of Prajāpati, while being one he rules over many'. Here the position of the *rājanya* appears to be regarded as due to his being the representative of Prajāpati. In the *Śatapatha Brāhmaṇa* (5.4.3.4), the sacrificer in the Rājasūya is identified with Indra and it is said that position is due to two causes, viz., (1) his being a member of the kṣatriya order and (2) his participating in a solemn sacrifice. But passages like the last and *Śatapatha Brāhmaṇa* (5.1.3.4; 5.14, 5.2;2.14) should not be relied upon in support of the theory of the divine right of kings since every participant (whether a brāhmaṇa or a kṣatriya) in such solemn sacrifices as the Agniṣṭoma and Vājapeya was supposed to possess a celestial body after *dīkṣā* and *pravargya* and was often spoken of as identified with Indra and other gods. Viśvarūpa on Yājñavalkya (1.350) quotes as long Vedic passage (*āgama*) in which it is stated that the gods said to Prajāpati, 'We shall arrange for a king in human form by taking from the moon, the sun, Indra, Viṣṇu, Vaiśravaṇa (Kubera) and Yama respectively majesty, brilliance, valour, victoriousness liberty and control; and that the king thus formed asked the gods to give him *dharma* as his friend and that then, he would protect the people. The gods made *dharma* (i.e. *daṇḍa*) his friend, Kane, III, 32-3.

*Election of:* A king was often selected by the people though the choice was probably restricted to the royal family or, at best, to members of the nobles of the clans. The election of kings is clearly referred to in certain passages (*AV* 1.9.3; 4.4.22). Nevertheless, it is certain that in emergencies, people had the power of selecting one member of the royal family in preference to another who was incompetent. But whatever we might think of the election of kings as a means of popular control over them, there is no doubt that the people continued to play an important part in political life. Thus, particular stress is laid on the necessity of concord between the king, and his elector in a passage in the *Atharvaveda* (3.4) which, by the way, is a clear testimony of the prevalence of the system of some popular control over the kings. Besides, it is held by some scholars that an essential part of the coronation ceremony was a solemn oath taken by the king to the effect that if he opposed the people, he might lose all the merit he had accumulated in his life. There are hymns in the Saṃhitās and Brāhmaṇas to celebrate not only the coronation of kings but also the return of exiled kings. This implies that the people had the power to punish kings, if an emergency arose, by banishing them. Then in the *Pañcaviṃśa Brāhmaṇa* (6.6.5) a sacrifice is mentioned whereby the popular will could be exerted.

*Entourage:* The *ratnin* is a term applied to those people of the royal entourage in whose houses the *ratna-havis* rite was performed during royal consecration. They were *purohita* (priest), *mahiṣī, vāvātā, parivṛkti* (royal wives), *sūta* (reporter or charioteer), *grāmaṇī* (village headman), *kṣattṛ* (chamberlain), *samgrahitṛ* (treasurer or collector), *bhāgadugha* (collector of taxes and divider of shares), and *akṣāvāpa* (superintendent of dicing). Besides, *palāgala* (courier), *go-vikartana* (cattle-keeper), *vaiśyagrāmaṇī* (village headman belonging to the *vaiśya* caste), *takṣa-rathakārau* (carpenter and chariot maker) are mentioned. A shorter list of eight heros (*vīras*) comprises king's brother, the prince, the priest, the queen, the *sūta*, the *grāmaṇī*, the *kṣattṛ* and the *saṃgrahitṛ* (*TS* 1.8.9.1 ff; *TB* 1.7.3.1 ff; *ŚB* 5.3.1.1 ff; *MS* 2.6.5; 4.3.8; *KS* 15.4; *PB* 19.1-4)

*Family: Rājapitṛ,* father of the king, is mentioned in *Aitareya Brāhmaṇa* (8.12, 8.17). In view of the fact that he was or would be the father of the future king or crown prince, the ruling king was also thus addressed in the Rājasūya. The king's son or prince was known as *rājaputra* (*RV* 10.40.3; *AB* 7.17; *PB* 19.1.4; *TB* 3.8.5.1; *ŚB* 13.4.2.5; 13.5.2.5; *KS* 14.8; 28.1), but the term was later used in a wider sense, meaning anyone of aristocratic origin or having a place near the power-centre. The brothers of the king were known as *rājabhrātṛ* (*PB* 19.1.4; *AB* 1.13), and were counted as the king's defenders. The general term for the queens was *rājñī* (*TS* 4.3.6.2; 4.4.2.1; *MS* 2.8.3.9; *KS* 14.13; 15.10). For details see **Queen**.

*Glamour of:* The *Ṛgveda* (8.5.38) speaks of king Kasu making a gift of ten kings to *ṛsi* (sage), while other passages (2.41.5; 5.62.6) represent Mitra and Varuṇa as occupying a spacious palace with a thousand pillars and a thousand gates. Even allowing for poetic exaggeration, the description postulates the existence of a royal place of imposing proportions, and necessarily presupposes a fairly large kingdom that could boast of a capital capable of accommodating a palace of such dimensions. Again, we have to admit that the size of some kingdoms at least was large enough to enable the rulers to command that affluence which is so often described in the *dānastutis*. The presents conferred by the kings on their priests were gorgeous, ample and varied. They consisted of cows numbering thousands at times, horses, chariots, gold, dresses and beautifully attired female slaves. Hence, the wealth possessed at least by some of these rulers was considerable. Further, it is interesting to note that we meet with the expression *samrāṭ*, which meant an 'emperor' in later days, and also the idea of a universal monarch (*viśvasya bhuvanasya rājā*). As the *Śatapatha Brāhmaṇa* (12.9.3.3) and *Aitareya Brāhmaṇa* (8.12.17) speak of a *daśapuruṣaṃ rājyam* (a kingdom of ten generations) and as royal descent may be traced in several other cases, the monarchy may be said to be normally hereditary. The term *rājaputra*, which can be interpreted as 'king's son' in the majority of its occurrences in the texts of this period, bears testimony to the same fact.

*Ideals of:* The king's main function was the protection of the state and the people, and it was recognized that this required firmness and vigour on his part. In the absence of any authoritative principles of international law, hostility, tacit or avowed, was the normal relation between states, and the king had necessarily to be a great warlord, endowed, with ample military resources. These requisites of kingly office are reflected in a hymn of the *Atharvaveda* (6.87-88), which addresses a new king as follows: 'Here be you firm as a mountain and may you not come down. Be you firm here like Indra; remain you here and hold the realm'. . . . 'Firm is the heaven, firm is the earth, firm is the universe, firm are the mountains, let the king of the people be firm'. . . . 'Vanquish you firmly, without falling, the enemies, and those behaving like enemies crush you under your feet. All the quarters unanimously honour you, and for firmness the assembly here creates you.' This evolution of kingly power, out of sheer political necessity, made further progress by the enunciation of his divinity. The *Śatapatha Brāhmaṇa*, a strong exponent of this theory, upholds the doctrine that by performing certain rites in the Rājasūya sacrifice the king becomes not only exempt from punishment but also the lord of the law (*ŚB* 5.4.4.7). But these extreme theoretical assumptions were hardly applicable to real life. The actual instances of expulsion of the king, referred to above, belie these canonical statements. Besides, one fundamental principle which characterizes the political thought of the Hindus is the conception of *dharma*, or Sacred Law, which sustains the universe and to which both the king and all sections of the community owe allegiance. The sages, not the king had the power to interpret this law, which was included in the Sacred Canon, and it was the clearly recognized duty of the king to abide by, and give effect to it. The moral and spiritual sanctions behind this Sacred Law were a sufficiently powerful motive, more than we can possibly imagine today, for restraining the wilful exercise of authority by the king. The *Bṛhadāraṇyaka Upaniṣad*, which forms a part of the *Śatapatha Brāhmaṇa*, clearly enunciates this great principle, though it was elaborated at a later age. In assessing the true character—beneficent or otherwise of kingly rule in this age, we must take note of the high intellectual qualifications of the king. Though kṣatriyas, they were as well-versed, if not more than, as the brāhmaṇas in the Vedas and Upaniṣads. They took great interest in philosophical discussions. They not only patronized learning but were themselves teachers and had even brāhmaṇa disciples, although it was not normal for a brāhmaṇa to learn from a kṣatriya. Such highly cultured kings are thus addressed in the *Vājasaneyī Saṃhitā* (10.27): 'As a ruler, from this day onwards, judge the strong and the weak impartially and fairly. Strive unceasingly to do good to the people and above all, protect the country from all calamities.'

*Judicial Functions:* The *Śatapatha Brāhmaṇa* (5.4.4, etc.) tells us that the king wields the rod of punishment (*daṇḍa*), but is not subject to it. He himself, as a rule, appears to have administered criminal justice. That he was assisted by assessors is probable, though not certain. At any rate, in his absence, he could delegate his jurisdiction to a royal officer, because the *Kāṭhaka Saṃhitā* (27.4) mentions the *rājanya* as a overseer (*adhyakṣa*) when a śūdra is punished. Among the crimes enumerated or otherwise recognized are, theft, robbery, adultery, incest, abduction, the killing of an embryo, the killing of a man, the slaying of a brāhmaṇa (which alone amounts to murder proper and is expiable by the performance of an Aśvamedha), drinking liquor, and treachery, punishable by death.

*Kinds of:* The *Aitareya Brāhmaṇa* (8.14) refers to four kinds of rulership namely, *sāmrājya* (overlordship), *bhaujya* (paramount ruler), *svārājya* (self-ruler), and *vairājya* (sovereign) as representative rulers of the four directions. It is not easy to decide whether all these terms *sāmrājya, bhaujya, svārājya, vairājya* and *rājya* referred to essentially different forms of royal authority in the Brāhmaṇic period. But two terms at least, namely *sāmrājya* and *rājya*, are clearly distinguished from each other in the *Śatapatha Brāhmaṇa* (5.1.1.12-13, cf. *KŚS* 15.1.1.2). In the *Aitareya Brāhmaṇa* (8.17) a king consecrated with Indra's great auction is called *virāt* and worthy of *vairājya*. When a king consecrated with the *punarabhiṣeka* (renewed anointment) ascends his *āsandī* or throne, he prays for attaining *vairājya* as well as other kinds of royal dignity. 'By offering the Rājasūya he becomes *rāja* and by the Vājapeya he becomes *samrāj*, and the office of *rājan* is the lower than that of *samrāj*.

*Land, Ownership of:* The conception of the absolute royal ownership of all land does not seem to have arisen during this age. 'Grants' of land only implied transfer or privileges regarding revenue but no ownership. Similarly, when the king granted to his favourites his royal prerogatives over villages, the 'grant' is to be understood as the transfer of privileges in fiscal matters. That a gift of land in the sense of 'the conferring of ownership' was looked upon as unconstitutional may be inferred from a story in the *Śatapatha Brāhmaṇa* (13.7.1.15) and *Aitareya Brāhmaṇa* (8.21.8). When king Viśvakarman offered the earth (probably a piece of land) to his officiating priest, the earth refused to be given. Such gifts of land probably constituted a violation of customary law. The king certainly had the power to expel a brāhmaṇa and vaiśya (there is no mention of the kṣatriya) from his land, but this power drew its sanction not from his ownership of land but from his sovereignty and was recognized only as a royal prerogative.

*Makers of: Rājakartṛ* or *rājakṛt* 'king maker' is the term applied in the *Atharvaveda* (3.5.7), *Aitareya Brāhmaṇa* (8.17) and the *Śatapatha Brāhmaṇa* (3.4.1.7; 13.2.2.18) to those who sanction the king's supreme authority during his consecration. These officials were the *sūta* and the *grāmaṇī*. Besides, there were officials of the *ratnin* category who belonged to the royal entourage in those houses the *Ratna-havis*, a special rite was performed in the course of the Rājasūya or 'royal consecration'. See **Entourage**.

*Rain-making Function:* Domestic ease and comfort of the kingdom entirely depended upon an abundant supply of timely rain. They did not know how to ensure regular and timely rainfall, but there were some wise and thoughtful men among them who seemed to know the mysteries of the cosmic powers, and the means of propitiating the benevolent among them by magic utterances (*mantras*) and the performance of mysterious rites. This enabled them to overcome the baneful influence of the malevolent powers with a view to bringing down timely rains. These men were called Ṛṣis, or seers, whose help was eagerly sought by all classes, especially the leaders, and the rich and powerful. The rainmakers in the early stages of the Aryan evolution developed into priests and Ṛṣis, whose help was thought to be indispensable for the production of timely rain, and was sought by the grāmaṇīs, the kings, the nobles and the rich. They framed elaborate rules and formulae for the performance of sacrifices with a view to propitiating and strengthening Indra and his auxiliary deities, who alone could defeat the Demon of Draught (*Vṛtra*) and ensure regular rainfall. As the leaders and kings owed their power to the prosperity, happiness and commandment of the people, it was their main interest to requisition the services of the Ṛṣis and priests in the performance of year-long and periodical sacrifices that had 'water' or timely rainfall as their object. But none but the king and the rich could engage their services, as they and their families had to be supported by rich gifts of cattle, gold, grain, and other necessities of life. Thus, the Ṛṣis and priests became indispensable factors in Aryan society. The Ṛṣis were the seers to whom the mysterious *mantras* had been revealed who had ecstatic visions of the great cosmic powers; they regulated and controlled the affairs of the universe. At first, they had been priests also, performing the sacrifices and chanting the *mantras*. But these offices were afterwards relegated to a special class.

*Relations:* Besides the king's father (*rājapitṛ*), brothers (*rājabhrātṛ*), sons (*rājaputra*) and wives (*rājñī*), *rājanya* is the regular term in Vedic literature (*RV* 10.90.12; *AV* 5.17.9; 18.2; 6.38.4; 10.10.18; 12.4.32 ff; 15.8.1; 19.32.8; *TS* 2.4.13.1; 2.5.4.4; 2.5.10.1; 5.1.10.3) for a man of the royal family. In the *Śatapatha Brāhmaṇa* (13.1.6.2, 13.4.2.17), the *rājanya* is different from the *rājaputra*, who is literally the son of a king. The term *rājamātra* (*KB* 26.6, *SŚS* 17.5.3-4, 17.15.13) seems to denote persons belonging to the royal family. The term *rājanya* seems to have originally applied to all the nobles, irrespective of kingly power. In several passages (*RV* 1.40.8; 108.7; 10.42.10; 97.6; *TS* 4.6.8.3; 5.7.6.4; *KS* 11.13; *VS* 18.48; 26.2, *AV* 19.62.1) even the word *rājan* means no more than 'a noble of the ruling house.'

*Tribal Heritage:* From an historical point of view, the Ṛgvedic societies were ruled by the tribal chiefs. The term *rājan* may also refer to the tribal heads. The country which the Vedic Aryans occupied was split into numerous tribal principalities. One passage of the *Ṛgveda* (1.126.1) speaks of a chief living on the banks of the Sindhu, and another (8.21.18) refers to a chief Citra and other nobles as residing in the neighbourhood of the river Sarasvatī. Ten tribal chiefs are described as having fought in the historic battle against Sudās. In the *dānastutis* and elsewhere, a very large number of *rājās* are mentioned. This proves that here the *rājās* meant tribal chiefs and not the king of a monarchical system. It is stated that the *rājās* assembled in *samiti* (*rājānaḥ samitau iva*). Here also tribal chiefs are indicated and it was quite likely that such chiefs occasionally met in war councils. However, towards the close of the Ṛgvedic period the monarchical form began to be established. But in the *Ṛgveda* we come across terms which, in later times, were undoubtedly applied to non-monarchical constitutions. Thus, we have references to the *gaṇa* with the *gaṇapati* or *jyeṣṭha* (elder) at its head. Generally speaking, the kingdoms were small in extent and were units of a single tribe. Whether the confederacy of the five tribes, who attacked Sudās, actually involved a system of political organization or some sort of political collaboration cannot be definitely determined. But it is not altogether unlikely.

**Knife:** Various kinds of knives are mentioned in the *Jaiminīya Brāhmaṇa* (1.42,1,44). The word *śāsa* (*ŚB* 13.2.2.16) is used to denote knife. It is one of the slaughtering knives for the horse and it is made of gold, copper and iron. Another word *sphya* is found in the *Taittirīya Saṃhitā* (1.6.8.2), which means wooden knife. It is used for the purpose of ritual context, which is regarded as one of the ten sacrificial implements. *Svadhīti* may refer to the thunderbolt of Indra (*svadhītir vajraḥ*). In the *Ṛgveda* (1.162.9; 1.162.18; 1.162.20) the word used to denote axe or knife, was used for dissecting the sacrificial horse. In other passages (*RV* 2.29.7; 3.2.10; 5.7.8; 7.3.9; 8.102, 19, 10.89.7), the sense of cutting wood is adequate; reference may be made in one place (*RV* 2.39.7) to sharpening the axe. In the *Atharvaveda* (6.141.2) the term seems once to denote the copper (*lohita*) knife used to mark the ears of cattle. The carpenter's knife or axe is also referred to there. Later the word means 'axe' generally (*TS* 6.3.3.2; *VS* 2.15, 5.43).

**Krivi:** *Krivi* is asserted in the *Śatapatha Brāhmaṇa* (13.5.4.7) to have been the older name of the Pañcālas. This statement is supported by the name of the king mentioned there, Kraivya Pañcāla. The Krivis appear in the *Ṛgveda* (8.20.24, 22.12) as settled on the Sindhu and the Asiknī. The importance of the Pañcālas, and the insignificance of the Krivis, may be explained in part by the fact that the later Kuru-Pañcāla alliance included the Bharatas. It is also probable from the *Śatapatha Brāhmaṇa* (8.5.4.16), that the Turuvasas were included in the Pañcālas, and as the latter name indicates, probably other tribes also.

**Krumu:** *Krumu* is the name of a stream mentioned twice in the *Ṛgveda* once in the Nadī-stuti, or 'praise of rivers' (10.75.6). There can be little doubt that this river is identical with the modern Kurum, a western tributary of the Indus.

**Kṣatriya:** In the later Saṃhitās (*AV* 6.76.3; 6.76.4; 12.5.5; 12.5.5; 12.5.44; 12.5.46; *VS* 30.5) and the Brāhmaṇas (*AV* 7.24; *ŚB* 1.3.2.15; 4.1.4.5; 4.1.46), the kṣatriya stands as a definite member of the social body, distinct from the priest, the subject people, and the slaves, brāhmaṇas, vaiśya and śūdra. It is significant that Rājanya is a variant to kṣatriya, and an earlier one. Hence, it is reasonable to suppose that the kṣatriya and Rājanya are both of similar origin, being princely, or connected with royalty. Moreover, the early use of *kṣatriya* in the *Ṛgveda* (4.12.3; 4.42.1; 5.69.1; 7.64.2; 8.25.8; 8.56.1; 10.109.3, cf. *VS* 4.19; 10.4; *TB* 2.4.7.7) is exclusively connected with royal authority or divine authority. It is impossible to say exactly what persons would be included in the term kṣatriya. That it covered the royal house and the various branches of the royal family may be regarded as certain. No doubt, it also included the nobles and their families; this would explain the occasional apposition of Rājanya and kṣatriya as in the *Aitareya Brāhmaṇa* (7.20; *KS* 20.1), where a Rājanya asks a kṣatriya for a place for sacrifice (*deva-yajña*). Thus, when strictly applied, *kṣatriya* would have wider denotation than Rājanya. As a rule, however, the two expressions are identical, and both are used as evidence in what follows. That kṣatriya ever included the mere fighting man has not been proved; in the *Ṛgveda*, and later, people other than kṣatriyas regularly fought; but possibly if the nobles had retinues as the kings had, kṣatriya would embrace those retainers who had military functions. The term did not apply to all members of the royal entourage. The connection of the kṣatriyas with the brāhmaṇas was very close. The prosperity of the two is repeatedly asserted to be indissolubly associated, especially in the relation of king (*rājan*) and domestic priest (*purohita*). Sometimes there was a feud between kṣatriya and brāhmaṇa (*KS* 28.5; *AV* 5.18.19). His management of the sacrifice then gave the brāhmaṇa power to ruin the kṣatriya by embroiling him with the people (*TS* 2.2.11.2; *MS* 1.6.5; 2.1.9; 3.3.10; *KS* 29.8) or with other kṣatriyas (*MS* 3.3.10). Towards the common people, on the other hand, the kṣatriya stood in a relation of superiority (*KS* 16.4; 21.1; 22.9; 29.9; 20.10; *AB* 2.33; *ŚB* 11.2.7.15; 11.2.7.16; *MS* 4.4.9; 4.4.10; 4.6.8). There are, however, references to occasional feuds between the people and nobles (*TS* 5.4.6.7; *MS* 4.6.7) in which, no doubt, the smaller numbers of the latter were compensated by their superior arms and prowess. No doubt the king granted to them the right, which may have been hereditary, to be supported by common people, they thus became superior to them in return for these privileges. The kṣatriyas had probably duties of protection to perform, as well as some judicial functions, to judge from an obscure passage of the *KS* (27.4). The main duty of the kṣatriya in the small states of the Vedic periods was readiness for war. The bow is thus his special attribute. (*AV* 18.2.60; *KS* 18.9; 37.1; *ŚB* 5.3.5.30; *TA* 6.1.3; *AB* 7.19; *TS* 7.5.18.1; *MS* 3.12.6; *VS* 22.2), just as the goad is that of the agriculturist. There is evidence to show that the kṣatriyas also paid attention to mental occupations. In the latest stratum of the Brāhmaṇa literature there are references to learned princes like Janaka of Videha, who is said to have become a brāhmaṇa (*brahma*), apparently in the sense that he had the full knowledge which a brāhmaṇa should possess (*ŚB* 11.6.2.1; *KU* 4.1). Other learned kṣatriyas of this period were Pravāhna Jaivali (*BU* 6.1.1; *CU* 1.8.1; 5.3.1). Aśvapati Kaikeya (*ŚB* 10.6.1.1) and Ajātaśatru (*BU* 2.1.1; *KU* 4.1). Of the training and education of a kṣatriya we have no record; presumably, as in fact if not in theory later on, he was mainly instructed in the art of war, besides some knowledge in the Vedas.

Rudimentary administrative functions also devolved on him. At the early state of the development of the nobility which appears to be represented in the *Ṛgveda*, it was probably not unusual or impossible for a vaiśya to become a kṣatriya; at least, this assumption best explains the phrase (*RV* 7.104.13) 'claiming falsely a kṣatriya's rank' (*kṣatriyaṃ mithuyā dhārayantam*). In fact, kṣatriyahood was always a matter of claim. Those who became rulers or were close to the centre of political power, claimed the status of kṣatriya and received it. In fact, all the ruling dynasties of ancient India belonged to the category of 'consecrated kṣatriya'. The king and the kṣatriyas must have stood in a particularly close relation. The former being kṣatriya *par excellence*, it is to him rather than to the ordinary kṣatriya that we must refer passages like that in the *Śatapatha Brāhmaṇa* (7.1.1.8), where it is said that the kṣatriya, with the consent of the clansmen, gives a settlement to a man; clearly, a parallel to the rule found among many peoples that the chief but only with the consent of the people, can make a grant of unoccupied land. In the same *Brāhmaṇa* (12.8.3.19) it is said that a kṣatriya consecrates a kṣatriya, a clear reference, as the commentators explain, to the practice of the old king consecrating the prince (*kumāra*) who is to succeed him and. The ksatriya and the *purohita* are regarded as alone complete in contrast with other people, the parallel with the *purohita* here suggesting that the kṣatriya *par excellence* is meant. On the other hand, the king is sometimes contrasted with Rājanya (*ŚB* 13.4.2.17).

**Kṣattṛ:** The term for a chamberlain is *kṣattṛ*. The word appears frequently in the later Saṃhitās and Brāhmaṇas, denoting a member of the royal entourage, but the sense is somewhat uncertain. In the *Ṛgveda* (6.13.2) it is used for a god as the 'distributor' of good things to his worshipper; the same sense seems to be found in the *Atharvaveda* (3.24.7; 5.17.4) and elsewhere (*ŚB* 13.5.4.6; *SSS* 16.9.16). In one passage of the *Vājasaneyī Saṃhitā* (30.13; *TB* 1.7.3.5), it is interpreted as 'doorkeeper' by the commentator Mahīdhara, a sense which seems possible in other passages (*TS* 4.5.4.2; *MS* 2.9.4; *KS* 17.13; *CU* 4.1.5; *PB* 19.1.4), while Sāyaṇa ascribes to it in one passage of the *Śatapatha Brāhmaṇa* (5.3.1.7) the more dignified meaning of *antaḥpurādhyakṣa*, 'a chamberlain'. In other passages (*VS* 16.26; *TB* 3.4.7.1; *SSS* 16.1.20), again, the sense of 'charioteer' is not unlikely. Later the *kṣattṛ* was regarded as a man of mixed caste.

**Kṣetra:** *Kṣetra* (neuter) is derived from the verbal root *kṣi* or *kṣay*, which means to dwell (*Nir.* 14), to abide, to reside, to remain (*AV* 19.10.10), and to inhabit (*ŚB* 10.2.3.2). It is used to denote the field, ground, land, region and country, even from the Ṛgvedic period. As a first part of a compound, for it mostly occurs in *kṣetrapati* the lord of the soil or grounding the *Ṛgveda* (4.57.1). In later texts *Kṣetrapati* is worshipped as god; it is also used to denote property and in the *Yajurveda Saṃhitā* it means 'belonging to the lord of the soil'. Again *Kṣetrapatya* is used in the *Atharvaveda* (1.99.4) to denote landlordship. As a derivative of *kṣetra*, the adjective form *kṣetriya* is used in the *Atharvaveda* to denote an organic and incurable disease; its plural form means the environs of a place. Again *kṣetriya-nāśana* is used in the *Atharvaveda* (2.8.5) to denote removing a chronic diseases. *Kṣetra* and its derivatives occurs one hundred seventy-five times in the Vedic texts alone with wide-ranging meanings. In the *Ṛgveda* it is geographical space, land, field, region or expanse of country. Distinct from the ordinary land is the *bhadrakṣetra* 'auspicious land' (*RV* 5.62.7), and the *mahīkṣetra*, 'great, splendid, rich dominion' (*RV* 3.31.15). The country void of pasture is also mentioned (*RV* 6.47.20). *Kṣetra* stands for the field and not the forest (*AV* 4.2.7). We find the following expressions: *kṣetrāsām* 'procuring land' (*RV* 4.38.1), *kṣetrapatyam*, 'possession or ownership of land' (*TS* 1.8.20.1), *kṣetrajeṣe* 'contest for landed property' (*RV* 1.33.15) and *kṣetrasata,* 'acquisition of land' (*RV* 7.19.3), etc. There are indications of 'fertile field' (*apnasvati*) and barren land (*RV* 1.127.6), properly irrigated and manured agricultural field (*RV* 7.49.2; *AV* 1.6.4; 19.2.2; 3.14.3; 19.31.3). The other related terms are *kṣetra-tara,* 'a good fertile field' (*ŚB* 1.4.1.16), *kṣetra-sadhas* 'one making the field fertile', he who divides the field' (*RV* 3.8.7; 8.31.4), etc.

**Kula:** From the evidences of the *Ṛgveda*, however meagre, we learn distinctly that the social and political organization of the Aryans rested on their patriarchal family. The very use of the term *kula,* which does not occur as an uncompounded word before the period to the Brāhmaṇas, suggests a system of individual families, each consisting of several members under the headship of the father or eldest brother to whom the *kula* belongs. The family life underwent subsequent changes in course of natural progress of the Aryan society by means of the formation of larger and still larger groups, as for example, the clans (*viśaḥ*) tribes, (*jana*) and the villages (*grāma*) culminating in the formation of states. As head of the family, the father controlled all activities of his children, sometimes even their marriage. The relation between the father and his children was, as a rule, that of deep love and affection and the father was, as he is still today, regarded as the foundation of all that is good and kind (*RV* 1.1.4). Though loving, the father did not fail to be strict to his sons, as shown in the chastisement of his gambler sons in the *Ṛgveda* (2.29.5). Of course, the *Ṛgveda* records the cruel act of Ṛjrāśva being blinded by his father for slaying one hundred rams, which may be passed over as unusual or isolated facts. The tale of the sale of Śunaḥśepa in the *Aitareya Brāhmaṇa* (7.13-18) suggests how the son was under the absolute control of his father and it also reflects the father's heartless treatment of his son. From this story we also learn that adoption was admitted even where there were natural sons, for the sake of adding a qualified member to the family as Viśvāmitra adopted Śunaḥśepa. The *Atharvaveda* (3.30) speaks of the family which was highly stressed upon. It shows how the members of a family were eager to live united, with common interests and mutual love and respect among themselves. The joint family system was the order of the day in the Vedic period and three generations might have lived under the same roof. Sons or daughters had free choice in their marriage affairs (*JUB* 3.12.2) and the son lived with his parents even after marriage (*MS* 4.1.9; *VS* 30.9; *AV* 6.112.3; *TB* 3.2.8.11). The bride was taken by her groom to her new house as its mistress, the *Ṛgveda* (10.85.26), and the term *grahapatnī* shows how she forced will with her position and prestige in the administration of the whole family. The new bride is blessed to be treated like an empress over her father-in-law, mother-in-law, sister-in-law and brother-in-law (*RV* 10.85.47). The *RV* (10.179.2) shows that the chief of the family (*kula-pā*) was inferior to and attendant on the *vrājapatis*, at least in war. The *Atharvaveda* (7.72.2) states the same fact as the above *Ṛgveda*. The above refers to the heads of families being subordinate in war to the village headman (*grāmaṇī*).

**Kuru:** The Kurus appear as by far the most important people in the Brāhmaṇa literature. There is clear evidence that it was in the country of the Kurus, or the allied Kuru-Pāñcālas, that the great Brāhmaṇas were composed (*TB* 1.8.4, 1.1.2; *MS* 4.2.6). The Kurus are comparatively seldom mentioned alone, their name being usually coupled with that of the Pāñcālas on account of the intimate connection of the two peoples. The Kuru-Pāñcālas are often expressly referred to as a united nation (*JUB* 3.7.6, 8.7, 4.7.2; *KauU* 4.1; *GB* 1.2.9; *VS* 11.3.3). In the land of the Kuru-Pāñcālas speech is said to have its particular home (*ŚB* 3.2.3.15); the mode of sacrifice among them is proclaimed to be the best (*ŚŚS* 15.3.15; *LŚS* 8.11.18); the Kuru-Pāñcāla kings perform the Rājasūya or royal sacrifice (*ŚB* 5.5, 2, 3.5); their princes march forth on raids in the dewy seasons, and return in the hot season (*TB* 1.8, 4, 12). Later on the Kuru-Pāñcāla brāhmaṇas are famous in the Upaniṣads (*JB* 2.78; *JUB* 3.30.6,4.6.2; *BU* 3.1.1.,9.20 etc.). The Kurus alone are chiefly mentioned in connection with the locality which they occupied, Kurukṣetra. We are told, however, of a domestic priest (*purohita*) in the service of both the Kurus and the Sṛñjayas (*ŚB* 2.4.4.5), who must therefore at one time have been closely connected. In the *Ṛgveda* the Kurus do not appear under that name as a people. But mention is made of a prince, Kuruśravaṇa (Glory of the Kurus) in the *Ṛgveda* (10.33.4), and of a Pākasthaman Kaurāyana (*RV* 8.3.21). In the *Atharvaveda* (20.127.7) there is a mention of a king of the Kurus, Parīkṣit, whose son, Janamejaya, is mentioned in the *Śatapatha Brāhmaṇa* (13.5.4) as one of the great performers of the horse sacrifice. The Kuru people, as known later, included some of the tribes referred to by other names in the *Ṛgveda*. Since the Bharatas appear so prominently in the Brāhmaṇa texts as a great people of the past, while the later literature ignores them in its list of nations, it is difficult to avoid the conclusion that they became merged in some other tribes. Moreover, there is evidence that the Bharatas occupied the territory in which the Kurus were later found. The territory of the Kuru-Pāñcālas is declared in the *Aitareya Brāhmaṇa* to be the middle country (Madhyadesa *AB* 8.14).

**Kurukṣetra:** The main centre of life in the period of later Saṃhitās and Brāhmaṇas was Kurukṣetra, in the country of the Kuru-Pāñcālas, which was regarded as particularly a sacred area (*ŚB* 4.15.13; 11.5.1.4; 14.1.1.2; *AB* 7.30; *PB* 25.10; *JB* 3.126; *MS* 2.1.4; 4.5.9). Within its boundaries flowed the rivers Dṛṣadvatī (q.v.) and Sarasvatī (q.v.) as well as the Āpayā (q.v.). Here too, was situated Śaryānavant which appears to have been a lake. The boundaries of Kurukṣetra, as given in the *Taittirīya Āraṇyaka* (5.1.1) are Khāṇḍava in the south, the Turghna in the north and the Parinaḥ in the west. The areas roughly corresponds with the modern districts Thanesar, Kurukṣetra and Ambala of Haryana.

# L

**Lace:** The word *śleṣman* is used to denote lace or cord which is mentioned in the *Kāṭhaka Saṃhitā* (34.9; *AB* 5.32.6; *PB* 16.1.14). Lace or cord is intended for fastening in the chariot.

**Ladle:** A sort of ladle is termed *sruva* (*MS* 4.1.11; *KS* 31.14; *VS* 2.6; *TS* 4.2.7.4; *AB* 1.11.8; *TB* 1.4.1.5; *ŚB* 1.4.5-6, 1.3.3.2, 4.2.4.24); it was used as the offering spoon in the morning and evening oblations. *Mekṣana* (*TB* 1.3.10.4; 3.7.4.9; *ŚB* 2.4.2.13) was wooden ladle used to stir up the oblation. A tongue-shaped ladle or spoon, indicated by the term *juhū* (*RV* 8.44.5; 10.21.3; *AV* 18.4.5-6; *JB* 1.49; 1.53), was used to offer butter to the gods. *Upabhṛt* (*MS* 1.1.12; 1.4.13; 4.1.14; *KS* 31.9, 31.4; *TS* 1.1.11.2; 2.5.9.5; *VS* 2.6; *JB* 1.48; *TB* 3.3.1.1-2; *ŚB* 1.3.2.2; 1.3.4.14; 11.4.2.1; 12.5.2.7) is the name of the ladle made of Aśvattha wood, which was held in the left hand under *juhū*, to save the oblations from slipping down. *Śruva* (*RV* 1.116.24, 1.21.6) denotes a small ladle used as a dipping-spoon for soma libation. In the *Jaiminīya Brāhmaṇa* (1.48) it designates a long handled, cup-shaped spoon for serving or transferring liquids. *Sruc* (*RV* 1.84.18; 1.110.6; 1.144.1; *AV* 5.27.5; 6.114.3; 9.6.17) is a large wooden sacrificial ladle used as an offering spoon. It is of an arm's length, with a bowl of the size of the hand and is spout-shaped. There is a ladle of a special type named *agnihotrahavanī* (*TS* 1.6.8.3), which is made of Vikankaṭa wood. It was used to offer libations in the Agnihotra rite and regarded as one of ten sacrificial weapons.

**Lagenaria Vulgaris:** Alāpu, Alābu, the bottle-gourd (Lagenaria vulgaris). Vessels made of it are referred to in the *Atharvaveda* (8.10.29; 8.10.30; 20.132.1; 20.132.2 cf. *alāpu* in *MS* 4.2.13).

**Laghurudra:** Recital of *ekādaśinī* Rudra *mantras,* (*TS* 4.5.1.11). It is prescribed for averting evil and for obtaining peace.

**Lakṣaṇa:** The term *Lakṣaṇa* has a wide significance. On the one hand, it denotes observation, sight, and seeing and on the other mark, sign, symbol, characteristic lineament, attribute and quality. In philosophical terms such as *lakṣaṇa-pariṇāma* (change in time-variation), *sāmānyalakṣana* and *jñānalakṣaṇa* (knowledge-marked sense-object contacts), *svalakṣaṇa* and *lakṣaṇa-śūnyatā, lakṣaṇa* refers to a specific and distinguishing characteristic. In the arts it refers to iconographic requirement, sign, symbol, attribute, lineament and so forth. In literature, thirty-six *lakṣaṇas* are spoken of. *Lakṣmī* denoting a mark, sign, token and fortune occurs in the Vedas (cf. *RV* 10.71.2) and classical Sanskrit literature (See **Lakṣmī**). Lakṣaṇa occurs in the sense of mark, sign, characteristic, etc., in the *Atharvaveda* (4.141.2). Lakṣaṇa denotes the mark made on cattle by branding, to distinguish ownership (*MS* 4.2.9). According to the *Maitrāyaṇī Saṃhitā* (4.2.9) it was to be made under the *nakṣatra* Revatī.

**Lakṣmī:** Lakṣmī is not found in the *Ṛgveda* in the sense which the word bears in the later mythology, of a goddess personifying good fortune, though the word itself occurs in the *Ṛgveda* 10.71.2. In the *Atharvaveda*, however, we have the hymn which speaks of a plurality of Lakṣmīs, actually denoting Alakṣmī or evil Lakṣmī (7.115.1). 'Fly away hence, O unlucky (or miserable) Lakṣmī, perish hence, fly away from hence; with an iron hook we fasten thee to our enemy. Savitṛ, do thou who art golden-handed, bestowing on us wealth, send away from us to some other quarter the flying and hateful Lakṣmī, who amounts upon me as a creeper upon a tree. A hundred Lakṣmīs are born together with the body of a mortal at his birth. Of these we chase away hence the most unlucky. Do thou, Jātavedas, retain for us those which are fortunate. Thus, I divide them like cows standing upon barren ground. May those Lakṣmīs which are unlucky I destroy.' (The expression *pūjya* Lakṣmī occurs also in the *Atharvaveda* (12.5.6.) Śrī and Lakṣmī occur in the Śrī Sūkta, which is a supplement of the *Ṛgveda* composed at a later period. In *Vājasaneyī Saṃhitā* (32.12) Śrī and Lakṣmī are described as the two wives of Āditya.

**Lance:** *Sṛka* in *Ṛgveda* (1.32.12, 10.180.2) denotes a weapon of Indra, perhaps a lance. Sāyaṇa in his commentary on the *Ṛgveda* (1.132.12) says '*sṛka* is *vajra*', as *Nirukta* (2.20.6) says *sṛkaḥ vṛkah iti vajranāmasu paṭhitatvāt. Pavira* also denotes lance (*Nirukta* 12.30).

**Land Tenures:** There are doubtful traces in Vedic literature of communal property in the sense of ownership by a community of any sort. The same holds good in the case of communal cultivation. Again, the precise nature of ownership is not determined by the expression 'individual ownership'. The legal relationship of the head of a family and its members is nowhere explained and can only be conjectured. Very often a family lived together with undivided shares in the land. The rules about the inheritance of landed property do not occur before the Sūtras. In the *Śatapatha Brāhmaṇa*, however, the giving of land as a fee to priests is mentioned, which shows that even at that time land was a special type of property (*ŚB* 13.6.2.18). Since the *Ṛgveda* (1.110.5) says that the fields are to be carefully measured, it somehow points to individual ownership of land for the plough. Such a conclusion is supported by a hymn in the *Ṛgveda* (8.91.5), which refers to Apālā's father's field (*urvara*) by putting it on the same level as his hand or hair, as a personal possession. Consistent with this are the epithets 'winning fields' (*urvara-sa, urvara-hit, kṣetra-sa*), the *Ṛgveda* (4.38.1, 6.20.1, 2.21.1, 4.38.1), while lord of fields, which is used as a god (*RV* 8.21.3), is presumably a transfer of a human epithet (*urvara-pati*). Moreover, fields are spoken of in the same connection as children (*RV* 4.41.6, etc.), and the conquest of fields (*kṣetrāni saṃ-ji*) is often referred to in the Saṃhitās (*TS* 3.2.8.5; *KS* 5.2, *MS* 4.12.3). The expression 'desirous of a village' (*grāmakāma*), which occurs frequently in the later *Saṃhitās* (*TS* 2.1.1.2, 3.2; 3.9.2, etc.), points, however, to the practice of the king granting his royal prerogatives over villages to his favourites as far as fiscal matters were concerned. Later (*ŚB* 7.1.1.8), the idea developed that the king was the owner of all the land, and parallel with that idea the view that the holders of such grants were landlords. But of either idea there is no trace in Vedic literature beyond the word *grāma-kāma*, which is a more probable reference to the grant of regalia than to the grant of land.

**Laughing Woman:** In the *Ṛgveda* (1.124.7) the word, *hasrā*, is found as an adjective for a woman. A laughing woman denotes a courtesan. Sāyaṇa and Yāska (Nir. 3.5) suggest this word as *hasana* in the sense of a laughing woman specially engaged in the business of courtesanship.

**Law of Contract:** The law of contract binds men and regulates their mutual relationship. The *Ṛgveda* (1.126.1-2) refers to a contract between Bhavayavya and Kakṣivan, wherein the latter would prepare *stoma* for the former and for this the latter would pay the former a hundred *niṣkas*, horses and oxen. The transaction of a sale or purchase was also determined by the law of contract, as evidenced by the *Ṛgveda* (4.24.9), which states that when the price for a thing of value was not adequate and hence the thing was not sold, the seller, unable to get a higher amount from the purchaser, agreed upon a price by means of bargaining with his customer. Once the bargain was made it was binding on both the purchaser and seller. The *Ṛgveda* (4.24.10) shows how letting or hiring was considered a temporary transaction by which the purchaser became the owner of the thing for a temporary period and for a specific purpose. When the purpose was served, he had to return the thing. The term *śulka* often meant a 'price' fixed with mutual agreement. In purchase, if nothing was specifically noted, the unit of value was evidently, the cow. Sometimes *hiraṇya* and *śatamāna* (*ŚB* 12.7.2.13; 9.1.4; *KS* 8.5; 14.8; 22.8) are found to be used to denote 'some standard' other that cows. The *Vājasaneyī Saṃhitā* (30) and *Taittirīya Brāhmaṇa* (3.4) give us a long list of technical workers in a village, who probably worked on contract basis. The Vedic literature refers little to any law of deposit. The *Atharvaveda* (19.48.1 ff) refers to something like a trust prevailing among Vedic Aryans. The term *paridānam* means deposit or trust of an article to somebody else, i.e. loan for a fixed period, to be returned in future. Another term *nidhi* is met with in the place of deposit or store and then treasure (*RV* 2.24.6; 8.29.6; 10.68.6). The *Śatapatha Brāhmaṇa* (1.1.1) shows how a contract was sanctified with a ceremonial practice. The *Aitareya Brāhmaṇa* indicates the same practice and speaks of the inviolability of the contract.

**Law: Dharma:** In early Indian tradition *dharma* did not mean religion. It was same as Law and as such it was connected with the law-governed universe (*ṛta*) and the reality behind all appearances (*satya*). *Ṛta*, *satya*, and *dharma* were held to be distinct in the age of the *Atharvaveda*, as evidenced by the hymn of the *Atharvaveda* (11.7.17). The commentator explains *ṛtam* as *mānasa yathārtha saṃkalpanam*, i.e. right conception. The *Atharvaveda* refers to *dhāma* (2.1.3), *vrata* (18.1.5) and *dharma* (7.5.1; cf. 18.3.1). These concepts of cosmic order (*ṛta*), divine ordinance and ancient custom acted as moral checks on the power of the king during the period of the *Atharvaveda*. In the Vedic age the word *dharma* denoted only ordinance or law. *Ṛta* lost its moral significance in the later period when *dharma* came to be used more frequently, signifying the sense of *ṛta* as well. In the *Aitareya Brāhmaṇa* (8.13 & 26), *dharmasya goptā*, the king is noted as the protector of *dharma*. The connection of the state with *dharma* in the Brahmanic period was of a limited kind. The religious rites and ceremonies and the ethical rules of conduct were settled and declared by the brāhmaṇas in which the state did not interfere. But it was the responsibility of the state to enforce the observance of their duties by the people. The king was thus the protector of *dharma*, which means no more than the idea that the king was considered to be the protector of social and moral principles. Notwithstanding his limitations, the king by virtue of his sovereignty was the guardian of law and as such wielded the rod of punishment (*daṇḍa*). Thus, as the upholder of law, he was the upholder of *dharma* as well.

**Law of Gift:** Dakṣiṇā was an important part of the Vedic ritual, as reflected in the *Ṛgveda* and later Vedic texts, which refer to gifts to priests performing the sacrifice. It consisted mostly in gold, but if the gift itself was gold then *dakṣiṇā*, which was to be received by the donee, may be of silver. Among other articles for gifts the best is the cow. The sacrificer or any other individual may also give goats, sheep, horses, elephants, clothes, chariots, slaves, corns, etc. (*ŚB* 4.3.4.1 ff; *GDS* 5, 16-17; *ĀpŚS* 13.5-7). But specific rules for making and receiving gifts, as given in the Dharmaśāstras, are absent in the Vedic texts. With reference to the gifts of Naciketa to Yama, mentioned in the *Kaṭha Upaniṣad*

(3.16), it is doubtful to say whether the term *sarvasva*, frequently used in connection to gifts, meant all properties including one's own son and wife. The same problem persists in the case of the gift of land. Though the practice of making land grants later became a socio-econmic feature of Indian history, it is difficult to say whether it was theoretically valid. Theoretically, earth cannot be gifted (*ŚB* 13.7.1.14-15; *AB* 8.2), as she herself explained when Viśvakarman was about to give her to Kaśyapa: 'No mortal can give me away, thou art foolish, O Viśvakarman.' According to Jaimini, however, the *devatās* were not a corporeal being and hence incapable of accepting gifts.

**Law of Inheritance:** *Dāya* is mentioned in the *Ṛgveda* (2.32.4) and explained by Sāyaṇa as 'possessed of plentiful heritage of wealth'. In the *Ṛgveda* (10.114.10) we find *dāya* in the sense of 'reward' of exertion, as Sāyaṇa explains it as *ebhyaḥ asyebhyaḥ śramasya nāsakaṃ ghasādikaṃ vi bhajanti devāḥ prayacohanti*. But later it means 'inheritance', i.e. a father's property which is to be divided among his sons either during his lifetime or after his death. Another word *riktha* is found in the *Ṛgveda* (3.31.2; *Nir* 3.5) and *AB* (7.18), denoting inheritance. The word *dāya* has been mentioned in the *Taittirīya Saṃhitā* and the Brāhmaṇas in the sense of 'Paternal Wealth' or wealth in general. The *Taittirīya Saṃhitā* (3.4.9.4) refers to the tale of Nābhānediṣṭha, who was deprived of his share of paternal property which his elder sons divided among themselves in the presence of Manu. In the *Aitareya Brāhmaṇa* (5.14) version, the division was made during Manu's lifetime. The property Manu divided seems to be movable property and not land. The *Taittirīya Saṃhitā* (2.5.2.7) shows that the eldest son received the lion's share. Thus *dāya* in the Vedic period was used to denote *dhana* or wealth inherited from the father. The *Taittirīya Brāhmaṇa* (16.4.3-5) states about the importance of the eldest son in matter of inheritance. The *Ṛgveda* (3.32.2) has been explained in the *Nirukta* (3.9) as follows: 'Not to sisters should the begotten son give the *riktha* or inheritance.' She is made the receptacle for the child of her husband; and thus we learn clearly that in the Ṛgvedic society woman were excluded from partition or inheritance (cf. *ŚB* 4.4.2.13). 'The story of Abhyagni Aitasāyaṇa in the *Aitareya Brāhmaṇa* (6.33) shows the right of the father to disinherit his sons.' He could bestow the largest share to any one of his chosen sons, not necessarily the eldest (*PB* 16.4.4). Another school of thought lays down a special share to be given to the eldest son, after which the rest is to be equally divided. Such an arrangement is obviously to be made by a man dividing his wealth before death, as indicated in the *Ṛgveda* (1.116.3). The heir is called *dāyāda* (*ŚB* 7.4.3.9; *AV* 5.18.6 ff *Nir.* 3.4).

**Law of Joint Undertaking:** Joint undertakings are indicated by the existence and functions of the corporate bodies, as evidenced by the functions like the *sabhā, samiti, vidatha, gaṇa*, etc. The last hymn of the *Ṛgveda* (10.191.3) speaks of such a spirit. The joint undertaking of priests in the Vedic sacrifices, like the *jyotiṣṭoma* and the mode of distribution of sacrificial fees, shows, how the principle of partnership was already formulated. The words *śreṣṭhin* and *śraiṣṭhya* in Vedic literature indicate the formation of trade-guilds. But we have little information about the laws of different associations. Even the earlier Dharmasūtras are silent on the law of joint undertaking. No detailed account of the laws pertaining to partnership or joint undertakings are found. However, we find the germs of such contributions of groups, as indicated by words like *śreṇī* in *Ṛgveda* (1.163.10), *vrāta* and *gaṇa* in *RV* (3.26.6 and 5.53.11) and *puga* in the *Kauṣītakai Brāhmaṇa* (16.7). The *Gautama Dharma Sūtra* (11.21) enjoins that cultivators, traders, herdsmen, money lenders and artisans may work jointly or in association for their respective classes. These classes of people formed guilds, which subsequently became powerful enough to extract the privilege of formulating laws for their own groups from the king.

**Law of Properties:** The *Ṛgveda* refers to various terms for properties of different classes. *Rayī* (*RV* 1.73.1; 4.36.9; 2.21.6; 6.6.7; 3.1.9; 6.31.1; *AV* 3.14.1; 6.33.3; 7.80.2; *TS* 7.1.72; *VS* 9.22) is the most common word for wealth. Wealth is also heard of in the shape of heroes (*vīra*), good sons (*RV* 2.11.13; 2.30.11; 4.51.10), horses (*RV* 4.4.1), slaves and slave-girls, bipeds and quadrupeds (*RV* 10.97.20). Besides, we hear of wealth in terms of *ratna* (*RV* 1.20.7; 35.8; 41.6; 125.1; 140.11; 141.10; 2.38.1; *AV* 5.1.7; 7-14.4; *ŚB* 5.3.1.1), *hiraṇya Ṛgveda* (1.162.16) meaning gold and gold coins, i.e. jewels and ornaments like necklaces and ear-ring, etc. (*RV* 10.78.1; 1.85.3), immovable property like fertile land (*RV* 6.25.4; cf.) *kṣetra* in *RV* (4.57.1-3; 8.35.10; *AV* 2.82.12.1; 8.21.3), tanks, wells and houses (*RV* 10.107.7-11), palaces (*RV* 2.41.5), carts, chariots, boats and ships and painted gift cars (*RV* 10.85.20) are also frequently referred to. The *Ṛgveda* (10.62.11; 107.5) draws our attention to family and village-ownership as well. Collective or communal ownership in the initial stage is evidenced by the common pasture, which the Ṛgvedic Aryans cared for at their pastoral stage, and subsequently followed by individual ownership of the things they needed most for the sustenance of physical life. That is why they recognized ownership in all their movable necessities of live, as evidenced by the *Ṛgveda* (6.25.4). The Vedic people were initially pastoral and hence interested in common pasture land (*RV* 1.25.16). Gradually, they became interested in agriculture and craved for possession of land. They, of course, recognized the right of transfer by sale, gift or otherwise. Gift was highly eulogized in the *Ṛgveda*

(10.107.5). The Vedic sages (*RV* 6.1.13) conceived of Agni as the owner of all wealth, from whom the worshippers received it as a matter of gift. In the course of the evolution of property relations, individual devolved on the head of the family or the clan. Individual earnings went to the head of the family as evidenced by the *Ṛgveda* (1.126.3), which states that Kakṣivan gave over to his father whatever he had received as gifts from Svanaya. The father, however, could give any of his sons property during his lifetime. The law relating to land-tenure in the Vedic age is difficult to determine. The *Ṛgveda* (1.100.18) refers to the division of land into well-defined plots. The Vedic literature refers to different modes of acquisition of properties: (i) *dakṣiṇā*, (ii) gain in war (*RV* 10.107.7-11), (iii) presents at marriage, (iv) purchase, (v) inheritance, (vi) labour, (vii) gambling, and (viii) races (*AB* 2.25). Treasure-troves (*nidhi*) are also mentioned in the *Ṛgveda* (1.116.11; 1.117.12; 2.24.6) but no detailed rules are mentioned in regard to them.

**Lead:** The Vedic term for lead is *sīsā*. It occurs first in the *Atharvaveda* (12.2.1.19), where it is mentioned as used for amulets (1.16.2.4). The word is amply found in later Saṃhitās and Brāhmaṇas (*MS* 2.4.2; *VS* 18.13; *TB* 3.12.6.5; *ŚB* 5.1.14, 12.7.1.7; *CU* 4.17.7). The use of lead by the weaver as a weight is perhaps also referred to (*VS* 19.80; *MS* 3.11.9; *TB* 2.6.4).

**Leather-bag:** Leather-bag is mentioned as *dṛti* in the *Ṛgveda* (1.19.110; 4.51.1; 4.51.3; 5.83.7; 6.48.18; 6.48.103; 6.48.2; 8.5.19, 8.9.18), *Atharvaveda* (7.18.1), *Taittirīya Saṃhitā* (1.8.19.1), *Vājasaneyī Saṃhitā* (26.18.26.19), *Pañcaviṃśa Brāhmaṇa* (5.10.2) and *Taittirīya Brāhmaṇa* (1.8.3.4). It means a leather bag to hold fluids. In the *Ṛgveda* (7.89.2) it is termed as *dhmata*, meaning, inflated; a patient of dropsy was compared with such as bag. It is used for containing drinks like milk, wine, etc. (*PB* 14.11.26, 16, 13, 13). The word *bhastrā* means leather bag, leather bottle or leather pouch in the *Śatapatha Brāhmaṇa* (1.1.2.7; 1.6.3.16). It was used to keep grains.

**Leather Industry:** The word *carmamnā* meaning a tanner, is used in the *Ṛgveda* (8.5.38) and indicates the prevalence of the art of tanning hides in the Ṛgvedic society. Wetting of the hide is referred to in the *Ṛgveda* (1.85.5). Sūrya is depicted as rolling up darkness like a piece of leather. The *Ṛgveda* mentioned different articles of hide (6.75.11); bowstrings (6.75.14), slings (1.121.9), thongs (6.47.26), reins for horses (6.46.14) and lash of a whip (6.53.9). It refers to skin vessels for storing soma juice (8.1.17; 9.66.28-29); honey (8.5.19), curd (6.48.18) and wine (*dṛti*) (1.191.10). The *Ṛgveda* (6.75.14) mentions leather-guard of the forearm for warriors. Chariots were girt with leather straps (6.47.26-27). Leather troughs are also noted in the *Ṛgveda* (10.101.7). Others (5.61.2-3) refer to reins, bridle, saddle and whip of the Maruts. Wardrums are heard in the *Ṛgveda* (6.47.29). *Carmamnā* is mentioned also in the *Vājasaneyī Saṃhitā* (30.15). The *Ṛgveda* (2.1.1.9-10) speaks of the process of tanning and stretching out of a hide with pegs (*śaṃkubhiḥ*). The *Śvetāśvatara Upaniṣad* (6.20) refers to rolling up of hides. The importance of this industry was due to the use of various articles made of skin, for daily use and for ritual purposes. The religious student wore the black antelope skin (*AV* 11.5.6). In the *Atharvaveda* (5.21.7) the gods are said to have alarmed the enemies by the drum and the skin of the gazele. Goat's skin was used as garment by a brāhmaṇa priest, (*Śatapatha Brāhmaṇa* 3.9.1.12) and also as coverlet for *āsandīs* (*ŚB* 5.2.1.22). The skin of the black antelope was also used for covering the āsandīs (*ŚB* 12.8.3.4-10) and for pressing *soma* (*AV* 11.1.8). Tiger-skin was also used for covering the *āsandī* (*ŚB* 5.4.4.1 ff). The *Taittirīya Saṃhitā* (5.4.4.4.) states that 'the fire is death; the black antelope skin is the form of holy power; he puts on a pair of black sandals'. The *Śatapatha Brāhmaṇa* (5.4.3.19) refers to boar-skin used for ritual shoes. Shoes of boar-skin were used by the sacrificer at Rājasūya (*BŚS* 12.12; & *KŚS* 15.6.23). Leather-garments were used in the Sūtra period as the *Pāraskara Gṛhya Sūtra* (2.5.17-18) enjoins that a brāhmaṇa should use an upper garment made of antelope-skin, a kṣatriya that of a spotted deer and vaiśya that of a goat or cow. The *Baudhāyana Śrautasūtra* (15.16) mentions storing of ghee, honey, oil grain, etc., in leather-bags. The *Āśvalāyana Gṛhyasūtra* (3.12.11) refers to traps of leather for protecting a warrior's arm against the bow string.

**Lesser Arts:** In the *Chāndogya Upaniṣad* (7.1.2.4) a few subjects are enlisted which, according to Śaṅkara, devote the arts associated with the lesser gods, such as the making of perfumes like *gandhadravyayukti*. Sometimes it is explained as *kunkumādisampadānāṃ* to mean dyeing, dancing, singing, playing on musical instruments and other fine arts, such as *nṛtyagītavādyaśilpādivijñānāni*. Raṅgarāmānuja splits up the compound into two parts as Devavidyā, the arts of the Gandharvas and Janavidyā, popular arts. The arts of dancing, singing, playing by musical instruments were especially favoured by people.

**Liberation:** The desire to escape the unending succession of births and rebirths, and a longing for a repose, is associated with the doctrine of transmigration (q.v.). This is not however a necessary corollary of that doctrine. If a pious believer is satisfied with his present lot, and is told that, by virtue of his *karma*, he is to have another lease of a similar or even a better life, there is no reason why he should seek liberation or *mukti* from his *saṃsāra* or round of existence. But there was something grand and inspiring in their search for *Brahman* or the ultimate cause and goal of existence, something to attract and ensure their imagination. The Brāhmaṇa texts went to the length of incorporating the newer doctrines into the scriptures, giving them a place on par with the older texts on condition that these newer doctrines would not impugn the authority of the older canon and of the philosophy of the *āśrama* or stages of life. If the newer philosophy was willing to allow full scope to the cult of the Vedic sacrifice during the first two stages, then Brahmanism was prepared to give full scope for abstract meditation of *Brahman* and on the other problems of life as propounded by the new school. This compromise was largely successful because the ideas, for the most part, fell in a line with those already to a certain extent developed by Brahmanism. Amongst the new ideas occurring in the Upaniṣads there is hardly one that is not implicit in, and logically deducible from, the ideas present in the different portions of the Brāhmaṇas (cf. *CU* 3.17.1). This is not exactly a new thought of the Āraṇyakas or the Upaniṣads. We have already many passages of a like import in the Brāhmaṇas (*ŚB* 11.3.1.1.ff). Yet the Āraṇyakas might have emphasized this tendency and, to that extent, freed men from too absolute a bondage to sacrificial worship. Finally, the Āraṇyakas laid stress upon the necessity of penance and meditation as a prerequisite for the purpose of several *upāsanās* or courses of concentered meditation upon specific symbols as representing and impersonating the highest Absolute. And, as some of these symbols came directly from the sacrifices in the Brāhmaṇas, the opposition between the dogma of *karma* and the dogma of *jñāna* was to that extent somewhat palliated. The doctrine of *devayāna* held that those who were faithful and performed asceticism (*tapas*) went by the way of the gods through successive stages, never to return to the world and suffer rebirth. This could be contrasted with the way of the fathers (*pitṛyāna*), where the dead were recompensed for a time in another world and then had to suffer rebirth. Liberation or Mukti means in the Upaniṣads the state of infiniteness that a man attains when he knows his own self and thus becomes *Brahman*. In this infinite and true self there is no difference, no diversity. It is like an ocean in which all our phenomenal existence dissolves like salt in water (*BU* 2.4.12). It seems evident from a consideration of *Kaṭha* (2.3.5) which maintains a kind of *kramamukti* or liberation by stages. It tells that there are different grades of God-vision in different worlds and that the ultimate stage of realization may be reached only through a process of gradual spiritual evolution. One may be able to realize *Brahman* only as in a mirror, that is to say, contrary-wise, right being to the left and left being to the right. In the world of the Fathers one experiences the Godhead as in a dream, where the earlier defect is removed, but the vision of God yet lacks substance. In the world of the Gandharvas, there is a further improvement and one is able to visualize divinity like a pebble under a sheet of clear water, the image being true and yet defective owing to refraction. It is only when one reaches the Brahmaloka that the vision of the reality becomes as clear as daylight. It is also not impossible to see in the *Kaṭhopaniṣad* (2.3.14-15) a leaning towards the doctrine of *jīvanmukti*, or full liberation, in this very life, when it is said that the moment the *ātman* is seen the knots of the heart are broken and the desires are at an end. As pure water may be poured into pure water, similarly does the individual spirit live in communion with the Universal Spirit (2.1.15), and an experience of identity (*tattva-bhāva*) follows (2.3.13). When a man is able to realize this identity he becomes *jīvanmukta*. Again, a passage like *Muṇḍaka* (3.2.6) teaches the doctrine of *kramamukti*, inasmuch as it tells us that the good souls are finally liberated in the Brahmaloka, which they have attained by a life of steady philosophical learning and a practical life of renunciation. Then again, we have in *Muṇḍaka* (1.2.5.11) a suggestion of the approach to god through the doorway of the sun. Different again from either of these conceptions is the conception of the 'assimilation' (*paramaṃ samyaṃ*) of the mystic's soul with god, after the death of the human body as even during (3.1.3). A fourth conception of immortality occurs in the *Muṇḍaka* (3.2.8) where we are told that just as the rivers flowing to the ocean are finally merged in it and lose their name and form, similarly does the soul which has realized God lose all name and form and become merged in the Highest Person. Finally, we have in the *Muṇḍaka* the conception of a right impersonal immortality, almost in the spirit of the poet who tells us that the liberated souls enter the All which is present everywhere (3.2.5), and become unified, along with their works, in the imperishable mass of the Absolute (3.2.7). In the *Maitrāyaṇī Upaniṣad* (6.34) it is stated that when a man is thus absorbed in the *ātman*, he becomes indistinguishable like fire in fire, water in water, or ether in ether; and attains final liberation. Belvalkar and Ranade 83 ff. Dasgupta 58 ff.

**Life Principle:** **See Prāṇa.**

**Lineage:** The word *Kula* which appears in the Vedas and is referred to in the *Śatapatha Brāhmaṇa* (1.1.2.22; 2.1.4.4; 11.5.3.11; 13.4.2.27); *Bṛhadāraṇyaka Upaniṣad* (1.5.32) and *Chāndogya Upaniṣad* (3.13.6) denotes home and lineage. Its use clearly points out a system of individual families undoubtedly consisting of several members under the headship of the father or, in his absence, the eldest brother dwelling in one undivided family. Being distinct from *gotra*, it seems to mean family in a narrower sense of the members still living in one undivided family. The term *vaṃśa* is also used in the sense of lineage. The stream of a family regarding the genealogy is to be construed from the *kulya* in *Ṛgveda* (7.49.2). The term *kulpā* in *Ṛgveda* (10.179.2) denotes the chief of family. *Vrājapati* in *Ṛgveda* (10.179.2) means a leader of a group of families (*grāma*) or clan.

**Liquid Container:** The term *asecana* is used to denote a container of *ghee* which is mentioned in the *Śatapatha Brāhmaṇa* (2.1.9.5). It is also used as a container for meat juice (*ŚB* 1.62.13).

**Living Being:** The term *Prāṇabhṛt* means man, i.e. a living being, and is found in the *Śatapatha Brāhmaṇa* (11.2.6.2) and the *Bṛhadāraṇyaka Upaniṣad* (1.5.22, 3.1.12). The term *Prāṇin* is to be noted in *Aitareya Brāhmaṇa* (7.13); *Śatapatha Brāhmaṇa* (7.4.2.2, 10.4.2.2); *Atharvaveda* (3.3.3.); *Chāndogya Upaniṣad* (2.11.2); *Nirukta* (6.36). Though being is meant as a 'living being', it goes for a person generally termed 'a conscious man' as suggested in the *Brāhmaṇa* and the Upaniṣads.

**Loka:** Loka is derived from *lok* or *loc*; 'to see, to behold, to perceive', 'to know, to recognize'. *Lokyate iti lokaḥ*, means 'that which is perceived is the world. It has developed a vast field or connotation, such as *loka* and *aloka* (the world of light and darkness), *bhūloka, bhuvarloka* and *svarloka* or the earth, the middle region and the heavens; *ihaloka* and *paraloka* (this world and the other); seven spheres, viz., *bhūloka, bhuvarloka, svarloka, maharloka, jñānaloka, tapoloka* and *satyaloka* (the seven successively higher regions); seven successively lower regions, viz., *atala, vit ala, sutala, rasātala, talātala, mahātala* and *pātāla*; inhabitants of this world and mankind in general; vast space (*uruloka*), etc. Heaven, earth, and atmosphere have been invariably grouped as *lokas*. Loka in the Creation Hymn (*RV* 10.129) seems to mean a stage in the frame of infinite time and space, and in *Puruṣa Sūkta* (*RV* 10.90) *nabhya asid*, etc., as the middle regions coming into existence from the navel of the great Being. Various notions about *loka* make it as one whole divided into mutually related spheres of existence or appearance of manifestation. On one hand *loka* appears to be a spatial concern, on the other it is a mental construct of the objective view of the Vedic ritual. *Loka* is not *deśa*, which is purely a spatial concept, though it is inclusive of *deśa*, in its non-particularized sense. Vedic reference of *loka* could be grouped in two categories, where the ideational divisions of space—both human and divine—are indicated such as *manuṣyaloka, devaloka* or *bhūloka*, etc., and where *loka* is the idealistic construct of a realm of bliss, peace and enjoyment. The first category is usually indicated by some particular division such as *bhūloka* (earth, this *loka*), *bhuvarloka* or *antarīkṣa* (mid-space), *svarloka* or *dyuloka* (heavens as referring to the region beyond). In the second category, *loka* is usually referred to as a non-spatial entity (cf. *ŚB* 2.1.4.11, 25). In the *Śatapatha Brāhmaṇa* (2.2.1.14 and 16) the sacrificer is supposed to lay down in three worlds, his three bodies, the blowing (*pavamāna*) one on this earth, the purifying one (*pāvaka*) in the ether, and that bright one (*suci*) in the sky. In the *Śatapatha Brāhmaṇa* (4.6.7.2) by the *ṛk* is conquered the worldly region, by the *Yajus* the airy and by the *sāman* the heavenly (cf. *ŚB* 4.3.4.8). The heavenly is something which has been committed or sought as *mokṣa*, or liberation from pain and misery. Loka is a cherished goal of the ritual activities. The later words formed of *loka* show the further extension of its meaning. Vatsyayan (ed) *Kalātattvakośa*, Vol. I. s.v. **loka**.

**Lokapāla:** In the Vedic tradition the four deities—Kubera, Varuṇa, Indra and Yama—who are supposed to be the guardians of the world. Certain texts have reference to eight *lokpālas* and include, in addition to the four mentioned above, Vāyu, Agni, Sūrya and Soma.

**Lords:** *Śatapati* (Lord of a hundred villages) occurs in a verse of the *Maitrāyaṇī Saṃhitā* (4.14.12) and the *Taittirīya Brāhmaṇa* (2.8.4.2) as an epithet of Indra, who is described as, alone, the lord of a hundred among men. To interpret the expression as lord of a hundred gods, as does the commentary on the *Taittirīya Brāhmaṇa*, is obviously impossible. It seems clear that there is a reference to an analogous human functionary, viz., the lord of a hundred villages, known in the later law, who was probably at once a judicial deputy of the sovereign and a revenue collector, an ancient magistrate and collector. *Rāja-pati* 'lord of kings', is found in the *Śatapatha Brāhmaṇa* (11.4.3.9) as an epithet of Soma. It is not used elsewhere as a title of imperial temporal supremacy. *Viś-pati* (Lord of subjects) is a word of somewhat uncertain significance, reflecting in this respect the nature of *viś*. Zimmer holds that in its strict sense it denotes the head of a canton, but he admits that there is not passage requiring this sense, the only one quoted by him (*RV* 1.37.8) being certainly indecisive. In the great majority of passages the world simply means the 'Lord of the dwelling', whether used of a man or of the god Agni as the householder *par excellence,* or possibly as the fire of the *sabhā* or assembly house of the people. This sense suits even the passage of the *Ṛgveda* (7.55.5; *AV* 4.5.6) in which the Viśpati, as well as the father and the mother of a maiden are to be lulled to sleep in order to allow her lover to approach her, for the household may well be deemed to have been a joint family, in which the Viśpati could easily be different from the father of the girl, e.g. a grandfather or uncle. In other passages *Atharvaveda* (3.4.1, 4.22.3) the Viśpati is the king as 'Lord of the subject people' (Viśaḥ). Or again, the *Viśpati* is chief of the *viś*, probably in the sense of subjects. Macdonell and Keith II, 217, 308, 351.

**Lotus:** *Puṇḍarīka* denotes the blossom of the lotus in

the *Ṛgveda* (10.142.8) and later (*TB* 1.8.3.1; *ŚB* 5.5.5.6; *BU* 2.3.10, 6.3.14; *CU* 1.6.7; *AA* 3.2.4). The *Pañcaviṃśa Brāhmaṇa* (18.9.6) states that the lotus flower is born of the light of the Nakṣatras, and the *Atharvaveda* (10.8.43; *CU* 8.1.1) compares the human heart to the lotus. *Bisa* denotes the radical fibres of the lotus, which like *śāluka* (*AV* 4.34.5) seem to have been eaten as a delicacy as early as the times of the *Atharvaveda* (4.34.5). It is also mentioned in the *Aitareya Brāhmaṇa* (5.10) and the *Aitareya Āraṇyaka* (3.2.4; *SĀ* 11.4). *Puṣkara* is the name in the *Ṛgveda* (6.16.13; 7.33.11) and later (*AV* 11.3.8; 12.1.24; *TS* 5.1.4, 1, 5.2.6.5, 5.6.4.2; *VS* 11.29; *TB* 1.2.1.4; *ŚB* 4.5.1.16; *MS* 3.1.5) of the blue lotus flower. The *Atharvaveda* (12.1.24) mentions its sweet perfume. The lotus grew in lakes, which were thence called *puṣkariṇī*, 'lotus-bearing' (*RV* 5.78.7; 10.107.10; *AV* 4.34.5; 5.16.17; *BU* 4.3.11). That the flower was early used for personal adornment is shown by an apithet of the Aśvins, 'lotus-crowned' (*puṣkara-sraj*) (*RV* 10.184.2; *AV* 3.32.4; *ŚB* 4.1.5.16). Presumably because of its likeness in shape to the flower of the lotus, the bowl of the ladle is called *puṣkara*, perhaps already in the *Ṛgveda* (5.72.11), and certainly in the *Aitareya Brāhmaṇa* (7.5). Moreover, according to the *Nirukta* (5.14), *puṣkara* means 'water', a sense actually found in the *Śatapatha Brāhmaṇa* (6.4.2.2).

**Love:** See **Kāma**.

**Low Profession:** A very comprehensive list of the professions, occupations, arts, crafts and industries of this period is to be found in the list of victims at the Puruṣamedha, as given in the *Vājasaneyī Saṃhitā* (30.11) and the *Taittirīya Brāhmaṇa* (3.4.9.1). The *anukṣattṛ*, a special type of attendant or the door keeper or on the charioteer, the *anucara*, an attendant in general, a drummer, a worker in thorns cut up and used to plait mats, a smith, a ploughman, an astrologer, a cow-killer (or butcher), a herdsman, a maker of bow-strings, a carpenter, a gatherer of wood, a fire-watcher (*dāva-pa*), a hand-clapper, who presumably scared away birds from the fields by making noise, a female embroiderer or a basket-maker, a jeweller, the yoker and unyoker of horses, the maker of Śurā, an elephant-keeper and a worker in gold—all these figure in the list. In the other texts are mentioned a few additional callings, viz., a ferry man or poleman, a washerman (*male-ga*), a menial (*Puruṣa*), a potter, a usuer or moneylender, a blower, a barber, a boat propeller, a cook, a messenger, and a footman running by the side of a chariot. See **Occupations**.

**Lower Deities:** Among the lower deities, besides the Gendharvas, Apsarases and tutelary deities (q.q.v.) the Ṛbhus are celebrated in eleven hymns of the *Ṛgveda* and are mentioned by name over a hundred times. They form a triad. Their individual names, which oftern occur, are Ṛbhu or less commonly Ṛbhukṣan (chief of the Ṛbhus), Vāja, and Vibhvan. They are most often spoken of in the plural as *ṛbhavaḥ*. Occasionally, an indefinite group seems to be meant, as all (*viśva*) the Ṛbhus (*RV* 7.51.3), or Ṛbhu with the Ṛbhus, Vibhvan with the Vibhus (*RV* 7.48.2) are invoked. In the latter passages Ṛbhu and Vibhvan are evidently thought of as cheifs of groups of the same name. The three Ṛbhus are once distinguished as eldest, younger and youngest (*RV* 4.33.5). They are also once collectively addressed as the son (*sūno*) of Indra (*RV* 4.37.4). In the same verse they are invoked as 'children of might' (*savaso napātaḥ*), as if a play on the meaning of *napāt* (also 'grandson') were intended, in contrast with the epithet 'son of might' (*savasaḥ sūnu*), which is applied exclusively to Indra. They are very frequently invoked to come to the sacrifice (*RV* 4.34.1.3; 37.1). Being high in heaven they are besought to come to Soma in the lower abodes (4.37.3). In this they are generally with Indra (*RV* 3, 60, 4-6; 4, 33,3, 34.6, 35.7), a few times with the Maruts (*RV* 1. 20.5; 111,4; 4.34.11), and once with the Ādityas, Saviṭr, Mountains, and Rivers (*RV* 4.34.8). In other respects also they are closely connected with Indra. The references to the physical aspect or the equipment of the Ṛbhus are scanty. They are of sunlike appearance (*RV* 1, 110.4). They have a car (*RV* 1, 161.7), which is drawn by steeds (*RV* 7.48.1). Their car is bright, and their steeds are fat; they wear metal helmets and fair necklaces (*RV* 4.37.4). Ṛbhu is a possessor of steeds (*aśvin RV* 4,37.5). The Ṛbhu are characteristically deft-handed (*suhastaḥ*) and skilful (*apas, suapas: RV* 4.33.1.8, etc.), their skilful deeds being incomparable (*RV* 3,60.4). They are frequently said to have acquired the rank of gods in consequence of their marvellous skill. They rejoiced so greatly in their work, that Vāja became the artificer of the gods, Ṛbhukṣan of Indra, and Vibhavan of Varuṇa (*RV* 4, 33,9). Like the higher gods, they are besought to give prosperity and wealth (*RV* 4,33.8, 37.5), in cattle, horses, heroes (*RV* 4, 34.10) and to grant vigour, nourishment, offspring, dexterity (*RV* 1.111.2). They further fashioned or made a cow (*RV* 1.20.3) and are all-stimulating and omniform (*RV* 4, 33.8). The Ṛbhu also rejuvenated their parents (*RV* 1.20.4; 111.1; 4.35.5), who were frail and lay like decaying posts (*RV* 1.110.8; 4.33.2.3). They made the two, who were old, young again (*RV* 1, 161.3.7). The exhibition of skill which is most frequently mentioned and appears to have been thought the greatest, as showing the Ṛbhus in the character of successful rivals of Tvaṣṭṛ, consists in their having made the one cup, the work of Tvaṣṭṛ, into four (*RV* 1, 20.6.1.10.3; 4.35.2.3.36.4). This cup is the drinking vessel of the gods (*RV* 1, 161, 5; 4, 35.5) or of the Asura (*RV* 1.110.3). The Ṛbhus were commissioned by the gods through their messenger Agni, to make the one cup, which was of wood, into four, promising as a reward that they should receive worship equally with the gods (*RV* 1, 161.1.2). The skill of the Ṛbhus is incidentally exemplified by the statement that they fashioned prayer (*RV* 10.80.7), sacrifice (*RV* 3, 54, 12), and the two worlds (*RV* 10.66.10). The word *ṛbhu* is apparently derived from the root *rabh*, to grasp (cf. *RV* 2,'3.8), thus meaning 'handy', 'dexterous'. It frequently occurs in the *Ṛgveda* as aṇ adjective and is several times used thus as an attribute of Indra, Agni, and the Ādityas. It is clear that they were regarded as not having been gods from the beginning. It is, however, most probable that their parent who are mentioned so often, represent heaven and earth. The notion that they produce fertility is connected with their sojourn of twelve days in the house of Savitṛ or Agohya, the sun 'who cannot be concealed'. They have, therefore, been taken to be genii of the three seasons, which are at a standstill during the twelve days of the winter solstice. On the whole, it seems probable that the Ṛbhus were originally terrestrial of aerial elves, whose dexterity gradually attracted to them various myths illustrative of marvellous skill. But the evidence furnished by the *Ṛgveda* is hardly sufficient to warrant any certain conclusion. Macdonell 131-3; Keith 178.

**Lust:** See **Kāma**.

**Lute, Lute-player:** The word *vīṇā* (*TS* 6.1.4.1; *KS* 34.5; *MS* 3.6.8; *ŚB* 3.2.4.6, 13.1.5.1; *JB* 1.42) stands for lute. The instrument was covered with hairy skin, head (*śiras*), cavity (*udara*), sounding board (*ambhana*), strings (*tantra*) and plectrum (*vadana*) are its various parts (*Saṅkh A* 8.9; *AĀ* 3.2.5). The term *uttaramandra* indicated either a tune or another kind of lute. *Karkari* is the name of a musical instrument probably lute. It is referred to in *Ṛgveda* (2.43.3), *Atharvaveda* (4.37.4 [5], 20.132.3; 20.132.8). A sort of lute (*kanda-vīṇā*) is made out of the joints of reed (*KS* 34.5) used at Mahāvrata ceremony. The word '*vīṇā-gāthin*' indicates 'lute-player' (*TB* 3.9.14.1; *ŚB* 13.1.5.1, 13.4.2.8, 13.4.2.11, 13.4.2.14, 13.4.3.5). It also means a leader of the band in *ŚB* (13.4.33, 13.4.4.2). A lute player is enumerated in the list of victims at the *puruṣamedha* in *Vājasaneyī Saṃhitā* (30.20), *Taittirīya Brāhmaṇa* (3.4.15.1) and *Bṛhadāraṇyaka Upaniṣad* (2.4.3, 4.5.9). They were employed as the accompanists of the singer in the *Śatapatha Brāhmaṇa* (13.1.5.3). *Vīṇā-vāda* (*VS* 30.20; *TB* 3.4.15.1; 2.4.8 [9]) is also the term for lute-player. At the Mahāvrata rite a hundred stringed as *śatatantrī* like the Vīṇā is used. A *Vīṇāvāda* or *Vīṇāgāthin* in the *Śatapatha Brāhmaṇa* (13.4.3.3) goes together with the word *vīṇāgaṇagin*, denoting the leader of a band.

# M

**Madantī:** Water heated on gārhapatya and used for making dough from pounded grains in connection with *darśapūrṇamāsa ĀpŚS* (1.21.8-9). Bhattacharyya 1990, 93.

**Madhumatī:** Hymn of the *Ṛgveda* (1.90-5-7) which shows succinctly the yearnings of the devotee for an equipoise between the elemental forces and material comforts. The former is concerned with the ingredients of matter and the latter with material objects produced for meeting human needs. Bhattacharyya 1990, 93.

**Madhuparka:** A mixture of honey and curds or clarified butter which is offered to honoured and distinguished guests: *ṛtvik, ācārya*, bridegroom, king, *snātaka* and to someone who is dear to one. *MGS* (1.9.1), *KhaGS* (4.2.21); *BGS* (1.2.65), etc. The procedure for *madhuparka* is set out in *ĀGS* (1.24.5-26).

**Madhuvidyā:** Madhuvidyā is expounded by Dadhyañc Atharvana in *Bṛhadāraṇyaka Upaniṣad* (2.5). It is a form of esoteric knowledge which the Aśvins received from him (*RV* 4.39.6; 4.40.5). The *Chāndogya Upaniṣad* (3.11.5) defines it as knowledge of highest excellence. It is the doctrine of the mutual interdependence of things because all are indissolubly connected in, and through, the Self. 'The earth', says Dadhyach, 'is the honey (*madhu*) of all beings, and all beings are the honey of the earth, just because the same lustrous immortal Self inhabits them both. The fire is the essence of all things, and all things are the essence of fire, just because the immortal Self is the essence of both.' And so it is with the wind, the sun, the space, the moon, the lightning, the thunder, the ether, and even law and truth and humanity the essence of all things whatsoever and all things are the essence of these. Finally, the individual Self is itself the essence of all things and all things are the essence of the individual Self, inasmuch as both of them are held together by the same Universal Spirit. 'As all the spokes are contained in the axle and the felly of a wheel, so are all things and all Selves connected in the Supreme Self.' Thus, does Dadhyañc teach the doctrine of the supreme existence of the One, and the apparent existence of the Many? Belvalkar and Ranade 122.

**Madra:** A people who are mentioned in the *Bṛhadāraṇyaka Upaniṣad* (3.3.1, 3.7.1). Kāpya Patañcala was then living among them. Their name appears elsewhere in Vedic literature, only in that of a branch, the Uttara Madras, the 'northern Madras', who are referred to in the *Aitareya Brāhmaṇa* (8.14) as living beyond the Himalaya (*pāreṇa himavantam*) in the neighbourhood of the Uttara Kurus, probably, in the land beyond Kashmir. The Madras mentioned in the Upaniṣad were probably settled somewhere near the Madhyadeśa 'Middle Land' or in the Punjab region.

**Māgadha:** Name of a people who appear throughout Vedic literature as of little repute. Though the name is not actually found in the *Ṛgveda*, it occurs in the *Atharvaveda* (5.22.14), where fever is asked to go to the Gandharis and Mujavants, northern peoples, and to the Aṅgas and Magadhas, peoples of the east. Again, in the list of victims at the Puruṣamedha (human sacrifice) in the *Yajurveda Saṃhitā* (*VS* 30.5.22; *TB* 3.4.1.1), a Māgadha, or man of Magadha, is included as dedicated to *ati-kruṣṭa*, 'loud noise', while in the Vrātya hymn of the *Atharvaveda* (15/2/1-4) the Megadha is said to be connected with the Vrātya as his mitra, mantra, his laughter and his thunder in the four quarters. The Māgadhas were treated contemptuously since the days of the *Ṛgveda*, in which they are mentioned as Kīkatas. This was due to the fact that they were not really brahmanized. This is attested to by the evidence of the *Śatapatha Brāhmaṇa* (1.4.1.4ff) that neither Kosala nor Videha were fully brahmanized at an early date, much less Magadha. The Māgadhas were evidently a people in the Baudhāyana and other sūtras (*BDS* 1.2.13; *BŚS* 20.13; *ĀŚS* 22.6.13; *HŚS* 17.6). In later literature and in the legal texts the tribal name Māgadha is given to a mixed caste.

**Magic:** Originally the sacrifices were simple rituals, magical rather than propitiatory. 'The majority of the sacrificial ceremonies as also the Yajus formula do not aim at worshipping the gods, but at influencing them, at compelling them to fulfil the wishes of the sacrificer' (Winternitz, I, 181). Keith also has to admit in connection with the sacrifices, as described in the *Brāhmaṇa* literature, that, 'In the vast majority of the cases the nature of the ritual can be solved at once by the application of the concept of sympathetic magic, and this is one of the most obvious and undeniable facts in the whole of the Vedic sacrifice, it is, from the beginning to end, full of magic elements' (Keith, 158-9). Similar views are held by Bergaigne, Geldner, Weber and others. Macdonell writes, 'It is thus impossible to suppose that the sacrificial priests of the *Ṛgveda*, the composers of the old hymns, should have occupied an isolated position, untouched by magical practices derived from a much earlier age and afterwards continued throughout the priestly literature of later times. In fact, a close examination of the hymns of the *Ṛgveda* actually affords the evidence that even then the belief in magical power independently of the gods is to be found. . . . Every page of the Brāhmaṇas and the Sūtras shows that the whole sacrificial ceremonial was overgrown with the union that the sacrifice exercised power over gods and going beyond them, could directly influence things and events without their intervention. An incipient from of this notion already appears in the *Ṛgveda* where exaggerated sacrificial powers are attributed to ancient priests' (*ERE*. VIII. 312). Primitive magic is founded on the notion that by creating an illusion of reality one may control it. It is the association of ideas in terms of similarity and contiguity. It is the art of influencing nature or the course of events by symbolic imitations of the desiring result. As a guide to action, magic embodies the valuable truth that the external world can in fact be changed by means of subjective attitude towards it. The oldest name of the *Atharvaveda* in Vedic literature is *Atharvāṅgirasaḥ*, that is, 'the Atharvans and the Aṅgirasaḥ'. The two words denote two different species of magic formulae. *Atharvan* is, 'holy magic bringing happiness' and *aṅgiras* is 'hostile or black magic'. The former includes, among others, formulae for the healing of diseases, while the latter includes cures against enemies, rivals, malicious magicians, etc. These two kinds of magic formulae than form the chief contents of the *Atharvaveda* but these ancient magic songs, which were originally popular poetry, appear in the *Saṃhitā* in a brahmanized form because of the priestly outlook of the compilers, which betrays itself in the similes and epithets. The gods are the same as in the *Ṛgveda*, Agni, Indra, etc. But their characters have become quite colourless, and their natural basis is utterly forgotten. The theosophical and cosmogonic speculations of the *Atharvaveda* indicate a later stage of development than in the *Ṛgveda*. It contains more theosophic matter than the earlier *Saṃhitā*. The philosophical terminology is of an advanced type, and the pantheistic thought is practically the same as in the Upaniṣads. But there is a magical twist given to the philosophical hymns. For example, the *Atharvaveda* (4.9.6) employs the conception of *asat*, 'the non-existent', as a spell to destroy enemies, demons, etc. Magical performances were originally collective in nature. When the mode of production was in the elementary stage, it was impossible to do a work without collective endeavour and collective impetus. The purpose of the Vedic sacrifices was the same. The *sattra-yāga* may be regarded as one of the earliest forms of the Vedic sacrifices in which collectivity of the performers is the basic feature. One of the significant rituals of this *sattra* was called Mahāvrata (Keith, 130). Since Mahāvrata means *anna*, or food, it may be assumed that the purpose of the *sattra-yāga* was originally connected with food (*ŚB* 4.6.4.2; *PB* 4.10.2). Another ancient Vedic sacrifice was called Vājapeya (*SBE* 41, intro. 23 ff. also Ch. III), which means food and drink'. Though in subsequent ages it came to be looked upon as a ceremony of royal consecration, like the Aśvamedha and the Rājasūya, it was originally an agricultural ritual, as Keith has rightly pointed out. This transformation of primitive magical rituals pertaining to the facts of daily life into grand sacrifices under the patronage of monarchs with a formidable array of priesthood, was evidently due to a corresponding socio-economic and political transformation. The first and tenth Maṇḍalas of the *Ṛgveda* contain many charms, which are found in the *Atharvaveda*. Generally speaking the *Ṛgveda* is not innocent of the magical practices (Oldenberg, *Die Religion des Veda*, 59). The *Taittirīya Saṃhitā* contains many magical formulae, which are like those found in the *Atharvaveda*. In the magical formulas of the *Atharvaveda*, mere verbal similarity is sometimes enough to connect the magical object with the desired effect. Thus, on account of the root *ruh* (to ascend) in the word, Rohita (the sun) is employed in a charm to bring sovereignty to a king, who ascends the throne (*rohati*, *AV* 13.1.4-5). In the same way in the *Taittirīya Saṃhitā*, the yoke of a cart (*dhur*) is asked 'to injure him who injures us (*dhruva*) and to injure him whom we injure' (1.1.4). The *Taittirīya Saṃhitā* often mentions the formula, viz., he who hates us and whom we hate should be killed, etc. (1.1.9). In the same manner, the *Atharvaveda* repeats it often in the magical rite for relieving one of distress, etc. (10.5.15-35). The *Vājasaneyī Saṃhitā* contains many ideas which are common to the *Atharvaveda*. The *Vājasaneyī Saṃhitā* (5.23) mentions demons and the witchcraft (*valga, kṛtyā*) as concealed in the holes, dug in the ground for erecting the sacrificial post (*yūpa*). These are to be thrown out by means of the charm. The destruction of the enemy is the common object of many sacrifices (*VS* 9.37; 15.4). The *Vājasaneyī Saṃhitā* (26.1) has a regular magical formula to kill rivals or enemies. Similarly, it (15.16-19) contains special magical formulas. It (11.77-82) asks Agni to kill the advancing enemies during battle, thieves and robbers, a debtor who refuses to pay and one who censures. The *Aitareya Brāhmaṇa* describes the magical power of the fire and the importance of the *purohita* in wielding those powers for the destruction of the enemies of a king (*AB* 8.24-28). Symbolical rites are common in magic and sacrifice. In the symbolical rite for curing fever, water made hot by dipping red-hot iron axe in it, is given to the patient for drinking (*AV* 1.25.1). Similarly, the *Aitareya Brahmaṇa* (8.8) describes the symbolical meaning of the different implements and liquids required in the coronation ceremony of a king. See **Mimetic Magic**.

**Magical Disease-creating:** Black magic performed by one's enemy is considered to be a cause of disease in many parts of the world. A person cursed (*abhiśapta*) by one's enemy may suffer from some diseases. In *Kauśika Sūtra* (29.15-17), a rite is prescribed for curing a person who is suffering from a disease magically transmitted to him. In the Vedic literature we get some descriptions of black magic for creating diseases for one's enemy. In the *Atharvaveda* (7.90 ff) there is a prayer for destroying someone's virility. Sending disease to enemy kingdom is mentioned in *Taittirīya Saṃhitā* (4.5.1.11). A person who wants to get the power of disease-creating, should at the time of midday mutter selected *mantras* ten thousand times. Thite 33.

**Mahāvṛṣa:** Name of a tribe mentioned along with the Mujavants in the *Atharvaveda* (5.22; 4.5.8). They were northerners, though Bloomfield suggests that the name may be chosen more for its sound and sense (as 'of mighty strength' to resist the disease) than for its geographical position. In the *Chāndogya Upaniṣad* (4.2.5) the place Raikvaparṇa is said to be in the country of the Mahāvṛṣas. The king of the Mahāvṛṣa in the *JUB* (3.40,2) is said to be Hṛtsvāśaya. The Mahāvṛṣas are also known in *Baudhāyana Śrautasūtra* (2.5).

**Mahāyajña:** The five daily observances or performances. They are Brahmayajña, Devayajña, Pitṛyajña, Bhūtayajña, and Manuṣyayajña. These differ from the Śrauta sacrifices in two respects. Firstly, the chief agent is the householder himself who does not need the help of a professional priest. Secondly, the central point of the five yajñas is the discharge of duty to the creator, to the ancient sages, to the Manes and to the whole universe with its myriads of creatures of various grades and intelligence. In the Śrauta sacrifices the main spring of action is the desire to secure some specific ends. *ŚB* 11.5.6.1; *TĀ* 1.10; *ĀGS* 3.1.1-4; *ĀpDS* 1.4.12-13; *BDS* 2.6.1-8, etc.

**Mahāvrata:** Functions on the second day in a *sattva* ritual, in which certain features of primitive collective life can be clearly observed. A *mahāvrata* cup of Soma is offered and *mahāvratāsāman* is chanted while the priests sway in tune with the rhythmic chanting during the ritual. An Ārya and a śūdra should engage themselves in a mock fight while a harlot and a brahmacārī should abuse each other. Sexual intercourse between a selected man and woman should take place in a screened shed after which there is drumbeating, singing and dancing. *JB* 10.4.8; *ŚB* 26.6.21 ff; *KŚS* 13.3.9; *ŚŚS* 18.15; *ĀpŚS*. 21.10-20; *AĀ* 1.5; *PB* 5.5.14-17.

**Mahī:** Mahī is frequently invited to the sacrifices along with Sarasvatī and several other goddesses. 'Ilā, Sarasvatī, Mahī, three goddesses who bring delight, be seated, peaceful, on the grass (*RV* 1.13.9). Let Hotrā pure, set among gods, amid the Maruts, Bhāratī, Ilā, Sarasvatī, Mahī, rest on the grass, adorable' (*RV* 1.142.9). 'Let Ilā, Sarasvatī, Mahī, three goddesses who bring us wealth, be seated harmless on the grass' (*RV* 5.5.8).

**Maidens:** A maiden growing old at her father's abode without finding husband is known as *amājur* in the *Ṛgveda* (2.17.1; 10.39.3). Similarly, a maiden dwelling at her father's abode without being married upto an old age is called *jūryantī*. In *Ṛgveda* (1.117.8) a lightened maiden is denoted as *ruśatī*. Maidens bowing before the youthful gallants come with love to them are frequently described (*RV* 10.30.6). Gatherings known as *samana* visited by well-dressed maidens are found in *Ṛgveda* (7.2.5). An ordinary expression is *yuvati*, suggesting a woman attaining a stage of growing maidenhood in the Vedic texts (*RV* 1.118.5, 2.35.4, 3.54.14, 4.18.8, 5.2.1, 9.86.16, 10.30.6; *AV* 14.2.61; *TB* 3.1.1.9, 3.1.2.4; *SB* 13.1.9.6, 13.4.3.8). *Kanīnakā* is a maiden or young women also termed *Kanyā* in *Ṛgveda* (1.123.10, 1.161.5, 3.23.10; *AV* 1.14.2, 11.5.18, 12.1.25, etc.). A rare form as *kanā* is found in the *Ṛgveda* (10.61.5). There are other terms as *kanyanā* in the *Ṛgveda* (8.35.5) and *Kanyalā* in the *Atharvaveda* (5.5.3, 14.2.52). *Kairātikā* is a maiden of the Kirāta people in the *Atharvaveda* (10.4.14) described as digging up roots for medicinal use.

**Mail:** Defensive armour, or mail *varman*, is mentioned in the *Ṛgveda* 6.75.1 and is referred to in numerous other passages (*RV* 6.75.18-19, 6.27.6, etc.). Varuṇa and Savitṛ are mentioned as being clad in golden or yellow mail, as the word *drāpi* is interpreted by Sāyaṇa. The *Ṛgveda* 1.116.10 refer to military garment, as it does in the *Ṛgveda* 9.100.9. *Drāpi* means coat of mail, as it occurs in the *Ṛgveda* 9.86.14. It may also mean robe in a general sense.

**Maināka:** Mainaka, descendant of Menakā, is the name of a mountain in the Himalayas in the *Taittirīya Āraṇyaka* (1.31.2). There is a variant reading Maināga.

**Male Principle:** See **Puruṣa**.

**Mallet:** The word *mallet* means a long-handled wooden hammer for striking a croquet or polo ball. The term *vṛṣā-rava* used for mallet, denotes an animal roaring like a bull (*RV* 10.146.2; *TS* 2.5.5.6). In some cases it indicates a drumstick (*ŚB* 12.5.2.7).

**Mammals:** See under **Carnivores and Herbivores**.

**Man:** The general name for man in the *Ṛgveda* (1.25.5; 2.34.6; 3.16.4); *Atharvaveda* (2.9.2; 9.1.3; 14.2.9); *Aitareya Brāhmaṇa* (3.34; 6/27), etc., is found to be *ṇr*; otherwise *nara* is occasionally mentioned in the *Taittirīya Saṃhitā* (7.1.12.1); *Śatapatha Brāhmaṇa* (9.3.1.3), and also in the *Nirukta* (5.1). *Nārva* in the sense of a person is found in the *Ṛgveda* (1.54.6, 1.112.9; 8.24.29). Māna is also a term for man while *nārī* and *mānavī* stand for woman.

**Manā:** Manā is found in one passage of the *Ṛgveda* (8.78.2) in an enumeration of gifts, where it is described as 'golden'. Therefore, it seems to designate some ornament or possibly a weight. The identification as regards *manā* is very conjectural. It may be identical with the word *manā,* which occurs several times in the *Ṛgveda* (1.173.2; 4.33.2; 10.6.3) and *Vājasaneyī Saṃhitā* (4.19) in the sense of desire and desirable object.

**Manor Avasarpana:** Name in the *Śatapatha Brāhmaṇa* (1.8.1.8) of the mountain on which the vessel of Manu rested. In the epic the name is *Naubandhana*.

**Mantle:** *Drāpi* denotes mantle in the *Ṛgveda* 1.116.10; 5.23.2. *Sāyaṇa* interprets it by coat of mail, termed *kavaca*. The use of this garment by god Varuṇa occurs in the *Ṛgveda* 1.25.13. Hence, seemingly it was worn by the prominent men of the society. In the *Atharvaveda* 5.7.10 a woman is described as golden mantled, termed *hiraṇyadrāpi* proving the use of this raiment by female. The term *adhivāsa* in the *Ṛgveda* 1.140.9; 1.162.16 denotes a kind of upper garment. According to the *Śatapatha Brāhmaṇa* 5.3.5.22 the king put on this raiment after an undergarment and a garment. Thus, it denotes some kind of mantle or cloak. In the *Ṛgveda* 5.55.1 *atka* denotes the garment, as wearing mantles adorned with gold entitled to the Maruts. In the *Ṛgveda* 2.35.14 and 5.74.5 it is a long garment as it covered the whole body. The body is closely fitted by this garment (*RV* 9.29.3), which looks bright and beautiful (*RV* 9.107.13). Often the mantle was embroidered (*RV* 1.122.2; 5.55.6).

**Mantra:** From the root *man* (to think), *mantra* denotes in the *Ṛgveda* (1.31.15, 1.40.5, 1.67.4, 1.74.1, 1.152.2, 2.35.2, etc.) and later (*AV* 15.2.1, 19.54.3, *TS* 1.5.4.1) the 'hymn' as the product of the singer's creative thought. In the Brāhmaṇas (*AB* 5.14; 16.1, *KB* 26.3.5; *ŚB* 1.4.4.6, 11.2.1.6, etc.) the term denotes the utterances of the holy persons, incantations, spells, charms, etc. *Mantras* are products of spiritual mentation, says Yāska (*Nirukta* 7.12). In the *Brāhmaṇa* texts and also in the Mīmāṃsā tradition, the sole import of the *mantras* lies in the urge to perform ritualistic action alone. *Mantra* is also an inspired utterance with an esoteric meaning (*rahasya*), which has been clearly stated in the *GB* 1.2.20. Even the *Ṛgveda* 1.164, 39, 4.3, 16, 8.100.10, 10.71, 3-5, 10.114.8, 10.125.7, etc., draw attention to the esoteric meaning of the *mantras*. In commenting on the *Ṛgveda* 10.71.5 Yāska says that, esoterically, the knowledge of the gods and of the self is the flower and fruit of *mantra*. (*Nirukta* 1.20).

**Manu:** As the appellation Manu or Manus is often used in the sense of man', there is sometimes an uncertainty as to when it has the value of a proper name in the *Ṛgveda*. Manu was the institutor of sacrifice. The sacrifice of Manu is the prototype of the present sacrifice. Soma is prayed to flow as he once flowed for Manu (*RV* 9.96.12). Manu established Agni as a light for all people (*RV* 1.36.19). Indra is said to have drunk Soma beside Manu Vivasvat in the *Ṛgveda*. In the *Atharvaveda* (8.10.24) and the *Śatapatha Brāhmaṇa* (13.4.3.3), as well as in post-Vedic literature, he bears the regular patronymic Vaivasvata. Manu is regarded as the first of men living on earth, while Yama, as the first of men who dies, became the king of the dead in the other world. Hence in the *Śatapatha Brāhmaṇa* (13.4.3.3-5) Manu Vaivasvata is described as ruler of men, and Yama Vaivasvata as ruler of the dead. The *Śatapatha Brāhmaṇa* (1.8.1.1-10) relates a legend of how Manu was saved in a ship from a deluge, which swept away all other creatures, by a fish (in post-Vedic mythology an Avatāra of Viṣṇu). Manu is then said to have become the progenitor of mankind through his daughter Iḍā, who was produced from his offerings.

**Manuṣya-yajña:** One of the five *mahāyajñas* for householders, it is performed for honouring guests. Also known as *nṛyajña*. *ĀpDS* 2.4.9.2-4, *BGS* 2.9.1-2.

**Manyu:** See **Subjective Deities**.

**Marital Relations:** Despite polygamy, however, there is ample evidence that the marriage tie was not lightly regarded as far as the fidelity of the wife was concerned. The term *patnī* regularly applies to the wife, while *jāyā* designates her in her conjugal capacity. There is, however, little trace that the husband was expected to be faithful in the matter of morality. Several passages (*TS* 5.6.8.3; *MS* 3.4.7), indeed, forbid with reference to ritual abstinence, intercourse with the women other than the wife. This may imply that adultery on the husband's part was otherwise regarded as venial. The ritual of the Varuṇapraghāsas (*MS* 1.10.11; *ŚB* 2.5.2.20; *TB* 1.6.5.2), in which the wife of the sacrificer is questioned about lovers, is a part of a rite meant to expiate unchastity on the part of a wife. Again, Yājñavalkya's doctrine in the *Śatapatha Brāhmaṇa* (1.3.1.21), which seems to assert that no one cares if a wife is unchaste (*paraḥpuṃsā*) or not, really means, that no one cares if the wife is away from the men who are sacrificing, as the wives of the gods are apart from them during the particular rite in question. Monogamy was also evidently approved (*RV* 1.124.7, 4.3.2, 10.71.4). On the other hand, no Vedic text gives us the rule that the adulterer taken in the act can be killed with impunity, though the later legal literature has traces of this rule. There is also evidence that the standard of ordinary sexual morality was not always high, but in most cases it was evenly maintained. The laws evolved and regulated the institution of marriage, on which the foundations of Vedic homes were laid. It is true, indeed, that the family institutions depended on sex, reproduction and economy. That woman played a prominent role as an embodiment of moral and spiritual force in originating the life at home and thereby a cultured society elsewhere cannot be gainsaid. The Vedic sage Viśvāmitra (*RV* 3.53.4) sang highly of the wife, equated with home, source of all wealth and pleasure. The dialogue hymn (*Ṛgveda* 10.10) of Yama and Yamī shows how the concept of marriage had already grown up in the Vedic society and incest and other abnormalities were condemned. Another dialogue (*Ṛgveda* 10.95) between Purūravas and Urvaśī shows how one of the conditions of the continuance of their union being broken, the nymph vanished forever, implying thereby that marriage during this period would in some cases have dissolved on the occurrence of an agreed event. The ceremony of *vahatu* (*RV* 1.184.3; 4.58.9; *AV* 10.1.1; 14.2.9; *AB* 4.7.1; *TB* 1.5.1.2), by which the bride is conducted from the house of her parents to her husband's house with all presents carried before, forms the normal process of marriage in the early Vedic period. The father or brother of the girl gave her, well-dressed and decked with ornaments, to the suitor who held her by the hand and took her home (*RV* 10.19.3). The *Ṛgveda* (1.116.1, 10.39.7) refers to capture of girls. In this way, the bride was carried even against the will of her father, as for example, the carrying away of the daughter of Purumitra by Vimada, to her lover's house where she would be married to him. It (*RV* 1.10.9.2) speaks of another form in which the bride's father took money from the bridegroom as her price before giving him his daughter. It (*RV* 10.27.12; *AV* 2.36.1) speaks of the later system of *svayamvara* by which the girl herself chose her husband. This may be treated as an example of gandharva form, in which love causes the pair to be united.

**Marriage, Forms of:** See **Marital Relations**, Wedding. Marriage in the early Vedic texts appears essentially as a union of two adult persons, which is proved by the numerous references (*RV* 1.117.7, 2.17.7, 10.39.3; *AV* 2.36.1, 14.2.59) to unmarried girls who grow old in their father's house (*amā-jur*). They adorn themselves in desire of marriage as well as to the paraphernalia of spells and aphrodisiac, used in the *Atharvaveda* tradition (3.18, 6.89.120, 7.36.37, 7.45) to compel the love of man or woman respectively, while even the *RV* (9.32.5, 10.34.5) itself seems to present us with a spell by which a lover seeks to send all the household to sleep when he visits his beloved. Child wives first occur regularly in the Sūtra period, though it is still uncertain to what extent the rule of marriage before puberty was in vogue. The Sūtras refer to *ṛtusaṅgamana* or *niṣeka*, which probably indicates a ceremonial defloration at puberty. The marriage was frequently arranged through an intermediary (*RV* 10.78.4, 10.85, 15, 10.85. 23), presumably after those concerned had in effect come to an agreement. The sale of a daughter was not unknown (*MS* 1.10.11, *KS* 36.5; *TS* 2.3.4.1; *TB* 1.1.2.4), but a certain amount of discredit would seem to have attached to it. (*RV* 1.109.2), and sons-in-law in such cases were sometimes stingy. On the other hand, dowries were not infrequently given, especially no doubt when damsels suffered from bodily defects (*RV* 6.28.5.10.27.12; *AV* 5.17.12). Occasionally marriages by capture may have taken place, but only as knightly feats, as when Vimada carried off Purumitra's daughter against her father's wish, but very possibly with her own consent (*RV* 1.112.19, 1.116.1, 1.117.20, 10.39, 10.65.12). The later law-books and the epic describe in much detail various forms of marriage but they all seem reducible to three types: (a) that which is based on mutual consent, the *prājāpātya* (connected with Prajāpati); (b) that in which a price is paid for the bride or the groom, the *āsura* (Asura like), *ārsạ* (connected with the Rsis), *brahma* (relating to *brahman*) or *daiva* (divine); (c) those which involve stealing the bride, the *kṣatra* (warrior like) or the *rākṣasa* (demon like) mode. The gift of a maiden for services rendered or other object is exemplified in the story of Cyavana in the *Jaiminīya Brāhmaṇa* (3.122), and in that of Syavasva in the *Bṛhaddevatā*.

**Marud-vṛdhā:** Name of a stream mentioned in the Nadīstuti (praise of rivers) in the *Ṛgveda* (10.75.5) along with the Asiknī (Akesines) and the Vitastā (Hydaspes). Roth considers that the *marudvṛdhā* denotes the stream formed by the combined waters of these two rivers down to its junction with the Paruṣṇī (Ravi), a view accepted by Zimmer. On the other hand, modern scholars identify it with a stream of Kashmir.

**Maruts:** The Maruts—the storm-gods from an important group of deities. They are the sons of Rudra and Pṛsṇi, the cow (representing the mottled storm cloud), also of Vāyu, and are sometimes described as self-born. They are all brothers of equal age, having the same birth-place and abode. They are golden, ruddy and self-luminous and are associated with *vidyut*, particularly having the epithet lightning-spread (*riṣṭi-vidyut*); the cars on which they ride, beam with lightning. Among their personal decorations, such as helmets, mantles, garlands, etc., armlets and anklets are peculiar. They make a loud noise represented by thunder and the roaring of the winds, and as such are pre-eminently the singers of heaven, their songs inspiring Indra. Their chief function is to shed rain, which is figuratively called either milk, honey, or ghee, and which is connected with the thunderstorm. At the same time, they produce light and make a path for the sun. They are the constant allies of Indra, in whose company they are addressed as 'priests', their songs representing hymns of praise. Indra achieves all his exploits in their company. Like Rudra, they are invoked to avert evils and also to bring healing remedies. *Ṛgveda* 1.64.2; 1.85.1 f; 1.114.6; 1.168.9; 2.33.1; 2.3.2; 5.42.15; 5.52.16; 5.60.5; 5.59.6; 6.50.4; 6.66.3; 7.56.1; 8.7.3; 8.17.17; 8.20.17; 8.83.1; 10.73.1; 10.77.2; 10.78.6; 10.99.5; 10.113.3.

**Maṣṇāra:** Name of a locality, the scene of the victory of a Kuru king mentioned in the *Aitareya Brāhmaṇa* (8.23).

**Masses:** A term *janatā* frequently found in the later Saṃhitās (*AV* 5.18.12; *KS* 9.17; *TS* 2.2.1.4, etc.) and the Brāhmaṇas (*AB* 1.7; 3.31; 5.9; *TB* 1.4.6.1; 2.3.1.3, etc.) denotes the people as a community.

**Mātariśvan:** Mātariśvan is not celebrated in any hymn of the *Ṛgveda*, and the name is found there only twenty-seven times. In the six older passages, Mātariśvan is always either identified with Agni or is the producer of fire. Mātariśvan is a name of Agni in three passages (3.5.9; 3.26.6; 1.96.4). This is probably also the case where the name occurs in the vocative, at the end of an Agni hymn (9.88.19). In another verse, where an etymological explanation of the name is given, he is spoken of as one of the forms of Agni (1.141.5). Elsewhere, he became the swift flight of wind (3.29.11). In some cases Mātariśvan is distinguished from Agni. 'He (Agni) being born in the highest heaven appeared to Mātariśvan (1.143.2), the messenger of Vivasvat, whom the mighty seized in the lap of the creators (6, 8-4). He brought from the hidden Agni, produced by friction, from the gods (3. 9-5). Mātariśvan would thus appear to be a personification of a celestial form of Agni, who at the same time is thought of as having, like Prometheus, brought down the hidden fire from heaven to earth. Hardly any thing but lightning can be his natural basis. Macdonell, 71-2.

**Mathematics:** There was highly developed numerical system from the early Vedic period (*RV* 3.6.15; 4.32.18; 8.1.5; 8.2.4.1; 8.21.18; *AV* 7.2.22; 7.8.7; 10.8.24). *Daśan* or ten forms the basis of the numerical system. It was developed unprecedently at a very early date. It seems likely that the Vedic Indians had the knowledge of signs of numerals (*RV* 10.62.7). Some fractions, such as *ardha, pāda, śapha* and *kalā* denoting 1/2, 1/4, 1/8 and 1/16 respectively, were known in the Vedic period. The fraction tripad denoting 3/4 also occurs in the *Ṛgveda* (10.90.4). In the Vedic texts (*VS* 17.2; 22.34; *KS* 39.6; *TS* 4.4.11.4; 7.2.20.1; *PB* 2.8.14; *JUB* 1.10.28.29, etc.) we come across names for very high numerals beyond 1,000. Thus 10,000 is *ayuta*, the latter multiplied by ten is *niyuta* and its subsequent multiplicands by ten constitute, respectively, *prayuta, arbuda, nyarbuda, samudra, madhya, anta* and *parārdha*. An arithmetical progression is found in *Pañcaviṃśa Brāhmaṇa* (18.3), where a list of sacrificial gifts is featured in which each successive figure doubles the amount of the preceding one. It begins with 'gold to the value of 12' followed by to the value of 24, 48, 96, 192, 384, 768, 1,536, 3,072 then *dve aṣṭāviṃśatiśatamāna*, which means 2 x 128 x 24 (the last unit being not a single *māna*, but a number of 24 *mānas*) 6,144, then 12,228, 24,576, 49,152, 98,304, 1, 96, 608, 3, 93,216. The *Ṛgveda* has the phrase *śata-sahasrāṇi* or 100,000 several times (4,32,18, 7.32.18). With these large numbers may be compared the minute theoretical subdivision of time in the *Śatapatha Brāhmaṇa* 12.3.2.1 ff, where a day is divided into 15 *muhūrtas* ( 1*muhūrta*, =15 *kṣipras*, 1*ksipra* = 15 *etarhis*, 1 *etarhis* = 15 *idānis*, 1 *idāni* = 15 *prāṇas*. The *Śāṅkhāyana Śrautasūtra* (14.75) and *Śāṅkhāyana Āraṇyaka* (7.20) have a decimal division: 1 *muhūrta* = 10 *nimeṣas*, 1 *nimeṣa* = 10 *dhvaṃsis*. Some specialized crafts, such as making the chariots and carts, must have required careful measurement of dimensions of their various parts. The Vedic period also required some units of value and weight. The exchange of commodities of the principle of barter system, with cow as a unit of value, is recorded in the *Ṛgveda* (4.24.10). The *niṣka*, originally a gold ornament (*RV* 5.19.3) at a later time became a unit of value. In the period of the later Saṃhitās, the *māna* became a measure of weight equivalent to the *Kṛṣṇala* (the berry), which was a unit of weight. The *śatamāna*, a piece of gold in weight, equivalent to a hundred *kṛṣṇalas*, might have evolved into a currency. The *Chāndogya Upaniṣad* (2.1.2; 2.1.4) mentions the science of numbers (*rāśi*). *Śulva* or geometry was used in Vedic times to solve propositions about the construction of various rectinitial figures, combination, transformation and application of areas, mensuration of areas and volumes; squaring of the circles and vice versa, etc. The authors of the Śulvasūtras obtained the complete jovial solutions of the rational right angled triangles. The texts also contain the elementary treatment of surds.

**Matsya:** Name of a people in one passage of the *Ṛgveda* (7.18.6), where they are ranged with the enemies of Sudās. In the list of Aśvamedhins, 'offerers of the sacrifice', in the *Śatapatha Brāhmaṇa* (13.5.4.9), Dhvaṣan Dvaitavana is mentioned as a Matsya king. The Matsyas as a people occur also in the *Kauṣītaki Upaniṣad* (4.1) in connection with the Vaśas, and in the *GS* (1.2.9) in connection with Śālvas. In Manu (2.19.7.193) the Kurukṣetra, the Matsyas, the Pañcālas and the Śūrasenakas comprise the land of the Brahmarṣideśa. The Matsays occupied much the same territory as in epic times, Alwar, Jaipur and Bharatupur in Rajasthan. Macdonell and Keith II, 121-2.

**Measure:** The lowest measure was *aṅguli* or finger-breadth (*ŚB* 10.2.1.2). *Anguṣtha* or thumb was also a unit of measure (*KU* 4.12; 6.17). *Bāhu* or arm as a measure of length is found in the *Taittirīya Saṃhitā* (6.2.11.1). *Pradeśa* occurs in the *Aitareya Brāhmaṇa* (8.5) and the *Śatapatha Brāhmaṇa* (3.5.4.5) as a measure of length, being the span between the thumb and the forefingers. *Prakrama* or stride is mentioned as a measure of distance in the *Śatapatha Brāhmaṇa* (10.2.3.1) but its exact length is unknown, *Prasṛta* is found in the *Śatapatha Brāhmaṇa* (4.5.10.7, 13.4.1.5) as a measure of capacity meaning a handful, while *sthivi* (*RV* 10.68.3) means 'bushel'. *Pāda* as a measure of length, denotes 'foot' in the *Śatapatha Brāhmaṇa* (6.5.3.2; 7.2.1.7; 8.7.2.17), which was also occassionally used to express a measure of weight. As a fraction it means a 'quarter' a sense derived from that of 'foot' of a quadruped, just as *sapha*, the divided hoof, comes to mean an eighth. *Aratni* is cubit. According to the Śulvasūtra or Baudhāyana (*JRAS*, 1912, 231), this measure is equal to 24 *aṅgulas* or finger-breadths. This measure is also mentioned in the

*Śatapatha Brāhmaṇa* (10.2.1.3). Measure of longer distance is indicated by the term *krośa* (*PB* 16.13.12), lit 'a shout', as expressing the range of the voice. The term is still valid and denotes a distance of about two miles, though this measure varies from place to place. *Yojana* occurs in the *Ṛgveda* (1.123.8; 2.16.3; 10.76.7; 10.86.20), *Atharvaveda* (4.26.1), *Maitrāyaṇī Saṃhitā* (2.9.9; 3.8.4), *Taittirīya Brāhmaṇa* (2.4.2.7), etc., as a measure of distance but there is no reference defining its real length.

**Meat Eating:** The term *māṃsa* denotes 'flesh'. The eating of flesh appears as something quite regular in the Vedic texts. Fire is called the eater of ox and barren cows (*RV* 8.43.11). A goat is offered to fire to be carried to forefathers (*RV* 10.16.4). A barren cow was also killed at the time of marriage (*RV* 10.75.3), obviously for food. The ritual offerings of flesh contemplate that the gods will eat it. Again, 'the brāhmaṇas ate the offerings' (*RV* 8.43.11; *AV* 3.21.6; *TS* 1.3.14.7). The slaying of a 'great ox' (*mahokṣa*) or a 'great goat (*mahāja*) for a guest was regularly prescribed (*ŚB* 3.4.1.2). The flesh of horse, rams, barren cows, sheep and buffaloes was cooked (*RV* 5.29.7-8); 6.17.11-12; 8.12.8). Probably flesh of birds was also eatern (*RV* 1.92.10). Fish is mentioned in the *Ṛgveda* (10.68.8) and words denoting fishermen (*VS* 13.12; 26.27; 30.16; *AV* 18.1; *TS* 4.5.42, *MS* 2.9.5, *TB* 3.4.12.1, etc.) make us infer that the Vedic Indians had included fish in their diet. Sometimes a cow that miscarried, or a sterile cow, was killed (*AV* 12.4.10); and the name *atithigva* probably means 'slaying cows for guests (*RV* 10.68.3). The great sage Yājñavalkya was wont to eat the meat of milch cows and bullock if only it was *aṃsala* ('firm' or 'tender', *ŚB* 3.1.2.21). The slaughter of a hundred bulls (*ukṣan*) was credited to one sacrificer, Agastya (*TB* 2.7.11.1; *PB* 21.14.5). A slaughterhouse is also mentioned (*RV* 10.89.14). The flesh of the sacrificial victims were eaten by the participants (*MS* 3.14; *VS* 13.47-51; *TS* 1.3.8, *GB* 3.13.18). The marriage ceremony was accompanied by the slaying of oxen, clearly for food (*RV* 10.85.13). Sometimes it is forbidden, as when a man is performing a vow (*ŚB* 14.1.1.29; *KŚS* 2.1.8), or its use is disapproved, as in a passage of the *Atharvaveda* (6.70.1), where meat is classed with *surā*, or intoxicating liquor, as a bad thing. Again, in the *Ṛgveda* (10.85.13; *AV* 14.1.13) the slaying of the cows is said to take place in the *aghās*, a deliberate variation for *maghās*; but this may merely be the outcome of a natural association of death with gloom, even when cows alone are the victims in question. The Brāhmaṇas also contain the doctrine of the eater in this world being eaten in the next (*ŚB* 1.6.1.1; *JB* 1.42-44; *AĀ* 2.1.1), but this is not to be regarded as a moral or religious disapproval of eating flesh. However, there is no doubt that it contains the germ of such a view, which is also in harmony with the persuasion of the unity of existence, which becomes marked in the Brāhmaṇas. But *ahiṃsā* as a developed and articulate doctrine would seem to have arisen from the acceptance of the doctrine of transmigration, which in its fundamentals is later than the *Brāhmaṇa* period. On the other hand, it is to be noted that the cow was on the road to acquiring special sanctity in the *Ṛgveda* (8.101.15; *VS* 4.19.20; *AV* 10.10, 12.4.5), as is shown by the name *aghnyā*, not to be slain, applied to it in several passages. But this fact cannot be regarded as showing that meat eating generally was condemned. Apart from mythical considerations, such as the identification of the cow with earth or Aditi, the value of the cow for purposes other than eating was so great as to account adequately for its sanctity. The usual food of the Vedic Indian, as far as flesh was concerned, can be gathered from the list of sacrificial victims: What man ate he presented to the gods-that is, the sheep, the goat, and the ox. The horse sacrifice was of infrequent occurrence. It is, however, more likely that the aim of this sacrifice was to impart magic strength, the speed and vigour of the horse, to the god and his worshippers Flesh was roasted on spits (*RV* 1.162.11, *AV* 9.6.17) or boiled in pots. Meat cooked with rice was much valued as food in the Vedic period (*BU* 6.4.18).

**Medhāyajña:** A sacrament for a child, which consists in muttering the word *Vāk* thrice in its right ear. (*ŚGS* 1.24.9; *BGS* 2.1.7; *TB* 2.5.1). Again, on the fourth day after *upanayana* a rite called *medhāyajña* is performed, which is supposed to make the student capable of mastering the Vedas. cf. *ĀGS* 1.22.18-9.

**Mediator:** The term *madhyamāśi* is found in the *Ṛgveda* (10.97.12), *Atharvaveda* (4.9.4) and *Vājasaneyī Saṃhitā* (12.86) to which Roth assigns the meaning of intercessor. Zimmer accepts it in the sense of 'mediator' or 'arbiter', as a legal term. Lanman suggests that it was intended to express adversary or preventer of the disease referred to in the hymn. Whitney thinks that it means 'midmost man' or chief, as the one around whom his followers encamp. Geldner, however, thinks that a third king, who is neutral between to enemies, is intended, which reminds us of the *maṇḍala* theory of diplomacy of later times. Macdonell and Keith II, 127-8.

**Medical Science:** The Vedic texts refer to a good number of diseases such as *apacit* (scrofulous swellings, *AV* 6.25.1; 83/1; 7.75.1.77.1) *apvā* and *viṣucikā* (dysentry, *RV* 10.103.12; *AV* 9.8.9; *VS* 19.10; *MS* 3.11.7; *KS* 37.18; *TB* 2.6.1.5; *ŚB* 12.7.3.2), *arśas* (haemorrhoids, *VS* 12.98); *alaji* and *duṣīkā* (eye disease, *AV* 9.8.20; 16.6.8; *KS* 34.12; *VS* 25.9; *ŚB* 3.1.3.10), *āśarikā*, *pṛṣṭyamaya* and *viśara* (pain in various limbs of the body (*RV* 1.105.18; *AV* 2.4.2; 19.34.10), *āsrāva* (diarrhoea, *AV* 1.2.4; 2.3.2; 6.44.2), *galunta* (swelling, *AV* 6.83.3), *graivya* (tumours on the neck, *AV* 6.25.2; 7.76.2) *glau* boil, (*AV* 6.83.3; *AB* 1.25), *jambha* (convulsion, *AV*

2.4.2; 8.1.16), *takman* (fever, *AV* 1.25; 5.22; 6.20; 7.116; 19.39), *pākāru* (ulcers, *VS* 12.97), *pāpayakṣma, balāsa, yakṣma, rājayakṣma* (consumptions of various types *RV* 1.122.9; 161.1; 10.85.31; 97.11; 137-4; 163.1-6; *AV* 2.10.56; 3.31.1; 4.9.8; 5.4.9; 22.1; 30.6; 6.14.1; 177.1; 8.7.2; 9.8.3-10; 11.3.29; 12.2.1-2; 4.8; 19.34.10; 36.1; 38.3; *VS* 12.97; *KS* 11.3; 17.11; 27.3; *TS* 2.3.5.2; *MS* 2.2.7; *SB* 4.1.2.9), *pāman* (scab, *AV* 5.22.12) *viklindu* (*catarrh, AV* 12.4.5); *vidradha* (abcesses, *AV* 6.127.1; 9.8.20), *viṣkandha* (rheumatism, *AV* 1.16.3; 2.4.1 ff; 3.9.2-6; 4.9.5; 19.34.5; *TS* 7.3.11.1), *visras* (senility, *AV* 19.34.3), *visalya* (nuralgia, *AV* 6.127.1 ff; 9.8.2 ff, 19.44.2), *śirṣakti, śirṣaśoka* and *śīrṣāmaya* (headache and disease of the head, *AV* 1.12.3; 5.4.10; 9.8.1; 12.2.19; 5.23; *AB* 8.5), *sloṇya* (lameness, *TB* 3.9.17.2; *TS* 6.1.6.7), *śvitra* (leukoderma, *PB* 12.11.11), *surāma* (alcoholism, *RV* 10.131.5; *VS* 21.42; *MS* 3.11.4; 4.12.3), *hariman* (jaundice, *RV* 1.50.11 ff, 1.22.1; 9.8.9; 19.44.2), *hṛdayāmaya, hṛddyota* and *hṛdroga* (heart disease, *RV* 1.50.11; *AV* 1.22.1; 6.24.1) and *hrūḍu* (*cramp, AV* 1.25.2-3). Besides, the Vedic Indians had recorded names of a few more diseases which have not been identified yet. These are *akṣata* (*AV* 7.76.4), *upacit* (*VS* 12.97), *kiśmīla* (*AV* 19.4.8), *kṣetriya* (*AV* 2.8.10; 14.5; 3.7.1 ff; 4.18.7; *KS* 15.1), *grāha* (*ŚB* 3.5.3.25; 3.6.1.25; *AV* 11.9.12), *grāhī* (*RV* 10.161.1; *AV* 2.9.1; 10.6; 6.112.1, etc.) *nirāla* (*AV* 6.16.3), *śipada* (*RV* 7.50.4), *śimida* (*RV* 7.50.4; *AV* 4.25.4; *ŚB* 7.4.1.27), *saṃskandha* (*AV* 19.34.5), *skandhyā* (*AV* 6.25.1.27), etc. *Bheṣaja*, denoting remedial agent or medicine, is mentioned (*RV* 1.89.4; 2.33.2; *AV* 5.29.1; 6.21.2, etc.) along with its numerous ingredients. It is generally held that the system of treatment as laid down in *Atharvaveda* is magical and not scientific. This is a mistaken idea. First of all, in the *Atharvaveda* we find specification of diseases, which is not possible without any scientific approach. Secondly, in all cases specific medicine is given to the patient. Many such medicines, prepared from herbs and other natural products, are effective even today. The only notable feature in the case of Atharvavedic medicines is that these were given to the patients along with certain incantations or spells as well as curative rituals. It has two significances. The physician did not ignore the primitive tribal practices which were ingrained in the mind of average people. Secondly, such spells and rituals were required for a psychological boost because people had faith in them. One should not fail to recall in this connection that the interest of the Vedic Indians seems early to have been attracted to the consideration of the questions connected with the anatomy (q.v.) of the body. Thus, a hymn of the *Atharvaveda* (10.2) enumerates parts of human body with accuracy and in orderly arrangement (cf. *VS* 19.81-93; 20.5.13; *MS* 3.11.8-9; *KS* 38.3-4; *TB* 2.6.4-5; *ŚB* 10.5.4.12; 12.2.4.9-14; 12.3.2.3-4, etc.). *Bhiṣaj* or physician is a word of common occurrence (*RV* 2.33.4; 6.50.7; 9.112.1; *AV* 5.29.1; 6.24.2; *TS* 6.4.9.2; *VS* 16.5; 19.12). Aśvins (*RV* 1.116.16; 157.6; 8.18.8; 86.1; 10.39.3-5; *AV* 7.53.1; *AB* 1.18), Varuṇa (*RV* 1.24.9) and Rudra (*RV* 2.33.4-7) are all called physicians. But it should be observed in this connection that the social position of the physicians was not high. This dislike is found in later Saṃhitās (*TS* 6.4.9.3; *MS* 4.6.2, *SB* 4.1.5.14), where the Aśvins are condemned on the grounds that the practice of medicine brought them too much among men. The physicians could not follow, for the sake of their profession, the rules relating to the sacred and the profane. Moreover, medical science directly contradicted the doctrine of *karma*, which is why the profession is utterly despised (*ĀpDS* 1.6.18.20; 19.15; *GDS* 17.17; *VDS* 14.2.19, etc.). The apathy towards medicinal science and the physicians was a worldwide phenomenon in ancient world. See **Aetiology, Amulets, Anatomy, Aśvins, Bacilius, Biology, Body, Breath, Diseases, Embryology, Fire-therapy, Hair-treatment, Herbs, Hot-water treatment, Medicinal Plants, Medicinal charms, Ointment, Pacificatory Herbs, Physicians, Physiology, plants, Quacks, Sin, Smearing, Smoke-therapy, Veterinary charms, Vital Airs, Wind-therapy.**

**Medicinal Plants:** An entire hymn of the *Ṛgveda* (10.97) is addressed to the Oṣadhis, or medicinal plants, with special reference to their curative power. Relevant verses are quoted here, 'Herbs that sprang up in time of old, three ages earlier than the gods, of these, whose hue is brown, will I declare the hundred powers and seven': (1) 'Ye, mothers, have a hundred homes, yes, and a thousand are your growth. Do ye who have a thousand powers free this my patient from disease.' (2) 'He who hath store of herbs at hand like kings amid a crowd of men, physician is that sage's name, find, slayer, chaser of disease.' (6) 'The healing virtues of the plants stream forth like cattle from the stall, plants that shall win me store of wealth, and save thy vital breath, O man. (8) 'When, bringing back the vanished strength, I hold these herbs within my hand. The spirit of disease departs ere, he can seize upon the life.'-(11) 'Fly, Spirit of Disease, begone, with the blue jay and kingfisher. Fly with the wind's impetuous speed, vanish together with the storm'. (13) 'Of all the many plants whose king is Soma, plants of hundred forms, thou art the plant most excellent, prompt to the wish, sweet to the hear.' (18) Griffith's translation.

**Medicinal Charms:** Quite a number of medicinal charms are included in the *Atharvaveda*. The chief malady that was sought to be treated magically was *takman* (this term does not occur outside of the *AV*). From the symptoms described it is almost certain that it was nothing but malarial fever. The plant *kuṣṭha* is mentioned as potent in fighting *takman*, but whether as medicine or as amulet, is not quite clear. That the *Atharvaveda* should contain charms against snakebite is quite obvious. One of them (*AV* 5.13) deserves special mention.

**Meditation:** The *Chāndogya Upaniṣad* (1.3.8-9) says, 'One should reflect on the *sāman* with which one would eulogize, on the *ṛc* on which the *sāman* rests, on the seer who saw the *ṛc* (verse), and one should reflect on the deity which one would eulogize'. In the *Taittirīya Upaniṣad* (1.3.1-4), we read of the *saṃhitā-upaniṣad*, or the meditation based on the conjunction of letters, where the idea is to lead the pupil's mind from the mere composition of words to the universal fact of four factors involved in all conjunctions, viz., the two component parts of a pair, their actual association, and the resulting whole. The *Chāndogya Upaniṣad* gives a practical hint as to how one can be in the constant presence of Reality in the midst of daily duties: 'The *ātman* is in the heart . . . who meditates thus goes to heaven every day' (8.3.3). Surely, it does not cost one much to bear constantly in mind that the heart is the temple of god, from which he is directing and watching all our activities. The same idea is involved in the *Bṛhadāraṇyaka Upaniṣad* (3.7) conception of *antar-yāmin*, the inner ruler. *Cultural Heritage of India* I, 375-7.

**Mehatnū:** Name of a stream in the Nadīstuti (praise of Rivers) in the *Ṛgveda* (10.75.6). Apparently it was a tributary of the Sindhu (Indus), entering that river before the Krumu (Kurum) and Gomati (Gomal). It may conceivably have been a tributary of the Krumu.

**Melody:** The word *sāman*, although frequently used for the designation of the *Sāmaveda*, which had been either made or destined for singing, originally means one tune or melody. Nowadays a verse is sung to a certain tune but in the Vedic period it was reverse. A particular melody (*sāman*) was sung upon a particular stanza. The Vedic seers conceived the relationship of melody and stanza as that between progeny and womb. The *ṛc* is, therefore, called the *yoni*, i.e. the womb, out of which the melody comes forth. There were various classes of *sāman* and each had a distinct application (*viniyoga*) to a specific ritual.

**Menial:** *Preṣya*, 'to be sent' on an errand, denotes a menial servant or slave, being applied in the *Aitareya Brāhmaṇa* (7.29), *KB* (17.1) and other texts. In the *Atharvaveda* (5.22.14) the adjective *praiṣya* 'menial', occurs (6.2.53). Another term for menial is *puruṣa*, which is found in the *Ṛgveda* (6.39.5); *Atharvaveda* (4.9.7; 10.1.17); *Śatapatha Brāhmaṇa* (6.3.1.22) and other texts.

**Merchant:** Merchants are described in the Vedic texts as *vaṇij* and *vaṇija*. The former denotes simple merchant in the *Ṛgveda* (1.112.11; 5.45.6); *Atharvaveda* (3.15.1). *Vaṇija* denotes a merchant as a hereditary profession (son of a *vaṇij*) in the *Vājasaneyī Saṃhitā* 30.17 and *Taittirīya Brāhmaṇa* 3.4.14.1. The word *śreṣthin* occurs in several passages of the Brāhmaṇas (*AB* 3.30.3; *KB* 28.6; *KU* 4.20). Macdonell and Keith write 'It is, however, possible that the word may already have the sense of the 'headman of a guild', the modern seth. There is a similar doubt in the use of *sraiṣṭhya* (*AV* 1.9.3; *TS* 3.5.4.2; *KS* 5.6; *MS* 1.4.3), which is perhaps not merely 'the foremost place' as usually assumed but definitely 'the presidency of a guild'. Guilds are referred to in the Dharma Sūtras and they play a considerable part in the Buddhist texts and the epic. But the Vedic evidence is inadequate to afford any grounds for positive assertion or denial of their instance of organization in Vedic times. Macdonell and Keith II, 403-4.

**Mess:** The term *odana* is a common expression (*RV* 8.69.14; *AV* 4.14.7), denoting a mess, usually of grain cooked with milk (*kṣīra-pākam odanam RV* 8.77.10). Special varieties are mentioned, such as the 'milk-mess' (*kṣīraudana SB* 2.5.3.4; 11.5.7.5; *BU* 6.4.13), 'the curd-mess' (*dadhy-odana, BU* 6.4.14), the 'bean-mess' (*mudgaudana, ŚāṅkhĀ* 12.8), the sesame-mess (*tilaudana, BU* 6.4.15), the 'meat-mess' (*māṃsaudana, BU* 6.4.16; *ŚB* 11.5.7.5; *ŚāṅkhĀ* 12.8), the 'ghee-mess' (*ghṛtaudana, ŚāṅkhĀ* 12.8), etc.

**Messenger:** *Pālāgala* occurs in the *Śatapatha Brāhmaṇa* (5.3.1.11), apparently in the sense of messenger of bearer of news.

**Metals:** *Bronze:* The exact metal denoted by the word *ayas* when used by itself in the *Ṛgveda* (1.57.3; 163.9; 4.2.17; 6.3.5) is uncertain. Macdonell and Keith, in accordance with the view of Zimmer, favour the sense of bronze rather than of iron. Agni is called *ayo-damṣṭra* (*RV* 1.88.5; 10.87.2), 'with teeth of Ayas', in reference to the colour of his flames. Likewise, the car-seat of Mitra and Varuna is called *ayaḥ-sthūna* (*RV* 5.62.8), 'with pillars of Ayas'. Both the colour resemble that of bronze. However, *ayas* has a wider denotation as its references, prefixed by various adjectives, clearly demonstrate.

*Copper:* In the *Vājasaneyī Saṃhitā* 918.13), *ayas, śyāma, loha, siśa, hiraṇya* and *trapu* are mentioned as six important metals. Considering *ayas* as suggestive of bronze, *śyāma* (swarthy) and *loha* (red) may mean iron and copper respectively. In the *Atharvaveda* (11.3.1.7); and the *Maitrāyaṇī Saṃhitā* (4.2.9), *lohita ayas*, as distinguished from *śyāma*, denotes copper. It may also denote bronze (cf. *SB* 5.4.1.2). Copper is *lohāyasa* or *lohitāyasa* (*ŚB* 5.4.1.1-2). It is simply called *loha* in the *Vājasaneyī Saṃhitā* (18.13; cf. *ŚB* 13.2.2.18; *CU* 4.17.7; 6.1-5; *JUB* 4.1.4). In the *Atharvaveda* (11.3.7) it is called *lohita*, while *lohamaṇi* in the *Chāndogya Upaniṣad* (6.2.5) denotes a copper amulet.

*Gold:* See **Gold**. Among the various names of gold the Vedic texts refer to *candra* (*RV* 2.2.4; 3.31.5; *AV* 12.2.53; *TS* 1.2.7.1; *VS* 16.26; 19-93; *PB* 6.6 *ŚB* 3.3.3.4), *jātarūpa* (*AB* 8.13; *BU* 6.4.25), *suvarṇa* (*AV* 15.1.2; *TB* 1.4.7.4; 3.12.6.6; *ŚB* 11.4.1.8; *CU* 1.6.6; 3.19.1; 4.17.7), *harita* (*AV* 5.28.5 ff, 11.3.8; *KS* 8.5) and *hiraṇya* (*RV* 1.43.5; 3.34.9; 4.10.6; 17.11; 6.61.7; 8.26.18; 78.9; 10.75.8; *AV* 1.9.2; 3.36.7; 5.28.6; 6.38.2; *TS* 6.1.7.1; *ŚB* 2.1.1.5, etc.

*Iron:* Among the six metal mentioned in the *Vājasaneyī Saṃhitā* (18.13), *śyāma* seems to denote iron. In the *Atharvaveda* (11.3.1 ff) and *Maitrāyaṇī Saṃhitā* (4.2.9) *ayas* is divided into two species—the *śyāma* (iron) and *lohita* (copper or bronze). In the *Atharvaveda* (5.28.1) *ayas*, without any attribute, denotes iron. And so the arrow of the *Ṛgveda* (6.75.15), which had a tip of *ayas* pointed with iron, *yasyā ayo mukham.* In the *Atharvaveda* (9.5.4) iron is called *śyāma ayas* or *śyāma* alone. Iron was known as *kṛṣnāyasa* in the Upaniṣads (*CU* 4.17.7; 6.1.5; *JUB* 3.17.3) which also refer to *loha.*

*Lead: Siśa* occurs first in the *Atharvaveda* (12.2.1 ff). It was used for amulets (*AV* 1.16.2-4) and also by the weavers (*VS* 19.80; *MS* 3.11.9; *TB* 2.6.4.1 ff). Siśa is frequently mentioned in later Saṃhitās, and Brāhmaṇas (*MS* 2.4.2; *VS* 18.13; *TB* 3.12.6.5; *ŚB* 5.1.2.14; 5.4.1.9; 12.7.1.7; 12.7.2.10; *CU* 4.17.7).

*Silver:* The Vedic term for silver is *rajata.* Ornaments (*rukma, ŚB* 12.8.3.11), dishes (*pātra, TB* 2.2.9.7; 3.9.6.5) and coins (*niṣka, PB* 17.1.14) made of silver are mentioned. The word is also used alone to denote the metal itself (*AV* 5.28.1; 13.4.51; *AB* 7.12.2; *CU* 4.17.7; *JUB* 3.17.3). *Rajata* is often mentioned with *hiraṇya* (*TS* 1.5.1.2; *KS* 10.4; *ŚB* 12.4.4.7; 13.4.2.10; 14.1.3.4).

*Tin: Trapu* denotes tin in later Saṃhitās and Brāhmaṇas. Its quality of being easily smelted is indicated by its name, which is derived from the root *trap* (*AV* 11.3.8; *KS* 18.10; *MS* 2.11.5; *VS* 18.13; *TB* 3.12.6.5; *JUB* 3.17.5; *CU* 4.17.7).

**Metempsychosis:** See **Karma**.

**Methonica Superba:** *Amūlā* (without root) is the name in the *Atharvaveda* (5.31.4) of a plant (*methonica superba*), which was used for poisoning arrows.

**Metrics:** In the *Ṛgveda* (10.14.16; 10.130.4-5), we meet with several terms which latter became well-known as technical designations of metres. Gāyatrī is said to be born of Agni, Uṣṇiḥ of Savitṛ, Anuṣṭubh of Soma, Bṛahatī or Bṛhaspati, and Virāṭ of Mitrāvaruṇa. Indra, the god praised most often, invented the Triṣṭubh, the metre employed most often. The Viśvedevas (all gods) created the Jagatī. The Śakvari is mentioned when we are told that the Vasiṣṭhas strengthened Indra by loudly chanting in that metre. A hymn in the eighth kāṇḍa of the *Atharvaveda* gives the number of syllables in these seven chief metres of Vedic poetry as increasing by four successively, i.e. from 24 in the Gāyatrī to 48 in the Jāgatī. These seven metres are often mentioned with names in the other Saṃhitās (*VS* 5.2; cf. *ŚB* 3.4.1; 8.5.2). Fascinated by the charming rhythm of the metres, the authors of the Brāhmaṇas ingeniously show that their harmony is, in some mystical and mysterious fashion, the fundamental cause of the harmony of the world. The *Śatapatha Brāhmaṇa* (8.1.1.2) tells us that metres, like other beings, were created by Prajāpati. In 3.9.4.10 it mentions Gāyatrī as a mystical name of Agni who carries off the *soma.* Gāyatrī, in the form of a bird, fetches the *soma* from heaven. In the *Brāhmaṇa* and *Upaniṣad* speculations on the mystical significance of metres, numbers play a great part. The *Bṛhadāraṇyaka Upaniṣad* (5.15) says: 'The word *bhūmi*, *antarīkṣa* and *dyu* (to be pronounced as di-u) make up 8 syllables; a *gāyatrī pāda* (foot) consists of 8 syllables; therefore, he who knows the Gāyatrī gains the three worlds'. In the *Śāṅkhāyana Śrauta Sūtra* (7.27) inquiries into the beginning of the science of metrics lead to the formulation of the principles of verification. In the *Vāsiṣṭha Dharmā Sūtra* (13.3 and elsewhere) the metres are deified enough to have sacrifices offered to them. In the *Śākala Prātiśākhya* of Śaunaka, the last three *paṭalas* (chapters) are on metres. The *Nidāna-Sūtra* of the *Sāma Veda* discusses the metrical aspect of the various parts of that musical Veda, such as the *uktha, stoma* and *gāṇa*. It explains the nature and different names of all the Vedic metres and gives an index to the metres of hymns employed in the *ekāha, ahīna* and *satra* sacrifices. Among the five or six extant *Anukramaṇis* (Indices), which are attached to the *Ṛgveda*, the *Chando'nukramaṇi* (of about 300 stanzas in the Anuṣṭubh and Triṣṭubh metres) enumerates the metres of the Ṛgvedic hymns and states the number of verses in each metre. The extensive *Sarvānukramaṇi* (General Index) epitomizes, in Sūtra style, the data of the *Anukramaṇis*. It contains some metrical *pādas*, and borrows a number of passages from the *Ārṣānukramaṇi* and the *Bṛhaddevatā* in their metrical wording, with or without additions. To Kātyāyana is also attributed the *Anukramaṇi* of the White *Yajurveda* in the Mādhyandina recension, consisting of five sections, the fifth section of which gives a brief account of the metres occurring in the white *Yajurveda*. V.M. Apte in *CHI*, I, 285-6.

**Migration:** There is a difference of opinion among the scholars as to the part of India where the bulk of the *Ṛgveda* was composed. Max Müller, Weber, Muir and others held that the Punjab was the main scene of the activity of the *Ṛgveda*. The view put forth by Hopkins and Keith is that it was composed in the country round the Sarasvatī river, south of modern Ambala. Brunnhofer, Hertel, Hunsing and others, however, argue that the scene of the *Ṛgveda* is laid not in the Punjab, but in Afghanistan and Iran. These and other theories need not be discussed in detail. Keith has rightly observed that 'conclusions can be drawn only with much caution. It is easy to frame and support by plausible evidence various hypothesis, to which the only effective objection is that other hypotheses are equally legitimate, and that the facts are too imperfect to allow conclusions from being drawn' (Rapson I, pp. 78-9). Whether the Aryans at all came from outside India is difficult to say at the present stage of our knowledge and there is a great scholarly controversy on this point but within India there was a migration of the Aryan-speaking tribes in different waves. We may conclude that the extent of the country as reflected in the hymns of the *Ṛgveda* is Afghanistan, the Punjab, parts of Sind and Rajasthan, the North-West Frontier Province, Kashmir and eastern India upto the Sarayu. Roughly speaking, the extreme North-west was occupied by the Gandhāris, Pakthas, Alinas, Bhalānases, and Viṣāṇins, some of whom probably contained non-Aryan elements. In Sind and the Punjab were settled the Śivas, Parśus, Kekayas, Vṛcivants, Yadus, Anus, Turvaśas and Druhyus. Further east, towards the region of the Madhyadeśa, were the settlements of the Tritsus, Bharatas, Purus, and Sṛñjayas, with the eastern-most part being in the occupation of the Kīkaṭas. The Matsyas and Cedis were settled to the south of the Punjab, in the region of Rajputana and Malwa. It may thus be reasonably concluded that the Aryan settlements during the period of the *Ṛgveda* were practically coterminous with the extent of the geographical knowledge of the period. The later Vedic literature refers to the three broad divisions-Brahmāvarta or Āryāvarta, Madhyadeśa, Dakṣiṇāpatha. There is also a fivefold division with the enumeration therein, which we come across for the first time in the *Aitareya Brāhmaṇa* (8.14), though it has, in a way, been anticipated by the *Atharvaveda* (19.17.1). The *Aitareya Brāhmaṇa* divides the whole country into five parts, viz., (1) Dhruvā Madhyamā Pratiṣṭhādiś or Madhyadeśa or middle country; (2) Prācīdiś, or the eastern quarter, (3) Dakṣiṇādiś or the southern quarter; (4) Praticīdiś or the western quarter, and (5) Udichīdiś or the northern quarter. The extent and limits of these divisions cannot be defined with any degree of plausibility. The disappearance of the Sarasvatī, referred to in the *Pañcaviṃśa Brāhmaṇa* (25.10.6) is an important geographical landmark in this period. The main centre of the life of the period is Kurukṣetra, in the country of the Kuru-Pañcālas, bounded by the Khāṇḍava on the South, Tūrghna on the north, and Parīṇāh on the west. It is noteworthy that the sphere of civilization is gradually shifting eastward and its localization in the region to the east of the land of five rivers is an accomplished fact. The Punjab and the west not only recede in importance, but the tribes of the west are looked upon with disapproval in the Ṛgvedic period, and many new tribes emerged during this period. The Bharatas do not occupy the premier position, but are merged in the Kurus who, with their allies the Pañcālas, are the tribe *par excellence.* With Vaśas and Uśīnaras, the Kuru-Pañcālas occupy the Madhyadeśa. The Uttarakurus and the Uttaramadras lay to the north beyond the Himalayas, and Satvats to the south. To the east Kosala, Videha, Magadha, and Aṅga rise into prominence. The Andhras, Puṇḍras, Mutibas, Pulindas and Śabaras, as also the Niṣādas, are the outcast tribes which were not fully brahmanized. The territory comprised within the sphere of Aryan influence down to the period of the Upaniṣads may thus be roughly described as the whole of India to the north of the Narmada, and some regions even to the south of that river. A.D. Pusalker in Majumdar I, 254-6.

**Milk:** *Kṣīra*, 'milk', also called *go* or *payas*, played a large part in the economy of the Vedic Indians (*RV* 1.109.3; 1.164.7; 8.2.9; 9.67.32; 10.87.16, *AV* 2.26.4, 5.19.5, 8.3.15, 10.9.12; *TS* 3.4.8.7, etc). It was warm as it came from the cow, or was used with grain to make a 'mess cooked with milk' (*RV* 8.77.10; *AV* 13.2.20; *TS* 4.4.9.1; *VS* 8.57). It was also used for mixing with *soma* (*abhiśrī, āśir*). From it butter (*ghṛta*) was made. Milk was also curdled, the *pūtikā* and *kvala* plants, among others, being used for the purpose (*TS* 2.5.3.5). The curdled milk (*dadhi*) was undoubtedly used for food; and, a kind of cheese is perhaps referred to in one passage of the *Ṛgveda* (6.48.18). Goat's milk (*aja-kṣīra*) is also mentioned (*ŚB* 14.1.2.13). The term *go* is often applied to express the products of the cow. It frequently means the milk (*RV* 1.33.10, 2.30.7, 4.27.5. 9.46.4), but rarely the flesh (*RV* 10.16.7) of the animal. In many passages it designates leather used as the material of various objects, as a bowstring (*RV* 6.75.11, 10.27.22; *AV* 1.2.3), or a sling (*RV* 1.121.9) or thongs to fasten part of the chariot (*RV* 6.47.26, 8.59.5), or reins (*RV* 6.46.14), or the lash of a whip (*RV* 6.53.9). The term *payas* denotes 'milk' of the cow in the *Ṛgveda* (1.164.28, 2.14.10, 4.3.9, 5.85.2 etc.) and later (*AV* 4.11.4, 12.1.10; *VS* 4.3). More generally it has also the sense of 'sap' or 'fluid' found in plants (*AV* 3.5.1, 10.1.12, 13.1.9; *VS* 17.1, 18.36), and giving them life and strength. In another passage it denotes the water' of heaven (*RV* 1.64.5, 4.27.8). A vow of life for a time on milk alone occurs in the *Śatapatha Brāhmaṇa* (9.5.1.1). Macdonell and Keith I, 208, 234, 490-1.

**Milk-pot:** *Gharma* (*RV* 3.53.14; 5. 30.15; 5.43.7; 5.73.6; 5.76.1; *AV* 7.73.6; *VS* 8.61; *AB* 1.18; 1.22) denotes a milk-boiling pot to offer oblations to the gods, specially the Aśvins.

**Milky Way:** The word *aryamṇaḥ panthā* occurs only in the Brāhmaṇas; cf. *Taittirīya Brāhmaṇa* 1.7.66; *Pañcaviṃśa Brāhmaṇa* 2.12.3; *Śatapatha Brāhmaṇa* 5.3.1.2. The word literally means Aryamans' way'. Weber thinks it is the 'milky way'. Hillebrant means it to be 'the ecliptic'. Macdonell and Keith I, 37.

**Milk-therapy:** Sometimes the loss of the vital milk (*payas*) or sap (*rasa*) was regarded as the cause of disease. The way of curing was naturally in the form of giving fresh milk or sap to the patient. Thus, according to the *Maitrāyaṇī Saṃhitā* (2.1.6), an offering of a milk-mess (*āmikṣā*) to Soma and Rudra is to be offered for the sake of curing a diseased sacrificer (cf. *KS* 11.5). In another offering, *payasya* (whey) is to offered to Mitra and Varuṇa if the sacrificer is a brāhmaṇa to Indra and Varuṇa, if he is a kṣatriya and to Agni and Varuṇa, if he is a vaiśya (cf. *MS* 2.3.1; *KS* 12.1). In the *Taittirīya Saṃhitā* 2.3.13.3 it is said, 'Verily mile leaves him who is caught by evil (diseased); because there is *payasya*. Milk is put in him.' Instead of the word *payas* (milk), sometimes the word *rasa* (sap) is used but the underlying idea is not very different. For, when one becomes ill, one's sap (*rasa*) goes to Soma and body to Agni (Rudra). By means of this offering, the sap and the body (of the patient) are redeemed (*TS* 2.2.10.4 f). Thite 271-8.

**Millet:** A cultivated grain named *aṇu* is referred to in the *Maitrāyaṇī Saṃhitā* (2.11.4), *Kāṭhaka Saṃhitā* (18.9), *Taittirīya Saṃhitā* (4.7.4.2) and *Vājasaneyī Saṃhitā* (18.12). Apparently, it seems to be the *Panicum miliaceum*.

**Mimetic Magic:** Magic is used to produce the desired event through an imitation of it. Thus, when an enemy is to be defeated his effigy is to be destroyed. When rain is desired its symbolic miming is performed. More elaborate instances are, of course, the ceremonies of Vedic sacrifices. In the ritual of Mahāvrata the water thrown on the fire is symbolic of rain; the winning of the white round skin which represents the sun is a spell representing the recovery of the sun from the hostile powers affecting it. In the royal consecration the victory of the king over his rival is graphically depicted in mimic form; his success in dicing (*ĀpŚS* 5.19.2; 20.1 ff) is a picture of his success in the position of king on earth. The fertility of the earth and of the crops is produced by the mimicry of sexual relationships at the Soma sacrifice, at the horse sacrifice, and by the actual performance of ritual intercourse at the Mahāvrata offering. At the Vājapeya the chariot race is a magic performance to secure the pre-eminence of the sacrificer, just as in the rite he is made to be the victor in the race in question. The Sautrāmaṇi offering is a clear imitation of the story of the healing of Indra from his intoxication with *Soma*, after the slaying of the demon Namuci; it is used to secure the sacrificer the success for which he is anxious in whatever sphere of life he may live. This sort of magic is particularly common in rain magic: herbs are often dipped in water, black garments assumed, black victims offered. One rite is of interest, the heads of a dog and a ram, hairs, and old shoes are fastened to the end of a bamboo, and passes are made in the air as if in combat with a demon. The animals may be intended to aid in the breaking open of the sky, presumably, to let the waters flow down to the earth, just as at the Mahāvrata the shooting of arrows through, but not so as to penetrate, a skin. The footmark of a maiden can be used as a means of winning her love; the footmark of a beleaguered king is scattered to the winds. Worms are generally to be banished by the crushing and the burning of twenty-one selected Uśīra worms (*KB* 29.24). The running away of a slave or some other persons may be prevented by the rite of pouring urine round the horn of an animal. The urine represents the person, in dog-symbolism, to whom the slave belongs. His living presence in the vicinity, symbolized by the urine, prevents the slave from running away (*HGS* 1.14; *PGS* 3.7). The destruction of misfortune of any king often takes the shape of the burning or throwing away of old things such as garments, sunshades or shoes in water. To destroy the borer insect, which damages crops, one of the species is buried, head downwards, the mouth closed with thread, to prevent further depredations (*AV* 6.50.1). When Soma is being pressed, he who desires to destroy a foe should think of him as he pounds with the pressing stone; the pounding will directly affect the foe. More in is the device to be adopted to secure the transfer of a stream from one course to another; the new bed desired is watered, plants like the *avakā* are put along it, and a frog is also put there. The stream will therefore follow the path thus laid down. The same principle is at work in the rule by which objects to be attained are often expressed in a speech as so won. See **Magic**. Keith II, 388-90.

**Mirror:** Mirror is suggested by the term *ādarśa*, which is found in the *Aitareya Āraṇyaka* (3.2.4), *Śāṅkhāyana Āraṇyaka* (8.7), *Bṛhadāraṇyaka Upaniṣad* (2.1.9. 3.9.15); *Chāndogya Upaniṣad* (8.7.4), *Kaṭha Upaniṣad* (4.2).

**Miscarriage:** See **Abortion**.

**Misogyny:** It is true that sometimes high praise is showered on women in the Vedic texts. Thus, it is said that she is half her husband and completes him (*ŚB* 5.2.1.10). But in spite of this praise there was a marked decline in the attitude towards women. In later Vedic period they were not allowed to take part in political life and attend the assembly like men. They were classed with dice and wine as one of the three chief evils (*MS* 3.6.3). According to the *Aitareya Brāhmaṇa* (3.24.7), a good woman is one who does not talk back. In the *Śatapatha Brāhmaṇa*, there is actually the rule that the wife should dine after her husband. The relative position of the two sexes is reflected in keen desire for male progeny. This may be regarded as natural in a patriarchal society, where relationship was recognized through the father. But this natural predilection exceeds all bounds of propriety or morality when we read in the *Aitareya Brāhmaṇa* (7.15) that a daughter is a source of misery and a son alone can be the saviour of the family. The *Atharvaveda* (6.11.3) also deplores the birth of daughters.

**Missile:** *Didyu* (*RV* 1.71.5, 4.41.4, 7.56.9, 7.85.2; *AV* 1.2.3; *VS* 2.20, 10.17) and *didyut* (*RV* 1.66.7, 5.86.3,

7.25.1). In the *Ṛgveda* both denote missile, arrow, whether divine or human.

**Mitra:** Mitra is so closely associated with Varuṇa, that only one hymn (3.59) is addressed to him separately and his individual character cannot be definitely established. His distinctly peculiar epithet is *yātayaj-jana* the 'bestirrer of the people', because he marshalls people into activity. As the great Āditya, Mitra is a sun-god, the guardian of faithfulness. The Avestan and Ṛgvedic evidence points to Mitra as a solar deity in the aspect of a benevolent power of nature, as suggested by the name Mitra which originally meant 'an ally', *Ṛgveda* 1.136.3; 3.5.4; 3.5.9; 5.3.1; 5.72.2; 5.81.4; 7.36.2; 7.60.6; 8.91.12; 10.8.4; *Atharvaveda* 9.3.18; 13.3.13; *Maitrāyaṇī Saṃhitā* 2.5.7; *Taittirīya Saṃhitā* 2.1.74. For detailed references see Macdonell 29-30.

**Mixed Caste:** The problem of the writers of the Dharmasūtras was to incorporate innumerable functional and endogamous castes into the idealized scheme of fourfold social division. In order to achieve this end they devised an imaginary and unreaslistic, but effective, theory which was known as a theory of *varṇasaṅkara*, or mixed caste. They tried to explain the origin of different occupational castes by describing them as descendants of persons born of jypergamic (*anuloma*) and hypogamic (*pratiloma*) matrimonial union among the four idealized castes. Thus, the offsprings of a brāhmaṇa male and a kṣatriya female is Murdhābhiṣikta, that of a kṣatriya male and vaiśya female is Māhiṣya, that of a vaiśya male and śūdra female is Karaṇa, that of a brāhmaṇa male and śūdra female is Ugra and so on. The hybrid castes thus emerged from morganatic and reverse forms of marriages produce many other hybrid castes of the second rank and they, in their turn, produce mixed castes of the third rank. Following this system, innumerable functional social groups can be accommodated as mixed castes within the structure of the fourfold system. But since the formation of such mixed castes through intercaste marriages was not practically possible, what the writers of the Dharmasutras really did was to classify the existing numerous castes, mostly belonging to the śūdra category, on the basis of their occupations and placed them in the scheme of the mixed castes. Some of the castes which later became despised for their performing lower grade occupations, such as sweeping, carrying corpses, dealing in flesh, handling filthy materials, etc., are foreshadowed in the Vedic texts as mixed castes of the lowest order. Thus, Caṇḍāla is a name of the despised caste to be victimized in the human sacrifice called Puruṣamedha, occurring in the *Vājasaneyī Saṃhitā* (30.21), and also in the *Śatapatha Brāhmaṇa* (14.4.1.22), simultaneously treated by the *Bṛhadāraṇyaka Upaniṣad* (4.3.22). It has been frequently referred to in the various Saṃhitās of the Veda (*VS* 30.17; *TB* 3.4.14.1). A son being born of a maiden kṣatriya by a male śūdra is called Paulkasa, relieved from the duties worthy of being performed in a hermitage. In the *Maitrāyaṇī Saṃhitā* (1.6.11) the two variant readings are found as *pulkaka* and *puklaka*, simultaneously referring to the same sense of Pulkasa. Subsequently, the number of mixed castes increased owing to the process of detribalization, which has been a constant feature of Indian social history. Many so-called mixed castes are named after tribes and places. See **Detribalization**.

**Mollusc:** In zoology mollusc means any invertebrate of the phylum Mollusca, with a soft body and usually a hard shell, including limpets, snails, cuttlefish, oysters, mussels, etc. *Śaṅkha* in the *Atharvaveda* (4.10.1), with the epithet *kṛśana*, denotes a pearl-shell used as an amulet. In the later literature (*BU* 2.4.9; 4.5.10) it denotes a 'shell' or 'conch', used for blowing as a wind instrument. *Kakuṭha*, a word occurring in the *Maitrāyaṇī Saṃhitā* (3.14.13), presumably denotes some kind of mollusc. According to Böhtlingk, it is identical with *kakkaṭa* which denotes the crab in the *Yajurveda Saṃhitā* (*TS* 5.5.15.1; *VS* 24.32) being a Prakritized form of *Karkaṭa*, which is common in the later literature.

**Moment:** Although the word *kṣaṇa* is conspicuously absent its synonyms, namely, *muhūrta* and *nimeṣa* appear in the Vedic Saṃhitās. Its use clearly shows that it originally denoted winking of the eyes and was later associated with the time required for the winking. In the *Taittirīya Saṃhitā* (7.5.25.1) various parts of the sacrificial horse, which is identified with a *saṃvatsara* 'year', are compared to different divisions of time. Its closing and opening of eyes are both the day and the night. The word *nimeṣa* originally refers to the closing of eyes, but since it is immediately followed by opening, *nimeṣa* denotes both the actions together. Various divisions of time, to its smallest part, appear to have been already found in the period of the Saṃhitās (*VS* 32.2). Mahīdhara comments that all *nimeṣas* were born of him who illuminates brightly. The word *muhūrta* is found in the *Ṛgveda* (3.33.5) in the sense of 'a short while'. Yāska makes *kṣaṇa* a synonym of *muhūrta*. The first attested reference two *kṣaṇa* appears in the *Gopatha Brāhmaṇa* (1.5.5). The word *muhūrta* is also used there, denoting specific time in relation to other parts of time.

**Momordica Monadelpha:** *Bimba* appears in one passage of the *Jaiminīya Upaniṣad Brāhmaṇa* (3.5.6) to denote the plant *momordica monadelpha*.

**Monarchy:** The term *eka-rāj*, or sole ruler, is found in the *Ṛgveda* (8.37.3) but used rather metaphorically. However the term is found in literal sense in the *Atharvaveda* (3.4.1) and the *Aitareya Brāhmaṇa* (8.15). The notion of a *rāṣtra* or a territorial state, however, was being gradually evolved in the later Vedic period. We find it clearly referred to in the *Atharvaveda*• (20.127.9-10; 19.30.3-4-4-2; 5-98-2). The *Taittirīya*

*Saṃhitā* (2.3.3-4) refers to a ritual, a partial performance of which could secure a king lordship over his tribe (*viś*) but not over the country (*rāṣtra*). The *Brāhmaṇa* literature, however, frequently refers to the emperors as the rulers not over all the tribes but over the whole earth, bounded by the sea. It is clear that the notion of the territorial state was fully established at this time. Monarchy was the formal form of the state in the Vedic period, *rājan* (a king), *mahārāja* (a great king), and *samrāṭ* (an emperor) being the different terms by which kings were designated according to their power and prestige. Some of them were also called *svarājas* and *bhojas*. In the description of the coronation, the ritual is sometimes described as securing *rājya, svārājya, bhaujya, vairājya* and *sāmrājya* to one and the same individual (*AB* 8.2.6, 8.3.13). A doubt, therefore, naturally arises as to whether these terms really denoted different types of states or monarchies. It is, however, not unlikely that it is the desire to emphasize the omnipotence of the ritual that the priest claims that the king who is receiving the holy coronation from him, can attain all the different positions referred to above. This conjecture becomes more probable when we remember that a passage in the *Aitareya Brāhmaṇa* states that the different types of states like *rājya, bhaujya, vairājya* and *sāmrājya* flourished in different regions of the country (*AB* 8.3.14). In the later Indian history we always come across a large number of kings enjoying different degrees of autonomy and ruling as feudatories of an emperor (*samrāṭ*). It is not unlikely that such feudatories existed in the Vedic period as well; they may have been known as *bhojas* and *svarājas* and their feudal lords as *samrāṭs*. The terrirotial extent of the dominion of a *samrāṭ*, as compared to that of *svarāṭ*, cannot be definitely determined. Most of the states in the Vedic period being small, it is doubtful whether there was one big enough to extend over the Punjab. The dominion of a *samrāṭ* was perhaps not much bigger than that of an ordinary king. Military glory and achievements were probably more responsible for his higher title than the extent of his dominion. *Rājya* probably denoted a smaller but independent kingdom. The statement in the *Aitareya Brāhmaṇa* that kings were common in the Madhyadeśa and emperors in eastern India would support this interpretation. *Vairājya* according to some scholars denoted a republic state, which had no king, but it does not seem likely.

**Moneylending:** *Ṛṇa* (debt) is frequently mentioned in the *Ṛgveda* though in a metaphorical sense in the majority of passages where it occurs. Indebtedness seems to be a fairly well-known condition. The loan (*ṛṇa*), thus, was the only contract known and that was, chiefly, at gambling. A debtor was punished with a period of servitude to the creditor and was bound by the creditor to a post (*dru-pada*), to bring pressure on him for payment. Some kind of reference to a rate of interest or instalment of principal may be traced in one passage, but this is not certain. The interest was presumably paid in kind. In the *Ṛgveda* (10.34.10; *AV* 6.119.1) reference is often made to debts contracted at dicing. To pay off a debt was called *ṛṇam sam-ni* (*RV* 8.47.17; *AV* 6.46.3). Allusion is made to debt contracted without intension of payment (*AV* 6.119.1). The result of non-payment of a debt could be very serious and the dicer could fall into slavery (*RV* 10.34). In one passage of the *Ṛgveda* (10.34.4) and *Atharvaveda* (6.46.3; 19.57.1), an eighth (*śapha*) and a sixteenth (*kalā*) are mentioned as paid but it is quite uncertain whether an interest or an instalment of the principal is meant. Presumably, the interest was to be paid in kind. How far a debt was a heritable interest or obligation does not appear. The *Kauśika Sūtra* regards three hymns of the *Atharvaveda* (6.117-19) as applicable to the occasion of the payment of a debt after the creditor's demise. For the payment of a debt by a relation of the debtor the evidence is still less clear. Macdonell and Keith I, 109-10.

**Monotheism:** The plurality of gods could not satisfy the intellect of the Ṛgvedic seers. One god was, therefore, identified with another. Or, gods were invoked in pairs or conjointly in groups of three or more. Systematization took the form of the classification of the gods into different categories or of the amalgamation of them all into one comprehensive group of the 'all-gods'. This systematization was but a step forward towards the more logical monotheism. There cannot be more than one supreme and unlimited Being. The appearance of what Max Müller calls henotheism is due to this unconscious urge towards monotheism, imperfectly moulding polytheistic tendencies and thus presenting an inconsistent picture. When individual gods are alternately regarded as the 'highest', a large number of attributes, personal characteristics and functions become common to all the gods. The merging of all these qualities into one divine figure becomes easy and, thus, polytheistic anthropomorphism evolves into a kind of spiritual monotheism. But the *Ṛgveda* betrays discontent even with this monotheistic development and the single, supreme anthropomorphic deity that should follow from it. The *Ṛgveda* (1.164.4) asks 'Who has seen the first-born, when the boneless one bore the one with bones? Where is the life, the blood, the self of this *bhūmi* (universe)? Has anyone approached the knowing one to ask this question?' As if in answer to this question, verse 46 of the same hymn affirms that the central principle was the sexless *sat* (the 'real') which, though one, was called by various names, Indra, Mitra, Varuṇa, Agni, Yama, Matāriśvan, etc. Thus, in some of the late hymns of the *Ṛgveda*, which designate indifferently the Supreme of Absolute as 'He' or 'It', is reflected the usual vacillation between monotheism and monism met with in all philosophies.

The transition from monotheism to monism was effected smoothly and almost unconsciously, owing to the growing influence of the conception of *ṛta* (V.M. Apte in Majumdar I, 382). Against the henotheistic theory of Max Müller, Macdonell says that the Vedic deities are not represented 'as independent of all the rest', since no religion brings its gods into more frequent and varied juxtaposition and combination, and that even the mightiest gods of the Veda are made dependent on others. Thus, Varuṇa and Sūrya are subordinate to Indra (1.101), Varuṇa and the Aśvins submit to the power of Viṣṇu (1.156). . . . Even when a god is spoken of a unique or chief (*eka*), as is natural enough in laudations, such statements lose their temporarily monotheistic force through the modifications or connections supplied by the context, or even by the same verse (Macdonell 16-7). 'Henotheism is therefore an appearance, rather than a reality, an appearance produced by the indefiniteness due to undeveloped anthropomorphism, by the lack of any Vedic god occupying the position of a Zeus as the constant head of the pantheon, by the nature tendency of the priest or singer in extolling a particular god to exaggerate his greatness and to ignore other gods and by the growing belief in the unity of the gods, each of whom might be regarded as a type of the divine'. (Macdonell 17). But whether we call it Henotheism or the mere temporary exaggeration of the powers of the deity in question, it is evident that this stage can neither be properly called polytheistic nor monotheistic, but one which had a tendency towards them both, although it was not sufficiently developed to be identified with either of them. The tendency towards extreme exaggeration could be called a monotheistic bias in germ, whereas the correlation of different deities as independent of one another and yet existing side by side was a tendency towards polytheism. This tendency towards extolling a god as the greatest and highest gradually brought forth the conception of a supreme Lord of all beings (Prajāpati), not by a process of conscious generalization but as a necessary stage of development of the mind, able to imagine a deity as the repository of the highest moral and physical power, though its direct manifestation cannot be perceived. Thus, the epithet Prajāpati or the Lord of beings, which was originally an epithet for other deities, came to be recognized as a separate deity, the highest and the greatest. It has been generally held that the Ṛgvedic religion is essentially a polytheistic one, taking on a pantheistic colouring only in a few of its latest hymns. Yet a deeply abstract philosophizing crops up unexpectedly in some hymns as a reminder of the long journey made from primitive ploytheism to systematic philosophy, through the stages of naturalistic polytheism, monotheism, and monism.

**Month:** The word *māsa* denotes month. The name of the twelve months are given in the *Taittirīya Saṃhitā* (4.4.11.1). They are as follows-Madhu, Māthava, Śukra, Śuci, Nabha, Nabhasya, Īṣa, Urja, Saha, Sahasya, Tapa and Tapasya. Months regularly had thirty days, according to the *Atharvaveda* (13.3.8), or thirty-five days according to the *Śatapatha Brāhmaṇa* (10.5.4.5), or thirty-six days according to the *Śatapatha Brāhmaṇa* (9.1.1.43, 9.3.3.18, etc. Lists are also given in the *Kāṭhaka Saṃhitā* (17.10; 35.9), *Maitrāyaṇī Saṃhitā* (2.8.12) *Vājasaneyī Saṃhitā* (13.25.14.6 ff. 15.57), etc. In some of these lists the intercalary month is mentioned, which is Amhasaspati in the *Vājasaneyī Saṃhitā* (7.30; 22-31), Samsarpa in the *Taittirīya Saṃhitā* (1.4.14.1) and *Maitrāyaṇī Saṃhitā* (3.12.13), Malimluca in the *Kāṭhaka Saṃhitā* (38.4) and Sanisrasa in the *Atharvaveda* (5.6.4). The naming of months is also done from the names of *nakṣatras* and we see it first in the Brāhmaṇas. The characteristic days of the month are the new moon day Amāvasyā; full moon day Paurṇamāsī; Sinīvālī, the day before the new moon; Anumati, the day before the full moon; Kuhū, the new moon day; and, Rākā, the full moon day.

**Moon-phase:** The characteristic days (or rather nights) of the month were those of the new moon, Amāvasyā, home-staying' (night), and 'of the full moon', Paurṇamāsī. Two hymns of the *Atharvaveda* (7.79-80; cf. *TS* 3.5.1.1; *TB* 3.7.5.13) celebrate these days respectively. A personification of the phases of the moon is seen in the four names, Sinīvālī (*TS* 1.8.1.1, 3.4.9.1; *RV* 2.32.6; *AV* 2.26.2, 6.11.3; *VS* 11.55.56; *KS* 12.8), the day before new moon; Kuhū (*AV* 7.47; *TS* 1.8.8.1, 3.4.9.1; *KS* 12.8), also called Guṅgu (*RV* 2.32.8), the new moon day; Anumati (*TS* 1.8.8.1, 3.4.9.1; *KS* 12.8; *VS* 29.60, 34.8.9; *ṢaḍB* 5.6), the day before full moon; and Rākā (*RV* 2.32.4, 5.42.12; *TS* 1.8.8.1, 3.4.9.1; *Nirukta* 11.31), the day of full moon. The importance of the new and full moon days is seen in the Darśapūrṇamāsau, or festivals of the new and full moon days respectively.

**Mortar:** The term *ulūkhala* indicated mortar which was frequently used in combination with *muṣala*. Its exact construction is unknown (*RV* 1.28.6; *TS* 5.3.8.7, 7.2.1.3; *AV* 9.6.15; *ŚB* 1.1.4.6-7; 1.1.1.22). '*ulūkhala muṣala yaśca carmani yo be śurpa taṇḍulaḥ kaṇaḥ*'. *AV* 10.9.26.

**Mountain:** Giri, 'mountain' or 'height', is a word that occurs repeatedly in the *Ṛgveda* (1.56.3, 1.61.14, 1.63.1, 4.20.6, 6.24.8). Thus, reference is made to the trees on the hills, hence called 'tree-haired' (*vṛkṣakeśaḥ*, *RV*, 5.41.11), and to the streams proceeding from the hills to the sea (*RV* 7.95.2). The term is frequently coupled with the adjectival *parvata* (*RV* 1.56.4, 8.64.5; *AV* 4.7.8, 6.12.3, 6.17.3; 9.1.18). The *Ṛgveda* mentions the waters from the hills (*RV* 6.66.11) and the *Atharvaveda* (12.1.11) refers to the snowy mountains. Of the mountains the *Ṛgveda* mentions only a few, such as Himavat (10.121.4, the Himalayas together with other systems, such as the Suleiman range), and the Mujavat (10.34.1, called Muñjavat in later works and located in the Himalayas). The later Saṃhitās and the Brāhmaṇas (*AV* 4.9.8; *ŚB* 3.1.12; *MS* 3.6.3; *KS* 23.1; *VS* 15.4; *PB* 22.14) speak of Trikakud or Trikakubh (modern Trikota in the Himalayas) while the *Taittirīya Āraṇyaka* (1.31.2) refers to Krañca, Mahāmeru (i.e. Meru or Sumeru) and Maināka, all of them located in or about the Himalayan region. The mountain on which Manu's vessel rested after the subsedence of the Great Deluge is called Manu's Avasarpaṇa in the *Śatapatha Brāhmaṇa* (1.8.1.8). The *Kauṣītaki Upaniṣad* (2.8) mentions the Dakṣiṇāpatha, which shows that the Vindhya range and other mountain ranges of peninsular India were known.

**Mowing:** *Lavaṇa* in the Nirukta (2.2) denotes the 'mowing' or 'reaping' of corn.

**Mūcīpa, Mūtība, Mūvīpa:** *Mūcīpa* or *Mūvīpa* is the variant in the *Śāṅkhāyana Śrauta Sūtra* (15.26.6) of the *Mūtība* of the *Aitareya Brāhmaṇa* (7.18), as the name of a southern tribe.

**Mujavant:** *Mujavant* is the name of a people who, along with the Mahāvṛṣas, the Gandhāris, and the Bālhīkas, are mentioned in the *Atharvaveda* (5.22, 55.7.8.14) as dwelling far away, and to whom fever is to be banished. Similarly in the *Yajurveda Saṃhitā* (*TS* 1.8.6, 2; *KS* 9.7, 36.14; *MS* 1.4, 10.20; *VS* 3.61; *ŚB* 2.6, 2, 17) the Mujavants are chosen as a type of distant folk, beyond which Rudra with his bow is entreated to depart. In the *Ṛgveda* (10.34.1) Soma is described as Maujavata, 'coming from the Mujavants', or, as Yāska (*Nirukta* 9.8) takes it, 'from Mount Mujavant'. The Indian commentators agree with Yāska in taking Mujavant as the name of a mountain from which the people took their name. Yāska suggests that Mujavant is equivalent to Muñjavant, which actually occurs later, in the *Mahābhārata* as the name of a mountain in the Himalays. Macdonell and Keith II, 169-70.

**Mundane Knowledge:** Mundane knowledge is known as *aparā vidyā* as contrasted to the spiritual knowledge, which was known as *parā vidyā*. It is said in the *Muṇḍakopaniṣad* (1.1.4-5), which includes even the Vedas and Vedāṅgas into the *aparā-vidyā* category that, knowledge other than the knowledge of the ultimate reality is of no value. On account of the emphasis thus laid upon this particular type of knowledge, all other subjects of study are thrown into the background and branded as *avidyā* in some of the Upaniṣads. The *Kaṭhopaniṣad* (1.2.4-5) regards even *aparā vidyā* and *avidyā* as emphasizing its essential inferiority and worthlessness.

**Mustard Plant:** *Ābayu* is apparently the name of the mustard plant in the *Atharvaveda* (6.16.1). *Sarṣapa* denoting 'mustard' or 'mustard seed' occurs only a few times in later Vedic texts (*CU* 3.14.3; cf. *ṢaḍB* 5.2; *ŚŚS* 4.15.8). *Bāja* (*AV* 8.6.3; 8.6.6; 8.6.7; 8.6.24) also probably means some sort of mustard plant.

**Music:** Music, both vocal and instrumental, was well known. The Frog-hymn (*RV* 7.103.7-9) refers to the musical chanting of the students engaged in reciting sacred texts. Different vocal sounds are carefully analyzed in the Vedic hymns. Singing is often mentioned as adapted to different ends, such as chanting', 'reciting', 'hymning', etc. Among instruments, we find references to the *vīṇā* (lute or string-instrument), and the drum. The *Sāmaveda* is a standing monument to the wonderful skill and originality of the ancients in the science of vocal music. Several professional musicians are known, and the variety of instrumental music in vogue can be inferred from the types of musicians enumerated, such as lute-players, flute-players, conch-blowers, drummers, etc. Among the musical instruments known are the *āghāṭi* (cymbal) to accompany dancing (*RV* 10.146.2; *AV* 4.37.4), drums (*āḍambara, VS* 30.19; *ŚB* 14.4.8.1; *dundubhi RV* 1.28.5; 6-47. 29.31; *AV* 5.20.1 ff; 21.7; 31.7; 6.38.4; 12.1.41; *TB* 1.3.6.2; *ŚB* 5.1.5.6; *lambana, BU* 5.10.1; *vanaspati AV* 12.3.15; *VS* 9.12), flutes (*tūnava, TS* 6.1.41; *MS* 3.6.8; *KS* 23.4; 34.5; *PB* 6.5.13; *TB* 3.4.13.1; 15.1, *VS* 30.19-20; *Nir.* 13.9) *karkari* (*RV* 2.43.3; *AV* 4.37.4; 20.132.3-8; *MS* 4.2.9), *kaṇḍavīṇā, KS* 34.5; *LŚS* 4.2.6; *vīṇā, TS* 6.1.4.1; *KS* 34.5; *MS* 3.6.8; *ŚB* 3.2.4.6; 13.1.5.1; *VS* 30.20; *TB* 3.4.15.1; *BU* 2.4.8; 4.5.9), and the harp (*Vāṇa, RV* 1.85.10; 8.20.8; 9.87.8; 10.32.4; *AV* 10.2.17; *TS* 7.5.9.2; *KS* 34.5; *PB* 5.6.12; 14.7.8). While singing, the Samavedic priests rigidly followed the rules and regulations laid by the liturgical texts. The Mahāvrata sacrifice may be cited as an example where the dance by the maidens and playing of the seven-stringed lute were performed for the sake of ritual (*KS* 34.5; *AĀ* 5.1.1). In the Mahāvrata, a special sort of drum *bhūmidundhbhi*, which was made by digging a hole in the ground and covering it with a hide was employed. In this ceremony *vāṇa*, a harp or lyre with a hundred strings (*śatatantu*), was used. The *Ṛgveda* (10.32.4) refers to seven notes (*dhātu*) of the instrument, which are called seven *vaṇis* elsewhere (*RV* 1.164.24; 3.1.6; 3.7.1; 9.103.3). The basic aspects of Vedic music were later canonized in the texts of the Śikṣā category.

**Mysticism:** It is not until the age of the Upaniṣads that mysticism became a regular feature in spiritual apprehension beyond ordinary understanding. The mysticism of the Upaniṣads as a whole is contained in a peculiar description of the self which they give and which goes very much beyond a mere metaphysical treatment of it. All the mystical theories of the Upaniṣads try to lay the axe at the roots of the merely intellectual disputes between monism and pluralism. There is the same gulf between metaphysics and mysticism as there is between theory and practice. One of the chief functions of mysticism is to annihilate the merely intellectual conceptions of reality. The *Kaṭha Upaniṣad* (2.3.4) contains, in miniature, the quintessence of all the mystical teachings of the Upaniṣads. The mystic way may be difficult to tread as verily on the edge of a razor *kṣurasya dhārā* (1.3.14). The *ātman* shines before the mystic like a smokeless flame and appears to be only as large as the size of a thumb (2.1.13). The *Muṇḍaka* like the *Kaṭha* is an epitome of the entire mystical teaching presented by the *Upaniṣad* (1.2-3; 2.1; 3.1.-2). The mystic who realizes god finds him everywhere and in such full possession of god he looks upon the world as the best of all possible worlds (*Muṇḍaka* 2.2.9-11). The mysticism of the *Śvetāśvatara* (1.8 ff) holds that the perishable and imperishable, the manifest and the unmanifest, the knowing and the not knowing the powerful and the powerless, the enjoyer and the enjoyed, ignorance and knowledge, are all synthesized into a higher unity. In the *Maitrāyaṇī* (6.18 ff) the sixfold *yoga* and especially meditation (*dhyāna*) and concentration (*dhāraṇa*) are recognized as the chief means for the realization of the ultimate reality. See also the *Taittirīya Upaniṣad* 2.9; 3.10.6; *Bṛhadāraṇyaka Upaniṣad* 2.4.10; 4.12.2; 4.5.11; *Chāndogya Upaniṣad* 3.5.2, etc.

**Mythology:** The earliest stage of Vedic mythology is not so primitive as it was supposed at one time, but it is sufficiently primitive to enable us to see clearly enough the process of personification by which natural phenomena developed into gods, a process not apparent in other literatures. The mythology, no less than the language, is still transparent enough in many cases to show the connection both of the god and his name with a physical basis. Nay, in several instances the anthropomorphism is only incipient. Thus, Uṣā, the dawn, is also a goddess wearing but a thin veil of personification, and when Agni, fire, designates the god, the personality of the deity is thoroughly interpenetrated by the physical element. The towering snow-peaks of the Himalayas, vast green meadows, gigantic rivers, boundless seas encircling the land on three sides, the ineffable splendour of the seasons . . . all produced an abiding effect upon them. Nurtured amid such environments, the Aryans in Indian must have been developing, from a very early period, a poetic and spiritual temperament and a deep introspective mind, which separated them from the rest of the world. They began to feel in these outstanding natural phenomena expressions and emblems of some spiritual beings offered and worship unto them with awe and reverence. Mitra, the sun; Varuṇa, the god of the night or blue sky; Dyu and Pṛthivī, the sky and the earth; and Agni or fire- all these are Vedic deities who were worshipped with simple and complex rites from the most ancient days of Aryan history. The Vedic sage, while contemplating upon the true significance of Dyaus and Pṛthivī, caught a glimpse of the Infinite, and he called it Aditi. She is considered the mother of all other gods, the Ādityas. The root meaning of the word *aditi* is unbroken, indivisible, or infinite. Yāska describes Aditi as 'mother of gods'. It is very significant that the Vedic bards could intuitively understand the one indivisible, immanent principle even in the early period of the Ṛgvedic age, and could feel its existence not only as a reality, but also as the progenitor of all other spiritual entities controlling this inscrutable physical universe around us, which we loosely call nature. Next we notice that the *ṛṣis* of the *Ṛgveda* looked upon the Universe as possessed of three different strata or planes of existence: Topmost plane is called *dyuloka* or celestial sphere; next comes the *antarīkṣaloka*, the sphere of intermediary space; and the Pṛthivīsthāna, the terrestrial sphere. In these spheres there are three presiding deities: Savitṛ or Sūrya (Sun) is the god of the celestial world; Indra or Vāyu (Air), is the god of the intermediary space; and Agni (Fire) is the god of the terrestrial region. These three gods were again multiplied into thirty-three, there being eleven in each sphere (*TS* 1.4.10; *RV* 1.239.11). There are numerous passages in the *Ṛgveda* as well as in the other Vedas, indicating the existence of these thirty-three gods. According to the *Śatapatha Brāhmaṇa* (4.5.7.2), they consist of eight Vasus, the eleven Rudras, the twelve Adityas, Dyu (sky), and Pṛthivi (earth). The following are the eight Vasus: Dhava, Dhruva, Soma, Āpa, Anila, Anala, Pratyūṣa and Prabhāsa. The twelve Ādityas are: Dhātṛ, Mitra, Aryaman, Rudra, Varuṇa, Sūrya, Bhaga, Vivasat, Pūṣan, Savitṛ, Tvaṣṭṛ, and Viṣṇu. The name of the eleven Rudras are not clearly mentioned in the Vedas; but they have been variously referred to in the *Yajurveda* and the *Taittirīya Āraṇyaka*. These thirty-three gods were augmented again into three thousand three hundred and thirty-nine gods, as we read in the *Ṛgveda* (3.9.9). The great Sāyaṇa while commenting on this passage, tells us that the original gods are only three, and these three thousand three hundred and thirty-nine gods are but enumerations of the glories of the thirty-three gods referred to above. The Vedic sages, while contemplating upon the different aspects of nature and the workings of the mighty elemental forces, might have conceived individualized spiritual principles or beings behind inert matter. Of all the natural phenomena, the sun is the most engaging and dominant expression of grandeur. In the Vedic India, we find the Sun-god of the primitive age transformed and sublimated. It was imagined that the celestial god, i.e. Āditya (Sun), one of the Trinity, had twelve aspects, according to the twelve months of the year. Or it may be, as some hold, according to the different hours of the day. Of these the most important ones are Mitra, Varuṇa, Bhaga, Savitṛ, Viṣṇu and Indra. In the *Ṛgveda* we meet with the names of six Ādityas only. But in other Vedas sometimes different names are given to these sun-gods. Some of the most sublime hymns of the *Ṛgveda* are dedicated to Mitra and Varuṇa. Mitra symbolized light, and was considered to be the god of day, and Varuṇa, the deity of the deep blue sky; the root meaning of the word *varuṇa* is 'one that covers'. If Mitra was the god of light and the day, Varuṇa became his counterpart, the god of the blue sky or night (nocturnal heaven). Here are a few specimens of the beautiful hymns addressed to these two deities: 'O Mitra and Varuṇa, you are mighty ones and increase the might (of the devotees). You hold the three celestial regions, the three shining worlds, and the three terrestrial worlds. O Mitra and Vauṇa, it is under your command that the cows give milk, the rivers give sweet waters, and the three shining gods (Agni, Vāyu and Āditya) exist while carrying and raining waters' (*RV* 5.69.1-2). Another very beautiful hymn to Varuṇa appears in the *AV* (4.16): 'The mighty ruler of these worlds beholds as though from close at hand the man who thinks he acts by stealth; all this the god perceives and knows. If a man stands or walks in secret, goes to his bed or rises, or what two men whisper as they sit together, king Varuṇa knows; he as the third is present. This earth, too, is king Varuṇa's possession, and the high heaven whose ends are far as under the loins of Varuṇa. Both the oceans, and this small drop of water, too, contains him. If one should flee afar beyond the heaven, king Varuṇa would still be round about him.' The god next in importance among the Ādityas is Savitṛ. Though the commentators Yāska and Sāyaṇa try to differentiate between Savitr and Sūrya, calling them two different aspects of the Sun, yet in the whole of the *Ṛgveda* both the terms were used for one identical god. But just like Varuṇa, Mitra, and other gods, even the conception of Sūrya or Savitṛ was sublimated into a transcendental principle as indicated in the following Gāyatrī mantra of the *Ṛgveda*: 'We meditate upon the glorious effulgence of that Savitṛ; may He direct our intellects towards Him' (3.52.10). This *mantra* occurs also in the White *Yajurveda* (4.35) and the *Sāmaveda* (2.8.12), and is regarded as the most sacred formula for meditation. Another Āditya who occupies a prominent place in the *Ṛgveda*, and whose worship has become a matter of very great importance in the subsequent development of the Vedic religion, is Viṣṇu. Viṣṇu is often described as covering the whole universe in three strides. Max Müller tells us that 'the stepping of Viṣṇu is emblematic of the rising, the culminating, and the setting of the sun' (*RV* Eng. trans. I, p. 117). But it signifies also the immanence of Viṣṇu. Yāska, quoting Śākapuni, comments on this passage: 'All this is the expression of the power of Viṣṇu. His three strides are the threefold aspects of existence, namely, the terrestrial, the ethereal, and the celestial' (*Nir.* 12.19). Another commentator, Durgācārya, says: 'Viṣṇu is not other than sun. His three strides are but his three aspects providing over the three spheres. He exists in the terrestrial region as Agni, in the ethereal region as lightning, and in the celestial region as the god Savitṛ'. By far the most important god of the *Ṛgveda* is Indra, and he is a purely Indo-Aryan god. Though he is included among the twelve Ādityas, and as such is a celestial deity, still he is always conceived as associated with Maruts, the Wind-gods, whose chief sphere of action is the etherial middle region. Indra is the mighty god who kills the demon Vṛtra, the *asura* to the intermediary space. Besides these, the Viśvadevas are regarded as the gods responsible for rain, as such they also belong to the etherial region. The goddess Uṣas (Dawn) was considered to be the deity that interlinks both the celestial and the etherial regions. Ṛbhus were originally men, but were subsequently changed into gods of space for their good deeds. Agni, the god of fire, is the greatest of the terrestrial gods. Perhaps next to Indra, he got the largest number of prayers from the Vedic *ṛṣis*. In this passage Agni has been called lord of the house, that is the terrestrial abode of men. He was conceived to be the mouth of all gods, as the oblations poured into fire reached them through his aid. The Vedic deities have but very few distinguishing features, while many attributes and powers are shared by all alike. This is partly due to the fact that the departments of nature which they represent have often much in common, while their anthropomorphism is comparatively undeveloped. Thus, the activity of a thunder-god, of the fire-god in his lightening form, and of the storm-gods might easily be described in similar language. their main function in the eyes of the Vedic poets being the discharge of rain. Again, it cannot be doubted that various Vedic deities have started from the same source but have become differentiated by an appellative denoting a particular attribute, having gradually assumed an independent character. Such is the case with the solar gods. There is, moreover, often a want of clarity in the statements of the Vedic poets about the deeds of the gods; for, owing to character of the literature, myths are not related but only alluded to. Nor can thorough consistency be expected in such mythological allusions when it is remembered that they are made by a number of different poets, whose production extend over a prolonged literary period. See **Celestial Gods, Atmospheric Gods, Terrestrial Gods, Abstract Gods; Lower Deities, Tutelary Deities, Animal Worship, Demonology**. Macdonell, 2-3.

# N

**Naming:** Not before the Sūtra period do we come across any well-defined method of naming a child. On the basis of the Gṛhyasūtras, the following may be suggested. The child had two names, one secret for the knowledge of father and mother alone, and apparently given immediately on birth at the life-giving ceremony. This name, from its close connection with the life of the child, was not allowed to be known in order to prevent injury through its use by enemies. The second normal name was given on the tenth day in agreement with the Brāhmaṇas, or on the twelfth day or even a year later. It should be of an even number, different merits being connected with the diverse numbers, begin with a soft letter, contain a semi-vowel, and end is 's' or a long vowel; for a brāhmaṇa it should be a compound in *śarman*, protection for a kṣatriya in *varman*, 'armour' and for a vaisya in *gupta* 'protected'. A girl's name should have an uneven number of syllables. The name giving is accompanied by offerings to Prajāpati, the day of birth the *nakṣatra* of that day, and the god of the *nakṣatra*. Another name is *nakṣatra* name, derived from a lunar mansion such as Rauhina. The notices regarding it are confused with that of the name by which the boy is to designate himself when he becomes a student and announces his name in greeting others. One or both of these names seem to be made out to be the secret name. A Soma sacrificer may have yet another name in due course. Birthday offerings to Agni, Indra, Heaven and Earth, the all-gods, the day and constellation of birth, and the deities of both, are prescribed every year. *GGS* 2.7.15. ff; *ĀGS* 1.15.4 ff., *SGS* 1.25; *PGS* 1.17; *ĀpGS* 15.8; *HGS* 2.4; Keith II. 368.

**Nard:** *Nalada*, *naladī*, i.e. nard which is an automatic balsam or the plant yielding it, is mentioned in the *Atharvaveda* (6.102.3), in the *Aitareya* (3.2.4) and the *Śāṅkhyāyana* (11.4) *Āraṇyakas* (where it is mentioned as being used for a garland), as well as in the Sūtras. In the *Atharvaveda* (4.37/3) the feminine form of the word, *naladī*, occurs as the name of an Apsaras, or celestial nymph.

**Narrative Verses:** The term *gāthā* in the *Ṛgveda* (8.12.1, 9.99.4, 9.11.4) usually means only 'song', 'verse' (1.151.2, 2.20.5, 3.4.4, 4.4.6, 5.87.8, 10.20.4). In one passage (10.85.6), however, it already has a more special sense, as it is classed with *nārāsāṃśī* and *raibhī*, a collocation repeatedly found later (*TS* 7.5.11.2; *KS* 5.3; *AB* 6.32; *KauB* 30.5; *ŚB* 11.5.6.8; *GB* 2.6.12). Gāthās are often mentioned elsewhere (*AV* 10.10.20, 15.6.4; *ŚB* 3.2.16, 11.5.7.10, 13.1.5.6; *CU* 4.17.9, etc.) and are referred to as metrical in the *Aitareya Āraṇyaka* (2.3.6), where the *ṛc kumbya*, and *gāthā* are classed as forms of verse. The *Aitareya Brāhmaṇa* (7.18) distinguishes between *ṛc* and *gāthā* as divine and human respectively. According to the usage of the Brāhmaṇas and the liturgical literature, the *gāthās* are, though religious in content, distinguished from *ṛc*, *yajus* and *sāman*. They are not *mantras*. The *Śatapatha Brāhmaṇa* (13.5.4) preserves several *gāthās*, which generally accord with this description as epitomizing the sacrifices of famous kings. Sometimes (*TB* 1.3.2.6) *gāthā* is qualified as *nārāsāṃśī*, where it must be a eulogy of a generous donor.

**Naturalism:** The doctrine of nature as the first principle is recorded in the *Śvetāśvatara Upaniṣad* (1.2). The doctrine of Nature as the First Principle probably makes reference to certain forerunners of Jain and Buddhist thought. The full implications of Nature as the substratum of things may be brought out, as later, when an inquiry was set afoot as to what it was that gave pointedness to the thorns, and variegated colours of woods and birds. As against this naturalistic way of looking at things, we can assert the later theistic manner of regarding the white colour of the swan, and the green colour of the parrot, and the variegated colour of the peacocks, as due not to Nature working independently, but the Nature as supervised by god. But the Svabhāvavādins reject the idea and hold that all variations are due to the inherent nature of things which have nothing to do with any intelligent agent from outside. The sharpness of thorns, the sweetness of sugarcane, the bitterness of *neem*, all are their inherent nature. These require no external interference. All beings are created through sexual union, by means of semen and blood, and this is the act of nature itself by which things are produced. There is no role for any creator-God. The Svabhāvavādins do not also believe in chance. Nothing can happen accidentally because the nature is governed by certain rules which are immutable. The doctrine of Svabhāva was later accepted by the Sāṅkhya philosophy. Nīlakaṇṭha, the commentator on the *Mahābhārata* equates Svabhāva with Sāṅkhya. The doctrine of Svabhāva also supplied the infrastructure of the Lokāyata or Cārvāka doctrine.

**Natural Calamities:** There are references to excessive rains (*vidyut*), or drought (*raśmi sūryasya*) and other natural calamities in the Vedic texts. In the *Atharvaveda* 7.11 there is a spell to prevent all these (*kṣetreṣu uptāḥ śālyādayaḥ ativṛṣtya-nāvṛṣṭibhyāṃ bādhyante*-Sāyaṇa). Foretelling of weather and recording of spells to counteract the evil effect of drought, flood and lightning are also referred to in the *Atharvaveda* 6.12.1-4, 7.18.

**Naval Warfare:** Boats and ships are frequently mentioned in the *Ṛgveda* (1.116.5; 10.101.2) and the *Vājasaneyī Saṃhitā* 21.7. There is an example of naval expedition for rescuing Bhujyu caught in a shipwreck. There is no reference to naval battles fought in the Vedic period. The merchant vessels of India, of course, carried a small body of trained archers armed with bows and arrows to repulse the attacks of the pirates. Nāvaprabhraṃśana, the sliding of the ship is read in the *Atharvaveda* (19.39.8) and has been connected by some scholars with *Manor Avasarpaṇa* (q.v.), the name in the *Śatapatha Brāhmaṇa* (1.8.1.6) of the northern mountain on which Manu's ship was tied during the deluge.

**Necklace:** *Niṣka* is frequently found in the *Ṛgveda* (2.33.10; 8.47.15) and later (*AV* 5.14.3; 7.99.1; 20.131.8; *CU* 4.2.1-2; 5.13.2; *JUB* 1.36.7-8; *ŚB* 13.4.1.7; 13.4.1.11) denoting a gold ornament worn around the neck, as is shown by the two epithets *niṣka-kaṇṭha* (*AB* 8.22) and *niṣka-grīva* (*RV* 5.19.3; *AV* 5.17.14), having a gold ornament on the neck. A *niṣka* of silver is mentioned in the *Pañcaviṃśa Brāhmaṇa* (17.1.14 cf. *AV* 15.3).

**Needle:** The word *sūcī* means needle. It is referred to in the *Ṛgveda* (2.32.4), *Atharvaveda* (11.10.3); *Vājasaneyī Saṃhitā* (18.33), *Aitareya Brāhmaṇa* (3.18.6), *Taittirīya Brāhmaṇa* (3.9.6.4, 3.9.6.5), *Jaiminīya Brāhmaṇa* (2.10), *Śatapatha Brāhmaṇa* (13.2.10, 13.2.10.3), *JUB* (1.10.3). It was used to sew up the clothes. There are three sorts of needles, made of gold, silver and iron. The word *veśi* also means needle in the *Ṛgveda* (7.18.17).

**Net:** The world *mukṣija* is used to denote the net used to catch animals *ṚV* (1.125.2). *Jāla* (*AV* 8.8.5; 8.8.8), *jālaka* (*BU* 4.2.3) is used to denote a covering of something woven. It was used to capture animals (*AB* 10.1.30). Another term *pāśa* denotes the meaning for fastening or tying up the animals (*RV* and *AV passim*; *TS* 2.2.5.1; *VS* 6.8; *AB* 4.10; *ŚB* 1.8.1.5). *Nidhā* means a sort of net, for the purpose of catching the birds (*RV* 9.83.4; 10.73.11; *AV* 8.8.5; *AB* 3.19). *Saṃdana* means bond or halter or fetter (*RV* 1.162.8; 1.162.16); (*AV* 6.103.1, 6.10.4.1, 11.9.3); (*TS* 2.4.7.2) and (*ŚB* 14.3.1.22).

**New Moon Day:** The term *sinīvālī* denotes the day of new moon and its presiding spirit, which, in accordance with widespread ideas concerning the connection of the moon and vegetation, is one of fertility and growth. It occurs very frequently from the *Ṛgveda* (2.32, 7;8; 10.184.2) onwards (*AV* 2.26.2, 6.11.3; 9.4.14, 14.2.15, 19.31.10; *TS* 2.4.6.2, 3.4.9, 1.6, 5.5.17.1; *KS* 35.2).

**Nigama:** Pure Vedic tradition. The second part of the *Nirukta* (4-6) is called *Naigamakāṇḍa* which includes the etymologies of a large number of *nigama* words, i.e. words extracted from Vedic passages. The Vedānta is known as *nigamānta-vidyā*. The Smṛtis of Dharma-śāstras also belong to the category of *nigama*.

**Night:** Rātri is the most usual word in the *Ṛgveda* (1.35.1) and later (*AV* 1.16.1, 5.5.1) for 'night'. The term *naktam* denoting 'at night', is found frequently in the *Ṛgveda* (1.13.7; 7.2.6; 10.70.6).

**Nirṛti:** Personification of forces which are opposed to that of *ṛta* or the law-governed universe. Maddened by the grim forces of this Nirṛti, the Vedic poet exclaims, 'I ask this, o Yajña . . . where the *ṛta* of the past has gone? Who is the new one that holds it' (*RV* 1.105.4-6). The concept of evil propensities of mind, of diseases, of sins and all those which are opposed to order (*ṛta*) is manifested in that of *Nirṛti*. Naturally, removal of *Nirṛti* is equivalent to the removal of disease, ruptures, and the like. Thus, in the *Ṛgveda* (1.24.9) Varuṇa is requested to remove *Nirṛti*; in the *Ṛgveda* (6.74.2) Soma and Rudra are also requested to remove *Nirṛti*. In the *Atharvaveda* (2.10.1), the medicine-man says, 'I release you from *Nirṛti* (disease)'. In the *Ṛgveda* (10.59.1 ff) it is expected. 'May *Nirṛti* go away far'. In the *Ṛgveda* (1.23.22) waters are requested to carry away the *Anṛta* (cf. *RV* 10.9.8; *AV* 8.89.3). Elsewhere, Varuṇa is requested to free the devotees from the sin of speaking *anṛta* (false), which is the cause of all evils (*AV* 19.44.8).

**Niṣāda:** *Niṣāda* is found in the later Saṃhitās and the Brāhmaṇas (*TS* 4.5.4.2; *KS* 17.13; *MS* 2.9.5; *VS* 1.27; *AB* 8.11; *PB* 16.6.8, etc.). It seems to denote not so much a particular tribe, but the general term for the non-Vedic tribes Aupamanyava (in Yāska, *Nirukta* 3.8) took the five peoples (*pañca janāḥ*) to be the four castes (*catvāro varṇāḥ*) and the Niṣādas as the fifth. The commentator Mahīdhara explains the word where it occurs in the *Vājasaneyī Saṃhitā* (16.27. cf. 30.8) as meaning a Bhilla, or Bhil. Of the eight people associated with the Niṣāda, as we find in the Rudrādhyāya of the *Yajurveda*, the Vrātas, Puñjiṣṭhas, Śvanins and Mṛgāyus were hunters while the Takṣan, Rathakāras, Kulālas and Karmāras left the tribal fold and settled in Vedic society as members of the lower castes, having undertaken the professions of carpenter, chariot-maker, potter and blacksmith respectively. A village of Niṣādas is mentioned in the *Lāṭyāyana Śrautasūtra* (8.2.8), and a Niṣāda sthapati, a leader of some kind, is referred to in the *Kātyāyana Śrautasūtra* (1.1.12). The Niṣādas were the settled local tribes (from *ni*, 'down', and *sad* 'settle'), a view supported by the fact that the ritual of the Viśvajit sacrifice (*KauB* 25.15) requires a temporary residence with Niṣādas. The name, thus, might easily be applied to the whole body of indigenous tribes outside the pale of Vedic culture. Some scholars think that the Niṣādas were most probably identical with the Nysæans who, according to the Greek account, sent an embassy to Alexander when he was in the territory of the Aśvakas. But this identification is doubtful. One of their settlement according to the *Vājasaneyī Saṃhitā* (3.10) was situated beyond Vinaśana, the 'place of disappearance' of the Sarasvatī.

**Niṣkramaṇa:** The minor rite of taking the child out of the house into the open for the first time. This rite is not found in the earlier Vedic texts. According to most authorities it should be performed in the fourth month after birth. *PGS* 1.17; *GGS* 2.8.1-7; *KhaGs* 2.3.1-5; *BGS* 2.2; *MGS* 1.19. It is also known as *Ādityadarśana*, *Nirṇayana* and *Upaniṣkramaṇa*.

**Niyati:** See **Chance, First Principles**.

**Nobles:** *Rājanya* is the regular term in Vedic literature (*RV* 10.90.12; *AV* 10.90.12; *AV* 5.17.9, 6.38.4, 10.40.48, 12.4.32, 15.8.1, 19.32.8; *TS* 2.4.13.1, 5.1.10.3) for a man of royal family, probably including those who were not actually members of that family, but war-nobles. In reality, the term was originally applied to all the nobles irrespective of kingly power. In the *Śatapatha Brāhmaṇa* (13.4.2.17) the *rājanya* is different from the *rājaputra*, who is literally a son of the king. The functions and place of the *rājanyas* were the same as those of the *kṣatriyas*, the expression which later took the place of *rājanya* as a designation for the ruling class. His high place is shown by the fact that in the *Taittirīya Saṃhitā* (2.5.4.4) he is ranked with the learned brāhmaṇa and the *grāmaṇī* (village headman) as having reached the height of power and prosperity.

**Non-dualism:** Even a philosophic monotheism failed to satisfy finally the inquiring mind of the ancient thinkers. Anthropomorphism in some form or other may be inevitable so long as one suffers from the limitations of finitude consequent on identification with a human organism and the human kind. Man is not destined to end as man. When he reaches the higher regions of experience, where all distinctions disappear, he realizes that any attempt to limit reality is virtually to negate it. The Vedic seer succeeded in rising to heights of unified vision, where there is no duality whatsoever. A glimpse of that vision is to be had in the Ṛgvedic conception of Aditi, the Boundless. Aditi is identified with all that has been and all that shall be (*RV* 1.89.10). A clearer insight into the conception of unity is to be found in what is known as the Nāsadīya hymn (*RV* 10.129), inadequately described as the 'Song of Creation'. In spite of the obscure nature of some of the expressions in the hymn, one can easily see that the philosopher poet is making the best possible use of words to express the nature of a Reality which is essentially inexpressible. This beautiful poem contains the essence of monism, or to use a better expression, non-daulism, couched in exquisite words. The ultimate Reality is not named here; it is not identified with any of the gods. No gods had then been born. It is spoken of as 'that one' (*tad-ekam*) in the neuter gender, thus at once lifting us to a region beyond all anthropomorphic conceptions of the deity. The inadequacy of intellectual categories to give a description of it is brought out by saying that it is beyond all opposites like being and non-being, death and life, night and day. We are also told that there is nothing other than it, that it is self-sustained. It is not to be identified with an inert mass, for it 'breathed calmly'. What we refer to as creation is not an extraneous process added on to that one. In fact, all questions regarding creation, when properly framed, will turn out to be absurd. All that one can say of the universe, adopting the well-known Vedantic term, is that it is Māyā. Thus, we find in the Nāsadīya hymn the foundations, well and truly laid, for Vedantic nondualism. 'We are here', as it has been aptly remarked 'on the threshold of Upanisadic monism'. T.M.P. Mahadevan in *Cultural Heritage of India* I, 167-9.

**Non-Vedic Tribes:** The dark complexion of the *dāsa* or *dasyu* is emphasized in the *Ṛgveda* (1.101.1). The Āryas are characterized by their *varṇa* in the *Ṛgveda* (3.34.9) being contrasted with *dasyus*. The distinction of the *dāsas* or *dasyus* from the Āryas in cultural matters is enshrined in the epithets used to characterize itself. There are some features as *abrahman*, devoid of devotion; *akarman*, riteless; *avrata*, lawless, etc. The *dāsas* have been described as enemies of the Vedic people. They lived in fortified towns (*āyasīḥ puraḥ*) and were divided into classes (*viśaḥ*). The *dāsas* owned considerable wealth, and Ilibisa, Dhuni, Cumuri, Sambara, Varcin, Pipru, etc., have been mentioned as individual *dāsa* kings. The Kirātas, Kīkaṭas, Parṇakas, Simyus, etc., were *dāsa* tribes which mostly inhabited the Gangetic valley. Kuyava is a non-Aryan chief, a member of the *dāsa* or *dasyu* people of the country. He appears as a demon in the *Ṛgveda* (1.104.3) by drawing attention on the stress of the luxurious nature in a laconic description of Kuyava's household. *Kuyavac* means evil-speaking and it appears in the *Ṛgveda* (1.174.7) to denote a demon personified by those opposed to the Aryans. In the *Ṛgveda* (5.29.10) it has an expression, *mṛdhravāc*, which is insultingly used similar to the barbarians. *Anās* is used as an epithet of the *dasyus* in the *Ṛgveda* (5.29.10), which is determined as speechless dumb by Sāyaṇa. The rendering, to mean a noseless person, is supported as the native tribes. Thus, the term accords well with the flat-nosed tribes of the Dravidian type, like those of the modern Brahui speaking peoples, who have traditionally preserved in the Dravidian settlements over north India, specially the north-west, through their language. In accordance with *anās* in the *Ṛgveda* (5.29.10) *mṛdhravāk* as an epithet of the *dasyus* is rendered by a meaning of unitelligible speech. Such an epithet is also applied to Paṇis and hostile persons in the *Ṛgveda* (7.18.13; 7.6.3; 10.23.5) respectively. Among the non-Vedic tribes, the *Aitareya Brāhmaṇa* refers to the Andhras who lived between the Krishnā and the Godāvarī, the Puṇḍras, located in Bengal, Śabaras of mid-India and south-eastern India and Mutibas on the Musi river, Pulindas and Niṣādas denoted a wide range of peoples. In the *Śatapatha Brāhmaṇa* (3.2.1.24) *mleccha* occurs as having the sense of a barbarian in speech. Such a speech is prohibited to be spoken by a brāhmaṇa. There is an instance of a barbarian speech in the *Śatapatha Brāhmaṇa* (3.2.1.23).

**Nuptial Relation:** The term *dampatī* is found in the *Ṛgveda* (2.3.9; 5.3.2; 8.21.5) to show the function of both the husband and wife as householders with one-mindedness. Perfect harmony and happiness are prayed for in conjugal life which, it is hoped, will be long enough to bless the couple with sons and grandsons (*RV* 5.3.2; 8.21.5; 10.5.68; 10.85.32, 10.85.12, etc). The *Ṛgveda* (10.85.46) describes the newly married wife as taking up a most respected position as the mistress of her new household, wielding authority over the husband's father, brother, and unmarried sisters. This verse envisages the case, very probably of the marriage of the eldest son in the family, when the old father has retired from active life. The authority exercised must have been more or less the rule of love. The wife participated regularly in the sacrificial offerings with her husband.

**Nymphoea Esculenta:** *Kumuda* is the name of a plant mentioned with other water plants in one passage of the *Atharvaveda* (4.34.5). It is no doubt the white water lily (*nymphoea esculents*), being the name of that plant in the post-Vedic Sanskrit also.

# O

**Oar:** Oar (*aritra*) of a boat, used for propelling, is referred to in the *Ṛgveda* (10.101.2) and the *Śatapatha Brāhmaṇa* (4.2.5.10). Description of a vessel with a hundred oars (*śataritra, RV* 1.116.5; *VS* 21.7) is found.

**Oath:** The general term for Oath (*śapatha*) in the *Ṛgveda* (10.87.15; *Nirukta* 7.3) and later the *Atharvaveda* (3.9.5; 4.9.5; 4.19.7) denotes a 'curse' not an oath as a judicial process. That an oath of such a kind was in vogue is shown at least in one passage of the *Ṛgveda* (7.104.15) where the speaker, possibly Vasiṣṭha, imprecates death on himself if he was a wizard, and death on his foes if he was not.

**Obedience:** Obedience to the elders, family, clan, tribe or state, the departed ancestors, teachers, sages and the deities was a basic feature of the partriarchal social organization of the Vedic Indians. That family discipline was strict is illustrated by the case of *Ṛjrāśva* who was deprived of his sight as a punishment by his father (*RV* 1.116.16). The case of the sale of Śunaḥśepa in the *Aitareya Brāhmaṇa* (7.12-18) suggests that the son was under the absolute control of the father. The *Taittirīya Saṃhitā* (3.1.9.4) has the famous episode of Manu's division of property among his sons. Nābhānediṣṭha was excluded from the inheritance, but he did not revolt or protest. He maintained obedience to his father, for which Manu compensated him, teaching him how to appease the Aṅgirases and secure cows from them. How far in actual practice the ideal of obedience was maintained is difficult to say, especially in regard to family life, but it was certainly maintained in the case of social norms and religious life. Absolute obedience to the teacher was an essential requirement for success in the student life, and the *brahmacārins* have been warned not to offend their teacher in any way.

**Obeisance:** See **Ethics**.

**Obligations:** That life is a duty and a responsibility is the central ethical teaching of the Vedas. Man is born with certain obligatory duties. For details see **Ethics**.

**Observance:** See **Rituals, Sacrifices**.

**Obstacle:** The term *pari-panthin* denotes a person besetting someone's path with obstacle. But in the *Ṛgveda* (1.42.3; 1.103.6; 10.85.32) and later (*AV* 1.27.1; 3.15.1; 12.1.32; *VS* 4.34, etc.) it appears as a robber, or enemy. Sāyaṇa also interprets the term as denoting some kind of enemy. Literally, the term means 'one who is opposed to'.

**Occasional Sacrifices:** Numerous variations of the *iṣṭi* type, modelled on the new and full moon sacrifices, with appropriate changes in the materials of the offerings, can be performed for the fulfilment of particular wishes. The animal sacrifice is a fairly frequent one, both as an independent sacrifice and as part of the *Soma* sacrifice, either of which may be looked upon as the *prakṛti* or norm of the other. As an independent sacrifice called the *nirūḍhapaśubandha* (or *paśubandha* briefly), it can be performed by an *āhitāgni* (one who has established the three fires). *Paryāgnikaraṇa*, which follows it, is an important ceremony. A fire torch is carried three times round the animal by way of describing a magic circle around it, to keep off evil spirits. The *Soma* sacrifice is the most important of all sacrifices. Though performed by kings and wealthy people, it was attended by lay spectators to such an extent as to make it a public event. It was a spring festival (it is plausibly suggested) performed originally at the beginning of the year, falling on the new or full moon day. The *Agniṣṭoma* is the model and fundamental form of the *Soma* sacrifice. The *soma* is offered strictly within the framework of the three pressings (*savanas*) of the *soma* (morning, midday, and evening) and to a prescribed series of gods; Indra is the most important of them, the midday *savana* belonging to him exclusively in addition to his share of the morning and evening pressings. Of the seven *Soma* sacrifices, entitled *jyotiṣṭoma*, the *vājapeya* (q.v.) shows some traces of a popular origin. It could be performed for the attainment of victory and power not only by kings, but also by any well-to-do member of the three higher castes. A conventional chariot race was a characteristic feature of it. The *agni-cayana* or piling of the fire-altar with the heads of five victims, built into the lowest stratum of the altar, is so elaborate and complicated a rite that it could not be a frequent one. In the *sattrayāgas* all the officiating priests are jointly and individually sacrificers. The model is the *dvādasāha* or the *ahīna* sacrifice which has twelve pressing days, the rules only showing how it is to be built up to the *sattra* pattern. The most interesting *sattra* is the *gavāmayana* (cow's walk) which lasts for one year, the astronomical landmarks in which correspond to the stages of the sacrifice. The *Sautrāmaṇi* is classified as a *havir-yajña,* as it is not a *Soma* sacrifice, *surā* being used as an offering in it, instead of the *soma.* Finally, there are any number of expiatory rites, simple as well as elaborate, for grave sins as well as negligible errors.

**Occupations:** The Vedic *varṇa* system is in itself a classification and gradation of occupations. Priestly, administrative and military occupations were probably at par, though within each of these categories there was a gradation. At least sixteen kinds of priests of different ranks and status are known. Such ranking is also found in the case of royal and military officials. See **Administration, Army, Priests**. Trading was another important occupation as is attested to by the terms *vaṇij*, *vaṇija* and *śreṣṭhin,* though the Vedic texts do not supply us sufficient data relating to varius kinds of traders, their specialization according to the articles of their commerce and professional ranking. Agriculture and cattle-rearing (q.v.) were however, the basic occupations. The agriculturalists were known as *kināsa* (*RV* 4.57.8, *AV* 4.11.10, 6.30.2; *VS* 30.11, *TB* 2.4.8.7), *kṛṣīvala* (*RV* 10.34.13, 10.117.7, 10.146.6) and *vapa* (*VS* 30.7.7, *TB* 3.4.3.1). The general terms to denote the herdsmen were *paśupa* (*RV* 1.114.9, 1.144.6, 4.6.4, 6.58.2, 10.142.2, *TB* 3.1.2.12), *gopa* (*RV* 1.164.21, 2.23.6, 3.10.2, 5.12.4) and *gopāla* (*VS* 30.11, *ŚB* 4.21.5.3). Huntsmen and fishermen were known as *mṛgāyu* (*AV* 10.1.26, *VS* 16.27, 30.7, *TB* 1.5.1.1, 3.4.3.1, *PB* 14.9.12), *dāsa* (*VS* 30.16, *TB* 3.4.12.1), *dhīvan* (*AV* 3.5.6), *kevarta, Kaivarta* (*VS* 30.15, *TB* 3.4.12.1), *dhaivara* (*VS* 30.16, *TB* 3.4.15.1), *pāśin* (*RV* 3.45.1, 9.73.4, *AV* 17.1.8), *puñjiṣṭha* (*VS* 16.27. *TS* 4.5.4.2, *MS* 2.9.5, *KS* 17.13), *bainda* (*VS* 30.16, *TB* 2.4.12.1), *mārgāra* (*VS* 30.16, *TB* 3.4.12.1), *maināla* (*VS* 30.16, *TB* 3.4.12.1), etc. Among other occupations, the attendants were denoted by the terms *anukṣatṛ* (*VS* 30.11, *TB* 3.4.9.1), *anucara* (30.13, *TB* 3.4.7.1) and *paricara* (*ŚB* 13.5.4.7), rower by *aritra* (*RV* 1.116.3, *VS* 21.7), drum-beater by *āḍambaraghātā* (*VS* 30.19, *ŚB* 14.4.8.1) and *dundubhyāghāta* (*TB* 3.4.13.1), police officer by *ugra* (*RV* 7.38.6, *BU* 3.37-38) and *jīvagṛbh* (*RV* 10.97.11-12), grinder of a meal by *upalaprakṣiṇī* (*RV* 9.122.3); worker in thorns by *kaṇṭakīkārī* (*VS* 30.8, *TB* 3.4.5.1), smith by *karmāra* (*RV* 10.72.2, *AV* 3.5.6, *KS* 17.13, *MS* 2.9.5, *VS* 16.27, 30.7), potter by *kaulāla* (*VS* 30.7, *MS* 2.9.5, *KS* 17.13), door-keeper by *kṣattṛ* (*RV* 6.13.2; *AV* 3.24.7, 5.17.4, *ŚB* 13.5.4.6), and *dvārapā* (*AB* 1.30; *CU* .13.6), astrologer by *gaṇaka* (*VS* 30.20, *TB* 3.4.15.1) and *nakṣatradarśa* (*VS* 30.10, *TB* 3.4.4.1, *ŚB* 2.1.1.19), village·judge by *grāmyavādhin* (*TS* 2.3.1.3, *KS* 2.2.1), reciter by *chandoga* (*ŚB* 10.5.2.10), bow-maker by *jyākāra* (*VS* 30.7, *TB* 3.4.3.1), carpenter by *takṣan* (*RV* 9.112.1, *AV* 10.6.3, *KS* 12.10.18, 13, *MS* 2.9.5, *VS* 16.27, 30.6, *TB* 3.4.2.1, *ŚB* 1.1.3.12, 3.6.6.4) and *tvaṣṭṛ* (*AV* 12.3.33), musician by *tālava* (*VS* 30.20, *TB* 3.4.15.1), gatherer of wood by *dāryāhāra* (*VS* 30.12, *TB* 3.4.11.1), charioteer by *dhurṣad* (*RV* 1.143.7, 2.2.1, 2.34.14), *vantṛ* (*RV* 1.162.19, 10.22.5), *rathagṛṣṭa* (*VS* 15.15, *AB* 3.48), *tathin* (*RV* 1.122.8, 5.83.3, 6.47.32, etc., *AV* 4.34.4, 7.62.1, etc.), *sārathi* (*RV* 1.55.7, 1.144.3, 2.19.6, 6.20.5, 6.57.6, *AV* 15.2.1, *TB* 1.7.9.1, *MS* 4.3.18), smelter by *dhmātṛ* (*RV* 5.9.5), barber by *nāpita* (*ŚB* 3.1.2.2) and *vaptṛ* (10.142.4), boatman by *nāvaja* (*ŚB* 2.3.5.3), cook by *paktṛ* (*AV* 10.9.7 ff, 11.1.17, 12.3.17, *ŚB* 3.3.4.17), waiter by *pariyeṣṭṛ* (*AV* 9.6.51, *TS* 6.3.1.3, *MS* 1.2.16), footman by *pariskanda* (*AV* 15.2.1 ff), messenger by *pālāgala* (*ŚB* 5.3.1.11), menial by *puruṣa* (*RV* 5.39.5, 10.97.4, *AV* 4.9.7; 10.1.17, *ŚB* 6.3.1.22), female embroider by *peśakārī* (*TB* 3.3.4.5), basket-maker by *bidalakārī* (*VS* 30.8, *TB* 3.4.5.1), jeweller by *maṇikāra* (*VS* 30.7, *TB* 3.4.3.1), washerman by *malaga* (*AV* 12.3.21), dyer by *rajayitrī* (*VS* 30.8, *TB* 3.4.5.1), chariot-maker by *rathakāra* (*AV* 3.5.6., *KS* 2.9.5, *VS* 16, 17, 30.6, *TB* 1.1.4.8, *ŚB* 13.4.2.17), acrobat by *vaṃśanartin* (*VS* 30.21, *TB* 3.4.17.1), forest-guard by *vanapā* (*VS* 30.19, *TB* 3.4.11.1), weaver by *vayitrī* (*TB* 3.9.14.1, *ŚB* 13.1.5.1), slaughterer by *śastṛ* (*RV* 1.162.2, *AV* 9.3.3), wine-maker by *surākāra* (*VS* 30.11, *TB* 3.4.7.1), elephant-keeper by *hastipa* (*VS* 30.11, *TB* 3.4.9.1) and worker in gold by *hiraṇyakāra* (*VS* 30.17, *TB* 3.4.14.1).

**Ocean:** The word *samudra*, meaning the sea, is found in the *Taittirīya Saṃhitā* (2.4.8.2, 7.5.1.2). It is described as unfailing in the *Aitareya Brāhmaṇa* (3.39.5.16), which also says that it encircles the earth (8.25). The eastern and western oceans are mentioned in the *Śatapatha Brāhmaṇa* (1.6.3.11, 10.6.4.1), though metaphorically. Allusions to oceans are found even in the *Ṛgveda* (7.6.7, 10.98.5, 10.136.5) and the *Atharvaveda* (11.5.6). There are references to the treasures of the ocean (*RV* 1.47.6, 7.6.7, 9.47.44), perhaps pearls or gains of trade (*RV* 1.48.3, 1.56.2, 4.55.6) and the story of Bhujyu (*RV* 1.112.6 ff, 1,116.3, 1.117.14, 1,119.4, 6,62.6, 7.68.7, 7.69.7, 10.40.7, 10.65.12, 10.143.5) seem to allude to marine navigation.

**Offsprings:** The fulfilment of the desire for offspring, and male offspring in particular, was the chief aim of marriage. Abundance of sons is constantly prayed for along with cattle and land, but no desire for daughters is expressed. This desire for a son is natural in a partriarchal organization of society. The son alone could perform the funeral rites for the father and continue the line. Sonlessness was as much deplored as poverty (*RV* 3.16.3). The adoption of sons was recognized though not favoured in the *Ṛgveda* (7.4.7, 8). The term *tanaya* denotes offspring as descendant in the *Ṛgveda* 1.96.4; 2.23.19; 7.1.21, etc. It is used, sometimes adjectively, with *toka* in the *Ṛgveda* 10.64.14, 2.30.5, etc., and the *Aitareya Brāhmaṇa* 2.7.10. *Toka* means children in the *Ṛgveda* 1.43.2; 2.2.11; 7.62.6; 8.5.20, etc. and later (*AV* 1.13.2; 5.19.2; *KS* 36.7; *ŚB* 7.5.3.39, etc.). Terms like *tan, tana, tanas* have the same sense of *tanaya*, which often denotes a grandson in the *Ṛgveda* 8.18.8; 6.48.9, but occasionally occurs denoting children. It also is compared with *tuj* having a same sense in the *Ṛgveda* 3.45.4; 4.1.3; 5.41.9; 8.4.15.

**Oil:** In some magico-medicinal rites and practices, oil was prescribed to be used for curing the neck-swellings. Sesame-oil was to be smeared on the swollen part, after consecrating it with the *Atharvaveda* 6.53, (*KauSū* 31.9). Likewise, when someone is possessed by evil beings and suffers from epilepsy Iṅgida-oil (*KauSū*

25.30) was required. Sesame oil was used as edible oil (*VS* 18.12; TS 7.2.10.2; *AV* 4.7.3; 2.8.3; 6.140.2; 18.3.69; 18.4.32; *ŚB* 9.1.1.3). Sesamum was used in preparing gruel (*AV* 4.7.3) and porridge (*BU* 6.4.16). A wild variety of sesamum (*jartila*) was also used in preparing some kind of food (*TS* 5.4.3.2; *ŚB* 9.1.1.3). Sesamum oil is not mentioned in the *Ṛgveda* but is mentioned in the *Atharvaveda* (20.136.16). Mustard is mentioned in the Upaniṣads and Brāhmaṇas (*ṢaḍB.* 5.2; *CU* 3.14.3).

**Ointments:** Ointments were of medicinal significance and their application was useful in curing and preventing diseases. In the *Atharvaveda* (19.44.1) an ointment is praised as all-healing and excellent. '(1) Thou art an extender of lifetime; all healing art thou called; O ye waters, weal and fearlessness, (2) What the jaundice is, the *jayanya* (a disease which comes as a result of excessive intercourse), the limb-splitter, the *visalpaka* all *yakṣmas* (diseases) from thy limbs let the ointment expel out . . . (diseases). (7) The demon-slayer, disease-expeller, hath crept down over the middle here, expelling all diseases making portents vanish from here' (*AV* 4.9.3). Special powers of ointment are mentioned. 'Both art thou, a protection, grinder up of familiar demons, O ointment, and of what is immortal thou knowest, likewise art thou gratification of the living, likewise remedy of jaundice (*harita*)'. In a rite to be performed against miscarriage and for getting a male progeny, the physician gave ointment and eye-ointment to the woman concerned, with the mantra of the *Atharvaveda* (1.1). *Añjana-kārī* denotes ointment-maker, specially female (*VS* 30.14; *TB* 3.4.10.1).

**Oligarchy:** The Vedic literature sometimes refers to kings meeting together in war *samagmata rājānaḥ . . . samitāviva, RV* 10.97.6. We are also told that person alone can become a king who is permitted to become so by other kings (*yasmai vai rājāno rājyamanumanyante sa rājā bhavati na sa yasmai no, ŚB* 9.3.2.5). These passages probably refer to the existence of an oligarchy, where power was vested in a council of nobles, each member of which was entitled to call himself a king and had a right to elect the chief of the state, who was also called a king. But it is more probable that the presence of many *rājās* in samiti, which appears to be a war-council, refers to the assemblage of tribal chiefs. See **Administration, Kingship**.

**Om:** A sacred syllable which is identified with *brahman* in the *Taittirīya Upaniṣad* 1.8 'Om is the bow, the soul is the arrow and *brahman* is the target' (*PU* 5.5). *Om* is the most prominent among the symbols (*pratīkas*) under which the *upāsanā* of the supra-sensible *brahman* is possible (*CU* 1.1.1). According to the *Yogasūtra* (1.23 ff), this mystic syllable is expressive of God, the *japa* of which leads to the one-pointedness of mind. It may be called a *bīja* in Tantric language. As the mystic syllable *par excellence*, it proved attractive because its repetition had the effect of inducting concentration. Thus, it was made the subject of meditation while it was also regarded as the most natural expression for God. The Buddhists place *Om* at the beginning of their mystical formulary. Bhattacharyya 1990, 115.

**Omens:** Belief in omens and protents pervades throughout the whole of Vedic literature. It is held that certain stars are unlucky (*KauB* 46.25 ff). Many sights foretell evil, such as when the sun seems as the moon, when one's shadow appears upside down in a mirror or water, or when one's head smells like a crow's nest. Evil is further foreshadowed by meteors and lightning. Of ominous birds, the main classes are those which are black or whose appearance or utterance is horrible: the pigeon, the owl, the vulture, the *dīrghamukhī*, etc. The bird is also generally called the mouth of dissolution. Birds (*AB* 2.15; *BDS* 2.8.14.9.10) are said to go about in the semblance of the panthers. The horse on several occasions is supposed to bring prosperity or other good results. It is rather due to its connection with the offering than to its intrinsic nature as ominous. Other omens are the appearance of a beehive in the house, scream of a jackal, the drinking of one cow from another, the cows giving blood for milk, and so on. The existence of men skilled in the interpretation of omens is natural and is also recorded. The man who could tell the marks of a woman in the choice of a wife was in great demand. We hear also of a prophet who made his prophecies on the basis of the smoke of dung, the *sakadhūma* of the *Atharvaveda*. It is made to forecast the weather. We learn also of men who, by the means of plants such as the *ṣaḍasupuṣpa* (*KauB* 28.7), were able to behold sorcerers male and female, whether they went to the sky or on the earth. The idea of the power of sorcerers to assume various forms is found in the *Ṛgveda* (7.104.18), where it asks for the destruction of the demons, who fly about the village at night in the forms of birds.

**Ontology:** Ontology is the branch of metaphysics dealing with nature of being. The earliest speculations on the question are, as is natural, mainly poetic and mythological with hardly an attempt at system-building. They name one god or gods-Indra, Varuṇa, Savitṛ, or Dyāva-Pṛthivī and credit him or them with the work of creating the world, its rivers, mountains, trees, the sun, the moon and the stars, simultaneously or in succession. The creative process is often compared to the art of the carpenter, or the smith, but is more often described as a procreative process. Thus, we find Kavaṣa Aituṣa posing the problem (*RV* 10.31.7)-what was the wood, and what the tree? Wherefrom they have fashioned the Heaven and the Earth? And, in accordance with this sentiment we find *vana* (wood) raised to the dignity of a first principle and later, when water came to be regarded as such, we find the word *vana* listed in the *Nighaṇṭus* (1.12.9) as a synonym for water. In the *Ṛgveda* (10.72.2) the creative process is likened to the art of the smith who smelts the metal; but the favourite metaphor of the late Vedic period introduces words like *jan*, to beget, or *srj*, to pour out, *aṇḍa* or the egg, *garbha* or embryo, and *retas* or semen virile. This led to the conception of some one specific god as the Father (*asuraḥ pitā naḥ*), who creates the world and rules over it. There are passages in the *Ṛgveda* (1.96.4, 1.160.4, 4.56.3, 8.36.4, 9.90.1, 10.66.9. etc.) where the Heaven and the Earth are spoken of as created beings. Elsewhere, these two become themselves the Original Parents. As a direct result of this conflicting speculation, the problem takes on the aspect of a riddle in which the poets of the later Veda merrily introduce still further complications, regarding the creation as the *māyā* of the gods which, as such, is beyond human comprehension. We find, for instance, Indra credited with the miracle of generating from his body his own father and mother (10.54.3); or Aditi spoken of as producing Dakṣa, and herself in turn being produced by him (10.72.4), this dogma being later received into regular philosophy under the guise of the *bījāṅkuranyāya*, or the maxim of the seed and the sprout. A further advance in this metaphysical speculations consists, first, in the gradual progress towards the idea of one god. This progress was facilitated by the tendency of Vedic poetry towards the so-called Henotheism or the readiness to regard, for the time, one god-Indra, Agni, Varuṇa, Savitṛ, etc., as the all-highest and transfer to him all the powers and attributes of the other gods. The oftquoted stanza (1.164.46) Indra, Mitra, Varuṇa, Agni, they style him. He is also the Heavenly Bird the winged Garutman. This 'one' which belongs to the last phase of Vedic cosmogony was not considered as a person, nor was he endowed with definite characteristics. On the other hand, the Vedic poets delight to leave It in a nebulous condition, assigning It contradictory qualities and uncertain functions. Sometimes the One becomes not an individuality but a principle; a something which is both Being and Non-Being, Life and Death, Active and Acted upon. The best illustration of this is the famous *Nāsadīya Sūkta* (10.129). The *Viśvakarman* (10.82) and the *Hiraṇyagarbha* (10.121) *Suktas* also form instructive reading in this connection. Belvalkar and Ranade 22-4.

**Orator:** According to the *Taittirīya Saṃhitā* (7.1.10.2), an orator is an official speaker on specific occasions having rhetorical power conducive to impressive effect. Orators were called *vācaspati.*

**Ordeals:** *Divya*, ordeal, is a term not found until the later literature, but several references to the practice have been seen in Vedic literature. The fire ordeal has been seen in the *Atharvaveda* (2.12) by some scholars. Such an ordeal appears in the *Pañcaviṃśa Brāhmaṇa* (14.6.6), while an ordeal with a glowing axe appears in the *Chāndogya Upaniṣad* (6.16) as applied in an accusation of theft. Geldner suggests that this usages is referred to even in the *Ṛgveda* (3.53.22) but that is doubtful. In another passage of the *Ṛgveda* (1.158.4) Ludwing and Griffith discover references to Dīrghatamas having been subjected to the fire and water ordeals. In the *Ṛgveda* (1.158.4-5), Dīrghatamas prays that the fire of faggots heaped tenfold may not burn him and that the rivers in which he was thrown, bound hand and foot, may not engulf him. It seems that in these verses there is probably no reference to ordeals, but to the cruel treatment of Dīrghatamas by Dāsas headed by Traitana. In the *Ṛgveda* (3.53.2.2.) also, where it is said 'he heats the axe'; it does not contain a clear or certain reference to the ordeal of holding the heated axe. The *Atharvaveda* (2.12) is held by several western scholars to contain a reference to the fire ordeal. This also is far from certain, though verse 8 may lend some support to that view. The *Pañcaviṃśa Brāhmaṇa* (14.6.6) refers to the story of Vatsa, who was abused by his stepbrother of being the son of a śūdra woman, against which Vatsa protested. He urged that he was a brāhmaṇa, entered the fire to prove the truth of his assertion and came out unscathed. This is referred to by Manu (8.116). This is probably the earliest and clearest reference in ancient Sanskrit literature to the fire ordeal. Next comes the reference to holding the heated head of an axe by a person accused of theft, to prove his innocence, contained in the *Chāndogya Upaniṣad* (6.16.1). The *ĀpDS* (2.11.29.6; 2.5.11.3) states that after carefully considering (the charge before him), by means of definite proof and questioning (of witnesses), the king should set about awarding punishment. Kane III, 361-2.

**Origins:** See **Cosmogony**.

**Ornament:** Several ornaments are mentioned in the *Ṛgveda*. The *karṇaśobhana* was an ornament for the ear, apparently for the use of man (*RV* 8.78.3). It may have been a gold ornament as is suggested by the *Ṛgveda* (1.122.14) which refers to a deity as gold-eared (*hiraṇyakarṇa*). The *kurīra* (10.85.8) was some kind of head-ornament worn by females, specially brides. The same may be said of a kind of ring worn as an armlet (*RV* 1.166.9; 7.56.13). *Niṣka* was a gold ornament worn round the neck and it must have been of a size suitable for its use as a sort of currency too. *Maṇi* was some kind of jewel worn round the neck (*RV* 1.122.14). *Rukma* was an ornament worn on the breast (*RV* 2.34.2; 8). Garlands were often worn by men desiring to appear to advantage (*RV* 4.38.6; 5.53.4). One hymn (10.184.3) refers to Aśvins as lotus-wreathed. The *Jaiminīya Brāhmaṇa* mentions an article called *sthāgāra*, probably an ornament made of a fragrant substance. *Śalalī*, the quill of the porcupine, was used for parting the hair and anointing the eyes. The *śaṅkha* or conch-shell was used as an amulet (*AV*). The *Ṣaḍviṃśa Brāhmaṇa* (5.6) mentions the pearls (*vi-mukta*). A jewel (*maṇi*) strung on a thread was worn round the neck as an amulet. The *prakāśa*, an ornament of metal mirror, is often mentioned in the Brāhmaṇas. The *pravarta* in the *Atharvaveda* (15.2.5) probably means an ear-ring. A *niṣka* of silver was worn by the Vrātyas as mentioned in the *Pañcaviṃśa Brāhmaṇa.*

**Ornamented Garments:** Wearing of ornamented or decorated garments (*peśas*) was in vogue in the society. Uṣas is described as a female dancer dressed in with this garment (*RV* 1.92.4, 5). In a *mantra* of the *Ṛgveda* (10.1.6) god Agni is specified by a well-decorated garment (*peśana*). In the *Aitareya Brāhmaṇa* (3.11) ornamentation in dress is reported frequently by the term *peśas*.

**Oṣadhi:** Herb, plant, etc., conceived of in terms of divinity. *Nirukta* 9.27, *Śatapatha Brāhmaṇa* 2.2.4.5. *Oṣadhigarbha* means producer of herbs, which is thought to represent the moon and the sun. (cf. the *Ṛgveda* 1.164.52; the *Atharvaveda* 10.4.23.)

**Outcast:** Caṇḍāla (*VS* 30.24; *TB* 3.4.17.1; *BU* 4.1.22) is the name of a despised caste, which in origin was probably a tribal body, but which in the brahminical theory was the offspring of śūdra fathers and brāhmaṇa mothers. The references to the caste in the *Yajurveda Saṃhitās* and in the Upaniṣads (cf. *CU* 5.10.7) clearly show that it was a degraded one, but they give no particulars about the caste. Paulkasa is the name of one of the victims at the Puruṣamedha in the *Yajurveda Saṃhitā* (*VS* 30.17; *TB* 3.4.14.1). The name also occurs in the *Bṛhadāraṇyaka Upaniṣad* (4.3.22), as that of a despised race of men, together with the Caṇḍāla. The *Maitrāyaṇī Saṃhitā* (1.6.11) has the variant Uklaka or Pulakaka, clearly the same as Pulkasa, of which Paulakasa is a derivative form, showing that a caste is meant (cf. Kaulāla, Pauñjiṣṭha). In the accepted theory the Paulkasa is the son of a Niṣāda, or śūdra by a *kṣatriya* women, but this is merely speculative; the Paulkasa may either have been a functional caste, or, as Fick believes, an aboriginal clan living by catching wild beasts, and only occasionally reduced to menial tasks. *Vṛṣala* in the dicing hymn of the *Ṛgveda* (10.34.11) denotes an 'outcast', the same sense appears in the *Bṛhadāraṇyaka Upaniṣad* (6.4.12), where the touch of either a Vṛṣala or a Vṛṣalī is to be avoided.

**Outer-Garment:** *Paridhāna* seems to have meant an outergarment in the *Atharvaveda* (8.2.16). Whitney translates it as an enveloping garment but according to Macdonell and Keith it was probably 'undergarment'. This garment was even dyed with saffron colour (*kausumbhaparidhāna*; *Śāṅkh Ā* 11.4) and signified as a 'silken garment'.

**Overlordship:** In the *Aitareya Brāhmaṇa* (8.14), four kinds of rulership have been described, among which *sāmrājya* or overlordship pertained to the countries of the eastern quarters. Not only do we find the germs of an imperialistic idea in the Vedic hymns but there is a clear evidence of the struggle for overlordship. Details are lacking, but the hymns contain a number of words and facts, which clearly speak of higher type of sovereign power for which the princes and chiefs fought. Of such, we have the word *ekarāja* (*RV* 8.37.3) both in the *Ṛgveda* and in the *Atharvaveda*, which meant nothing but a 'sole ruler' dominating over a vast area. We have next the word *samrāj* which meant, according to the Brāhmaṇas, a higher type of sovereignty than that exercised by the ordinary king. As a result of the reflection of the anthropomorphic idea, this word is even applied to some of the divine rulers. Varuṇa especially is called a *samrāṭ* more than once (*RV* 3.55.7, 3.56.5; 4.17.8, 8.19.32). The same word occurs in the *Vājasaneyī Saṃhitā* and the other texts. In addition to this, we have another word, e.g. *adhirāja*, which in later literature undoubtedly meant a suzerain ruler of higher authority. It appears in the *Ṛgveda* (10.128.9), where the speaker claims higher sovereign power. The same word appears in the *Atharvaveda* (6.98.1, 9.10.24), and in the *Yajurveda Saṃhitās* (*TS* 2.4.14.2; *MS* 4.12.3; *KS* 8.17).

# P

**Pacificatory Herbs:** There are certain trees and herbs called *śānta* (pacificatory) and one is advised to make use of them in certain magico-religious medicinal rites. Diseases are considered to be caused by evil beings and these herbs are supposed to pacify or appease the evil beings. The *śānta* trees are *palāśa* (*Butea frondosa*), *udumbara* (*Ficus glomerata*), and *jambu* (*Eugeni a Jomolana*). Preparations from these trees were required in the treatment of sexually caused and phelgmatic diseases, for stopping of miscarriages and for bringing mental peace and tranquillity (*KauSū.* 27.33; 29.30; 34.1; 39.28, etc.). The medicine is to be given by chanting verses from the *Atharvaveda*.

**Paddy:** See **Agriculture, Grains**.

**Paediatrics:** See **Medical Science**.

**Painful Urination:** The *Atharvaveda* (1.2.4) refers to *mutrātisāra*, which means diabetes or some form of painful urination caused by the enlargement of the prostate gland.

**Pākayajña:** See **Yajña**.

**Paktha:** *Paktha* is the name of a people in the *Ṛgveda* (7.18.7), where they appear as one of the tribes that opposed the Tṛtsu-Bharatas in the *dāsarājña*, or 'battle of the ten kings'. Their descendants seem to be the modern Pakhtuns of India-Afghanistan border. In three passages in the *Ṛgveda* (8.22.10, 49.10. 10.61.1) they are referred to. In one passage, a Paktha is referred to as a protege of the Aśvins. The second connects him with Trāsadasyu, whose tribe, the Purus, were aided by the Pakthas in their unsuccessful onslaught on Sudās. In the third passage he seems specified as Turvayana, and appears as an opponent of Cyavana.

**Palace:** In the *Ṛgveda* (7.88.5) there is a reference to Varuṇa's *mana* as a palace with a thousand doors, which was visited by Vasiṣṭha. In the *Atharvaveda* (3.12.5) in the reference to *manasya-patnī*, Lady of the Palace, the word *mana* suggests a house that was being inaugurated. The same expression is found in another hymn of the *Atharvaveda* (9.3.9). In later texts *mana* is not a common word for house, unlike *śālā, gṛha, āgāra, śarana,* and *vāstu*. In the *Ṛgveda*, the connection between building and construction is most clearly alluded to in one hymn (3.15.3), where the poet extols the great deeds of Indra with measures like those of a house he had measured. *Prāsāda* in the sense of palace does not occur until the late *Adbhuta Brāhmaṇa*. The *harmya* was also a palace (*RV* 7.56.16, 10.106.5) that had a unity of structure and was surrounded by a wall (*RV* 8.55.6, 7.56.16, 9.71.4, 10.73.10, *AV* 18.4.53; *TB* 3.6.3).

**Palisade:** See **Rampart**.

**Pañcāla:** Later name (*ŚB* 13.5.4.7) of the people called Krivi in the *Ṛgveda*. The Pañcālas are rarely referred to except in connection with the Kurus. Kings of the Kuru-Pañcālas are mentioned in the *Aitareya Brāhmaṇa* (8.14). In the *Kāṭhaka Saṃhitā* (30.2) the Pañcālas appear as the people of Kesin Dālbhya. In the Upaniṣads and later (*BU* 6.1.1; *CU* 5.3.1; *ŚSS* 12.13.6, etc.) the brāhmaṇas of the Pañcalas figure as taking part in philosophical discussions. The *Saṃhitopaniṣad Brāhmaṇa* (2. cf. 4.375, 8.92), a late text, makes mention of the Prācya-Pañcālas. The Pañcālas, no doubt, included other tribes besides the Krivis. There is no trace in Vedic literature of the epic division of the Pañcālas into northern (*uttara*) and southern (*dakṣiṇa*). The *Śatapatha Brāhmaṇa* (13.5.4.7) mentions their town Paricakrā. Other towns to which allusion seems to be made were Kāmpila and Kauśāmbī. Of their kings and chiefs, we hear of Kraivya, Durmukha, Pravāhaṇa Jaivali and Sona. The territory of the Pañcālas roughly corresponded to the Bareilly, Badaun and Farrukhabad districts of Uttar Pradesh.

**Panegyric:** Panegyrics were a regular feature of the Vedic royal sacrifices, in which laudatory songs praising the king or his ancestors were sung by the priests along with the tales of the past (*pariplava ākhyāna*). For example, in the Aśvamedha, everyday during the year that the horse was absent, a brāhmaṇa with a *vīṇā* chanted three laudatory *gāthās* in honour of the king, which he had composed himself. The features of the rite also included panegyrics of the sacrifice along with righteous kings of yore by a kṣatriya lute player, who sang the songs composed by himself, 'such war he waged, such battle he won', etc. *Śatapatha Brāhmaṇa* (13.1.5, 1 ff; 13.4.2.8 ff), *Taittirīya Brāhmaṇa* (3.9.14, *ĀpŚS* 20.6; *KŚS* 20.2).

**Paṇi:** The term Paṇi in the *Ṛgveda* appears to denote a person who is rich, but who does not give offerings to the gods, or bestow *dakṣiṇās* on the priests, and who is therefore an object of intense dislike to the composers of the *Saṃhitā* (*RV* 1.33.3, 5.34.7; *AV* 20, 128.4; *VS* 3.1). They seem to be a tribe or people, rich in cattle wealth, who were opposed to the Vedic Indians. Hence, the gods are asked to attack the Paṇis, who are also referred to as being defeated and slaughtered (*RV* 1.83.4, 3.58.2, 5.34.7, 6.13.3, 8.64.11). The Paṇi is opposed to the pious sacrificer as a niggard (*RV* 1.124.10, 4.51.3, 8.45.14), and is spoken of as a wolf (*RV* 6.51.14), the symbol of enmity. In some passages (*RV* 1.32.11, 2.24.6, 4.58.4, 6.44.22, 7.9.2, 10.67.6; *AV*

4.23.5, 19.46.2; *ŚB* 13.8.2.3), the Paṇis definitely appear as mythological figures, demons who withhold the cows of waters of heaven, and to whom Saramā goes on a mission from Indra (*RV* 10.108). Among the Paṇis, Bṛhu was apparently important. In one passage of the *Ṛgveda* (8.66.10) they are described as usurers. In another (*RV* 7.6.3) they are called Dasyus, and styled *mṛdhravāc* or of hostile speech, the *grathin,* a word of uncertain meaning. In two passages (*RV* 5.34.5-7; *AV* 5.11.6), the Paṇis appear as Dāsas, and in one (*RV* 5.61.8) a Paṇi is mentioned in connection with wergeld (*vaira*) being apparently regarded as equal to a man merely in the price put on his life, but inferior in other respects. The Paṇis are often mentioned with the Dāsas and Dasyus as the enemies of the Aryans. Though opulent and rich, the Paṇis never worshipped the gods or rewarded the priests. They have been described as selfish, non-sacrificing, with hostile speech, greedy like the wolf, niggardly, of cruel speech, Dasyus, Dāsas of inferior status. They were cattle-owners and notorious cattle-lifters, and in some passages definitely figure as demons who withheld the cows or waters of the heavens. Vala, whom Indra pierced when he robbed the Paṇis of their cows, appears to be their patron god. Bribu is mentioned as one of their kings. The question of the identity of the Paṇis has not yet been settled with any degree of certainty. The words *paṇik* or *vaṇik, paṇya*, and *vipaṇi*, found in Sanskrit, suggest that the Paṇis should be identified with a trading people rich in cattle and other forms of wealth. Some scholars have tried to identify them with the Babylonians and Iranians. Some prefer to identify them with the Phonecians on the basis of phonetic correspondence. But such identifications have no historical basis.

**Pantheism:** The term pantheism is difficult to define, although it is very frequently used by the writers on religion. The lexicons define pantheism as the belief that god is identifiable with the forces of nature and with natural substance. But it is a narrow definition. Pantheism has an element of theism in it. The theistic conception tries to find out a supreme being which is not anthropomorphic. Not in any concrete or personified form it pervades the world as the force of creation, preservation and destruction. The latter form is described as deism. For example, Viṣṇu, Śiva or Śakti of the later religious systems are not concrete beings with any material form, though they are worshipped by devotees in their iconic form for the comprehension of ordinary people. They are theistic entities. On the other hand, Indra, although endowed with superhuman qualities is modelled after a man, a tribal leader. His connection is rather deistic. Polytheism on the other hand is a cult of many gods, though the gods of a polytheistic pantheon are more of deistic nature than theistic. Monotheism is the cult of one single deity as the supreme being, who may have anthropomorphic form like the supreme being of the Jews, or a formless entity like the supreme being of the Muslims. Pantheism represents an intermediary stage. The plurality of the Vedic gods may lead a superficial enquirer to think that the faith of the Vedic people was polytheistic. But an intelligent reader will find here neither polytheism nor monotheism but a simple primitive stage of belief, to which both of these may be said to owe their origin. The gods here do not preserve their proper places as in a polytheistic faith, but each one of them shrinks into insignificance or shines as supreme according to its being the object of adoration. The Vedic poets were children of nature. Every natural phenomenon excited their wonder, admiration or veneration. The poet is struck with wonder that 'the rough red cow gives soft white milk'. The appearance of the setting of the sun sends a thrill into the minds of the Vedic sage and with wonder-gazing eyes he exclaims: 'Updropped beneath, not fastened firm, how comes it/That downward turned he falls not downward? The guide of his ascending path-who saw?' (*RV* 3.13.5). The sages wonder how 'the sparkling waters of all rivers flow into one ocean without overfilling it.' The minds of the Vedic people, as we find in the hymns, were highly impressionable and fresh. At this state the time was not ripe enough for them to accord a consistent and well-defined existence to the multitude of gods nor to universalize them in a monotheistic creed. They adopted unconsciously any force of nature that overawed them or filled them with gratefulness and joy by its beneficent or aesthetic character, and adored it. The deity which moved the devotion or admiration or their mind was the most supreme for the time being. This peculiar trait of the Vedic hymns Max Müller has called Henotheism or Kathenotheism, 'a belief in single gods, each in turn standing out as the highest. And since the gods are thought of as specially ruling in their own spheres, the singers, in their special concerns and desires, call most of all on that god to whom they ascribe the most power in the matters, to whose department their wish belongs. This god alone is present to the mind of the suppliant; with him for the time being is associated everything that can be said of a divine being; he is the highest, the only god, before whom all others disappear, there being in this, however, no offence or depreciation of any other god.' (A. Kaegi, *The Ṛgveda*, 27). There are attempts in the hymns to bring together the various gods under one conception. Prayers are offered not only to the different deities severally, but also to all of them together as Viśve-devas (all-gods). Certain characteristic features of the gods, like creation of the world and lordship over the creatures, are abstracted, and are themselves regarded as god. Thus, we have the conceptions of Viśvakarman (world-maker) and Prajāpati (lord of beings). In the hymn, the *Ṛgveda* declares repeatedly that the great divinity of the gods is one: *mahat-devānām-asurāt-vam-ekam* (3.55). Another famous passage reads: 'What is but one Reality, sages call it by different names-as Agni, Yama and Mātariśvan' (*RV* 1.164.46). The Upaniṣadic cosmism should be distinguished from pantheism with which it is sometimes confused. A distinction is made between two types of pantheism, the one which believes that all is God, and the other which thinks that God is all. If we begin with the 'all' or Nature and consider it to be absolute and designate it as God, we have pancosmism. If we start with the postulate that God is infinite and eternal and resolve the world in Him, we have acosmism. The former of these views is not, in the strict sense, a philosohical view. The word 'God' is used here, as it has been said, only as a figleaf to hide the nakedness of a type of materialism. The other variety or pantheism may be the result of either a religious belief or a philosophical view. In fact, the joint exercise of various powers, functions, and notable deeds by two or more or all the gods is almost a favourite theme in the *Ṛgveda* hymnology. In a thorough impartial spirit, the mutual co-operation, interdependence, and subordination of the various deities in pairs or larger groups are often described. There is hardly a god in the *Ṛgveda* so insignificant as not to receive homage from others, not excluding the highest. Henotheism, in the strict sense of the term, is not to be thought of because the divine host of the *Ṛgveda* is not a pantheon (technically speaking) with an acknowledged overlord. Various explanations have been offered to account for this apparently inconsistent evaluation of divine ranks and dignities in the *Ṛgveda*. It has been urged, for example, that the inconsistency may be due to the partiality of a particular *Ṛsi* or Vedic *śākhā* to a particular god. But the force of this argument is considerably weakened by the large number of Ṛgvedic repetitions and (on the whole) their even distribution throughout the text. As Bloomfield observes, 'No theory as to the character and origin of the *RV*. can pass by these facts. They mark the entire Mantra-literature as, in a sense, epigonal, and they forbid pungent theories about profound differences between the family books, their authors, and their geographical provenience.' It has also been contended, as Macdonell points out, that 'in the frequent hymns addressed to the Viśvedevas of all-gods, all the deities, even the lesser ones, are praised in succession, and that as the great mass of the Vedic hymns was composed for the ritual of the Soma-offering, which included the worship of almost the entire pantheon, the technical priest could not but know that the exact rests on the unwarranted assumption that the ritualists of a later age, when sacrifical technique was enormously developed, had to, and could, preserve very scrupulously the mythological values of Ṛgvedic poetry.' Another approach to the problem of introducing order and system into this apparent chaos has been through classification. There is, first of all, the traditional classification hinted at in the *Ṛgveda* (1.139.11) and followed by Yāska, giving us a triple division of the Vedic gods corresponding to the three orders, namely terrestrial (*pṛthivīsthāna*), aerial or intermediate (*antarīkṣasthāna* or *madhyamasthāna*) and celestial (*dyusthāna*). Pṛthivī, Agni, Soma, Bṛhaspati and the rivers belong to the first order; Indra, Apāṃnapāt, Rudra, Vāyu-Vāta, Parjanya, Āpah and Mātariśvan to the second; and Dyaus, Varuṇa, Mitra, Sūrya, Savitṛ, Pūṣan, Viṣṇu and Ādityas, Uṣas and the Aśvins to the third. This classification is founded on the natural basis which the deities represent, and is thus the most practical and least not open to objection (comparatively speaking). The *Ṛgveda* (10.158.1) which invokes, Sūrya, Vāta, and Agni for protection from heaven, air and earth respectively is apparently the lead followed by the predecessors of Yāska whose views are quoted in the *Nirukta*, and who hold that there are only three representative deities, Sūrya in heaven, Vāyu or Indra in air and Agni on earth, each of these having various appellation according to differences of function.

**Pantheon:** See **Abstract gods, Atmospheric gods, Celestial gods, Pantheism, Terrestrial gods**.

**Parables:** In the Saṃhitās there is no dearth of similies, metaphors and allegories, though parables and fables rarely occur. In the *Śatapatha Brāhmaṇa* (11.6.1) we have the parable of proud Bhṛgu and in the *Jaiminīya Upaniṣad Brāhmaṇa* (3.1.1-2) we have the story of the dispute of the deities for precedence. It is in the Upaniṣads, however, that we come across a good number of parables. In the *Kena Upaniṣad* for example, we have the parable of Indra and the damsel. In the sixth *adhyāya* of the *Bṛhadāraṇyaka Upaniṣad* there is the parable of the senses. In the third *prapāṭhaka* of the *Chāndogya Upaniṣad* there is the parable of the sun and two cosmological parables. The myth of Indra and Vairocana given in the eighth *prapāṭhaka* of the same text is of the nature of a parable. In the *Kaṭha Upaniṣad* (1.3.3 ff, 2.2.1), we have the interesting eschatological parable of the chariot.

**Paradise:** See **Eschatology, Heaven**.

**Parents:** See **Family**.

**Paramountcy:** See **House Sacrifice, Kingship, Rājasūya, Royal Ceremonies, Sovereignty**.

**Paramour:** Paramours of women are mentioned in the Vedic literature as *upapati*, along with a term of similar significance which is *jāra*. See *Vājasaneyī Saṃhitā* 30.9; *Taittirīya Brāhmaṇa* 3.4.4.1.

**Pārāvata:** *Pārāvata* occurs in several passages of the *Ṛgveda*. In some places (*RV* 5.52.11, 8.100.6; *AV* 20.135.14) it means 'coming from distance', but elsewhere (cf. *RV* 8.34.18) it is the proper name of a people on the Yamunā (Jumna). It is certain that in the

*Pañcaviṃśa Brāhmaṇa* the Pārāvatas are a people on that river. The mention of the Sarasvatī in connection with the Pārāvatas (*RV* 5.52.11, 8.100.6, 6.61.2; *AV* 20.135.14) in the *Ṛgveda* accords generally with their position on the Yamunā in the *Pañcaviṃśa Brāhmaṇa* (9.4.11). The said people had a totemic name made after turtle-dove (*RV* 5.52.11, 8.100.6, *AV* 20.135.14).

**Pariṣad:** This term which literally means 'sitting round', is available in the earlier Vedic literature. Indra is mentioned as destroying with his thunderbolt the *pariṣads* (companions) of the Asuras, who obstructed rain in the *Ṛgveda* (3.33.7). Similarly in another *Ṛgvedic* passage (10.61.13) we hear of Indra surrounded by his *pariṣads* while killing his enemy. These passages show the military function of the *pariṣad*, of both the Aryans and the Asuras. In the *Ṛgveda* (4.2.17) the gods are praised as making a wide conclave, rich in kine. Here the term *pariṣadantaḥ* has been explained as *paritaḥ sīdantaḥ santaḥ* by Sāyaṇa to mean those good souls who, being seated round for worshipping Agni and Indra, obtained a large herd of kine. Thus, *gabyam* meaning only 'a herd of kine', if we accept Sāyaṇa's explanation, is only the accusative case of 'agman' and hence it is hard to accept it as the adjective of '*pariṣad*'. However, there is no doubt about the fact that *pariṣad* means an assembly because, it is derived from *pari sad*, i.e. sitting around. This expresses the fact that the worshippers of Agni and Indra who had assembled together, were rewarded with a herd of kine. The first line of the hymn of the *Ṛgveda* (7.4.7) is quoted here for careful consideration, *pariṣadyaṃ hyaraṇasya rekṇo nityasya rāyaḥ patayaḥ syāma*. Sāyaṇa explains it as *aṇṛṇasya dhanaṃ paryāptaṃ bhavati*, i.e. he who is free from debt and has enough wealth. In the *Vājasaneyī Saṃhitā* (5.32) Agni is said to have been present in the *pariṣad*, as indicated by his epithet *pariṣadya*. This shows that the fire-god was pleased to grace the assembly known as *pariṣad* as he did the *vidatha*, and that the *pariṣad* was also a religious or distributive assembly like *vidatha* in which Agni was worshipped. We hear of a *daivī pariṣad* along with *sabhā* and *samiti* in the *Jaiminīya Upaniṣad Brāhmaṇa* (2.2.13-14). The *Taittirīya Brāhmaṇa* (3.1.2.9) also refers to Ahirbudhnya, a form of Rudra as *pāriṣadya*, explained by Sāyaṇa as worthy of attending the *sabhā*. These references to the divine assembly suggest a similar assembly among the Aryans and this is corroborated by a later *Brāhmaṇa*, *Sāmavidhāna Brāhmaṇa* (2.7.5), which speaks of royal assembly in the passage *pariṣadirajani, chottara-vadi bhvatyuttara-vadi bhavati*. Pariṣad is used in the *Bṛhadāraṇyaka Upaniṣad* (6.1.1) and the *Jaiminīya Upaniṣad Brāhmaṇa* (2.11.13.14) as an 'assemblage' of advisers on questions of philosophy. Hence, the term means an assembly of only learned men rather than of ordinary people. The *pariṣad* appears as an alternative designation of the *samiti* only in the older *Upaniṣad* texts, where it has the form of an aristocratic council attended by the king and the learned brāhmaṇas and is not specifically created with any public functions. There can be, therefore, no question of the *pariṣad* of the late or post-Vedic times inheriting the popular tradition or retaining the representative character of the old Vedic *samiti*. It is worthy of note that the military character of the *pariṣad*, indicated by the Vedic references mentioned above, is confirmed by the epics and the Purāṇas. The association of women with the *pariṣad* in the later Vedic age, as with the *vidatha* in the earlier Vedic period, is clearly corroborated by the term *pariṣadī* in the *Baudhāyana Dharma Sūtra* (2.5.12). From the earlier Vedic references, however, limited, we may suppose that *pariṣad* was originally a tribal assembly, military in character and this feature is also confirmed by the epic and puranic traditions. With the increase of the power of kingship in the later Vedic society the *pariṣad* evolved itself into a select body of scholars and partly into a royal council dominated by priests, as evidenced by the texts of the later Vedic literature.

**Parish:** See **Administration**.

**Parjanya:** Parjanya, like *Vāta*, is a god whose natural character is obvious and undeniable. He has three hymns in the *Ṛgveda* and his name occurs some thirty times, but in other passages it has beyond doubt the simple sense of rain cloud. More often, however, the rain cloud is made into a real person, often in theriomorphic shape, thus, he is a bull who roars and impregnates the plants, and his roaring waters delight the earth. But, as the waters are normally conceived as feminine, in other cases he becomes a barren cow, or even a productive cow. He is the rain giver, and is besought to bestow rain, but in his actions he is subject to the control of Mitra and Varuṇa. He also thunders and smites trees and evildoers in anger and, when he quickens the earth with his seed, the winds blow, and the lightning flashes. He is often associated with Vāta and Indra. As a rain god plants spring up through him, he is also credited with the increase of cattle and mares, and of women. He is even exalted as an independent monarch, the ruler of all the world, in whom are established the three worlds and all beings. From another point of view he is essentially the father, and even the divine father. In one place Dyaus is stated to be his father, and in his character, especially in the stress laid on his paternity, and his bull shape, he is likened to his father. His wife is the earth, though once (*AV* 10.10.6) she is called Vācā. He has a son (*RV* 7.101.1) who may be Soma, for that god is called son of Parjanya (*RV* 9.82.3), but the lightning may also be meant. He is not rarely connected with Indra, but rarely with Agni, and occasionally with the Maruts. In an interesting hymn (*RV* 7.103), the frogs are spoken of as raising their voices when aroused by Parjanya, though it is uncertain if the god of the cloud is meant.

**Parliament:** See **Pariṣad, Popular Assembly, Sabhā, Samiti** and **Vidatha.**

**Parlour:** See **House**.

**Paruṣṇī:** Name of a river mentioned in the Nadī-stuti (*RV* 10.75.5) and in the song of the victory of Sudās over the ten kings (*RV* 7.18.8-9). In one passage of the *Ṛgveda* (8.74.15) it is called a 'great stream'. It has been identified with Ravi or Irāvatī, as recognized by Yāska (*Nir.* 9.26). There is a doubtful reference to Paruṣṇī in the *Atharvaveda* (6.12.3).

**Parśu:** *Parśu* occurs in one passage in a Dānastuti (praise of gifts) in the *Ṛgveda* (8.6.46) as the name of a man. It is not certain that he is identical with Tirindira, but the *Śāṅkhāyana Śrauta Sūtra* (16.11.20) mentions Tirindira Pāraśavya as the patron of Vatsa Kanya. In another passage in the *Ṛgveda* (10.46.23), Parśu Mānavī occurs, apparently a woman, probably a daughter of Manu. Excepting these two, there are no other occurrences in which the word has with any probability the value of a proper name in the *Ṛgveda*. In several other places there is allusion to the Parśus as a tribe. Thus, in one passage of the *Ṛgveda* (10.33.2) we find a reference to the defeat of Kuruśrvaṇa by the Parśus; in another (7.83.1) we find a reference to the Pṛthus and Parśus. In a passage (*RV* 8.6.46) Parśus are brought in connection with Yadus. The Parśus must have been a frontier tribe but their identification with the Persians, as suggested by some scholars, is doubtful.

**Partition:** It is not certain whether the sons had any share of the ancestral property during their father's lifetime in the Ṛgvedic age. In the age of the later Saṃhitās and Brāhmaṇas, the word *dāya* had come to mean inheritance in the sense of a father's property, which was to be divided among his sons either during his life or after his death. For details see **Inheritance.**

**Passion:** See **Kāma**.

**Pastime:** See **Entertainment**.

**Pastoral Economy:** The Vedic economy was predominantly pastoral. Although agriculture had a significant role to play in the post-Ṛgvedic period, the importance of cattle rearing and pastoral economy was not at all minimized. Cattle was an important form of wealth, which could be accumulated and increased by reproduction as also by wars and raids. It was the best medium of exchange prior to the development of money economy, which did not squarely take place in India before the sixth century BC. Out of more than ten thousands verses of the *Ṛgveda* only twenty-five refer to agriculture whereas there is scarcely any hymn which does not refer to cattle. The term *go*, which denotes cattle in the broad sense, has been made a synonym of the earth. 'The chief source of income was cattle rearing, and the chief cattle was the bullock. The horse also was greatly valued and harnessed before the chariot, and bore the warrior to the glory for the victor'. Again and again in the songs and invocations to the gods, the prayer for the cattle and horses occurs. Also, the strife amongst the hostile aboriginal inhabitants turns on the possession of cattle. Therefore, too, the old word for 'war' or battle is originally 'desire for cattle' (*gaviṣṭi*). In the most extravagant expressions cows and bullocks are praised as the most precious possessions. The lowing of cows hastening to the calves is looked on by the ancient Indian as the sweetest music. 'The singers are shouting to the god Indra', says a poet, 'as mother cows low to the calf'. Gods are readily compared with bullocks, goddesses with cows. 'The milk of the cow was not only one of the chief articles of food, but milk and butter formed an essential part of the sacrifices to the gods (Winternitz I, pp. 53-4). The high esteem in which cattle were held, however, proved no obstacles to the slaughtering of cows, especially bullocks, at the sacrifices, and to the eating of their flesh. An absolute prohibition of cow killing did not exist in the oldest times, although the word *aghnyā*, 'she who is not to be killed', for 'cow' indicated that cows were killed under exceptional circumstances. In fact, a sacrifice like the Aśvamedha required as many as five hundred cattle to be killed. That is why, a theory has been put forward by some scholars that the Buddha's and Mahāvīra's insistence on non-violence and not-killing had an economic perspective, because they did not want senseless destruction of cattle wealth, in the sacrifices. The skin of the oxen was used for preparing numerous articles. The tanner worked it up into leather bottles, strings of bows, straps, boxes and so forth. Cattle not only constituted the chief form of wealth but they were also the original form of *dakṣiṇā* or sacrificial fee. The word *dakṣiṇā* is in fact an adjective meaning 'right' or 'valuable' with an eclipse of *go* (cow), because the sacrificial fee was a cow placed on the right side of the singer to be rewarded. In the later Saṃhitās and Brāhmaṇas we find that 6, 8, 12 or even 24 oxen were used to drag the plough. The oxen were yoked and harassed with traces and guided by the goad of the ploughman. This denotes what the sociologists describe as 'higher pastoralism', in which agriculture was supplemented by cattle raising as well as the latter was supplemented by the former. A fairly long hymn in the *Atharvaveda* shows the reverence inspired by the cow. The occasional mythological identifications of the cow with the earth or Aditi indicate the importance of the pastoral economy and also the process which culminated in the full-fledged deification of the cow in later times. The importance of pastoral economy was not diminished even in the age of the Sūtras. The Gṛhyasūtras prescribe as number of minor rights on the following occasions: (1) When the cows are led to the pastoral land; (2) When they run about; (3) When they return, and (4) Before and after their entry into the cowpen. Prayers and rites for prosperity in cattle and their good health abound in the Gṛhya-sūtras. There is a ceremony for cattle breeding, called Vṛṣotsarga, on the release of a stud-bull among the cows. Yakṣma, a disease affecting cattle, was very much dreaded. The feeling of reverence for the cow went on gathering volume steadily and this accounts for the importance of pastoral economy in the Vedic age.

**Pasture:** The term *goṣṭha*, lit, 'standing place for cows', denotes not so much a 'cowstall' as the 'grazing ground of cows' as may be shown from a passage of the *Aitareya Brāhmaṇa* (3.18) and from a note of Mahīdhara on *Vājasaneyī Saṃhitā* (3.21). This sense suits adequately all the passages of the *Ṛgveda* (1.191.4, 6.28.1, 8.43.17) and other texts (*AV* 2.26.2, 3.14.1. ff, *ŚB* 11.8.3.2, *KS* 7.3, *MS* 4.2.11). Suyavasa denotes a 'good pasture' in the *Ṛgveda* (1.42.8, 6.28.7, 7.18.4) and the *Taittirīya Saṃhitā* (1.7.5.2).

**Paternity:** See **Family**.

**Pathways:** In a spiritual sense, two separate pathways along which all moving creatures travel, namely the Path of the Fathers (*pitṛyāna*) and that of the gods (*devayāna*) is spoken of in the *Ṛgveda* (10.88.15), and it is supposed that there is a reference here to the ways of the other world. The former leads the departed one to the realm of Yama, where the Fathers live in the midst of the joys of immortality. The latter leads to a world even superior to the former, where the departed one lives in the company of gods. For details see **Eschatoloy**.

**Pathology:** See **Medical Science**.

**Patient:** In order to understand why in the ancient Indian medicine a particular thing is considered to be a cause of disease, or why a particular way of curing is adopted for a particular disease, one has to take into account the concepts about the patient, about the disease and about the curing. The state of being diseased is considered to be something 'wholly other'. Thus, a person who is ill, is supposed to be neither living nor dead (*naisa jīvo na mṛto ya āmayāvī- KS* (11.5.8). His wholly otherness causes a patient to be treated differently.

**Patriarchy:** Patriarchy means a male-dominated society in which descent, inheritance, succession, marriage, residence and social relations are traced through father or agnates and in which political, economic and religious life of the people are dominated by males. Such a system is the outcome of the consolidation of economic power in the hands of the males. Patriarchal tendencies find more favourable expression in pastoral societies than the agricultural societies. The most pronounced form of patriarchy was foreshadowed in the *Ṛgveda* which had an all-round development in the age of the later Saṃhitās and Brāhmaṇas. In the Vedic texts there is no reference of daughters inheriting paternal property. Even as late as in the Sūtra period, it is said that a daughter cannot by right inherit the property of her father, on whose death the inheritance is to be passed to the patrilineal agnates and cognates. The deterioration of her status and dignity went as far as to result in women being classed with dice and wine, as one of the three chief evils (*MS* 3.6.3). Insignificance of women is stressed in the *Taittirīya Saṃhitā* (6.5.8.2). The relative position of the two sexes is reflected in the keen desire for male progeny. This predilection exceeds all bounds of propriety or morality when we read in the *Aitareya Brāhmaṇa* (7.15) that a daughter is a source of misery and a son alone can be saviour of the family. The *Atharvaveda* (6.1.3) also deplores the birth of daughters. The Vedic pantheon is also male dominated, goddesses occupying only a very subordinate position. Even after death a man is supposed to go to the abode of the Fathers. The patriarchal social norms established in the Vedic age have persisted in India through subsequent ages and is a social reality even today.

**Patrimony:** See **Inheritance**.

**Patronage:** Though in almost all the hymns of the *Ṛgveda* patronage of gods for material prosperity is sought, human patronage to various causes has also been repeatedly sought. To quote from the *Ṛgveda* 10.117, 'The wealth of liberal is never exhausted, but a miserly person never finds a friend. He who, though possessing food, refuses a morsel to the destitute likewise never finds a friend. He indeed is a patron who gives. . . . Let the wealth in person be generous to the applicant. . . . He who eats alone bears the burden of his sins alone. . . . A liberal friend is better than an illiberal one'. In fact, the *dānastutis*, 'praises of givers' exaggerate immensely the donations of the patrons.

**Pavilion:** Pavilions (*śālā*) were made for sacrifical purposes. The word in the *Atharvaveda* (5.21.5, 6.106.3, 8.6.10, 9.3.1, 14.1.63), and later (*TB* 1.2.3.1, *ŚB* 3.1.1.6, etc.), means shade or stall. The owner or maker was called *śālāpati* (*AV* 2.3.12).

**Payment:** The term for payment is *dakṣiṇā*, which appears repeatedly in the *Ṛgveda* (1.168.7, 6.27.8, 8.24.29, 8.39.5, 10.17.9, 10.62.1) and later (*AV* 4.11.4, 5.7.11, 11-7.9, 13.1.52, etc., *TS* 1.7.7.1, 1.8.1.1, *VS* 4.19, 19.30, *TB* 1.7.3.3, etc., *ŚB* 1.9.3.1, etc.), as the designation of the gift presented to priests as fee for conducting sacrifices. *Dakṣiṇā* consisted of articles or personal property such as kine, horses, buffaloes or camels, ornaments and so forth, but not land. Reference is, however, made in the *Śatapatha Brāhmaṇa* (13.7.1.13) to land as a *dakṣiṇā*, but with disapproval because it came to be regarded as inalienable without the consent of the clansmen. Clothes and gold are mentioned as *dakṣiṇā* in the *Atharvaveda* (9.5.14). Gold, cow, clothes and a horse are referred to as four *dakṣiṇās* in the *Śatapatha Brāhmaṇa* (4.3.4.7).

**Pearl:** In the *Ṛgveda* (1.35.4, 10.68.1) pearls are mentioned as adorning the car of Savitṛ, and also being used for the adornment of a horse. Henceforth, the horse is called the pearled-one or *kṛśanavant* in the *Ṛgveda* (1.126.4) as well as *kṛśanin* in the *Ṛgveda* (7.18.23). Pearls or precious stones have figured in the Vedic concept of wealth. *Kṛśana* denotes 'Pearl'. *Vimukta*, another term for pearl, is found in the late *Ṣaḍviṃśa Brāhmaṇa* (5.6). *Śaṅkha* in the *Atharvaveda* (4.10.1), with the epithet *kṛśana*, denotes a pearl-shell used as an amulet.

**Peasant:** See **Agriculture**.

**Peg:** *Mayukha* (*RV* 7.99.3; *KS* 11.6; *TS* 2.3.1.5, *AB* 5.15.9) signifies a peg. It was probably used to stretch out a web (*RV* 10.130.2; *AV* 10.7.42; *KS* 26.6; *TB* 2.5.5.3). *Samya* (*RV* 10.31.10; *AV* 138.4; 20.136.9; *TS* 6.2.7.1; *PB* 25.10.4; *ŚB* 12.5.2.7) denotes the same. But more precisely it is a pin (*RV* 3.33.13; *TS* 1.6.8.3; *ŚB* 3.3.4.25) attached to the yoke, in order to keep it properly on the ox's neck (*PB* 6.5.20). Śaṅku is another term used in the *Ṛgveda* (1.164.48), *Aitareya Brāhmaṇa* (3.18.6), *Śatapatha Brāhmaṇa*. (3.5.1.2-6; 3.5.2.2; 3.6.1.3; 13.8.4.1) to designate a wooden peg by which a skin could be stretched out (*ŚB* 2.1.1.10).

**Penalty:** See **Wergeld**.

**Penance:** In the *Brāhmaṇa* literature, it is found that prior to each act of creation, Prajāpati was believed to have practised penance (*tapas*) and the gods, face to face with some obstacle or difficulty, we are told, went on worshipping and toiling. Again, prior to and during the continuance of the sacrifice, a life of more or less exacting discipline was always enjoined upon the sacrificer; and, during the stage of studenthood, the pupil who lived with his preceptor for a number of years was expected to do menial work of all kinds and to undergo a rigorous training of body and mind. Yet, the idea of a wholehearted life of mere penance, or of meditation in the recesses of some mountain away from the haunts of the people was, we might say, essentially foreign to the religious code of the Brāhmaṇas, which on the contrary, called upon the pious householder to perform the *agnihotra* to the very end of his days. However, in the later *Brāhmaṇa* texts we do find a life of penance in the forest recognized and recommended, and we have texts called the Āraṇyakas or forest-portions that seem to have been specially designed for the purpose. In the Upaniṣads we come across a class of persons taking a wandering life and making penances from some positive and irresistable impulse. The *Bṛhadāraṇyaka Upaniṣad* (4.4.22) says, Desirous of regarding their very *ātman* as a (self-sufficient) world in itself, the mendicants step out into the life of houselessness. The ancients knowing this very fact desired not offspring, saying, What shall we do with offspring-we who have in this *ātman* our world (*loka*)? They, verily rising above the desire for worlds, lived a mendicant life. Also, the *Muṇḍaka Upaniṣad* (1.2.11) says they who practise austerity and faith in the forests, the peaceful knowers who live a beggar's life, etc. The story of Yājñavalkya renouncing his two wives and all the worldly interests, saying, 'I am about to wander forth from this (*āśrama*), my dear', is quite familiar; and other instances of people, well-situated in life, deliberately turning their back upon their homes in the interest of the pure knowledge of highest reality, are not very far to seek. In the *Brāhmaṇa* literature, *tapas* or penance has sometimes been conceived as a creative force. In the *Ṛgveda* 10.100.90, it is said: 'From *tapas*, mightily kindled Law and Truth were born; thence the Night was born and the Billowy Ocean. From the Billowy Ocean the Year was produced; And Nights, the Sun and the Moon, as of old, the Creator formed, the Heaven, the Earth, the Mid-World and the Light.' In the Brāhmaṇa literature, this idea has been given a greater dimension. For a mechanical and an easily intelligible conception of the process of creation, like the one put forth by primitive philosophy, the Brāhmaṇas substituted a far-fetched ritualistic process grounded upon etymological aetiology, in which '*tapas*' plays the chief role. The term *tapas* of the Nāsadīya hymn appears abundantly in the post-Ṛgvedic literature in the sense of fervour. In the *Śatapatha Brāhmaṇa* (11.5.8.1) Prajāpati, who is described as being the universe, is said to have desired to propagate (13.7.1.1); the self-existent *Brahman* himself is similarly related to have practised *tapas*. In the *Taittirīya Brāhmaṇa* (3.12.3.1), we come across the following statement: Let us worship the first born god by whom the universe is encompassed, the self-existent *Brahman*, who is the highest *tapas*. He is at the same time father, mother and son. *Tapas* was produced as the first object. In the *Atharvaveda* (17.1.24), however, *tapas* means the heat of the sun. There it is also connected with Agni (*AV* 7.61) and also with Karman (*AV* 11.8.2).

**People:** If the *grāma* was the smallest, the *jana* was the highest political and social union among the Vedic communities. The word comes from a very ancient root, which is found in many other Indo-European languages. It meant both, an individual and a body of men claiming birth from a common ancestor. That it signified such a body is apparent from its use in the *Ṛgveda*, where we find almost all the important Vedic tribes were designated as *janāsah*. Thus, in 3.53.12 of the *Ṛgveda*, in which Viśvāmitra prays for the Bharatas, the latter are described as forming a *janāḥ* (*RV* 3.53.12) (*bhāratam janam*). In another hymn by Kaṇva, in praise of gifts (*RV* 8.6.46-8), the Yādavas are described both as Yadava *jana*, or are designated in the plural (*yadvānām*), a practice supported by the rules of grammar (*RV* 8.6.46-8). The word *jana* is also applied to designate the five great divisions of the Vedic peoples (*pañca janāḥ* or *janāsaḥ*). This *jana* was intimately connected with the *rājan* or the king. This would appear from the evidence of a number of passages. One of these, in course of a prayer, expressly asks for providing the tribe with a king (*RV* 5.58.4). In another (*RV* 6.43.5), we find the king described as *gopa janasya*, while in the *Ṛgveda* (9.35.5), Soma is described as *gopatim janasya*. Lastly, we have one passage in the tenth Maṇḍala, which throws more light on this point and establishes the closest possible relation between the king (*rājan*) and the *jana*. The hymn in question is the *Ṛgveda* 10.159 and in that we find a queen, Sacī Paulomī, uttering a magical formula for counteracting the influence of co-wives over her husband; to prevent any harm arising out of their influence; to retain the highest place in her husband's eyes; to enable her son to be the master some time afterwards; and, to bestow honour on her daughter. The conjuration ends with the following utterance: 'I have displayed rival wives, risen superior to them and thereby I rule over this man and the *jana*.' In another (*RV* 10.174.5), a victorious king speaks of his success over enemies and his lordship over the *jana*. The *jana*, therefore, we may take and regard as having been synonymous with the tribe. Apart from *jana kṛṣṭi*, it denotes 'people' in a general sense from the *Ṛgveda* (1.52.11; 1.100.10; 1.160.5; 1.189.3; 3.49.1; 4.21.2), and onwards (*AV* 12.1.3; 12.1.4). Indra is the lord of men in the *Ṛgveda* (1.77.1; 4.17.5; 7.26.5; 8.13.9) as is Agni (*RV* 1.59.5; 6.18.2; 7.5.5). There men are termed by *kṛṣṭi*. Sometimes, such a word is further defined by the addition of an adjective for the sense of 'belonging to mankind' in the *Ṛgveda* (1.59.5, 6.18.2) and of men' in *Atharvaveda* (3.24.3) as soon as found in *mānuṣī* and *mānavī* respectively. Five peoples are specially mentioned in the *Ṛgveda* (2.2.10; 3.53.16; 4.38.10; 10. 60.4; 10.119.6; 10.178, 3; the *Atharvaveda* (3.24.2; 12.1.42). Here five peoples termed by *pañcakṛṣṭayaḥ* are mentioned variously as the four castes and the Niṣādas. Sāyaṇa is of the same opinion. According to the *Aitareya Brāhmaṇa* (3.31) the five are: gods, men, *gandharvas* and *apsarases*, snakes and the Fathers. According to Yāska, the five are mentioned in the *Nirukta* (3.8), with the reference to the view of Upamanyu as follows: the Gandharvas, Fathers, gods, Asuras and Rāksaṣas.

**Perception:** In the early Vedic texts we do not come across clear references to the sources of valid knowledge, like perception, inference and testimony from a philosophical point of view, though from the description of the Vedic deities, as found in the *Ṛgveda*, it is certain that the early Vedic Indians had much trust in perception. Philosophically, the incipient form of perception as a source of valid knowledge, as contrasted with the intellectual levels of experience, is found in *Bṛhadāraṇyaka Upaniṣad* (1.5). In it, a distinction of perception on the one hand, and understanding on the other, is drawn where it is said that we often hear people say, 'As our mind was elsewhere, we did not see or hear'. It is clear from such statements, says the writer, that one is able to see and hear not with one's eye or ear respectively, but with the mind. This is an exaltation of the fact of mental understanding over the mere physiological processes of perception.

**Perfumes:** See **Aphrodisiacs**.

**Pessimism:** Pessimism was unknown to the seers of the early Vedic texts. As the Ṛgvedic Indians were full of the *joie de vivre*, they were particularly interested in worldly joys and pleasures. 'We have drunk *soma*; we have known the gods; we have become immortal', this is what they wanted to convey to others. The entire sacrificial cult was meant for material gains and pleasure. By performing rituals they tried to influence the course of nature to work in their favour. But later, with the development of the doctrine of transmigration, a tinge of pessimism expressing itself in the desire to escape the unending succession of births and rebirths, and a longing for repose, can be observed. This tinge became more pronounced in certain Upaniṣads and eventually led to an absolutely pessimistic view of life, which subsequently found philosophical expression in Buddhism and allied systems. In fact, the Buddhist pessimism is foreshadowed in the utterance of king Bṛhadratha in the *Maitrāyaṇī Upaniṣad*. 'We see that all beings do ultimately perish. . . . The mighty warriors, the great kings and emperors have to pass away from this earth. Even demigods, like the Gandharvas, demons and spirits, orges and ghosts are all alike ultimately destroyed. What of these? Even the greatest oceans dry, the loftiest mountains crumble, the steadiest of stars fall down; the earth is submerged, and even the gods are displaced from their stations. Worldly pleasures merely involve a man in the cycles of births and deaths'.

**Pestle:** *Upala* in the Brāhmaṇas (*ŚB* 1.1.1.22) may denote the upper and smaller 'stone', which was used as a pestle with the *dṛṣad* as the mortar, whereas *upara* in the Saṃhitās denotes rather the mortar and *dṛṣad* the pestle. *Musala* (*AV* 10.9.26, 11.3.3, 12.3.13; *JB* 1.42; 1.44, *ŚB* 12.5.2.7; *Śāṅkh Ā* 12.8) is also pestle, used to grind grains or to pound Soma-plant. According to the *Taittirīya Saṃhitā* (1.6.8.3), it is one of the ten sacrificial weapons.

**Phantom:** See **Animism**.

**Phallic Worship:** Phallic worship was known in the early Vedic period, as is shown by the occurrance in two passages of the word *śiśnadevāḥ*, 'those who have a phallus for their deity'. Such worship was, however, repugnant to the religious ideas of the *Ṛgveda*, for Indra is besought not to let the *śiśnadevāḥ* approach the sacrifice (*RV* 7.21.5). He is said to have slain the *śiśnadevāḥ* when he won the treasure of the hundred-gated fort (*RV* 10.99.3). In the post-Vedic period, the phallus or *liṅga* became symbolical of Śiva's generative power and its worship is widely diffused in India even at the present day. Macdonell, 1887, 155.

**Phenomenalism:** See **Atheism, Cosmogony, Naturalism, Svabhāvavāda.**

**Philosophy:** See **Absolute, Aesthetics, Agnosticism, Akṣara, Ātman, Atheism, Brahman, Breath, Categories, Causation, Chance, Consciousness, Cosmology, Cosmo-psychology, Cosmogony, Devayāna, Devotion, Elements, Epistemology, Emancipation, Eschatology, Ethics, First Principle, Henotheism, Hiraṇyagarbha, Karma, Knowledge, Liberation, Life Principle, Madhuvidyā, Naturalism, Negativism, Niyati, Non-Dualism, Ontology, Pantheism, Perception, Pessimism, Polytheism, Prāṇa, Prajāpati, Primitive Chaos, Puruṣa, Reality, Rebirth, Renunciation, Ṛta, Scepticism, Solipsism, Theogony, Transmigration, Yadṛcchā, Yoga.**

**Phonetics:** The traditional list enumerating the six Vedāṅgas assigns the first place to Śikṣā, or the science of phonetics. The word originally means only 'instruction', and then specially such instruction as is imparted for the correct pronunciation, accentuation, etc., of the Vedic texts. The *Taittirīya Upaniṣad* (1.2) mentions this Vedāṅga for the first time and the Sūtra texts belonging to it are at least as old as the Kalpasūtras. The oldest text-books dealing with this science are the Prātiśākhyas which, as their name suggests, belonged to every *śākhā* or recension of a Vedic Saṃhitā. Thus, we have at present a *Ṛgveda Prātiśākhya* ascribed to Śaunaka, perhaps a later revision in verse born of an earlier Sūtra text, a *Taittrirīya Prātiśākhya Sūtra*, ascribed to Kātyāyana and an *Atharvaveda Prātiśākhya Sūtra*, supposed to belong to the school of the Śaunakas. The *Pañcavidha Sūtra* shows the manner in which the *sāmans* are to be sung at the sacrifice, and the *Puṣpasūtra*, a kind of *Prātiśākhya* is meant for the *Uttaragāna* of the *Sāmaveda*. All these works instruct the students in the correct pronunciation, accent, and euphonic changes which the sounds undergoing the composition of words and such other topics as came under Vedic phonetics of later origin and of much less importance are some short treatise or phonetics ascribed to such important persons as Bharadvāja, Vyāsa, Vasiṣṭha and Yājñavalkya. The *Vyāsa-śikṣā*, which is directly connected with the *Taittirīya Prātiśākhya*, is comparatively older than the other works of similar nature. The *Pāṇinīya-śikṣā* may be old in its contents though its present form is rather late. Phonetic rules do not always mean a treatise on the phonetic peculiarities of each Veda, but a collection of phonetic rules peculiar to one of the different *śākhās* of the four Vedas, i.e. to one of those different texts in which each of the Vedas had been handed down for ages in different families and different parts of India. The Śākhās denote the texts, their propagators or *pravartakas* were the *caranas*. *caraṇaśabdaḥ śākhāviśeṣādhyayana-paraikatāpannajana-sanghavacī.*

**Physician:** *Bhiṣaj*, 'physician', is a word of common occurrence in the *Ṛgveda* (2.33.4; 6.50.7; 9.112.1) and later (*AV* 5.29.1; 6.24.2; *TS* 6.4.9.2; *VS* 16.5, 19.12, 30.10). In the former text, there is no trace of the profession being held in disrepute. The Aśvins (*RV* 1.116.16; 8.18.8; 10.39.3; *AV* 7.53.1; *AB*.18), Varuṇa (*RV* 1.24.9), and Rudra (*RV* 2.33.4-7) are all called physicians. In the early Vedic period the medical profession was not hereditary. In the *Ṛgveda* (9.112.3) the poet says that his father is a physician and his mother a grinder of corns and that they all work for wealth. On the other hand, in the Dharma literature (*ĀpDS* 1.6.18.20; *GDS* 17.17), this profession is utterly despised. This dislike is found as early as the *Yajurveda Saṃhitā* (*TS* 6.4.9.3; *MS* 4.6.2; *ŚB* 4.1.5.14), where the Aśvins are condemned because of their practise of medicine (*bheṣaja*) brings them too much among men, an allusion to the caste dislike of promiscuous contact. The *Ṛgveda* (10.9.7) contains a hymn in which a physician celebrates his plants and their powers. Moreover, wonderful cures are referred to as performed by the Aśvins: the healing of the lame (*RV* 1.112.8, 10.39.3) and of the blind (*RV* 10.39.4) and of Puraṃdhi's husband (1.116.18); the giving of an iron leg (*jaṅghā āyasī*) to Viśpalā (*RV* 1.116.15), a deed only more wonderful if we assume that Viśpalā was a mare. That the practise of medicine was a means of livelihood is attested by the following verse: 'We have various hopes and plans and many are the ways of men, the craftsman seeks a job to do, the priest his flock, the leech the sick', (*RV* 9.11.1). The profession, however, gradually came to disrepute till the rise of the classical Indian medicine, the 'Āyurveda', That the profession came to be disliked by the priestly class is attested by the inclusion of a physician in the list of victims in the *Vājasaneyī Saṃhitā* (30.10), and *Taittirīya Brāhmaṇa* (3.4.4.1) at the Puruṣamedha. In the *Atharvaveda* (2.9.3-5) we read that there were hundreds of medical practitioners and thousands of medicinal herbs, as distinct from priest-magicians. But one priest-magician is said to be equal in power with hundreds of ordinary physicians and his amulet was no less in potency than that of the thousands of herbs together. Most of the medical practices of the *Atharvaveda* are merely magical in nature. The transition from magical treatment to scientific treatment is foreshadowed in the Vedic texts.

**Physiology:** See **Anatomy**.

**Pigeon:** See **Birds**.

**Pilgrimage:** The Vedic texts refer to certain regions in the plains of northern India inhabited by cultured (*śiṣṭa*) peoples and certain impure regions, especially in the eastern zone, inhabited by *vrātyas* and non-Vedic tribes, as well as holy rivers like Sarasvatī, Gaṅgā and Yamunā, on the banks of which numerous sacrifices were performed. The idea of pilgrimage, however, was an idea of later times.

**Pillars:** Pillars on which buildings were erected are described in the *Ṛgveda* as *upamit* (1.59.1; 4.5.1). The *Atharvaveda* (9.3.1) also mentions them as the designation of some part of a house. In the *Atharvaveda*, *upamit* is coupled with *parimit,* which denotes angles. The term *stambha* occurs in the *Kāṭhaka Saṃhitā* (30.9, 31.1) and means 'pillar'. The term *akambha* is referred to in the *Ṛgveda* (1.34.2, 4.13.5) to designate 'pillar' only metaphorically.

**Pillow:** *Upa-barhaṇa* denotes a 'pillow' or 'cushion' especially of a seat (*āsandī*), and appears in the *Ṛgveda* (10.85.7) the *Atharvaveda* (9.5.28; 12.2.19 12.2.20; 15.3.7) and the Brāhmaṇas (*AV* 8.12; *ŚB* 13.8.4.10; 1.6.8.9; *KS* 28.4). The feminine *upabarhaṇī* is found in the *Ṛgveda* with the same sense, but it is used metaphorically.

**Pisciculture:** Artificial rearing of fish or fish cultivation in ponds appears to have been known to the Vedic Indians. This is proved by the existence in the Vedic texts of numerous fisherman-castes, like *kevarta* or *kaivarta, dāsa, dhīvara, dhaivara, puñjiṣṭha, bainda, mārgāra, maināla*, etc., which indicate a specialization in this job. But surprisingly enough, except the general terms *matsya* and *mahāmatsya*, meaning fish and great fish respectively, we do not come across name of the variety of fishes in the Vedic texts.

**Places:** Among the specific places mentioned in the Vedic texts, besides the tribal territories, we have Kampila (*TS* 7.4.19.1, *MS* 3.12.20, *KS* 4.8; *VS* 23.18, *TB* 3.9.6, *ŚB* 13.2.8.3) as the capital city of the Pañcālas in the Madhyadeśa; Karapacava (*PB* 25.10.23) on the Yamunā; Karoti (*ŚB* 9.5.2.15) of uncertain location; Kurukṣetra (*PB* 25.10, *ŚB* 4.1.5.13; 11.5.1.4; 14.1.1.2; *AB* 7.30; *MS* 2.1.4; *JB* 3.12.6) between Khāṇḍava on the south, the Trughna on the north and the Parinaḥ on the west (*TA* 5.1.1), watered by the Dṛṣadvatī, Sarasvatī and the Āpayā (*RV* 3.23.4); Kauśāmbeya near modern Allahabad; Trughna (*TA* 5.1) on the eastern part of Kurukṣetra; Triplakṣa (*PB* 25.13.4), where the Dṛsadvatī disappeared near the Yamunā; Nadapit (*ŚB* 13.5.4.13) in the middle country; Parinaḥ (*PB* 25.13.1, *TA* 5.1.1) near Kurukṣetra; Plakṣaprasravaṇa (*PB* 15.10.16, 22, *JUB* 4.26.12), forty-four days' journey from the spot where the Sarasvatī disappeared; Maru (*TA* 5.1.1), the desert region of Rajasthan; Masnara (*AB* 7.23), the place of victory of a Kuru king in Madhyadeśa; Raikvaparṇa (*CU* 4.2.5), in the Mahāvṛṣa country; Rohitakakula (*PB* 14.3.12), having uncertain location; Vinaśana (*PB* 25.10.6; *JUB* 4.26), where the Sarasvatī was lost in the sand of the desert (same as Adarśana of later times); and, Saciguṇa (*AB* 8.23), which was a territory of the Bharatas in the middle country.

**Plait:** The use of the word *opasa* indicates that plaits were worn by women in dressing the hair. There are undoubted references to the custom of wearing the hair in braids or plaits. A maiden had her hair made in four plaits (*RV* 10.114.3). It seems from the descriptions of Rudra and Puṣan that men also wore their hair plaited or braided.

**Plakṣa Prasravaṇa:** Plakṣa Prasravaṇa is the name of a locality, forty-four days journey from the spot where Sarasvatī disappears. It is mentioned in the *Pañcaviṃśa Brāhmaṇa* (25.10; 16; 22) and *JUB* (4.26.12). In the latter text it is said that the middle of the earth is only a span (*pradeśa*) to the north of it.

**Planets:** The term for planet is *graha*, but in the *Śatapatha Brāhmaṇa* (4.6.5.1) it is applied to the sun. The seven *ādityas* are often thought of to be the sun, moon and five planets. According to some scholars, the five *adhvaryus* mentioned in the *Ṛgveda* (3.7.7) are the five planets, which move about in the heavens like the Adhvaryu priests in the sacrificial ground. The five bulls (*ukṣaṇāḥ*) in another passage of the *Ṛgveda* (1.105.10), have received a similar interpretation. Durgācārya in his commentary on the *Nirukta* (1.14) explains the term *bhūmija*, 'earth born', as meaning the planet Mars. *Bṛhaspati* is Jupiter, which in the *Taittirīya Saṃhitā* (4.4.10.1) is made a regent of *tiṣya*. A reference to the planets is much more probable in the seven suns (*sapta sūryāḥ*) of the *Taittirīya Āraṇyaka* (1.7). In the *Muṇḍakopaniṣad* (6.16) we have a more concrete conceptualization of the planets. In one passage of the *Atharvaveda* (6.21.2), *Yama*, used in the plural, denotes the planets among which the sun (*bhaga*) moves. *Vena* of the *Ṛgveda* (10.123) may denote the planet Venus. *Śukra* in the *Ṛgveda* (3.32.2; 9.46.4) also means some planet.

**Plants:** Roughly speaking, the vegetable world is divided in Vedic literature between *oṣadhi* (*RV* 10.97) or *virudh* 'plants' and *vana* or *vṛkṣa* 'trees'. *Oṣadhi-vanaspati* is a frequent compound from the *Śatapatha Brāhmaṇa* (6.1.1.12) onwards. The medicinal properties of plants account for the epithet 'if manifold powers' (*nānā-vīrya*) applied to them in the *Atharvaveda* (12.1.2). *Oṣadhi* is employed in opposition to *virudh*, to denote plants as possessing a healing power or some other quality useful for men. On the other hand, *virudh* is rather a general term for minor vegetable growths, but sometimes (*TS* 2.5.3.2) when occurring beside *oṣadhi*, signifies those plants which do not possess medicinal properties. A list of parts of a plant is given in later Saṃhitās (*TS* 7.3.19.1, *VS* 22.28). It comprises the root (*mūla*), the stem (*kāṇḍa*), the twig (*valśa*), the flower (*puṣpa*), and the fruit (*phala*), while trees (*TS* 7.3.20.1; *RV* 1.32.5; *AV* 10.7.38) have in addition a corona (*skandha*), branches (*śākhā*) and leaves (*parṇa*). The *Atharvaveda* (8.7.4) gives an elaborate division of plants into those which expand (*prastirṇatiḥ*), are bushy (*stambiniḥ*), have only one (*ekaśrṅgaḥ*), are creepers (*pratanvatiḥ*), have many stalks (*aṃśumatiḥ*), are jointed (*kuṇḍiniḥ*) or have spreading branches (*viśākhaḥ*). In the *Ṛgveda* (10.97.3; 15), plants are termed 'fruitful' (*phalinaḥ*), 'blossoming' (*puṣpavatiḥ*) and having flowers (*prasuvariḥ*). Among various plants *ajaśrṅgi* (*prosopis spicigera or mimosa suma*) is celebrated as demon-destroyer (*AV* 4.37.6). Its other name is *arāṭaki*. *Arundhatī* (*AV* 4.22.1; 5.5.5; 6.59.1-2; 8.7.6; 19.38.1) had healing properties. It was a climber which attached itself to trees like Plakṣa, Aśvattha, Nyagrodha, and Parṇa. It was golden in colour and had a hairy stem (*AV* 5.5.7). It was also called *silāci*, and the *lākṣā* (lac) appears to have been a product of it. *Adhyāṇḍā* is an unidentified plant mentioned in the *Śatapatha Brāhmaṇa* (13.8.1.16). *Apāmārga* (*Achyranthes aspera*), used frequently in witchcraft and medical purposes, is described as revertive (*AV* 4.17.6), 4.18.7, 4.19.4, 7.65, 2; *VS* 35.11, *TB* 1.7.1.8, *ŚB* 5.2.4.14, 13.8.4.4). *Amalā*, also called *āmalaka* or *amālaka* was *emblica officinalis* or *myrolalan* tree (*JUB* 1.38.6). *Amūlā* is *methonica superba*, which was used for poisoning arrows (*AV* 5.31.4). *Araṭu* was *Colosanthes indica* from whose wood the axle of chariot was sometimes made (*RV* 8.46.27, *AV* 20.131.17). *Arka* was the name of the tree *Calotropis gigantea* (*AV* 6.72.1). *Alasāla* (*AV* 6.16.4) denoted a grain-creeper. Alābu bottle-gourd (*Lagenaria vulgaris*) is mentioned in the *Atharvaveda* (8.10.29-30; 20.13.2.1-2), from which vessels were made. *Avakā* was an aquatic plant (*Blyxa octandra*) known as *śaivāla* or *sipala* (*AV* 4.37.8; 8.7.9; 8.37. 8-10, *TS* 4.6.1.1, *VS* 17.4, *MS* 2.10.1, *ŚB* 7.5.1.11). *Aśmagandhā*, probably identical with the late *aśvagandhā*, was the same as *Physalis flexuosa* (*ŚB* 13.8.6.16). *Aśvavāra* or *aśvavāla* denoted a species of reed, *Saccharum spontaneum* (*MS* 3.7.9; *KS* 24.8, *ŚB* 3.4.1.7). *Āṇḍīka* (*AV* 4.34.5; 5.17.16) was an edible plant, apparently with egg-shaped fruit or leaves. *Ādāra* was a kind of plant which was prescribed as a substitute for *soma* (*ŚB* 4.5.10.4). It was the same as *putikā* (*ŚB* 14.1.2.12). *Ābayu* (*AV* 6.16.1) was the mustard plant. *Āla* appears to mean weed in the *Atharvaveda* (6.16.3), while *urvāru* was the cucumber plant (*AV* 6.14.2). *Uśanā* (*ŚB* 3.4.3.13; 4.2.5.15) was a plant from which *soma* was prepared. *Eraṇḍa*, the castor-oil plant, is first mentioned in the *Śāṅkhāyana Āraṇyaka* (12.8), while *aukṣagandhi* appears as a fragrant plant (*AV* 4.37.3; 2.36.7). *Karira* (*Capparis aphylla*) is a leafless shrub (*TS* 2.4.9.2). *Kiyāmbu* (*RV* 10.16.13) appears to be water plant, while *kumuda* (*AV* 4.54.5) denotes the white waterlily. *Kuṣṭha* (*AV* 5.4, 6.102, 19.138) is *Costus speciosus*, which grows on the mountains and cures headache, diseases of the eyes and bodily afflictions. *Jaṅgiḍa* (*AV* 2.4, 19.34-5) was a healing plant meant for curing such diseases as *takman, balāsa, āśarīkā, viśarīka, pṛṣṭyāmaya, fevers*. *Jāmbila* (*MS* 3.15.3; *VS* 5.13) was the citron plant while *tājadbhaṅga* (*AV* 8.8.3) was a plant from which oil was extracted. *Tilvaka* (*SB* 13.8.1.16) was *Symplocos racemosa*, *taudī* (*AV* 10.4.24) was an unidentified plant, and so was *trāyamāṇā* (*AV* 8.2-6). *Narācī* (*AV* 5.31.4) was a poisonous plant, *nalada* (*AV* 6.102.3) was *Nardastachys Jatamansi*, *nīlāgalasāla* (*AV* 6.16.4) was a grain creeper, *nyastikā* (*AV* 6.139.1) was *Andropogon aciculatus* and *pākadūrvā* (*RV* 10.16.13, *TĀ* 6.4.1.2, *AV* 18.3.6) was a plant for edible millet. *Pāṭā* (*AV* 2.27.4) was *Clypea hernandifolia*, *pīlā* (*AV* 4.37.3) a fragrant plant and *puṇḍarīka* (*RV* 10.142.8; *TB* 5.5.5.6; *PB* 10.8.43) the lotus plant. *Pūtirajju* (*AV* 8.8.2) was an unknown plant while *pūtīka* (*KS* 34.3, *TS* 2.5.3.5) was a substitute for soma. *Pṛśniparṇi* (*AV* 2.25.1 ff) was *Hermionitis cordifolia* used for medicinal purposes, *praprotha* (*PB* 8.4.1) a substitute for soma, *pramandanī* (*AV* 4.37) a sweet-scented herbal plant, and *baja* (*AV* 8.6.3, etc.) and *sarṣapa* (*CU* 3.14.3) were some sort of mustard plants. *Bimba* (*JUB* 3.5.6) was *Momordica monadelpha*, *bhaṅga* and *śana* (*AV* 2.4.5; 11.6.15) the hemp-plant, *madāvatī* (*AV* 6.16.2) an intoxicating plant and *madugha* (*AV* 1.34.4, etc.) a honey-plant. *Viṣāṇakā* (*AV* 6.44.3) was used as a remedy against the disease *vatikara*, *vihahha* (*AV* 6.16.2) an unspecified plant, *vratati* (*RV* 8.40.6; *TB* 1.5.1.3) a general name for creepers, *saphaka* (*AV* 4.34.3) an edible water-plant, *sipāla* (*RV* 10.68.5) the *Blyxa octandra* and *sahamāna* (*AV* 2.35.2, etc.) an unspecified plant. *Silāci* (*AV* 5.3.1 ff) and *silāñjālā* (*AV* 6.16.4) were healing plants.

**Plank:** The term *phalaka* means plank which was used to make a cart (*PB* 17.1.4) to pound *soma* (*AB* 7.30; 32; *ŚB* 3.3.4.9) or to serve other purposes (*ŚB* 13.4.3.1). According to Eggeling it is 'a gold stool' or a thing of gold, used as a seat'.

**Pleading:** Pleading (*praśna*) denotes generally enquiry or disputed question, the phrase *praśnaṃ eti* having the sense 'he asks a person for the decision of a disputed point' in the *Taittirīya Saṃhitā* (2.5.8.5; 2.9); *Taittirīya Brāhmaṇa* (2.1.6.2), *Aitareya Brāhmaṇa* (3.38). Thus, *praśna* comes to have the definite meaning of decision in the *Aitareya Brāhmaṇa* (5.14). The *praśnin*, the *abhi-praśnin* and *praśna-vivaka* are included in the list of victims at the Purusamedha in the *Vājasaneyī Saṃhitā* (30.10; *TB* 3.4.6.1); it is quite likely that the three parties to a civil case—the plaintiff, the defendant, and the arbitrator or judge (*madhyamasi*) are meant here.

**Pleiades:** The *Kṛttikās* are the Pleiades in the Vedic literature. The names of the seven stars forming this constellation are given in the *Taittirīya Saṃhitā* (4.4.5.1), *Kāṭhaka Saṃhitā* (40.4) and the *Taittirīya Brāhmaṇa* (3.1.4.1). *Abhrayantī*, 'forming cloud', *meghayantī*, 'making cloudy', and *varṣayantī* as appellations of the stars, clearly refer to the rainy Pleiades. The word *kṛttikā* probably means web', from the root *kṛt*, 'spin'. Macdonell and Keith I, 415.

**Plough:** In the Vedic text the word *laṅgala* is the regular term for plough. Its origin may be traced to *liṅga*, or male generative organ which, according to J. Przylusky and P.C. Bagchi, was basically of Austric origin. The world is found in the *Ṛgveda* (4.57.4) and later (*AV* 2.8.4; *TS* 6.6.7.4). It is described in a series of passages (*AV* 3.17.3, *TS* 4.2.5.6 = *KS* 16.11 = *MS* 2.7.12 = *VS* 12.71) as 'lance-pointed' (*pavīravam* or *pavīravat*), 'well-lying' (*suśīmam*) and 'having a well-smoothed handle' (*sumati-tsaru*). *Lāṅgala* is referred to in the *Jaiminīya Brāhmaṇa* (2.84), in which it is described as an instrument of land, which is used in the field for cultivation. In the same text (3.72-4) it is stated, 'Get up, wake up, yoke your ploughs (*lāṅgala*), it's day-break'. Apart from *lāṅgala, sīra* 'plough' is mentioned in the *Ṛgveda* (4.57.8; 10.101.3,4) and often later (*AV* 6.30.1; 6.91.1; 8.9.16; *TB* 1.7.1.2; 2.5.8.12; *VS* 18.7; *MS* 2.11.4). It was large and heavy as is suggested by the fact that six oxen (*AV* 6.91.1; 8.9.16; *TS* 5.2.5.2; *KS* 15.2; 20.3; *ŚB* 7.2.26; *KS* 15.2; 20.3; *ŚB* 7.2.26; 13.8.2.6) or eight (*AV* 6.91.1), or twelve (*TS* 1.8.71; 5.2.5.2; *KS* 15.2; *MS* 2.6.2), or even twenty-four (*KS* 15.2) were used to drag it. The animals that drew the plough were oxen, which were, no doubt, yoked and harnessed with straps (*varatrā* in *RV* 4.5.57.4; c.f. the Mudgala story in 10.102.8). It may denote the fastening of the ox to the yoke by the *asira* or 'goad' of the polughman. *Sīla* plough, is found in the *Kātyāyana Śrautasūtra* (28.8). In the *Śatapatha Brāhmaṇa* (7.2.2.2 ff) plough is referred to as *sīra* or *sera*, which is said to be made of *udumbara* wood. 'He yokes the right (ox) first, then the left one; thus, it is done with the gods differently in human practice. It is a team of six oxen or one of twelve oxen or one of the twenty-four oxen; it is the year (he obtains) as the consummation.' The term of the handle of a plough is *tsaru*, which appears in the *Ṛgveda* 7.50.1; *Atharvaveda* 3.17.3; *Maitrāyaṇī Saṃhitā* 2.7.12; *Kāṭhaka Saṃhitā* 16.12; *Taittirīya Saṃhitā* 4.2.5. The *Atharvaveda* 3.17.3 says, 'Let the plough (*lāṅgala*), lance-pointed, well-lying, with well smoothed handle (*tsaru*) turn up.' According to Whitney, the term *tsaru* may be derived from the root *tsar*, which means 'to be held by the ploughman's hand'. The term *kināsa* denotes the ploughman or cultivator of the soil (*RV* 4.57.8; *AV* 4.11.10, 6.20.1, *VS* 30.11; *TB* 2.4.8.7). Other terms for ploughman is *kṛṣivala*; (6.116.1) refers specially to *karṣīvāna* as a plougher. The word *phāla* occurs in the *Ṛgveda* 4.57.8; 10.117.7; *Kāṭhaka Saṃhitā* 19.1 in the sense of ploughshare. The *Atharvaveda* 3.17.5; *Maitrāyaṇī Saṃhitā* 2.7.12; *Kāṭhaka Saṃhitā* 12.7; *Kauṣitakī Brāhmaṇa* 25.15 use another term *suphāla* to denote the same. Another word for ploughshare is *stega* which occurs in the *Ṛgveda* 10.31.9; *Atharvaveda* 18.1.39.

**Pole-Dancer:** *Vaṃśa-nartin* denotes a pole-dancer or acrobat. They are referred to in the *Vājasaneyī Saṃhitā* (30.21 and *TB* 3.4.17.1).

**Police:** In the *Bṛhadāraṇyaka Upaniṣad* (4.3.27 ff) the term *ugra* denotes a 'man in authority', which according to Max Müller means a policeman. Roth (*St. Petersburg Dictionary*) compared a passage in the *Ṛgveda* (7.38.6), where the word has simply the general sense of 'mighty man'. *Jīva-gṛbh*, 'seizing alive', is according to Roth (*St. Petersburg Dictionary*), the term for a police official in the *Ṛgveda* (10.97.11). But although this sense is rendered possible by the mention of *madhyamasi*, perhaps, 'arbitrator', in the same passage, it is neither necessary nor probable. *Pratyenas* may also denote an officer of police. The sense, however, may be that of the humbler 'servants' of the king rather than 'magistrates', as Max Müller, in his translation, has taken it. Macdonell and Keith I, 288.

**Polity:** The family (*gṛha* or *kula*) was the ultimate basis of the Vedic state. A number of families, connected with the ties of kinship, formed the *grāma*. An aggregate of villages made up *vis* composed the *jana* (tribe). The tribe was under the rule of its chief (*rājan*). The term *rājan*, which is of frequent occurrence in the *Ṛgveda*, originally denoted tribal chieftain and not a monarchical king. The country which the Vedic Indians occupied was split up into numerous tribal principalities. The 'five peoples' (*pañcajanāḥ*) were perhaps a comprehensive term for the Vedic tribes. References to several *rājās* attending the assemblies can only be explained in terms of the attendance of a number of tribal chiefs at a meeting In the *Ṛgveda* (10.34) it is clearly stated that *rājā* is the commander (*senānī*) of the tribe (*gaṇa*) and the first (*prathama*) among the group (*vrāta*). He is the protector of the tribe (*gopo janasya*) and his function was basically that of a warlord. He led the tribe in battle and ensured their protection, in return for which the people rendered him obedience or presented voluntary gifts. In the earliest period, the chief probably did not raise only fixed taxes for maintenance of territory. When free from fighting he dispensed justice or performed sacrifices for material prosperity. In the *Ṛgveda* popular assemblies and institutions like Sabhā, Samiti and Vidatha (q.v) are mentioned. The chiefs went to the Samiti just as they went to the Sabhā (*RV* 9.92.6; 10.97.6), which had multifarious activities. The Samiti, however, was mainly a war-council, which the tribal chiefs had to attend: *rājānaḥ samitau iva*. In the later period of the Ṛgvedic age the tribal system began to disintegrate, giving rise to regular kingship and organized statehood. Originally the states were usually small, but due to wars and Dasyu menace, the tendency to coalesce under an overlord, or evolve bigger territorial units, had already stated. With the emergence of the larger realms, the importance of the royal rank also grew. This is reflected in the importance attached to, and elaboration of, the consecration ceremony itself, in which important state functionaries figured prominently. Kingship became hereditary in many cases. Even in the scanty notices of the *Ṛgveda* lines of succession, such as that of Vadhṛyaśva, Divodāsa, Pijavana and Sudās or Durgaha, Girikṣit, Purukutsa, and Trāsadasyu or Mitrātithi, Kuruśravaṇa and Upamaśravas can be traced. The activity of the king on which much stress is laid is his duty of protecting his subjects; and, even the *Ṛgveda*, despite sacerdotal and poetic character allows us to catch some glimpses of the warlike deeds of such men as Divodāsa, Sudās and Trāsadasyu. In the *Ṛgveda* we also come across terms which in later times were undoubtedly applied to non-monarchical constitutions. Thus, we have references to the *gaṇa* with the *gaṇapati* or *jyeṣṭha* (elder) at its head. The last probably corresponds to the *jetthaka* of the Pali texts, and it is not impossible that there were even in this early period the germs of the republican states of the type we meet with in the early Buddhist times. The word *bali* occurs several times in the *Ṛgveda*, in the sense of a tribute to the gods (1.70.9, 5.1.10, etc.) and to the king (7.6.5; 10.173.6). In some cases, election of the king by the cantons (*viśaḥ*) is indicated. The *viś* played a vital part in the political organization. In a geographical sense, the term means settlement or colonies and a group of these probably made up the *jana* or people. Politically, the *viśaḥ* were the subjects who constituted the *rāṣṭra* and who, foregathering a formal assembly, could unseat an incapable ruler or set the seal of approval on the coronation of a worthy one in an emergency. In a socio-economic sense, the *viśaḥ* represented the third class of the Vedic society, engaged in agriculture and commerce. It may be more safe to conclude that the members of a tribal unit were the *viśaḥ* constituting the *rāṣṭra* or tribal territory, later developed into kingdoms. Reference is also sometimes made to *jana*, another unit whose precise nature is not known. Below the *viś* came the *grāma* or village, which was the basic administrative unit. The *grāma* was probably made up of little knots of houses of several branches of one family (*kula*). The part played by the *kula* in the administrative organization is perhaps indicated by the description (*RV* 10.179.2-3) of a *kulapā* forming the entourage of a *vrājapati* (probably the same as the *grāmaṇī*) and fighting under his banner. The *grāmaṇī* exercised both civil and military functions. The *senānī* whose military authority at times of war is undeniable, probably discharged civil functions in times of peace, ranking higher than the *grāmaṇī*. Of other functionaries of the Ṛgvedic king, the *purohita* or priest should be mentioned. He accompanied the king to battle and seconded his efforts for victory by his prayers and spells. In the age of the later Saṃhitās and Brāhmaṇas, with a further development of organized statehood and monarchical form of government, as well as the concept of sovereignty, various theories were invented to rationalize the institution of kingship. Some kings of this period were styled *mahārāja* and *samrāṭ*. A few were described as great conquerers who celebrated their victories by performing Aśvamedha (q.v.), Rājasūya (q.v.) and Vājapeya (q.v.) sacrifices. The growing power of the king is illustrated by the tendency to attribute divinity to him. He was *adaṇḍya*, i.e. above ordinary punishment. He could rely upon regular taxation for the upkeep of the administration and could supplement it with extra exactions. Even then, in this age, in some cases kings were elected, as is attested by the *Atharvaveda* (1.9; 3.4; 4.22) which clearly refers to the election of the kings. But in most cases kingship was hereditary. The *Śatapatha Brāhmaṇa* (12.9.3.3) and *Aitareya Brāhmaṇa* (8.12) speak of a *daśa-puruṣamrājyam* or a kingdom of ten generations. There are hymns indicating that people had the power to punish a king (*PB* 6.5.5). The Sṛñjayas expelled their king Duṣṭaritu Pauṃsāyana from the kingdom inspite of his ten generations of royal descent. The popular control in the affairs of states was exercised as in the Ṛgvedic period, through the popular assemblies, Sabhā and Samiti, referred to in the later Saṃhitās and Brāhmaṇas in terms of which indicate an effective exercise of authority not only in the general administration but also over the person of the king (*AV* 7.12, *ŚB* 4.1.4.1-6, etc.). Various forms of royal dignity were known by such terms as Rājya, Sāmrājya, Vairājya, Svārājya, Bhaujya, Pārameṣṭhya, Māhārājya, Ādhipatya, Svāvasya and Atiṣṭhātva (*AB* 8.15). The monarch capable of lording over the whole subcontinent was to be known as Ekarāt. Frequent references to a large body of royal officials indicate the development of the administrative system during this period. Those who aided in the consecration of the king (see, Aśvamedha, Rājasūya and Vājapeya) were called Rājakartṛ or Rajakṛt, i.e. king-maker. In *Śatapatha Brāhmaṇa* (3.4.1.7, 13.2.18) the persons meant and specified are the *suta* (ministrel, chronicler of charioteer) and the *grāmaṇī* (leader of the host or of the village). The chief members of the royal household and the king's civil and military service were the *senānī* (commander of the army), *purohita* (royal chaplain), *mahiṣī* (chief queen), *kṣattṛ* (chamberlain), *samgrahitṛ* (treasurer), *bhāgadugha* (collector of royal share), *akṣāvāpa* (keeper of the dice), *govikartana* (king's companion in the chase), *pālāgala* (courier), *sūta* and *grāmaṇī* (*ŚB* 5.3.1.5). The *sthapati* was either the chief judge or a local chief. For the maintenance of the machinery of administration the king had the right to receive contributions and loyal service from his subjects. The reference to the 'share of village, horses and kine' in the *Atharvaveda* (4.22.2) and the frequent description of the king as 'devourer of the people' show that the extraction of *bali* or tax was quite in vogue and that the king's retinue was maintained by the contributions of, and extraction from, the people in the form of food grains and other necessities of life. The brāhmaṇas, however, claimed to be exempt from the normal exercise of royal authority, particularly in respect to taxation. In the later Vedic age, the Dharmasūtras prescribed a high intellectual and moral discipline and a sound military training for the king. Except legal taxes, the king was not authorized to take the property for his own use from the inhabitants of his realm (*VDS* 19.14). The taxes were regarded as 'pay' received the by king for protecting his subjects. It amounted to one-sixth of their income (*BDS* 1.10.18.19). The high position of the brāhmaṇas is indicated by several injunctions (*GDS* 8.1.11.1) In religious and many other matters, the king had to act according to the advice of the *Purohita*. We also hear of an influential body of brāhmaṇas forming a Pariṣad. Although its chief function was to advise the king on intricate and disputed points of law, it was probably a general body of advisers on all matters. The king's supreme duty was the protection of the people and maintenance of the rules of caste and order. According to *ĀpDS* (2.10.26.4), the king should 'appoint men of the first three castes, who are pure and truthful, over villages and towns.'

**Polyandry:** There is no clear passage in the *Ṛgveda* containing any clear reference to polyandry as a recognized social custom. The most that can be said is that occasionally verses are found in the *Ṛgveda* (10.85.37; 10.85.38) and the *Atharvaveda* (14.1.44.52.61; 14.2.14; 14.2.27), in which husbands are mentioned in relation to a single wife. It is difficult to be certain of the correct explanation of each separate instance of this mode of expression. In some passages (*ŚB* 2.6.2.14) the plural is simply generic.

**Polygamy:** *Vadhu* is a frequent term used for wife in the *Ṛgveda* (5.37.3; 5.47.6; 7.69.3; 8.26.13; 10.27.12; 10.85.30; 10.107.9) and the *Atharvaveda* (1.14.2, 4.20.3, 10.1.1, 14.2.9, etc.). But *vadhu* also denoted a woman either married or seeking a husband. The term *vahatu,* found in the same source, means the bridal procession. It also denotes a woman having been conducted to her home. The *Ṛgveda* (8.19.36) refers to a gift of fifty *vadhus* to the singer of hymns by Paurukutsa Trāsadasyu. Polygamy was recognized in the Vedic society. The first wife of the king was termed *mahiṣī* in the *Ṛgveda* (5.2.2; 5.37.3). According to the *Śatapatha Brāhmaṇa* (6.5.3.1), such a wife appears chiefly as one being first married. It is frequently mentioned in *Maitrāyaṇī Saṃhitā* (2.6.5; *KS* 15.4; *TS* 1.8.9.1; *PB* 19.1.4; *SB* 7.5.1.6, etc.). The *brahmā* addressed the queen *mahiṣī* in *Vājasaneyī Saṃhitā* (23.24). In *Śatapatha Brāhmaṇa* (13.2.9.7) there is a reference to a chief queen also. The woman first wedded had the greatest respect socially as per the views in *Maitrāyaṇī Saṃhitā* (3.3.1) and *Taittirīya Saṃhitā* (2.5.6.4). *Vāvātā* was a favourite category of wives and is frequently found in the *Aitareya Brāhmaṇa* (3.22; *TB* 1.7.3.3, 3.9.4.4; *ŚB* 13.2.6.5, 13.4.1.8). She is inferior to the *mahiṣī* only. Pālāgalī is a type of wives of the king in the *Taittirīya Brāhmaṇa* (1.7.3.3, 3.9.4.5; *ŚB* 13.4.1.8; 13.5.2.8). She might have been the daughter of a court official. A discarded wife is a former favourite of the king, but subsequently neglected. Owing to the low-caste origin, she did not take part in the ceremony, though her presence at the sacrifice as the daughter of a messenger of courier was required. According to another interpretation, *pālāgalī* meant one who had no son. *Parivṛkta, parivṛkti* and *parivṛtti* are the variant forms of the name of a rejected one among the royal wives. A Vedic Indian could have more than one wife. This is proved clearly by many passages in the *Ṛgveda* (1.62.11; 1.71.1; 1.104.3; 1.105.8; 1.112.19; 1.186.7; 6.53.4; 7.18.2; 7.26.3; 10.43.1; 10.101.11; cf. *AV* 3.4; *TS* 6.5.1.4); Manu, according to the *Maitrāyaṇī Saṃhitā* (1.5.8), had ten wives; and, the *Śatapatha Brāhmaṇa* (9.1.4.6) explains polygamy by a characteristic legend. But in the sacrifices the *patnī* is usually mentioned in the singular, apparent exceptions being due to some mythological reason (*TS* 2.5.6.4; *MS* 3.3.1).

**Polytheism:** The different parts of the *Ṛgveda* were composed at different times and it should not be regarded as a single text by one author, but rather as a whole literature accumulating for centuries; a library, as it were, in the making for years. No wonder then that we should find in the *Ṛgveda* thoughts, beliefs, and practices that one would associate with the most primitive grades of society and with an unsophisticated technique and advanced metaphysical speculation, indicating the deepest apprehension of the godhead and its relation to man. The *Ṛgveda* poets were deeply affected by the apparently mysterious working of the awe-inspiring forces of nature. In places, their hymns reflect that primitive attitude of mind which looks upon all nature as a living presence, or an aggregate of animated entities. The luminaries who follow a fixed course across the sky are the *devas* (lit, the shining ones) or gods. Naturally, the sense of the dependence of human welfare on the powers of nature gave them a 'supernatural' or divine character. At the same time the attempt of the human mind, more poetic than scientific, to account for the various forces and phenomena of nature with which man is confronted, led to the rise of myths when the imagination interprets a natural event as the action of a personified being resembling a human agent. The creative fancy of the Ṛgvedic poets goes on adding new touches to the picture, so that a natural phenomenon ultimately appears as a drama of human passions and not as an unintelligible and chaotic happening. The stage of anthropomorphism is thus reached. Ṛgvedic mythology is not as primitive as some scholars once believed it to be. In no other literary monuments of the world do we come across this primitive phase of the evolution of religious beliefs, which reveals the very process of personification by which natural phenomena developed into gods. In many cases the myths that have grown up around a deity are transparent enough to keep the physical basis almost in full view all the time. The name of the god often hides but little. Nevertheless, in cases where such a clear view of the original nature of a god is not possible, the etymological equations of comparative mythology have not proved to be the reliable guides that they were once supposed to be. In the hymns to the Dawn, the Sun and the Fire, among others, we are face to face with the corresponding physical phenomena directly exercising their powers. The process of personification makes gradual progress, and the personified phenomenon is deities and thus emerge the concrete figures of Uṣas, Sūrya, and Agni with whom the poet holds as it were, direct communion. We are not so fortunate in the case of the greatest figures of the Ṛgvedic pantheon, namely Varuṇa and Indra, regarding whose physical basis no certain conclusions have yet been arrived at. But in the case of a large number of Ṛgvedic gods, we are able to trace the original forces or agents in nature where the personification does not dominate the conception. The name of the deity is identical with that of the natural phenomenon, as in the case of Uṣas and Sūrya. Where the names differ, the personification is evidently advanced to the stage of anthropomorphism and apotheosis. V.M. Apte in Majumdar 363-4.

**Popular Assemblies:** See **Kingship, Pariṣad, Sabhā, Samiti, Vidatha**.

**Porcupine Quill:** Śalalī denotes the quill of the porcupine, used for parting the hair and anointing the eyes (*KS* 23.1; *TB* 1.5.6.6; *ŚB* 2.6.4.5).

**Porridge:** See **Food**.

**Portents:** See **Omens**.

**Post:** Post is indicated by the term *sthunā*. It is referred to in the *Ṛgveda* (1.59.1; 5.45.21; 5.62.7; 8.17.14; 10.18.13) and later (*AV* 3.12.6; 14.1.63; *ŚB* 14.1.3.7; 14.3.1.22). *Durya* (*RV* 1.91.19, *TS* 1.6.3.1, *VS* 1.11) is a door-post while *pakṣa* (*AV* 9.3.4) denotes side-post.

**Potsherd:** The word *kapāla* denotes a potsherd. It means to represent the fragments of a broken dish. The sacrificial cake was no doubt to be baked on a dish, but for symbolic reason the dish was to be broken up into a number of pieces (*JB* 1.94).

**Pottery:** The art of pottery was well-known in India in the Vedic age. The *Ṛgveda* (7.104.21; cf. 10.89.7) refers to the fact that Indra smashed the enemies like earthen pots, as an axe cut down trees. We hear of women carrying water in their jars, evidently earthen vessels in another place (*RV* 1.191.14). Vessels (*kalasāḥ*), obviously made of earth were used for offering *Soma* to Indra, as noted in the *Ṛgveda* (3.42.16; cf. 1.116.7-*śataṃ kumbhān*). Vessels (*RV* 1.117.6) were also used for storing honey and also gold (*RV* 1.117.12). It is interesting to note that the word *kulāla*, meaning a potter, is conspicuous by its absence in the *Ṛgveda*, but it appears in the Śatarudrīya hymn of the *Yajurveda* (*VS* 16.27; *MS* 1.8.3). The *Ṛgveda* (1.162.13) refers to vessels for holding meatjuice (*yuṣan*) and also to *ukhā*, a cooking pot which is distinctly mentioned as earthen (*mṛnmayī*) in the *Vājasaneyī Saṃhitā* (11.59) and *Taittirīya Saṃhitā* (4.1.5.4). The *Atharvaveda* (9.6.17) refers to earthen vessels more clearly. The word *kāṃsa* denotes a pot or vessel of metal. It is referred to in the *Atharvaveda* (10.10.5), *Aitareya Brāhmaṇa* (8.10), *Śāṅkhāyana Āraṇyaka* (12.8) and *Bṛhadāraṇyaka Upaniṣad* (6.3.1). *Kalasa* is referred to in the *Atharvaveda* (4.17.4), *Taittirīya Saṃhitā* (1.1.8.1, 4.1.54, 5.1.7.2) and *Vājasaneyī Saṃhitā* (22.11.59). *Kumbha* is referred to in the *Ṛgveda* (1.116.7, 1.117.6, 7.33.13), *Atharvaveda* (1.6.4, 3.12,7) and *Vājasaneyī Saṃhitā* (19.87).

**Pounding Stone:** A pounding stone to grind corn is mentioned as *dṛṣad* in the *Ṛgveda* (7.104.22, 8.7.4) and the *Atharvaveda* (2.31.2, 5.23.8). It is used together with *upala*, lower and upper stone or mortar pestle in the *Taittirīya Saṃhitā* (1.6.8.3, 1.6.9.3) and *Śatapatha Brāhmaṇa* (1.1.1.22, 32.6.1.9). The word *upala* means stone, on which *soma* was kept to be pressed by another stone, i.e. *adri* in the *Ṛgveda* (1.79.3, 10.94.5, 10.175.3) and the *Atharvaveda* (6.49.3).

**Prajāpati:** In the *Taittirīya Saṃhitā* it is stated that, in the beginning there was nothing but waters and Prajāpati as wind went over them or floated on a lotus leaf. According to a story found in the *Taittirīya Brāhmaṇa*, the urinary bladder of Prajāpati burst open and produced the ocean. One should not fail to recall in this connection the Hesodic version of the story of the emasculation of Uranus. Chronus, the youngest Titan, cut off his father's generative organ with a huge, sharp sickle, and the fluid that gushed out became the ocean. In the *Aitareya Brāhmaṇa* (5.32), it is stated that Prajāpati created the three worlds; the earth, the atmosphere and the sky. From these worlds three luminaries were born: Agni was born from the earth, Vāyu from the atmosphere and Āditya from the sky. Chronus of the Greek mythology also produced from his seed Fire, Air and Water, who in their turn begot the five families of gods. The personality of Prajāpati thus developed to a considerable extent in the Brāhmaṇa literature and he came to be identified with Rohita, the Ruddy-one or the Sun, (*AV* 13, 1-3; *TB* 2.52.2.1-3), with the Virile Bull (*AV* 4.11), and with other mythological conceptions. According to the *Taittirīya Saṃhitā* (7.1.5.1) Prajāpati, as wind, produced movement into waters and therein he saw the earth. Then, having taken the form of a boar, he seized the earth and, as Viśvakarman, laboured upon it and thus produced the gods, Vasus, Rudras and Ādityas. Elsewhere in the same text, he is explicitly mentioned as the supreme creator (1.7.1.5). The word Prajāpati, lord of creatures, was originally employed as an epithet of Savitṛ, Soma and Hiraṇyagarbha. It afterwards came to denote a separate deity who appears in three passages of the *Ṛgveda* (10.85.43; 169.4; 184.1). In the *Vājasaneyī Saṃhitā* (31.19.32.5), the god is referred to as a creative entity. It is said that he moves within the womb; before him nothing was born and in him all the worlds stand. Frequent mention of Prajāpati is found in the *Atharvaveda* (10.7.7 ff; 10.8.13) in which he is described as the founder of the world, which he produced by the half of his body. In one place of the same text, he is said to have formed thirty-three worlds out of the oblations of boiled rice (11.3.52), while in another he is identified with Prāṇa or breath (11.4.12). Still it appears that in the *Atharvaveda* he is not regarded as the supreme or primal deity; he is said to have been generated by the Brahmacārin (11.5.7) or by Kāla, i.e. time (19.53.8-10), and is declared to exist in the *ucchiṣṭa* or remnant of the sacrifice. However, in the *Brāhmaṇa* literature we have the fullest development of the conception of Prajāpati. In the *Śatapatha Brāhmaṇa* (2.2.4.1; 7.5.2.6; 1.5.8.1, etc.) Prajāpati is identified with the universe, and described as having alone existed in the beginning as the source out of which the creation was evolved. In the cosmogonic conception of Prajāpati, the principle of sexual dualism also has something to do. Vāk is associated with Prajāpati as his consort through whom he completes his work of creation. In the *Kāṭhaka Saṃhitā* (12.5; 27.1) in which Prajāpati is identified with the universe is stated that Vāk was his consort and out of their sexual union all beings were produced. The same theme is repeated in the *Pañcaviṃśa Brāhmaṇa* (20.14.2). In the Brāhmaṇa literature we have a variety of creation legends associated with Prajāpati. Thus, the *Aitareya Brāhmaṇa* (5.32) narrates; Prajāpati desired, 'May I be multiplied, may I be propagated.' He practised *tapas*, as a result of which he created the three worlds—the earth, the atmosphere and the sky. He brooded over these worlds, so three luminaries were born: Agni from the earth, Vāyu from the atmosphere and Āditya from the sky. He brooded over these luminaries, and so the *Ṛgveda* was born from Agni, the *Yajurveda* from Vāyu and the *Sāmaveda* from Āditya. He brooded over these Vedas, and so *bhūh* was born from the *Ṛgveda*, *bhuvaḥ* from the *Sāmaveda*. The creative activities of Prajāpati are sometimes regarded as a continuous process of sacrifice which exhausted him. Here we may refer to the following account from the *Pañcaviṃśa Brāhmaṇa* (4.10.1). Prajāpati, having created all creatures, became exhausted and lay down. The gods approached him and said, let us prepare for him a great ritual which will restore him. They offered unto him all food, cooked throughout the year, which restored him once again. In another passage of the same text (24.11.2), we find that Prajāpati faces calamity after completing his creation and somehow avoided the situation with the help of a sacrifice. In other texts also the creative process is described in terms of sacrifice or self-immolation. In the *Taittirīya Saṃhitā* (2.1.1) we come across the following legend: Prajāpati was alone. He desired to create and so took out the omentum from his body and offered it to the fire. From this a hornless goat was produced, which was offered as a sacrificial victim. Then he created men and beasts. In the *Taittirīya Brāhmaṇa* (2.2.9) we find a creation legend, which has some similarity with Heseoidic legend of the emasculation of Uranus: There was no existence of the Universe in the beginning. The non-existing entity desired to have a form and began to practise fervour, as a result of which smoke was produced. Then fire, flames and rays were produced in succession. All these again produced vapours, which were condensed like a cloud. That burst open the urinary bladder of Prajāpati, which produced the ocean. Then Prajāpati wept and his hot tears fell into the waters and became solid earth. In the *Śatapatha Brāhmaṇa* we have a number of creation legends. According to one (6.1.1.8 ff), Prajāpati wanted to become numerous, and practising fervour he created at first *Brahman* and then the triple science, which became his support. Resting on that support, he produced waters and entered them with that triple science. Thence arose an egg, which he touched. He said, let it exist, let it multiply. Then he created the earth out of the waters. He toiled and practised fervour and thus created foam, clay and saline, soil and sand, gravel, rock, ore, gold and plants, and with these he clothed the earth. In another passage of the same text (11.1.6), the waters seem to have believed to be coeval with Prajāpati or to have preceded him. In the beginning this universe was nothing but water. The waters desired, How can we reproduce? So saying, they toiled and performed austerity. While they were performing austerity, a Golden Egg came into existence. Being produced, it then became a year, wherefore this Golden Egg floated about for the period of a year. From it, Prajāpati came into existence. The impersonal *Brahman* took the place of the personal and more or less ritualistic figure of Prajāpati, the latter being absorbed in the former. The process of such an absorption is found even in the Brāhmaṇa literature. Although elevated to the position of the world creator, Prajāpati was yet conceived of as the Golden Germ floating upon waters, the eternally pre-existing substance. In the *Taittirīya*

*Saṃhitā* we are told that the waters were everything in the beginning. In them, Prajāpati produced movement as wind. Therein he saw the earth and, becoming a boar, he seized it and then, as Viśvakarman, he laboured upon it. In the next stage of the development of the cosmogonic conceptions, we find that Prajāpati is raised to the positions of the first principle. The *Taittirīya Brāhmaṇa* says that the body of Prajāpati formed the substance out of which everything was produced. But there are other passages which show that something must have existed independent of Prajāpati's creative activities. We have already quoted a passage from the *Śatapatha Brāhmaṇa* (10.3.5.11), which tells that there was nothing earlier and higher than the *Brahman*. In other passages of the same text (11.2.3.1 ff; 13.6.2.8), Prajāpati is identified with the *Brahman*. Bhattacharyya 1971. 25-32.

**Prāṇa:** Among the cosmogonic principle of the *Atharvaveda*, we have a reference to the abstract conception of *prāṇa* or breath (2.4). *Prāṇa* is described as the lord of all to whom the universe is subject and on whom all is supported. *Prāṇa* is identified with Prajāpati and other deities. *Prāṇa* of the earlier texts continued to develop as a cosmogonic principle in the *Upaniṣad* until it became identical with the *Brahman* (cf. *KauU* 2.1.12). The *Bṛhadāraṇyaka Upaniṣad* (1.4.7) speaks of the formless creator as having entered the body right upto the tips of the nails and assumed therein the name and function of *prāna*. In the *MaitU* (2.6) it is stated that in the beginning Prajāpati stood alone and they, by meditating upon himself, created numerous offsprings and animated them by dividing himself into five winds-*prāṇa, apāna, samāna, udāna* and *vyāna*. Several elements of the cosmos are found in the nature of the individual. Man is the meeting-point of the various stages of reality. *Prāṇa* corresponds to Vāyu, the breath of the body to the wind of the world. *Manas* or *ākāśa*, the mind of man to the space of the universe, the gross body to the physical elements. In the earlier elemental cosmologies what was demanded in the first cause was the ability to produce the effect, like water hardening itself into the earth. Pursuing this line of thinking, there was a steady but multifarious advance from a concrete physical cause like earth or water to an abstract cause like the *ākāśa* or the *Brahman*; to a ritualistic and thence a theistic principle like Prajāpati; but ultimately to a physiological first principle, like the *prāṇa* and the *ātman*-the last being the culminating point of the process.

**Precession:** Precession is an astronomical phenomenon, describing the motion of the pole of the equator in a small circle around the pole of the ecliptic. As a result, the equinoxes are not fixed and the first point of Aries has a backward motion along the equator, at the rate of 50.2″ annually. Due to precession, the first point of Aries of the vernal equinox moved and this fact has been stated in the *Ṛgveda* in the form of a story. Prajāpati fell in love with Rohinī (Aldebaran) and chased her, but the gods dissuaded him with their arrows. Ultimately, the sun gave shelter to this beautiful lady. Analyzing this story, we can recognize the knowledge Vedic seers had about precession. Prajāpati is a star at the apex of the constellation Orion, which is known as *kālapuruṣa*. The mighty personage who calculates time was introduced when Prajāpati was at the vernal equinox which, due to precession, shifted to the bright star Rohinī, the beautiful lady described in that story. The appearance of the sun and the shelter given to Rohinī clearly, indicate its association with the vernal equinox. This is also confirmed by the fact that Prajāpati chased Rohinī, i.e. the vernal equinox shifted towards Aldebaran.

**Presentation:** In the *Ṛgveda* (10.78.4) the term *vareyu* denotes a giving of presentation or boon to anybody. Sāyaṇa suggests this word to mean presentation of something to anybody. But relating to the *Ṛgveda* (10.78.4) this term indicates a law in a ritual sacrifice. The wealth is presented as a sacrificial process through the water sprinkled on the recipient.

**Price:** The two words used to denote price or value in the Ṛgvedic society are *śulka* and *vasna*. In the *Ṛgveda* (8.1.5) *śulka* clearly denotes a price. But from before Pāṇini's time it comes to be restricted to denote tax. According to the Dharma-sūtras it expresses a tax. The term is also found in a passage of the *Atharvaveda* (3.29.3). In the *Ṛgveda* (4.24.9) *vasna* means a greater price to be obtained on a thing of a lesser value. In the *Atharvaveda* (12.2.36), *Maitrāyaṇī Saṃhitā* (1.10.2), *Kāṭhaka Saṃhitā* (9.5), *Taittirīya Saṃhitā* (1.8.41) and *Vājasaneyī Saṃhitā* (3.49) the word seems to mean a price paid for anything. *Vasnika*, as formed from *vasna*, denotes a price in the *Pañcaviṃśa Brāhmaṇa* (14.3.13). It also denotes value or the thing itself or the object of purchase. In the *Ṛgveda* (10.34.3), we find at least one derivative form of the word *vasna* and that is *vasnya*, meaning costly. Pāṇini has recorded for posterity that the extended use of derivatives from it used to meet the more complex needs of the economic situation. By Kauṭilya's time, however, *vasna* was replaced by *mutya*.

**Priesthood:** *Ṛtv-ij* is the regular term for sacrificial 'priest', covering all the different kinds of priests employed at the sacrifice. The number of priests officiating at a sacrifice, with different functions, was mostly seven. The oldest list, in one passage of the *Ṛgveda* (2.1.2), enumerates their names as *hotṛ, potṛ, neṣṭṛ, agnidhra, praśāstṛ, adhvaryu, brahman*, besides the institutor of the sacrifice. The chief of the seven priests was the *hotṛ*, who was the singer of the hymns, and in the early times their composer also. The *adhvaryu* performed the practical work of the sacrifice, and accompanied his performance with muttered formulas of prayer and deprecation of evil. His chief assistance was derived from the *agnidhra*, the two performing the smaller sacrifices without the other's help in practical matters. The *praśāstṛ, upavaktṛ* or *maitrāvaruṇa*, as he was variously called, appeared only in the greater sacrifices as giving instructions to the *hotṛ* and as entrusted with certain litanies. The *potṛ, neṣṭṛ* and *brahman* belonged to the ritual of the *Soma* sacrifice, the latter being later styled *brāhmaṇācchaṃsin* to distinguish him from the priest who, in the later ritual, acted as supervisor. Other priests referred to in the *Ṛgveda* (8.81.5) are the singers of *sāmans* or chants, the *udgātṛ* and his assistant the *prastotṛ*, while the *pratihartṛ*, though not mentioned, may quite will have featured at a later stage of the ritual. In the development of the elaborate series of sacrificial calls on the one hand, and use of long hymns addressed to the Soma-plant on the other, there arose offices of other priests, such as the *acchāvāka* (*KB* 28.4; *AB* 6.14.8), the *grāvastut,* the *unnestṛ* and the *subrahmanya*, as known in a later ritual of the brāhmaṇas, making in all sixteen priests, being technically and artificially classed in four groups-*hotṛ, maitrāvaruṇa, acchāvāka* and *grāvastut*; *udgātṛ prastotṛ, pratihartṛ* and *subrahmnya, adhvaryu, pratiprasthātṛ, neṣṭṛ* and *unnetṛ; brahman, brāhmaṇācchaṃsin, agnīdhra* and *potṛ*. Apart from all these priests was the *purohita*, who was the spiritual adviser of the king in all his religious duties (*RV* 1.44.10, 1.94.8, 8.27.1). As a rule the *purohita* took the part of the *brahman*, i.e. as supervisor in all the great royal sacrifices. In the *Ṛgveda* (2.24.9), Bṛhaspati is the *purohita* of the gods. In the *Ṛgveda* (10.150.5) Vasiṣṭha is the *purohita* of Sudās Paijavana, and in the *Śāṅkhāyana Śrautasūtra* (15.21) he was the *brahman* of the Śunaḥśepa sacrifice. The *purohita* was normally the hotṛ, the singer of the most important song. It was only later that the *brahman,* in his capacity as the supervisor of the rite, acquired the function of general supervisor, which was for long exercised by the *purohita*, who was endowed with skill and power of guarding the sacrifice against any evil. In this sense Agni is designated pre-eminently as a *hotṛ* and also a *purohita* in the *Ṛgveda* (1.1.1; 3.3.2; 3.11.1; 5.11.2). In the Āprī hymns (*RV* 10.66.13 and 10.70.7), Agni's two divine *hotṛs* are called the divine *purohitas.* The *Aitareya Brāhmaṇa* (7.20) recognizes explicitly the rule that a king should have a *brahman* as a *purohita*. The *Taittirīya Saṃhitā* (3.5.2.1) confirms the special claim of the Vasiṣṭha family to the office of *brahman-purohita*, which proves that the *purohitas* first exchanged the function of *hotṛ* for that of *brahman* in the sacrificial ritual. Examples of *purohitas* in the *Ṛgveda* are Viśvāmitra in (3.33.53) and Vasiṣṭha in (7.18.83), in the service of the Bharata king Sudās of the Tṛtsu family. The function of the office of the *purohita* was to advise the king in all religious matters as his alter ego, to ensure the king's safety and victory in battle by his prayers, to procure rain for the crops and also to arrange for protection of the kingdom. As a general rule, a *purohita* was to serve one king at a time. But in some cases one *purohita* served more than one king, as for instance Devabhāga. Śrautarṣa was the *purohita* of the Kurus and the Sṛñjayas at the same time (*ŚB* 2.4.4.5). There is no certain proof that the office of the *purohitas* was hereditary in a family, though it was probably so. King Kuruśravaṇa and his son Upamasravas in the *Ṛgveda* (10.33) kept the same *purohita*, Kavaṣa. The influence of the priesthood was great, of which the Dānastutis bear indirect testimony. Special reference may also be made to the following verses (*RV* 4.59.7-9). That king, indeed, overpowers all opposing forces with his valour and might who maintains Bṛhaspati (the brāhmaṇa priest) well attended, and praises and honours him as (a deity) deserving the first share (of the homage due). He (that king) verily abides, well established in his own place; to him, the holy food flows forever; to him the *viśaḥ* bow down of their own accord, the king with whom the brāhmaṇa takes precedence. Irresistible, he wins the riches of his enemies and his kinsmen; the king who provides protection for the brāhmaṇa desiring help from him, the gods help. There is hardly any material difference in this passage and the power of the *purohita* over a king, which is associated in our minds with the later stages of political history when the caste system was fully developed. Eventually, under diverse historical conditions, royalty was glorified and regal authority deified through priestly support. This brought the latter to the forefront. The representative of the sacerdotal order, the *purohita* came to the front rank of the state functionaries and, as a class, brāhmaṇas came to be regarded with veneration and styled as mundane gods (*ŚB* 2.2.2.6). This was due to their close connection with the ceremony which brought moral sanction to royal authority and gave the anointed prince a sacred character. Allusions to the fixation of the king's becoming the son of the sacrificial priest show the importance of priesthood. The *purohita* stood out foremost and was regarded as the alter ego of the king. If the king was the counterpart of Indra and Varuṇa, he was the incarnation of Bṛhaspti and performed the Bṛhaspatisava (*TB* 2.7.2). He was regarded as half of the king and his blessings brought victory in war. He appeased the gods and without him they did not accept the food offered by a king. At the intercession of the *purohita*, the gods protected the kingdom (*AB* 8.26). So a king was to consecrate a *purohita* and this man was to be looked upon as protector of the kingdom (*rāṣṭra gopa*), the one who conferred energy, granted success and made the people loyal and prosperous (*AB* 8.25). Thus, the *purohita* was not a mere priest. He presented moral authority and was an adviser on important affairs of state. He seems to have accompanied the king in battle on his chariot and it was he who, on behalf of the common people, administered the oath, both in the ordinary coronation and in the Aindra Mahābhiṣeka. As such, he was honoured by the king who accepted him as a superior and washed his feet in submission to his authority. Privileges were conferred on him as well as on the brāhmaṇas. His life was sacred, like the Tribunes in Rome. Transgression meant death or deposition to kings. As champion of the moral principle, he exercised co-ordinate authority with the king and he, together with the brāhmaṇas, claimed absolution from regal authority which embraced everything else in this world. This would appear from the formula uttered by the brāhmaṇas at the end of royal consecration that the king was lord of everything but not of the brāhmaṇas.

**Primitive Chaos:** Perceiving light and form and colour and beauty emerge slowly every morning out of a gloom in which all objects had before appeared to be confounded. The early speculator might conceive that, in like manner, the brightness and order of the world around him had sprung necessarily out of an antecedent night, in which the elements of all things had existed together in indistinguishable water. That One which lay in void, and wrapped in nothingness, was developed by the power of fervour. Desire, first arose in it, which was the primal germ of mind. The creative *kāma*, the conception of which is further developed in the *Atharvaveda* (9.2, etc.) corresponds strikingly and curiously with the cosmogonic Eros of the Greeks. Almost in the same language of the *Ṛgveda*, Hesiod writes: From chaos were generated Erebos and Black Night, and from Night again were generated Ether and Day whom she brought forth, having conceived from the embrace of Erebos **Theogony**, 143 ff.

**Princes:** The term *rāja-putra*, which denotes 'king's son' or prince, seems to be capable of being interpreted literally in every passage of the older literature (*RV* 10.40.3; *AB* 7.17.6; *PB* 19.1.4; *KS* 14.8; *TB* 3.8.51.1; *ŚB* 13.4.2.5) in which it is found, though it may also be capable of a wider interpretation (*KS* 28.1). Later the term *rājaputra* degenerated into a mere land-owner'.

**Procreation:** In the *Ṛgveda* (10.129.4) *kāma*, denoting desire, is said to have been the first movement arising in the One. It is, mentioned as a great cosmogonic force in the *Atharvaveda* (9.2). The conception of sexual dualism, in terms of procreative process, has given much importance to the *kāma* doctrine as a principle of the creative process frequently formed by such terms as *jan, sṛj, garbha*, etc. In the *Śatapatha Brāhmaṇa* we come across numerous passages in which sexual union is identified with sacrifice (1.9.2.7; 1.9.2.11; 6.4.3.7; 6.6.2.8; 6.6.1.11; etc.). In the *Chāndogya Upaniṣad* (2.1-3) it is said that, 'He who knows thus this *vāmadvya sāman* as woven upon coupulation, comes to copulation, procreates himself with every copulation, reaches a full length of life, lives long, becomes great in offspring and cattle, great in fame' (Hume's tr.). The *Bṛhadāraṇyaka Upaniṣad* (6.4.3) says that the lower portion of a woman is to be considered as the sacrificial alter, the pubic hairs as the sacrificial grass, the outer-skin as the flow for the pressing of the *soma* plant, and the two labia of the vulva as the innermost fire. He who remembers this during copulation gets the reward of Vājapeya sacrifice. These are the sources of later Tantric *dehavāda* and Sāṅkhya dualism. The primitive empirical and analogical belief, and the equation of earth and woman, of natural and human fertility invariably connects the mystery of nature with that of human body, from which it transpires that the birth of the universe is the result of the same or similar process as the birth of the human beings.

**Pronunciation:** The *Śikṣā* texts of Vedāṅga are devoted to the means of instruction particularly in reciting as well as the correct pronunciation and accentuation of the Saṃhitā texts. In the *Taittirīya Upaniṣad* (1.2) there is a mention of this Vedāṅga, wherein the teaching of the letters, the accounts of the quantity of syllables, the stress, the melody and the compilation of words in continuous recitation are enumerated.

**Propitiatory Verses:** The propitiatory verses, called *āprīs*, are the offering formulas of the eleven or twelve fore-offerings as *prayāja* of the animal sacrifice. The twelve verses accounted in the *Vājasaneyī Saṃhitā* (20.55-66) are used on the occasion, there being in the second and third places fore-offerings both in Tanūnapāt or Narāsaṃśa. In each of these verses, again three deities, Aśvins, Sarasvatī and Indra, are referred to. The *āprī*-formulas are in *anuṣṭubha* verses and pronounced at the offerings of the animal sacrifice.

**Prostitution:** See **Hetairai**.

**Protective Armour:** The use of protective armour can be found in the *Ṛgveda* as well as the later texts. The common word denoting a coat of mails in the *Ṛgveda* 1.31.15 is *varman*. References may also be found to the wearing of the armour in the *Ṛgveda* (10.101.8), though the material it was made from has not been specified. It may have been in the form of a leather corselet reinforced with metal. The *Ṛgveda* (6.27.6) speaks of a mailed warrior falling before the arrows, like bursting vessels. The *Jaiminīya Upaniṣad Brāhmaṇa* (4.1.3) mentions corselets of *ayas, loha* or *rajata*, whether it was of leather or metal or both. The armour of the early Aryans was considered to be of great importance to provide protection against the weapons of the day. In the *Atharvaveda* 11.10.22 and *Vājasaneyī Saṃhitā* 16.45 *kavacin* (in *AB* 13.1.6.3. 2.2.7; 4.1.5) the word *kavaca* is used for a corselet or breast-plate. A *kavaca pāśa* or corselet-strap was used to keep *kavaca* in a particular place of the body, as laid down in the *Atharvaveda* (11.10.22).

**Pṛthivī:** Among the terrestrial deities Pṛthivī is so closely associated with Dyaus that, generally, they are celebrated conjointly. Dyaus is never lauded alone in any hymn, while Pṛthivī is invoked alone only in one short hymn of three stanzas (*RV* 5.84). The personification is so slight that the attributes are mainly those of the physical earth. In the *Atharvaveda* an entire hymn (12.1) is dedicated to Pṛthivī. The hymn runs sixty-three verses and at the end, the poet, dissolving in rapture and gratitude, pours out his heart in these simple words: 'O Mother Earth, settle me down and kindly make me well-established; In concord with heaven, O sage, settle me in splendour and glory'. There are many passages in which all the terrestrial objects are described as being sprung from Heaven and Earth (*RV* 1.106.3; 1.58.1; 1.185.4; 4.56.2; 6.17.7; 7.53.1; 7.97.8; 10.2.7; 10.11.9). Heaven and Earth (Dyaus and Pṛthivī) are regarded as the parents not only of the gods, but of the men also (*RV* 1.159.2; 1.160.2; 1.185.1).

**Pulinda:** Name of a people mentioned with the Andhras in the *Aitareya Brāhmaṇa* (7.18). Like Niṣādas, Kirātas, etc., the Pulindas was the generic name of some indigenous tribes. The Pulindas again appear associated with the Andhras in the time of Aśoka.

**Pulses:** See **Grains**.

**Puṇḍra:** Name of the people that lived outside the area of Vedic culture, mentioned in the *Aitareya Brāhmaṇa* (7.18., *ŚŚS* 12.26). Their name occurs in the Sūtras (*BDS* 1.2.14). In the epic tradition, they were classed with the eastern tribes and were located in northern Bengal.

**Puru:** Name of a people and their king in the *Ṛgveda*. They are mentioned with the Anus, Druhyus, Turvaśas, and Yadus in one passage (1.108.8). They also occur as enemies of the Tṛtsus in the hymn of the victory of Sudās. In another hymn (*RV* 7.8.4), Agni of the Bharatas is celebrated as victorious over the Purus, probably a reference to the same decisive victory. On the other hand, victories of the Purus over the indigenous tribes seem to be referred to in several passages (*RV* 1.50.6, 131.4, 174.2, 4.21.10, 38.1, 6.20.10, 7.5.3, 19.3). The great kings of the Purus were Purukutsa and his son Trāsadasyu, whose names bear testimony to their prowess against local foes, while a later prince was Tṛkṣī Trāsadasyava. In the *Ṛgveda* the Purus are expressly (7.96.2) mentioned as residing along the Sarasvatī, most probably eastern Sarasvatī in the Kurukṣetra region. This view accords well with the sudden disappearance of the name of the Purus from Vedic tradition, as disappearance that accounted for the Purus becoming part of the great Kuru people, just as Turvaśa and Krivi disappear on their being merged in the Pañcāla nation. Trāsadasyava, the patronymic of Kuruśravaṇa in the *Ṛgveda* 910.33.4), shows that the royal families of the Kurus and the Purus were allied by inter-marriage. In later times the Purus lived in the eastern country round the Sarasvatī and in earlier days they were to be found to the west of the Indus with Divodāsa. It might, however, be held to be supported by the fact that Alexander found a Puruva prince on the Hydaspes, a sort of halfway locality between the Sarasvatī and the west. In several other passages of the *Ṛgveda* (1.36.1; 1.129.5; 4.39.2; 5.17.1; 6.46.8; 10.4.1; 48.5) the Purus are also found.

**Puruṣa:** In the *Puruṣa-sūkta* of the *Ṛgveda* (10.90) we have the conception of a male spirit, who is transformed or who transforms himself into the world, like the giant Yimer of the Teutons. The Ṛgvedic conception of Puruṣa was originally that of a human shape, from whose limbs all the constituents of the universe emanated. In later works Puruṣa began to be identified at first with Prāṇa or breath (*ŚB* 13.6.2.1, etc.), the sign of life, and then with some elementary concepts of soul (*Kaṭha* 2.1.12-3; 2.31.17; *Śvet* 3.13; 5.8; etc.). Further, when the idea of a World-Soul or Virāṭ-Puruṣa in the macrocosm came to be formulated, the individual existences in the world were looked upon as issuing from the dismembered limbs of that Puruṣa in the act of primordial sacrificial immolation. This idea may be traced in the *Puruṣa-sūkta* mentioned above, but it is further developed in the Upaniṣads (cf. *CU* 3.16.1). The Puruṣa-sūkta equates the cosmic elements, such as fire, sun, etc., with the head, eye and other limbs of the Puruṣa, while later passages found in some Upaniṣads turn each limb into a Puruṣa. It is in the *Puruṣa-sūkta* (10.90) that we come across the most thorough-going elevation of the sacrifice into a world-principle. Besides the said hymn, as the subject of sacrifice, there are two other hymns in which the deity is represented as either the agent or the object (*RV* 10.81.5; 10.130.2-3; cf. *Nirukta* 10.26 on the sacrifice of Viśvakarman). It is not very easy to find out the precise idea in the *Puruṣa-sūkta*. It was written at a period when the sacrificial ceremony had largely developed and when a mystical meaning was attached to the various materials and instruments of the ritual. The Puruṣa is described as having a thousand heads and eyes and a thousand feet and is equated with the universe. This is, in all probability, a secondary development of the original conception. Then, we are told that all the regions sprang from this Puruṣa, who became diffused everywhere among things animate and inanimate. Then, we have a myth of reciprocal generation of Virāj from Puruṣa and again of Puruṣa from Virāj. This *vījāṅkura-nyāya* (the maxim of seed and plant) has also been applied to Aditi and Dakṣa (10.72.4). Virāj is another cosmogonic principle whose better conception is found in later works. The above myth is evidently to harmonize more than one principles arising from different sources. In the second part of the *Puruṣa-sūkta* it is stated that the gods offered upon this Puruṣa as the victim for a sacrifice. His body was divided in many parts. The brāhmaṇa was his mouth, the rājanya his arms, the vaiśya his thigh and the śūdra his feet. The moon was produced from his soul; the sun from his eye; Indra and Agni from his mouth; Vāyu from his breath; atmosphere from his naval; sky from his head; earth from his feet; and the four quarters from his ear. The conception of Puruṣa has an interesting history. The *Puruṣa-sūkta* was evidently composed at a period when the ceremony of sacrifice had largely developed and a mystical meaning had come to be attached to the ritualistic implements and to the different members of the victim. The *Atharvaveda* (10.2) contains a long hymn on the conception of Puruṣa. Here Puruṣa is conceived as a Man, the embodiment of the male principle that has probably some part to play in the matter of creation. In the *Vājasaneyī Saṃhitā* (31.18; 32.2), Puruṣa is described as a resplendent principle pervading the universe. In the *Śatapatha Brāhmaṇa* (13.6.1.1) the word Nārāyaṇa is coupled with Puruṣa and it is said that this being desired to surpass all and become the entire universe. In Yāska's *Nirukta* (2.3) it is stated that universe is filled up by the Puruṣa, to whom there is nothing superior and from whom there is nothing different. In the Brāhmaṇa literature, however, we do not find that Puruṣa is equated with *Brahman* although in one place he is identified with Prajāpati. The distinct denotation of Puruṣa is more clearly brought out by certain ritualistic and other statements made about him in the Brāhmaṇas. Thus in the *Śatapatha Brāhmaṇa* (6.2.2.9), Puruṣa is described as a human being with ten Prāṇas, four limbs, a trunk, a neck and a head. In the *Aitareya Brāhmaṇa* (2.14) and the *Gopatha Brāhmaṇa* (6.6.8), the brain, hair, skin, flesh, etc., of the Puruṣa are mentioned. In the *Pañcaviṃśa Brāhmaṇa* (23.14.5) we have reference to his hand and feet. This clearly shows that Puruṣa was conceived in the form of a human being and as an agent of creation he served the purpose of a male principle. The conception of Puruṣa as the male principle of creation finds its best expression in the Sāṅkhya. In the *Bṛhadāraṇyaka Upaniṣad* (1.4) it is stated that in the beginning this world was *ātman* alone in the form of Puruṣa; he was afraid of his lonely existence and so divided himself into two parts, male and female and as a result of their copulation human beings were produced. The *ātman* is called Puruṣa because he had the capacity to burn (*us*) all sins (*pāpman*). A passage in the *Kaṭha*, which gives us a gradation of existences, tells that beyond the senses is the mind; beyond the mind is intellect; beyond intellect is the *mahat ātman*; beyond the *mahat ātman* is the *avyakta*; beyond the *avyakta* is the great Puruṣa; and beyond the Puruṣa is nothing else (3.10.1). Puruṣa is generally conceived in the Upaniṣads as consisting of sixteen parts. In the *Muṇḍaka* (2.1-10), Puruṣa is conceived as a primeval person who is heavenly (*divya*), formless (*amūrta*), breathless (*aprāṇa*) and pure (*śubhra*). From him are born in order Prāṇa, mind, the senses, ether, air, light, water and earth. It is from this macrocosmic person that the Vedas are born. He is the source of the world and the individual, of all religions, of all religious rites, of all forms of existence and of all activities of senses. In fact, all the earthly and celestial existences, along with all moral physical and psychical qualities are described as having proceeded from the primeval bodiless Puruṣa. In the *Śvetāśvatara*, Puruṣa is mentioned as the first principle (1.2) and is described as the macrocosmic person with superhuman powers (3.11-19). Side by side with the macrocosmic conception of the Puruṣa, we come across another animistic conception. Thus, in the *Kaṭha*, Puruṣa is endowed with a subtle, corporeal appearance of the sizes of the thumb. In the *Śvetāśvatara* (3.13; 5.8) Puruṣa is also described as having the measure of a thumb and as being identical with the inner soul (*antarātman*). However, the idea of a world soul or *Virāṭ-Puruṣa* came to be formulated even earlier than the Upaniṣads. The earlier passages equate the cosmic elements like fire, sun, etc., with the head, eye and other limbs of the *Virāṭ-Puruṣa*. The later passages turn each of the elements into a Puruṣa controlled by the *ātman* residing in all of them. The transmission from the category of Puruṣa to that of *atman* is clearly shown in many passages of the Upaniṣads. For example, in the *Bṛhadāraṇyaka Upaniṣad* (3.9.26), *ātman* is designated as the 'Upaniṣadic Puruṣa'. Elsewhere in the same text (2.5.1. ff), the shining immortal Puruṣa, who is in this earth and the shining immortal Puruṣa who is in the body, are both declared to be other than the immortal *ātman* or *Brahman*. Similarly in the *Chāndogya Upaniṣad* (3.12.7), the space within the Puruṣa is equated with that within the heart. In two other passages of the said work (4.15.5-6; 5.10.1), Puruṣa is described to be a non-human (a-*mānava*) entity, leading everything on to the *Brahman*.

**Pūṣan:** Pūṣan is a god with a very interesting personality, the anthropomorphic details being very few. He has a beard and braided hair. His chariot is drawn by goats and he carries a golden spear, an awl and a goad. His favourite food is *karambha* (gruel). He is connected with marriage in the wedding hymn (*RV* 10.35). He acts as the envoy of Sūrya with his golden aerial ships, and as a charioteer drives downward the golden wheel of the sun. He is a guardian of the roads, the deliverer, *par excellence*, from danger, and takes care of cattle. *Aghriṇī* (shining) is an exclusive epithet of his. It is very probable that he was originally a solar deity, standing for the beneficent power of the sun, manifested chiefly in its pastoral aspect. The *Ṛgveda* 1.38.4; 1.7.47; 1.42.1-3; 1.115.2; 1.162.2.3; 1.115.1; 2.40.4; 2.40.6; 3.52.1; 3.52.7; 3.55.19; 3.56.6; 3.62.9; 6.17.6; 6.57; 6.55.2; 6.55.3.4; 6.58.2; 7.60.2; 9.67.10; 10.85; 10.187.4; the *Atharvaveda* 16.9.2; 18.2.53; 6.112.3; the *Taittirīya Brāhmaṇa* 1.7.2.4.

# Q

**Quack:** Quack means ignorant pretender to skill, especially in relation to medical practice. The physicians of the *Atharvaveda* apparently seem to be quacks, but they were not really pretenders. Their philosophy of medicine and treatment was magical. Notwithstanding their shortcomings, one has to admit that the magical system of treatment of diseases had its historical role, and it supplied the basis, however primitive and fanciful it might have been, for the later development of medical science, which was elaborated in the Saṃhitās of Caraka and Suśruta.

**Quadrupeds:** See **Animals**.

**Quail:** Quails are known as *laba* in the Vedic literature (*MS* 3.14.3; *VS* 24.24; *Nirukta* 7.3) They are mentioned as victims in the Aśvamedha or horse sacrifice. There is a Ṛgvedic legend that the Aśvina rescued a quail from the mouth of a wolf, the symbolism of which is not clear. May be the quail represents the diseased person, and the wolf the disease.

**Quarters:** The worship of the guardian deities of the quarters is mentioned in the Sūtra literature. The cardinal points lead very slowly upto more adequate conceptions of space and time. The idea of the quarters is found in the Upaniṣads. In the *Jaiminīya Upaniṣad Brāhmaṇa* (3.2) it is stated that Ka or Prajāpati swallows fire, moon, sun and the Quarters. There are the cosmic parallels and the Quarters are equated with space. The *Maitrāyanī Upaniṣad* (6.2) describes *ākāśa* as a lotus whose leaves are the four quarters and the four intermediate quarters or cardinal points. Keith 213 ff.

**Queen:** The monarch during the *Brāhmaṇa* period was usually allowed to have four queens, viz., the Mahiṣī, the Parivṛkti, the Vāvātā and the Pālāgalī. The Mahiṣī was the chief wife, being the first one married according to the *Śatapatha Brāhmaṇa* (6.5.3.1). The Parivṛkti was the neglected or discarded wife, probably one that had no son. The Vāvātā was the favourite, while the Pālāgalī was the daughter of a court official. The *Aitareya Brāhmaṇa* (7.13), however, refers to the 'hundred' wives of the king Hariścandra. In the sacrifices of royal inauguration such as the Rājasūya, the Aśvamedha and the Vājapeya the queens had important parts to play. In the Aśvamedha, on the return of the horses, the victim was anointed by the chief of the queens. The horse was covered with a garment and slain. The queens went round it from left to right thrice, and thrice the other way round; the chief queen went near the horse; both were covered with a garment, and the queen united with it. Meanwhile, the priest and the maidens and the other wives indulged in ribald dialogue. In the Rājasūya, each of the four queens represents a class of woman in the sacrificial assembly. In the Vājapeya the priest brought the sacrificer's wife, who was wrapped in a garment of *darbha* and caused her to propitiate the sacrifice. The company of the wife was intended to make the sacrifice perfect. A ladder was fixed in which the king and the queen ascended thereafter they touched a wheaten head-piece and muttered, 'we have gone to the light, to the gods, we have become immortal'. Apart from this the queens had many other minor rituals to perform in connection with the grand sacrifices of royal inauguration.

**Quiver:** The quiver was called *iṣudhi* in the *Ṛgveda* and later (1.33.3; 6.75.5; 10.95.3; *AV* 2.33; 4.10.6). The *Ṛgveda* shows how it was slung on the back, though the later practice of carrying two quivers is nowhere in evidence.

# R

**Race:** Racing, especially horse-racing, was a favourite sport of the Vedic Indians and the term by which it is denoted is *āji*, which is frequently used in the *Ṛgveda* (5.37.7; 6.24.6; etc.,). The race course was called *kāṣṭhā* in the *Ṛgveda* (8.80.8) and *Atharvaveda* (2.14.6) or *āji* itself in the *Ṛgveda* (4.24.8) and *Atharvaveda* (13.2.4). It is described in the *Atharvaveda* (2.14.6; 13.2.4) as quasi-circular. In the *Ṛgveda* the course is described as broad (*urvi*) and the distance is measured out. Prizes for victory were offered and eagerly competed for the *Ṛgveda* (1.81.3, etc.). Other words for victory and the prize were *kara Ṛgveda* (5.29.8, 9.14.1) and *bhara*. To run a race is described by various expressions (*AS* 2.25; *ŚB* 2.4.3.4, etc.). A person who instituted a race is referred to as *āji-kṛt* (*ŚB* 5.1.5.10, etc.). Indra is called *āji-kṛt* or race-maker and *āji-pati* or lord of the race (*RV* 8.53.6, 8.53.14). The swift steeds (*vājin, ātya*) used for race were often washed and adorned (*RV* 2.34.3, 9.109.10, 10.68.11). A formal race was a feature of the ritual of Rājasūya.

**Racism:** See **Asuras, Dāsas, Dasyus, Non-Vedic Tribes**.

**Raikvaparṇa:** Name of a locality in the Mahāvṛṣa country according to the *Chāndogya Upaniṣad* (4.2.5).

**Raiments:** See **Clothings**.

**Rainy Season:** The term *varṣā* denotes primarily 'rain' (*RV* 5.58; 7.83.10; *AV* 3.27.6, 4.15.2, etc.), then 'rainy season' (*AV* 6.55.2; *TS* 1.6.2.3, 2.6.1.1, 5.6.10.1; *VS* 10.12, etc.) and 'year' (*AB* 4.17.5; *ŚB* 1.9.19 etc.). *Prāvṛs* is the name of the 'rainy season' in the *Ṛgveda* (7.103.3, 9) and later (*AV* 12.1.46; *KS* 3.6.2; *TB* 1.8.4.2; *ŚB* 5.5.2.3, 7.2.4, etc.). The term *madhya-varṣā*, which denotes the 'middle of the rains', is specially mentioned as a time of the year in the *Kauṣitaki Brāhmaṇa* (1.3) and in the *Sūtras* (*ŚŚS* 3.5.5.7).

**Rākā:** A goddess with an unfailing needle, who is invoked in the *Ṛgveda* (2.32.4) to bestow wealthy heroic sons, various kinds of food (2.32.5) and benevolence (*RV* 2.32.8) , along with Sinīvālī, Guṅgu, Sarasvatī, Indrāṇī, Varuṇāṇī and Bṛhaddivā, Sāyaṇa says that Rākā is the full moon. (*Ṛgveda* 5.42.12; *Taittirīya Saṃhitā* 1.8.1.1; 3.4.9.1, 4; *Kāṭhaka Saṃhitā* 12.8, *Aitareya Brāhmaṇa* 3.37, *Pañcaviṃśa Brāhmaṇa* 16.13.1.)

**Rākṣasa:** The term normally refers to demons, and is only metaphorically (*Ṛgveda* 3.30.15-17; 7.104.1) applied to human foes. In the Vedic texts the term *rākṣasas*, however, has not been applied with reference to any particular tribe whose cults and rituals were opposed to those of the Vedic Indians. In later literature the term came to denote demonical beings. Since the term is derived from *rakṣ*, meaning 'protection', they were probably a people who claimed to have been the protectors of indigenous cults and rituals.

**Rampart:** The term for rampart is *pur*, which appears frequently in the *Ṛgveda* (1.53.7; 1.58.8; 1.131.4; 1.160.8; 3.15.4; 4.27.1) and later (*TB* 1.7.7.5; *AB* 1.23, 2.11; *ŚB* 3.4.4.3; 6.3.3.25; 11.1.1.2-3). Such fortifications were occasionally of considerable size as one is called *pṛthvī* or broad and *urvī* or wide (*RV* 1.189.2). Elsewhere (*RV* 4.30.20), a fort made of stone (*aśmanmayī*) is mentioned. Sometimes 'strongholds of iron' (*āyasi*) are referred to (*RV* 1.58.8; 2.20.8; 4.27.1; 7.8.7; 7.15.4; 7.95.1; 10.101.8). A fort full of cattle is mentioned (*AV* 8.6.23), as also autumnal forts (*śāradī*) are named. Forts 'with a hundred walls' (*śatabhujī*) are spoken of (*RV* 1.166.8; 7.15.14). The siege of forts is also mentioned (*RV* 7.5.3; *TS* 6.2.3.1; *AB* 1.23; *ŚB* 3.4.4.3-5; *GB* 2.2.7). *Dehī* in two passages of the *Ṛgveda* 96.47.2, 7.6.5) also refers to rampart.

**Rank:** See **War**. For social hierarchy see **Caste**. For Administration see **Royal Officers**.

**Ransom:** See **Wergeld**.

**Rape:** In the *Ṛgveda* (4.30.8-11) the poet does not hesitate to admire the heroism of Indra in raping Uṣas: 'This Indra, was a deed of might and manliness which thou didst achieve that thou didst smite the daughter of the sky (Uṣas), a woman who was bent on evil. Thou Indra, the great (god) didst crush Uṣas, though the daughter of the sky, who was exalting herself. Uṣas fled away in terror from her shattered car, when the vigorous (Indra) had crushed it. This chariot of hers lies broken and dissolved while she herself has fled afar'. (Muir's trans.). The story of the rape of Uṣas by Indra is repeated in many passages of the *Ṛgveda* (2.15.6; 10.73.3; 10.138.5).

**Rasā:** Found in the three passages of the *Ṛgveda* (1.112.12; 5.53.9; 10.75.6), clearly as the name of a real stream in the extreme north-west, of the Vedic territory. It is the Jaxartes; *Vendidad* mention it as Ranhā, which is the Avestan form of the Rasā.

**Rātri:** Rātri, Night, is invoked in one hymn of the *Ṛgveda* (10.127). Like her sister Dawn, she is called the daughter of Heaven. She is not conceived as dark, but as the bright starlit night. She shines manifold with her eyes. Decked with all splendour, she fills the valleys and heights, driving away the darkness with light. At her approach men return home like birds to their nests. She is invoked to keep away the wolf and the thief, guiding her worshippers to safety. Night probably became a goddess by way of being the antithesis of Dawn, with whom she is invoked in several verses as a dual divinity. Macdonell, 124.

**Real, Reality:** The term *sat* or 'existent' has been used in the *Ṛgveda* to denote the Real. In the later Saṃhitās and Brāhmaṇas, we come across a few interesting physical, physiological and psychological approaches, but eventually it is in the Upaniṣads that the concept of Reality has acquired a wider dimension in terms of the doctrine of the identification of the psychical Self (*ātman*), with the cosmic Self (*Brahman*). In the third chapter of the *Aitareya*, the highest Reality has been identified with intellect. In the second chapter of the *Bṛhadāraṇyaka Upaniṣad* Ajātaśatru tells Bālāki that the ultimate Reality lies in pure consciousness, while Yājñavalkya characterized it in negative terms. In the *Chāndogya Upaniṣad* (*Prapāṭhakas* 5 and 7) Aśvapati upholds the doctrine of *ātman* as the supreme Reality, while Sanatkumāra says that happiness resulting from the realization of the Self is conducive to the understanding of the highest reality in which there is no distinction between the subjects and the object. The essence of the individual is intelligence or consciousness and the same essence is also at the bottom of the whole creation. See **Absolute, Ātman, Brahman**.

**Reason:** See **Ethics**.

**Rebirth:** There is no explicit mention of rebirth or transmigration in the *Ṛgveda.* We come across only a few doubtful passages. According to the *Ṛgveda* 1.164.30, 'the soul (*jīvah*) of the dead one moves in its own power, the immortal one moves in its own power, with the latter having a common origin with the former (the body).' But this translation is not certain. The reference in the *Ṛgveda* 10.15.2 to *pitṛs*, who reside in the earth region or in the dwellings of men, need not imply belief in the soul as a ghost revisiting the haunts of men. It may only be the germ of the idea of the acceptance of the funeral (*śrāddha*) offerings by them, which became a regular practice at a later time. The *Ṛgveda* 10.16.3 exports the soul of the dead to go over to heaven or earth, to the waters or to the plants, along with all its physical parts. In the *Ṛgveda* 10.58 the departing spirit of a dying person is called back from Yama, from heaven, earth, the quarters, the sea, the waters, the sun, the dawn or the mountains, i.e. from wheresoever it may have gone to. So we may conclude that only the germs of the conception of rebirth were there, and these developed either naturally, or through the influence of ideas prevalent among the original tribes with whom the Vedic people came into contact. The idea of reward and punishment, after death, in exact correspondence to the good and bad deeds of a person in this life, gained a firm hold in the age of the later Saṃhitās and Brāhmaṇas. This is considerable advance over the view of the *Ṛgveda*. The *Brāhmaṇa* doctrine, that whatever food a man consumes in this world in return consumes him in the next (*ŚB* 13.9.1.1), is but the transfer from the physical to the moral plane of the law that action and reaction are equal and opposite. Similarly, the enjoyment of the rewards, which is in exact measure to the good deeds performed, must come to an end at sometime. Thus, there is the prospect of rebirth for both the pious and the wicked. The *Bṛhadāraṇyaka Upaniṣad* (4.3-4) tells us of the fortune of the soul and incidentally develops the doctrine of the transmigration of souls, and in close connection with it, the ethical doctrine of *karman* (action) which, with the infallibility of a law of nature, must produce its consequences and regulate the new birth. This, therefore, depends on a man's own deeds and truly makes him 'an architect of his own fate'. The *Chāndogya Upaniṣad* gives us the most detailed account of this theory of transmigration. The forest ascetic, equipped with knowledge and faith, enters the *devayāna* (the path of the gods) after death, which leads to absorption in (i.e. oneness with) *Brahman* on deliverance. The householder who performs sacrifices and works, goes by the *pitṛyāna* (the path of the fathers), where he abides till the consequences of his actions are exhausted. He then returns to the earth, where he is first born as a plant and then as a member of one of the *dvija* (or three higher) classes. This is a kind of double retribution, first in the next world (which is traceable to a survival of the old Vedic belief about future life), and then by transmigration in this. The wicked are born again as outcastes, dogs, or swine. The *Bṛhadāraṇyaka Upaniṣad* (6.2.15-16) gives a similar account. The *Kauṣītaki Upaniṣad* (1.2-3) gives a somewhat different itinerary, according to which, after death, all first go to the moon. From there, some go by the path of the Fathers to *Brahman,* while others return to various forms of earthy existence, from men to worm. The earliest form of this theory is found in the *Śatapatha Brāhmaṇa*, which speaks of repeated births and deaths in the next world, both for the man who has correct knowledge and performs a certain sacrifice, resulting in attainment of immortality, and for the ignorant defaulter, who ultimately becomes the prey of death. In the Upaniṣadic version, the rebirth takes place in this world. V.M. Apte in Majumdar 385, 450, 500-1.

**Recensions:** The *Ṛgveda* has five recensions, namely, *Śākala, Bāskala, Āśvalāyana, Śāṅkhyāyana* and *Maṇduka*, of which the *Śākala* has come down to us in an apparently complete form. Eleven hymns, usually placed in the middle of the eighth *maṇḍala* of the *śākala* recension, are known as *Vālakhilya* while thirty-six hymns in the Aundh edition of the *Ṛgveda*, inserted at several places of the *Śākala* recension, are the so-called *Khila Sūktas*. The recensions of the *Atharvaveda* which survive are known as *Śaunaka* and *Paippalāda*. The

*Sāmaveda* has three recensions, namely, *Kauthuma, Rāṇāyanīya* and *Jaiminīya*. There are no less than six recensions of the *Yajurveda* of which two (*Mādhyandina* and *Kāṇva*) constitute the White *Yajurveda* and the rest (*Taittirīya, Kāṭhaka, Maitrāyaṇī* and *Kapiṣṭhala*), the Black *Yajurveda*. The *Śatapatha Brāhmaṇa* has two recensions, *Kānva* and *Mādhyandina*.

**Recitation:** The Vedic hymns were recited or chanted by the priests with appropriate solemnity at sacrifices. Sāyaṇa explains the term *stotra* as referring to the recited verses, usually chanted thrice, by certain repetitions of words. Chando-gā, metre-singing, is the term applied to reciters of the Sāmans, no doubt because these were sung according to their order in the *Chanda ārcika* of the *Sāmaveda*. It is only found in the *Śatapatha Brāhmaṇa* (10.5.2.10) and often in the Sūtras.

**Recluses:** See **Asceticism**.

**Reed Flute:** *Nāḍi* denotes reed-flute. It is a name of a musical instrument. It is referred to in the *Ṛgveda* (10.135.7; *KS* 23.4; 34.5).

**Refined Speech:** In the *Ṛgveda* (10.71) the Vedic speech is described as a refined speech, on which the goddess Vāk dwells. The best speech of the times seems to have been prevalent in the country of the Kuru-Pañcālas and probably also among the Uttara-Kurus. Among subjects of study, there was an emphasis on learning decent and faultless language. Sāyaṇa cites a text, *tasmād brāhmaṇa ubhayaṃ vācaṃ vadanti, yāca devānāṃ iti*, which shows that *devabhāṣā*, or pure speech, was already seperated from the spoken tongue.

**Regalia:** See **Kingship, Royal Officers**.

**Regions:** The concept of *deśa* (space, region) is a part of the total space-time (*deśa-kāla*) dimension. In a narrow sense, the word *deśa* denotes a country or a region irrespective of the notion of time. In the Puruṣa-Sūkta (*RV* 10.90), both *diś* and *loka* occur in the space-time sequence. In the *Yajurveda Saṃhitā* regions, fore-regions, by-regions, intermediary and the upper regions are lauded. The *Śatapatha Brāhmaṇa* (10.2.6.3) says: 'By the regions it (Prajāpati) is sevenfold—the rays which are in the eastern region are one part, and those in the southern are one, and those in the western are one, and those in the northern are one, and those in the upper (region) are one, and those in the lower (region) are one, and the disc itself is the seventh part' (Eggeling's trans.). The word *deśa* features a few times in Vedic literature. In the *Aitareya Brāhmaṇa* (8.10) *deśa* is the intervening place between two directions. Apart from the metaphysical concepts of regions, we have pure geographical conception of five regions of the country with the enumeration of the residents therein which we come across for the first time in the *Aitareya Brāhmaṇa* (8.14), though it has in a way anticipated in the *Atharvaveda* (19.17.1.9). The *Aitareya Brāhmaṇa* division is Dhruvā Madhyamā Pratiṣṭhā Diś or Madhyadeśa or middle country, Prāci Diś or the eastern quarter, Dikṣiṇa Diś or the southern quarter, Pratīcī-Diś or western quarter and Udicī-Diś or northern quarter.

**Reincarnation:** See **Eschatology, Rebirth, Transmigration**.

**Reins:** The warlike people of the *Ṛgveda* were closely acquainted with horses and used the word *abhiṣu* to denote the reins or bridle of the chariot horses. (*RV* 1.38.12; 5.44.4; 6.75.6; 8.33.11; *AV* 6.137.2; 8.8.22; *VS* 34.6; *ŚB* 5.4.3.14). There are terms like *daśābhiṣu*, which denote 'ten bridled' horses yoked to the car (*RV* 10.94.7).

**Rejected Wife:** *Pari-vṛkta, pari-vṛkti, pari-vṛtti* are various forms of the name of the rejected one among the royal wives. *Pari-vṛkta* appears in the *Ṛgveda* (10.102.11; *Atharvaveda* 7.113.2; 20.128.10-1), *Śatapatha Brāhmaṇa* (13.2.6.6; 4.1.8; 5, 2,7); *parivṛkti* in the *Taittirīya Saṃhitā* 1.7.3.4; 3.9.4,4; *KS* 10; 15.4; *ŚB* 5.3.1.13).

**Relations:** *Bandhu* appears in the *Ṛgveda* (5.73.4; 7.72.2; 8.73.12, etc.) *Atharvaveda* 5.11.10), *Taittirīya Saṃhitā* (1.5.1.4), *Taittirīya Brāhmaṇa* (3.7.55) and so on, signifying 'relationship' as a concrete feature of the society, tracing it to friendship connected with an individual and a family. *Sabandhu* denotes a person of the same kin in the *Ṛgveda* (3.1.10; 5.47.5; 8.70.21; etc.). Later on, i.e. in the *Atharvaveda* (6.15.2; 8.2.26; 15.8.2, etc.) it means 'related'. *Sajāta* (born together) is found once in the *Ṛgveda* (1.109.1), and very often later (*AV* 1.9.3; 1.19.3; 2.6.4; 3.3.6; 6.5.2; 7.73.1; 10.1.6; 11.1.7; *TS* 2.1.3.2; 2.2.1.2; 2.6.9.7; *MS* 2.1.8; *KS* 11.12; 11.13; 12.1; *VS* 5.23; 10.29; 27.5 and often in the Brāhmaṇas). The word must clearly mean a 'relative' and, more widely, a man of the same position or rank, but the senses cannot be distinguished so much as they merge into each other. The disputes of *sajātas* are also mentioned (*TB* 3.7.12.2). In Sūtra literature we come across *Sapiṇḍa* (agnates) and *Sakulya* (distant agnates) relations. For specific relations see **Family**.

**Remarriage of Women:** Marriage of a widow to the brother-in-law or near agnate was apparently permitted. The ceremony is alluded to in a funeral hymn of the *Ṛgveda* (10.8.8) and also in another passage (10.40.2). In the *Atharvaveda* (9.5.27-8), a verse refers to a charm that would secure the reunion, in the next world, of a wife and her second husband. The verse uses the term *punarbhū* to refer to the remarried woman. There is also a hint in the *Ṛgveda* (6.49.8) that a woman could remarry if her husband disappeared and could not be found or remained unheard of. The later Dharma Sūtras (*VDS* 17.19.20; 72,74, *BDS* 4.1.16) recognized ordinary remarriage in case of the death of the first husband.

**Renewed Anointment:** The *punar-abhiṣeka*, or

Renewed Anointment, is described in the *Aitareya Brāhmaṇa* (8.5-11). It was intended for kṣatriya-conquering monarchs. The first interesting part of the ceremony was the king's ascent to the throne, or *āsanadī*, which was made of *udumbara* wood, with the exception of the interwoven part (*vivāyana*) which consisted of *muñja* grass. Then came the besprinkling. Among other things the priest said, 'Do thou become here the overking of kings; the great of the great people, the supreme ruler of the people' (*AB* 8.7). The king was next required to get down from the throne and make obeisance to the holy power (*Brahman*). 'Verily thus the influence of the holy power, that kingdom is prosperous'. Janamejaya, the son of Parikṣit, was evidently consecrated with the *punarabhiṣeka* (*AB* 8.11).

**Renunciation:** See **Asceticism**. The idea of renunciation does not feature in the Saṃhitās and Brāhmaṇas. It is in the Āraṇyakas that a life of penance in the forest is recognized and recommended. In the third chapter of the *Bṛhadāraṇyaka Upaniṣad*, Yājāvalkya says that he who is able to bear the extremes of hunger and thirst, of grief, infatuation, age and death, he who rises higher than all desires, he who takes up to a mendicant's life, leading the guiltless life of a child, alone is able to realise the *ātman*. The great urge that came in the Upaniṣadic period for a life of renunciation and meditation upon the mystery of the *ātman* in the recesses of mountains, and in the solitude of the forests, was evidently the precurser of later Buddhist and Jain concepts of detachment from worldly affairs for reaching the highest stage of liberation.

**Reptiles:** In the Vedic texts such reptiles as snakes, crocodiles, lizards, chameleon, etc., are mentioned. The general Vedic term for reptile is *sarīsṛpa* (*RV* 10.162.3; *AV* 3.10.6; 14.7.1; 19.7.1; 19.48.3). *Nakra* is the name of an aquatic animal (*TS* 5.5.13.1; *MS* 3.14.2; *VS* 24.35), which seems to be the crocodile. *Makara* is also the name of the crocodile (*TS* 5.5.13.1; *MS* 3.14.16; *VS* 24.35). *Śiṃśumāra* or *Śiśumāra* is the name of an aquatic creature in the *Ṛgveda* and the later Saṃhitās. It could mean crocodile, dolphin, alligator or porpoise. The word *śiṃśumāra* is referred to in the *Ṛgveda* (1.116.18), *Taittirīya Saṃhitā* (5.5.11), *Atharvaveda* (11.2.25) and *śiśumāra* in *Maitrāyaṇī Saṃhitā* (3.14.2) and *Vājasaneyī Saṃhitā* (24.30) and *Taittirīya Āraṇyaka* (2.19). The word *godhā* means iguana. *Kaśyapa*, a word denoting tortoise, appears in the *Atharvaveda* (4.20.7) and other Saṃhitās and Brāhmaṇas (*MS* 3.14.18; *VS* 24.37; *ŚB* 7.5.1.5; *AB* 2.6). *Kūrma*, the tortoise, is mentioned frequently in the later Saṃhitās (*AV* 9.4.16; *TS* 2.6.3.3; 5.2.8.4; 5.2.8.5; 5.7.13.1; *MS* 3.15.3; *VS* 24.34) and Brāhmaṇas (*ŚB* 1.6.2.3.; 6.1.1.12), but nothing is said of its characteristics. *Vṛścika* in the *Ṛgveda* (1.191.16) and the *Atharvaveda* (10.4.9; 10.4.15; 12.1.46; *Śāṅkh Ā* 12.27) denotes scorpion. Its poison, like that of the serpents was feared (*AV* 10.4.9; 10.4.15; *RV* 1.191.16). It is described as lying torpid in the earth during winter (*AV* 12.1.46). *Nakula*, ichnanmon, is mentioned in the *Atharvaveda* (6.139.5) as being able to cut a snake in two and then join it up again. Its knowledge (*AV* 8.7.23) of a remedy against snake poison is also mentioned. See under **Serpents**.

**Republics:** Some scholars are of the opinion that, along with monarchical and oligarchical states, republican governments could also have existed in India during the Vedic age. They refer to a passage in the *Aitareya Brāhmaṇa* (8.12), which states that the people in the vicinity of the Himalayas, like the Uttarakurus and the Uttaramadras, had a kingless type of state and were therefore called *vi-rāṭ*, or kingless. But it may be asked how the same passage that earlier refers to the kings of the easterners and the southerners, and the titles that were borne by them, could state that it was among the people of Uttarakurus and Uttarmadras that monarchy did not exist? In fact, there is no clear allusion in the Vedic texts with regard to republicanism. The tribal character of the early Vedic polity must have some democratic elements. It may also be argued that the tribal chiefs were natural leaders and had the consent of the entire tribe behind their selection or that, at least in some cases, the Vedic kings were elected directly or indirectly. All this does not, however, amount to the existence of a republican system of administration, though it is a fact that a great monarchy of the Maurya or Gupta type never existed in the Vedic age. We do not, however, have any idea of the internal administrative system of each and every Vedic state or settlement. Though textual evidence is lacking, it is not improbable that a few Vedic states might have had republican constitutions because, according to the later Buddhist and Greek evidence, the existence of republican states in north-western India was an historical reality, whose origin can be traced to a remote antiquity.

**Requiem:** In the funeral hymns of the *Ṛgveda* a gentle and sophisticated spirit is revealed. To quote from one such hymn (10.16), 'When thou hast made him ready, Jātavedas, then do thou give him over to the Fathers? When he attains unto the life that waits him, he shall become the deities' controller. The Sun receives thine eye, the wind thy spirit; go as thy merit is, to earth or heaven. Go, if it be thy lot, unto the waters; go, make thine home in plants with all thy members', Winternitz, 97.

**Respect:** The traditional Indian maxim that *śraddhayā labhate jñānam,* knowledge is obtained by the feeling of respect, has been foreshadowed in the Vedic texts, which insist on *tapas* (practising austerities), *śraddhā* (respect to others), *satya* (seeking for truth), *brah-*

*macarya* (abstinence from sensual pleasure) and *vidhi* (following the code of conduct) as the basic requirements for an enlightened person. These values are stressed especially in the Upaniṣads (cf. *MU* 2.1.7, *PU* 1.2, etc.).

**Restrictions:** See **Taboos**.

**Retinue, Royal:** See **Administration, Kingship, Rājasūya**.

**Retirement:** See **Renunciation**.

**Retribution:** See **Reward**.

**Revelation:** The whole Vedic literature is a long succession of works that belong to different successive periods of time, but which represent a unity. The entire bulk is thought of as a *śruti* 'hearing' because the revealed texts are not supposed to be written and read but only spoken and heard. 'The whole history of Indian philosophy bears witness that not only were the ancient hymns of the *Ṛgveda* looked upon as "breathed out" by the *Brahman*, and "visioned" by the ancient seers, but that also every word in the Upaniṣads, the latest productions of the Vedic literature, was looked upon as indisputable wisdom emanating from the *Brahman* itself. However much the different systems of Indian philosophy may vary, they are all nearly agreed in considering the Veda as revealed, and in appealing to the Veda, especially to the Upaniṣads—although great freedom and arbitrariness prevail in regard to the explanation of these texts—every philosopher gleans from them just what he wishes to,' Winternitz, I, 55.

**Reward:** Material reward comes from pious activities and performance of specific sacrifice. After death the soul of the good or pious man goes to the realm of the blessed where Yama, or Yama and Varuṇa, rule as kings, where the worlds are full of light, where are eager wishes and strong desires, where are food and full delight, where are joys and transports and happiness and felicity and where the longings of desire are fulfilled (*RV* 9.113.7 ff). Elsewhere (*RV* 1.154), we read of Viṣṇu's realm where are 'fleet of many-horned kine and where is a spring of unfailing mead', and of Varuṇa's brilliant and hundred-portalled house (*RV* 7.88.5). This realm of the pious dead is said to be in the highest heaven (*RV* 10.14.4; 10.19.7), where all imperfections of the world are at an end and where one lives in the companionship of the gods, drinking celestial drink with them and listening to heavenly songs (*RV* 10.154.1). In the post-Ṛgvedic period a change in the concept of reward and retribution is observed with the development of the ideas of *karma*, metempsychosis, rebirth and transmigration (q.v.).

**Rheumatism:** *Vi-skandha* occurs several times in the *Atharvaveda* (1.16.3; 2.4.1; 3.9.2; 3.9.6; 4.9.5, 19.34.5, 15.7.3, 11.1) as the name of a disease. As remedies against it, a lead amulet (*AV* 1.16.3), or hemp (*AV* 2.4.5) or a salve (*AV* 2.4.1; 2.4.5; 19.34.5; 19.35.1) are mentioned. The disease is probably rheumatism, because it drew the shoulders apart (*vi-skandha*). Possibly *karṣapha* and *viṣapha*, mentioned in one hymn (*AV* 3.9.1), are plants used to cure the disease.

**Rhythm:** See **Metre**.

**Rice:** *Vrīhi* nowhere occurs in the *Ṛgveda*, but frequently in later literature (*AV* 6.14.1.2; 8.17.20; 9.6.14; *MS* 2.1.6; 2.11.4; 4.3.2; *TS* 1.8.10.1; 4.7.4.2; *VS* 18.12; *TB* 1.3.2; 1.3.7; *JB* 1.1.9; 1.43.1; 263.2.228; *ŚB* 1.1.4.20; 16.6.3.2; 12.7.1.9; *CU* 5.10.6) denoting 'rice' or 'paddy'. The *Atharvaveda* (11.4.13) distinguishes between dark and swift growing (*āśu*) and large rice (*mahāvrīhi*) is referred to in the *Maitrāyaṇī Saṃhitā* (2.1.6), which is contrasted with white rice in the *Taittirīya Saṃhitā* (1.8.10.1). *Plāsuka* is an epithet of *vrīhi* to mean growing rapidly, alluded to in the *Śatapatha Brāhmaṇa* (5.3.3.2). *Taṇḍula* is another term, which designates any type of grain specially rice (*AV* 10.9.26; 11.1.18; *MS* 2.6.6; *KS* 10.1; 15.5; *TS* 1.8.9.3; *ŚB* 1.1.4.3; 2.5.3.4; 5.2.3.2). A wild rice is termed as *nīvāra* (*MS* 2.11.4; *KS* 10.5; *TS* 4.7.3; *VS* 1.8.12; *TB* 1.3.6.7; *ŚB* 5.1.4.14; 5.3.3.5). The term *kṣīraudana*, 'rice cooked with milk' is mentioned frequently in the *Śatapatha Brāhmaṇa* (2.5.3.4; 11.5.7.5). Other preparations of rice are also known.

**Riddles:** Riddle poetry was very popular with the Vedic Indians. The *Ṛgveda* (1.114) contains a large number of riddles, such as, 'Seven harness a one-wheeled cart; it is drawn by one horse with seven names; three naves have the immortal never-stopping wheel, on which all these beings stand.' In content, the *Kuntapa* hymns (*AV* 20.127-36) are partly riddles and their solutions are partly obscene songs and coarse jokes. The *Vājasaneyī Saṃhitā* (32) contains a number or riddles with which the priests amused themselves at the horse-sacrifice. These riddle games form an equally important part of the prayers and sacrificial formulae. The Vedic texts frequently assure us that gods wish to be not only fed but entertained as well as they take a particular pleasure in the mysterious and the enigmatic.

**Riding:** The *Ṛgveda* (1.62.17; 1.163.9; 5-61.3) and the *Taittirīya Brāhmaṇa* (3.4-7.1) contain clear reference to horse-riding, while the *Aitareya Āraṇyaka* (1.2.4) and the *Śatapatha Brāhmaṇa* (7.3.2.17) refer to mounting a horse sideways. The word *sādin* in the *Atharvaveda* (11.10.24) denotes the rider of a horse as opposed to *asāda*, a pedestrian. An *aśva-sādin*, or horse-rider, is mentioned in the *Vājasaneyī Saṃhitā* (30.13).

**Rituals:** The beliefs and ideals of Vedic civilization are often formulated in its general rituals than in other culture traits. Rites are magical rather than propitiatory. In other words, the desired objects are attained by ceremonies which are believed to influence the course of nature. It is ritual that also generates and sustains myth. At the simplest level of life, the rites employed are instinctive in character and are concerned with birth, puberty, marriage, parentage, eldership, death, etc. Just as there are seasons in the arc of man's days, so there are seasons of the natural year which man must observe, such as the rites of seed time and harvest. Above this level comes the cultural grade, wherein ritualism is modified to reflect and sustain social organization. That is why the study of rituals should not only be restricted to that of classifying their contents, with a view to making out their distribution in geography and history, but the motives by which they are characterized, are to be detected as well. It is possible also to make a distinction between the original and sophisticated forms of Vedic rituals. For example, it may be shown how the simple agricultural rites, originally based upon the primitive conception of the identity of earth and woman were fabricated step by step, how their original kernel was gradually thrown aside leading to the development of accretions, which ultimately came to take the bad, and how the primitive techniques, by which the agricultural rites were originally characterized, having assumed sophisticated tone and colour, became decorative features of grand royal ceremonies. The Vedic texts, barring some portions of the *Ṛgveda* and the Upaniṣads, are ritualistic texts that convey information on all kinds of Vedic rituals. For details see **Sacrifices**.

**Rivers:** See **Ārjikiyā, Asmanvatī, Gaṅgā, Gomatī, Hariyūpiyā Krumu, Marudvṛdhā, Mehātnu, Paruṣṇī, Rasā, Revā, Sadānīrā, Sarayu, Sarasvatī, Silamavatī, Sindhu, Siphā, Sudaman, Susartu, Susomā, Śutudri, Suvāstu, Śvetyā, Tristamā, Urṇāvatī, Vibali, Varaṇavatī, Vipāś, Vitastā, Yamunā, Yavyavatī.**

**Roads:** Good roads and thoroughfares were essential for communication and hence the art of road-construction gradually improved. Royal thoroughfare was called *rājapatha* or *śruti* whereas the national highways were called *mahāpatha*. The *Aitareya Brāhmaṇa* (18.3) mentions both *śruti* and *mahāpatha*. It seems that the latter was connected with, and fed by, many minor throughfares leading to different parts of the country. The former was comparatively free from dangers and its construction was better than the *mahāpatha*. *Rājapatha* was comfortable and short, whereas *mahāpatha* led to various directions. Roads connected villages with one another. Roads making the boundaries of villages used to run parallel to each other (*ŚB* 13.2.4.2).

**Robbers:** In one passage of the *Ṛgveda* (1.42.3), the term *muṣivan* denotes a robber or thief. It is a synonym of the word *taskara*. This meaning is attested by Yāska in his *Nirukta* in a sense of *malimlu* as *muṣivan malimlucaḥ* (*Nir.* 3.14.11). In the *Yajurveda Saṃhitā* (*TS* 6.3.2.6; *VS* 11.78-9), the term *malimlu* denotes a robber, a burglar or housebreaker, according to Mahīdhara, the commentator on the *Vājasaneyī Saṃhitā*. The term *malimlu* (*devamalimluc*) suggests a god of the god of the robbers. In the *Taittirīya Saṃhitā* (6.3.2.6) and the *Vājasaneyī Saṃhitā* (11.78-9) it denotes a robber. So, *deva-malimluc* is an epithet of Rahasya or Rahasyu who is said in the *Pañcaviṃśa Brāhmaṇa* (14.4.7) as having slain the pious Vaikhānasas. Other terms for robbers are *tayu* and *stena*.

**Rodasī:** Agnāyī, Varuṇānī, Aśvinī and Rodasī are Ṛgvedic minor goddesses. According to Sāyaṇa (on 1.167.5), Rodasī is *marut-patnī*, 'the wife of the Maruts, or Lightning' though ordinarily she is the wife of Rudra. Rodasī is invoked in the *Ṛgveda* (5.46.8) to grant boons along with Aśvinī, Agnāyī, Indraṇī and Varuṇāṇī (7.34.22). In one verse it is stated, 'To whom the goddess Rodasī clings closely, whom Puṣan follows bringing ample bounty' (*RV* 5.50.5). Her company with the warriors is described in the *Ṛgveda* (6.66.6). Still Rodasī is not a distinct personality.

**Rower:** The term *Aritṛ* means rower of a boat which is found in the *Ṛgveda* (2.42.1; 9.95.2).

**Royal Ceremonies:** *Abhiṣeka:* See **Besprinkling Ceremony**.

*Aindra Mahābhiṣeka:* Indra's great unction (AB 8.12.23) consisted of five important ceremonies. In the first place, an oath is administered by the priest to the king-elect: 'From the night of thy birth to that of thy death for the space between these two, the sacrifice, and thy gifts, the place, thy good deeds, thy life, and thine offspring let me take, if thou play me false (*AB* 8.15).' Next follows the *ārohana* or enthronement. When the king is seated on the throne, there is the *utkrośana* (*AB* 8.17) or proclamation. The king-makers should say: 'The kṣatriya, if not proclaimed, cannot show his strength, let us proclaim him'. 'Be it so', (the people reply). Him the king makers proclaim saying: 'Him do ye proclaim, O men (janāḥ) as king and father of kings. . . . The sovereign lord of all beings (*viśvasya bhūtasya adhipati*) hath been born, the eater of the folk (*visamatta*) hath been born, the destroyer of enemies (*amitrānām hantā*) hath been born, the protector of the brāhmaṇas (*brāhmaṇānām goptā*) hath been born, the guardian of the law (*dharmasya goptā*) hath been born'. Here, we have the important attributes of kingship. In the words *viśvasya bhūtasya adhipati* (supreme lord of all beings), we have a reference to the king's sovereignty and imperium. The expression *visamattā*, devourer of the folk, alludes to his power of taxation. As *amitrānāṃ hantā*, he exercises supreme command to weed out enemies. The epithet *brāhmaṇānām goptā* gives expression to his special relations with the hierarchy, while the style *dharmasya goptā* points to his duties in connection with the preservation of the laws and their proper administration for the promotion of the common weal (*yoga-kṣema*). The king is proclaimed in an address with the formula, *abhimantraṇa* (*AB* 8.18). Varuṇa the wise one, is supposed to set him down for preserving order. Then comes the anointment (*abhiṣecana*). The following kings are said to have been consecrated with the *Aindra Mahābhiṣeka:* Janamejaya Parīkṣita, Śaryāta, Mānava, Śatānīka Satrājita, Ambaṣṭhya, Yudhāmsrausti Augrasainya, Viśvakarma Bhauvana, Sudāsa Paijavana, Marutta Avikṣita, Aṅga Vairocana and Bharata Dauḥṣyanti (*AB* 8.21-3). The first mentioned king, and probably the third, fourth, fifth and ninth also, belonged to the post-Parīkṣit period. Durmukha Pañcāla and Atyārati Janantapi were informed of the efficacy of the rite. The first made good use of the advice. But the latter who neglected his priest, and wanted to conquer the Uttara Kurus, whom 'no mortal man could vanquish', perished at the hands of a king of the Śibis.

*Aśvamedha:* Horse sacrifice. It was originally a fertility-cum-agricultural ritual, which later became transformed into a ceremony for royal paramountcy. From the *Atharvaveda* (11.7.7-8), the *Taittirīya Saṃhitā* (5.4.12.3) and the *Śatapatha Brāhmaṇa* (13.3.3.6) it appears that even in ancient times this sacrifice was rare. Details of its procedure are given in the Śrautasūtras (*ĀŚS* 10; *ĀpŚS* 20; *KŚS* 20; *LŚS* 9; *SŚS* 16, etc.), from which it is known that women in general and queens in particular had an important role in it and that the mantras connected to the killing of the horse are all quoted from the *Ṛgveda* (1.162-3), and those connected to the chief queen's ceremonial union with the horse from the *Vājasaneyī Saṃhitā* (22-3). The *Vājasaneyī Saṃhitā* verses, which were exchanged in the form of dialogue between the priests and the queens, indicate that the Vedic Aśvamedha was a relic or rather a transformation of an older ritual in which a man, who might have been a chief or priest, was put to death after his ceremonial intercourse with the queen. The sophisticated form of Aśvamedha, which lasted for three days, required the presence of four queens. The sacrificial horse roamed over the country for the period of one year, during which three *iṣtis* were to be offered to Savitṛ every day, followed by chants by a brāhmaṇa and also by a kṣatriya lute-player. The hotṛ priest recited the narrative called *pāriplava* in the royal court. At the final ceremony the horse was anointed by the four queens. After the horse was killed, the crowned queen lay embracing the horse. Dialogues dealing with the archaic and antiquated ritual of the queen's sexual intercourse with the priest were now repeated between hotṛ and the crowned queen (Mahiṣī), between the brāhmaṇa and the favourite wife (Vāvātā), and between the four principal priests and chamberlain on the side and the queens and the attendants on the other. The fat and blood of the horse were offered to the deities and a theological dialogue of questions and riddles took place. Soma was pressed on all the three days. Bhattacharyya 1990, 27-8.

*Rājasūya:* The Rajasūya consisted of a long succession of sacrificial performances, which began on the first day of Phālguṇa and spread over a period of two years. The rite is described at great length in the *Śatapatha Brāhmaṇa* 5.2.1.25 ff. Besides mere priestly elaboration, the ritual contains traces of popular ceremony. The popular features are: (a) the presents of the bejewelled ones to the divinities or those possessed of the jewel, viz., the chief queen and court officials; (b) the *abhiṣecanīya* or besprinkling ceremony; (c) the *digvyasthāpana* or the king's symbolical walking towards the various quarters as an indication of his universal rule; (d) treading upon a tiger skin, thus gaining the strength and the pre-eminence of the animal; (e) the *hotṛ* priest's narration of the story of Śunaḥśepa; (f) a mock cow raid against a relative; or a sham fight with a member of the ruling aristocracy; (g) enthronement; (h) and, a game of dice in which the king is made to be the victor. The recipients of the sacrificial honours called *ratninām havīṃṣi* were the divinities in the houses of the *ratnins,* i.e. of the chief members of the royal household and of the king's civil and military service, viz., (1) the senānī, commander of the army, (2) the purohita, royal chaplain, (3) the mahiṣī, chief queen, (4) the sūta, charioteer and bard, (5) the grāmaṇī, leader of the host or village headman, (6) the kṣattṛ, chamberlain, (7) the saṃgrahitṛ, treasurer, (8) the bhāgadugha, collector of the royal share, i.e. taxes, (9) the akṣāvāpa, keeper of the dice; (10) the go-vikartana, the king's companion in the chase, and (11) pālāgala, courier. On the day of the *abhiṣeka* (anointing), his anointment with an appropriate formula was announced. He then stepped forth in each of the different quarters and sat on a seat made from the wood of *udumbara,* tree covered with a tiger-skin. He was then libated with a fluid-made of butter, honey, different kinds of holy water and other ingredients poured over him from a cup of *udumbara* wood. Some libations and offerings followed next, after which he enacted a mock raid on the cattle of his kinsfolk from his chariot. He also played a mock-game of dice, with a cow as the stake, in which his victory was guaranteed. The final rite was a ceremonial bath. The *TS* 1.8.1-22; *TB* 1.4.9-10; *ŚB* 5.2.3-5; *AB* 7.13; 8; *PB* 18.8-11; *ĀpŚS* 18.8-22, *KŚS* 15.1-9; *ĀŚS* 9.3-4; *SŚS* 15.12 ff.

*Vājapeya:* Primitive sacrifice for food (*vāja*) and drink (*peya*), which was later transformed into the consecration for overlordship. It may be regarded as an independent sacrifice to be performed by a brāhmaṇa or kṣatriya desiring supereminence. The number 17 predominates in it. It requires 17 cups of *soma*, 17 cups of *surā*, 17 chariots and 17 drums. A mock chariot race is held in which the sacrificer is declared victorious. A ladder is raised against the *yūpa* on which the scrificer climbs and holds a ritual dialogue with his wife. Animals are offered to Prajāpati at the time of mid-day soma-pressing. The *adhvaryu* declares the Yajamāna to be *samrāṭ* (universal monarch). The fees distributed are 1,700 cows, 17 chariots with four horses yoked to each, 17 maid-servants, etc. After Vājapeya a king should perform Rājasūya (q.v.) and a brāhmaṇa Bṛhaspatisava. For details see *Taittirīya Saṃhitā* 1.7.7-12; *Taittirīya Brāhmaṇa* 1.3.2-9; *Pañcaviṃśa Brāhmaṇa* 18.6-7; *Śatapatha Brāhmaṇa* 5.1.2.

**Royal Functions:** Besides offensive war, defence was a chief duty of the king. He is emphatically the 'protector of the tribe' (*gopa janasya*) or, as it is said in the Rājasūya, 'protector of the brāhmaṇas' (*RV* 3.43.5; *KS* 9.17.10; *ŚB* 2.6.4.2). In return for his war like services, the king received the obedience (*MS* 1.6.10)—sometimes forced (*TB* 2.7.18.2)—of the people, and in particular their contributions for maintenance of royalty. The king is often (*AV* 4.22.7; *AB* 7.29; 8.12; *ŚB* 1.8.2.17; 4.2.1.3.5) regarded as the 'devourer of the people' but this phrase must not be explained as meaning that he necessarily oppressed them. It is also probably that the king could assign the royal right of maintenance to a kṣatriya, thus developing a nobility supported by the people. The king performed the duties of judge. Himself immune from punishment (*a-daṇḍya*), he wields the rod of punishment (*ŚB* 5.4.4.7). Possibly the jurisdiction could be extended to a royal officer, or even to a delegate, for a *rājanya* is mentioned as an overseer (*adhyakṣa*) of the punishment (*KS* 27.4). In civil justice it may be that the king played a much less prominent part, save as a court of final appeal, but evidence is lacking on this count. A wide criminal jurisdiction is, however, to some extent supported (*RV* 1.25.13; 4.4.3; 6.67.5; 7.61.3; 10.10.8; *AV* 4.36.4) by the frequent mention of Varuṇa as the divine counterpart of the human king. In early Vedic literature, there is no reference to the exercise of legislative activity by the king. In all his acts the king was regularly advised by his *purohita*; he also had the advantage of the advice of the royal ministers and attendants. The local administration was entrusted to the *grāmaṇī*, or village chief, who may have been selected or appointed by the king. See **kingship**.

**Royal Herald:** Among the *ratnins* or electors of the king mentioned in connection with the Rājasūya, there is a court official under the designation *sūta*, who is often mentioned with the *grāmaṇī*. It appears that in later Vedic period, *sūta* denoted the royal herald, and his elevation was due to his original occupation of the ministerial. He is one of the eight *vīras* in the *Pañcaviṃśa Brāhmaṇa* (9.1.4), and of the eleven *ratnins* in other texts (*KS* 15.4; *MS* 2.6.5; 4.3.8; *TB* 1.7.3.1; *TS* 1.8.9.1; *ŚB* 5.3.1.5). He also appears in the *Atharvaveda* (3.5.7), among the kingmakers (*rājakṛt*), and in the *Śatarudrīya*, in the section dealing with the hundred Rudras (*TB* 4.5.3.1; *KS* 17.2; *MS* 2.9.3; *VS* 16.18). The commentators are agreed in seeing in him the 'charioteer' (*sārathi*) or 'master of the horse' of the king. In the epic the *sūta* serves as a royal herald and bard. Perhaps, the curious words *ahanti* (*VS* 16.18), *ahantvya* (*TS* 4.5.2.1) or *ahantyva* (*KS* 17.2; *MS* 2.9.3) applied to him in the *Śatarudrīya*, denote his sacred character at once as ministerial and as herald—a combination of functions not known elsewhere.

**Royal Inauguration:** See **Rājasūya, Royal Ceremonies**.

**Royal Income:** Vedic literature, owing to its predominantly religious nature, naturally supplies meagre information about the revenues of the state in the contemporary times. In the earliest period, the king's power was not well established and taxation seems to have been occasional and voluntary. The king probably supported himself, his retinue and meagre administrative staff out of the proceeds of his own lands, pastures and herds. The term *bali*, originally used to denote voluntary offerings made to gods for securing their favour (*RV* 5.1.10), came to be applied later to the presents and taxes offered to the king, more or less voluntarily. It is also significant to note that a prayer is often offered on behalf of a king, restored to the throne after an earlier desposition, that Indra may compel his subjects to pay him his dues and taxes (*RV* 10.173.6). Or, that he may have the good fortune to see ample presents brought to him by his subjects (*AV* 3.4.3). These prayers suggest that people were not yet quite accustomed to paying regular taxes to the state as a matter of normal liability. There was a change in the situation in the coronation ritual of the later Vedic literature, where the king is described as the 'eater of the subjects' (*Aitareya Brāhmaṇa* 7.29). This metaphor was obviously suggested by the regular payment of taxes by the people to the king, which enabled him and his officers to live in dignity and pomp. In the Vedic period, brāhmaṇas were engaged in the unproductive profession of priesthood, and the kṣatriyas were mostly occupied in conquering and annexing new territories, the śūdras were not very wealthy. The burden of taxation, therefore, naturally fell heavily on the vaiśyas who were engaged in the productive profession of agriculture, trade and cattle rearing. The vaiśya is, therefore, often described as the payer of tributes and taxes (*AB* 7.29; *ŚB* 11.2.6.14). It is not, however, to be supposed that the other classes escaped altogether; for the king is often described as taxing all his subjects (*Atharvaveda* 4.22.7). They paid taxes in the form of cows, bulls, and horses, (*Atharvaveda* 4.22.2), a certain percent of the herds being claimed by the state. Apart from taxes from their subjects, Vedic kings often used to receive tributes from conquered chieftains (*RV* 7.18.19). Trade and commerce were not held in high esteem in the Vedic age and do not seem to have made any appreciable contribution to the royal exchequer. Whether mines were actively worked and were regarded as state property, we do not know.

**Royal Officers:** In the Vedic texts we come across the

term *ratnin*, which means people of the royal entourage in whose houses the *ratna-havis*, a special rite, was performed in the course of the Rājasūya or 'royal consecration'. The list given in the *Taittirīya Saṃhitā* (1.8.9.1) and the *Taittirīya Brāhmaṇa* (1.7.3.1) consists of the brāhmaṇa (priest), the rājanya (royal kinsman), the mahiṣī, (chief queen), the vāvātā (favourite wife), the parivṛkti (discarded wife), the senānī (commander of the army), the sūta (charioteer), the grāmaṇī (village headman), the kṣattṛ (chamberlain), the saṃgrahitṛ (charioteer or treasurer), the bhāgadugha (collector of taxes) and the akṣāvāpa (superintendent of dicing). In the *Śatapatha Brāhmaṇa* (5.3.1.1) the order is senāni; purohita; mahiṣī; śūta; grāmaṇī; ksattṛ; saṃgrahitṛ; bhāgadugha; akṣāvāpa; go-vikartana (huntsman) and pālāgala (courier). In the *Maitrāyaṇī Saṃhitā* (2.6.5; 4.3.8) the list is brāhmaṇa (i.e. purohita); rājan; mahīṣi; parivṛkti; senānī; saṃgrahitṛ; ksattṛ; sūta; vaiśya grāmaṇi; bhāgadugha; takṣa-rathakārau (carpenter and chariot-maker); akṣāvāpa; and go-vikarta. The *Kāṭhaka Saṃhitā* (15.4) substitutes go-vyaccha for go-vikarta, and omits takṣa-rathakārau. It will be seen that the list is essentially that of the royal household and of the king's servants in the administration of the country. The exact sense of saṃgrahitṛ, bhāgadugha, sūta, grāmaṇī, kṣattṛ, however, is open to reasonable doubt, mainly as to whether public officers or private servants are meant for the names of uncertain significance. A briefer list of eight *vīras*, 'heroes', as among the friends of the king, is given in the *Pañcaviṃśa Brāhmaṇa* (19.1.4): brother, son, purohita, mahiṣī, sūta, grāmaṇi, kṣattṛ and saṃgrahitṛ.

**Royal ownership:** The concept of the absolute royal ownership of all lands does not seem to have arisen during the Vedic age. 'Grants' of land only implied transfer of privileges regarding revenue, but not ownership. Similarly, when the king granted his royal prerogatives over villages to his favourites, 'the grant' is to be understood as the transfer of privileges in fiscal matters. That a gift of land in the sense of 'the conferring of ownership' was looked upon as beyond the royal prerogative, may be inferred from a story in the *Śatapatha Brāhmaṇa* (13.7.1.13-15) and the *Aitareya Brāhmaṇa* (8.21.8) where, when king Viśvāmitra offered the earth (probably a piece of land) to his officiating priest, the earth refused to be given. Such gifts of land probably constituted a violation of customary law. The king certainly had the power to expel a brāhmaṇa or vaiśya (there is no mention of the kṣatriya) from his land, but this power drew its sanction not from his ownership of the land but from his sovereignty, and was recognized only as a royal prerogative.

**Royal Priest:** *Pruro-hita* 'placed in front', 'appointed' is the name of a priest in the *Ṛgveda* (1.1.1; 1.44.10; 1.44.12; 2.24.9; 2.8; 3.3.2; 5.11.2; 6.70.4) and later (*AV* 8.5.5; *VS* 9.23.11.81; 31.20; *AB* 8.24; *Nirukta* 1.12.7.15). The office of *purohita* is called *purohiti* (*RV* 7.6.12; 7.83.4) and *purodhā*. It is clear that the primary function of the *purohita* was that of 'domestic priest' of a king, or perhaps a great noble. His quite exceptional position is shown by the fact that only one *purohita* seems ever to be mentioned in Vedic literature. Examples of purohitas in the Ṛgvedic age are Viśvāmitra (3.33.53) and Vasiṣṭha (*RV* 7.18.83) in the service of the Bharata king Sudās of the Tṛtsu family; the *purohita* of Kuruśravaṇa (*RV* 10.33); and Devāpi, the *purohita* of Śantanu (*RV* 10.98). In all religious matters, the *purohita* was the alter ego of the king. In the ritual (*AB* 8.24) it is laid down that a king must have a *purohita*, else the god will not accept his offerings. His prayer ensures the king's safety and victory in battle (*RV* 7.18.13; *AV* 3.19); he procures the fall of rain for the crops (*RV* 10.98); he is the flaming fire that guards the kingdom (*AB* 8.24; 8.25). At any rate, it seems clear from the relations of the *purohita* with king Kuruśravaṇa, and with his son Upamaśravas (*RV* 10.33), that a king would retain the *purohita* of his father. The king might act as his own *purohita*, as shown by the case of a king who performed sacrifice without the help of the priest (*AB* 7.27), and that a *purohita* need not be a professional priest, as shown by case of Devāpi and Śantanu (*RV* 10.98). From the beginning the *purohita* acted as the brāhmaṇa priest in the sacrificial ritual, being there as the general superintendent of the sacrifice. Vasiṣṭha is mentioned both as *purohita* (*RV* 10.150.5) and as brāhmaṇa (*RV* 7.33.11). The *purohitas* also exercised great influence in public affairs, in the administration of justice and the king's conduct of business. See **Priesthood**.

**Ṛta:** The three fundamental concepts of *ṛta, satya* and *dharma*, are so closely interrelated that exact demarcation of their meanings is very difficult. For determining the original significance of *ṛta*, two cognate words are helpful. One is the Avestan *asa*, meaning a holy order of which Āhura is the guardian (cf. in the Vedas Varuṇa is the guardian of *ṛta*). The other is Latin *ratus*, conveying a fixed order. The original meaning of *ṛta*, thus, appears to be settled order, the cosmic order which is holy and universal. It is concealed in itself. (*RV* 5.62), those who know it are *ṛtajña*; they were sages who guarded the seat of *ṛta* (*RV* 10.177-2), in praise of which the Vedic seers are eloquent (*RV* 4.3.9-12; 4.23.8-10). The wheel of *ṛta* rolls round the heaven (*RV*1.164.11), manifold are its bounties. Firm are the foundations of *ṛta*, and as the cosmic order yields harmony and symmetry, it has an aesthetic aspect too (*RV* 4.23.9). The vast earth and heaven belong to *ṛta*, by its force the Aṅgirasas cleft the mountains asunder; by *ṛta* the divine waters continue to flow (*RV* 4.3.8-12). *Ṛta* is personified in the *Ṛgveda* (1.75.5; 10.66.4). The earth, the atmosphere, the sky, the quarters and the world of heaven are respectively described as the realm, the might, the circumference, truth and light of *ṛta* (*TS* 3.3.5). Mitra-Varuṇa are guardians of *ṛta* (*RV* 5.63.1) and they govern the whole world by *ṛta* (*RV* 6.63.7). The Vedic gods are associated with *ṛta* in various capacities (*RV* 2.23.3; 4.40.5; 10.85.1; *AV* 7.6.2, etc.) but *ṛta* does not depend on the will of personal gods. Sacrifice is said to be the way of *ṛta* (*MS* 4.8.2). The cosmic order has its counterpart in moral order. At the personal level, therefore, *ṛta* thus also expresses moral order. The seer prays to Indra, 'Lead us along the path of *ṛta*' (*RV* 10.133.6).

**Rudra:** Though a subordinate deity in the *Ṛgveda*, Rudra is interesting from the point of view of later mythology. He has braided hair and a brown complexion. He wears golden ornaments and a glorious necklace (*niṣka*). He is the father of the Maruts whom he brought forth from the shining Pṛśni. He is fierce like a terrible beast and is called a bull as well as the ruddy boar of heaven. He is exalted and the mightiest of the mighty. He is the lord (Īśāna) and father of the world. He is easily invoked and auspicious (Śiva), but in many passages is looked upon as malevolent. He is implored to save his worshippers from his bolt which destroys cows and men. Dread of his wrath and shafts is frequently expressed. The beneficent side of his character, however, comes out in other passages. His two exclusive epithets *jalāsa* (cooling) and *jalāsa-bheṣaja* (possessing cooling remedies) suggest his healing powers. He is a great physician. The physical basis is not certain. It is suggested that the storm in its destructive aspect may explain the malevolent side of his nature, while the fertilizing and purifying function of the thunderstorm may well be the basis of his healing power. The *Ṛgveda* 1.27.10; 1.64.2; 1.85.1; 1.114.1 ff; 8.26.5; 10.70.2, *Nir.* 10.8, *Vājasaneyī Saṃhitā* 16.48; *Taittirīya Saṃhitā* 4.5.10.1, etc.

# S

**Śabara:** Name of a tribe which in the *Aitareya Brāhmaṇa* (7.18.2; *ŚŚS* 15.26.6) are classed as Dasyus and also with the Andhras, Pulindas, Mutibas and Puṇḍas. They were inhabitants of the wild tracts of Orissa and Madhya Pradesh and also of the Eastern Ghats region. The Śabaras are mentioned by Pliny as Suari and by Ptolemy as Sabarae.

**Sabhā:** In a general sense *sabhā* denoted an assembly house in which important persons met and discussed matters of public interest (*RV* 6.28.6; 8.4.9; 10.34.6; 7.12.1-2; 8.10.5; 12.1.56; 19.55.6; etc). It is also mentioned in the later Saṃhitās and Brāhmaṇas (*AV* 5.31.6; 7.12.1-2; 8.10.5; 12.1.56; 19.55.6; *TS* 1.7.6.7; *MS* 4.7.4; *VS* 3.45; 16.24; 20.17; *TB* 1.1.10.6; *SB* 2.3.2.3; 5.3.1.1; *KB* 7.9) but its exact character is not very precisely known to us. Those who achieved prominence in discussions were known as *sabhāsaha* (*RV*). The assembly-hall was also used for dicing (*RV* 10.34.6; *AV* 5.31.6; 12.3.46), presumably when the assembly was not transacting public business, and its director was known as *sabhāsthānu*, 'pillar of the assembly-hall', doubtless because of his constant presence there (*VS* 30.18; *TB* 3.4.16.1). Apart from entertainment, this dice-play had other purposes as well. It was also a means of distribution of wealth among clans: The hall also served as the meeting-place for social itntercourse and general conversations and debates were also held there (*RV* 2.24.13). In his commentary on *Vājasaneyī Saṃhitā* (20.27), Mahīdhara says that disputes were also solved and mitigated in the *sabhā*. Financial affairs like cattle-wealth were also discussed and settled in the *sabhā* (*RV* 6.28.6; 8.4.9). Higher subjects were also discussed (*AV* 7.12.3). That *sabhā* might have also been as assembly of the affluents (*maghvan*) has been suggested by some scholars. Domestic use of *sabhā* is recognized in several passages of the later saṃhitās and brāhmaṇas (*AV* 8.10.5; *TS* 3.4.8.6; *TB* 1.1.10.3). It could also have been the meeting place of the village council. A trace of fire used in sacrifice, on behalf of the assembly, is met with in the *Atharvaveda* (8.10.5; 19.55.6). Care was taken to maintain the standard of speech in the *sabhā*. Important participants were known as *sabheya* or 'fit for assembly' (*RV* 2.24.13; *AV* 20.12.8; *VS* 22.22), *rayiḥ sabhāvān* 'the wealth of assembly' (*RV* 4.2.5), and so forth (*RV* 2.24.13; 4.2.5). The term *sabhāvatī* meant female members in the *Rgveda* (1.167.3), in which it is said that the female member utters fitting words in the *sabhā*. It is also said that a woman who protects *ṛta* or law comes thrice to the *sabhā* (*RV* 3.56.5). In the *Chāndogya Upaniṣad* (5.3.6) the presence of the king in the *sabhā* is recorded. The chairperson of the *sabhā* was known as *sabhāpāla* (*TB* 3.7.46). Members were also known as *sabhācara* (*VS* 30.6; *TB* 3.4.2.1) and *sabhāsada* (*AV* 1.12.2; 3.29.1; 19.55.6; *KS* 8.1; *MS* 1.6.11; *AB* 8.21). Both *sabhā* and *samiti* (q.v.) are described as the twin daughters of Prajāpati (*AV* 7.12; *ŚB* 4.1.4.1-6).

**Sacerdotalism:** See **Priesthood, Yajña**.

**Sacraments:** See **Saṃskāras**.

**Sacred Thread:** See **Initiation, Yajñopavīta**.

**Sacrifice:** See **Yajña**.

**Sacrificers:** See **Yajamāna**.

**Sadānīrā:** *Sadānīrā*, always having water (perennial), is the name of a stream which, according to the *Śatapatha Brāhmaṇa* (1.4.1.14), was the boundary between the Kosalas and the Videhas. The river is identified by Sāyaṇa with the Karotoyā, which is retained in the *Amarakośa*. It is identified with the Gaṇḍakī but the identification fits better with the Rāptī.

**Sages:** See **Seers**.

**Sailor:** The term *nāvāja* indicates a sailor in the *Śatapatha Brāhmaṇa* (2.3.3.5) *Nau* is the regular word for a boat or ship in the *Ṛgveda* (1.131.2; 2.39.2; 8.42.3; 8.83.3; *AV* 2.36.5; 5.19.8; *TS* 5.3.10.1; *VS* 10.19). The word *nāva* also means ship in the *Ṛgveda*.

**Saints:** See **Seers**.

**Śākalya:** A philosopher of the Upaniṣadic period whose full name was Vidagdha Śākalya. The theological queries of Śākalya feature in the *Bṛhadāraṇyaka Upaniṣad* (3.9). Vidagdha Śākalya wanted to inquire of Yājñavalkya as to how many gods really existed in the world. To Vidagdha's first query releasing to the number of gods Yājñavalkya replied that there were 'three and three hundred', and yet again 'three and thousand'. Vidagdha was not satisfied with this answer and pressed him again. Yājñavalkya said in return that there were thirty-three gods, then there were six, and three, and two, and one-and-a half God. Vidagdha was eminently dissatisfied and asked him again. Yājñavalkya replied that there was only one God. Śākalya again asked him who were the different three and three hundred gods and three hundred gods and three thousand gods, and yet again the thirty-three Gods, whom he mentioned. Eventually Yājñavalkya said that there were five gods of earth, air, the inter-mundia, the sun and heaven. When Vidagdha asked him who the one God was, Yājñavalkya replied that it was *prāṇa* that was identical with the *Brahman* immanent in the earth and the sky, darkness and the light, water and seed, and all forms of the world.

**Śākamedha:** Vedic sacrifice for *pitṛyajña*. It was performed in autumn in which the *dakṣiṇāgni* (southern-fire) was prominent. A sacrificial feast was given to the participants. Another important element in this sacrifice was an offering to Rudra Tryambaka for the protection of the flocks. It is followed by an offering to *sunaśīrau*, the two deited parts of the plough, which shows the agricultural affiliation of the rituals. *TS* 1.8.4-6; *TB* 1.6.10; *ŚB* 2.5.3 ff, 2.6.1.2; *ĀŚS*. 2.18-19; *ĀpŚS* 8.9-19; *KŚS* 5.6-10; *BŚS* 6.10-17.

**Sale:** The term for sale as well as for purchase is *kraya* in the *Ṛgveda* (4.24.10) and also in later saṃhitās and brāhmaṇas (*TS* 3.1.2.1; 6.1.3.3; *VS* 7.55; 19.13; *ŚB* 3.3.2.10, etc.). Sale appears to have regularly consisted in barter in the *Ṛgveda* (4.24.10). The haggling of the market was already familiar (*RV* 4.24.9). The price was called *vasna* (*RV* 1.33.3). See **Trade**.

**Salt:** Salt is considered to be a very great power-substance and, as such, supposed to have many significances, useful as well as harmful, according to the situation. In the magico-religious medicine, therefore, it is sometimes prescribed and sometimes prohibited. Thus, when a patient is suffering from scrupulous swelling, the medicine-man powders stone salt, consecrates it with the *Atharvaveda* (6.83) and (7.76), besmears it on the tumour (*KauSū*. 31.17). On the other hand, if a man wants to get a son who will study the Vedas, he and his wife have to undergo a vow for three days, during which they are not supposed to eat salt and observe celibacy. Salt is not mentioned in the *Ṛgveda* but in the rest of the Vedic literature it is frequently mentioned (*AV* 7.76.1; *ŚB* 5.2.1.16; *GB* 1.14; *BU* 4.12; *CU* 4.17.7).

**Salutation:** Though in the early Vedic texts salutation to the gods, kings, teachers and Brāhmaṇas are mentioned while describing various sacrifices, often by bodily postures or by exclamation of laudatory verses, it is in the Dharmasūtras that we come across detailed rules laid down about *pratyutthāna* (rising from one's seat to receive a person), *abhivādana* (saluting a man), *upasaṃgrahaṇa* (saluting by clasping the feet of the teacher or another with one's hands), *pratyabhivāda* (returning a salutation) and *namaskāra* (bowing with the word *namaḥ*). Salutation is of three kinds, viz., *nitya* (obligatory everyday), *naimittika* (to be done only on certain occasion) and *kāmya* (to be done when a person has certain rewards in view). A brāhmaṇa shall salute stretching forward his right arm on a level with his ear, a kṣatriya holding it on the level with the chest, a vaiśya holding it on the level with the waist, and the sūdra holding it low upto his feet. The general salutation will be made by joining the palms while in case one has to show honour, only by rising up from his seat. *ĀpDS* 1.2.5; *BDS* 1.2.24.

**Śālva:** Name of a people which is found in the *Gopatha Brāhmaṇa* (1.2.9), and coupled with that of the Matsyas Sālva is mentioned in a passage of the *Śatapatha Brāhmaṇa* (10.4.1.10). These people also appear to be alluded to as *śālviḥ* (prajāḥ) in the *mantrapātha* (2.11.12), where they are said to have declared that their king was Yaugandharī when they stayed with their chariots on the banks of the Yamuna. The Śālvas were closely connected with the Kuru-Pañcālas, and apparently lived near the banks of the Yamuna.

**Samāvartana:** Taking the ceremonial bath after finishing Vedic study. It literally means 'return from the teacher's house to one's home'. *Samāvartana* is mentioned in the *Chāndogya Upaniṣad* (4.10.1) in connection with Upakośala's education. Elsewhere in the same text (8.15), it is stated that 'having studied the Veda according to the rules in the time that was left after doing work for the teacher and having returned from his teacher's house to his own family'. For details see **Snātaka**.

**Samiti:** In the *Ṛgveda* 1.95.8 the meaning of Samiti is entirely metaphorical and hardly gives a clue to finding out its real character. But in the *Ṛgveda* 9.92.6, it gives an idea of a collective body. Elsewhere, the *Ṛgveda* 10.97.6 refers to kings coming to the Samiti. The *Ṛgveda* 10.191.3 shows its importance of the business transacted there. In the *Atharvaveda* 7.12 (cf. *ŚB* 4.1.4.1-6) the *samiti* along with the *sabhā* is described as one of the two daughters of Prajāpati. The same hymn further describes the *sabhā* and the *samiti* as deliberative bodies, where the opinion of the many was expressed and carried weight with the community. In the *Atharvaveda* 8.10, we hear of the *samiti* and of the polite and courtly men coming as guests to the assembly. In the *Atharvaveda* 12.1.56, in a hymn addressed to Pṛthivī, her praise is said to be sung in all gatherings of men. *Samiti* is mentioned along with other such gatherings as *sabhā*. It was an assembly of the people and accord with it was vitally important to the king. Further importance of the *samiti* is apparent from a consideration of the *Atharvaveda* 5.19, which enables us to come to the conclusions that it was a gathering of the whole folk of the community, that it was the assembly of the *rāṣṭra*, and that it had a close connection with the royal person and met on all important occasions, especially in times of war or national calamity. It was conveyed to elect and accept the king or to approve of his acts. A critical review of the sources (*RV* 1.95.8; 9.92.6; 10.97.6; 10.166.4; 10.191.3; *AV* 5.19.15; 6.88.3; 7.12.1; 12.1.56, etc.), however, suggests that compared to *sabhā*, it was a smaller assembly intended exclusively for political and war purposes. Sāyaṇa categorically states that *samiti* was a war-council (*saṅgrāma*), where kings or tribal chiefs assembled to discuss the course of action.

**Saṃskāras:** Etymologically the term signifies 'putting together', forming well, 'making perfect', 'accomplishment', 'embellishment', 'purification', 'cleansing', 'preparation', 'dressing', 'refining', 'polishing', etc. From the religious point of view, it denotes sacraments, rituals, purificatory acts, etc. Śabara on *Jaimini* 3.1.3 explains *saṃskāra* as that, which being effected, makes a certain thing or person fit for a certain purpose. More precisely, in the Hindu tradition it denotes a sacred or sanctifying ceremony, one which purifies from the taint of sin contracted in the womb and which leads to regeneration. Twelve such ceremonies are enjoined on the first three or twice-born classes. They are, *Garbhādhāna*, *Puṃsavana*, *Cuḍākaraṇa*, *Upanayana*, *Keśānta*, *Samāvartana* and *Vivāha*. The *Gautama Dharmasūtra* speaks of forty *saṃskāras* (8.14-4). Early Vedic texts mention only *upanayana* and *vivāha*, i.e. initiation and marriage.

**Sanctuary:** The term *pratiṣṭhā* in the *Atharvaveda* (6.32.3; 8.8.21) seems to denote a 'sanctuary'. The word also appears in the same sense in the *Śāṅkhāyana Āraṇyaka* (12.14). One desirous of a sanctuary is mentioned in the *Taittirīya Saṃhitā* (2.1.3.4) and *Pañcaviṃśa Brāhmaṇa* (23.18.1) as *pratiṣṭhākāma*.

**Saptasindhu:** The term Saptasindhu means a definite country in the *Ṛgveda* (8.24.27) whereas at other places even streams themselves are intended. 'According to Max Müller, the seven rivers are the five rivers of the Punjab along with Indus and Sarasvatī. Ludwig, Lassen and Whitney substitute Kubhā for the Sarasvatī and think that originally the Oxus also must have been one of the seven. Considering that the *Ṛgveda* mentions the Kubhā (Kabul), Gomati (Gumal), Krumu (Kurram), Suvāstu (Swat), etc., which lie to the west of the Indus, it is possible that the Ṛgvedic people knew of the existence of the Oxus. The reasonable view, however, appears to be to take the seven streams to be the Indus, the five streams of the Punjab and the Sarasvatī.

**Sarasvatī:** The Sarasvatī is the river *par excellence* (*nadītamā*, *RV* 2.41.16), and appears most frequently in the *Ṛgveda*. It seems to have been the holy stream of the Vedic age. In the enumeration of rivers in the Nadīstuti (*RV* 10.75.5), Sarasvatī comes between the Yamunā and Śutudri, and is generally identified with the modern Sarasvati, which is lost in the desert and Bhatnair. Roth, Zimmer, Griffith, and Ludwig hold that in many passages of the *Ṛgveda* Sarasvatī means the sindhu. It maybe observed in this connection that it is possible that the Sarasvatī was as large as the Sutlej in the Vedic age, and actually reached the sea, as the *Ṛgveda* (6.61.2; 6.61.8; 7.85.2) describes it as going to the ocean. It was the first of the Vedic rivers (2.41.16) and its banks witnessed the development of the Vedic sacrifices. In many passages (*TS* 7.2.1.40; *PB* 25.10.1; *KB* 12.2.3; *ŚB* 1.4.1.14; *AB* 2.19.1.2) of the later texts it is certain that the river meant is the modern Sarasvatī, which loses itself in the sands of Patiala. It formed the western boundary of Brahmāvarta with the Dṛṣadvati. It is the holy stream of early Vedic India. The Sūtras (*KŚS* 12.3.20; 24.6.22; *LŚS* 10.15.1; 18.13; 19.4; *AŚS* 12.6.2.3; *SŚS* 13.29) mention sacrifices held on its banks as being of great importance and sanctity. In the post-Ṛgvedic period the most striking fact is the disappearance of the Sarasvatī. The place where the river vanished in the desert was known as Vinaśana (Patiala district), and it reappeared at Plakṣa Prasravaṇa at a distance of forty-four days' jouney from Vinaśana. In the laudatory passages of the *Ṛgveda*, Sarasvatī is described as surpassing all other waters in greatness; of all rivers she alone appears pure, flowing from the mountains, from the (celestial) ocean (7.95.1, 2). She tears away with her mighty waves the peaks of mountains, and her immense and impetuous flood moves roaring (6.61.2, 8). She is distinguished by greatness among the great, most active of the active and is implored not to withhold her milk (6.61.13). She has seven sisters and is sevenfold (6.61.10, 12). She is one of seven, a mother of streams (7.36.6). She is the mother of rivers and of goddesses (2.41.16). She is called *paviravi*, an epithet probably meaning 'daughter of lightning', and is said (6.49.7) to be the wife of a hero (probably Sarasvat). Also as a personified goddess, she is frequently invoked in the form of Vāk. She fills the terrestrial regions and the wide atmospheric space and occupies three abodes (6.61.11-12). She is invoked to descend from the sky, from the great mountain, to the sacrifice (5.43.11). She is besought to come 'swelling with streams' (6.52.6) and, alongwith the waters, the bestowers of wealth, progeny, and immortality, to grant vitality (10.30.12). She is often said to bestow wealth, plenty, and nourishment (7.95.2; 8.21, 17; 9.67.32; 10.17, 8-9), receives the epithet *subhagā*, bountiful (1.89.3; 7.95.4; 6, 8.21-17). As a mother (*ambā*), she grants reputation to the unrenowned (2.41.16). She stimulates, directs, and makes the devotions of her worshippers prosper (1.3.10-11, 2.3.8; 6.61.4). She is invoked along with the goddesses of prayer (7.37.11; 10.65.13). She destroys the revilers of the gods, is terrible, and a Vṛtra-slayer (6.61.3, 7). But to her worshippers she affords protection and conquers their enemies (7.95.4-5; 2.30.8; 6.49.7). See **Vāk**.

**Sarayu:** Sarayu is mentioned thrice in the *Ṛgveda* as the name of a river. Citraratha and Arṇa are said to have been defeated apparently by the Turvaśas and Yadus, who crossed the Sarayu (4.30.18). Sarayu appears in one passage with Sarasvatī and Sindhu (10.64.9), and in another with Rasā, Anitabhā and Kubhā (5.53.9). Later, in the post-Vedic period, Sarayu is the name of a river in Oudh, the modern Sarayu. It appears that this Sarayu is the river meant in all the Vedic passages. But some scholars have tried to locate the Sarayu in the Punjab. There are others who identify it with the Kurum (*Krumu*) and with the united course of the Śutudri (Sutlej) and Vipās (Beas).

**Sarvamedha:** Vedic sacrifice (*VS* 32.33), so called because at its conclusion the sacrificer gives away all his possessions as *dakṣiṇā* and retires to the forest as a hermit. It belongs to the *ahīna* category of sacrifices prescribed in the *Yajurveda*, Brāhmaṇas and Śrautasūtras.

**Śaryanavant:** This name appears in several passages of the *Ṛgveda* (1-84, 14; 8.6.39; 8.7, 29; 8.64.11; 9.25.22; 9.113.1; 10.35.2) as that of a lake not far from the region near (*jaghana*) Kurukṣetra.

**Satī:** See **Widow**.

**Satvant:** Satvant is the name of a people who are stated in the *Aitareya Brāhmaṇa* (8.14.3) to belong to the south. In the *Śatapatha Brāhmaṇa* (13.5.4.21) Satvants' defeat at the hands of Bharata, and his taking away the horse, which they had prepared for an Aśvamedha (horse sacrifice), are referred to in this. In a passage of the *Aitareya Brāhmaṇa* (2.25) also they are mentioned. They were not on friendly terms with the Bharatas.

**Sautrāmaṇi:** Vedic sacrifice belonging to the *haviryajña* group. It is not a Soma-sacrifice, *surā* being used instead. The other offerings are a bull, a sheep and a goat dedicated to Indra, Sarasvatī and the Aśvins respectively. *Vājasaneyī Saṃhitā* 19-21, *Taittirīya Saṃhitā* 1.8.2, *Taittirīya Brāhmaṇa* 1.4.2; 1.8.5-6; 2.6-7.

**Savana:** Pressing of Soma-juice which used to take place in the morning, at midday and in the evening. The three metres—*gāyatrī*, *triṣṭubh* and *jagatī* are assigned to the three *savanas*. The juice was extracted by pounding the *soma* plant with the pressing stones (*adri*), mixed with water in a vat (*kośa*), poured into two bowls (*camu*), mixed with milk, and finally transferred to the special vessel (*kalasa*).

**Savitṛ:** Savitṛ is pre-eminently a golden deity. His eyes, arms, hands, and tongue are golden, as are his car and its pole. He diffuses golden splendour. He removes evil dreams and drives away demons and sorcerers. In the famous Gāyatrī stanza (3.62.10), which has remained the sacred morning prayer of the Hindus for more than two thousand years, he is invoked to confer his splendour on, and stimulate the thoughts of, the worshipper. When Savitṛ is said to shine with the rays of the sun, to urge the sun or to announce men as sinless to the sun, he is evidently distinguished from Sūrya as in the *Ṛgveda* 7.63. But there are a large number of passages where it is difficult to distinguish between the two. The poets love to play on the name of the god, derived as it is from *su*, which means 'to stimulate'. It is to be noted that he is connected with evening as well as with the morning time. *Ṛgveda* 1.35.9; 10.1.110, 2-3; 1.95.7; 2.38, 7-9; 4.14.2; 4.43.2; 5.82.2; 5.82.2; 5.82, 4; 5.81.4; 6.71.4; 7.79.2; 7.38.7; 7.45.1; 10.158. 1-4; 10.100.8.

**Scabbard:** The word *koṣa-kāri* indicates a scabbard-maker, who is enumerated in the list of victims of Puruṣa-medha. The term appears in the *Vājasaneyī Saṃhitā* 30.14 and *Taittirīya Brāhmaṇa* 3.4.10.1.

**Scepticism:** See **Agnosticism**.

**Science:** See **Anatomy, Astronomy, Botany, Implements, Medical Science, Measures, Metals, Occupations, Warfare, Zoology**.

**Scissors:** Scissors are termed as *bhurija*, having two arms only, used for cutting (*RV* 4.1.14; 9.26.4; 9.71.5). The term *parśu* is denoting the sickle (*AV* 7.28.1; 12.3.31; *TS* 3.2.4.1; *AB* 2.25; *Śāṅkh.B* 10.1; *ŚB* 3.6.4.10, *BU* 6.4.26; *CU* 6.16.1).

**Schools:** Even in early Vedic times centres of Vedic learning, presided over by celebrated Vedic teachers, were scattered all over the country. The *Sāmaveda Sūtras* refer to as many as fifteen *caraṇas* (schools) of the Vājasaneyins, including the *Kānva* and *Mādhyandina* ones. Apart from the *Brāhmaṇa caraṇas*, *Saṃhitā-caraṇas* were also known. Later Sūtra *caraṇas* were established. These schools were mostly concerned with the teaching and interpretations of the texts. The Upaniṣads refer to various philosophical schools receiving royal patronage.

**Sculpture:** Though the description of the Vedic gods has an iconological approach, sculptural evidence has been found which may be confidently called Vedic. A small gold tablet, representing a naked woman standing on her leg in symmetrical rigidity, with exaggerated hips and sexual organs, heavy and clumpy ornaments and in a rigidly angular composition, was dug out near Lauriya Nandangarh. This little plaque supposed to represent Pṛthivī, found in a burial mound regarded as 'Vedic', was identified by Bloch as the iconic representation of the Earth Goddess and was ascribed by him to about the eighth or seventh century BC. A.K. Coomaraswamy, *History of Indian and Indonesian Art*, London 1927, rep. New Delhi 1972, 42; Th. Block in *Archaeological Survey of India*, Annal Review, 1906-7, 122 ff, L. Bachhofar, *Early Indian Sculptures*, Paris 1929, rep. New Delhi 1973, I, 14-15.

**Sea:** See **Ocean**.

**Seaborne Trade:** It is a controversial question whether the Vedic tribes in the days of the *Ṛgveda* had reached the ocean and had knowledge of sea navigation. Keith and many other Western scholars hold that there is no clear indication that sea navigation was known during this period. Max Müller, Lassen and Zimmer on the other hand assert that ocean was known to the Ṛgvedic people. This seems to be the more probable view. The Sarasvatī is stated to have reached the sea and the *Ṛgveda* 10.136.5 *dvausamudrāvā* seem to refer clearly to the Western and Eastern oceans. References to the treasures of the ocean and to Bhujyu's story appear to allude to marine navigation. The knowledge of high tide may be inferred from the *Ṛgveda* (1.48.3). All these references suggest that the Ṛgvedic people not only knew the sea, but were mariners and had trade relations with the outside world. The view that the Ṛgvedic Indians took part in ocean-shipping is however opposed on the following grounds: (1) The *nau* (boat or ship) was, in the majority of cases, merely a boat for crossing rivers, and there may have been large boats in use for crossing the broad rivers of the Punjab. These boats were so simple in their construction that only the paddle or oar (*aritra*) was needed to propel them. There is no mention of masts or sails or rudder or anchor. Thus, the Vedic Indian was not much of a navigator. (2) Metaphors used by a people familiar with the ocean are lacking in the *Ṛgveda*. (3) The numerous mouths of the Indus are ignored, although that river was the convenient natural outlet to the sea. Against these arguments are set down the following facts: (1) The *Ṛgveda* mentions men who go to the ocean (*samudra*) eager for gain (1.56.2 and 4.55.6) and *samudra* can not be explained away in these passages as standing for the very broad and wide stream of the lower Indus. (2) There are some allusions to a trade more extensive than that implied by boats for crossing rivers. (3) Verses (*RV* 1.116.3) tell us that the Aśvins rescued Bhujyu in the ocean with a ship of a hundred oars (*śataritra*). A ship of this type could be needed only for a sea-voyage. (4) the *Ṛgveda* (10.136.5) refers to 'Eastern and Western oceans'. These passages seem to indicate that sea-trade was carried on during this age. The sea was undoubtedly known and there was probably some amount of sea-borne trade. In the texts of this period, *samudra* is frequently used in the definite sense of the 'sea'. The texts speak of the 'inexhaustible sea' (*RV* 5.16.7) and 'the sea as encircling the earth'. The Eastern and Western oceans (mentioned in the *ŚB*) are probably references to the Indian ocean and the Arabian Sea.

**Seasons:** *Ṛtu* 'season', is a term repeatedly mentioned from the *Ṛgveda* (1.49.3) onwards. Three seasons of the year are often allued to (*RV* 1.164.2; *ŚB* 14.1.1.28), but the names are not usually specified. In one passage of the *Ṛgveda* (10.90.6), spring (*vasanta*), summer (*grīṣma*) and autumn (śarad) are given. The *Ṛgveda* also knows the rainy season (*prā-vṛs*) and the winter (*hima, hemanta*). A more usual (*AV* 8.2.22; 13.1.18; *TS* 1.6.2.3, 4.3.3; 1-2; 5.1.10.3, etc.; *MS* 1.7.3; 3.4.8; *KS* 4.14.9.16; *VS* 10.10-14; *ŚB* 1.3.5.11; 6.2.2.3; *TB* 3.10.4.1, etc.) division (not found in the *Ṛgveda*) is into five seasons: *vasanta, grīṣma, varṣā, śarad, hemanta-śiśira;* but occasionally the five are otherwise divided, *varṣā-śarad* being made one season (*ŚB* 13.6.1). Sometimes six (*AV* 6.55.2; 12.1.36; *TS* 5.1.5.2; 7.3, 2.5.1; *MS* 1.7.3; 3.11.12; *KS* 8.6; *VS* 21.23-28; *ŚB* 1.7.2.21; 2.4.2.24; 12.8.2.34; *TB* 2.6.19, etc.) seasons are reckoned, *hemanta* and *śiśira* being divided, so that the six seasons can be with equated to the twelve months of the year. A still more artificial arrangement (*AV* 6.61.2; 8.9.18; *ŚB* 8.5.1.15; 9.1.2.31; 2.3.45; 3.1.19; 5.2.8) makes the seasons seven, possibly by reckoning the intercalary month as a season, as Weber and Zimmer held, or more probably because of the predilection for the number seven, as Roth suggests. Occasionally the word *ṛtu* is applied to the months (*AV* 15.4; *TS* 4.4.11.1; *VS* 13.25.15.57, etc.). The last season, according to the *Śatapatha Brāhmaṇa* (1.5.3.13), is *hemanta*. The growth of the division of the seasons from three to five is rightly explained by Zimmer as indicating the advance of the Vedic Indians towards the east. Though not a Ṛgvedic concept, it dominates the later Saṃhitās. Traces of an earlier division of the year into winter and summer do not appear clearly in the *Ṛgveda*, where the appropriate words *hima* and *sama* are merely general appellations of the year and where *śarad* is commoner than either as a designation of the year, because it denotes the harvest, a time of the overwhelming importance to an early agricultural people. The division of the year in one passage of the *Atharvaveda* (8.9.17) into two periods of six months is merely formal, and in no way an indication of old tradition. The term *ārtava* denotes a portion of the year consisting of more seasons than one. But it does not bear the exact sense of 'half-year', as suggested by Zimmer. This is shown by the fact that it occurs regularly in the plural, not in the dual. In the *Atharvaveda* (3.10.9) it appears between seasons and years (*hāyana*) but also in the combinations, 'seasons, *ārtavas*, months, years (3.10.10); 'half-months, months, *ārtavas*, seasons (11.7.20)'; 'seasons, *ārtavas*, months half-months, days and nights, day (16.8.18)'; and, in the *Vājasaneyī Saṃhitā* 'months, seasons, *ārtavas*, the year (22.28)'; or simply with the seasons (*AV* 10.6.18; 11.3.17; *TS* 7.2.6, 1, 3; *KauU.* 1.3). Macdonell and Keith, I. 63-4, 110-11.

**Seasoner:** A seasoner or sprinkler is denoted by the term *prakaritṛ*, which is found in the *Vājasaneyī Saṃhitā* 30.12 and *Taittirīya Brāhmaṇa* 3.4.8.1.

**Seats:** The generic term for a seat of some sort is *āsandī* (*AV* 14.2.65; 1.5.3.2; *TS* 7.5.8.5; *VS* 8.56, 19.16, etc.). A general description of a seat is found in the *Atharvaveda* (15.3.2), which was two feet square and made of wood. It was often covered with a cushion (*āstaraṇa*) and a pillow (*upabarhaṇa*) and also a support (*upaśraya*), which made the whole thing a form of modern chair. Similar seats are described in the *KauU* (1.5) and *the Jaiminīya Brāhmaṇa* (2.24). The seat for the king at the royal consecration is described in very similar terms in the *Aitareya Brāhmaṇa* (8.5 ff), where the height of the feet is placed at a span, and the lengthwise and cross-pieces are each to be a cubit, while the interwoven part (*vivayana*) is to be made of *muñja*-grass, and the seat of *udumbara*-wood. In another passage of the *Atharvaveda* (14.2.65), there is reference to a long reclining chair. A cushion (*upādhāna*) and coverlet (*upavāsana*) are mentioned. According to the *Śatapatha Brāhmaṇa* (5.4.4.1), the *āsandi* should be made of *khadira*-wood, perforated and joined with straps. The imperial seat (*ŚB* 14.1.3.8) is to be shoulder-high, of *udumbara*-wood, and wound all over the cords of *balvaja*-grass. Elsewhere in the same text (6.7.1.12), the seat is a span-high and a cubit in width and depth. A tiger-skin serves as the *āstaraṇa* or coverlet of the king's seat in the royal consecration (*AB* 8.5).

**Seclusion, of Women:** Seclusion of women during the time of their menstruation, which is so much stressed in the Dharmaśāstras and Purāṇas, has no mention in the early Vedic texts. It is only in the Gṛhyasūtras that it is stated that a student must not see a woman in her courses. After the *samāvartana* he must be careful at least for three days so that he may not come across a menstruating woman. The vedas must not be recited before a woman who is in her monthly impurity. Those who have retired from family should not also see a menstruating woman. A student must not talk or play with girls in their menses. *ŚGS* 2.12.10, 4.7.48, 4.11.6, 6.1.3, *PGS* 4.7.48, *GGS* 3.5.6, *KhDS* 3.1.36.

**Secret Paramours:** *Upapati* denoting secret paramour occurs in the *Vājasaneyī Saṃhitā* (30.9) and *Taittirīya Brāhmaṇa* (3.4.4.1). In the *Ṛgveda* 1.134.3, 1.117.18, 1.134.3, 1.52.4, 9.31.5, *jāra* means simply lover, though in special cases the word means an illegitimate lover (*BU* 6.4.11). According to Sāyaṇa, *jāra* is suggested in the *Ṛgveda* (1.134.3) in the sense of *upapatyāgaman-adhyānena*, i.e. meditation for meeting a lover, akin to husband. See **Sexual Laxity**.

**Security, Royal:** The chief obstacles to the irresponsible exercise of royal authority were: (a) the vested rights of the king's own kinsmen, who were ever ready to displace the ruling princes, by taking advantage of enemy attacks, or the discontent of the subjects. This importance of the royal kinsmen, who remained 'equals' to the king, is to be inferred from various passages. These speak of *rājānaḥ* by the side of king. In one passage, Yama is said to have his *sabhāsadarājānaḥ* (*AV* 3.20). (b) The alertness on the part of the people, ready to take up arms, whenever the king proved tyrannical or whenever his exactions injured them. At the same time, they could be used by any ambitious prince, who could win them over with promises. In the body-politic, the personal element predominated and personal relation between the king and the subjects was only a political bond. The *rāṣṭra* or the community was not considerable and, as such, popular anger or discontent was fatal to the king. Therefore, the king was bound to take popular opinion into consideration. They had not yet sunk into the position of *prajāḥ* (meaning both children and subjects, but originally meaning only the former) but were the free *viśaḥ*. The king, therefore, was bound to rely on the goodwill and support of both these elements. The influence of the former was immense and this is confirmed by the evidence of the hymns of the *Ṛgveda* or the *Atharvaveda*. While the evidence is rather scanty in the former, in the latter, we find that the kinsmen of the king, his own relatives together with a number of other important personages, had formed a body of men that selected the ruling prince and probably guided his conduct. The following passages from the *Atharvaveda* fully illustrate the point. Thus, in one passage of the *Atharvaveda* (1.9.3), the priest clearly invokes the help of Indra, Agni, Varuṇa and other gods to save the king from his enemies and rivals and to exalt him high above his kinsmen. In a large number of hymns we find the same idea. Thus, in another hymn (3.4) of the *Atharvaveda*, on the occasion of royal inauguration, the king is told that the tribesmen shall elect him for kingship and that kinsmen (*sajātaḥ*) should support him. The person of the king thus required safety and security because he had to live with ambitious rivals.

**Seed:** *Bīja* is seed which occurs in the *Ṛgveda* (10.85.37; 10.94.13; 10.101.3; *ŚB* 7.2.2.54). *Dhānyaṃ bījam* (*RV* 5.53.13) means the seed of corn. See **Agriculture, Grains**.

**Seer:** The term *ṛṣi*, which means 'seer', primarily denotes a composer of hymns to the gods (*RV* 1.1-2; 1.45.3; 8.43.13, etc.). Old poems were inherited and refurnished by members of the composer's family (*RV* 1.89.3; 1.96.2; 3.39.2; 8.6.11, etc.), but the emergence of new seers was desired (*RV* 1.109.2; 2.18.3; 3.62.7; 6.50.6; 7.14.4; 7.93.1; 8.23.14). The *ṛṣi* or seer was the most exalted of brāhmaṇas (*RV* 9.96.6; *ŚB* 12.4.4.6) and was regarded as heaven-sent (*RV* 1.37.4; 7.36.1; 8.32.27, etc.). A *rājanya-ṛṣi*, the prototype of the later *rājarṣi* or 'royal seer', appears in the *Pañcaviṃśa Brāhmaṇa* (12.12.6). In later literature a seer is regularly cited when a Vedic Saṃhitā is quoted. The seers become the representatives of a sacred past and are regarded as holy sages, whose deeds are narrated as if they were the deeds of gods or Asuras (*AB* 1.27, 2.19; *ŚB* 1.6.2.7). They are typified by a particular group of seven, mentioned in the *Ṛgveda* (4.42.8; 10.109.4; 10.130.7) and the later Saṃhitās (*VS* 14.24; *AV* 11.1.1; 12.1.39, etc.) and enumerated in the Upaniṣads (cf. *BU* 2.2.6 ff). The *Atharvaveda* (4.29) contains a long list of their names.

**Self:** See **Ātman**.

**Semen:** The idea of *retas*, the germ of life, is equated in the Veda with *soma*. The father's sperm and mother's ovum are both two forms of *soma*: *reto vai somaḥ* (*ŚB* 1.9.2.9). The forms of *retas* or semen may be different in the two parents, but they are essentially one and the same principles: *ubhayataḥ parigṛhitaṃ vai retaḥ prajāyate* (*ŚB* 2.3.1.32). The seed is the same as birth. Both *retas* and *soma*, whatever be their material form in the male and the female, are but the same life-principle. In the Vedas it is prayed that the person of excellent vigour may procreate offspring with his semen. May the vigorous male moisten your womb with the semen in pulsating more and create offspring so that they may live hundred autumns (*AV* 3.14.7). The cycle of creation has been excellently described in the following extract from the Āraṇyaka: *athāto retasaḥ sṛṣṭi*, etc. 'Then comes the origin of seed. The seed of Prajāpati are the gods. The seed of the gods is rain. The seed of rain is herbs. The seed of herbs is food. The seed of food is seed (see **Sex Rites**). The seed of seed is creatures' (*AĀ* 2.1.3; tr. A.B. Keith). In the Upaniṣads the term *retas* has been used to mean *bīja*. 'Woman, verily, O Gautama is a sacrificial fire'. In this case the sexual organ is the fuel. When one invites the smoke, the vulva, the flame; when one inserts, the coals, the sexual pleasure, the sparks. In this fire the gods offer semen. From this oblation arises the foetus (*CU* 5.8.1-2; tr. Hume). Both the sperm and ovum have some spiritual significance. To the seers they represent Agni and Āditya. 'The blood in the woman is the form of Agni, therefore one should despise it not. The seed in the man is the form of Āditya, therefore one should despise it not' (*AB* 2.3.7; tr. A.B. Keith).

**Serpents:** *Aghāśva* is the name of a serpent in the *Atharvaveda* (10.4.10). *ajagara* (goat-swallower) appears in the *Atharvaveda* (11.2.25; 20.129.17) and in the list of animals at the horse sacrifice as the boa-constrictor. Elsewhere (*TS* 5.5.13.1; *VS* 24.34), it is called *vāhasa*. It denotes a person at the snake feast in the *Pañcaviṃśa Brāhmaṇa* (25.14). *Asita* is a name of the black snake, referred to in the later Saṃhitās (*AV* 3.27.1; 5.13.5; 5.13.6; 6.56.2, *TS* 5.5.10.1; *MS* 3.14.18). *Āligī* is the name of a kind of serpent in the *Atharvaveda* (5.13.7). *Āśī-viṣa* appearing only in the *Aitareya Brāhmaṇa* (6.1), means 'having poison (*viṣa*) in its fangs' (*āśī*). *Kanikrada* or *karikrata* denotes a snake in the *Atharvaveda* (10.4.13). *Kalmāṣagrīva* (speckled neck) is the name of a snake in the *Atharvaveda* (3.27.5; 12.3.59; cf. *TS* 5.5.10.2). *Kasarṇīla* is the name of a kind of snake in the *Atharvaveda* (10.4.5). It appears also in the form *kasarṇīra*, personified as the seer *Kasarnira Kādraveya* in the *Taittirīya Saṃhitā* (1.5.4.1). *Jūrṇi* is one of the names given to serpents in a hymn of the *Atharvaveda* (2.24.5), perhaps from their habit of casting their slough. *Tiraścarāji* (*TS* 5.5.10.2) or *tiraśei-rāji* (*AV* 3.27.2; 6.56.2; 7.56.1; 10.4.13; 12.3.56, *tiraścīna-rāji* (*MS* 2.13.21; *SA* 12.27) are variant forms of a name for 'snake' (lit. striped across), found in the later Saṃhitās. *Taimāta* is twice mentioned as a species of snake in the *Atharvaveda* (5.13.6; 5.18.4). *Darvī* properly denotes a ladle, in which sense it is found in the *Ṛgveda* (5.6.9; 10.105.10) and later (*AV* 3.10.7; 4.14.7; 9.6.17). But the word also means a serpent's hood in the *Atharvaveda* (10.1.13), though Zimmer regards it as the name of a serpent. *Daśonasi* or *Naśonaśī* are the names of a kind of snake in the *Atharvaveda* (10.4.17). *Nāga* appears once in the *Śatapatha Brāhmaṇa* (11.2.7.12), in the form *mahānāga*, where great snake or 'great elephant' may be meant. In the *Bṛhadāraṇyaka Upaniṣad* (1.3.24) and in a citation found in the *Aitareya Brāhmaṇa* (8.22) the sense of 'elephant' is clearly intended. In the Sūtras the mythic *Nāga* already occurs. *Ratharvī* is the name of a snake in the *Atharvaveda* (10.4.5). *Lohitāhi*, red snake is the name of a variety of serpent mentioned in the list of victims of the horse sacrifice in the *Yajurveda Saṃhitās* (*TS* 5.5.14.1; *MS* 3.14.12; *VS* 24.31). *Viligī* denotes a kind of snake in the *Atharvaveda* (5.13.7). Śerabha or *śerabhaka* is the name of some snake or demon (2.24.1). *Śevṛdha* or *Sevṛdhaka* also denotes the same in the *Atharvaveda* (2.24.1). *Svitra* (white) is the name of a species of serpent in the *Atharvaveda* (3.27.6; 10.4.5.13) and the later *Saṃhitās* (*TS* 5.5.10.2; *MS* 2.13.21). *Satīna-Kaṅkata* in the *Ṛgveda* (1.191.1), is the name of some animal, perhaps an aquatic snake according to Sāyaṇa. *Sarpa*, general name of serpent, appears once in the *Ṛgveda* (10.16.6), where *ahi* is the usual word, but often later (*AV* 10.4.23; 11.3.47; *TS* 1.5.4.1; 3.1.1.1). *Svaja* in the *Atharvaveda* (3.27.4; 5.14.10; 10; 6.56.2; 10.4.10; 10.4.15; 10.4.17; 12.3.58) and later (*TS* 5.5.10.2; 5.5.14.1; *AB* 3.26.3) denotes the viper. The word is explained by the commentators as *sva-ja*, 'self-born', or it may be derived from the root *svaj*, clasp, encircle. In the *Maitrāyaṇī Saṃhitā* (3.9.3) the *hariṇa* is said to kill the viper.

**Serpent Lore:** The most common animal used for symbolic purpose is the serpent (*ahi*-Avestan, *azhi*). This is another designation of the demon Vṛtra, who probably received his name as a formidable enemy of mankind, enveloping his prey like a serpent in his coils. The Vṛtra-slayer Indra is also called the serpent slayer (*RV* 8.82.2; cf. 4, 14.1); the identity of Ahi and Vṛtra is clear when the terms interchange (*RV* 1.32.1, 2, 4-14); and by the first born of the serpents (16.3.4) none other than Vṛtra can be meant. In several passages too, the words are in opposition and may be translated as the serpent Vṛtra. When Ahi is mentioned alone, the result of Indra's victory over him is the same as in the case of Vṛtra, the god causing the waters to flow, delivering the seven stream, or winning the chaos. The waters are also described as encompassed by the serpent. The action being expressed by the root *vṛ* (*RV* 2.19.2) among others. They are said to be similarly swallowed by the serpent (*RV* 4.14.1; 10. 111.9). Ahi is armed with lightning, thunder and hail (*RV* 1.32.13). He is bright, for the Maruts are called *ahibhānavaḥ*, shining like *ahi* (1.172.1); and the term *ahi* is applied to Agni, who is described as a 'raging serpent like the rushing wind' (*RV* 1.79.1); Soma is besought to deliver an enemy as *ahi* (7.104.9). The plural of the word is occasionally used to express a race of demons (9.88.4; 10, 139.6), as whom the Ahi is the first born (1.32.9.4). However, the serpent also appears as a divine being in the form of Ahi Budhnya, who seems to represent the beneficent side of the character of Ahivṛtra. In the later Saṃhitās, the serpents (*sarpāḥ*) are found as a class of semi-divine beings beside the Gandharvas and others. They are spoken of as being in earth, air, and heaven (*VS* 13.6; cf. *TB* 3.1.4). They are often mentioned in the the *Atharvaveda*, one hymn of which (11.9) is sometimes interpreted as invocation of certain serpent divinities.

**Sesamum:** *Tila,* 'sesamum' of cultivated variety, as a food grain, occurs in the *Atharvaveda* (2.8.3; 6.140.2; 18.3.69; 18.4.32), *Maitrāyaṇī Saṃhitā* (4.3.2); *Taittirīya Saṃhitā* (2.7.10.2); *Vājasaneyī Saṃhitā* (18.12); *Śatapatha Brāhmaṇa* (1.236, 2.310). From this a rich oil was extracted. It is attributed to the cool season (*TS* 7.2.10.2). *Tilaudana* is mentioned in *Śāṅkhāyana Āraṇyaka* (12.8). A wild variety of sesamum grain is called by the name *jartila*. It is *akṛṣṭapācya* (*ŚB* 9.1.1.3; *TS* 5.4.3.2), that is uncultivated, and hence is unfit for sacrificial offering. Sesamum plant was also used for fuel.

**Settlement Pattern:** The whole of the territory known to the Vedic settlers was divided into a number of tribal principalities, normally ruled by chiefs. The Bharatas, who gave their name to the whole country, are the most important of the Ṛgvedic tribes. In the Ṛgvedic age, they were settled in the region between the Sarasvatī and Yamunā. They appeared prominently in the *Ṛgveda*, in relationship with Sudās and the Tṛtsus, and were enemies of the Purus. Their princes carried out sacrifices on the Sarasvatī, Dṛṣadvatī, and Āpayā, i.e. Kurukṣetra of later times. The exact relation of the Tṛtsus and Bharatas cannot be determined and there is a sharp differences of opinion among scholars on this subject. The Tṛtsus occupied the country to the east of the Paruṣṇī. The Tṛtsus and their kinsfolk, the Bharatas, were at war with the various tribes on both sides of the Paruṣṇī and Yamunā, as already stated. In post-Ṛgvedic times, however, they coalesced with the Purus, their erstwhile enemies, to form the Kuru people of later times. The *Ṛgveda* refers to the Sṛñjayas as being the allies of the Tṛtsus. The Purus have been mentioned in the *Ṛgveda* along with Kurus, Druhyus, Turvaśas and Yadus. Though defeated in the Dāsarājña, the Purus were a very important tribe in the days of the *Ṛgveda*. They were closely connected with the Tṛtsus and the Bharatas, and lived on either side of the Sarasvatī. The unusually large number of kings of the Purus suggests the importance of the tribe. The name Kuru is not directly mentioned in the *Ṛgveda*, but the amalgamation of these rival tribes in later Vedic period under Kuru is implied by the name Kuruśravaṇa, a king of the Puru line as shown by his Patronymic Trāsadasyava (*RV* 10.33.4). Connected with the Kurus were the Krivis, a comparatively unimportant tribe who possibly lived on the Sindhu (Indus) and the Asiknī (Chenab), and later moved to the east, across the Yamunā to the land later known as Pañcāla. The insignificance of the Krivis in later literature as compared with the importance of the Pañcālas is probably due to the fact that the later Kuru-Pañcāla alliance included not only the Bharatas and other tribes but Krivis also. The *Śatapatha Brāhmaṇa* (13.5.4.7) asserts that Krivi was the older name of the Pañcālas. Closely allied with the Tṛtsus was the tribe of the Sṛñjayas, who lived in their neighbourhood, probably in Pañcāla. The Anus, Druhyus, Yadus and Turvaśas were the allies of the Purus against the Bharatas. The Druhyus, Turvaśas and Anus lived between the Asiknī and Paruṣṇī. The names Yadu and Turvaśa normally appear together in the *Ṛgveda*. These two closely allied tribes lived in the southern Punjab and probably further south. The name Turvasa disappears from later Vedic literature, possibly because they became merged in the Pañcāla people. In the epic age the Matsyas lived to the west of the Surasenas of Mathurā, i.e. in modern Alwar, Bharatpur, and Jaipur, which was probably their home in the Ṛgvedic age also. The Ajas, Sigrus and Yakṣus were probably the eastern people. They are generally regarded as non-Aryan, though there is no definite information on this point. The Pakthas, Bhalānases, Viṣāṇins, Alinas, and Śivas were the five frontier tribes. The Pakthas lived in the hills from which the Krumu originated. South of the Pakthas stretched the Bhalānases, for whom some scholars suggest east Kabulistan as original home. So-called probably because their helmets were horn-shaped or ornamented with horns, the Viṣānins were like their allies, a tribe of the north-west, located farther down between the Krumu and the Gomatī. North-east of Kafiristan has been suggested as the location of the Alinas, who were closely allied with the Pakthas. The Śivas lay between the Sindhu and Vitastā in the Vedic period. The Cedis, who dwelt probably between the Yamunā and the Vindhyas, had a very powerful king named Kasu. The Uśīnaras are mentioned in the *Aitareya Brāhmaṇa* as dwelling in the middle country, along with the Vasa and the Kuru-Pañcālas. The Gandhāris, one of the frontier peoples, lived to the extreme north-west of India. The good wool of the sheep of the Gandhāri has been referred to in the *Ṛgveda* (1.126.7). The Pārāvatas appearing in several passages of the *Ṛgveda* have been rightly taken as a people on the Yamunā on the strength of the mention of the Sarasvatī in their location in the *Pañcaviṃśa Brāhmaṇa*. The Kīkaṭas occur in the *Ṛgveda* (3.53.14) as a people under Pramaganda's leadership. They are taken as non-Aryans and located in the country later known as Magadha.

**Sex Rites:** In many passages in Vedic literature, sexual union is identified with *Yajña* or sacrifice or with some of its aspects. In the *Atharvaveda* (6.11.1-3), for example, the rubbing of the two pieces of woods (*aśvattha* and *śamī*) to churn fire, used as an expedient to ensure the birth of a male child, is thought of in terms of sexual intercourse. In the *Taittirīya Saṃhitā* (4.2.5.5) the act of sowing seed in the field is likewise thought of in terms of sowing seed in the womb: 'Yoke the ploughs, stretch apart the yokes, here, sew in the womb, make ready the seed (Keith, *Vedas of the Black Yajus School*, Cambridge, 1914, 315). In the *Aitareya Brāhmaṇa* (1.1) a Soma ritual intended to generate offspring and cattle among those who are unsupported by all these, requires mixing of clarified butter with rice grain, the former standing for female blood and the latter for the male semen. We quote from Keith's translation: 'A pap in ghee should he offer, who considers himself unsupported; in this (earth) does he not find support who does not find support. *Ghee* is the milk (blood) of the woman and rice grains that of the man; that is a pairing; with a paring verily does he propagated with offspring and cattle, for generation; he is propagated with horse and cattle who knows thus' (Keith, *Ṛgveda Brāhmaṇas*, HOS XXV, London, 1920, 107). In other passages of the *Aitareya Brāhmaṇa* (2.35), greatest importance is attached to symbolic copulation as a means of generating offspring and cattle. 'Forward to your god Agni are Anuṣṭubh (verses). He separates the two first *pādas*; therefore a woman separates her thighs. He creates the last two Padas; therefore a man unites his things. That is a pairing; verily thus he makes a pairing at the beginning of the litany, for generation; he is propagated with offspring, with cattle who knows thus' (Keith, *Ṛgveda Brāhmaṇas*, London, 1920, 159). The same is repeated in the *KauB* (14.1). 'The *anuṣṭubh* is speech; whatever is described by speech, the *anuṣṭubh*, all that he obtains. He separates the two *pādas*; that is a symbol of generation; a man takes apart as it were (the limbs) of his wife. Further in that he takes apart, that is a symbol of support' (*Ibid.*). In the *Śatapatha Brāhmaṇa* (1.9.27; 1.9.2.11; 6.4.3.7; 6.6.1.11; 6.6.2.8) we come across numerous passages in which sexual union is identified with sacrifice. There are more than one hundred passages and sometimes deal with 'productive pairs', in which symbolic and sometimes direct emphasis on sexual intercourse is found (*SBE* 12, 194 ff; 26.61 ff; 44.15 ff). Here we reproduce some specimens from the *Patnīsaṃyāja* section. The mistress then unites the Veda-bunch. The altar (*vedi*) assuredly is female and the Veda is male. For the Veda is male; and, accordingly, when he touches the altar with it during the sacrifice, a union productive of offspring is thereby effected. And (the reason) why it is the mistress who unites the Veda (is thus): the mistress is female and the Veda is male; consequently a union productive of offspring is thereby effected; this is why the mistress unites the Veda (*ŚB* 1.9.2.21-2; *SBE* 12, 194). In the *Chāndogya Upaniṣad* (2.13) we have the following passage: 'One summons; that is a *hiṃkāra*. He makes request; that is a *prastāva*. Together with the woman he lies down; that is an *udgītha*. He lies upon the woman that is a *pratihāra*. He comes to the end; that is a *nidhāna*. He comes to the finish; that is a *nidhāna*. This is the *Vāmadevya sāman* as woven upon copulation. He who knows thus this *Vāmadevya sāman* as woven upon copulation, comes to copulation, procreates himself from every copulation, reaches a full length of life, lives long, becomes great in offspring and in cattle, great in fame. One should never abstain from any woman. That is his rule' (Hume's trans.). In many scattered passages of the Upaniṣads, the woman is conceived as the sacrificial fire, her lower portion as the sacrificial woods, the genitalia as the flames, the penetration as the carbon and the copulation as the spark (*CU* 5.8.1-2). 'Woman, verily, O Gautama, is a sacrificial fire. In this case the sexual organ is the fuel; when one invites, the smoke; the vulva, the flame; when one inserts, the coals; the sexual pleasure, the sparks. In this fire the gods offer semen. From this oblation arises the foetus' (Hume's trans. cf. *BU* 6.2.13). The *Bṛhadāraṇyaka Upaniṣad* (6.4.6-7) says that the lower portion of a woman (*upastha*) is to be conceived as the sacrificial altar, her skin (*habiścarman*) as the floor for the pressing of the *soma* plants (*adhisavana*), and the two labia of the vulva (*muṣkau*) as the innermost fire. He who remembers this during copulation gets the reward of the Vājapeya sacrifice. The same Upaniṣad goes on so far as to state that if a woman refuses sexual union she must be forced to do so (*BU* 4.4.6.7).

**Sexual Laxity:** As sexual desire leads to the procreation and birth of beings, so the Vedic thinkers considered sexual desire as the primal source of all existence (10.129). The term *mārya* is regarded as a young lover in the *Ṛgveda* (3.31.7; 3.33.10; 4.20.5, etc.), who is constantly mentioned as in the company with maidens (*yuvati*). In the *Ṛgveda* (2.10.5) the word *maryaśrī* denotes a virile person. The term *jāra*, frequently used in the *Ṛgveda* (1.66.8; 1.117.18; 1.152.4; 9.32.5), leads to the assumption that women sometimes kept connections with unlawful lovers. The presumption is based on a domestic ritual formula in the *Ṛgveda* (10.162.5; 10.162.6), which indicates women having illegitimate lovers. In the *Ṛgveda* (9.32.5, 9.56.3, 10.34.5) a society permissive towards sexual matters may be presupposed in the *Vājasaneyī Saṃhitā* (30.9). Illegitimate sexual relation is found in the *Vājasaneyī Saṃhitā* (30.9; *TB* 3.4.4.1) and *Bṛhadāraṇyaka Upaniṣad* (6.4.11). Indra's illicit relation with Ahalyā, wife of Gautama, is foreshadowed in the *Bṛhadāraṇyaka Upaniṣad* (6.4.11).

**Shampoo:** See **Hair-dressing**.

**Share:** See **Distribution.**

**Shaving:** The term *vapana* means the process of shaving (*TS* 2.7.17.1; *ŚB* 3.1.2.1) and the term *vaptṛ* denotes shaver, barber (*RV* 10.142.4; *AV* 8.2.17; *TB* 1.5.6.3). Razor (*kṣura*), an implement of shaving, was used for this purpose (*AV* 6.68.1, 3).

**Sheaf:** *Parṣa* occurs in the *Ṛgveda* (10.48.7, *Nirukta* 3.10, *ŚB* 13.4.2.5) denoting the plural 'sheaves' strewn over the threshing floor.

**Shed:** Sheds, meant for various purposes of roofing, are denoted by the term *śālā* found in the *Atharvaveda* (5.31.5; 6.106.3; 8.6.10; 9.3.1; 14.1.63); *Taittirīya Brāhmaṇa* (1.2.3.1), *Śatapatha Brāhmaṇa* (3.1.1.6), etc.

**Sheep:** The terms for sheep are *meṣa* and *meṣī* (*RV* 1.43.6; 1.116.16; 8.2.40; 10.27.17); *Atharvaveda* (6.49.2), *Vājasaneyī Saṃhitā* (3.59, 19.90), *Taittirīya Saṃhitā* (4.12.1); *Śatapatha Brāhmaṇa* (3.4.4.18). Both words are also used to denote the wool of the sheep, especially employed for some filter. The sheep of Gandhāra are very much praised in the *Ṛgveda* for their nice quality of wool.

**Shell:** *Śaṅkha* in the *Atharvaveda* (4.10.1) denotes a shell. In the *Bṛhadāraṇyaka Upaniṣad* (3.4.9, 4.5.10) it denotes a conch, used for blowing a wind instrument. *Kakkata* denotes crab in the *Taittirīya Saṃhitā* (5.5.15.1) and the *Vājasaneyī Saṃhitā* (24.32).

**Ship:** Since the Vedic Indians had knowledge of sea, they must have used ships for travelling to distant lands. But there were no separate terms for boat and ship, and the word *nau* denoted boat. In fact, prior to the invention of steam-run ships, sea-faring ships were nothing but bigger forms of boat. The term *nau* is frequently mentioned in the *Ṛgveda* (1.131.2; 2.39; 4.8.42.3; 8.83, 3); *Atharvaveda* (92.36.5; 5.19.8); *Taittirīya Saṃhitā* (5.3.10.1); *Vājasaneyī Saṃhitā* (10.19) and the *Śatapatha Brāhmaṇa* (18.1.4, 4.2.5-10) in the meaning of ship or boat. Sea-voyage is referred to in the *Ṛgveda* (1.116.5). Aśvins rescued Bhujyu in the ocean with a ship having a hundred oars (*śataritra*). Destruction of a kingdom where brāhmaṇas are harassed is compared with shipwreck in the *Atharvaveda* (5.19.8). The term *nāva* denotes ship (*RV* 1.97.8). The word *sairavati* denotes a particular type of vessel used in connection with sea (*AB* 6.29.5). *Dyumna* is a term which perhaps denotes raft or a lifeboat or small boat (*RV* 8.19, 14). The term *maṇḍa* denotes part of a boat or rudder. *Maṇḍa* indicates two rudders of a ship (*ŚB* 2.3.3.15). The term *naumaṇḍa* denotes the deck of the ship (*JB* 1.125). A word for boatman is *nāvāja* (*ŚB* 2.3.3.5). It is mentioned that merchants journeyed across the ocean to distant countries in pursuit of wealth (*RV* 1.48.3). One passage refers to a well-rigged ship in which Varuṇa and Vasiṣṭha sailed to mid-ocean (*RV* 7.8.3-4). A prayer for prosperity in distant lands is also found in the *Ṛgveda* (1.97.8). 'O Lord, take us in a ship across the oceans for our well-being', a kind of vessel called a *plava* is described in some detail (1.24.35-36). It is said to be strongly constructed and able to withstand the battering of storms. It is also described as having 'wings' which are perhaps some sort of archaic stabilizers. The *Śatapatha Brāhmaṇa* (2.3.3.15) refers to a clear reference to maritime navigation. This also occurs in the *Baudhāyana Dharmasūtra* (1.2.4; 2.2.2).

**Shovel:** *Khanitra* 'shovel', 'spade' for digging occurs in *Ṛgveda* 1.179.6; *Taittirīya Brāhmaṇa* 2.182; *Taittirīya Brāhmaṇa* 1.6.6.3, etc. See **Implements.**

**Sickle:** The word for sickle is *dātra*, which appears in the *Ṛgveda* 8.78.10; *Maitrāyaṇī Saṃhitā* 4.29. Another word for sickle is *sṛṇi*, which appears in the *Ṛgveda* 1.58.4, 10.101.3, 4, 106.6; *Śatapatha Brāhmaṇa* 7.2.2.5. *Sṛṇi* in the *Ṛgveda* 4.20.5 also means hook.

**Side Post:** Side posts (*pakṣa*) in the *Atharvaveda* (9.3.4), are specially mentioned for the construction of a house. The *pakṣas* were required for holding the roof. The description of the roof (*chandas*) as *catus-pakṣa*, four-sides, in the *Atharvaveda* (3.7.3) tells in favour of this explanation. In the *Kāṭhaka Saṃhitā* (30.5) and the *Taittirīya Brāhmaṇa* (1.2.3.1) the term is used to denote the side posts of a hut or chamber (*śālā*).

**Sieve:** The word for sieve is *titau* (*RV* 10.71.2), which also denotes a 'winnowing fan' used for purifying corn (*śaktu*). The term *pavitra* used for sieve, denotes the soma-filter. It is probably made of fleece of the sheep (or cowhide), but whether woven or plaited is uncertain because of obscure expressions (*RV* 9.16.2; 9.81-47; 9.107.11; *ŚB* 1.1.3.1-3). Another term for sieve is *pavana*, which is used as a purifier of grains (*AV* 4.34.2, 18.3.11). *Putaḥ pavitraiḥ abhad dibañcayanti—AV.* 12.3.25).

**Śigru:** Name of a tribe appearing in the passage of the *Ṛgveda* (7.18.19), in which they are mentioned with the Ajas and the Yakṣus as having been defeated by the Tṛtsus and king Sudās. It is not possible to say whether they were under the leadership of Bheda in their battle against the Tṛtsus. The Śigrus were probably eastern peoples.

**Silamavatī:** In the *Ṛgveda* (10.75.8), Silamavatī is thought by some scholars to be the name of a river. Sāyaṇa thinks that the word means 'rich in hemp'.

**Silver:** *Rajata* in the sense of silver appears in the *Taittirīya Saṃhitā* (1.5.1.2). Ornaments (*rukma ŚB* (12.8.3.11), dishes (*pātra*) *TB* 2.2.9, 7) and coins (*niṣka PB* 7.1.14) all made of silver are also mentioned. The *Atharvaveda* (5.28.1 and 5) refers to silver amulets, bestowing on the warrior 'dexterity with favouring mind'. The *Bṛhadāraṇyaka Upaniṣad* (1.1.2) refers to two vessels called *mahima*, one of gold and another of silver to be placed on two sides of the horse in the Aśvamedha sacrifice. The *Chāndogya Upaniṣad* (4.17.1) speaks of union of gold with silver and of tin with silver. From the above reference we may assume that silver was also manufactured into different articles in the Vedic age.

**Simyu:** *Simyu* occurs in the *Ṛgveda* (7.18.5) as the name of a people who were defeated by Sudās in the Dāsarājña (battle of the ten kings). Being coupled with the Dasyus in another passage (1.100.18) Zimmer concludes that Simyus were non-Aryans. They were probably a non-Aryan tribe of the Gangetic valley.

**Sin:** In the magico-religious doctrine of disease and cure according to the Vedic and later literature, sins are not only supposed to be causes of diseases but identical with diseases and efforts for curing and not different from those of expiating or confessing the sins. Thus, in the *Ṛgveda* (1.24.9) Varuṇa is requested to remove sins (*enas*) committed by the invokers. Elsewhere, Soma and Rudra are requested to remove the sin (*enas*) in the bodies of the diseased person (*RV* 6.74.3). In the *Ṛgveda* (10.97.16) there is a prayer for being free from, among others, sin (*kilbisa*). In the *Atharvaveda* (2.10.1) it is said that various diseases are caused by sin, which binds a man like Varuṇa's fetters. In the *Atharvaveda* (6.26.1 ff) the evil (*pāpman*) is deified and requested to leave the devotees and go to the enemies. In *Kāṭhaka Saṃhitā* (13.2 and 6) it is said that the diseased person is caught by evil (*pāpman*). In order to free him from *pāpman*, evil in the form of disease, a black he-goat is to be offered to Varuṇa, as black is the colour of *pāpman* (*KS* 13.2). In the *Śatapatha Brāhmaṇa* (4.1.3.9) disease and *pāpman* are identified.

**Sindhu:** *Sindhu* in the *Ṛgveda* (1.97.8; 125.5; 2.11.9; 2.25.3; 2.25.5; 3.53.9, etc.) and the *Atharvaveda* (3.13.1; 4.24.2; 10.4.15; 13.3.50; etc.) often means merely 'stream' (cf. *sapta sindhavaḥ*), but it also has (*RV* 1.122.6; 126.1; 4.54.6; 455.3; 5.53.9; 7.95.1; 8.12.3; 8.20.25; 8.25.14; 8.26.18; 10.64.9; *AV* 12.1.3; 14.1.43; *VS* 8.59) the more exact sense of 'the stream' par excellence, the Indus. The name is, however, rarely mentioned after the period of the Saṃhitās, always then appearing in such a way as to suggest distance. The horses from the Indus (*saindhava*) were famous (*BU* 6.2.15).

**Sinīvālī:** Goddess referred to in two hymns of the *Ṛgveda* (2.32; 10.184). She is a sister of the gods, broad-hipped, fair-armed, fair-figured, prolific, a mistress of the family and is implored to grant offsprings. She is invoked with Rākā, Sarasvatī and Guṅgu. In the *Atharvaveda* (8.46.3) she is called the wife of Viṣṇu.

**Sipha:** *Sipha* is found in one passage of the *Ṛgveda* (1.104.3), Sāyaṇa explains the word as the name of a river. It has not been identified.

**Śiva:** Śiva as the name of a people appears once in the *Ṛgveda* (7.18.7), where they share with the Alinas, Pakthas, Bhalānases, and Viṣāṇins the same fate of being defeated by Sudās. There can hardly be any doubt of their identified with the Siboi of the Greeks, who dwelt between the Indus and the Akesines (Asiknī) in Alexander's time. Subsequently, they inhabited the Shorkot region in Jheng in the Punjab, lying between the Ravi and the Chenab. The village of Śivapura, mentioned by the scholiast on Pāṇini (4.2.109) as situated in the northern country, may also preserve the name.

**Skambha:** Principle of 'support' mentioned in the *Atharvaveda* 10.7, 10.8, as a cosmogonic principle within which both entity exist. It is described as a great being, like *puruṣa* with whom it is identified, and is equated with the universe. It is regarded as superior to Prajāpati, who found the world upon it. The sky and the earth are said to be supported on it.

**Skin-garment:** Skin of animals was used as garment in the Vedic period of India. As termed *ajina*, a clothing, it denotes not only skin of deer in the *Atharvaveda* 5.2.1.21, 25. In the *Śatapatha Brāhmaṇa* 3.9.1.12 the term *ajina-vāsin* denoting 'clothed in skin', indicates the use of skin as raiment. The furriers' trade, as *ajina-saṃdha*, appears in the *Vājasaneyī Saṃhitā* 30.15; *ajina-saṃdhaya* in the *Taittirīya Brāhmaṇa* 3.4.13.1; and, *kṛṣṇājina* in the *Atharvaveda* 9.6.17; *Taittirīya Saṃhitā* 2.4.9.21; 5.4.4.4; the *Śatapatha Brāhmaṇa* 1.1.1.22; 1.9.2.35 in respect of use during rituals, it means skin of black antelope. The term *ajina* stands for *brahmacarya*, as a dress of brahmacārins during their student-life in the *Aitareya Brāhmaṇa* 7.3.3.1. *Kṛtti* is used as a robe of skin in the *Maitrāyaṇī Saṃhitā* 2.9.9; *Kāṭhaka Saṃhitā* 17.16; *Taittirīya Saṃhitā* 4.5.10.4 and *Vājasaneyī Saṃhitā* 16.51. In the *Ṛgveda* 10.136.2 *mala* is stated as the raiment of the sages, as denoted by leather. The word *mala*, however, appears with *ajina* in the *Aitareya Brāhmaṇa* 7.33.1, indicating difference in meaning. Cowskin is mentioned in connection with the consecration of the Agniṣṭoma in the *Śatapatha Brāhmaṇa* 3.1.2.13-16 as a garment.

**Slaughterer:** *Śamitṛ* means butcher who cuts up the slaughtered animal to pieces (*RV* 1.162-9-2-3-10; 3.4.10; 5.43.4; *VS* 17.57, 21.21; 23.39; *AB* 2.6.2.7). The term *goghāta* means a cow-killer. The name is mentioned in the list of victims at the human-sacrifice in the *Vājasaneyī Saṃhitā* (30.18) and *Taittirīya Brāhmaṇa* (3.4.18.1). An animal-slaughterer is also termed as *śastṛ* (*RV* 1.162.5; *AV* 9.3.3).

**Slavery:** According to the Marxist historiography, there was an invariable stage of slavery in the process of social evolution. Whether such a stage is really found in India is a matter of great controversy, even among the Marxist historians themselves. While D.R. Chanana and R.S. Sharma admit the existence of such a stage of slavery, D.D. Kosambi rejects it downright. It had been argued by certain scholars, on the basis of the Vedic term *dāsa*, that slavery was prevalent in the Vedic age. Macdonell and Keith (I. 357) write: 'Since the *dāsa* has the sense of 'slave' in several passages of the *Ṛgveda* (7.86.7; 8.56.3; 10.62.10), Roth (*St.*

*Petersburg Dictionary,* s.v.) suggests that in the *Ṛgveda* 8.46.32 the word *dāsān*, 'slave', should be read in place of *dāse*, qualifying *balbūtha*. Zimmer quotes the passage to indicate the admixture of Aryan and *dāsa* blood. See also the *Atharvaveda* 4.9.8; *Chāndogya Upaniṣad* 7.24.2. It is uncertain whether *dāsapravarga*, as an epithet of *rayi*, 'wealth' in the *Ṛgveda* 1.92.8 means 'consisting of troop of slaves'. So Geldner takes the expression in *RV* (1.158.5). *Dāsī*, the feminine, always has this sense from the *Atharvaveda* onwards (*AV* 5.2.26; 12.3.13; 12.4.9; *CU* 5.13.2; *BU* 6.1.10). Aboriginal women were, no doubt, slaves, for on their husbands being slain in battle they would naturally have been taken as servants. They would sometimes also become concubines; thus Kavaṣa was taunted with being the son of a female slave (*dāsyāḥ putraḥ*) in the *Aitareya Brāhmaṇa* (2.19; *KB* 12.3). But on historical ground the *dāsas* meant certain tribes that were regarded as hostile to the Vedic Aryans. Moreover, the *dāsas* were invariably associated with the *dasyus*. S.K. Chatterji (in Majumdar 159) writes: 'The Dāsa-Dasyu people evidently had ramifications or extensions in Iran as well. We have in the south-east of the Caspian the Dahai people noted by the Greeks, and Daha is but the Iranian modification of *dāsa*. In Iranian the word *Dahyu* (whence Modern Persian *dih*) was in use, meaning "country" or "the countryside", which would only appear to have been originally a tribal name, the Iranian equivalent of the Indo-Aryan *dasyu*, generalized to mean the "country" only. In India the words *dāsa* and *dasyu* changed their meaning as names of the enemies of the Aryans, offering them resistance. They were conquered frequently enough and enslaved, and these words came respectively to mean "slaves" and "robbers". The two names appear originally to be related, both being from a root or base *das* or *dās*; the words may after all be Aryan or Indo-European in origin, cf. Sanskrit *dāsati* "follows up", and likely equivalents of this Indo-Aryan root occur in other Indo-European languages. . . .' *Dāsa*, like *dasyu*, sometimes denotes enemies of a demoniac character in the *Ṛgveda* (cf. Macdonell, 157), but in many passages (cf. *Ṛgveda* 5.34.63; 6.22.10; 6.33.3; 6.60.6; 7.83.1; 10.38.3; 10.69.6; 10.83.1; *AV* 5.11.3) the word refers to human foes of the Aryans. The Dāsas are described as having forts (*puraḥ* 2.20.8, called *āyasiḥ*, made of iron; 1.103.3; 3.12.6; 32.10. They are called *śāradih* 'autumnal', in 1.131.4; 1.174.2; 6.20.10; cf. also *dehyas*, 'ramparts', in 6.47.2), and their clans (*viśaḥ*) are mentioned (2.11.4; 4.28.4; 6.25.2). It is possible that the forts, which are called 'autumnal' (*śāradih*) (cf. Macdonell, 60), may be mythical, but it is not necessarily so for the epithet that may allude to their being restored in the autumn season. The *dāsa* colour (*varṇa*) (*RV* 1.101.1; 1.130.8; 2.20.7; 4.16.13; 6.47.21; 7.5.3) is referred to. In the *Vājasaneyī Saṃhitā* (24.30) the day and night (*ahorātri*) are paralleled with the Śūdrārya, which is probably the Aryan and śūdra (the compound is not to be taken as giving the words in the correct order), as an allusion to the black skin of the aborigines, which is also directly mentioned (*kṛṣṇa tvac*, 'black skin' *RV* 1.130.8; 9.41.1). The aborigines (as Dasyus) are called *anās*, 'noseless' and *mṛdhra-vāc*, 'of hostile speech' (5.29.10), and are probably meant as the Phallus worshippers (*śiśna-davāḥ*, whose deity is a phallus) of the *Ṛgveda* (7.21.5, 10.99.3). It is significant that constant reference is made to the differences in religion between Ārya and *dāsa* or *dasyu* (*RV* 1.33.4-5; 4.16.9; 5.7.10; 5.42.9; 6.14.3; 8.70.10; 10.22.7-8, etc.). P.V. Kane writes: In the *Ṛgveda*, however, there are not many passages where the word "*dāsa*" can be said to have been used in the sense of slave.' In the *Ṛgveda* 8.56.3 we read, 'Thou madest a gift to me of one hundred donkeys, of one hundred fleece bearing ewes and one hundred *dāsas*'. It appears that here *dāsa* means slaves or serfs. In the *Ṛgveda* 8.5.38 the sage praises his patron Caidya Kasu: 'The common people sit down at the feet of Caidya Kasu like men crowding round tanners of hides, (*caidya*) who honoured me by giving me ten noblemen that were like gold in appearance.' Here probably the allusion is to a gift of ten captured nobles, made to the sage by Caidya Kasu, the victor. A sage declared in the *Ṛgveda* 8.19.36 'Trāsadasyu, son of Purukutsa, gave me fifty young women'. This probably refers to the gift of female slaves (*dāsīs*). The *Taittirīya Saṃhitā* 7.5.10.1 says, '*dāsīs*' (girl slaves) place jars full of water on their heads and, singing songs and beating their feet against the ground, dance round the mārjālīya. The *Taittirīya Saṃhitā* 2.2.6.3. refers to the gift of a horse or a male (slave). He obtains a portion of himself who accepts (in gift) a being with two rows of teeth, (such as) a horse or a human male; on accepting an animal with two rows of teeth one should offer to Vaiśvānara a mess cooked on twelve potsherds. The *Aitareya Brāhmaṇa* (39.8) mentions large gifts, such as 10,000 girls (*dāsī*) and 10,000 elephants, made by a king to his purohita performing coronation. When the angel of Death tries to dissuade Naciketas from his curiosity to know the destiny of a person after death, he tempts the inquirer (*KU* 1.1.25). 'Here are such handsome women with chariots and musical instruments as cannot be secured (ordinarily) by men; take them, when gifts by me, serve you; do not ask me what happens after death.' The women referred to were probably meant to be serving (or slave) girls who attended on a man as maids and who could dance and sing (Kane II, 180-1).

**Sleep:** In the Upaniṣads, sleep has been considered as physiological and psychological factor conducive to the realization of the self. It implies the complete overcoming of the light, while during dreams—where man only revives the already-experienced impression of wakeful life-there is only a partial overcoming. The separate existence of the individual soul (*vijñānātmā puruṣaḥ*) belongs only to the wakeful and the dreaming states; in the state of deep sleep he is merged into the highest immutable *ātman*, which is the *Brahman.* That in sound sleep the *ātman* rests within the *ākāśa* in the heart, covered up by the 72,000 *nāḍis* called *hitās*, which stretch outwards from the heart to the *purītāt*, is a detail supplied by the *Bṛhadāraṇyaka Upaniṣad* 2.1.16-20. This is also confirmed by the *Kauṣitakī* 4.19 and *Bṛhadāraṇyaka Upaniṣad* 4.3.20. The clearest exposition of the differences between the three states is, of course, afforded by the story of Indra and Virocana in the *Chāndogya Upaniṣad* 8.7 ff., wherein the wakeful state of the *Ātman* is said to be susceptible to all the external and physical affectations of the body, the dream state to transcend these but yet remain liable to afflictions, while the state of sound-sleep is declared to be beyond the physical and the mental mishaps, but not yet completely realizing one's ideal of the true *Ātman* inasmuch as it retains no consciousness as such and may as well be said to be not existing. Belvalkar and Ranade, 372-3. See **Dream, Waking State**.

**Slings:** *Adri* (*RV* 1.51.3) and *aśani* (*RV* 6.6.5, cf. *RV* 1.121.9) meaning 'rock' or 'stone' in the *Ṛgveda* signified sling stones. According to Zimmer, the slings were known and used in the Vedic age.

**Smearing:** In order to cure the swellings on the neck, the physician used to make a paste of *paraśu*-leaves and smeared it on the swollen part of the body reciting the *Atharvaveda* (6.26). He smeared the swollen part with other ointments too (*KauSū*. 30.14 ff).

**Smelter:** That the Vedic Indians were conversant with metallurgy is attested to by various terms pertaining to the occupations of iron-smiths, goldsmiths, coppersmiths and so forth. Since metallurgy required smelting of metals there were professional smelters. In the *Ṛgveda* (5.9.5) we come across a term *dhmātṛ*, which literally means blower. The word *dhmātṛ* in nominative means the smelter and its derivative form *dhmātarī* probably denotes the smelting furnace. Use of birds's wings for the purpose of blowing by the smelter is recorded in the *Ṛgveda* (4.2.17; 9.112.2). The references to fan the flames indicate that the art of smelting was widely applied. That iron-smelting or copper-smelting was widely in vogue is amply testified with reference to arrows pointed with *ayas*, kettle fashioned with the same and *soma*-cups made from metal (*RV* 5.30.15; 6.75.15; 9.1.12).

**Smith:** *Karmāra* denotes smith in Vedic literature (*RV* 9.112.2; 10.72.2; *AV* 3.5.6; *MS* 2.9.5; *KS* 17.13; *VS* 16.27, 30.7; *TB* 3.4.3.1). The *karmāras* are mentioned along with fishermen and chariot-builders, as expert workers (*AV* 3.5.6). But their working method and tools can hardly be known. His other name *dhmātṛ*, 'smelter', proves that he smelted ore on the fire. Bellow of birds' feather (*RV* 5.9.5) was used for blowing the fire. He mostly made vessels of metal (*ayasmaya*). Hammered metal (*aya-hata*) is also mentioned. See Smelter.

**Smoke Therapy:** Smoke was used against the evil beings (causes of diseases) in order to remove them. It was treated as a curing substance. In the *Atharvaveda* (19.38,1-2) *yakṣma* (disease) is said to be cured by the agreeable fragrance of smoke of the healing *guggulu*. According to *KauSū* (31.22), when a patient suffers from dropsy, or is caught by evil, the physician should give smoke of *soma*-stalks consecrated with the *Atharvaveda* (6.96). Similarly, when a patient suffers from hemiplegia, smoke is to be given to the bleeding place, and consecrated with the *Atharvaveda* 6.80, (*KauSū*. 31.19). When a patient is troubled by red worms, smoke was applied. This held good also in the case of cattle disease. A person troubled by worms should smell the smoke of *karīra* (crappairs aphylla) with the *Atharvaveda* 5.53 (*KauSū* 29.20). In most cases smoke prepared from pacificatory (*śānta*) woods were used.

**Social Contract Theory:** The social contract theory of the origin of state and kingship seems to have been foreshadowed in the Vedic texts. Reference may be made in this connection to a short passage in the *Śatapatha Brāhmaṇa* (11.1.6-24): Whenever there is drought, then the stronger seizes the weaker, for the waters are the law. 'Although somewhat enigmatic and mystical, it seems to foreshadow the later theory of the state of nature resulting in anarchy and confusion, which led to the foundation of state and monarchy.'

**Social Dance:** Social dances were held on such occasions as sacraments, marriages, religious rites, harvest festivals, sacrifices, royal coronations, communical gatherings and so forth. In short, whenever people following any happy occurrence demanded expression in the happy rhythmic movements of the limbs, men and women of the community joined in the celebration of mirth. The funeral hymn (*RV* 10.18.3) advises the relatives of the dead, after he had been laid to the rest, to go forth, sing and dance and laugh and prolong their own span of life (*RV* 10.18.3). Laughter and dance are associated with each other. We find a fair picture of community dance in all its vigour and vivacity in the *Ṛgveda* (10.94.4-5). The atmosphere resounded with the cries of dancers. The humming sound of this dance and song has been termed as *nyunikha*. This collective social dance in couple formation, the call for embracing each other, makes us pre-suppose a festive occasion of a happy society. The meeting place for this collective festival was *samāja*. Women went there to enjoy themselves and the courtesans to make a profit by the occasion.

**Socio-Political Division:** The Aryans originally seem to have been nomadic tribes, invading lands and constantly moving from one place to another. Gradually they gave up their nomadic habits and settled down in the land they wrested from their enemies. In the course of time these regions became dotted with their settlements, which were known as the *viś* or *viśaḥ*. Thus, we hear of the Tṛṇaskanda Viś (*RV* 7.5.3). In other places we hear of *viśaḥ* called after the tribe to which they belonged and as an example we may mention the *viś* of the Tṛtsus (*RV* 7.33.6). In many other places the word is used rather in a general sense and designates people at large. Thus, the *Ṛgveda* 10.11.4 speaks of the Ārya Viś. Similarly the *Ṛgveda* 4.28.4 speaks of the Dasyu-Viś. In another place we hear of the Dāsa-Viś, which is contrasted with the Ārya-Viś (*RV* 6.25.2). We have no further details of the *viś* or its organization. The task is made difficult by various circumstances, with the modification that the social fabric was rapidly undergoing being one of these. The rise of the caste system was of immense influence. Each of these *viśaḥ* or settlements seems to have had a chief of its own. This man dominated over the inhabitants of the settlement, either by virtue of his being the patriarchal head of the clan that had settled therein or by virtue of his being vested with authority by the people who recognized him as leader. Probably different types of settlements existed and, in some cases, these belonged to men of the same blood. In these the patriarch or the agnatic elder was also the head of the settlement, the two offices vesting in the same person. Such settlements are to be pre-supposed from the evidence of the *Taittirīya Saṃhitā*, which describes *viśaḥ* as *sajātas* (*TS* 2.1.3.2, 3 etc.) in more than one place. Or, of that passage of the *Atharvaveda* which mentions *viśaḥ* along with the *bāndhavaḥ* (15.8.2.3). On the other hand the separate existence of a *viśpati*, apart from the head of the family, is also found (*RV* 7.55.5).

**Solar Motion:** The sun's annual and daily motions are described in Vedic hymns. According to the *Ṛgveda* (1.35.2) the sky remains black before sunrise: Savitṛ comes out in the sky daily and awakens men and the gods. The Vedic Indians knew that the diurnal motion of the sun is a spinning motion, different from its annual motion. The *Ṛgveda* (1.22.16) states: the Gods be gracious unto us even from the place whence Viṣṇu strode through the seven regions of the earth.

Though the word *śaptadhāma* often indicated the seven prosodies, it also means the seven regions, representing the whole sky. It also denotes the seven places or paths of the sun in the course of its annual motion. This division of layers is based on the division of a year into twelve months. In the *Ṛgveda* (1.22.17) reference is made of Viṣṇu's traversing the whole world in three strides. These strides, or ways are indicated by two different motions of the sun, from winter solstice to summer solstice (*uttarāyaṇa*) and from summer solstice (*dakṣiṇāyana*) to the winter one. The daily motion of the sun represents the third course of its motion. The expression encompasses the orbital as well as diurnal course of the sun.

**Solipsism:** The fourth section of the second chapter of the *Bṛhadāraṇyaka Upaniṣad* refers to certain views of Yājñavalkya, which recall solipsism of contemporary philosophical thought. In his own words: 'As the sole repository of all tastes is the tongue: as the sole repository of all smells is the nose and of all colours the eye; as the sole repository of all desires is the mind and of all learning the intellect; as, finally, the sole repository of all actions are the hands and of all motions the feet; verily, as all the waters rest in the sea and Vedas in speech, similarly the self is *summum bonus* of all. Using a similar metaphor Yājñavalkya further says, 'As a lump of salt when thrown into water dissolves into it and we are unable to find it anymore, similarly, does this Great Being, endless, infinite, and the quintessence of all knowledge, rise from out of all these elements and vanish after them.' 'When a man is departed', says Yājñavalkya, 'no consciousness remains'. This last assertion was sufficient to confound the intellect of his wife Maitreyī. 'You do bewilder me', says she to her husband, 'when you say that when a man is departed, no consciousness remains'. This surprises Yājñavalkya and he only hastily excuses himself by saying that what he had already said was enough for her knowledge. It is rather hard for us to understand exactly what Yājñavalkya must have meant when he said that. Does he mean that when a man dies there is an end of the matter; the curtain falls, never to rise anymore? Or, does he take his stand on the pedestal of absolute monism, from which point of view re-incarnation, consciousness, post mortem, and immortality are alike a delusion and a farce? It seems that Yājñavalkya chooses to resort to the second alternative because he immediately goes on to say, 'When there is a duality between subject and object, one perceives while the other is perceived; one smells while the other is smelt; one hears while the other is heard; one says while the other is said; one thinks while the other is thought; one meditates, while the other is meditated upon, one sees while other is seen; how can one hear; how can one think while the other is thought, how can one meditate, while the other is meditated upon? 'All processes of perception and understanding were possible. But, by hypothesis, there is no duality; and consequently, there is no distinction between subject and object, between perceiver and perceived. If perceiver alone exists, would it be possible that he himself may be perceived? For who may perceive the only perceiver? Into such solipsistic approach does Yājñavalkya's absolute monism lead us. Belvalkar and Ranade 189, 359.

**Soma:** Next in importance to Indra and Agni comes Soma, because the Soma sacrifice was the centre of the Ṛgvedic ritual. As the *soma* plant and its juice were ever present before the Ṛgvedic poets, the anthropomorphism is less developed than that of Indra or Varuṇa. The weapons of *soma*, such as the bow, his car, and his team are described. An entire book-the ninth-is devoted to *soma* (the deity and the plant) and the preparation of the Soma juice. The *aṃśu* (shoot or stalk) is pounded between stones called *adri*. The passed juice, in the act of passing through the filter of sheep's wool, is called *pavamāna* (or *punāna*) 'flowing clear'. The juice thus purified, and as yet unmixed, is called *śukra* or *suci* (bright), also *śuddha* (pure). This filtered *soma* next flows into jars (*kalasa*) or vats (*droṇa*), where it is mixed (technically 'cleansed') with water and milk to sweeten it. The *soma* has three kinds of admixture (*asir*), with milk (*go*), sour milk (*dadhi*) or barley (*yava*). The admixture is poetically described as a bright robe. Soma is thus pressed three times a day; the morning libation is the first drink of Indra, the midday one belongs to him exclusively, while the third pressing is for the Ṛbhus. Then admixture of *soma* brings him into a special relation with the waters, who are called his 'mothers' and 'sisters'. Soma is also the lord of streams. The exhilarating power of *soma* is appreciated. It is a divine drink, conferring immortality on gods and men. It is called *amṛta,* the 'draught of immortality'. *Soma* has curative powers also. As a deity, Soma is a wise seer, a poet who stimulates thought and inspires hymns. The fact that Soma invigorates Indra in his fight with Vṛtra is repeated so often that Indra's exploits and cosmic actions come to be attributed to him. Like the corresponding *haoma* in the *Avesta, soma* grows on the mountains, but his true origin is said to be in heaven, from which he was brought to earth by an eagle. Soma is a king, the lord of plants or lord of the wood (*vanaspati*). In a few of the latest hymns of the *Ṛgveda*, Soma is mystically identified with the moon. The preparation and offering of the Soma was a feature of Indo-Iranian worship. There were numerous similarities between the *soma* and the *haoma* (Avestan) cults. The belief in an intoxicating beverage of the gods, a kind of honey or mead, may probably go back even to the Indo-European period (*RV* 1.94.14; 3.48.2; 4.27.5; 5.45.9; 8.32.28; 8.43.11; 9.51.3; 9.61.10; 10.94.8; 10.115.3; *ŚB* 9.5.1.8; *TS* 6.1.6.7; *VS* 19.72; *TB* 3.7.13.1; 3.10.5.1; *CU* 5.10.1).

**Soma Sacrifices:** By far the most important of the Vedic sacrifices are the Soma-Yāgas. They are divided into three classes, the *Ekāhas* or those of one day's duration, the *Ahīnas* or those lasting from two to twelve days, and the *sattras* or those of more than twelve days in duration. The *Agniṣṭoma* is regarded as the norm for all the Soma sacrifices. It is technically an *Ekāha* but generally extends over five days, the first four days being devoted to introducing ceremonies like the *dīkṣā* or initiation, *soma-kraya* or the purchase of *soma* (which appears to have been a short ritualistic drama, probably symbolical of the original winning of the heavenly *soma* by the bird-shaped Gāyatrī), the *pravargya*, the *agnipraṇayana*, etc. The squeezing, offering, and the drinking of the *soma* at the morning, mid-days, and evening libations take place on the last or the fifth day, when the ceremonies end with an *avabhṛtha* or ablutionary bath. The original significance of the Agniṣṭoma has been variously explained. It is supposed by some to be a spring or New-Year festival, symbolical of the drinking of the nectar in the moon (Soma means both the moon and the plant) by the gods; as a rain-charm to induce rain by means of straining the Soma through the sieve (which works as a sympathetic magic); or, seeing that the God Soma is himself killed in the act and is partaken of by the worshipper as a totem ritual in the shape of a formal sacrifice of communion, with a view to renew the kingship between the god and his votaries as well as that of the votaries amongst themselves. The point is however debatable. The other Soma sacrifices are: the Pravargya, which although included amongst the introductory ceremonial of the Agniṣṭoma, was originally very probably an independent Yāga. Its principal feature is the libation of milk and ghee heated together in a pot called the Mahāvīra. The pot with its covering golden plate is explained as an emblem of the Sun, while the whole ceremony represents a symbolic renewal of the Sun's heat and the restoration of the sacrificer's own energy and vigour. Then comes the Ekādaśīna-kratupaśu, the Atyagniṣṭoma, the Ukthya, the Ṣoḍaśin, the Vājapeya, the Atirātra, and the Āptaryāma, all of which vary from the norm only in unessential particulars. Deserving of special mention amongst these, however, is the Vājapeya, which is more important than the Rājasuya (q.v.) though earlier texts do not show this indication of its pre-eminence. Finally, the Rājasūya (q.v.) is a coronation and consecration ritual, which seems to have been a symbolic reproduction of the attainment of divine kingship by Indra (or by Varuṇa).

**Sowing:** The work of sowing is mentioned in the *Ṛgveda* (10.85.37; 10.94.13; 10.101.3; 1.117.21) and subsequent Saṃhitās and Brāhmaṇas. The *Atharvaveda* refers to the application of charms during the sowing of seeds. The *Atharvaveda* (6.142.1-3) was recited while barley (or grain in general, *yava*) mixed with *ghee*, was scattered in the field. Three handfuls of seeds were first thrown, one with each stanza of the hymn, and then the rest. There was a special time of sowing and reaping the harvest, which varied according to the nature of the crops. The use of manure was well known, so also irrigation. But the dependence was greater on the monsoons. Prayers for fertilizing rains occur frequently in the Vedic texts. Sacrifices were performed also for the same purpose. For details see **Agriculture**.

**Songs:** *Sāman*, chanting the hymns in the form of songs

is repeatedly referred to in the *Ṛgveda* (1.62.1; 1.107.2; 1.164.24, etc.). The *Sāmaveda* itself is a collection of such songs, to be sung either in the village (*grāmageya*) or in the forest (*araṇyageya*). *Stotṛ* denotes 'praiser' or 'panegyrist' in the *Ṛgveda* (1.11.3; 1.38.4; 3.18.5; 6.34.3) and later (*AV* 6.2.1; 19.48.4). The word often (*Ṛgveda* 1.24.10; 2.1.16; 5.64.1; 7.7.7) appears in connection with patrons, the Maghavan or Sūri. *Stotra* denotes the 'song' of the Udgātṛ and his assistant priests, just as *śastra* denotes the 'recitation' of the Hotṛ and his assistants. The word is used in this technical sense quite frequently in the later Saṃhitās and the Brāhmaṇas (*TS* 3.1.2.4; *KS* 29.2; *AB* 2.37-4; 3.46.8; 4.12.6; *KB* 17.7; *ŚB* 4.1.1.7; 8.1.3.4). *Stoma* denotes 'song of praise' in the *Ṛgveda* (1.114.9; 3.5.2; 3.5.8.1). later (*TS* 3.1.2.4; *VS* 9.33; 1.10), the term has the technical sense of the typical forms in which the *stotras* are chanted. *Gāthā* in the *Ṛgveda* (8.32.1; 8.71.14; 8.98.9; 9.99.4, etc.), *chandas* in the *Ṛgveda* (10.85.8; 10.114.5; *AV* 4.34.1; 5.26.5; 6.124.1; 11.7.8) usually denote metre.

**Sound:** When the breath in the mouth comes in the form of sound it is called *svara* in the *Chāndogya Upaniṣad* (1.3.2). *Pratyasvara* is reflected sound, the echo of the former. The metaphysical articulation of sound in the form of *Om* itself is called *svara* in *Kaṭha Upaniṣad* 1.4.3 and *prasvara* in the *Ṛgveda-Prātiśākhya.*

**Sour Milk:** The term *mastu* in the *Yajurveda Saṃhitā* (*TS* 6.1.1.4; *KS* 36.1) and the Brāhmaṇas (*ŚB* 1.8.1.7; 3.3.3.2) denotes curds. The word *dadhi* 'sour milk', is repeatedly mentioned in the *Ṛgveda* (8.2.9; 9.87.1) and later (*AV* 3.12.7; 4.34.6; *TS* 2.5.3.4; *PB* 18.5.12, etc.). The *Śatapatha Brāhmaṇa* (1.8.1.7) mentions in order *ghṛta* (clarified butter), and *amīkṣā* 'curds'. It was used for mixing with Soma (*RV* 1.5.5; 5.51.7; 7.32.4).

**Sovereignty:** In the *Aitareya Brāhmaṇa* (8.14) four kinds of rulership have been described, among which *vairājya* or sovereignty pertained to the countries of the northern quarters. Next to the consolidation of royal power, ideas about the nature of the sovereign authority became more definite. From the primary warlord and collector of *bali* or tribute the king came to be regarded as a sovereign ruling over his people, the lord of the territory in which the people lived and of the material resources of the locality, the sole judge wielding the rod of punishment and the protector of *dharma*. When the nomadic tribes gave up their nomadic habits, of which we find traces in the earlier literature, and settled down, it led to the idea of territorial sovereignty. Tribal names gave rise to place names and almost all the kingdoms came to have fixed boundaries. In the case of the Kuru country, we have a clear account of its territorial limits. Territorial epithets came to be applied to princes. We have numerous instances of this in the Brahman literature. A king Prātipīya of the Kurus is described as Bālhika (*ŚB* 12.9.3.3); a second prince Bhīma is described Vaidarbha or ruler of the Vairdarbha region; two other princes Dhṛtarāṣṭra and Ajatāśatru are designated Kāśya or ruler of the Kāśi Kingdom; two princess of Kośala are described as Kauśalya, i.e. Para Atnara and Hairaṇyanābha. Such local epithets are very common and we find them applied even to ordinary people, to distinguish them from others of the same name. Thus, Proti is called Kauśāmbeya. Citra is called Gaṅgāyani, Āśvalāyana is called Kauśalya, while one more is called Naimiṣya. The importance of this conception of territorial sovereignty is also felt in the coronation ritual. The king, as we have seen, is made to ascend the steps in four quarters, i.e. the north, south, east and west, symbolic of his supremacy over these regions. Furthermore, the suzerain overlord's ideal of conquest embraced the whole region of the country then known, extending from the hills to the sea. In regard to the newer ideas about the nature of sovereignty, some further light is thrown by the Rājasūya ritual. In *abhiṣecanīya* the king was made to make offerings to Savitṛ Satyaprasava, Agni Gṛhapati, Soma Vanaspati, Bṛhaspati Vākpati, Rudra Paśupati, Mitra Satya, and Varuṇa Dharmapati, with a view to his investment with their authority and functions. We need not stretch our imagination, but the text as well as the interpretation is so clear that it gives a full import of the ceremonies and their constitutional significances. The priest himself, thus addressed the king and prayed: 'May Savitṛ quicken thee for ruling, Agni for house-holders, Soma for trees, Bṛhaspati for speech, Indra for lordship, Rudra for cattle, Mitra for truth and Varuṇa for the lord of the law.' The meaning is apparent; the prince was vested with supreme ruling authority and this comprised the general overlordship of the people, full governing authority, general superintendence over plants and animals (i.e. agriculture and cattle) and the power of administering the laws as the Vicegerent of Lord Varuṇa, the divine judge *par excellence*. The consummation of investiture was attained by the king-elect's stepping over a tiger skin (symbolic of his greatness and conquest over enemies; of the epithet *vyāghrapratīka*). His investment with the wooden sacrificial sword symbolized regal and legal authority, his identification with Indra and Varuṇa and the proclamation of his immunity from punishment (*adaṇḍya*), which in those days made him free from the jealousy or intrigue of rivals and factions.

**Spears:** Archaeological discoveries show that the spears and lances were used in India both before and after the arrival of the Aryans (*RV* 1.31.1; 1.37.1; 1.37.1; 1.37.2; 1.64.4; 1.64.8; 1.64.11; 1.89.4; 1.88.1; 1.166.4; 5.22.6; 5.54.11; 5.57.2; 5.57.6; 8.20.11). In the term *ṛṣṭi*, denoting a weapon held in the Marut's hands, an equivalent of the spear in warfare, can be found. The term certainly signifies a spear in later Sanskrit and its metaphorical use presupposes the popularity of the weapon among the Ṛgvedic Aryans. In different regions, the spear came to resemble thunder and lightning, like the trident and the axe. The term *rambhini*, a weapon on the shoulders of the Maruts, denotes a spear (*RV* 1.168.3). In the Battle of the Ten Kings, spears can be recognized in the word *srakti* (*RV* 7.18.7). The term *sṛka* is used in a couple of the *Ṛgveda* the passages to designate a weapon of Indra, a lance (*RV* 1.32.12, 10.180.2). The terms *sṛkavi* and *sṛka-hasta* mean 'one bearing a lance in his (Indra's) hand' (*VS* 16.21, 61). See **Weapons**.

**Specialization:** Besides the traditional vocation ascribed to the four *varṇas*, the Vedic texts amply show that there were specializations in various crafts and industries. It appears from the large numbers of similes and metaphors drawn from the art of fashioning chariots for war and race, and carts for agriculture and transport, that carpentry was an honoured profession, with the carpenter also being a wheelwright and joiner. He did all sorts of work in wood, and even carved works of a finer type were not beyond his skill (*RV* 10.7.86; 51. 16; 1.9, 3; 7.60.2). The workers in metal smelted ore in the furnace, using the wing of a bird as a bellows to fan the flames. That household utensils like kettles were made of metal but it is uncertain that *ayas* means iron. If we suppose that the word is consistently used in the same sense it may have been either copper, bronze or iron; but it is also possible that it is used in more senses than one. Its colour is to be inferred from the epithets used with it, such as 'reddish'. As the use of copper precedes that of iron in the development of civilization, *ayas* may have indicated 'copper' or its alloy 'bronze'; but this is by no means certain, and iron may have been known. Earthenware and wooden vessels, along with those of metal, were used for eating and drinking. The art of the tanner (*carmamnā* in *RV* 8.5.38) and the use of hide are well known. Ox-hide was used to manufacture bowstrings, thongs (to fasten parts of the chariots), reins and the lash of the whip (*RV* 6.75.11; 6.47.26, etc.). It was also placed above the boards on which the *soma* was pressed with the stones. It is not unlikely that spin bags were also made with it (*RV* 10.106.10). Among the home and cottage industries may be mentioned sewing, the plaiting of mats from grass or reeds, and the spinning and weaving of cloth, chiefly done by women. Among the other professions may be mentioned those of the dancers, both male and female, barbers, physicians, goldsmiths, wine-makers, weapon-makers, masons, priests, soldiers, traders, and such like. See **Occupations**.

**Spices:** Some spices such as brassica (*baja*, *AV* 8.6.6), *jambīla* (*citrus aurantum MS* 3.15.3; *KS* 5.2.1; *VS* 15.3), turmeric (*haridrā AV* 12.24.2) and long pepper (*pippati*, i.e. epuloides, *AV* 6.109) were used in the preparation of food articles and are mentioned in the Vedic texts.

**Spies:** Spies appear frequently in the *Ṛgveda* and elsewhere. We find references to Varuṇa's spies (*RV* 1.25.13; 4.4.3; 6.67.5; 7.61.3; 7.87.3; 10.10.8; *AV* 18.1.9), who testify to the early organization of state intelligence. The *Atharvaveda* (4.16.4) refers to the thousand-eyed spies (*spaśaḥ*) of Varuṇa looking at even the earth beneath them. Soma's rays are compared to omnipresent and unwinking spies, ready with fetters for tying the offender (*AV* 5.6.3). There can be no doubt in understanding that these spies and their work had military significance. The *Ṛgveda* speaks of spies, or presumably surveying troops, going forward in an unambiguous content of war, and this is corroborated by another passage (*RV* 4.4.3; 8.87.11; *TS* 1.2.14.1). The *Sāmāvidhāna Brāhmaṇa* (1.1.24) says that the spies try to find the exact position of the enemy as the opposing armies approach each other. Messengers kept the king informed of the latest happenings (*JB* 1.234). So *sūta* acted as an envoy or messenger and the term *dūta* was regularly used for an envoy (*RV* 3.3.2; 6.8.4; 7.3.3; 10. 14.12; *AV* 8.8.10; *ŚB* 3.5.1.6; *KU* 2.1). We come across Saramā, a female envoy (*dūtī*), on a peace mission (*RV* 10.108.2-3). Saramā found her way to the Paṇis to demand the return of stolen cattle and to threaten them with destruction in the event of non-compliance. The latter tried to induce her to stay with them but the last verse seems to record the fulfilment of her prophecy (*RV* 10.108). Presumably the envoys visited the enemy camps to explore the possibility of peace before the actual outbreak of hostilities. The *prahita* was a simple messenger, a forerunner of the later *dūtas*. In ancient India the high development of the sciences of diplomacy can be sensed from the mention of spies, *dūtas*, *cāras* and ambassadors in the Saṃhitās. All important gods—Mitra (*AV* 8.61.3), Soma (*RV* 9.73.4), Varuṇa (*RV* 1.24.13), Agni (*RV* 4.4.3; *AV* 6.4.3) had a number of spies who looked about far and wide and went about in different directions, who were true to their duties, and were never confused in carrying out their tasks (*RV* 6.67.5; 8.87.3). Only men of wisdom, who were free from corruption and temptation of any sort, were sent to act as spies (*RV* 7.67.3). The term *prahita* is interpreted by Sāyaṇa (*TS* 4.7.1) as standing for the spy.

**Spit:** Spit or slender rod on which meat is skewed before being roasted on a fire is described as *śūla* (*RV* 1.162.11; *ŚB* 11.4.2.4; 11.7.3.2; 11.7.4.3; *Ṣaḍ.B.* 5.11). *Śūla* is the weapon of Rudra. Another word for spit is *nekṣaṇa*, 'whether the food is ready'. (*pākaparīkṣāsādhanaṃ kāṣṭham*).

**Spirituous Liquor:** *Surā* is the name of an intoxicating 'spirituous liquor', often mentioned in Vedic literature. In some passages (*RV* 1.116.7, 10.131.4; *AV* 4.34.6, 10.6.5; *TS* 1.3.3.2; *ŚB* 12.7.3.8), it is referred to favourably, in others with distinct disapproval (*RV* 7.46.6; 8.2.12; *MS* 1.1.6; 2.4.2; 4.2.1). It is classed with the use of meat and with dicing as an evil in the

*Atharvaveda* (6.70.1), and often with dicing (*RV* 7.86.6; *AV* 14.1.35, 15.9.1). It was, as opposed to Soma, essentially a drink of ordinary life (*TB* 1.3.3.2). It was the drink of men in the *sabhā* and gave rise to broils (*RV* 8.2.12). Its exact nature is not certain. It may have been a strong spirit prepared from fermented grains and plants, as Eggeling holds, or, as Whitney thought, a kind of beer or ale. Geldner renders it 'brandy'. It is sometimes mentioned in connection with *madhu* (*AV* 6.69.1; 9.1.18). It was kept in skin-vessels (*PB* 14.11.26).

**Spoken Language:** Spoken language was known as *bhāṣā*. Vedic Sanskrit has grown out of the spoken tongue of the times as its root. The point is discussed by Yāska in the *Nirukta* (1.16). Non-Aryan speakers are referred to in the *Ṛgveda* as *mṛdhṛavāc*. The *Śatapatha Brāhmaṇa* (3.2.1, 23; 24) refers to barbarisms in speech which are to be avoided, being probably characteristic of the Vrātyas, who are also described in the *Pañcaviṃśa Brāhmaṇa* (17.1.9) as speaking the language of the initiated by the uninitiated people as they felt it difficult to utter.

**Spoon:** See under **Ladle**. The terms *camasa, śruva* and *śruca* are also sometimes used to denote spoon. These are the three implements of sacrifice (*TB* 1.39, 1,351). The *Ṛgveda* 1.161.1 refers to *camasa* as denoting cup, spoon and bowl.

**Spouted Jar:** A typical water pot used in religious purposes, which is mentioned as *kamaṇḍalu* in the *Jaiminīya Brāhmaṇa* (1.52). There is also another term *udakamaṇḍalu* (*JB* 1.52) used in the same sense, with which the religious performer should pour water in the Gārhapatya and Āhavanīya fires for a purificatory ceremony addressed to Viṣṇu.

**Śraddhā:** One short hymn of the *Ṛgveda* (10.151) is devoted to the praise of Śraddhā, 'Faith'. She is said to be invoked at morning, noon and night. Through Faith fire is kindled and *ghee* offered. Through Faith wealth is obtained. In the Brāhmaṇas, Śraddhā is the daughter of the Sun (*ŚB* 12.7, 3.11) or of Prajāpati (*TB* 2, 3, 10.1). Her relationships are still further worked out in the epics and Purāṇas.

**Śrauta Ceremonies:** The Vedic sacrifice is part of an exchange of a nourishing gift preferred to the god by the worshipper with a motive followed by a reward, a perfectly voluntary act of the gladdened deity. The attitude of the worshipper is not one of extreme humility or of deep emotion, but one of confident friendship, though full of reverence towards the maker of the universe. As a rule, ritual accompanies prayer, with a few exceptions, like during the recitation of the prayers to Agni, Uṣas and the Aśvins in the morning litany of the *soma* sacrifice and the muttering of the daily *sandhyā* or twilight devotions, morning and evening. Agni, called the mouth of the gods, because he receives the sacrificial offerings not only for himself but also for transmission to the gods, is the centre of the Vedic ritual. Earth, air and water were also used as instruments of transmission in certain cases, when offerings intended for water-divinities were thrown into water, those intended for the Dead were deposited in small pits, and oblations to Rudra and the demons were scattered in the air, suspended on trees, buried, thrown on the hills, or disposed of in some secret manner. A dual practice is hinted at when we find that the oblations, before being consigned to the fire to be conducted to the gods in heaven, are placed for some time on a liter of sacred grass (*barhis*) which is spread on the *vedi* (an ablong, shallow excavation). Therefore, in the same breath of the sacrifice, offerings are conveyed by Agni to the gods in heaven and of the gods borne by Agni to the sacrifice on earth (7.2.5). The preparation of the offerings for the sacrifice takes place in the *gārhapatya* fire; the *ahavanīya*, installed in the east, receives the offerings intended for the gods; and, the *dakṣiṇa* fire, being established in the south, that for the *pitṛs* and demons, the quarter being associated with these beings. The fire produced either by the friction of the two *araṇis* (a lower slab of soft wood and an upper drill of hard wood) or borrowed from the house of a wealthy owner of cows, or a reputed sacrificer. A rejuvenation of the old *ahavanīya* fire, by adding to it a new fire wood, took place at the *soma* sacrifices and at the four-monthly seasonal sacrifices. Oblations (solid or liquid) consisting of the products of the cow, believed to have a sacred and mystical quality, namely milk in all its forms and butter in varying degrees of temperature, were offered into the fire. Barley and rice, cooked or baked, were made into cakes that were offered on potsherds or tablets, the number of which depended on the character of the god in question. Libations of water mixed with sesame were peculiar to the *śrāddha* offerings to the *pitṛs*. In the animal sacrifice, the flesh of cattle, sheep, and (especially) the he-goat were the common offerings. Roughly speaking, two or three principles seem to have determined the choice of the material of the sacrifice: (i) The worshipper offered his own favourite food (including flesh) and drink to the deity. (ii) That which corresponded to the individuality of the god was offered to him, e.g. the milk of a black cow with a white calf was offered to the twin goddesses of night and morning. The correspondence extended to the colour and other qualities of the deity and the victim, a white goat offered to Sūrya being another example. (iii) The particular wishes, for the fulfilment of which the sacrifice was undertaken, determined the character and the material of the sacrifice. For example, in the *śyena* (a *soma*) sacrifice, if the life of an enemy is aimed at, the priests wear a red *frontlet* and the sacrificial butter is made from the milk of a sick cow. Further, in all *soma* sacrifices *soma*-juice was offered, the drink being more invigorating than inebriating. In a few cases, honey and *surā* (wine) were offered. The sacrifice of non-edible and non-potable objects (like iron-nails) was a feature of magic rites (to secure, say, deadly weapons) on the principle that the means should be analogous in character to the end in view. A convenient and very practical classification of Vedic sacrifices is the one into (a) periodic or regularly recurrent (*nitya*); and (b) occasional or special (*naimittika*). The time for the setting up of the sacred fires (*agnyādhāna*) is either a particular season (according to the taste of the performer) or a *parvan* (new or full moon). It is a two-day ceremony. On the first day, two sheds are erected, one for the *gārhapatya* with a round altar, a spot to the south of it being marked out for the *dakṣiṇā* fire with a semi-circular altar, and the other shed for the *āhavanīya* with a square altar. The sacrificer and his wife keep awake the whole night, listening to the music of lutes and flutes. The next morning, the fire is either produced or borrowed and placed on the *gārhapatya* altar, fuel is added, and it is addressed in the name of the ancestors of the sacrificer. When it blazes up, a brand is taken from it and transferred to the *āhavanīya* fire. The *dakṣiṇā* fire is lighted in the same way, before or after the *āhavanīya*. When the fires are found to bring no luck to the sacrificer, they are allowed to go out, and after a break of three days to one year, new fires are established, feeding the fire with *kuśa* grass instead of wood. This is the *punarādhana* or re-establishment of the fires. V.M. Apte in *Cultural Heritage of India* I, 244-5.

**Śrī:** In the *Vājasaneyī Saṃhitā* 31.22 (*śrīśca te lakṣmīśca patnyau*), Śrī and Lakṣmī are said to be the two wives of Āditya, according to the commentator's explanation. In the *Śatapatha Brāhmaṇa* (11.4.3.1) Śrī is described as issuing forth from Prajāpati when he was performing intense austerity. Beholding her then, standing resplendent and trembling, the gods were covetous of her, and proposed to Prajāpati that they should be allowed to kill her and appropriate her gifts. His response was that she was female, and that males did not generally kill females. Therefore, they should take away her gifts without depriving her of life. In consequence, Agni took from her food; Soma, kingly authority; Varuṇa, imperial authority; Mitra, martial energy; Indra, force; Bṛhaspati priestly glory; Sāvitrī dominion; Puṣan, splendour; Sarasvatī, nourishment and Tvaṣṭṛ, forms.

**Sṛñjaya:** Sṛñjaya is the name of a people mentioned as early as the *Ṛgveda*. Sṛñjaya Daivavāta is celebrated as victorious over the Turvasas and the Vṛcīvants (*RV* 6.27.7). In connection with Daivavāta, Sahadevya Somaka, no doubt another prince, is also mentioned (*RV* 4.15.7). The *Ṛgveda* (6.47.22, 25) also has a Dānastuti (praise and gifts) of Praśloka a Sṛñjaya. It seems probable that the Sṛñjayas and the Tṛtsus were closely allied, for Divodāsa and a Sṛñjaya princes are celebrated together, and the Turvasas were enemies of both. This view is borne out by the *Śatapatha Brāhmaṇa* (2.4.4.5), which recognizes Devabhāga Śrautarsa as *purohita* of the Kurus and the Sṛñjayas. The geographical position of the Sṛñjayas is uncertain. They might have inhabited the west of the Indus, or the upper Indus; but it is difficult to decide definitely in favour of any particular location. They might well have settled farther east than the Indus, since their allies, the Tṛtsus, were in the Madhyadeśa and were certainly absorbed in the Kurus. Of the history of this clan we have one example (*ŚB* 12.9.3). They expelled Duṣṭaritu Pauṃsāyana, one of their kings from the hereditary monarchy-of ten generations-and also drove out his minister.

**State:** The term *rājya* in the *Atharvaveda* (3.4.2; 4.8.1; 11.6.15; 12.3.31; 18.4.31) and later (*TS* 2.1.3.2, 7.5.8.3; *AB* 7.23; *JUB* 1.4.5) regularly denotes state or sovereign power. In addition to *rājya*, the texts give other expressions of sovereign power. Thus, the *Śatapatha Brāhmaṇa* (5.1.1.3) contends that the Rājasūya sacrifice is that of a king, the Vājapeya that of a *samrāj* or emperor, the status of the latter (*sāmrājya*) being superior to that of the former (*rājya*). In the same text (12.8.3.4), sitting on a throne (*āsandī*) is given as one of the characteristics of the *samrāj*. Elsewhere (*KS* 14.5; *MS* 1.11.5; *TB* 1.3.2.2), *svārājya* means uncontrolled dominion. In the ritual of the Rājasūya, the *Aitareya Brāhmaṇa* (8.12) gives a whole series of terms: *rājya, sāmrājya, bhaujya, svārājya, vairājya, pārameṣṭhya,* and *māhārājya*, while *ādhipatya*, supreme power, is found elsewhere *Pañcaviṃśa Brāhmaṇa* (15.3.35) *Chāndogya Upaniṣad* (5.2.6). But there is no reason to believe that these terms refer to essentially different forms of authority. A king might be called a *mahārāja* or a *samrāj* without really being an overlord of king; he would be so termed if he were an important sovereign, as a compliment by his own entourage, as was Janaka of Videha, (*ŚB* 11.3.1.2). That a really great monarchy of the Aśoka or Gupta type ever existed in the Vedic period seems highly improbable.

**Stool:** The Vedic term for stool is *pīṭha* (*VS* 30.21; *TB* 3.4.17.1). Its derivative *pīṭha-sarpin* denotes a cripple and hump-backed person as a sacrificial victim in the aforesaid texts of *Vājasaneyī Saṃhitā* and *Taittirīya Brāhmaṇa*. The *Śatapatha Brāhmaṇa* (13.4.3.1) refers to a golden stool (*vediṃ hiraṇmayam*) with special reference to *rurca*, which also denotes a form of seat.

**Story-cycle:** The revolving legends or cycle of stories are known as *pāriplava ākhyānas*. *Pāri-plava*, 'cyclic', is a term applied to the *ākhyāna* or 'tale', which is to be recited at the Aśvamedha (horse sacrifice) and to be repeated at intervals throughout the year. It is mentioned in the *Śatapatha Brāhmaṇa* (10.13.4.3; 2.15) and the Sūtras (*ŚŚS* 16.1.26; 2.36; *LŚS* 9.9.11).

**Subjective Deities:** The clearest example of what may be called physical or subjective deities in the *Ṛgveda* is Manyu, 'wrath', who is invoked in two hymns (*RV* 10.83, 84). he is described as self-existent, irresistible. He slays Vṛtra, bestows wealth, grants victory like Indra, and is accompanied by the Maruts. Without a doubt, the conception is deducted from that of the wrath of Indra as a destructive force. Tapas, mentioned along with him, denotes ardour; his conception plays a part of the utmost importance in Vedic cosmogony, as a refined form of physical heat, but it is hardly directly deified. The *Ṛgveda* (10.151) also has deities like Śraddhā, 'faith', through whom the fire of the sacrifice is kindled, ghee offered, and wealth obtained, and who is invoked at morning, midday, and night. The brāhmaṇas (*TB* 2.3.10; *ŚB* 12.7.3.11) make her out to be the daughter of the sun or of Prajāpati. The conception clearly means belief in the existence and the generosity of the gods in its first appearance. In the *Atharvaveda* (9.2; 19.52) is found the conception of *kāma* 'desire' or 'love'. He is described as the first to be born, and he has arrows (*AV* 3.25.1) which pierce all hearts. He is not, however, as far as it appears from the scanty notices we have of him: a god primarily of human love, though that side of his character may have existed from the first or may have been soon attributed to him. In his cosmic aspect, which is in accordance with the theosophic tone of the *Atharvaveda,* the one in which he is described in, he is probably derived from the mention of *Kāma* in one of the most important cosmogonic hymns of the *Ṛgveda* (10.129.4) as the first seed of mind, regarded also as cosmic. It is not until the later literature in the last strata of the epic that we meet with the Indian cupid with his arrows, who is described as the disturber of the hearts of men whom he vexes with the pangs of love. Keith, I. 210.

**Śūdra:** *Śūdra* is the designation of the fourth caste in the Vedic texts. It is quite unknown in the *Ṛgveda* except in the *Puruṣasūkta* (10.90.12) in the tenth Maṇḍala, where the śūdra appears for the first time in the earliest version of the origin of the castes. The *Ṛgveda*, on the other hand, knows *dasyu* and *dāsa*, both as non-Aryan independent of Aryan control and as subjugated slaves. However, it is unreasonable to reckon the śūdra of the later texts as belonging to the non-Vedic peoples who had been reduced to subjection by the Aryans. The term śūdra would cover various professional castes (mixed-castes and subcastes of later tradition) other than the priests, warriors and traders (see **Caste**) that belonged to the lower grades of social hierarchy. The *Aitareya Brāhmaṇa* (7.29), in its account of the castes, declares that the śūdra is *anyasya preṣya* 'the servant of another', *kāmotthapya*, 'to be expelled at will; and *yathākāmavadhya*, 'to be slain at will'. All these terms describe their low position well enough. The *Pañcaviṃśa Brāhmaṇa* (6.1.11) explains that even if prosperous (*bahu-paśu*, 'having many cows'), a śūdra could not be other than a servant. His business was *padāvanejya* 'the washing of the feet' of his superiors. The slaying of a śūdra involved a wergeld of ten cows according to both *Baudhāyana Dharmasūtra* (1.10.19) and *Āśvalāyana Dharmasūtra* (1.9.24.3). It may, indeed, be held that his wergeld was only due in case of murder. The low status of the śūdra was, of course, specially marked. The texts (*ŚB* 2.1.4.2) do not hesitate to declare that the śūdra should not get the same privileges as are obtained by the higher *varṇas*. The śūdra is prohibited (*KS* 31.2; *MS* 4.1.3) from milking a cow if the milk is required at the Agnihotra (oblation to Agni); and the *Śatapatha Brāhmaṇa* (3.1.1.10) forbids a man who has been consecrated (*dīkṣita*) for a sacrifice to speak to a śūdra at all for the time being, though this rule (*KŚS* 7.5.7) seems to have been relaxed in some cases. At the sacrifice itself, the śūdra could not be presented in the *śālā*, 'hall'; he is definitely classed in the *Śatapatha Brāhmaṇa* (3.1.1.10; *MS* 7.1.1.6) and the *Pañcaviṃśa Brāhmaṇa* (4.1.11) as unfit for 'sacrifice' (*ayajñīya*); and declared in the *Kāṭhaka Saṃhitā* (11.10) not to be admitted to drink Soma. At the Pravargya (introductory Soma) rite the performer is not allowed to come in contact with a śūdra (*ŚB* 14.1.1.31), who here, as in the *Kāṭhaka Saṃhitā* (11.10), is reckoned as excluded from a share in one of the victims at the Puruṣamedha in the *Yajurveda Saṃhitā* (*VS* 30.5; *TB* 3.4.1.1; *ŚB* 13.6.2.10); and a fight between the Aryan and a śūdra in which, of course, the former wins, forms a part of the Mahāvrata rite, being perhaps a precursor of the Indian drama. Other indications, however, exists, showing that it would be undesirable to ignore the real importance of the śūdra, who, though legally restrained, still gradually won his way to the rank of a free man. Rich śūdras are mentioned in the early texts (*MS* 4.2.7.10; *PB* 6.1.11; *ŚB* 5.3.2.2), just as śūdra *gahapatis*, householders', appear in the Buddhist texts, and śūdra kings in the legal literature (*JUB* 1.4.5). Prayers for glory on behalf of śūdras, as well as of the other castes (*YS* 5.7.6.4; *KS* 11.13, *MS* 3.4.8; *VS* 18.48) appear; and the desire to be dear to śūdra as well as to Aryan is expressed (*AV* 19.328; *VS* 26.2). The Sūtras also, while they emphasize as general rules points earlier not insisted on, such as their inferiority in sitting, etc. (*GDS* 12.7; *ADS* 2.10.27.15), their exclusion from the study of the Vedas, the danger of contact with them (*ADS* 1.5.17.1; 2.2.3.4) or their food (*ADS* 1.5.16.2), still recognize that the śūdras can be merchants (*GDS* 10.60), or even exercise any trade. Moreover, the sūtras (*PGS* 1.4.11) permit the marriage of a śūdra woman with members of all castes. Though it was a reproach to Vatsa (*PB* 14.6.6) and to Kavasa (*AB* 2.19.1) that they were the sons of a śūdra and a dāsī respectively, still the possibility of such a reproach shows that marriage of this kind did take place. Moreover, illicit union of ārya and śūdra, or śūdra and ārya, are referred to in the Saṃhitās of the *Yajurveda* (*VS* 23.30; *TS* 7.4.19.3; *MS* 3.13.1; *KS* 4.8). Macdonell and Keith II, 388-92.

**Sūrya:** Sūrya is the most concrete of the solar deities, the name (which designates the orb of the sun as well as the god) showing that his character as a luminary was always present in the minds of the poets. As the all-seeing god, he is often called the eye of Mitra, Varuṇa, Agni, and other gods. The dawns produce Sūrya and he is to be the son of the goddess Aditi and of Dyaus. He is a ruddy bird or eagle that flies through space. He is cognate with the Avestic counterpart, who is the eye of Ahura Mazda. The *Ṛgveda* 1.24.8; 1.115.1; 1.191.9; 4.13.3; 4.25.4; 5. 29.5; 5.63.4; 5.62.2; 6.15.2; 6.72.2; 7.63.1, 5; 7.60.1; 8.35.13-15; 8.61.16; 8.90.12; 9.63.7; 9.96.5; 9.197.7; 10.85.1; 10.88.11.

**Susartu:** *Susartu* is the name of a river in the Nadī-Stuti (praise of rivers) in the *Ṛgveda* (10.75.6). That it was a tributary of the Indus is certain, but which one is unknown.

**Suṣomā:** Name of a river in the Nadīstuti (praise of rivers) in the *Ṛgveda* (10.75.5; *Nirukta* 9.26). In two other passages it would seem to be a proper name, once masculine (7.7.29) and once feminine (8.64.11). Its identification is quite uncertain, though it has been thought to be the modern Sohan.

**Sūta:** The Sūta or the charioteer, an important official figures as one of the kingmakers in the *Atharvaveda* 3.5.7; the *Śatapatha Brāhmaṇa* 13-2, 18; 3.4.1; 3.4.7.8. In the *Pañcaviṃśa Brāhmaṇa* (19.1.4) he holds his place among the eight *vīras* or dignitaries of the king and elsewhere (*KS* 15.4; *MS* 2.6.5; 4.3.8; *TS* 1.8.9.1; *TB* 1.7.3.1). A man of wit and wisdom, the royal charioteer was soon obliged to discharge many more functions, he often acted as a herald bard or ministrel or even as a messenger or envoy. The *Vājasaneyī Saṃhitā* (30.6) mentions the Sūta as a dancer. He is also occasionally described as unslayable in the *Taittirīya Saṃhitā* (5.2.1); *Maitrāyaṇī Saṃhitā* 2.9.3; *Vājasaneyī Saṃhitā* 16.18, seeming to denote his character as a herald or envoy, besides that of a charioteer, to be unworthy of being dishonoured.

**Śutudrī:** Śutudrī, twice mentioned in the *Ṛgveda* (3.33.1; 10.75.5 and *Nirukta* 9.26), is the name of the most easterly river of the Punjab, the modern Sutlej, the Zarodros or Ptolemy and Arrian. In the post-Vedic period the name of this river appears transformed to Śatadru (as flowing in a hundred channels). The Sutlej has changed its course very considerably within historical times.

**Suvāstu:** Suvāstu (having fair dwellings) is the name of a river in the *Ṛgveda* (8.19.37; *Nirukta* 4.15). It is clearly the Soastos of Arrian and the modern Swāt, a tributary of the Kubhā (Kabul river) which is itself an affluent of the Indus.

**Svetyā:** Svetyā appears in the Nadī-stuti (*RV* 10.75.6) to be a stream, probably a tributary of the Indus.

**Sword:** Swords were definitely known to the Aryans. The *Ṛgveda* (1.163.20; 10.79.6; 10.86.18) and the *Atharvaveda* (11.9.1) record the word *asi*, denoting a sacrificial sword or knife as well as a weapon of war. The word *niṣaṅgī* in the *Vājasaneyī Saṃhitā* means, according to Mahīdhara, 'having a sword' which is equally true of many other passages where it is found (*VS* 16.20; *KS* 17.12; 37.11; *MS* 2.9.3; *TS* 4.5.3.1; *ŚB* 13.4.2.5). Mention of a sheath (*vavri*) (a case for the blade of a sword or dagger) to which a belt (*vala*) was attached, can be found in *Kāṭhaka Saṃhitā* (15.4) and *Maitrāyaṇī Saṃhitā* (3.6.5). *Asi-dhara* in *Jaiminīya Upaniṣad Brāhmaṇa* (3.1.39) also denotes a sheath. The *Vājasaneyī Saṃhitā* (30.14) speaks of a female scabbard-maker.

# T

**Taxation:** The country which the Vedic Aryans occupied was split up into numerous tribal principalities. The tribe as a political unit was under a single ruler. Earlier kingdoms were small in extent and were units of a single tribe. Later, however, the institution or regular kingship (q.v.) was established; and the king was no longer merely a leader of a primitive tribe but occupied a position of pre-eminence, which was distinguished from the rest of the people. Necessity made him carry on bitter and prolonged fights with the Dāsas and Dasyus (q.v.), as also against other tribes who posed threat to his existence or whose territories he required for the sake of the fulfilment of his own ambition and the promotion of his tribal or territorial interest. In return for his warlike services the chief received the obedience of the people, and in particular their contributions for the maintenance of royalty. In the *Ṛgveda* the word *bali* has been variously understood. In one sense (*RV* 7.6.5; 10.173.6) it is a form of taxation. The king or chief was called *bali-hṛt* 'as one who subsists on payment of tribute'. It is possible that in the age of the *Ṛgveda* the chief of the tribe used to receive gifts in kind as presents, but not as a regular tribute. The prerogatives of monarchy in origin were due to voluntary action on the part of the tribesmen. But the Vedic people, who were basically warlike tribes, soon converted the original tribal society into organized states, and as such the voluntary gifts were converted into tributes. It is to this form of taxation that the share of village (*grāma*), horses (*aśveṣu*) and kine (*goṣu*) of the *Atharvaveda* (4.22.2) is to be referred. It is significant that the village and cattle are put on the same footing, as tending to refute the argument that the king was the supreme land owner. According to Macdonell and Keith (Vg. II, 213), the king is regularly regarded as 'devouring the people' but this phrase must not be explained as meaning that he necessarily oppressed them. It obviously has its origin in a custom by which the king and his retinue were fed by the people's contributions. It is also probable that the king could assign the royal right of maintenance to a kṣatriya, thus developing a nobility supported by the people. Taxation would not normally fall on kṣatriya or brāhmaṇa; the texts contain emphatic assertions of the exemption of the goods of the latter from the royal country. Among the revenue officials we come across a designation called *bhāga-dugha*, which apparently means the collector of the royal share or taxes. The word *bhāga-dugha* meaning dealer out of portions or distributor; is the name of one of the king's jewels (*ratnin*) in the *Taittirīya Saṃhitā* (1.8.9.2; *KS* 15.4; *MS* 2.6.5; 4.3.8; *VS* 30.13). What his functions exactly were is uncertain. In some places (*ŚB* 5.3.1.9) the word denotes tax-collector but in others (*ŚB* 1.12.17) an officer, thus making this functionary either a revenue officer or a mere court official. That taxation was a regular feature of state activities is attested by the fact that already in the post-Ṛgvedic age we come across names of such posts as denoting revenue officials. The term *saṃ-grahitṛ* is found in later Saṃhitās (*TS* 1.8.9.2; *KS* 15.4; *MS* 2.6.5; 5.3.8; *TB* 1.7.3.5; 9.6; 3.8.5.3; *AB* 2.25.6; *ŚB* 5.3.1.8; 4.3.23). He is an official who figures among the *ratnins* of the king. According to Sāyaṇa, in some passages it means the treasurer of the king. The incidence of taxation, however, did not fall equitably upon all classes of people. As the members of the royal family, the nobility and the kṣatriya class generally assisted the king in war, it was but natural that the right of maintenance should also be claimed by them. The brāhmaṇas also claimed to be exempt from the normal exercise of royal authority, particularly in respect to taxation. It appears that on the whole, the main burden of taxation fell on the 'people' who pursued peaceful occupations, such as agriculture, cattle-keeping, the arts, crafts, industries and trade. In the Sūtra period we come across a general statement that the king was entitled to a sixth part of the income or spiritual merit of his subjects (*BDS* 1.10.18.1; *VDS* 1.42). One-sixth, one-eighth, or one-tenth of the agricultural produce, the variation probably being due to the difference in the quality of land. One-fifth of cattle and gold, one-twentieth of merchandise and one-sixtieth of roots, fruits, flowers, medicinal herbs, honey, meat, grass and firewood were levied. The artisans and other manual workers had to do one day's work every month for the king and there were similar rules in respect to owners of the ships and carts (*GDS* 10.24-35; *BDS* 1.10.18.14).

**Tenant:** *Veśas* is a term apparently denoting 'vassal' or 'tenant' in the *Ṛgveda* (4.3.13; 5.85.7). In the verses the term *veśa* means neighbour and clothing respectively. Somehow, *veśa* (*RV* 10.49.5; *KS* 12.5; 31.12; *MS* 1.4.8; *AV* 2.32.5) collectively taken as *veśas* and *pari-veśas* indicate dependence. *Veśa* may also be related to the *vaiśya*. In the *Taittirīya Saṃhitā* 2.3.7 *vaiśya* has been explained as *vaiśyaṃ vittaṃ viśaḥ prajāḥ, kiṅkarādayaḥ*.

**Terrestrial Gods: See Rivers, Sarasvatī, Pṛthivī, Agni, Bṛhaspati, Soma.**

**Territorial Expansion:** The descriptions of the Aśvamedha and Rājasūya sacrifices in the texts show that ambitious kings strove to be all-powerful by extending their sway over neighbouring kingdoms, and seem to imply the existence of fairly large kingdoms. Although some of the tribal kingdoms of the Ṛgvedic days had probably grown in size through amalgamation and expansion, there were no great kingdoms even in this period and no empire as such. The fact that kings are often described in the *Atharvaveda* as fighting with their cousins (*bhrātṛvyas*), or with their non-Aryan enemies, appears to confirm this view, though not conclusive. On the other hand, the *Aitareya Brāhmaṇa* tells us that kings in the east were called *saṃrāṭs*, those in the south *bhojas*, those in the north *virāṭs*, and those in the famous middle country merely *rājans*, and that titles like *ekarāṭ* and *sārvabhaūma* could be claimed by a king who had conquered the kings in all the four directions. These specific references to imperialism, the flamboyant accounts of the imperial grandeur of kings who performed the Aśvamedha or the ceremony of royal consecration, and the titles like 'conquerors of the whole earth' assumed by them on these occasions, indicate the existence or large kingdoms and occasionally also of empires, even if we make full allowance for obvious poetic exaggerations. In the *Aitareya Brāhmaṇa* there is a fairly long list of kings who received the royal consecration at the Rājasūya, and it generally agrees with that in the *Śatapatha Brāhmaṇa*, listing those who had performed the horse-sacrifice. The very multiplicity of these 'imperial' monarchs, each of whom strides forth in the ceremony as a conqueror in all the four directions, perhaps shows that the performance of the Rājasūya often represented royal aspirations rather than actual conquests. Majumdar 431-2.

**Textile:** Cloth, made of linen or silk was known in the Vedic period. *Tārpya* is mentioned in the *Atharvaveda* (18.4.31) *Taittirīya Saṃhitā* (24.11.6) *Taittirīya Brāhmaṇa* (1.3.7.1) *Śatapatha Brāhmaṇa* (5.3.5.20), *Kātyāyana Śrauta Sūtra* (15.5.7) and *Śāṅkhāyana Śrauta Sūtra* (16.12.19) but scholars differ as to its meaning. By *tṛpa* plant we may mean mulberry leaves, suitable for silk cocoons. Textile industry was highly developed in the Sūtra period as reflected in *Pāraskara Gṛhya Sūtra* (1.4.13), which states that 'the goddess who had spun and woven, who stretched the wrap and who crossed the woof, may clothe you for old age. Blessed with long life you put on this garment'.

**Theft:** Theft may be traced even from the *Ṛgveda* and other Saṃhitās *RV* 1.191.5; 7.55.3; 8.29.6; *AV* 4.3.2; *VS* 11.77-78), which is denoted by the word *steya*. Thief was thus *steyakṛt* (*RV* 7.104.10). *Stena* and *taskara* mean thieves, whereas *malimlu*, as noted in the *Vājasaneyī Saṃhitā*, means a burglar or a house-breaker. *Malimlu* also appears in the sense of a highwayman, either among men or in the forest. The commentator on the *Taittirīya Saṃhitā* explains *stenaḥ guptacauraḥ, taskaraḥ prakaṭa-coraḥ ati-prakaṭa nirbhaya grāmeṣu vandikaraḥ malimluvah*, i.e. secret, open and more daring thieves respectively. The *Ṛgveda* (10.4.6) speaks distinctly of robbers who haunt the woods and risk their lives. They tie the wayfarers with ropes to a tree and rob all their belongings. The thieves are also reported to have stolen and killed cattle in the *Ṛgveda* (6.28.3). The *tāyu-s* (6.12.5) also stole clothes and cattle at night, under cover of darkness. The *Ṛgveda* (7.55.3) speaks of a dog barking at a thief and thus points to an attempt at house breaking. From another *Ṛgveda* passage (1.191.5), we learn that the thief does his business at night and from the *Ṛgveda* (8.29.6) it is clear that the thief knows where he has to attack his victim. The *Atharvaveda* (19.50.5) refers to robbers snatching away kine and horses. The *Ṛgveda* (4.38.5) speaks of thieves of a lesser category stealing clothes proves that thief was used to be scorched by kings. In the *Śatarudrīya* literary of the *Vājasaneyī Saṃhitā* (16.20-21) and *Taittirīya Saṃhitā* (4.5.3.4), Rudra has been called the lord of sailors, thieves, robbers and highwaymen, cheats, swindlers, burglars and other similar people. Keith opines that, 'The increased complexity of society seems to have been accompanied by an increase of crime and moral laxity, as appears from the curious literary in the *Yajurvedas*.' But V.M. Apte has justly remarked that this view 'does not appear to be correct'. However, there is no doubt that the *Ṛgveda* and the *Atharvaveda* refer to various crimes like theft, robbery, etc., and hence they contain many prayers for safety from these evils. But that does not suggest an increase in crimes and moral laxity in the Vedic age. The *Śatarudrīya* hymn points to Rudra's activity in almost every aspect of nature and hence we may find in him comprehensive control over all nature. The learned authors of the *Vedic Index* (1.304) think that 'the punishment of thieves appears primarily to have been left to the action of the robbed'. The practice of binding them is distinctly referred to in the *Ṛgveda* (1.24, 13 and 15). Sometimes thieves were brought to the king (*RV* 5.79.9). The *Ṛgveda* 7.86.5 is a prayer to Varuṇa to cleanse all sins of Vasiṣṭha. It speaks of a cattle thief who satisfies a cow with grass after performing the expiation ceremony and also of a calf which is freed from the rope with which it is bound. The *Atharvaveda* (19.47.8 and 50.1) similarly 'prays to Night to caste the thief into the snare'. The *Ṛgveda* (10.4.6) noted above, refers to cords for binding the thieves, when captured, or for binding the victim. The *Ṛgveda* 8.67.14 indicates that the thief, when caught, was bound with ropes. The *Atharvaveda* (4.3) contains charms against the wild beasts that may attack the thieves.

**Theogony:** In the philosophical hymns the origin of the gods is mostly connected with the element of water. In the *Atharvaveda* (10.7.25) they are said to have arisen from non-existence. According to one cosmogonic hymn of the *Ṛgveda* (10.129.6) they were born after the creation of the universe. Otherwise, in general, they are described as the children of Heaven and Earth. In one passage of the *Ṛgveda* (10.63.2) a triple origin, apparently corresponding to the triple division of the universe, is ascribed to the gods, when they are said to have been 'born from Aditi, from the waters, from the earth' (cf. 1.139.11). According to a secondary conception, certain individual gods are spoken of as having begotten others. Thus, the Dawn is called the mother of the gods (*RV* 1.113.19) and Brahmanaspati (*RV* 2.26.3), as well as Soma (*RV* 9.87.2), are said to be their father. A group of seven or eight gods, the Ādityas, are regarded as the son of Aditi. In the *Atharvaveda* some gods are spoken of as fathers, others as sons (*AV* 1.30.2). The Vedic conceptions on the subject of the origin of men are rather fluctuating, but the human race generally appears to have been regarded as descended from a first man. The latter is called either Vivasvat's son Manu, who was the first sacrificer (*RV* 10.63.7), and who is also spoken as father of the Manus (*RV* 1.80.16); or, he is Yama Vaivasvata, Vivasvat's son, who produced the human race with his twin sister Yamī. The origin of men, when thought of as going back beyond this first ancestor, seems to have been conceived as celestial. Vivasvat is the father of the primeval twins, while once the celestial Gandharvas and the water nymphs are designated as their highest kin in the *Ṛgveda* (10.10.4). Men's relationship with the gods is sometimes also alluded to; and men must have been thought of as included among the offspring of Heaven and Earth, the great parents of all that exists. Again, Agni is said to have begotten the offsprings of men (*RV* 1.96.2; 4), and the Aṅgirases, the semi-divine ancestors of later priestly families, are described as his sons. Various other human families are spoken of as independently descended from the gods through their founders Atri, Kaṇva, and others (*RV* 1.139.9). Vasiṣṭha (*RV* 7.33.11) was miraculously begotten by Mitra and Varuṇa, the divine nymph Urvaśī having been his mother. The conception of the origin of various classes of men from parts of the world giant, Puruṣa, belongs to a different order of ideas. Macdonell 14-5.

**Theriomorphism:** While most of the Vedic nature deities are normally conceived as anthropomorphic, there was no rigid exclusion of theriomorphic conceptions of the deities. It is often asserted, even by Oldenberg, that in earlier periods of religion, theriomorphic conceptions were more frequent than anthropomorphic, but the proof for such a theory seems to be wholly lacking. That the storm-god should be conceived in human form appears to be as natural and as primitive as that he should be ascribed an animal form, unless indeed we are asked to believe that religious conceptions of animal gods were formed before the development of man as such. Apart from theories such as these, however, there can be no question of the predominance of anthropomorphism in the *Ṛgveda*, while at the same time theriomorphism is not unknown, a condition which accords well with the observed fact that the distinction of man and beast is never drawn by early peoples with the definite precision of modern feeling. Two deities are recorded as in animal form only, the one-footed goat, Aja Ekapād, and the serpent of the deep, Ahi Budhnya. It is not likely that either is in origin an animal deity; the one-footed goat may be the lightning flash that descends to earth in a single streak, while the serpent has clear mythological meaning in its application to Vṛtra, the demon who is defeated by Indra, and who holds back the desired waters of the clouds. The mother of the Maruts, gods of the storm wind, is called the dappled cow, which seems to have been felt as a description of clouds whence sprang the rain. The Ādityas themselves, sons of Aditi, who is either a personification of freedom or an abstraction derived from their name, are also cow-born, reflecting perhaps-not probably—a conception of the birth of the luminaries from a celestial cow (cf. *AV* 8.9.1) where the two calves of Virāj may be the sun and the moon, the children of Dawn. The sacrificial food is personified as early in the *Ṛgveda* as a lady with hands full of butter, but she is also styled a cow, and in the ritual the cow is addressed with the words: 'Come, O Iḍā, O Aditi'. Agni is often conceived as a horse and Indra as a bull. When the rain is brought down, clouds are normally and usually styled the cows. Śaraṇyu, according to an old tradition, becomes a mare and in that condition brings forth the two Aśvins. Keith 61-2.

**Thongs:** The word *vardhra* means thongs. It is referred to in the *Atharvaveda* (14.1.60) and the *Śatapatha Brāhmaṇa* (5.4.4.1). It was used to fasten a woven couch. *Pari-carmanya* denotes a thong of leather in the *Kauṣitaki Brāhmaṇa* and the *Śāṅkhāyana Āraṇyaka* (2.1).

**Thorn-worker:** The word *kaṇṭakī-kārī* indicates the 'worker in thorns', an occupation mentioned in the *Yajurveda Saṃhitā* (*VS* 30.9; *TB* 3.4.5.1). Thorns were cut up and used to plait mats (*kaṭa*) or to stuff cushions.

**Threefold Knowledge:** *Vidyā* in the *Atharvaveda* (6.116.1; 11.7.10; 11.8.3) and later (*TS* 2.1.2.8; 5.1.7.2; *AB* 8.23.8; 8.23.9) denotes 'knowledge' especially that of the three Vedas, which are called the *trayī vidyā* 'the threefold knowledge', as early as the *Taittirīya Brāhmaṇa* (3.10.11.5; cf. *ŚB* 5.5.5.6). In a more special sense, *vidyā* appears in lists of subjects of study in the *Śatapatha Brāhmaṇa* (11.5.6.8) and the *Bṛhadāraṇyaka Upaniṣad* (2.4.10, 4.5.11). What exactly the expression here means is uncertain. A student of all the three Vedas is called *triśukrīya* (*KS* 37.1.7) or *triśukra*, thrice pure in the *Taittirīya Brāhmaṇa* (2.7.1.2).

**Time:** *Kāla*, the generic expression for 'time' appears

in the *Ṛgveda* (10.42.9). The concept of *kāla* is symbolically represented by the Great Night in the *Ṛgveda* (10.190.1-2). This symbolical Night is the infinite time, enveloping infinite space when creation takes place by cosmic actions, at both the macro and micro levels. The equation of infinite time with darkness, the space with the great primordial waters is further supported by the *Nāsadīya-Sūkta* (*RV* 10.129. 3-4). A fuller treatment of Time is found in the *Atharvaveda*, where *kāla* has been conceived as the prime mover and the cosmic principle, metaphorically represented as the horse with seven reins to control and thousand eyes (*AV* 19.53.1) carrying the chariot-wheel of the universe. The seven seasons and the whole year itself are the seven wheels (cf. *ŚB* 10.2.6.1) and seven are its naves. *kāla* gives shape to all manifestations. (First principle *AV* 19.53.2). The pitcher of fullness (*pūrṇa*) is placed on time which brings forth all becomings. Infinite time is wrapped in the great infinite space (*AV* 19.53.3), fills it and transcends it. No energy is higher than this time (*AV* 19.53.4). Another hymn (*AV* 19.54) is also devoted to *kāla*, wherein it is the substratum of all phases of creation. *Kāla* transcends this region and the region beyond by its power of pervasiveness. As a potent force, time is responsible for all cosmic activities so that the period taken by the earth to make the rotation of the sun, the cycle of seasons, the months, day and night, and dawn and twilight, have their successive appearances. In the Brāhmaṇas and Upaniṣads, five seasons are regarded as the changing rhythmic pattern of time, so much so that *kāla* came to be considered as the main cause of all creation or manifestations.

**Tin:** *Trapu* in the *Atharvaveda* (11.3.8; *KS* 18.19; *VS* 18.13; *MS* 2.11.5; *TB* 3.12; *CU* 4.17.7; *TS* 4.7.5.1) means tin.

**Tongs:** Tongs means an instrument with two hinged or sprung arms for grasping and holding, *aṅgāra-vakṣayaṇam* (*BU* 3.9.18) is a vessel or instrument in which coals are extinguished. *Ulmukavakṣayaṇam* means extinguishing a fire-brand (*ŚB* 4.6.8.7; 5.2.4.15; 11.6.3.3; *JB* 2.76). Another term for tongs is *parisasa*, which was used to lift the sacrificial kettle off the fire (*ŚB* 14.1.3.1, 14.2.1.16, 14.2.2.54, 14.3.1.20) and also used to serve domestic and ritual purposes, whether wooden or metal is not certain. The term *sapha* means a wooden implement and is used to lift up a pot from the fire (*AB* 1.22).

**Tonsure:** The ceremony of the tonsure is usually performed in the third year, or the fifth and seventh for a kṣatriya and vaiśya respectively. The essence of the ceremony is the formal wetting of the child's hair, putting bunches of *darbha* on it cutting the right and then back and then the left side with a razor, which is not to injure the child. The hair is thrown away with the *darbha* in the cow-stall, near water, or in a pool of water or elsewhere. For three days after, it seems, the barber must not use the razor; as often, in the case of girls the formulae used for boys are omitted. The hair is then arranged in the peculiar mode of the family, or in a number of tufts according to the number of seers hailed as belonging to the family tree in the *pravara* ceremony. As his fee, the barber receives rice and butter, or other gifts; the family teacher receives a cow. In the 16th year, or the 22nd and 24th for the kṣatriya and vaiśya, follows shaving of the beard based on the same model, but the cutting is extended to hair, beard, hair of the body and nails. The fee to the priest is a pair of cattle, and a goat to the barber. The youth should observe chastity for a year or at least three days, and not cut his hair again. Keith, 359.

**Totemism:** Some survivals of totemism, or the belief in the descent of the human race or of individual tribes or families from animals or plants, are found in Vedic literature. Kaśyapa, 'tortoise', the name of a seer (*RV* 9.1.14) and that of a priestly family (*AB* 7.27) is also frequently found in the *Atharvaveda* and the later Vedic literature as that of a cosmogonic power nearly related to, or identified with the creator Prajāpati. In a passage of the *Śatapatha Brāhmaṇa* (7.5.15) Prajāpati appears in the form of a tortoise (*kūrma*). Here it is remarked that, as *kūrma* is identical with *kaśyapa*, 'therefore men say: all beings are the children of the tortoise (*kaśyapa*)'. The *Ṛgveda* (7.18.6, 19) mentions as tribal names of Matsyas (fishes), the Ajas (goats), and the Śigrus (horse-radishes). As Vedic priestly families, names of the Gotamas (oxen), the Vatsas (calves), the Śunakas (dogs), the Kauśikas (owls), the Māṇḍūkeyas (frog-sons) also appear. The father of Samvaraṇa (a name occurring in *RV* 5.53.10), from whom the kings of the Kurus claimed descent, is called Ṛkṣa (bear) in the epic. There are various anthropological and psychological theories in relations to totemism. It is not merely the ancestor or tribal god conceived of in the form of an animal or any natural object, though it is very often connected with ancestor-worship. In fact, among primitive peoples the totem gave the tribal or clan identity. When life was collective and there was no individual names of persons, the entire clan introduced themselves by their totem names. Certain features of totemism may be discerned. The totem animal cannot be eaten by persons belonging to that totem (however, there are exceptions in certain cases when the totem animal is eaten for gathering strength from the ancestor). Secondly, a man must not kill a man belonging to his own totem and observe the social rules which emanate from the totem itself. Thus, totem is inseparable from certain taboos. Thirdly, a man must marry a girl outside his own totem and as such totemism is connected with exogamy. The Vedic concept of *gotra* is directly associated with totemistic beliefs. *Gotra* occurs several times in the *Ṛgveda* (1.51.3; 2.17.1;

3.39.1; 3.43.7; 8.74.5; 10.48.2; 10.103.7) in the account of the mythic exploits of Indra. Roth interprets the word as 'cowstall', while Geldner thinks it as 'herd'. The latter sense seems to explain best the employment which the term shows in the later literature as denoting the 'family' or 'clan', and which is found in the *Chāndogya Upaniṣad* (4.4.1). In the Gṛhya Sūtras stress is laid on the prohibition of marriage within a *gotra* or with a *sapiṇḍa* of the mother of the bridegroom, i.e. roughly, with agnates and cognates. Senart has emphasized this fact as a basis of caste, on the ground that marriage within a *curia, phratria,* or caste (*varṇa*) was Indo-European, as was marriage outside the circle of agnates and cognates. In the *Chāndogya Upaniṣad* (1.12), in which Glāva Dāllhya went for the acquisition of learning (*svādhyāya*), he came across a white dog surrounded by others who were requesting him to sing so that they might get food, must be a magical practice, and the gods associated with it are not dogs in the real sense of the term but they represent a totemic concept. Similar totemistic beliefs are found in the Ṛgvedic concepts of such horses as *dadhikrā*, who smites the *dasyus* and is victorious (*RV* 4.38.1-3, 7). His adversaries fear him as the thunder of heaven when he fights against a thousand; he wins booty in combats and against the hostile tribes (*RV* 8.5.4). Making himself (*kṛṇvana*) a garland, he tosses the dust and scatters it from his brows (*RV* 4.38.6-7). He belongs to all the tribes, pervades the five tribes with his power, as Sūrya he waters with his light, and observes the assemblies (*RV* 4.38.2, 4.38.10). This *dadhikrā* must be a totem horse. Nearly related to *dadhikrā* is Tārkṣya, whose name is mentioned only twice in the *Ṛgveda* (1.89.6; 10.178.1). He is described as a god—a mighty steed (*vājin*), a vanquisher of chariots, swift and speeding to battle. Another white steed of totemistic origin is that which the Aśvins are said to have brought (*RV* 1.119.10; 7.71.5) and which was called Paidva (*RV* 1.116.6; 9.88.4). This steed is spoken of as 'white', *śveta* (*RV* 1.116.6) several times. He is praiseworthy (*RV* 1.119.10; 10.39.10) and is to be invoked (*RV* 1.16.6; 1.119.10; 10.39.10) by men, like Bhaga (*RV* 10.39.10). He is compared with Indra (*RV* 1.119.10) and is called a 'dragon-slayer', *ahihan* (*RV* 1.117.9; 1.118.9), an epithet otherwise peculiar to Indra. He is conqueror, invincible in battles, and seeking heaven (*RV* 1.119.10). Among other totemic specimens the bull, the cow, the goat, the dog, the monkey and the birds may be taken into account. In the *Ṛgveda* Indra is constantly designated as a bull, a term applied much less frequently to Agni, and occasionally to other gods, such as Dyaus. In the *Atharvaveda* (9.4.9) a bull is addressed as Indra, and in the *Śatapatha Brāhmaṇa* (2.5.3.18) the bull is stated to be Indra's form. The terrestrial cow herself has already acquired a certain sanctity in the *Ṛgveda*, being addressed as Aditi and a goddess, while the poet impresses on his hearers that she should not be killed (*VS* 4.19.20). In the *Ṛgveda* the goat is specially connected with Pūṣan as drawing his car. It also appears there as a divine being in the form of Aja-Ekapād, the one-footed goat. The dog is found in the *Ṛgveda,* mythologically in the form of the two brindled hounds of Yama, called Sārameya. This name indicates that they were regarded as descendants of Saramā, the messenger of Indra. The boar appears in the *Ṛgveda*, as a figurative designation of Rudra, the Maruts, and Vṛtra. In the later Saṃhitās the tortoise is raised to a semi-divine position as 'lord of waters' (*VS* 13.31), or, it often appears beside or identical with Prajāpati as Kaśyapa in the *Atharvaveda* where he receives the epithet *svayambhū*, 'self-existent (*AV* 19.53.10). In the *Aitareya Brāhmaṇa* (8.21.10). Viśvakarmā is said to have promised the earth to Kaśyapa. A monkey appears in a late hymn of the *Ṛgveda* (10.86) as Indra's favourite. Soma is often compared with or called a bird. Agni in particular is frequently linked to or directly designated a bird, once being spoken of as the eagle of the sky. The sun is also sometimes conceived as a bird, twice under the name of *garutmat*. Ominous birds as well as beasts are occasionally connected with certain gods by whom they are supposed to seat. Some Vedic texts betray their totemic affiliations. There is at least one Saṃhitā, one Brāhmaṇa, one Āraṇyaka and one Upaniṣad which are named after the *tittira* bird (*taittirīya*). Two Upaniṣads are named after frog (*Muṇḍaka & Māṇḍukya*) and one after a white mule (*Śvetāśvatara*). Two of the recensions of the *Ṛgveda* are known as Āśvalāyana and Māṇḍukeya, each suggestive of the horse and the frog respectively. Name of three of the *sūtra* category (*Āśvalāyana*) also suggest the horse. One of the recensions of the *Atharvaveda* is named after the dog (*Śaunaka*).

**Town:** See **Cities**.

**Trade and Commerce:** In the *Ṛgveda* (1.56.2), there are clear references to trading in distant lands for profit. 'No him the guidance following songs of praise flow full, as those who seek gain go in company to the food.' (Grifitth, 1.78). The prayers and oblations offered for 'gaining a hundred treasures' are probably those of merchants seeking divine aid for success in trade. The *Ṛgveda* (3.18.3) says: 'With fuel, Agni, and with oil, desirous, mine offering I present for strength and conquest, with prayer, so far as I have power, adoring this hymn divine to gain a hundred treasures' (*ibid* 336). Apart from trade with foreign countries, or alien tribes, there must have been quite an extensive inland trade, but no definite details are available. Haggling in the market was, however, well known. The exchange of commodities on the principle of barter seems to have been in vogue, but the cow had already come to be regarded as a unit of value (*RV* 4.24.10). There might have been other recognized units of value. Great importance is attached to one such unit called *niṣka*. Originally it meant a gold ornament of the shape of a necklace or a necklet (*RV* 5.19.3). However, in the *Ṛgveda* 1.126.2, when the poet celebrates the receipt of a gift of a hundred *niṣkas* with a hundred horses, he could hardly be referring to a hundred necklaces. So it probably came to be used as a sort of currency even during the Ṛgvedic age. Booty in battle was one of the sources of wealth to the state, and consisted chiefly of flocks and herds. In individual economy, dowry and bride-price played no small part. Movable property could change hands by gift or sale which amounted to barter. Land was not an article of commerce, and does not seem to have presented any problems in connection with the transfer of immovable property in the case of the family or of the individual. The population being scanty and scattered over wide areas, fresh land could be easily obtained, if needed by a family which had grown to a very large size with several sons. The rivers of the North-West are referred to as yielding gold. In the age of the later Saṃhitās and the Brāhmaṇas, rich vaiśyas (*śreṣṭhins*), who had acquired wealth in trade or agriculture, and who were probably the headmen of guilds were often referred to. That moneylending was a flourishing business is indicated in various ways. *Kusīdin* is a designation of the usurer in the *Śatapatha Brāhmaṇa* and *kusīda* has the sense of a 'loan' in the *Taittirīya Saṃhitā*. The rate of interest is not specified. No regular system of currency or coinage appears to have been introduced yet, as no coins definitely belonging to this period have been unearthed and there is no specific and undoubted references to coins in the literature of the period. The *māna* is a measure of weight equivalent to the *kṛṣṇala* (i.e. the berry of the *guñja*), which was a unit of weight. The *śatamāna*, a piece of gold equivalent in weight to a hundred *kṛṣṇalas*, must have been in use as currency among the merchants. By now the *niṣka* had also become a unit of value in addition to the old-time unit, the cow. The profession of the merchant was often hereditary, as the term *vaṇija* (son of a *vaṇij*) in the sense of a merchant shows. Haggling, already known in the Ṛgvedic age, had now become such a pronounced feature of commerce that a whole hymn of the *Atharvaveda* (3.15) aims at procuring success in trade through clever bargaining. Garments, coverlets, and goat-skins were among the articles of commerce and market commodities. In the later Vedic period we come across a rite called *paṇyasiddhi* (ensuring success in trade), in which a portion of the particular article of trade is cut off and sacrificed in the fire with the prayer to Soma for carrying on trade in order to acquire wealth (*HGS* 1.15.1). The vaiśya class was engaged in trade and commerce. The *sūtras* of Pāṇini refer to imports from the north and his *vaṃśādhi yana* mentions several forest-products, such as *vaṃśa, kūṭaja, ikṣu* (sugar cane) and *madya* (liquor). The rule enjoined by the *Gṛhyasūtra* that the relatives of a deceased person are not to cook in the house, but to buy food during the period of the death-impurity, shows that food could be bought either from public eating houses or private individuals. A system of coinage or currency was probably in vogue in the later Vedic age though quite a large volume of trade was managed by way of exchanges in kind. Majumdar 399, 465, 530.

**Trade Routes:** While tracing the trade routes used by the Vedic Indians, the *Ṛgveda* (4.28.3) refers to numerous troubles like thieves on roads through remote regions or forests. Elsewhere (*RV* 10.5.6), we find mention of thieves lying in wait in forests for robbing travellers of their properties. The *Ṛgveda* (1.106.1) refers to bad conditions of roads causing chariots to move with great difficulty. That is why the seer prays to Puṣan for journeys by good paths (*RV* 1.42.7; 8). The *Ṛgveda* (5.54.6) is a similar prayer for good roads and a reliable leader to reach the land of riches. The *Ṛgveda* (1.91.1) is a prayer to 'Soma for direct route'. Again, the *Ṛgveda* (10.32.7) mentions how a traveller, not knowing the path, took advice from the local people who had full knowledge of it and reached his destination. The verse (*RV* 1.42.2) is an appeal to Pūṣan for saving one from a wicked person who misleads one to a wrong path and robs one of riches. The verse (*RV* 10.17.6, cf. *AV* 7.9.1) refers to roads, ordinary (paths) and superior (*prapatha*). The word *prapathin* (*RV* 10.63.16) also appears in another verse (*RV* 6.31.5) invoked to Indra, while passing by the road of the highest quality. The *Atharvaveda* (3.15) is pregnant with economic significance which deserves our minute study. This hymn is used by Kauśika in a ritual success in trade. Sāyaṇa also speaks of use for profit in commerce. It stresses on safe routes as essential for trade and commerce. The roads must run through the length and breadth of the country, fit for travel for decent persons. This hymn refers to enemies of trade, like thieves and wild animals, infesting the roads and causing loss of life and property to traders. Indra is addressed in this hymn as Vaṇija, explained by Sāyaṇa as *vāṇijya rartaram*, i.e. as a divine agent for making the routes safe. Obviously, the king is referred to as the political leader of the land, who is the lord like Indra (*Īśāna*) and is capable of removing obstructions. Another verse (no. 2) of this hymn mentions provisions like milk and *ghee*, including other articles of nourishment, to be available on roadsides for the maintenance of traders and also the two motives of traders like purchase and acquisition of riches. Oblations to Agni, with *ghee* and divine prayer as noted in its verse (no. 3), made by the trader indicate the objects of his undertaking, like winning a hundredfold profit and prayer for speed (both in travelling and the despatch of business) and physical strength, which is necessary for trade and commerce. Elsewhere (*AV* 12.1.47), we find a similar prayer for roads, 'free from enemies and free from robbers', and the roads are noted as open to 'men of both kinds, excellent and evil'. The word *parirathya* in the *Atharvaveda* (18.26) shows that some roads were suitable for chariots. Again, in the *Atharvaveda* (14.1.63) we learn of roads passing through pillars (gateways), evidently near the approaches of some towns through which the bride is depicted to have passed with the bridal procession. The *Ṛgveda* (1.166.9) refers to rest houses, provided with food or drink, on the routes. The *Atharvaveda* (7.53) is a charm for what is pleasant on the roads. The prayer of a traveller either on leaving or returning to his house is also found in the *Atharvaveda* (7.60). It is used for prosperity in a rite in *Kauśika Sūtra* by one setting out on journey, contemplating the house and its occupants. The *Aitareya Brāhmaṇa* (6.17.8) and *Chāndogya Upaniṣad* (8.6.2) mention *mahāpathas*, obviously high roads like the national highways of modern times, connecting different parts of the country, built and used for trade-purposes. S.C. Sarkar (*Some Aspects of the Earliest Social History of India*, London, 1928, p. 14) remarks that these *mahāpathas* of the Vedic period agree with *mahāpathas* of early Buddhist literature. We come across the term *badvan* in the *Pañcaviṃśa Brāhmaṇa* (1.1.4) and *Lāṭyāyana Śrautasūtra* (1.1.23), used in the sense of a spcieally prepared way, firmer than an ordinary road. The word *setu* is found in Vedic literature (*RV* 9.41.2; *KS* 27.4; *TS* 3.2.2.2; 6.1.4.9; *AB* 3.3.5.4; *ŚB* 13.2.10.1; *TB* 2.4.2.6; *BU* 4.4.22; *CU* 8.4.1-2). It means either a raised construction demarcating one field from another, or a raised bank or a bridge for crossing inundated land or a river. The *Chāndogya Upaniṣad* (8.4, 2) mentions it distinctly in the second sense of crossing, like a bridge to reach Brahmaloka. Whatever sense it may mean, it shows that the Vedic period witnessed the construction of raised ground or bridge for disconnecting or connecting one with the other, on roads passing through inundated land or rivers. B. Srivastava (*Trade and Commerce in Ancient India*, Varanasi, 1968, p. 120) thinks that the existence of bridges in the Vedic period cannot be substantiated, and that it may suggest any ordinary crossway. He refutes Dr. Sarkar's interpretation of the *Atharvaveda* (14.1.63), wherein the pillars standing in the way are taken as barrier-posts for collecting toll or octroi on the trade routs, On the basis of Sāyaṇa's interpretation, he holds that *prapatheṣu khadayo* means rest houses on the routes, providing food for travellers and the pillars of the hymn were meant for decoration, evidently for welcoming the bride on the bridal road. The *Chāndogya Upaniṣad* (4.1.1) refers to guest-houses on routes where weary travellers would have their meals and rest during the night. While prescribing the preferential treatment of various types of men, the *Āpastamba Dharmasūtra* (2.5.11.5-9) advises that all must make way for a laden vehicle. This shows how the traders carrying their goods in vehicles were also provided with all facilities for their smooth journey. Sarkar 14, Srivastava 120.

**Transference of Disease:** Among the magico-religious ways of curing, transference of disease to another individual or to an animal or to a plant or some inanimate object or to another country is a frequently adopted way. The person to whom the disease is transferred is sometimes a sinner or sometimes an enemy or sometimes some hateful person. Thus, in the *Atharvaveda* (4.16.6-8) a person caught by Varuṇa's fetters, i.e. the diseased one, requests him to transfer his disease to some villain. In the *Atharvaveda* (6.112.2 and 6.113.2) Pūṣan is so requested. In the *Atharvaveda* (8.6.26) a herb is requested to inflict childlessness, still birth and barrenness on the enemy. Elsewhere, the evil (*pāpmān*) is expected to go after another person (*AV* 6.26.2 f), to somebody who is hated by the disease and to kill the hated person (*AV* 6.26.3). Vasus are requested to send away the sin committed by their devotees to one who wants to harm them (*RV* 10.37.12). In the *Ṛgveda* (10.97.23) medicinal herbs are requested to make the person who threatens the devotees attacked by disease. The disease named *takman* is expected to go from the devotee to someone else (*AV* 6.20.1). The same disease is elsewhere asked to go and catch a slave-woman of a Śūdra class of bad behaviour (*AV* 5.22.6 f). The disease is also asked to go to the countries like Mujavat or Bālhīka (*AV* 5.22.7; 9), or among the Māhavṛṣa (*AV* 5.22.5). One also likes to send disease to peoples like the Gāndhāras, Aṅgas, and Magadhas (*AV* 5.22.14). These countries are generally considered as outside the 'Aryandom' and inhabited by heretic people. The god Rudra is asked to go to Mujavat country to cause disaster (*ŚB* 2.6.2.17; *VS* 3.61; *MS* 1.10.4; 20; *KS* 9.7; 35.14). Thite 74-5.

**Transmigration:** When the Vedic people witnessed the burning of a dead body they supposed that the eye of the man went to the fire, his limbs to the different parts of the universe. They also believed in the recompense of good and bad actions in worlds other than our own, and though we hear of such things as the passing of the human soul into trees, etc., the tendency towards transmigration had but little developed in the time of the earlier Saṃhitās. In the Upaniṣads, however, we find a clear development in the direction of transmigration in two distinct stages. In the one, the Vedic idea of a recompense in the other world is combined with the doctrine of transmigration, whereas in the other, the doctrine of transmigration comes to the forefront in supersession of the idea of a recompense in the other world. Thus, it is said that those who performed charitable deeds or such public works as the digging of wells, etc., after death follow the way of the fathers (*pitṛyāna*) which is meant for those who cultivate faith and asceticism (*tapas*). The other line of thought is a direct reference to the doctrine of transmigration, unmixed with the idea of reaping the fruits of one's deeds (*karma*) by passing through the other worlds and without reference to the doctrine of the ways of the fathers and gods, the *Yajñas* (*CU* 5.10). The tip of one's heart shines and by that shining this soul goes out. When it goes out either through the eye, the head, or through any other part of the body, the vital function (*prāṇa*) is coming out. It is then with determinate consciousness it comes out. Knowledge, the deeds as well as previous experience (*prajñā*) accompany it. Just as a goldsmith takes a small bit of gold and gives it a newer and fairer form, so the soul after destroying this body, and removing ignorance, fashions a newer and fairer form as of the *pitṛs*, the Gandharvas, the gods, Prajāpati or Brahmā or of any other being. As it acts and behaves so it becomes, good by good deeds, bad by bad deeds, virtuous by virtuous deeds and vicious by vice. As it desires so it wills, as it wills so it works as, the work is done so it happens (*BU* 4.4.1-7). At the time of death, the self collected within itself all senses and faculties and after death all its previous knowledge, work and experience accompanied it. The falling off of the body at the time of death is only for the building of a newer body, either in this world or in the other worlds. The self which thus takes rebirth is regarded as an aggregation of diverse categories. Thus, it is said that, 'He is of the essence of understanding, of the auditory sense, of the essence of the five elements (which would make up the physical body in accordance with its needs) or the essence of desires, of the essence of restraint of desires, of the essence of *adharma*, of the essence of all that is this (manifest) and that is unmanifest or latent (*BU* 4.4.5).' The self that undergoes rebirth is thus a unity not only of moral and psychological tendencies, but also of all the elements which compose the physical world. The whole logic of the genesis of *karma* and its fruits is held up within him, for he is a unity of the moral and psychological tendencies on the one hand and elements of the physical world on the other. The self that undergoes rebirth, being a combination of diverse psychological and moral tendencies and the physical elements, holds within itself the principles of all its transformations. The root of all this is the desire of the self and the consequent fruition of it through will and action. When the self continues to desire and act, it reaps the fruit and comes again to this world for performing acts. The most distinctive aspect refers to desires as the cause of rebirth and not *karma*. *Karma* only comes as the connecting link between desires and rebirth, for it is said that whatever a man desires he wills, and whatever he wills he acts. See **Re-birth** and **Karma**.

**Transport:** Being a necessary precondition for economic activities, trade and commerce, various means of transport are referred to in the Vedic texts. For the ordinary purpose of travelling, chariots and carts, drawn by oxen, mules or horses were extensively used in the Vedic period. Prayers were offered to the gods (*RV* 7.35.15) to 'give broad paths to travel'. Paths that should be straight in direction and thornless (*RV* 10.85.23). A solemn prayer to Indra for the safety of the journey (*RV* 3.53.17; 2.53.18; 2.53.19; 3.53.20) gives many interesting details of an oxen-driven cart in which the journey was made. In the age of the later Saṃhitās and Brāhmaṇas, the draft wagon (*anas*) is distinguished from the chariot (*ratha*) used for war and sport. The axle-box of a conveyance is mentioned. Chariots drawn either by horses or by mules and carts drawn by bullocks were the common forms of conveyance. Chariots drawn by horses were different in size and shape from those drawn by mules. Again, some chariots were drawn by a single horse while others by two horses. The chariot drawn by a single horse is mentioned in the *Aitareya Brāhmaṇa* (5.25.5). Chariots drawn by she-mules were used to run very fast. The *Aitareya Brāhmaṇa* refers to such chariots as *aśvatarī-ratha*. There is reference to a cart in the Soma-Yāga also. The different parts of a cart (*sakaṭa*), such as *yuga* or yoke, *samya* or yoke-pin, etc., are mentioned in the *Śatapatha Brāhmaṇa* (3.5.1.24). All wheeled vehicles were generally referred to by the term *cakra* alone. Thus we read in the *Śatapatha Brāhmaṇa* 'gods were driving about in wheels', meaning wheeled vehicles. The different parts of a chariot are described in the *Taittirīya Brāhmaṇa* (1.5.12.5), such as wheels, axle, yoke, the pole connecting the yoke with the chariot, the seat, etc. In this passage the journey of god Prajāpati is described. Ferry boats called *naukā* or *nāva* to cross rivers and sea-going strong-built vessels are referred to. The *Aitareya Brāhmaṇa* refers to boats in which one can cross easily (*sutarmā nauḥ* 1.3). The *Aitareya Brāhmaṇa* (6.29) makes an important observation with regard to sea-going vessels. It mentions a particular kind of vessel called *sairavatī* in which one can cross the sea. The mythological story of the great deluge appears in the *Śatapatha Brāhmaṇa* (1.8.1). There we read how Manu built himself a strong vessel able to stand the rage of wind and water and kept himself afloat in that vessel, which sailed over the mighty waters of the fathomless deep. Different part of a ship, such as spars, oars, mast, etc., have been described in the *Śatapatha Brāhmaṇa* (3.5.1.14). Since the *Atharvaveda* (15.2.1) mentions *u-patha*, a rough vehicle used for bad tracks, it can be inferred that there were some well-made roads. In later Vedic texts, bridges, roads, crossways and squares, where four roads meet, are referred to. Horses and oxen (even cows occasionally) were the common draught animals, the elephant being employed for a state journey or a procession. Horses, asses and camels were used for purposes of travel.

**Treasure:** The words for treasure or '*rayaḥ*' and treasure or store as place of deposit, i.e. *nidhi*. The former probably denotes 'richness' in wealth. The latter is found in the *Ṛgveda* (1.183.4; 15.43.8; 7.67.7) as store as well as treasure (*RV* 2.24.5; 8.29.6; 10.68.6, *AV* 10.7.23). Storing of treasure is mentioned in the *Ṛgveda* (10.108.17). A treasure house was called *dhanadhānī*. Wealth as well as gift is referred to in the *Ṛgveda* (1.42.6; 10.18.2; 10.84.7) and the *Atharvaveda* (1.15.3; 2.7.4; 3.15.2, 5.19.9), etc. *Dhānī* means a place, i.e. treasury. The conjunct term *dhanadhānī* is mentioned in the *Taittirīya Āraṇyaka* (10.67). In one passage of the *Ṛgveda* (10.73.4) *vasāvi* denotes a treasure-house. But Sāyaṇa interprets such a term as some form of property. *śevadhi* is also a term for treasure in the *Ṛgveda* (2.13.6), the *Atharvaveda* (5.22.14) and the *Vājasaneyī Saṃhitā* (18.59). *Vasu* is also treasure in the *Śatapatha Brāhmaṇa* (1.6.4.2). Indra is the chief of the Vasus. The term *vārya* means distributable wealth.

**Treasurer:** The term *saṃgrahitṛ* is found in the later Saṃhitās (*TB* 1.8.9.2; *KS* 15.4.4; *MS* 2.6.5, 4.3.8; *VS* 16.26) and the Brāhmaṇas (*TB* 1.7.3.5; 3.8.5.3; *AB* 2.25.6; *ŚB* 5.3.1.8). He is an official who figures among the *ratnins* of the king. Some scholars suggest that the term means 'charioteer'. In interpreting some passages (*TS* 1.8.9.2; *TB* 1.7.10.6), Sāyaṇa is inclined to think that the meaning is 'treasurer' of the king.

**Tribal Republics:** The tribal political life of the Ṛgvedic people was a sort of pre-class tribal republic, called *gaṇas*, living under several leaders or kings (*rājānaḥ*), of whom one was the *Jyeṣtha rāja*, i.e. senior king. The expression *rājānaḥ samitāviva* (*RV* 10.97.6), explained by Sāyaṇa as king in *samiti*, may be taken to refer to the existence of a political organization having a popular assembly and many leaders called *rājas*. D.P. Chattopadhyaya has rightly pointed out, 'Evidently the scholars who have discovered "monarchy" among Vedic tribes are misled by the word *rājan* . . . Even in the latest stratum of the *Ṛgveda* we come across the epithet '*rāja-vrātasya*' and this is a synonym for *gaṇasya senāniḥ*. This means nothing but the tribal chief' (*Lokayata*, Delhi, 1958, pp. 593-4). Thus, he argues that the word *rājan* does not always necessarily prove the existence of a monarchical form of government. *Gaṇa*, the technical term for a republic, is mentioned at least 46 times in the *Ṛgveda*, 9 times in the *Atharvaveda* and several times in the Brāhmaṇas. This term is used very often in the sense of hosts, with reference to Maruts and gods in general (*RV* 1.64.12; 5.52, 13-14; *AV* 13.4.8; *SB* 5.4.3.17). The Maruts are noted as sons of Rudra and so their *gaṇa* is evidently a republic of a tribal unit. Their number was forty-nine (*PB* 19.14.2) or sixty-three, divided into seven groups, with each having nine (*ŚB* 2.5.1.12; *RV* 8.96.8; *TB* 1.6.2.3). The verse (*RV* 2.23.1) refers to Brāhmaṇaspati, invoked as *ganānāṃ tvāṃ ganapatim* and as *jyeṣtharājam*, meaning 'lord or leader of heavenly hosts' and 'king senior' respectively. From this evidence we may say that the Vedic Aryans had been familiar with *gaṇas*, i.e. hosts of gods representing organized groups of people living under several leaders whom they called *rājans*. We have enough instances of *gaṇas* of devas in the Vedic literature (*RV* 4.35.3; cf. *TB* 2.8.6.4; *ŚB* 13.2.84). These divine *gaṇas* may be taken as reflections of human *gaṇas*. The *Atharvaveda* (19.22.16; 17) speaks of *gaṇa* and *mahāgaṇa*. Thus, we may hold that tribal groups lived an organized political life, not under any particular king but under many kings (*rājānaḥ*). Prof. R.S. Sharma opines that in Vedic literature *gaṇa* was a sort of organization, chiefly of Indo-Aryans and in most cases in Vedic literature, this term means 'a tribal organisation'. Griffith has rendered this term at various places of the *Ṛgveda* as 'an assembly of gods or men'. Jayaswal writes, 'The hymns of the *RK* and *Atharvan* . . . point to the fact that the republican form of government of India came long after monarchy and after the early Vedic age'. *Hindu Polity* 25. But it is more likely that the Āryans of even the Ṛgvedic age, when they had to fight out the pre-Aryans before settlement anywhere, engaged in a perpetual state of warfare, deeply interested in gaining cattle and others, grouped together and formed *gaṇas*. The verse (*RV* 5.61.13) speaks of the Marut *gaṇas* in the sense of the army and troops. The sun is extolled in the *Atharvaveda* (13.4.8) as having the troops of Maruts under his command. Indra, the god of war is also described in the verse (*RV* 3.35.9) as the leader of the *gaṇa* of Maruts. The *Atharvaveda* (4.13.4) states that the troops of Maruts are invoked to come to the rescue of man. The *gaṇas* are described as equipped with sniff steeds and weapons like bows, arrows and quivers. In the verse (*RV* 6.56.5) Pūṣan is invoked to satisfy the *gaṇa* of men with the acquisition of kine as spoils of war. So we may say that, as in other primitive societies, the Vedic *gaṇa* was a self-made organization, with each member being fully armed for both offensive and defensive purposes.

**Tribes:** The Bharatas (*RV* 3.53.9, 12, 24; 3.33.11-12; 7.8.4; 7.33.6) were the most important of the Ṛgvedic tribes. They were settled in the region between the Sarasvatī and Yamunā. Their exact relation with the Tṛtsus (*RV* 7.18.7, 15, 19; 7.33.5-6, 7.83.4, 6, 8), who occupied the country to the east of the Paruṣṇī, cannot be determined. Both were enemies of the Purus. In the post-Ṛgvedic period the Bharatas and Tṛtsus coalesced with the Purus, their erstwhile enemies, to form the Kuru people. The Purus have been mentioned in the *Ṛgveda* (7.18.13) along with Anus, Druhyus, Turvasas Yadus and lived on the either side of the Sarasvatī. The Anus (*RV* 1.108.8, 7.18.14, 8.10.5, 8.74.15) dwelt on the Paruṣṇī, the Druhyus (*RV* 1.108.1) and the Turvasas (*RV* 1.36.18; 1.54.6; 1.174.9; 6.45.1; 8.4.7; 8.7.18, etc.) lived beyond the Paruṣṇī, and the Yadus (*RV* 1.36.18; 1.54.6; 1.174.9; 4.30.17; 5.31.8; 6.45.1; 8.4.7; 8.7.18, etc.) lived in the southern Punjab. According to some scholars these five tribes—all living in or around the Punjab region—were the traditional *pañcajanāḥ* of the Vedas. The Krivis (*RV* 8.20.14; 8.22.12), a comparatively unimportant tribe, who possibly lived on the Sindhu (Indus) and Asiknī (Chenab), later moved to the east across the Yamunā to the land later known as Pañcāla. The Sṛñjayas (*RV* 4.15.4, 7; 6.16.5; 6.27.7; 6.31.4; 7.34.9) were closely allied with the Tṛtsus and lived in the neighbourhood of Pañcāla. The Matsyas (*RV* 7.18.6) lived in the modern Alwar, Bharatpur and Jaipur region. The Ajas, Śigrus and Yakṣus (*RV* 7.18.19) were probably eastern tribes. The Pakthas, Bhalānases, Alinas, Viṣānins and Śivas (*RV* 7.18.7) were five frontier peoples. The Pakthas lived in the hills from which the Krumu originates. South of the Pakthas stretched the Bhalānases. The Viṣāṇins were settled between the Krumu and the Gomatī. The Alinas were settled in the north-east of Kafiristan and the Śivas lived between the Sindhu and the Vitastā. The Cedis (*RV* 8.5.37-39) dwelt between the Yamunā and the Vindhyas. The Uśīnaras (*RV* 10.59.10) lived in the middle country, in or around the Gangetic divide. The Gandhāris (*RV* 1.126.7; *AV* 5.22.14), one of the frontier tribes lived to the extreme north-west of India. The Pṛthus and Parśus (*RV* 7.83.1) may refer to the Parthians and Parsians, but such identifications are purely hypothetical. The Pārāvatas (*RV* 6.62.2) dwelt on the Yamunā. The Kīkaṭas (*RV* 3.53.14) appear to be a hostile people of the Magadha region. The Paṇis (q.v.) are mentioned with the Dāsas (q.v.) and the Dasyus (q.v.) as the enemies of the Aryans. Though opulent the Paṇis were not respectful to the Vedic culture. Nothing is known about their geographical location. In the post Ṛgvedic period the Bharatas disappear as a tribe. The Kurus—the successors of the Bharatas, Tṛtsus and Purus—along with the Pañcālas, Vaśas and Uśīnaras occupied the Madhyadeśa. The Kuru-Pañcālas are the people *par excellence* in the Brāhmaṇa period and they are referred to as a united nation. The Sṛñjayas were also in the process of amalgamation as is indicated by their sharing of priest with the Kurus (*ŚB* 2.4.4.5). The five-tribes—Anus, Druhyus, Yadus, Turvaśas and Purus—are heard of no more. The *Gopatha Brāhmaṇa* (1.2.9) speaks of the union of the Vaśas and Uśīnaras, while the *Kaṭha Upaniṣad* (4.1) connects the Vaśas with the Matsyas. Kauśāmbi was the capital of the Vaśas. The Śibis were associated with the Uśīnaras and they inhabited the Shorkot region lying between the Ravi and the Chenab. The Śālvas (*ŚB* 10.4.1.10) were settled near the Yamunā and the Ikṣvākus (*ŚB* 13.5.4.5) in the Ayodhya region. The Kośalas and Videhas (*ŚB* 1.4.1.10 ff) were eastern tribes, the latter having their settlement across the Sadānīrā. The Kāśis were connected with the Kośalas and Videhas on account of their proximity. The Magadhas (*AV* 5.22.14, 15.2.3-4) were settled in southern Bihar and the Aṅgas in the Bhagalpur region. The Vaṅgas in Bengal proper are mentioned with the Vagadhas (Magadhas) in the *Aitareya Āraṇyaka* (2.1). In the southern region, the Satvants (*AB* 7.14; *ŚB* 13.5.4.21; 8.5.4.11) lived below the Gangetic divide and later moved beyond the river Chambal. The Vidarbhas (*AB* 7.34), famous for their special breed of hounds (*JUB* 2.440), lived in the modern Berar region. Contiguous to the Vidharvas was the settlement of the Naiṣadhas (*ŚB* 3.3.2.1). The settlement of the Kuntis (*KS* 26.9) is not precisely known to us. Under the Pratīcyas or Westerners come the Nicyas (*AB* 7.14), living in the Punjab region, Apācyas (*AB* 7.14) living near the territory of the former, Bāhīkas (*ŚB* 1.7.3.8) settling to the West of the Punjab and Ambaṣṭhas (*AB* 8.21) settled on the lower Āsiknī. Among the Udicyas or northerners we have Uttarakurus and Uttaramadras (*AB* 7.14; 8.23) located beyond the Himālayās. The Mujavants are mentioned as a distant people; the Mahāvṛṣas as northerners with no specific region ascribed; and the Bāhlīkas are mentioned along with the three foregoing tribes who were probably inhabitants of the distant Balkh region (*AV* 5.22.5-14, *AB* 8.34, *ŚB* 12.9.8.3). The Keśins (*ŚB* 11.8.4.6) were probably a branch of the Pañcālas. The Kekayas were settled in the north-west, between the Sindhu and the Vitastā. The *Śatapatha Brāhmaṇa* (11.6.1.2) and *Chāndogya Upaniṣad* (5.11.4) mention Aśvapati, king of the Kekayas as a man of learning. The Kambojas, mentioned in the *Vaṃśa Brāhmaṇa* settled in the north-west of the Indus and were the Kambujiya of the old Persian inscriptions. The *Aitareya Brāhmaṇa* (7.18) mentions the Andhras, Puṇḍras, Śabaras, Pulindas and Mutibas as being Dasyus living on the borders of Aryan settlements. The Andhras originally lived between the Kṛṣṇā and the Godāvarī. The Puṇḍras were settled in northern Bengal. The Pulindas is the name of a generic tribe of the Deccan, one of the branches of which had their stronghold in the Bhilsa region. The Śabaras were also a generic tribe, Suari of Pliny and Sabarae of Ptolemy. They settled in central and south-eastern India. The Mutibas, also known as Mucipas, settled on the banks of the river Musī on which modern Hyderabad stands. The Niṣādas, mentioned in the later Saṃhitās and Brāhmaṇas appears to be not the name of a particular tribe, but the generic term for non-Vedic tribes. In view of the above, it appears that in the Ṛgvedic age the extreme north-west was occupied by the Gandhārīs, Pakthas, Alinas, Bhalānases and Viṣāṇins. The Śivas, Parśus, Kekayas, Vṛcivants, Yadus, Anus, Turvaśas and Druhyus settled in Sind and the Punjab. In the middle region settled the Tṛtsus, Bharatas, Purus and Sṛñjayas. The Kīkaṭas occupied the Magadha region while the Matsyas and Ceḍis settled to the south of the Punjab in Rajasthan and Malva. In the age of the later Saṃhitās and Brāhmaṇas, the eastern region was occupied by the Kośalas, Videhas, Magadhas and Aṅgas. In the north and north-west, we come across the Uttarakurus and the Uttaramadras, Bāhlīkas, Mahāvṛṣas and Mujavants, showing the expansion along Kashmir and the Himālayās. Towards the south, the Vindhya appears for the first time in the *Kausītakī Upaniṣad* (2.8) and the Kuntis and Vītahavyas seem to have penetrated further south, and Narmadā and Vidarbha were also within the fold of Vedic culture.

**Tribute:** *Bali* appears several times in the *Ṛgveda* (1.70.9; 5.1.10; 8.100.9, 5.1.10; 8.100.9) and often later (*AV* 6.117.1; *TB* 1.2.3.2; *KS* 29.7; *TU* 1.5.3; *TB* 2.7.18.3; 3.12.2.7; *ŚB* 1.3.2.15; *PB* 15.7.4; *AB* 7.29; *KS* 29.9; *TS* 1.6.2.1) in the sense of tribute to a king or offering to a god. Some scholars think that the offerings were in both cases voluntary. They compare the notices of the Germans in Tacitus, where the kings of the tribes are said to receive gifts in kind, but not a regular tribute. No doubt, the origin of the prerogatives of monarchy was due to voluntary action on the part of the tribesmen, but this gradually developed into the system of elaborate taxation (q.v.).

**Trikakud:** *Tri-kakud* (*AV* 4.9.8; *ŚB* 3.1.3.12) or *Tri-kakubh* (*MS* 3.6.3; *KS* 23.2; *VS* 15.4; *PB* 22.14) 'having three peaks' appears in the *Atharvaveda* and later as the name of a mountain in the Himālayās, the modern Trikoṭa.

**Trita Āptya:** Trita Āptya is only incidentally mentioned in the *Ṛgveda* in forty passages. He is mentioned in connection with Indra. He is connected or identified with Agni seven times; he is spoken of several times with the Maruts and ten times with other deities. Trita is also mentioned alone (1.187.1). The Maruts aided Trita and Indra in the victory over Vṛtra (8.7.24). Trita Āptya knowing his paternal weapons, and urged by Indra, fought against and had slain the three-headed son of Tvaṣṭṛ and released the cows (10.7-8). At one place Trita is impelled by Indra, while in another Indra is inspired by Trita; and thrice Indra is said to have acted for Trita. He is associated with the Maruts in the thunderstorm. He finds and kindles Agni in heaven, and takes up his abode in human dwelling as a form of Agni. Macdonell, 67-8.

**Tṛṣṭamā:** *Tṛṣṭamā* is mentioned as a stream in the Nadīstuti in the *Ṛgveda* (10.75.6). It was a small stream in the Punjab region.

**Tuft:** 'Tuft' or 'lock' (*śikhaṇḍa*) a style of wearing hair on the head appears in the *Taittirīya Saṃhitā* (7.3.16.2). In the *Taittirīya Brāhmaṇa* (1.2.1.27; 3.7.6.4) a young lady is described as 'four tufted' (*catuḥ-śikhaṇḍā*) and figuratively interpreted as four-angled sacrificing altar by Sāyaṇa. 'Wearer of tuft' (*śikhaṇḍin*) is revealed in the *Atharvaveda* (4.37.7; 11.2.12). *Stūpa* in the *Taittirīya Saṃhitā* (1.1.11.1), *śikhā* in the *Śatapatha Brāhmaṇa* (1.3.3.5) and *stuka* (*ŚB* 3.2.1.13; *AV* 7.74.2) indicate tuft or lock.

**Turban:** Turban or head band (*uṣṇīṣa*) was used by both men and women in Vedic period. It was put on by the king at the Vājapeya (*ŚB* 5.35.23) and Rājasūya (*MS* 4.4.3) ceremonies. Vrātya's turban is alluded to in the *Atharvaveda* (15.2.1) and the *Pañcaviṃśa Brāhmaṇa* (17.1.14). A most multicoloured turban is pointed out in the *Śatapatha Brāhmaṇa* (14.2.1.8), which belongs to Indra's dear wife Indrāṇī (*indrānī ha vā indrasya priyā patnī tasya uṣṇīṣo viśvarūpa-tamaḥ*). This was not simply a piece of cloth to cover the head but something like a 'pagree', which the ladies did not usually wear for they arranged their hair in various decorative braids. Indrāṇī's turban indicates its use by the rich and aristocratic ladies of the Vedic age. Altekar 280, Chakraborty 162.

**Turghna:** Mentioned in the *Taittirīya Āraṇyaka* (5.1.1) as the northern part of Kurukṣetra. Its exact location is uncertain.

**Turvaśva:** A tribe living on the western bank of Paruṣṇī, mentioned in the *Ṛgveda* (1.36.18; 1.56.6; 1.174.9; 6.20.12; 6.45.1; 8.4.7; 8.7.18; 8.9.14; 8.45.27; 10.48.8; etc.) along with the Anus, Yadus, Druhyus and Purus. They lived in the southern Punjab. See **Tribes**.

**Tutelary Deities:** The name of Vāstospati appears only seven times in the *Ṛgveda*, and one hymn of three stanzas (7.54) is devoted to his praise. He is invoked there to grant a favourable entry, to remove disease, to bless man and beasts, to confer prosperity in cattle and horses, and to afford protection. In the first verse of the hymn immediately following (7.55.1), he is described as a destroyer of disease. He is once (7.54.2) identified with Soma, being addressed as Indu. In a verse of a hymn to the all-gods (*RV* 5.41.8), he is invoked in immediate juxtaposition with Tvaṣṭṛ and is perhaps identified with him as the great artificer. In another verse (*RV* 8.17.14) he is called a firm pillar, a friend of Soma-pressers, and seems to be identified with Indra. He is spoken of as the observer of ordinances who, along with prayer (*brahma*), was fashioned by the gods (*RV* 10.61.7). To the same order belongs Kṣetrasya patiḥ, the tutelary deity of the field. He is invoked, in the first three verses of 4.57, to grant cattle and horses as well as to fill heaven and earth, plants and waters with sweetness. In a verse of a hymn to the all-gods (*RV* 7.35.10) he is besought, along with Savitṛ, the Dawns and Parjanya, to bestow prosperity. In a similar hymn (*RV* 10.66.13), worshippers express a desire to have him as a neighbour. In one verse of a hymn addressed to agricultural deities (4.57.6), Sītā, the Furrow, is invoked to grant rich blessings and crops.

**Twice-born:** The term *dvija* applies to persons belonging to the first three *varṇas* as twice born, being consecrated in ritual performances. The concept was universally recognized as a consequence of puberty rites meant for a ritualistic rebirth, which was needed for the attainment of manhood. A man becomes twice-born owing to the initiation. The term *dvija* appears in the *Atharvaveda* (19.71.1). Its derivatives are *dvijanman* and *dvijāti*. The concept had a greater development in the later period, in the age of the Upaniṣads and Sūtras.

**Twin-Ādityas:** In the *Ṛgveda* Aśvins are distinguished as twin-Ādityas and are described as the physicians of the gods. According to Yāska, some held them to represent heaven and earth, others day and night, or the sun and moon. But the Nairuktas held that they were the morning stars or the two stars in the constellation of Gemini. In the *Ṛgveda* (1.45.2) the Aśvins are called the sons of the sea and are requested to appear thrice a day to accept sacrifices (1.34.1 ff) at sunrise, noon and sunset.

**Tvaṣṭṛ:** Tvaṣṭṛ is mentioned some sixty-five times in the *Ṛgveda*. Like the other gods of the *Ṛgveda* he goes to the heaven, and bestows blessings (*RV* 10.10.5). His characteristic feature is the iron axe which makes him the most skilled artificer. He forges the bolt of Indra, and the axe of Brahmaṇaspati, and especially the cup out of which the gods drink. Tvaṣṭṛ stands in special relation to the human race. His daughter Śaraṇyu, wife of Vivasvant, produced the twins, Yama and Yamī. He is also father of Bṛhaspati, of Agni, and even of Indra, who, however, seems to have slain him for withholding the Soma from him. In the *Ṛgveda* Tvaṣṭṛ is normally mentioned along with gods of similar character, such as Savitṛ, Dhātṛ, Prajāpati, and Pūṣan. He is twice identified with Savitṛ (*RV* 3.55.19; 10.10.5). The post-Vedic mythology regards him as an Āditya, Tvaṣṭṛ figures also in the myth of the Ṛbhus.

# U

**Uddālaka Āruṇi:** The epistemological queries of Uddālaka appear in *Bṛhadāraṇyaka Upaniṣad* (3.7). Uddālaka and Bhujyu refer to the house of one Patañcala, the son of Kapi, who lived in the Madra territory. Both of them mention a certain Gandharva who had seized in one case the daughter, and in the other the wife, of Patañcala. The question which Uddālaka had asked Yājñavalkya was as follows: 'What is the thread (*sūtra*) that holds this world and all the beings thereon in their places?' And again, 'Who is the inner ruler of this world and the next and all the beings thereon?' In his answer to Uddālaka, Yājñavalkya said that it was Air itself which must be regarded as the *Sūtra*, as the thread which had woven together the different worlds and the beings that lived in them. The *antaryāmin*, or the Being Immanent in the worlds regulating the motions and changes in them, said Yājñavalkya, could only be the *ātman* of a veritably immortal nature. The view expressed by Yājñavalkya is that of the immanence of the *ātman* that lies encased in very form of existence in the universe.

**Uktha:** The concept of *uktha* pervades the Upaniṣads. It is the innermost essence and symbol of the Universe. Etymologically *uktha* signifies that from which things arise, and therefore that whereto the things depart. Hence, the earth as the source of all produce, the atmosphere as the goal and limit of all upward motion, the sky as the bestower of life-giving moisture to the whole creation; all these are to be identified with *uktha*. The innermost essence of Prajāpati are the gods; the innermost essence of the gods, the rain; of rain, the herbs; of herbs, the food, of food, the semen; of semen, the off-spring; of off-spring, the heart; of heart, the mind; of mind, the speech; and of speech, action, constituting the be-all and end-all of man. In the second chapter of the *Kauṣītakī Upaniṣad* it is said that *uktha* is the same as *Brahman*.

**Unidentified Grains:** In the Vedic texts there are references to some grains which have not been identified. Among these *āmba* is a kind of wild-growing grain which appears in *Kāṭhaka Saṃhitā* 15.5 and *Taittirīya Saṃhitā* 1.8.10.1. *Masūsya* is a type of corn (*TB* 3.8.16.6) which, according to Sāyaṇa, are grown in northern countries. *Nāmba* is probably the same as *āmba* (*KS* 15.15, *TS* 1.8.10.1) and is used to prepare a porridge to be offered to Mitra, the lord of Truth (*ŚB* 5.3.3.8). *Palāla* is a straw of barley or likewise (*AV* 2.8.3; 8.6.2), which was probably animal fodder. *Pulya* or *Pulpa* apparently denotes shrivelled grain (*AV* 14.2.63). *Yayāsa* was a kind of grass (*RV* 1.38.5; 1.91.13; 3.45.3; 7.18.70; 7.87.2; 7.93.2; 7.102.1, etc., *VS* 21.43), which was probably used as animal fodder (*VS* 21.43; *RV* 1.38.5; 1.91.13; 7.87.2).

**Undergarments:** See **Dress**.

**Underworld:** See **Cosmography, Hell**.

**Unguent:** See **Aphrodisiacs**.

**Universe:** See **Cosmology**.

**University:** See **Education**.

**Unmarried Girls:** The frequent mention of unmarried girls like Ghoṣā, who grew up in their parents' houses (*RV* 1.117.7; 10.39.3; 10.40.5), the references to the ornaments worn by maidens at festive occasions in order to win lovers (*RV* 1.123.11; 8.2.5), to a youth's courtship with the maiden he loves (*RV* 1.115.2), to the lover's gifts (*RV* 1.117.18), to their mutual love (*RV* 1.167.3; 9.32.5), etc., and to the spell (*RV* 8.55.5-8) by which a lover hopes to lull the whole household to sleep while he visits his beloved, all this speaks in favour of the custom of girls normally marrying long after they had reached puberty. There seems to have been considerable freedom for young persons in the selection of a wife or husband, as they generally married at a mature age. There is no clear evidence that the consent of the parent or brother was essential. The latter appeared on the scene after the parties concerned had come to an understanding.

**Unmaried Mother:** *Kānīna* in the *Atharvaveda* (5.5.8) apparently denotes the son of a maiden. Such a son already spoken of in the *Vājasaneyī Saṃhitā* (30.6) was known as *kumārī-putra*. Such a person appearing with metronymic was Jābāla Satyakāma. Metronymics are found in the lists of teachers called Vaṃśas in the *Bṛhadāraṇyaka Upaniṣad* (4.1.14; 6.3.19) and *Chāndogya Upaniṣad* (4.4.1). In the *Vājasaneyī Saṃhitā* (30.6) Mahīdhara commented upon *kumārī-putra* as denoting a son of an unmarried daughter or *kanyā*. In the *Ṛgveda* (2.29.1) the term *rahasuḥ* has a bearing on unmarried mothers. According to Sāyaṇa it means a wanton woman. A woman without husband is called *agru* in the *Ṛgveda* (4.19.9; 4.30.16). The son of a maiden, i.e. unmarried girl was also known as *agruvaḥ putraḥ*.

**Upanayana:** The word *upanayana* means to bring (the student) near the teacher. The *Ṛgveda* (3.8.4) is a verse that clearly indicates that some of the characteristics of *upanayana* described in the Gṛhya Sūtras were well known in the earlier period. There the sacrificial post (*yūpa*) is praised as a young person. 'Here comes the youth, well dressed and encircled (the boy by his *mekhalā* and the post by its *raśanā*); he, when born, attains, eminence; wise sages, full of devotion to the gods in their hearts and entertaining happy thoughts, raise him up.' Here in *unnayanti* we have the same root that we have in *upanayana*. In the *Taittirīya Saṃhitā* (6.3.10.5) we have the famous passage referring to the three debts, where the words *brahmacārī* and *brahmacarya* occur. Every brāhmaṇa, when born, is indebted in three debts, viz., in *brahmacarya* to the sages, in sacrifice to the gods and in offspring to the manes; he indeed becomes free from debts who has a son, who sacrifices and who dwells (with the teacher) as a *brahmacārī*. In the other Vedas and in the Brāhmaṇa literature, there is ample material to show what the characteristic features of *upanayana* and *brahmacarya* were. The *Atharvaveda* (11.7) is a hymn containing hyperbolic praise to the *brahmācarins*, in which the earlier form of *upanayana* ceremony is found which was later elaborated in Sūtra literature. In the *Taittirīya Brāhmaṇa* (3.10.11) there is the story of Bharadvāja who remained a *brahmacārī* for three parts of his life (i.e. till 75), and to whom Indra said that in that long period of *brahmacarya* he had mastered only an insignificant portion (three handfuls of dust out of three mountains) of the Vedas, which were endless in extent. The fairly detailed description of the *upanayana* as a sacrament (*samṣkāra*) in the *Śatapatha Brāhmaṇa* (11.3.3.1-7) includes all the essential features of the same sacrament and life of studentship which are treated at length in the Gṛhya Sūtras. These are: (1) the formal acceptance of the pupil by the teacher at the former's request; (2) entrusting the pupil to the care of certain deities; (3) the vows and duties to be discharged by the pupil while residing at the house of the *guru*, such as putting fuel in the fire, sipping water, and begging alms; and, (4) the dress of the pupil consisting of the *ajina*, the girdle, etc. The description of young Aṅgirasa teaching his elders, in the *Pañcaviṃśa Brāhmaṇa* (13.3.23-24), and the stories of Nābhānediṣtha and Bharadvāja in the *Aitareya* and *Taittirīya* Brāhmaṇas, give us a vivid picture of the educational system of those days, with its insistence on truthfulness, observance of duty (*dharma*), devotion to the *ācārya* or *guru* (preceptor) and to one's parents, hospitality, faith, and generosity. The *Taittirīya Āraṇyaka* even anticipated some minute directions of the type given in the Gṛhya-Sūtras, such as: the pupil should not run while it is raining, nor urinate in water, nor bathe naked, etc. Kane II, 268 ff.

**Urbanism:** Unlike the pre-Vedic Harappa civilization, the Vedic society was rural, though we have references in the Vedic texts of a few cities like Asandivat, Kāmpilya, Paricakrā and so on. Archaeological evidence does not furnish us with clues in regard to the development of urbanism in the Vedic period. The Vedic states were seemingly small. There are no clear signs of any really large kingdoms, despite the mention of Mahārājas. The people engaged in agriculture, pastoral pursuits, other home industries, and trade (*vaṇij*) and paid tribute to the king for the protection afforded to them. But circumstantial evidence proves that, like other countries of the ancient world, there was a development of urbanism in Vedic India. At least in the age of the later Saṃhitās and Brāhmaṇas and also in the subsequent age of the Upaniṣads and Sūtras there must have been an elaborate development of urbanism. The Brāhmaṇa literature speaks of the great sacrifices like the Aśvamedha, the Rājasūya, the Vājapeya, the Aindra Mahābhiṣeka, etc., for the consecration of the king as sovereign emperors, which shows that the concept of empire was already popular in the post-Ṛgvedic period. The Vedic texts testify to various classes of people, and numerous occupations that are conducive to the growth of urbanism. The very concept of a society based on fourfold *varṇa* division is suggestive of a plural society, which would be accommodated in an urban setup. The legends like king Janaka offering a gift of thousands of cows with their horns plated in gold, prove that a great amount of social surplus was stored in the hand of the king. This phenomenon is not in accordance with a tribal or rural type of polity itself. The Vedic people penetrated into the Saptasindhu region upto the Śatadru and they established their supremacy over the Kabul Valley as well near about 1500 BC. Gradually they spread in Sarasvatī-Dṛṣadvatī valley. Indra, chief of Ṛgvedic gods is called Purandara, evidently because he helped the Vedic people in destroying 90 cities of the Saptasindhu region. Whether these cities or forts belonged to the Harappans or their descendants, it is not possible to say at the present state of our knowledge. That the Vedic Indians took interest in road-making is reflected in the *Ṛgveda* (2.34.5) in which the Maruts are invoked to come by strongly built paths. Elsewhere (*RV* 1.140.9), we find the praise of forest fire burning trees and thereby creating routes. The verse (*RV* 2.13.5) also mentions the river-routes, made navigable by Indra. Agni and Soma are also depicted as makers of roads, by which they give 'gods a pleasant treasure and world' (*AV* 18.2.53). The *Ṛgveda* (10.32.7) refers to the utility of the knowledge of routes, particularly direct routes, obviously for the convenience in trade and commerce. Puṣan is described in the *Ṛgveda* (8.29.6) as the guard of roads. Savitṛ is mentioned as the maker of roads free from dust (*RV* 1.35.11). These suggest that the Vedic Indians were highly conscious of the utility of roads, well-made and without dust in their socio-economic life. The *Atharvaveda* (14.1.34) also contains a prayer for roads 'free from obstacles and straight'. From the *Aitareya Brāhmaṇa* (38.3) we know that the Vedic people spread from the Sarasvatī region to that of Kuru-Pañcāla, where the Brāhmaṇa texts were composed. The *Śatapatha Brāhmaṇa* (14.11.17) refers to the transfer of Vedic fire by Videgha Māthava and his priest Gotama from the

Sarasvatī region to the river Sadānīrā, thereby indicating the Aryan colonization upto Bihar and obviously the opening of the route to this region. In this connection, the *Śatapatha Brāhmaṇa* mentions the towns of Āsandivat, Paricakrā, Kāmpilya and Nimiṣa. It deserves mention that Indraprastha, Hastināpura, Ahicchatra and Kāmpilya have yielded painted greyware assigned by archaeologists to the Aryans. Kāśi is mentioned in the *Atharvaveda* (5.22.14) and *Śatapatha Brāhmaṇa* (13.5.4.19-21). The *Śatapatha Brāhmaṇa* (13.5; 4.19) tells us of Dhṛtarāṣṭra, king of Kāśi who was defeated by Śatānīka Satrājita of the Bharata family. Kāśi-Videha in *Kauṣītakī Upaniṣad* (4.1) and *Bṛhadāraṇyaka Upaniṣad* (3.8.2) refers to closer connection between the Kāśis and Videhas. Excavations at Rajghat near Vārāṇasī (Kāśi) confirm the prevalence and stratigraphic position of the painted greyware in the Gangetic valley. The same ceramic industry of Rajghat is also found at Hastinapur and Ahicchatra. Archaeological finds have thus also some bearing on the process of urbanization that was taking place in the Vedic period.

**Usages:** See **Law, Rituals, Sacraments**.

**Uṣas:** The goddess of Dawn in the *Ṛgveda*. In her case the personification is slight, the poet never losing sight of the beautiful physical phenomena behind the deity. Gaily attired like a dancer, with a garment of light, she rises in the east and exhibits her graces. Though ancient, she is ever youthful, being born again and again. Her association with the sun is naturally very close. He is her lover, but as she precedes him, she is also said to be his mother. She is the sister of the night. She is also associated with Agni. (*RV* 1.48; 1.49; 1.92; 1.113; 1.123; 1.124; 3.61; 4.51; 4.52; 5.79; 5.80; 6.64; 6.65; 7.75-81; 10.172.)

**Usasta:** The metaphysical queries of Usasta appear in the *Bṛhadāraṇyaka Upaniṣad* (3.4). Usasta asked Yājñavalkya about the nature of the Ultimate Reality, the *ātman* and its relation with the perception of objects of sense. Yājñavalkya replied that *ātman* must be regarded as immanent in the whole world, which is why any perception of it in the ordinary sense of the term would be impossible.

**Uśīnara:** In the *Aitareya Brāhmaṇa* (8.14) the Kuru-Pañcālas are mentioned as dwelling together in the 'Middle Country' with the Vasas and the Uśīnaras. In the *Kauṣītakī Upaniṣad* (4.1) also the Uśīnaras are associated with the Kuru-Pacālas and Vasas, but in the *Gopatha Brāhmaṇa* (2.9) the Uśīnaras and Vasas are regarded as northerners. In the *Ṛgveda* (10.59.10) the people alluded to in one passage by reference to their queen, Uśīnarāṇī. Some scholars hold that the Uśīnaras originally lived in the north-west. The Anukramaṇi (Index) of the *Ṛgveda* ascribes one hymn (*RV* 10.179) to Śibi Auśīnara. The Śibis were known to Alexander's followers as Siboi, living between the Indus and the Akesines (Chenab). The Śibis in epic times occupied the land to the north of Kurukṣetra. The Vasas and Uśīnaras are spoken of as united in the *Gopatha Brāhmaṇa* (1.2.9).

**Usury:** Though in the *Ṛgveda* we have no direct evidence of money-lending, and receiving interest, in the later Saṃhitās and Brāhmaṇas we have reference to both money-lending and interest. *Kusīdin* is a designation of the 'usurer' found in the *Śatapatha Brāhmaṇa* (13.4.3.11) and the *Nirukta* (6.12) and often in the Sūtras. The expression *kusīda apratitta*, 'a loan not yet repaid', occurring in connection with *an-ṛṇa*, 'free from debt', indicates *kusīda* to have the sense of 'loan' in the *Taittirīya Saṃhitā*. The rate of interest on loans is not specified before the Sūtra period. Reference is often made (*RV* 10.34.10 and *AV* 6.119.1) to debts contracted at dicing. To pay off a debt was called *ṛṇaṃ saṃ-ni* (*RV* 8.47.17 and *AV* 6.46.3). Allusion is made to debt contracted without intention of repayment (*AV* 6.119.1). The result of non-payment of a debt might be very serious; the dicer might fall into slavery (*RV* 10.34.61). Debtors, like other malefactors, such as thieves, were frequently bound to posts by their creditors (*dru-pada*, *RV* 10.34.4), presumably as a means of putting pressure on them or their friends to pay up the debt. In one passage of the *Ṛgveda* (8.46.3) an eighth (*sapha*) and a sixteenth (*kalā*) are mentioned as paid, but it is quite uncertain whether interest or an instalment of the principal is meant. Presumably the interest would be paid in kind. The *Kauśika Sūtra* regards three hymns of the *Atharvaveda* (6.117-119) as applicable to the occasion of the payment of a debt after the creditor's demise. There is no evidence in regard to the payment of a debt by a relation of the debtor.

**Utensils:** Among the furniture the Vedic texts refer to is the use of *akṣu* or seat made of cane, *paryaṅka* and *proṣṭha*, each denoting a kind of wooden seat, *vahya* or coach, *śayana* or divan and *talpa* or bed. Among other household articles, a mention is made of buckets (*āhāva, udañcana*), cooking pots (*ukhā, sthālī, pacana*), stools (*pīṭha*), axes (*praśas*), scissors (*bhurij*), tongs (*aṅgārāvakṣayaṇa, ulmukāvakṣayaṇa, dhṛṣṭi, sapha, parīśāsa*), pounding stones (*upara, upalā, dṛṣad*), vessels (*amatra, āsecana, kadrū, kośa, capya, camasa, camū, pātra, pānnejana, pinvana*), pots (*kaṃsa, kalaśa, kumbha*), kettles (*carū*), ladles (*juhū, mekṣaṇa*), leather bags (*dṛti*), wooden pots (*dru, droṇa*), wooden dishes (*piśīla*), fans (*dhavitra*), sieves or winnowing fans (*paripavana, pavana, pavitra*), sickle (*parśu*) planks (*phalaka*), leathern bottles (*bhastrā*), mat of split reeds (*bhitti*), water-bottles (*maṇika*), nets (*mukṣījā*), pestles (*musala*), baskets (*mūta, mūtaka, śūrpa*), awls (*vāśī*), needles (*veśi, sūcī*), pegs (*śaṅku*), etc. Metallic utensils were also in use. See **Furniture, Implements, Village Economy**.

# V

**Vāc:** Personified speech is celebrated in one hymn of the *Ṛgveda* (10.12.5), in which she describes herself. She accompanies all the gods and supports Mitra-Varuṇa, Indra-Agni and the Aśvins. She bends Rudra's bow against the unbeliever. Her place is in the waters, the sea. She encompasses all beings. In another passage (*RV* 8.89.10-11), she is called the queen of the gods and divine. In the *Naighaṇṭuka* (5.5), Vāc is enumerated among the deities of the atmosphere, and thunder or *mādhyamikā vāc*, 'the voice of the middle region' in the terminology of the commentator (*Nirukta* 11.27), may have been the starting point of the personification. A legend of Vāc frequently referred to in the Brāhmaṇas is that of Soma being bought back from the Gandharvas at the price of Vāc transformed into a woman (*AB* 1.27). Macdonell 124.

**Vaiśvadeva:** First 'four-month' (*cāturmāya*) sacrifice in which the five common libations are followed by a cake to the Maruts: a milk preparation to all-gods (*Viśvadevas*), and a cake to Heaven and Earth. It took place in the spring. *Āśvalāyana Gṛhyasūtra* 1.2.21, *Vāsiṣṭha Dharmasūtra* 11.3, *Taittirīya Saṃhitā* 1.8, *Śatapatha Brāhmaṇa* 2.5.1.3.

**Vaiśvānara:** The sun in the sky, according to the view of the ancient Yājñikas, and terrestrial Agni or fire, according to Śākapuṇi. *Nirukta* 5.11, 7.4, 8.21-3.

**Vaiśya:** The term 'vaiśya' denotes a man, not so much of the people, as of the subject class, distinct from the ruling noble (*kṣatriya*) and the brāhmaṇa, the higher strata of the community on the one side, and from the śūdra on the other. The name is first found in the *Puruṣa-Sūkta* (*RV* 10.90) in the *Ṛgveda* onwards (*VS* 18.48; 30.5). Not much is written about the vaiśya in Vedic literature, which has much to say on the kṣatriyas and brāhmaṇas. His characteristics are admirably summed up in the *Aitareya Brāhmaṇa* (7.29) in the adjectives *anyasya balikṛt*, 'tributary to another'; *anyasyādya*, 'to be lived upon by another'; and *yathākāmajyeyaḥ*, 'to be oppressed at will'. He was unquestionably taxed by the king (*rājan*), who no doubt assigned to his retinue the right of support by the people, so that the kṣatriya grew to depend more and more on the services rendered to them by the vaiśyas. But the vaiśya was not a slave; he could not be killed by the king or anyone else without the slayer incurring risk and the payment of a wergeld (*vaira*), which in the Brāhmaṇa books extends to 100 cows for a vaiśya. Moreover, though the vaiśya could be expelled by the king, he cannot be said to have been without property in his hand. Since the vaiśyas were the class of producers in the economic sense and traders *par excellence*, their social importance could not be ignored. The kings had to depend on the wealth of the vaiśya. The Brāhmanical attitude towards this trading class was ambivalent, and hence, despite their great contribution to the cause of social mobility and progress, they were regarded as an inferior class and assigned the third rank in the social hierarchy. The socio-economic importance of this class was understood by the Buddha and Lord Mahāvīra, and that is why they were given special treatment by the Buddhist and the Jains. In post-Vedic age, Buddhism and Jainism received moral and financial support from the vaiśyas.

**Vajra:** There is a term *vidyut* used in the *Ṛgveda* for the thunderbolt associated alone with Parjanya, the real rain-god of the Veda. Indra is never called *vidyut-hasta*, but *vajra-hasta*. In the *Ṛgveda* 10.27.21 *vajra* is described as whirling about in different directions under the lofty light of the sun. In fact, the thunderbolt and the sun do not easily co-exist. *Vajra* here probably refers to a weapon. It is a fatal weapon (*RV* 1.52.5; 5.5.5) made of *ayas* or metal (*RV* 1.52.8; 8.96.3; 10.48.3, etc.). It is forged and fashioned by Tvaṣṭṛ, the smith-god (*RV* 1.52.7; 10.48.3, etc.). It is said to have been ground, whetted or polished (*RV* 1.130.4; 8.15.7; 8.76.9; 10.153.4). It has a hundred or a thousand joints, edges or spikes (*RV* 8.6.6; 76. 2; 89.3 etc.). Not transient like a bolt of thunder, it is a regular companion of Indra (*RV* 1.33.10; 6.21.7), who holds it in his arms (*RV* 1.63.2; 2.11.4; 3.44.4; 4.22.3; 6.23.1, etc.) but sometimes only in one (*RV* 6.20.9; 7.28.2, etc.). The metal *vajra* clings to Indra's person (*RV* 8.96.3). It is firmly held in his locked hands (*RV* 1.81.4). It is described as *sthavira* (*RV* 4.20.6) or stable being denoted and *dharṇasi* or durable (*RV* 8.6.14).

**Vaṅga:** Vaṅga, the designation of Bengal proper, is not found in the earlier Vedic literature, unless it is to be recognized in the curious word *vaṅgavagadhaḥ*, which occurs in the *Aitareya Āraṇyaka* (2.1-1), and which suggests amendment to Vaṅga-Magadhaḥ 'the Vaṅgas and the Magadhas', two neighbouring peoples. The name is certainly found in the *Baudhāyana Dharma-sūtra* (1.1.14).

**Varaṇāvatī:** Varaṇāvati is found in one passage of the *Atharvaveda* (4.7.1). It seems to be the name of a stream, a tributary of the Ganges. A plant may, as Sāyaṇa thinks, also be meant by this word but a river is more probable.

**Varṇa Concept:** A common origin, name, tutelary deity, occupation, and ceremonies generally distinguish one

Varṇa Concept

homogeneous caste-group from another, but today caste is rigidly fixed by birth, and exclusive commensality and connubium between the members of a caste-group to the exclusion of all others are its fundamental and outstanding characteristics. Again in the place of the four original *varṇas* or class-groups, today there are thousands of caste divisions and subdivisions and the number is still growing. This unique development of an ordinary social phenomenon naturally invests its history with a special importance. The extent to which caste had been developed in the age of the *Ṛgveda* has formed a subject of keen controversy among scholars. The uncertainty regarding the exact interpretation of the basic words and phrases in the *Ṛgveda*, and the relative chronology of the various relevant passages scattered throughout that Veda, make it difficult to arrive at any conclusion that is likely to meet with general acceptance. There are various speculations in later Brahmanical literature regarding the origin of castes. The most common is that which represents the brāhmaṇas, kṣatriyas, vaiśyas and śūdras to have been created respectively from the head, breast or arms, the thighs, and the feet of the Creator. An echo of this is found in a hymn of the *Ṛgveda* (10.90), the famous Puruṣa-sūkta, which describes the mythical legend of the sacrifice of a primeval giant called Puruṣa, the ideal 'Man' or World-Spirit. This passage refers to the first three castes as not having sprung from, but as being identical with, the mouth, arms and the thighs of the Creator. But in spite of this difference many regard this hymn of the *Ṛgveda* as the earliest exposition of the later Brahmanical view and regard the essential feature of the caste-system as existing even in the earliest Aryan society in India. This theory has been challenged by many scholars whose views may be briefly stated as follows: The evidence of the Puruṣa-sūkta, an admittedly late hymn, is not valid for the bulk of the *Ṛgveda*, which was produced by the as yet un-brahmanized tribes of Vedic Indians living in the Indus region and the Punjab. The caste system was developed only later, when a section of these Vedic tribes migrated farther east. The term *varṇa* (lit. Aryan colour) is used in the *Ṛgveda* of all the three highest castes of later times, being contrasted only with dāsa (the *dasyu-varṇa* or indigenous colour). The terms rājanya, vaiśya and śūdra appear only in the Puruṣa-sūkta, the term brāhmaṇa, also, being rare in the *Ṛgveda*. The term 'kṣatriya' of which rājanya is an earlier variant, appears but seldom in the *Ṛgveda*. The term *brahman* denotes a 'priest by profession' only in some passages, while in others it denotes any person who was distinguished by genius or virtue, or one who, for some reason, was deemed specially receptive of the divine inspiration. The necessity of carrying on a ceaseless fight with, and the conquest of the indigenous tribes called for an organization of the conquering people by the merger or fusion of petty tribes into centralized kingdoms. Thus emerged the powerful monarch, while the lesser tribal princes, deprived of their royal rank, sank to the position of nobles. Moreover, the monarchy now needed a standing armed force, prepared to meet all eventualities, such as resisting the sudden incursions of native or other Aryan tribes and quelling revolts on the part of the subdued original inhabitants. This standing army was naturally recruited from the ranks of the nobility of tribal princes and the chief armed retainers of the king. This is the genesis of the warrior class. At the same time, the 'people' of the Aryan masses, secure in the protection afforded by the warrior class, ceased to take interest in military matters and settled down to a peaceful life devoted to agriculture, pastoral pursuits, trade, and industry. They constituted the third class, which was later called vaiśya. When the size of the kingdom grew and military and administrative affairs kept the hands not only of the king but also of warrior class full, while, at the same time, the ritual tended to become more complicated and elaborate, the need was keenly felt of a hierarchic order, composed of the more intellectual elements among the non-fighters who could dedicate themselves, undisturbed by the distractions of war or peace to the faithful and exact performance of the highly developed ritual, and to the preservation (by order of mouth) of the traditional formulae and sacred hymnology of the Aryans. As regards the fourth class, the śūdra is mentioned for the first and only time in the 'Puruṣa-Sūkta'. But *dasyu* and *dāsa* are known to the *Ṛgveda* both as indigenous tribes independent of Aryan control and as conquered peoples. The latter may reasonably be supposed to represent the śūdras of the later texts. But all the defeated locals were not śūdras. Aryans with lower occupations also fell in this category. According to another set of arguments, (1) The term *brāhmaṇa*, 'son of a *brahman* or priest', suggests that the priesthood was normally hereditary. There is no definite instance of a person other than a priest exercising priestly functions. (2) The power of the *purohita* over the king in the *Ṛgveda*, derivable from the fact that the correct performance of the sacrifice demanded the services of a hereditary priest, is nearly as great as in the post-Ṛgvedic age. (3) The *Ṛgveda* knows of a ruling class—the kṣatriya—who, as a class of nobles, are appropriately named in the Puruṣa-sūkta as rājanya or 'man of kingly family'. As kingship was normally hereditary, the kṣatriyas were also in all probability a hereditary body. The śūdras were admittedly a separate group; so all the elements of the caste system were in existence in the age of the *Ṛgveda*. The existence of the four classes in Avestan literature certainly argues for the existence of somewhat similar classes in

Ṛgvedic society. According to some scholars the brāhmaṇas (far less the kṣatriya or vaiśyas) did not constitute an exclusive caste or race, and that the prerogatives of composing hymns and officiating at the services of the gods were not regarded, in the age of the *Ṛgveda*, as entirely confined to men of priestly families. The same thing was equally, or perhaps more, true of the minor professions, as a hymn refers to the father, mother and the son following three different vocations in life, viz., those of a poet, a grinder of corn, and a physician. The heredity of occupation was, therefore, not yet a recognized principle, far less an established fact. The utmost that can be said is that there were recognized professions like priesthood, or distinctions of nobility, and these had in many cases a tendency to become hereditary, but, as in other countries or societies, their ranks might have been recruited from all sections of the community. From the *Pañcaviṃśa Brāhmaṇa* (17.1) it appears that the Vedic Indians on the Indus were unbrahmanized. According to another view the term *varṇa* occurring in the Veda (*RV* 10.3.5; *VS* 4.2) to denote colour as a common word also expresses the classification of the Aryans being contrasted with the Dāsas. The brāhmaṇa termed by *brahman* in the *Ṛgveda* (9.112.1, 10.85.29) denotes a special class of priest. In some passage of the *Ṛgveda* (10.107.6; 10.125.5) this term denotes a priest by profession of sage to receive divine inspiration respectively. With the advance of the Vedic Indians to the east, the society of the *Ṛgveda* has been transformed gradually to the elaborate system of the *Yajurveda*. The conquering people needed a monarch for defence and protection of the place. The advantage thus won by the nobles including brāhmaṇa, rājanya, etc., over the people was shared by them with the priesthood. The origin of the power of priesthood is determined in the office of *purohita* laid down in the *Ṛgveda* (7.60.12; 7.83.4). Originally the prince could sacrifice for himself and the people. The right of the noble to act as purohita is acknowledged by Yāska in his *Nirukta* (2.10), explaining the *Ṛgveda* (10.98) in which Devāpi Ārṣṭisena sacrificed for his younger brother, king Śantanu, to bring down rain for removing vice of the king. The cases of Viśvāmitra and Vasiṣṭha illustrate the power of the Purohita as domestic priests of the kings. There had always been a tendency among some scholars to trace the caste system as being progressively developed, not appearing in the *Ṛgveda*. The supporters of the casteless Ṛgvedic system put forward the non-brahmanical character of the Vrātyas of the Indus and the Punjab and the theory that in the earlier period this system was unknown till the Vedic Aryans had migrated to further east, the Madhyadeśa which became the seat of Brahmanical culture. It has been argued that, in the *Ṛgveda*, even the idea of *brahman* as a 'poet' or 'sage' is not maintainable, because the Ṛgvedic tradition assumes *brahman* as the highest priest, i.e. *purohita* in charge of all round supervision in the sacrifice with other priests, generally seven Ṛtvijs as are enumerated in the *Ṛgveda* (2.1.2). In the *Ṛgveda* a regular term '*ṛtvij*' is used for a sacrificial priest covering the different kinds of priests employed at the sacrifice. All the priests were brāhmaṇas assumed throughout the Vedic texts. In the portion (*RV* 2.1.2) the oldest names of seven priests are enumerated as: Hotṛ, Potṛ, Neṣṭṛ, Agnīdhra, Praśaṣtr, Adhvaryu and Brahman besides the institutor of the sacrifice. In the *Ṛgveda* (8.35.16-18) there are traces of the three-fold division of the people into brahman, kṣatra and viś respectively. In the Bṛhaspati-hymn of the *Ṛgveda* (4.50.8) the king lives happily in his own abode. Where Bṛhaspati goes, the subjects, or 'viś', the term being generally used as common people, always obey him by paying homage to him (*RV* 4.50). Such a passage gives us an idea of brahman, rājan and viś revealed in the threefold caste. Notwithstanding such speculations, from an historical point of view it may be said that in all societies and at all ages, a fourfold social division consisting of the priestly and intellectual class, the ruling and warrior class, the producing and trading class, and the working class is admitted, and the Vedic society was no exception. See **Caste**.

**Varuṇa:** The comparatively small number of hymns addressed to Varuṇa hardly does justice to his importance in the *Ṛgveda*. The personification of Varuṇa has so advanced that his physical basis remains obscure. It has been suggested that the word Varuṇa is probably the same as the Greek word Ouranos (sky), though phonetic difficulties make the identification uncertain. Varuṇa is the upholder of the physical and moral order symbolized in *ṛta*, with which he is more intimately connected than any other god. He is a king and a universal monarch having a golden abode in which heaven is lofty and firm, and has a thousand columns and doors. He wears glistening garments. He has spies whom none can deceive. He is predominantly called the Asura, who rules by means of his *māya*. By this power he sends forth dawns and makes the sun (who is also described as his eye) traverse the sky. He supports heaven, earth, and air. He, with Mitra, is most frequently invoked as a bestower of rain. He regulates the seasons. Neither god nor mortals may violate his ordinances. Varuṇa's special connection with the waters is unmistakable. He is a regulator of the waters and causes the rivers to flow. He is above all the *dhṛtavrata*, the upholder of ordinances such as the fixed paths of the luminaries across the sky. He stands out pre-eminently as the moral governor among all the deities. The fetters (*pāśas*) with which he binds sinners are characteristic of him in this capacity. In every hymn to Varuṇa, there is a prayer for forgiveness of sin. There is uncertainty regarding the physical basis of the idea of Varuṇa. The view generally held is that it is the encompassing sky. This original conception, it is supposed, goes back at least to the Indo-Iranian period since Ahura Mazdah (the wise spirit) of the *Avesta* agrees with the Asura Varuṇa in character, though not in name. Keith 96-104, Macdonell 22-6.

**Varuṇāṇī:** Excepting Pṛthivī, Aditi, and Uṣas, most of the other goddesses mentioned in the *Ṛgveda* are of very little importance, Varuṇāṇī the wife of Varuṇa is only alluded to in a few passages (1.22.12; 2.32.8; 5.46,8; 7.34.22). She is invoked to drink *soma* juice, to bestow treasures and to be merciful to her devotees. Sinīvālī, Rākā, Sarasvatī, Indrāṇī, Rodasī, Agnāyī are her companions. No distinct function is assigned to her and she does not occupy positions at all corresponding to the rank of her husband.

**Vāyu-Vāta:** Vāyu and Vāta (wind) are almost interchangeable terms; when distinguished, the former is chiefly the god, the Vāyu is celebrated alone in a whole hymn besides parts of others, and in about half a dozen others, conjointly with Indra in the *Ṛgveda*. Vāta is invoked only in two hymns (10.168; 10.186). Generated by two worlds (7.90.3), or from the breath of the world-giant (10.90.13). Vāyu is the son-in-law of Tvaṣṭṛ (8.26.21-22). His car, in which Indra is his companion (4.46.2), has a golden seat. He is fond of *soma*, swiftest among the gods who grants fame, offspring and wealth, disperses foes and protects the weak. Vāta is the breath of the gods (7.87.2, 10.92.13) and like Rudra, causes healing and prolongs life (10.186).

**Vertibrates:** See under **Carnivores** and **Herbivores**.

**Vegetarianism:** Vegetarianism was perhaps not unknown to the Ṛgvedic Aryans. A devout offering of praise or of fuel stick or cooked food was considered as good as a more solemn sacrifice (*RV* 8.19.5). Then there is a whole hymn addressed to *pitu* (nutriment) which mentions all the articles of food except meat (*RV* 1.187. 8-10). Besides cereals and milk products, various kinds of vegetables must have been used as food by the Vedic Indian, but the Vedic texts mention very few compared to the variety of cereals. Of the vegetables cucumber (*urvāruka*) (*RV* 7.59.12; *AV* 6.14.2; *MS* 1.10.4; *TS* 1.8.62; *VS* 3.60) and lotus stalks or *bisa* (*RV* 6.61.2; *AV* 4.34.5; *AB* 5.30; *AĀ* 3.3.4; *SĀ* 11.4) were known to the Ṛgvedic Indians. The latter was probably in common use with the edible roots of lotus or *Śāluka* (*AV* 4.35.5) and *alābu* or bottle gourd (*AV* 8.10.29-30), *śaphaka* (*AV* 4.34.5) or *trapabispinosa* also seems to have been used as a food article. People of Maheśwar-Navdātolī used beans in about 1200 BC. In the later Vedic period a feeling of revulsion against meat eating, especially beef, is found in almost all our works (*ŚB* 3.1.2.21). The progeny of those who consume a cow (*AV* 12.4.38). The *Atharvaveda* regards beef eating as an offence against the forefathers (*pitṛs*). There was also an injunction against the slaughter of horses in a sacrifice (*VS* 13.48). People who observed a vow, generally, abstained from meat diet (*AV* 6.70.1; *ŚB* 14.1.1.29) and brāhmaṇas ate only sanctioned meat and that too of pure animals (*ŚB* 2.2.1.39; 12.1.2.39; cf. *AB* 6.8).

**Veterinary Charms:** In the *Ṛgveda* (1.43.6) it is said, 'Rudra gives happiness to horses, goats, men and cattle'. Elsewhere, Rudra is praised for the health of quadrupeds (*RV* 1.114). In the *Ṛgveda* (10.97.20), herbs are prayed to, 'May all the bipeds and quadrupeds be diseaseless'. Similarly in the *Atharvaveda* (8.7.11) we read, 'Let the purchased, very powerful plants that are praised, save the cow, horse, man, and beast in this village'. In the *Cāturmāsya*-sacrifices there is a group of offerings called *Śākamedhaparvan* and in it the Tryambaka-havir-yāga is performed. In this offering, as many cakes as there are the members in the sacrificer's family, added by one, are prepared. Except that additional one, the rest are offered to the fire. The additional cake is buried and it is hoped that animals will be free from Rudra (disease) (*ŚB* 2.6.2.10; *MS* 1.10.20; *KS* 36.14). After the cake is buried, the Adhvaryu returns to the fire and utters a formula, in which the following prayer is made: 'Thou (O Rudra) art the medicine for the cattle, a medicine for the horse, a medicine for the man, a blessing for the ram and ewe.' Thite 227.

**Vidarbha:** Vidarbha appears in the Vedic literature as the name of a region only in the *Jaiminīya Upaniṣad Brāhmaṇa* (2.440), where its Mācalas (perhaps a species of dog) are said to kill tigers. The region comprised parts of Maharashtra and Madhya Pradesh, modern Vidarbha or Berar region.

**Vidatha:** The term 'vidatha' is found in the *Ṛgveda* (1.31.6; 1.117.25; 3.1, 18; 3.27.7, 4.38.4; 10.85, 26; 10.92.2) and also in the *Atharvaveda* (4.25.1; 5.20.12; 18.3.70) but its meaning is not clear. According to Roth, the sense is primarily 'order', then the concrete body which gives orders, then assembly for secular purposes (*RV* 2.1.4; 2.27.12; 2.27.17; 3.38.5; 3.38, 6; 5.63.2; 7.66.10; *AV* 17.1.15), or religious ends (*RV* 1.60.1; 2.4.8; 2.39.1; 3.1.1; 3.56.8), or for war (*RV* 1.166.2; 1.167.6; 5.59.2). Whitney renders this term in the *Atharvaveda* (1.13.4) as council. Oldenberg first took it in the sense of 'ordinance' derived from *vidha*, dispose or ordain, but afterwards in the sense of 'sacrifice'. Zimmer thinks that sometimes it meant smaller assembly than the *samiti*. But the authors of the *Vedic Index* (II.297) find 'no ground to be certain that such smaller assemblies ever existed at an early date either in India or elsewhere among Aryan peoples.' Ludwig (*RV* tr. 3.259) thinks that, 'The root idea is an assembly; specially of the Maghavans and the Brāhmaṇa', i.e. equivalent to his conception of the *sabhā*. Elsewhere, he suggests that word denotes 'an asylum', like the house of the brāhmaṇa. Geldner considers that the word primarily means 'knowledge' 'wisdom' 'priestly love', then 'sacrifice' and spiritual authority. Bloomfield again thinks that the word means 'the house' as in the *Ṛgveda* (10.85.26-7 of the wife in the marriage ritual; *RV* 1.117.25; 2.1.6) and in the *Atharvaveda* (18.3.70) and also 'the sacrifice' in connection with the house. The authors of the *Vedic Index* (II.296) say that '*vidatha* is a word of obscure sense, confined mainly to the *Rigveda*'; but they hold that Bloomfield's interpretation noted above, 'at any rate, appears to suit all passages'. That '*vidathya*' (*RV* 4.27.2) once applied to the king might seem to be against this view, but it may refer to his being 'rich in homesteads'; and the connection of the woman with the *vidatha*, as opposed to the sabhā, tells in favour of Bloomfield's explanation (*AV* 7.38.4). They think that the word '*vidathya*' in the *Atharvaveda* (20.128.1) means 'having an establishment' and that this sense seems adequate. They opine that Ludwig's suggestion 'is doubtful', because the *Aitareya Brāhmaṇa* (1.30, 27, 28) certainly does not show this clearly. Jayaswal (*Hindu Polity* 20) remarks that 'the religious life was organized through the *vidatha* assembly (*AV* 1.13.4), which had existed even earlier than the *samiti*'. In the *Ṛgveda* (1.60) fire is called the flag of the *vidatha*. U.N. Ghosal admits that 'there is room for considerable difference of opinion' and concludes that 'in view of these differences it seems impossible to predicate any certain attribute of the Vedic *vidatha*'. V.P. Verma thinks that the *vidatha* seems to be a spontaneous and occasional assemblage rather than a regular and formal one like the other two. R.S. Sharma has drawn our attention to the importance of this institution in the early Vedic period, as reflected in the fact that *vidatha* is mentioned 122 times in the *Ṛgveda* and 22 times in the *Atharvaveda*. *Vidatha* appears 10 times in the *Vājasaneyī Saṃhitā*, 21 times in the Brāhmaṇas and once in the *Taittirīya Āraṇyaka*. From the relative references in Vedic literature we may say that *vidatha* was more important in the early Vedic period, whereas *sabhā* and *samiti* became so in the later Vedic age. It is interesting to note that the *vidatha* is found to be frequently associated with women in the hymns of the *Ṛgveda* and the *Atharvaveda* but less or rarely in the later Vedic literature. Oldenberg's opinion may be taken into consideration. He interprets *vidatha* as 'an act of disposing of any business'. The *Śatapatha Brāhmaṇa* (4.2) contains a passage: 'May we with valiant men mightily revise our voice at the determining (of ordinance)'. In the *Ṛgveda* (3.14.1), Agni is described as an ordinance when he comes to the *vidatha*. From these references of the *Ṛgveda* and the *Śatapatha Brāhmaṇa* we may assume that laws or ordinances were framed for the regulation of the tribe in the *vidatha*. Oldenberg gives another meaning of the term '*vidatha*' as 'distribution'. Some hymns of the *Ṛgveda* speak of the military character of the *vidatha*. The *Ṛgveda* refers to this institution as singing praises of the might of Agni. The religious character of the *vidatha* is also equally reflected in the Vedas. It loomed so large in the eye of Sāyaṇa that he explained the term *vidatha* always as sacrifice (*yajña*). Thus, from the above survey we may conclude that *vidatha* represents the 'forum' of the tribal life of the Vedic people, in which both secular and sacred interest were looked into. The *Nighaṇṭu* (3.17) take the term *vidatha* as sacrifice and *Nirukta* (1.7) as both 'sacrifice and assembly'.

**Videha:** *Videha* is the name of a people who are not mentioned before the Brāhmaṇa period. In the *Śatapatha Brāhmaṇa* (1.4.1.10) the legend of Videha Māthava clearly preserves a tradition that in Videha, culture came from the brāhmaṇas of the West, and that Kośala was brahminized before the Videhas. The Videhas, however, derived some fame later from the attainment of their king Janaka, who figures in the *Bṛhadāraṇyaka Upaniṣad* (3.8.2; *ŚB* 11.3.1.2, 6.2.1, 3.1; *TB* 3.10.9.9) as one of the leading patrons of the *brahman* doctrine. In the *Kauṣītakī Upaniṣad* (4.1) the Videhas are coupled with the Kāśis; in the list of peoples in the *Aitareya Brāhmaṇa* (8.14) the Videhas are passed over, probably because, with Kośala and Kāśī, they were included in the term Prācyas, 'easterners'. Again, in the *Śāṅkhāyana Śrautasūtra* (16.29.5) it is recorded that the Kāśī, Kośala, and Videha kingdoms each had the one purohita, Jala Jātukarṇya; and in another passage of the same text (16.9.11.13) the connection between the Videha king Para Atnara, and the Kośala king, Hiraṇyanābha, is explained, while the *Śatapatha Brāhmaṇa* (13.5.4.4) speaks of Para Atnara as the Kośala king, descendant of Hiraṇyanābha. Another king of Videha was Nami Sāpya, mentioned in the *Pañcaviṃśa Brāhmaṇa* (25.10.17). In the Saṃhitās of the *Yajurveda* (*TS* 2.1.4.5, *KS* 14.5) 'cows of Videha' seem to be alluded to, though the commentator on the *Taittirīya Saṃhitā* merely takes the adjective Vaidehī as 'having a splendid body' (*viśiṣṭadeha-sambandhinī*) and the point of a place's name in the expression is not very obvious. The Videhas also appear in the *Baudhāyana Śrautasūtra* (2.5, 21.13) in Brāhmaṇa-like passages. The boundary of Kosala and Videha was the Sadānīrā, probably the modern Gandak (or more probably Rapti) which, rising in Nepal, flows into the Ganges opposite Patna. Videha itself corresponds roughly to the modern Tirhut. Macdonell and Keith, II. 298-9.

**Village:** A lower sub-division of the *viś* was the *grāma* or the village. The word *grāma* also denoted a wandering body and we have even a tradition in the *Śatapatha Brāhmaṇa* (4.1.5.2-7), which speaks of Śaryāta Mānava wandering with his *grāma*. A Ṛgvedic passage (3.33.11), too, goes to confirm the above view, which describes the Bharatas as consisting of *grāmas* seeking cows. Zimmer explains *grāma* as 'horde', the armed force of the tribe. Hopkins on the term *grāmakāma* (*TS* 2.1.1.2; 2.1.3.2; 2.3.9.2; *MS* 2.1.9; 2.2.3) says that *grāma* here means 'herd of cattle'. But, gradually, the *grāma* became a settled body, and comprised a number of families (*kulas*) who were mainly engaged in agriculture. Furthermore, as agriculture later became the chief occupation of the Vedic peoples, the *grāma* became the basis of social life. As the number of villages increased, the *araṇya* (forest, which is contrasted with the *grāma* and was a sort of no man's land) was cleared, pastures and fields were extended and the activity of the people was directed to peaceful settled ways of life. Roads were constructed to connect distant villages. Lack of information stands in our way, when we try to ascertain the original basis of village life or its gradual development. We have no means of deciding whether originally the village was established on the basis of kinship or that its leader was the head of the agnatic group. Zimmer is inclined to take the *grāma* as a clan standing mid-way between the tribe and the family. We have no explicit statement to prove such blood-relationship among villagers but it is not improbable that originally newly-settled villages were mostly peopled by men of the same family, or that some villages arose out of the elaboration of the family of the original settler as well as his dependants and servants. Macdonell and Keith think that it was the royal prerogative of the king to villages to his favourites. The king's share in a village is clearly stated in the *Atharvaveda* (4.22.2), which proves the role of the village as an administrative unit and belies the assumption of the ownership of the entire village by the villagers alone. The judicial function of the village headman in the later Vedic period is attested to by the term *grāmyavādin* (*TS* 2.3.1.3). But royal control was to a great extent indirect. In many places the *Taittirīya Saṃhitā* gives us details about ceremonies which qualified men to become *grāmaṇīs*, or heads of villages, and in some places we are told of some such village-owners who rose to that position with the consent of *sajātas* or *samānas*. The mention of these words clearly points to the existence of village-types in which kinship prevailed as the bond of unity. Probably, out of these the later caste-villages arose. But in course of time, apart from the cultivating owners, the village included various professionals, as also *brāhmaṇas* and *kṣatriyas*, within its members. At the head of the villages, there was the *grāmaṇī* or the headman who formed a part of royal entourage, signifying the growing importance of the village. In villages far from the capital, it was more convenient for any rebel to hatch plots against the king and for any powerful headman to create difficulties in the way of administration. Hence, it was quite natural for the king to take so much interest in the development of villages and to keep their heads in good humour by treating them on equal terms with other officers. In many places we find him taking a prominent part in the coronation ritual described in the Brāhmaṇas. He is one of the *ratnins*, and is explained as the elected head of the villages by our Indian commentators (e.g. *grāmānāṃ netā*). The rights of the villagers or their duties to the heads of the tribe are not clearly known. The evidence of the *Atharvaveda* (4.22.2) mentioned above clearly shows that the king was entitled only to a share of the village. Whatever other rights the latter had are not clearly known. Bandyopahyay 26-8.

**Village Economy:** A Vedic *grāma* or village was self-contained. The wants of the people, which were few, were supplied by the people themselves. They cultivated corns like barley (*yava*, *RV* 5.83.3; 10.69.3, 131.2), rice (*dhāna* or *dhānya*, *RV* 5.53.13; 6.13.4; 10.94.13), beans (*mudga*, *māsa*), sesamum (*tila*), etc. The grains were stored in granaries (*sthivi*), from where it was taken as per requirement (*RV* 10.68.3). From the possession of large herds of cows by each family, we can easily infer that it had an abundant supply of milk from which curds, *ghee*, etc., were prepared. Meat was also supplied from the livestock. Sheep's wool was spun into yarns, and woollen clothes were woven with them (*RV* 10.26.60). There were men who learnt the art of weaving, took it up as a profession, and were called weavers (*vāya, RV* 10.26.6; 10.6.1). The loom was called *tantra* (*RV* 10.71.9). The cloth required use, and the weaving was usually entrusted to and done by the women (*RV* 2.3.6; 38.4; 5; 47.6, cf. *AV* 10.7.42; 14.25.1). It is distinctly said in one verse that the mother wove clothes for her sons (*RV* 5.47.6). There were carpenters (*tvaṣṭṛ, RV* 10.110.5, *takṣan*, *RV* 9.112.1) who made chariots, wheels, boats, and wooden vessels (*droṇa*, *RV* 9.65.6), and smiths who made implements and weapons for war. There were also potters who made pots and vessels of clay, which were easily broken (*RV* 5.89.7). There is frequent mention of *kalasa* or pots, either made of clay or wood (*RV* 1.117.12; 3.32.15), or *kumbha* or earthen jar or vessel (*RV* 1.116.7; 1.117.6, 7.33.13), as well as of *ukhā* or cooking pot (*RV* 1.162.13; 15.3.53.22), which was also 'made of clay' (*mṛnmaya, VS* 11.59; *TS* 4.1.5.4). There were also goldsmiths who made gold ornaments like *niṣka*, ear-rings, etc. (*RV* 8.57.15; 8.78.3). There were also men whose profession it was to make flowergarlands or wreaths (*RV* 8.47.15), which must have been in great demand among fashionable and luxurious men and women. We find numerous mention of skin-vessels (*RV* 6.48.17; 8.5.19; 9.66.29), which were manufactured by men who knew the art of tanning leathers (*RV* 8.55.3) and sewing them into shapes. The tanner was known by the name of *carmamnāḥ* (*RV* 8.5.38). Barbers (*vaptā*) are also mentioned in the *Ṛgveda* (10.142.4). There were also physicians (*bhiṣak*, *RV* 10.112.1, 3) who, it is jestingly said, were eager to see the outbreak of diseases. But their services were in great demand and valued, as one *ṛṣi* earnestly remarks that he would readily give a physician cows, horses, clothes, nay, his very person (*RV* 10.95.4). The physicians claimed a scientific knowledge, so far as it went in those days, of the properties of the various herbs and drugs, from which they prepared their nostrums and medicines (*RV* 10.95). Das 126-7.

**Village Headman:** At the head of the village was the *grāmaṇī*, or 'leader of the village', who is referred to in the *Ṛgveda* (10.62.11), and often in the later Saṃhitās and in the Brāhmaṇas (*AV* 3.5.7; 19, 31.12; *TS* 2.5.4.4; *MS* 1.6.5; *KS* 8.4.10.3; *VS* 15.15. 30.20; *TB* 1.1.4.8; 2.7.18.4; *SB* 3.4.1.7; 5.4.4.19; 8.6.2.1; *BU* 4.3.37-8). Often the *grāmaṇī* is regarded by scholars as having military functions only, as he is certainly often connected with the *senānī*, or 'leader of an army'. In ancient times civil and military departments were not compartmentalized and as such served defensive purposes as well, but basically he was the head of the village. He is ranked in the *Śatapatha Brāhmaṇa* (5.4.4.19) as inferior to the *sūta* or, 'charioteer', with whom, however, he is associated (*ŚB* 5.3.1.5) as one of the *ratnins*, the jewels of the royal establishement. The post was especially valuable to a *vaiśya*, who, if he attained it, was at the summit of prosperity (*gataśrī*) (*TS* 2.5.4.4; *MS* 1.6.5). The *grāmaṇī's* connection with the royal person does not, however, point to his having been a nominee of the king. He was either a popularly elected officer or the natural village leader, who was required for becoming a support-base of the king, which is why he was honoured in royal ceremonies. In those days centralized administration was not possible and, for his own survival in the royal position, the king required the support of as many village headmen as possible.

**Village Judge:** Village judge is termed by *grāmyavādin* (*KS* 11.4; *TS* 2.3.1.3). His court (*sabhā*) is referred to in the *Maitrāyaṇī Saṃhitā* (2.2.1). He might have been the *grāmaṇī* or village headman himself, or was a wise senior villager appointed by the *grāmaṇī*, or chosen by the villagers themselves. It does not appear that the village judges were appointed directly by the kings.

**Vinaśana:** Vinaśana, 'disappearance' is the name of the place where the Sarasvatī is lost in the sands of the desert. It is mentioned in the *Pañcaviṃśa Brāhmaṇa* (25.10.6) and the *Jaiminīya Upaniṣad Brāhmaṇa* (4.26). The locality was some where in lower district of the Punjab, or more probably northern Rajasthan.

**Vipāś:** Vipāś (fetterless) is the name of a river mentioned twice in the *Ṛgveda* (3.33.1; 4.30.11; *Nirukta* 11.48). It is the modern Beas in the Punjab, the Hyphasis, Hypanis or Bipasis of the Greeks. The *Nirukta* (9.26) preserves the notice that its earlier name was Uruñjirā. The *Gopatha Brāhmaṇa* (1.2.7) places in the middle of it the *vasiṣtha-śilāḥ*. Pāṇini (4.2.74) mentions the name, which otherwise in post-Vedic literature appears as Vipāśā. This river has changed its course considerably since ancient times.

**Viśaḥ:** *Viś* is an expression of somewhat doubtful significance. In many passages of the *Ṛgveda* (4.4.3; 4.37, 1; 5.3.5; 6.21.4; 6.48.8; 7.56.22; 7.61.3) the sense of settlement or 'dwelling' is adequate and probable, since the root *viś* means to 'enter' or 'settle'. In other passages, where the *viśaḥ* stand in relation to a prince, the term must mean 'subject' (*RV* 4.50.8; 6.8.4; 10.124.8; 10.173.6; *AV* 3.4.1; 4.8.4; *TS* 3.2.8.6; *VS* 8.46, *ŚB* 1.8.2.17; 4.2.1.3; 5.3.3.12; 5.4.2.3; 10.6.2.1), for example, when the people of Tṛṇaskanda (*RV* 1.172.3), or of the Tṛtsus (*RV* 7.33.6), are mentioned. Again, in some passages (*RV* 6.1.8; 6.26-1; 8.71.11, *manuṣo viśaḥ* in *RV* 6.14.2; 8.23.13; *mānuṣīḥ* in 10.80.6) the general sense of people is found as when the *Ṛgveda* speaks of 'the Aryan people' (*RV* 10.11.4) or the 'divine people' (*RV* 3.34.2; *AV* 6.98.2; *VS* 17.86). On the basis of the *Ṛgveda* (2.26.3) it may be argued that people were divided into cantons, into joint families or clans, or village committees and these again into single families. In the later Vedic period the sense of *viś* is definitely restricted, in some cases (*TS* 2.2.11.2; *MS* 2.1.9; 3.3.10; *PB* 18.10.9 and *ŚB* 2.1.3.5), to denote the third of the classes of the Vedic polity, the people or clansmen as opposed to the nobles and the priests. The *viśaḥ* may mean the peasantry on the basis of the later Vedic literature, which refers to the strife between the *viśaḥ* and the nobility and also sometimes to their combination and coordination. The word *viśaḥ* has been used in the Brāhmaṇas in the sense of common people, as opposed to two sections, brāhmaṇas and kṣatriyas. Macdonell and Keith, 305-06.

**Viṣāṇins:** Viṣāṇin occurs once in the *Ṛgveda* (7.18.7) as the name of a tribe in the list of the enemies of the Tṛtsus. The word seems to mean 'having horns', but in what sense, is not known; perhaps their helmets were horn-shaped or ornamented with horns. They may, like their allies, the Alinas, Bhalānasas, Śivas and Pakthas, be reckoned as belonging to the tribes of the north west.

**Viṣṇu:** The only prominent anthropomorphic trait, nay, the main characteristic of the nature of Viṣṇu—a minor deity in the *Ṛgveda*—is his three steps which give him the exclusive epithets *uru-gāya* (wide going) and *uru-krama* (wide-stepping). Two of his steps are visible, but the third or highest is invisible, far beyond the flight of birds, and is like an eye fixed in heaven, shining brightly down. Since he is described as setting in motion, like a revolving wheel, his ninety steeds (days) with their four names (seasons, an evident allusion to the three hundred and sixty days of the solar year), Viṣṇu probably is a personification of the activity of the sun, whose passage through the three divisions of the universe, namely, earth, air and heaven, is referred to in his three steps. Indra is the only deity most closely associated with him. He is celebrated in not more than five whole hymns and in part of another, while his name occurs only about 100 times altogether. Macdonnel 37-42.

**Vispati:** See **Lords**.

**Viśvajit:** An *ekāha* (one day sacrifice) in which the sacrificer gives a thousand cows or all his wealth. He has to stay for three days beneath an *udumbara* tree, for three days in a settlement of Niṣādas, for three days among vaiśyas and for three days with kṣatriyas. For a year he should not refuse what is offered but should not beg. Jaimini 4.3, 10-16; 6.7.1-20; 7.3.6-11; 10.6.13; *KSS* 22.1.91-11; *LSS* 8.2.1-13. The *viśvajit* sacrifice has also been recommended as expiation for murdering a brāhmaṇa. Bhattacharyya 1991, 169.

**Viśvakarman:** According to the *Taittirīya Saṃhitā* (7.1.5.1) Prajāpati as wind produced movement into waters and therein he saw the earth. Then, having taken the form of a boar, he seized the earth and as Viśvakarman laboured upon it and thus produced the gods, Vasus, Rudras and Ādityas. The god Tvaṣṭṛ, the divine artisan and the most skilful of workmen, is described in many passages (*RV* 2.23.17; 3.4.9; 3.55.19; 4.42.3; 10.2.7; 10.46.9; 10.11.9, etc.) as the creator of the world. He is said to have created Brahmaṇaspati above all creatures and along with heaven and earth, the waters and Bhṛgus, generated Agni. Even the Aśvins are described as the producers of fire, water and trees (*RV* 1.157.5). Incidentally various creative functions are also ascribed to Soma. He is said to be the generator of heaven and earth (2.40.1; cf. 9.42.4; 9.86.10; 9.87.2), and is given the epithet Prajāpati (9.5.9). In some of the representations of the character and functions of Tvaṣṭṛ, the divine artisan who shaped heaven and earth, we have an approach to the idea of a creator of the Viśvakarman type. The term Viśvakarman, 'the great architect of the universe', was originally an epithet applied to different gods believed to have been possessed with same creative functions. The sun-god Sūrya was designated as Viśvakarman (*RV* 10.170.4). The term 'the most skilful workman' is also attributed to Indra (*AV* 4.17.4). But in the later portion of the *Ṛgveda*, Viśvakarman is developed into a concrete personality. He is represented as the one all-seeing god who has on every side eyes, faces, arms and feet. He produced heaven and earth and threw them away with his arms and wings. He is regarded as the father, generator and disposer; he knows all worlds; he has given the gods their names; and he is beyond the comprehension of the mortals (*RV* 10.81; 10.82). The conception of Viśvakarman is the development of an idea that considers the function of creation in terms of that of the carpenter or the pot maker and, therefore, dependent upon the nature of the material and skill of the operator. In a verse we come across the question: what was the wood, and what the tree out of which they fashioned the heaven and earth? (*RV* 10.31.7). The same question is repeated in another hymn (*RV* 10.81), in which the creation of heaven and earth is ascribed to the sole agency of the god Viśvakarman. In accordance with this sentiment we find *vana* (wood) regarded as the first principle and, when water came to be regarded as such, we find the word *vana* listed in the *Nighaṇṭus* (1.12.9) as a synonym for water. In another passage of the *Ṛgveda* (10.72.2; cf. 4.2.27), the creative process is likened to the art of the smith. Here creation of the gods is ascribed to Brahmaṇaspati who brought them forth like a blacksmith. The character of this god does not belong to the earliest stage of the Vedic mythology. Identified with Bṛhaspati, he is styled the father of the gods (*RV* 2.63.3). A widely extended creative power is ascribed to him in a number of verses (*RV* 10.68.8 ff; 10.97.15). See **Cosmogony, Hiraṇyagarbha, Prajāpati, Puruṣa**.

**Vital Airs:** In the Vedic doctrine of medicine the concept of breath or vital airs (*prāṇa*) is very important. The word *prāṇa* is often equivalent to life itself. Thus, in the *Jaiminīya Brāhmaṇa* (1.212) it is said, 'There is nothing more desirable than *prāṇa* (life) (*na hi prāṇāt kiñcid asti*)'. To be diseased is often supposed to be defective in respect of *prāṇas*, the breaths. Thus, in the *Kāṭhaka Saṃhitā* (30.3) it is said, 'He lacks breath, who is ill' (cf. *PB* 16.13.2). Therefore, while drawing the cups of *soma* in the course of a Soma sacrifice, the Adhvaryu should invoke Indra and Vāyu, as they were regarded as the vital healing airs (*KS* 30.3; cf. *TS* 7.2.7.11). Elsewhere it is said, 'Pain approaches to his vital airs who is ill' (e.g. *KS* 30.3.), which is to be freed by rituals (*TS* 7.2.1.1; *KS* 30.3). Similarly, in the *Maitrāyaṇī Saṃhitā* (2.5.1) we read, 'His vital airs, verily, have gone away who is ill'. That is why deities are made identical with vital airs and by making offerings to them, vital airs are put in the diseased person (*MS* 2.3.5; *KS* 11.8). Thereby vital airs are also connected with speech (*TS* 2.2.4.2 f). Thite 215.

**Vitastā:** Vitastā, the most westerly of the five rivers of the Punjab, is mentioned in the *Ṛgveda* (10.75.5; *Nirukta* 9.26) in the *Nadīstuti* (praise of rivers). It is the Hydaspes of Alexander's historians, and mentioned by Ptolemy as Bidaspes. It is the modern Jhelum.

**Vivasvat:** Vivasvat is not the subject of any complete hymn in the *Ṛgveda*, although he is mentioned about thirty times. The most important thing about him is his relation to Manu, the ancestor of the human race, who thence bears the name Vaivasvata or Vivasvat, taking simply his father's name as a sign of paternity. Yama also is his son. The *Ṛgveda* ascribes to him the fathership of the gods. His wife is Śaraṇyu, the daughter of Tvastṛ, and he is the father of the Aśvins. Agni was first manifested to him and to Mātariśvan and he has Mātariśvan or Agni as his messenger. Soma again dwells with Vivasvat and is cleansed by his daughters, doubtless, in the ordinary mythical style of the Soma hymns, his fingers. In the prayer of Vivasvat, Indra rejoices and places his treasure beside him. Varuṇa is also mentioned along with him. In one passage the worshippers of the Ādityas pray that the well-wrought arrow of the god may not slay them before old age (*RV* 8.67.20). In the *Atharvaveda* (18.3.62) he is said to protect from Yama. The seat of Vivasvat is a special feat''re of the god. The word *vivasvat* is used occasionally as an epithet of Agni and Uṣas in the etymological sense of shining forth, which is specially appropriate in the goddess Dawn. The *Śatapatha Brāhmaṇa* (10.5.2.4) explains the god Vivasvat's name by the doctrine that he illumines night and day, which are connected with him in the *Ṛgveda* (*RV* 10.39.2). It calls him Āditya, and this name is found elsewhere in the *Yajurveda* (*MS* 1.6.12). In post-Vedic literature, Vivasvat is a name of the sun (*RV* 8.52.1). Keith 112-13.

**Vrātya:** Vrātya is included in the list of victims at the Puruṣamedha (human sacrifice) in the *Yajurveda* (*VS* 30.8; *TB* 3.4.5.1), although no further explanation of the name is given. Fuller information is furnished by the *Atharvaveda* (15.1.1), the *Pañcaviṃśa Brāhmaṇa* (17.1-4), and the Sūtras (*KŚS* 12.1; 22.4; *LŚS* 8.6; *ĀŚS* 22.5.4-14), which describe at length a certain rite intended for the use of Vrātyas. According to the *Pañcaviṃśa Brāhmaṇa*, there are four different kinds of 'outcasts', viz., the *hīna*, who are merely described as 'depressed'; those who have become outcasts at an early age, apparently by living among outcasts; and those old men who, being impotent, have gone to live with outcasts. The last three categories are by no means of the same importance as the first. The motive of the fourth is hard to understand. According to one view there were two categories of the first class, viz., the depressed (*hīna*), who were non-Aryan, and degraded Aryans. That they were non-Aryans is not improbable. Other particulars accord with the view that they were Aryans who did not practise agriculture or commerce (an allusion to a nomadic life), or observe the rules of Brahmacarya, i.e. the principle regulating the Brahminic order of life. They are also allowed to become members of the Brahminical community by performance of the prescribed ritual, which would hardly be so natural in the case of non-Aryans. Some details are given of the life and dress of the vrātyas. Their principles were opposed to those of the brāhmaṇas: they beat those unworthy of correction. Their leader (*gṛhapati*), or householder, wore a turban (*uṣṇīṣa*), carried a whip (*pratoda*), a kind of bow (*jyāhroḍa*), was clothed in a black (*kṛṣṇasa*) garment and two skins (*ajina*), black and white, and owned a rough wagon (*vipatha*) covered with planks (*phalakāstīrṇa*). The others, subordinate to the leader, had garments with fringes of red, two fringes on each, skins folded double and sandals (*upānaḥ*). The locality in which the Vrātyas lived cannot be stated with certainty, but their nomadic life suggests the western tribes beyond the Sarasvatī. But they may equally well have been in the east. This possibility is so far supported by the fact that the Sūtras make the brāhman receiving the gift of the Vrātya's outfit an inhabitant of Magadha. Macdonell and Keith, II, 342-4, Anirvān's *Veda Mīmāṅgsā*.

**Vrātyaṣṭoma:** See **Yajña**.

**Vṛcīvant:** *Vṛcīvant* is the name of a tribe referred to in the *Ṛgveda* (6.27.5), where it is clearly stated that the Sṛñjaya king, Daivavāta conquered the Turvaśa king and the Vṛcīvants. The Vṛcīvants appear again only in the strange legend in the *Pañcaviṃśa Brāhmaṇa* (21.12.2), according to which the Jahnus and the Vṛcīvants contended for sovereignty, Viśvāmitra, the Jahnu king, won by his knowledge of a certain rite. Hariyūpiyā is mentioned in a hymn of the *Ṛgveda* (6.27.5) as the scene of the defeat of the Vṛcīvants by Abhyāvartin Cayamāna. It may denote either a place or a river, since many battles seem to have been fought on the banks of rivers The Vṛcīvants were a tribe of north-western India.

# W

**Wagon:** Among the vehicles, as opposed to the chariot for war or sports, wagon was used in the Vedic age. The term for wagon was *anas* (*RV* 4.30.10; 10.85.10; 10.86.18; *ŚB* 1.1.2.5; *CU* 7.15.1; *KU* 3.8). Indra is once said to be seated in a wagon instead of on a chariot (*RV* 1.121.7). Wagon was the characteristic vehicle of Uṣas (*RV* 2.15.6; 4.30.11; 8.91.7; 10.73.6; 10.138.5). *Anas* referred to in the *Ṛgveda* (4.30.10; 10.85.10; 10.86.18; *ŚB* 1.1.2.5), reveals the draft wagon drawn by ruddy cows or bulls. This vehicle is contrasted to the chariot for war or sport (*RV* 3.33.9). Reference is also made to the bridal wagon of Sūryā (*RV* 10.85.10). In the *Atharvaveda* (15.2.1) *vipatha* appears to denote an ordinary vehicle used for bad tracks. Wagons or carts were usually drawn by oxen (*RV* 8.85.11). This cart was also used for carrying rice in connection with sacrificial ceremony (*ŚB* 1.1.2.5, 22).

**Waiter:** The term *pariveṣṭṛ* denotes attendant (*AV* 9.6.51; *TS* 6.3.1.3; *MS* 1.2.16; *VS* 6.13; 30.12-13; *TB* 3.4.8.1; *AB 8.21; ŚB* 13.5.4.6, 3.8.2.3; 6.2.13.3). The same term (*ŚB* 11.2.7.5; *Kau.U.* 2.1) indicates female attendant/ hand-maiden.

**Waking State:** The greatest contribution made by the Upaniṣadic theory of the *ātman* is their interpretation of the wakeful, dreaming, sleeping, and other states of the soul. The earliest passage to be noted in this connection is *Praśna* 4, where the functions of the sense-organs are compared to the rays of the sun and are said, during sleep, to become refunded back into the Highest Deity within us, as do the rays into the solar orb at sunset. The various movements of breath alone continue, and they are compared to the sacrificial fires which are not permitted to become extinguished during the sacrificer's life. Sleep implies the complete overcoming of the light of the individual rays by the central source of light, while during dreams—where man only revives the already—experienced impressions of wakeful life—there is only a partial overcoming. The separate existence of the individual soul (*vijñānātmā puruṣaḥ*) belongs only to the wakeful and the dreaming states; in the state of deep sleep he is merged into the highest immutable *ātman* which is *Brahman* (*CU* 6.8-10) amplifies the same doctrine by giving the similes of the juices of individual flowers merging into the totality known as honey, or the different rivers pouring their waters into the ocean, and adds that, upon the return from sleep to wakeful life, the whole phantasmagoria of sense and outward things is once more presented exactly as it was before sleep, although as long as the sleep lasted there was no consciousness of any individual distinctions whatsoever. See **Sleep, Dream**, Belvalkar and Ranade, 372-3.

**Wandering Ascetics:** Wandering ascetic (*parivrājaka*) literally means a person wandering about in spiritual quest. According to the *Nirukta* (1.14.2.8) a mendicant monk is meant by this term. According to the rules of four Āśramas the last stage is treated as sannyāsa. But this stage of life was that of complete renunciation, while the Parivrājakas, as we specially find them in the Buddhist and Jain texts, were a class of sophists who travelled from one place to another, debating philosophical issues among themselves. They belonged to different sectarian orders as well. The practice of *parivrajyā* or 'wandering about' was in the sphere of expounding knowledge in the ancient Indian tradition. The early Vedas do not explicitly refer to this tradition, though some of the Vedic seers might have been wandering ascetics. A life of *parivrājaka* is cited in *Bṛhadāraṇyaka Upaniṣad* (2.4.1; 4.5.1), with a reference to the case of Yājñavalkya in renouncing the world. The wandering ascetics of the Upanisadic age paved the rise of Buddhism, Jainism and other heterodox systems.

**War:** See **Army, Bow, Fort, War-ethics, Warrior class, Weapon**. The Vedic society and state were those of pastoral warriors. Since cattle were the best source of wealth, *gaviṣṭi* or fight for cattle was a basic feature of the time. Moreover, there was the problem of subduing the hostile indigenous peoples. At a later stage war for territorial expansion became imperative, which is why the warrior class formed an important section in the social hierarchy of the Vedic Indians. *Yuddha* in the *Ṛgveda* (10.54.2) and later (*TB* 1.5.4.1; *AB* 3.39; 6.36; *ŚB* 13.1.5.6) denoted battle. The more ancient term was *yudh* (*RV* 1.53.7; 1.59.1; 5.25.6; 6.46.11; *AV* 1.24.1; 4.24.7; 6.66.1; 6.103.3; *ŚB* 5.2.4.16). Another term for war was *raṇa* (*RV* 1.61.1 ff; 1.74.3; 1.119.3; 6.16.15; *AV* 5.2.4). *Saṃgrāma* also meant war (*AV* 5.21.7; 11.9.96; *TS* 2.1.3.1; 2.1.8.4). The general term for army was *senā* (*RV* 1.33.6; 7.25.1; 9.96.1; 10.103.1 ff; 10.156.2; *AV* 3.1.3; 3.19.6; 4.19.2; 5.21.9). *Senānī*, leader of an army, was the title of the royal general (*RV* 7.20.5; 9.96.1; 10.84.2). He was appointed by the king and an officer of the *ratnin* category (*TS* 1.8.9.1; *TB* 1.7.3.4; *MS* 2.6.5; 4.3.8; *KS* 15.4; *ŚB* 5.3.1.1). In the *Aitareya Brāhmaṇa* (8.23) this officer is called *senāpati*. A body of foot soldiers (*patti*) with charioteers composed the army (*RV* 2.12.8; *AV* 7.62.1), which was divided into several contingents (*pakṣas*). There were gradations like *rathī* and *mahārathī*, who were dressed in armour (*varman*), corselet *(kavaca)*, helmet (*śiprā*) and hand-guard (*hastaghna*). On the car was the charioteer (*sārathi, savyaṣṭhā*), siting below the warrior. Riding is never mentioned in connection with war. The offensive weapon (*āyudha*) was specially the bow. For defence forts (q.v.), *durga* and *mahādurga*, were constructed. These were besieged and invested (*upa-sad, pravid*) as a rule by blockade (*TS* 6.2.3.1; *ŚB* 3.4.4.3-5; *AB* 1.23.2; *GB* 2.2.7). Besides ordinary wars of defence and conquests, raids into neighbouring territories seem to have been frequent and normal (*RV* 10.142.4; *TB* 1.8.4.1), no doubt because of the booty (*udāja, nirāja*) that was to be won and which the king had to share with the people. *Pur* is a word that appears frequently in the *Ṛgveda* (1.53.7; 1.58.8; 1.131.4; 1.166.8; 3.15.4; 4.27.1) and later (*TB* 1.7.7.5; *AB* 1.2.3; 2.11; *ŚB* 3.4.4.3; 6.3.3.25; 11.1.1.2-3), meaning rampart, fort or stronghold. From the references to the forts of the Dāsa chiefs destroyed by Indra it appears that these belonged to the indigenous non-Vedic tribes. The Vedic gods are described as great fighters who defeated the Asuras, Dāsas and many other classes of their foes, who were undoubtedly mythical representations of their human enemies. There are also many references to stray battles in the Vedic texts. One of the great inter-tribal war described in the *Ṛgveda* was that of Dāśarājña (q.v.).

**War-ethics:** Since great battles cause the death of thousands, the Vedic texts are in favour of fair battle (*RV* 2.14.7). The famous battle hymn of the *Ṛgveda* states that the use of arrows smeared with poison (*RV* 6.75.15; *AV* 4.6.6) is against the code of ethics. Sacrifices as Aśvamedha, Rājasūya, Vājapeya, etc., meant for the glorification of the all-conquering king were recognized as a means of peaceful conquests. The word *kṣatra* in the *Aitareya Brāhmaṇa* 8.12 holds the wordly power in high esteem, mentioning the kings like Janamejaya, Parīkṣita, Sudās and many more as having performed the horse sacrifice (*AB* 8.21.23) and thus conquering in every direction. Such kings campaigned primarily perhaps to exact homage, and secondarily only to annex territories nearer home. Thus, the ideals of righteous conquest is evident though not explicitly stated in the later ethics of war. As a particularly effective means of promoting social cohesion, it provides an occasion when the members of the society untie and submerge their differences in the pursuit of a common purpose. The Vedic texts insists that prosperity depends on peaceful means, and there is no need of war which should be the last step for settling affairs. Notwithstanding the fierceness of spirit and unabashed prayers for cattle and booty in the *Ṛgveda* 1.74; 10.84, an incipient moral consciousness appears and gods like Indra and Agni are invoked to destroy the enemies with ruthless aggression in the *Ṛgveda* 1.51.8; 1.100.18, etc. This perhaps provides the first crude attempt at a moral justification of warfare. The horrors of war, however, have been taken into account. In the *Ṛgveda* 10.108 the person of an envoy is considered sacred; in the later Saṃhitās, i.e. *Maitrāyaṇī Saṃhitā* 2.9.3; *Kāṭhaka Saṃhitā* 17.12; *Taittirīya Saṃhitā* 4.5.2.1; *Vājasaneyī Saṃhitā* 16.18 the *sūta* acted as charioteer, bard, herald or envoy are regarded physically inviolable. In the *Ṛgveda* 3.59.1 Mitra causes people to make mutual arrangements conducive to peace. The *Ṛgveda* repeatedly calls on Indra to destroy the *amitra*. The later Saṃhitās refer to acts and agreements. We are told of an amnesty and truce in one, i.e. *Taittirīya Saṃhitā* 2.1.8.4 and a one-year treaty in another, i.e. *Maitrāyaṇī Saṃhitā* 2.1.2. The *Pañcaviṃśa Brāhmaṇa* (13.6.7) speaks of a pact between the gods and the Asuras. The cattle should belong to the party vanquishing the order at a mere tournament for winning a prize. There are, however, stories of the violation of war ethics by gods like Indra. But the higher qualities of a warrior are frequently praised. It is expressly said that war should be waged for the right cause, for defence and not for shameless aggression.

**War Music:** Music was a feature of ancient Indian warfare. *Dundubhi* 'the kettle drum' (*RV* 1.28.5; *AV* 5.20.1; 5.21.1; *KS* 34.5, *TS* 7.5.9.3; *PB* 5.5.19, *TB* 3.4.13.1) and the *bhūmi-dundubhi*, the earth drum, nothing but a hole in the ground covered with a hide, (*KS* 34.5; *TS* 7.5.9.3; *PB* 5.5.19), were used in war. There was the instrument *bakurā* with its variations in *Ṛgveda* 1.117.21. It was possibly an instrument for the purpose of war. It is the course of an expedition against the Dasyus, the Aśvins blew this musical instrument to help their army against their enemies. It could have meant trumpet.

**Warrior Class:** Kṣatra is a general sense of dominion, rule, power as exercised by gods and men in the *Ṛgveda* 1.24.11; 4.17.1; 5.62.6; *Atharvaveda* 3.5.2. *Kṣatraśrī* in the *Ṛgveda* 1.25.5; 6.26.8; *kṣatrabhṛt*, bringers of lordship in the *Taittirīya Saṃhitā* 2.4.7.2; *Vājasaneyī Saṃhitā* 27.7; *Taittirīya Brāhmaṇa* 2.4.6.12 are found in the concrete sense of ruler. *Kṣatrapati* is an equivalent of king in the *Taittirīya Saṃhitā* 1.8.14.2; *Vājasaneyī Saṃhitā* 10.17; *Taittirīya Brāhmaṇa* 1.7.8.5; *Śatapatha Brāhmaṇa* 5.4.2.2. *Kṣatriya* is a definite class of the social body distinct from the priest, the subject people and the working class in the *Atharvaveda* 6.76.3; 12.5.44; *Vājasaneyī Saṃhitā* 30.5; *Aitareya Brāhmaṇa* 7.24; *Śatapatha Brāhmaṇa* 1.3.2.15, etc. *Rājanya* is a variant of *kṣatriya*, and an earlier one. They are both of similar origin, being princely or connected with royality. Moreover, the early use of *kṣatriya* in the *Ṛgveda* is exclusively connected with royal authority or divine authority (*RV* 4, 12.3; 5.69.1; 7.64.2; 8.25.8; 10.103.3; *VS* 4.19; 10.4; *TB* 2.4.7.7). In the *Aitareya Brāhmaṇa* 7.20; *Pañcaviṃśa Brāhmaṇa* 24.18.2 a *rājanya* asks a *kṣatriya* for a place of sacrifice, *deva-yajana*. There were the royal houses and the various branches of the royal family, the nobles and their families to explain the occasional opposition of rājanya and kṣatriya. Thus, the *kṣatriya* has wider denotation than *rājanya*. The main duty of the *kṣatriya* in the small states of the Vedic period was readiness for war; bow is his special weapon in the *Atharvaveda* 18.2.60; *Kāṭhaka Saṃhitā* 19.9; 37.1; *Śatapatha Brāhmaṇa* 5.3.5.30; *Taittirīya Āraṇyaka* 6.1.3. In the *Aitareya Brāhmaṇa* 7.19 the list is longer: chariot, breast plate *kavaca*, bow and arrow; *iṣu-dhanvan*, and in the prayer for the prosperity of the *kṣatirya* at the Aśvamedha and the *rājanya* is to be an archer and a good chariot fighter in the *Kāṭhaka Saṃhitā* 5.14; *Maitrāyaṇī Saṃhitā* 3.12.6; *Taittirīya Saṃhitā* 7.5.18.1; *Vājasaneyī Saṃhitā* 22.2. So, Indra is the god of the *kṣātriyas* in the *Maitrāyaṇī Saṃhitā* 2.3.1; 4.5.8. The duties of a *kṣatriya* are administration and war, without any reference to engaging in agriculture or in trade and commerce. There is no record of the training and education in the art of war. But weapons are recorded in detail as also glimpses of administrative function. *Nṛpati*, a lord of men denotes a king or a man of the ruling class as *kṣatriya* in the *Ṛgveda* 2.1.1, 7; 4.20.1; 7.69.1; 10.44.2, 3; *Atharvaveda* 5.18.1, 15; *Taittirīya Āraṇyaka* 6.3.3, 6.10.77. The science of the ruling class is termed *kṣatravidyā* in the *Chāndogya Upaniṣad* 7.1.2.1, 4; 1.7.1. Saṅkara, the commentator of the Upaniṣads, explains it as the *dhanurveda*, the science of archery.

**Washerman/Woman:** The term *malaga* denotes a washerman. It is referred to in the *Atharvaveda* (12.3.21). The term *vasaḥpalpuli* means washerwoman, who is regarded as one of the sacrifical victims in the *Vājasaneyī Saṃhitā* (30.12) and *Taittirīya Brāhmaṇa* (3.4.71).

**Waste Land:** The term for waste land is *ārtanā* in the *Ṛgveda* 1.127.6. There are also terms like *khila* or *khilya* to denote wasteland lying between the two fields (*RV* 10.142.3; *AV* 7.115.4; *ŚB* 8.3.4.1). The expression *abhinne khilya* (*RV* 6.28.2) has been interpreted as broad pasture land, not broken up by cultivated fields, 'land between cultivated fields not necessarily unfertile', and so on.

**Water Plant:** *Kiyāmbu* is the name of one of the water-plants which are to grow, according to a funeral hymn in the *Ṛgveda* (10.10.13 = *AV* 18.3.6), on the place where the body of the dead was burnt. The word seems to mean 'having some water', possibly by popular etymology.

**Wealth:** See **Agriculture, Cattle, Metals, Animals, Forests, Gems, Ornaments, Occupations**. *Dhana* in the *Ṛgveda* (1.81.3; 6.45.2; 8.80.8; 9.53.2; 9.109.10) appears as a sense of wealth rather than booty in the battle. Besides denoting the stake at dicing in the *Ṛgveda* (10.34.10, *AV* 4.38.3), and meaning the contest itself in the *Ṛgveda* (1.31.6, 5.35.7, 7.38.8, 8.5.26, 10.48.5, etc.), it more generally appears as wealth, or gift in the *Ṛgveda* (91.42.6; 10.18.2; 10.34.7) and the *Atharvaveda* (1.15.3; 2.7.4; 3.15.2; 5.19.9; 6.81.1; 7.81.4; 8.5.16, etc.). In the *Ṛgveda* (1.74.3; 1.57.2, etc.) it expresses booty, seemingly from the notion of wealth rather than the prize. *Rekṇa* in the *Ṛgveda* (1.31.14; 1.121.5; 1.158.1; 1.162.2; 6.20.7; 7.4.7; 7.40.2; etc.) denotes inherited property. But generally it means property. In the *Ṛgveda* (4.17.11; 6.55.3; 8.13.22; *AV* 7.115.2; 9.4.3; 10.8.20; 14.2.8) *vasu* denotes property as an inheritable thing handed down from one heir to another. It appears as an inheritable property, from generation to generation in the *Ṛgveda* and onwards. *Vitta* in the *Ṛgveda* (5.42.9, 10.34.13; *AV* 12.3.52; *TS* 1.5.9.2; 6.2.4.3; *VS* 18.11.14, etc.) means wealth possessions. In the *Taittirīya Upaniṣad* (2.8) the earth is referred to as full of riches in connection with the name of *vasumatī* in the *Śāṅkhāyana Āraṇyaka* (13.1, cf *vittasya pūrna*). The greatness of a man depending on his wealth is found as doctrine in the *Taittirīya Brāhmaṇa* (1.4.7.7). The desire of wealth, after striving in the contemplation of knowledge, is mentioned by *vittaiṣanā* in the *Bṛhadāraṇyaka Upaniṣad* (3.5.1, 4.4.26) as one of the things abandoned by the sage. *Rayi* is a common word for wealth in the *Ṛgveda* (1.73.1; 1.59.5; 2.21.6; 3.1.19; 4.2.7; 4.34.10; 6.6.7, etc.) and in later literature (*Atharvaveda* (3.14.1; 6.33.3; 7.80.2; *TS* 7.1.7.2; *VS* 9.22; 14.22.27.6). It is often specially mentioned as hero and termed *vīra*, denoting good sons in the *Ṛgveda* (2.11.13; 4.51.10), horses in the *Ṛgveda* (5.41.5; 8.5.9) and cattle in the *Ṛgveda* (5.4.11). In the *Ṛgveda* (1.11.3; 1.104.5; 3.13.3; 4.17.8; 5.30.12; *VS* 20.67) *magha* denotes bounty. But in the *Ṛgveda* (1.31.12; 2.6.4; 5.39.4; 6.27.8, etc.), it is personified as the generous giver of bounties to the priests. There are several terms, viz., *maghatti* for giving gifts in the *Ṛgveda* (4.37.8; 5.79.5; 8.24.10, etc.) *maghadeya* is denoting the giving of gifts in the *Ṛgveda* (7.67.9, 10.156.2) *maghavattvā* for liberality in the *Ṛgveda* (6.27.3) in connection with the word. In the Vedic society whether the *maghavants* had any special rank as a class in the *Ṛgveda* (4.2.5) for the wealth fitting in the assembly. In the *Ṛgveda* (1.20.7, 2.38.1, etc.) and onwards, (i.e. *Atharvaveda* 5.1.7, 7.14.4; *ŚB* 5.3.1.1) *ratna* denotes as wealth. According to the proper sense it means well-inherited property. As in the post-Vedic literature, it specifically appears in the sense of jewel. The glorification of wealth implied in the *Ṛgveda* (5.51.14) bears testimony to the widespread existence of desire for accumulation. As such condition there are two terms adopted by *vasāvi* and *śevadhi*, denoting storehouse and treasure respectively, being traced by leading one to the conclusion. The bounteous paths are deified in the *Ṛgveda* (5.51.14). Such deification appears more frankly in the *Atharvaveda* (3.4.7).

**Weapons:** Various types of weapons used by a kṣatriya are mentioned in the *Aitareya Brāhmaṇa* 7.34. Among them, the most important were the bowstring and arrow, the sword and the spear. *Dhanus* and *dhanvan* were terms for bow; *godhā, jyā, jyāka* for bowstring and *piṅgā, niṣaṅgāthi* and *bāṇavant* for quiver; *paruṣa bāṇa, bunda, śara, śaru, śaryā, śāri* and *śāyaka* for arrow; *apāṣtha* and *śṛṅga* for barb and *ārtni, parṇa, parṇadhi, pyukṣna*, etc., for different parts of the arrow. The different parts of an arrow are described in the *Aitareya Brāhmaṇa* 1.48 as *anīka*, the head piece; *śalya*, the sharpened blade; *tejana*, the tip of the blade and *parṇa*, the feathered portion of the arrow. The *Śatapatha Brāhmaṇa* (1.2.4.6,7) refers to the thousand-spiked hundred-edged thunderbolt. According to the *Śatapatha Brāhmaṇa* an arrow measures five span in length. The carpenters's knife, the chopping knife and a razor called *svadhīti* are mentioned in the *Śatapatha Brāhmaṇa*. In the horse sacrifice the slaughter-knives are made of gold, iron and copper respectively, to serve different purposes as stated in the *Śatapatha Brāhmaṇa* 13.2.2.16. The hooked knife is termed *parsva. Asi*, the sword; *sāsa* scimiter; *daṇḍa* stones, *abhri*, sharp shove; *varma* armour are mentioned in the *Śatapatha Brāhmaṇa*. The axe termed *paraśu* is used to chop firewood and meant to kill people in battle (*ŚB* 8.6.1.16). In the *Vājasaneyī Saṃhitā* 16.53 names of many weapons of war are mentioned, viz., *heti* (weapons), *pināka* (colossal bow), *dhanu* (small bow), *iṣu* (arrow), *vajra* (thunderbolt), *khaḍga* (scimitar), *asi* (sword), *nisaṅga* (pointed sword), *iṣudhi* (quiver), *śara* (thin arrow), *āyudha* missile), *śatadhanu* (hundred bows). In the *Ṛgveda* 6.75, the famous battle hymn describes the warrior on his chariot, armed with bow and arrow. Clad in defensive armour, well-equipped with weapons and riding on a powerful steed are the usual features of a Vedic warrior as described in the texts. The term *āyudha* denotes the whole of a kṣatriya's warlike equipment. *Aśva-ratha* means horsechariot, *iṣu-dhanva* denotes bow and arrow and *kavaca* denotes corselet (*AB* 7.19.2). Specifically, bow and arrow (*iṣu, dhanvan*) were the main weapons of the Vedic fighter. The battle hymn in the *Ṛgveda* (6.75) presents to us the warrior armed with bow and arrow on his chariot, and clad in armour (*varman*), with a guard (*hastaghna*) on the left arm to avoid the friction of the bow-string. The warrior wore a helmet (*śiprā*). The use of sling-stones (*adri, aśani*) was in vogue in ordinary warfare. The hook (*aṅkuśa*) was also a weapon. The axe (*svadhiti, vasi, paraśu*), the spear (*ṛṣṭi, rambhinī, śakti, śaru*), the sword (*asi, kṛti*), and the club (*vajra*) were not considered ordinary in warfare. Corselet was denoted by *varman* (body-armour, coat of mail) and *kavaca* in the Vedas and later literature. Whether the corselet or breast-plate was made of metal, is not clearly known; there are references to sewing (*RV* 1.31.15, 10.101.8), which may be reckoned in favour of the use of linen corselet-strap (*kavaca-pāśa*), which may denote a linen corselet. Two forms of armour were known as *drāpi* and *atka*. Standards or banners, known as *dhvaja* and *patākā*, were also used. See **Army, Bow, Fort, War, Warrior Class.**

**Weaver/Weaving:** The terms *vayitrī*, and *sirī* indicate 'female weaver', occurring in the *Pañcaviṃśa Brāhmaṇa* 1.8.9; *Ṛgveda* 10.71.9. *Otu* in the Vedic literature (*RV* 6.9, 2.3; *AV* 14.2.5; *TS* 6.1.1.4, etc.) denotes the 'woof' in weaving, and corresponds to *tantu*, 'the warp', the roots *va* (*RV* 6.9.2), 'to weave', and *tan* (*VS* 19.80; *RV* 10.130.2; *AV* 10.7.43, etc.) to stretch, from which these two terms are derived being used in parallel senses. In the process of weaving, a shuttle (*tasara*) was used. In Vedic literature we find terms like *vaya* (weaver) (*RV* 10.26.6), *veman* (loom) *VS* (19.83) and *mayūkha-s* (wooden pegs *VS* 19.80) used for stretching the web. Weaving was entrusted to women as reflected in the *Ṛgveda* (2.3.6; cf. *AV* 10.7.42). In *Ṛgveda* (5.47.6) we find mothers weaving garments for their sons. The *Ṛgveda* (6.9.2 and cf. 6.9.3) states: 'I know not other warp or woof, I know not web they weave, when moving to the contest'. Here the Ṛṣi means to eulogize the greatness of Vaiśvānara in terms of the threads of the warp, which are the metres of the Vedas, these of the woof, prayers and ceremonies and their combination results in the weaving of a cloth, signifying the performance of a sacrifice. We come across terms *vāsas, vastra and vasana* to mean cloth in the *Ṛgveda* (1.34.1; 1.115.4; 8.3.24; 3.92.2; 1.95.7). Other types of garment called *adhivāsa, drāpi, atka* and *peśas* and woollen goods specially of Gandhāra are mentioned. In connection with the textile industry, terms like *otu, tantu, anuchāda* and *prācīnatāna, veman* and *mayūkha*, meaning woof, yarn, forward-stretched warp, loom and wooden pegs or shuttle respectively are found in later Vedic literature (*AV* 14.2.51; *KS* 23.1; *VS* 19.80, 83; *ŚB* 3.12.131, *TS* 6.1.1.3). *Vastra, vasana* and *vāsas* are also mentioned to mean cloth in later Vedic literature (*AV* 5.1.3; 9.5.25; *AV* 1.3). *Sic* appears in the *Atharvaveda* (14.3.50) in the sense of the skirt and *daśā* is noted in the *Aitareya Brāhmaṇa* (7.32; *ŚB* 3.3.2.9) as a border of the garment. *Praghāta* is referred to in the *Śatapatha Brāhmaṇa* (3.1.2.18) as the fore edge of cloth, apparently the closely woven parts at both ends. *Vātapā* occurs in the *Taittirīya Saṃhitā* (6.1.13 f) in the sense of the part of a cloth which protects it against winds, i.e. its lengthwise border. The *Śatapatha Brāhmaṇa* 1.3.3.6; 3.2.1.15 refers to *nīvi* or waist-guard. It also mentions *adhivāsa* (mantle *ŚB* 5.4.4.3) covering the upper part of the body. The *Ṛgveda* (1.140.9) also refers to it (*adhivāsam parimātū rihannaha*). *Uṣṇīṣa*, a turban, is referred to in the *Atharvaveda* (15.2.1; *ŚB* 5.3.5.23). *KŚS* 21.4. It is stated to have been tied with a tilt and cross-windings (*tīryaññaddham*). The loom was generally known as *Veman* (*VS* 19.83).

**Wedding:** *Vivāha* is mentioned in the *Atharvaveda* (12.1.24; 14.2.65) and later texts (*KS* 25.3; *TS* 7.2.8.7, *AB* 4.27.5; *PB* 7.10.4). The Ṛgvedic term *vahatu* denotes marriage (*RV* 10.5.14). The root *vah*, followed by the prefix '*vi*' is added to the suffix *ghañ* in formation of such a word. So, it means specially marriage of the bride by her husband through the wedding ceremony. The word *janya* means bridesman. In the *Ṛgveda* (4.38.6) and the *Atharvaveda* (11.8.1) it has a special sense of the bride's agnate who had an important role at a wedding ceremony. Sāyaṇa suggests the sense as *janebhyo hitaḥ*. The auspicious man being so termed is enlisted to a category of bridesman in giving the marriage of a woman. In normal marriages, the ceremony commenced at the bride's house, to which the bridegroom with his friends and relations repaired, and in which he met the friends and relations of the bride (*RV* 10.17.1; 4.58.9 *AV* 6.60; 14.2.59). A cow or cows were slain for the entertainment of the guests (*RV* 10.85.13). The bridegroom having caused the bride to mount a stone, formally grasped her hand, and led her round the household fire (*RV* 10.85.36, 10.85.38) and the *Atharvaveda* (14.1.47; 14.1.48). This act constituted the marriage, the husband being called 'he who takes by the hand' (*hasta-grābha*) (*AV* 14.1.51). The festivities being over (*AV* 14.2.59), the bridegroom took the bride to his home on a car, in a marriage procession (*RV* 10.85.7; 8; 10,24,25,26,27,42; *AV* 14.1.60). It is difficult to say with certainty within what limits marriage was allowed. The dialogue of Yama and Yamī in the *Ṛgveda* (10.10) seems clearly to point to a prohibition of the marriage between near relatives. In the *Gobhila Gṛhya Sūtra* (3.4.5) and the Dharmasūtras (*ĀpDS*. 2.5.15, 16, etc.) prohibitions against marriage in the *gotra* (family) or within six degrees on the mother's or father's side are found. In the *ŚB* (1.8.3.6), however, marriage is allowed in the third or fourth generation, the former being allowed, according to Harisvāmin (on *ŚB loc.cit*) by the Kāṇvas, and the second by the Saurāṣṭras, while the Dākṣiṇātyas allowed marriage with the daughter of the mother's brother or the son of the father's sister, but presumbaly not with the daughter of the mother's sister or the son of the father's brother. The prohibition of marriage within the *gotra* cannot then have existed, though naturally marriages outside the *gotra* were frequent. Sameness of castes was also not an essential to marriage, as hypergamy was permitted even by the Dharmasūtras (*GDS* 4.16; *BDS* 1.16.2-5; *VDS* 1.24; 25; *PGS* 1.4) so that a brāhmaṇa could marry women of any lower caste, a kṣatriya woman of the two lowest castes as well as of his own caste, a vaiśya, a śūdra as well as a vaiśya, although the śūdra marriages were later disapproved. Instances of such intermarriage are common in the epic, and are viewed as normal in the *Bṛhaddevatā* (5.79). It was considered proper that the younger brothers and sisters should not anticipate their elders by marrying before them. The later Saṃhitās and Brāhmaṇas present a series of names expressive of such anticipation, censuring as sinful those who bear them. These terms are the *pari-vividāna* who, (*MS* 4.1.9; *VS* 30.9) or perhaps agre-dadhus (*MS* 4.1.9) the man, who, though younger, marries before his elder brother; the latter being then called the *parivitta* (*AV* 6.112.3; *TB* 3.2.8.11; *ĀpŚS* 9.12.11; *ĀpDS* 2.5.12; 22), the *agre-didhiṣu* (*KS* has *agre-didhiṣu, Kapiṣṭhala, agre-dadhiṣu; TB* 3.2.8.11 *agra-didhiṣu*), the man who weds a younger daughter while her elder sister is still unmarried; and the *Didhiṣu-pati* (*KS* has *didhiṣu-pati*; *Kapiṣṭhala dadhiṣu-pati*, *VS* 30.9 has *edidhiṣuḥ-pati*), who is the husband of the latter. The passages do not explicitly say that the exact order of birth must always be followed, but the mention of the terms shows that the order was often broken.

**Weights and Measures:** In the field of business transactions, the sale and purchase of commodities have very much to do with weights and measures by which the proportion of the saleable commodity is characterized. The Vedic Indians evidently had the concepts of measures and weights. The unit of measures was evidently the length of hand or the span of stretched fingers, as they are now. Likewise, the primary unit of quantity was characterized by what was contained within the ambit of both the hands. It appears that the Vedic people did not use a mass of metal adjusted to a standard in weighing or calculating weight. They depended mostly on the bushel as a measures of capacity for corn, fruit, liquids and other products. Finger-breadth is referred to as the 'lowest measure' by the term *aṅguli* (*ŚB* 10.2.12). *Aṅguṣṭha* (*KU* 4.12; 6.17) is found as a measure of size. A measure of distance, 'stride' is termed by *prakrama* (*ŚB* 10.2. 31, etc.), though the actual length is unknown. *Bāhu* denotes 'arm', a measure of length in the *Taittirīya Saṃhitā* (6.2.11.1). Another measure of length is termed as *sala* (*AV* 8.7.28; *KS* 12.10; *TB* 1.5.10), *Pāda* (*SB* 6.5.3.2, 7.2.1.7, 8.7.2.17) means 'foot', a measure of length. It also denotes a measure of weight (*BU* 3.1.3.1.1). It signifies a 'quarter' as a fraction, a meaning derived from that of 'foot' of a quadruped. *Sapha* (*RV* 8.47.17; *AV* 6.46.3, 19.57.1; *TS* 6.1.10.1; *ŚB* 3.3.3.3) comes to mean 'one-eight'. *Pradeśa* (*AB* 8.5; *ŚB* 3.5.4.5; *CU* 5.18.1) means 'span' that which is between thumb and forefinger, a measure of length. The *māna* is a measure of weight, equivalent to a *kṛṣṇala* (that is the berry of the *guñja*), which was a unit of weight. This tradition was followed by Manu and is prevalent till today as the lowest unit of weighing gold. A measure of capacity, *prasṛta* means a 'handful' in the *Śatapatha Brāhmaṇa* (4.5.10.7, 13.4.1.5). The term *mṛḍa* (*KS* 11.1m 13.10;

*TS* 3.4.1.4), used only in compounds, seems to have meant a 'small weight of gold'. As a measure of corn, *sarava* is used in the *Taittirīya Brāhmaṇa* (1.3.4.5; 1.3.6.8) and *Śatapatha Brāhmaṇa* (5.1.4.12).

**Wergeld:** In the later Saṃhitās and the Brāhmaṇas, *vaira* and *variar-deya* (*PB* 16.1.12; cf. *TS* 1.5.2.1; *KS* 9.2; *MS* 1.7.5; and *RV* 5.61.8) seem to have the definite and technical sense of 'wergeld', the money to be paid for killing a man as a compensation to his relatives. This view is borne out by the Sūtras of Āpastamba (1.9.24, 1-4) and Baudhāyana (1.10, 19. 1.2). Both prescribed the scale of 1.000 cows for a kṣatriya, 100 for a vaiśya, 10 for a śūdra, and a bull over and above in each case. It is reasonable to suppose that the cows were intended for the relatives, and the bull was a present to the king for his intervention to induce the injured relatives to abandon the demand for the life of the offender. The *Āpastamba Dharmasūtra* (1.9.24.5) allows the same scale of wergeld for women, but the *Gautama Dharmasūtra* (1.10.19.3) puts them on a level with men of the śūdra caste only, except in one special case. The payment is made for the purpose of *vaira-yātana* or *vaira-niryātana*, 'requital of enmity', expiation. The *Ṛgveda* (2.32.4) preserves, also, the important notice that a man's wergeld was a hundred (cows), for it contains the epithet *śata-dāya*, 'one whose wergeld is a hundred'. No doubt the values varied, but in the case of Śunaḥśepa the amount is a hundred (cows) in the *Aitareya Brāhmaṇa* (7.15.7).

**Wheel:** Being both the centre of the wheel and the centre of the earth, *Nābhi* is conceived both physically and metaphysically. In an ordinary wheel, the hub occupies the central position and directs the energy in a balanced way through the spokes to its circumference, to move on. In the early Vedas the navel is considered to be the origin of rays of the sun, representing a wheel (*cakra*). The seven primal rays of the sun, symbolizing the spokes, have their source in the navel. The concept that the navel of the cosmic man is the source of the firmament (*antarīkṣa*) has been hinted at in the *Puruṣasūkta* (*RV* 10.90). When the cosmic Puruṣa is visualized as standing, his navel is imagined in the *antarīkṣa* above the earth (*ŚB* 5.1.5.2). Time is represented as a chariot with seven wheels (*AV* 19.53.2). While emphasizing the idea of the relation between the spokes and the circumference, the *Atharvaveda* states that both have their steady base in the central hub to which they remain firmly fixed. The nave of a wheel is the point of concentration. In the *Chāndogya Upaniṣad* (7.15) *prāṇa* is compared to the hub of the wheel to which the spokes are fastened, being the centre of life.

**Widow:** The term '*vidhavā*' is found in the *Ṛgveda* 10.40.2, denoting a female whose husband passed away. Sāyaṇa interprets this word as '*mṛtabhartṛkā nārī*'. On the other hand, Yāska also explains this term in the sense of a widow. She was not entitled to a social status without a husband. *Vidhavā* thus denotes 'widow' as the 'desolate one', from the root *vidh*, 'be bereft'. The custom of Suttee is implied in a reference in the *Atharvaveda* (18.3.1), but the *Ṛgveda* does not apparently contemplate the custom. The practice seems to have been mainly usual among families of the warrior class, to judge from the other Indo-European parallels. In other classes the survival of wives was more necessary. In the Vedic age there were widows who could be remarried (*RV* 1.124.7). In a reference to the *Ṛgveda* 10.18.8 such women get husbands according to their own liking, and after their own hearts, without feeling any affliction to widowhood. There are several instance in the *Ṛgveda* where widows lived after their husband's deaths. In the *Ṛgveda* 10.40.8 the Aśvins saved the life of a widow. In the *Ṛgveda* 10.102.2 and 10.102.11 warrior Mudgala's brave wife Mudgalāni Indrasena led her dead husband's army to win the booty of the war after his heroic death in the battlefield. In the *Ṛgveda* 1.124.7 a widow enters the house to get wealth. In the later period the duty of a widow was to lead a chaste life after her husband's deaths. Originally, a widow's remarriage seems to have taken the form of her marriage the brother or other nearest kinsman of the dead man in order to produce children. At any rate, the ceremony is apparently alluded to in a funeral hymn of the *Ṛgveda* (10.18.8). This is also supported by the Sūtra evidence (*AGS* 4.2.18). Moreover, another passage of the *Ṛgveda* (10.40.2) clearly refers to the marriage of the widow and the husband's brother (*devṛ*), which constitutes what the Indian later knew as *niyoga* (*Nirukta*, 3.15). This custom was probably not followed, except in cases where no son was already born. This custom was hardly remarriage in the strict sense, since the brother might already be married himself. In the *Atharvaveda* (9.5.27-28), a verse refers to a charm which would secure the reunion, in the next world, of a wife and her second husband. Though this very possibly refers to a case in which the first husband was still alive (*AV* 5.17.8), but was impotent or had lost caste (*patita BDS* 2.2.3.27), still it is certain that the later Dharma Sūtras (*VDS* 17.19.20; *BDS* 4.1.16; *MDS* 9.175) began to recognize ordinary remarriage in case of the death of the first husband. There is some evidence in the *Ṛgveda* (6.49.8) that a woman could remarry if her husband disappeared and could not be found or heard of.

**Wife:** Bhāryā, later a common expression for wife, does not appear in that sense at all in the Saṃhitās. It first appears in the *Aitareya Brāhmaṇa* (7.9) where, however merely a member of the household (who is to be maintained) may be meant. In the *Bṛhadāraṇyaka Upaniṣad* (3.4.1; 4.5.1) the two wives of Yājñavalkya are so designated. *Dāra* is another term for wife found in the Sūtras (usually as plural masculine), and once as a singular in the *Ṛgveda* (6.4.12). *Strī* is the ordinary word in poetry and prose for 'woman', without any special reference to her as a wife or as a maiden. *Nārī* has the same sense, but disappears in later prose. In the *Ṛgveda* (1.164.16; 5.61.8) *strī* stands opposed to *pumāṃs*, man. Not until the *Atharvaveda* (12.2.39) does it mean wife, as opposed to *pati*, husband and even in the Sūtras it is sharply opposed to *jāyā*. The wife was a regular participator in the offerings of the husband. In this connection the term *patnī* regularly applies to her in the Brāhmaṇas (*ŚB* 1.9.2.14), where *jāyā* designates her in her conjugal capacity, not in that of a sharer in the sacrifice. *Jani* or *Janī* appears to denote 'wife', usually applying to her in relation to her husband (*pati*). The more general sense of 'woman' is doubtful; for when Uṣas is called a fair *janī* (*RV* 4.52.1), 'wife' may be meant. The other passage (*RV* 5.61.3) cited for this sense refers to the begetting of children, and seems to demand the sense of 'wives'. Since the words usually appear in the plural (*RV* 1.85.1; 4.5.5; 4.19.5; 7.18.2; 7.26.3; 9.86.32, *VS* 12.35; 20.40; 20.43, cf. *RV* 10.43.1), it is possible they may refer not to 'wives' proper, but to Hetairai. This is, however, rendered unlikely because the *Ṛgveda* (10.18.8) used the phrase *patyur janitvaṃ*, denoting 'wifehood to a husband' as well as the expression *janayo na patnīḥ* (*RV* 1.62.10; 1.186.7), like wives (who are) mistresses, besides containing passages in which the word has reference to marriage (*RV* 5.61.3). The singular occurs in the dialogue of Yama and Yamī (*RV* 10.10.3). The word *jāyā* regularly denotes 'wife' and, as opposed to *patnī*, wife, as an object of marital affection, the source of the continuance of the race. So it is used of the wife of the gambler, and of the wife of the brāhmaṇa in the *Ṛgveda* (10.34.2; 10.34.3; 10.34.13; 10.109); it is also frequently combined with *pati*, 'husband' (*RV* 4.3.2; 10.149.4), also in the later literature (*AB* 3.23.1; cf. 7.13.10; *ŚB* 4.6.7.9; cf. *MS* 1.6.12). *Patnī*, on the other hand, is used to denote the wife as partner in the sacrifice (*ŚB* 1.9.2.14), when no share in it is assigned to her, is called *jāyā* (*ŚB* 1.1.4.13). The distinction is, of course, merely relative; hence, one text (*ŚB* 1.1.4.16) calls Manu's wife *jāyā*, another (*MS* 4.8.1) *patnī*. Later on *jāyā* is superseded by *dāra*. *Dampati* denotes 'the master of the house' in the *Ṛgveda* (1.127.8; 2.39.2; 5.22.4; 8.69.16; 8.84.7), but is more often used in the dual to designate 'the master and the mistress' (*RV* 5.3.2; 8.31.5; 10.10.5; 10.68.2; 10.85.32, etc. *AV* 6.123.3; 12.3.14; 14.2.9), an expression that may legitimately be deemed to show the high status of women at the time of the *Ṛgveda*. *Dāra*, 'wife', is found in the Sūtras (usually masculine and plural), and once (as a singular) in the *Bṛhadāraṇyaka Upaniṣad* (6.4.12). *Strī* is the ordinary word in poetry and prose for 'woman', without any special reference to her as a wife or as a maiden. *Nārī* has the same sense but disappears in later prose, while *gnā* refers only to the wives of the gods, and *yoṣit*, with its cognate words, denotes the young woman as ripe for marriage.

**Wind Therapy:** In the ancient Indian medicinal doctrine, wind is very significant (*RV* 10.137.3; *AV* 4.13.3), deified wind is thus requested: 'Blow as a medicine, O wind, blow up whatever rapture there is, you are a medicine of all'. Similarly in the *Ṛgveda* (10.186.1 ff), we read, 'May wind bring here medicine, blissful for our heart; may you lengthen our lives. Moreover, you are our father, also brother, and friend also, do thou make us live. What that, O wind, the treasure of ambrosia preserved in your house, give thereof to us for the sake of living'. In *Vājasaneyī Saṃhitā* (20.15) wind is requested to free the devotees from sin (*enas*) and distress (*aṃhas*). Thite 223.

**Winnowing Fan:** The term *paripavana* is an instrument suggestive of the winnowing fan (*Nirukta* 4.2.10). Another term for it is *śurpa* (*AV* 9.6.16; 10.9.26; 11.3.4; 12.3.19; 20.136.9; *TS* 1.6.5.4; 3.2.5.11), which named as *varṣā-vṛddha*, swellen by rain (*AV* 12.3.19), is made of reeds and not of dry wood.

**Winter:** The term *hima*, denoting 'cold', 'cold weather', is quite common in the *Ṛgveda* (1.116.8; 119.6; 8.32.26; etc.), but less frequent later (*AV* 7.18.2; 13.1.46; 19.49.5). As 'snow' the word appears as a masculine in the *Taittirīya Brāhmaṇa* (3.12.7.2), and often later as a neuter (*Ṣad.B.* 6.9). 'Hundred winters' are in the *Ṛgveda* (1.64.14; 2.33.2; 5.54.15; 6.48.8) and elsewhere (*AV* 2.28.4, 12.2.28; *TS* 1.6.6.3; *VS* 2.27). Another term for winter is *hemanta*, appearing only once in the *Ṛgveda* (10.161.4), but often in the later texts (*AV* 6.55.2; 8.2.22; 12.1.36; *TS* 5.7.2.4; *VS* 13.58; *PB* 21.15.2; *TB* 1.4.10.10; *ŚB* 10.4.5.2, etc.). Certain hymns (*RV* 7.103; 10.90), which ignore winter and insist on the rains, indicate a different place and time of origin from those which refer to the snowy mountains (*RV* 10.68.10; 121.4). The *Śatapatha Brāhmaṇa* (1.5.4.5) describes winter as the time when the plants wither, the leaves fall from the trees, the birds fly low and retire more and more. See **Seasons**.

**Witness:** Witness (*jñātṛ*) appears in two passages of the *Atharvaveda* (6.32.3; 8.8.21) and in one of the *Śāṅkhāyana Āraṇyaka* (12.14) with a somewhat obscure sense. The word is a technical term taken from law, meaning witness. The reference is, perhaps, to a custom of carrying on transactions of business before a witness, as practised in other ancient societies. The word may also have the sense of 'surety'.

**Woman:** See **Child-marriage, Common Women, Daughter, Daughter-in-law, Family, Female Education, Forms of Marriage, Hetairai, Illegitimate Lovers, Incest, Laughing Women, Maidens, Marital Relations, Misogyny, Nuptial Relations, Polyandry, Polygamy, Rape, Rejected Wife, Remarriage of Women, Seclusion of Women, Sexual Laxity, Unmarried Girls, Unmarried Mothers, Widow, Wife, Young Maidens.**

**Wood Craft:** The importance of this craft, even in hoary antiquity, is indicated by words like *takṣan* in Sanskrit, *tashan* in the *Zend Avesta* and *taktan* in Greek. Takṣan meaning a carpenter is mentioned in the *Ṛgveda* (9.112.1) and later Vedic texts (*KS* 12.10; *MS* 2.9.5; *VS* 16.27, 30.6; 30.6; *TB* 3.4.2.1; *SB* 1.1.3.12). The carpenter made carts (*śakaṭa* and *śakaṭī*) as referred to in the *Ṛgveda* (10.146.3) *Nirukta* (6.22; 11.47) and the *Chāndogya Upaniṣad* (4.1.8), chariots (*RV* 1.61.4) and boats and ships (*RV* 1.116.5; 5.25.9). *Kuliśa* (3.2.1), axe, was one of his tools far making chariots. The *ṛc* (1.105.18) refers to the fact that a carpenter bends over his work till his back aches. Sacrificial vessels were usually made of *palāsa* wood (10.97.5). That *droṇa* (*RV* 6.2.8), a particular wood was used for making the sacrificial ladle, used for pouring clarified butter on the fire, is mentioned in the *Ṛgveda* (1.84.18). Similarly *sruva*, a small ladle was used to convey the *ājya* (*ghee*) from the cooking pot to the large ladle, and the *Ṛgveda* (1.116.24) mentions it distinctly for *soma* libation. The carpenter made three types of bedsteads, *talpa*, *proṣṭha* and *vahya*, referred to in the *Ṛgveda* (7.55.8; cf. *AV* 5.17.12). The *Taittirīya Brāhmaṇa* (1.2.6.5) mentions it as being made of sacred *udumbara* wood. *Tālpya* noted in the *Śatapatha Brāhmaṇa* (12.1.6.2), meaning a legitimate son born in the nuptial couch, indicates that *talpa* was generally used in the sense of a bed or couch. Perhaps *vahya* was of a more comfortable type, as indicated by the *Atharvaveda* (4.20.3) referring to its use by a wearied bride. The *Vājasaneyī Saṃhitā* (1.29; 2.20; cf. *Bṛhadāraṇyaka Upaniṣad* 6.3.13) and *AV* (18.5; *TS* 3.5.7.2) refers to various sacrificial ladles like *sruc, sruva, dhruvā, juhū,* and *upabhṛt*. The *Taittirīya Saṃhitā* (3.2.4.1; cf. *AV* 7.28) mentions instruments of offering like *sphya, vighana, parśu* and *pareśu*. The carpenter made *yupa-s* (sacrificial posts), used for tying the sacrificial victims even from the Ṛgvedic age, as noted in the *Ṛgveda* (5.2.7) and later Vedic texts (*AV* 12.1.38; *VS* 19.17; *TS* 6.3.4.1; *PB* 9.10.2). We find mention of other posts like *svaru* (*RV* 1.92.5; 3.8.6; *AV* 4.24.4; *ŚB* 3.7.1.22) and *drupad* (*RV* 1.24.13; *AV* 6.63.3; *VS* 20.20). *Āsandī* is conspicuous by its absence in the *Ṛgveda* but it appears frequently in later Vedic texts, (*AV* 14.2.65; *TS* 7.5.8.5; *VS* 8.56). The *Atharvaveda* (15.3.9) describes the seat for the *vrātya*, made of wood; it was covered with a cushion and a pillow, and it had a seat and support. The *Aitareya Brāhmaṇa* (8.5; 6.12) also describes a seat for the king at the royal consecration with a seat of *udambara* wood. The *Śatapatha Brāhmaṇa* (5.4.4.1) refers to *āsandī*, 'a throne-seat', made of *khadira* wood. *Paryaṅka* is a later development, mentioned in the *Kaṭha Upaniṣad* (1.5) as having four legs, *śīrṣaṇya* (head-piece), *upaśrī* (soft garment on the couch), and *upavarhaṇa* (pillow for the head). Besides, we find a mention of *kośa* in the *Ṛgveda* (10.42.2; cf. *AV* 1.14.4), meaning a box and bowls (*RV* 6.8.3; *AV* 19.49.8), some of which were decorated with carvings. The *Atharvaveda* (9.6.16-17) refers to a sieve (*śūrpa*), a spoon, a stirring stick and the kettles, wooden vessels and domestic utensils. Other examples of carpentry works of the period were the musical instruments, like *vīṇā, piṅgā, gargara* and *godhā* (*RV* 8.69.9) and *vakura* (*RV* 1.117.21). We find the mention of the word *druhantara* in the *Ṛgveda* (1.127.3), meaning the destroyer of foes, which may be taken to mean a wood-cutter, as reflected in the simile here. The wood-cutter was then a very useful member of the society. He supplied wood as fuel to the people and as raw material to the carpenter and because he cut and felled trees with axes, as reflected in the *Ṛgveda* (10.28.8; 1.32.5), he helped in the making of roads in the country flush with forests. The word *pathikṛt* is referred to as an epithet of Bṛhaspati in the *Ṛgveda* (2.23.6) and in the *Atharvaveda* (18.2.53), of Agni and Soma. Carpenters were never looked down upon in the society. In fact, their works were ever appreciated in the rural societies for their usefulness in agriculture, as reflected in the *Taittirīya Saṃhitā* (4.5.4.2). The *Atharvaveda* (9.3.24) describes the different features of a dwelling house and the *mantra* no. 24, 'Like a woman, O dwelling we carry thee where we will', suggests that the house was made of wood, light enough to be carried whenever required. The houses were fixed in the ground with wooden pegs, as reflected in the *Ṛgveda* (7.99.3) and they rested on wooden pillars (*RV* 1.59.1). The *Atharvaveda* (9.3) gives us to understand the different parts of the house: beams, ties, binding grass, roofs, supported by props and cross-beams, consisting of 'thousand eyed net' (*akṣu*), stretched out as *opaśa* on the division line. The term *dāruāhāra* seems to have meant wood-gatherer. It is referred to in the *Vājasaneyī Saṃhitā* (30.12) and *Taittirīya Brāhmaṇa* (3.4.8.1). The term *prāśitra-haraṇa* denotes a pan, made of *khadira* wood (*acacea catechu*), either square or round, in the shape of a cow's ear (*JB* 1.48. *ŚB* 1.3.1.6; 12.5.2.7; *ASS* 1.13.1; *ŚŚS* 14.22; *BŚS* 20.10.3; *KŚS* 2.6.42; 25.7.27). It was also used for holding the brāhmaṇa's portion of the sacrificial cake. *Piśīla* is the term which designates a wooden plate (*ŚB* 2.5.6.3; 7.2.2.10). However, Sūtra literature meant a sort of guitar by the term *piśīla-vīṇā* which was made of wood and had strings. *Dru* (*RV* 1.161.1; 5.86.3; 8.66.2; 10.101.10) suggests an wooden vessel that was used as the container for soma-juice, particularly at the *soma* sacrifice (*RV* 9.1.2; 9.65.6; 9.98.2). *Droṇa* (*RV* 6.2.8; 6.37.2; 6.44.20; 9.93.1; *JB* 1.48) is another term for a wooden trough, specially a *soma*-container (*RV* 9.3.1; 9.15.7; 9.28.4; 9.30.4; 9.67.19). A reservoir of *soma* is termed *droṇa-kalaśa*. (*TS* 3.2.1.2; *VS* 18.21; 19.27; *AB* 7.17; 7.32; *ŚB* 1.6.3.7).

**Wool, Woollen Garments:** Woollen goods were in use, as reflected in the *Vājasaneyī Saṃhitā* (19.80);

*Maitrāyaṇī Saṃhitā* (3.11.9); *Kāṭhaka Saṃhitā* (38.3); and, also in the *Bṛhadāraṇyaka Upaniṣad* (2.3.6). The *Atharvaveda* refers to *kambala* (14.2.6) and *śāmulya* (14.1.25; cf. *RV* 10.85.29), i.e. blankets and woollen shirts. Wool was already known in the Ṛgvedic period, as evidenced by the *Ṛgveda* (1.126.7-Gandhāra wool, 4.22.2, wool of Paruṣṇī, 10.26.6 *vāsovāyo'vīnā mā vāsāṃsi mar mṛjata*) produced from sheep. Garments made of wool were worn by the Vedic Indians, as we find a mention of woollen thread (*ūrṇā-sūtra*) in the *Maitrāyaṇī Saṃhitā* (3.11.9), *Kāṭhaka Saṃhitā* (38.3), *Vājasaneyī Saṃhitā* (19.80), *Taittirīya Brāhmaṇa* (2.6.4) and *Śatapatha Brāhmaṇa* (12.7.2.11). The word *ūrṇā* denotes not only sheep's wool (*ŚB* 2.5.2.15). *Śāmulya* is a name of a garment, mentioned in the marriage hymn of the *Ṛgveda* (10.85.29) and described as 'woollen robe'. But Sāyaṇa interprets it as 'garment soiled by the body' (*śarīrāvacchannasya malasya dhārakaṃ vastraṃ. Śāmūla* (*JUB* 1.38.4) is assumed as a synonym of *śāmulya* and denotes 'woollen shirt'.

**World Egg:** See **Cosmogony, Hiraṇyagarbha**.

**World Soul:** The conception of a world soul related to the universe, as the soul of man to his body, is found for the first time in the *Ṛgveda* 10.121.1, where he is said to have sprung forth as the first born of creation from the primeval waters. This being has twice been referred to in the *Śvetāśvatara*, in 3.4 and 4.12. In the two passages in which this soul has been spoken of, its mythical character is apparent. The passage in the *Śvetāśvatara* clearly shows how from the supreme eminence that he had in the *Ṛgveda* 10.121, Hiraṇyagarbha had been brought to the level of one of the created beings. Explaining the philosophical significance of the Hiraṇyagarbha doctrine of the Upaniṣads, Deussen says that the 'entire objective universe is possible only in so far as it is sustained by a knowing subject. This subject as a sustainer of the objective universe is manifested in all individual objects but is by no means identical with them. For the individual objects pass away but the objective universe continues to exist without them; there exists therefore the eternal knowing subject also (*hiraṇyagarbha*) by whom it is sustained. Space and time are derived from this subject. It is itself accordingly not in space and does not belong to time, and therefore from an empirical point of view it is in general non-existent, it has no empirical but only a metaphysical reality'. (*Philosophy of the Upaniṣads*, 201). For details see **Cosmogony, Hiraṇyagarbha**.

**Worm:** Various worms have been mentioned in the Vedic texts but, unlike the insects, it is difficult to identify them. The general term for worms is *kīṭa* and for insects *pataṅga. Adṛṣṭa*, 'the unseen' is a term used in the *Ṛgveda* (1.191.4) and the *Atharvaveda* (6.52.3), to designate a species of vermin. The sun is also described as 'the slayer of the unseen' (*adṛṣṭa-han RV* 1.191.9; *AV* 6.52.1; 5.23.6) and as a counterpart a 'seen' (*dṛṣṭa*) is mentioned (*AV* 2.31.2; 8.8.15). In one passage (*AV* 5.23.6; 5.23.7) the epithets 'seen' and 'unseen' are applied to the worm (*kṛmi*), their use being no doubt due to the widespread theory of disease being due to worms, whether discernible by examination or not. *Alāṇḍu* (*AV* 2.31.2) is the name of a species of worm. *Avaskava* is a kind of worm, mentioned along with others in the *Atharvaveda* (2.31.4). *Kapanā*, from its solitary occurrence in the *Ṛgveda* (5.54.6), appears to mean a worm that destroys the leaves of trees, and is so interpreted in the *Nirukta* (6.4). *Kaṣkaṣa* designates a kind of worm in the *Atharvaveda* (5.23.7). *Kīṭa* is the name of a species of worm mentioned in the *Atharvaveda* (9.4.16) and frequently in the Upaniṣads (*BU* 6.1.19; 6.1.14; *CU* 6.9.3; 6.10.2; 7.2.1; 7.7.1; *KU* 1.2) *Kurūru*, apparently the name of a species of worm, is mentioned twice in the *Atharvaveda* (2.31.2; 9.2.22). In the later *Saṃhitās* (*TS* 5.5.11.1; *MS* 3.14.11; *VS* 24.30; *TĀ* 4.36; *ŚB* 5.4.1.2), and especially in the *Atharvaveda* (2.31.32; 5.23), worms play a considerable part. They are regarded as poisonous, and are spoken of as found in the mountains, in forests, in waters, in plants and in the human body. In accordance with widespread primitive ideas, they are considered to be the causes of disease in men and animals. The *Atharvaveda* contains three hymns as charms directed against them. The first of these hymns is of a general nature, the second is meant to destroy worms in cattle, and the third is intended to cure children of worms. When found in men, worms are said to have their place in the head and ribs (*AV* 2.31.4) and to creep into the eyes, nose and teeth (*AV* 5.23.3); they are described as dark brown, but white in the forepart of the body, with black ears, and as having three heads (*AV* 5.23.4). *Nīlaṅgu* is the name of a species of worm in the *Yajurveda Saṃhitās* (*TS* 5.5.11.1; *MS* 3.14.11; *VS* 24.30) in the list of victims at the horse sacrifice. *Yevāṣa* is the name of a destructive insect in the *Atharvaveda* (5.23.7/8). The form *Yavāṣa* is found in the *Kāṭhaka Saṃhitā* (30.1). *Vaghā* is the name of a noxious worm in the *Atharvaveda* (6.50.3; 9.2.22). *Vṛkṣa-sarpī*, tree-creeper, is the name of a species of worm or female serpent in the *Atharvaveda* (9.2.22). *Śaluna* is found in the *Atharvaveda* (2.31.2), denoting a 'worm'. The *Paippalāda* recension reads *śalūla* and Sāyaṇa *śalga*. *Śvavarta* is the name of a species of worm in the *Atharvaveda* (9.4.16) and the *Taittirīya Saṃhitā* (5.7.23.1). *Śipavitnuka* in the *Atharvaveda* (5.20.7) seems to denote a species of worm. *Śva-varta* in the *Atharvaveda* seems to denote a species of worm found in dogs (*AV* 9.4.16). *Samaṅka* occurring in two passages of the *Atharvaveda* (1.12.2; 6.50.1), denotes hookworm and also an insect destructive of grain.

**Worship:** Literally, *upāsanā* means sitting near, mentally approaching an ideal. It lays emphasis on meditation and devotion, a private or personal affair to be diligently protected as one's own, and not to be merely talked or argued about or exposed to others. It is a mental attitude with regard to the objects of devotion, which are not to be looked upon as detached entities, but are to be linked up with their higher aspects in a cosmic whole. It is to be changed into an experience, the whole personality getting transformed and elevated thereby. It is both an objective outlook and a subjective realization. The sacrifices which are calculated to heighten the results are said to be efficacious by themselves. But they do not provide spiritual merit unless they are conjoined with meditation (*CU* 1.1.10). Certain meditations, however, are neither connected with actual sacrifices nor with *Brahman*, but are calculated to lead to heaven or yield other cherished results. In the world of sorrow and suffering, *upāsanā* is a means to achieve grace (*BU* 5.11.1). From another point of view, there are two kinds of *upāsanās*—*brahma-upāsanā* (direct meditation of *Brahman*) and *pratīkopāsanā* (indirect meditation based on symbols). A *pratīka* is a symbol of an image, a name, etc., on which the ideas of the deities to be meditated on are fastened. In consonance with the rise of devotional schools, the Upaniṣads illustrate the state of realization through the imageries (*BU* 6.3.21). Devotion to a personal god capable of forgiving the frailties of the devotee and of bestowing grace, is foreshadowed in the Upaniṣads which hold: 'He is indeed the essence (love) and getting that essence all become happy' (*TU* 2.7); '*Brahman* is bliss, and they move towards and enter into bliss' (*TU* 3.6). An example of meditation on personality can be cited from the *Chāndogya Upaniṣad* (1.6.6-8), where the mind is directed towards the divine presence in the sun, who is the Golden Being above all impurities (cf. *BU* 5.5; 2.4). The *Muṇḍaka Upaniṣad* (2.1.4) speaks of the cosmic person as his head, the sun and moon as his eyes, the Vedas as his voice, the earth as his legs, and so on. There is also a mention of *tanmayatva*, i.e. absolute merger with the object of worship. The *Muṇḍaka Upaniṣad* (2.2.3-4) teaches a beautiful *upāsanā* based on *Om*, which reveals the process of concentration in which the Upaniṣads are conceived of as a bow, meditation as an arrow and the Supreme Being as the target. The *Om* is the bow, the mind is the arrow, and *Brahman* is the target. It is to be hit with concentration, and one should become unified with the target just like the arrow. *Om* is everything (*CU* 2.3.23). Devotional *upāsanā* is often combined with prayer to God, both in his personal and impersonal aspect. The *Śvetāśvatara Upaniṣad* (3.6) illustrates this: 'O Śiva, do thou make innocuous the arrow that thou has taken in hand for shooting?' 'From evil lead me to good; from darkness lead me to light; from death lead me to immortality' (*BU* 1.3.28). But if the Upaniṣads taught the *upāsanās* of infinite expansion, they were careful to prescribe meditations for probing into the subtlest of all subtle things, the *Brahman*. Reality in its immanent form is visualized in various ways on the personal, natural and supernatural planes. On the personal or individual plane, the series runs thus: gross body, vital force, thought, intelligence, and bliss; on the material planes, the progress lies from the smaller to the larger and from the grosser to the subtler; and, on the supernatural plane, the advance is from the individual presiding deities to their cosmic counterparts. On the cosmic plane, again, first comes the gross, Virāṭ; then the subtle, Hiraṇyagarbha; and lastly the causal, Īśvara—the immanent *Brahman* (Saguṇa Brahman), beyond which is the transcendetal Reality (Nirguṇa Brahman). Upāsanā thus consists in 'covering all this with God', as the *Īśā Upaniṣad* puts it, through progressive stages.

**Writing:** While there is no doubt that the instruction was orally imparted, it is debatable whether the art of writing was known at all to Vedic Indians. No actual specimens of any alphabets have been discovered in India which can be definitely dated before the fourth century BC. Consequently, some scholars are of opinion that the art of writing was unknown in Vedic India. Bühler sought to prove that the Indian merchants learnt this art in Western Asia and introduced it in their country some time around the eighth century BC. This view, which regarded the most ancient alphabet of India (the Brāhmī alphabet of Aśoka's inscriptions) as derived from the Western Semitic types of the ninth century BC, is no longer tenable after the discovery of the Harappan seals with pictographic writings. The Indus script appears to be the parent source of subsequent scripts. Some are even of opinion that when the *Ṛgveda* was finally arranged in its present form, it was written in a script which formed an intermediate stage between the Indus script and the Aśokan scripts. If we accept the old theory of Bühler, we have to presume that the vast Vedic literature was composed and preserved by oral transmission alone—a stupendous feat of memory which is nothing short of miraculous. On the other hand, if we believe that these voluminous texts were committed in those old days to writing, we are faced with the problem of writing materials, of which we definitely know nothing. The most sophisticated language of the Vedas, burdened with words containing double and triple and all conceivable form of vowels and consonants, must have required for its own justification its written form. One inference may, however, be drawn that Vedic writing were on perishable materials which is why they are all lost. The whole thing is surrounded in mystery, which cannot be solved until more definite facts come to light.

# Y

**Yadṛcchā:** See **Accidentalism, Chance, First Principles**.

**Yadu:** Name of a tribe of southern Punjab region mentioned repeatedly in the *Ṛgveda* (1.36.18; 1.54.6; 4.30.1; 5.31.8; 6.45.1; 8.4.7; 9.61.2; 10.49.8), normally in conjunction with Turvaśa. They seem to have taken part in the great battle against Sudās. The Yadu and the Turvaśa kings seem to have escaped with their lives, while the Anu and the Druhyu kings perished. At least this is the most natural explanation of several passages (*RV* 1.74.9; 4.30.17; 5.31.8; 6.20.12).

**Yajamāna:** Sacrificer, the person paying the cost of sacrifice (*yajña* q.v.), the institutor of a sacrifice (to perform which he employs priests), any patron, rich man, head of a family or tribe, and so on. In the *Ṛgveda* 1.27.12; 1.51.8; 1.82.2; 4.17.15, etc., there are references to Yajamānas performing the function of priests in their own sacrifices. In later times Yajamāna is the enjoyer of the fruit of sacrifice, but he does not perform it personally. The priests perform the act against remuneration.

**Yajña:** Generally translated as sacrifice in the sense of offering objects dear to gods, just as Abraham went to sacrifice his own son in order to please God. Modern scholars hold that at the root of Yajña is a king of reciprocal arrangement: to offer something to please god and to expect a favour in return. Such an idea also prevailed in the past. The Mīmāṃsakas hold that in believing that Yajña is a means to please the gods, their opponents utterly misunderstand its significance because, in reality, there are no gods. According to the Mīmāṃsakas, Yajña is for the sake of Yajña only and not for the gods. Ritual is the first and last word, the performance of which yields *apūrva*—'that which was not before'. It means that what did not exist before can be produced by ritual as an effect of performing it. Śabara on *Jaimini* 3.1.15; 6.1.2; 7.1.34; 10.4.23, says that, according to the Vedas, the cause of producing effect is sacrifice and not the gods, because the effect is *puruṣārtha* (ultimate aim) which is achieved through human efforts and not through the agency of gods. If it be said that sacrifice is to be offered to the gods, then the gods must necessarily possess a shape and eat the food offered to them at the sacrifice. But neither is possible. If it is hoped that, being satisfied, god will grant the desired object, this cannot be an argument because god's ownership of worldly objects is not proved. Therefore, Yajña is not prayer or propitiation. It simply consists of some definite rituals for the fulfilment of worldly desires, and these rituals are effective in themselves. These rituals are illusory techniques to control nature, to complement the deficiencies of real techniques. This explanation recalls the primitive magical beliefs and practices. The significance of Yajña can be understood only against the background of primitive, undifferentiated, collective life as is proved by rites pertaining to the *satrayāgas*. It is a fact that the original and sophisticated forms of the Vedic Yajñas are not the same and that in the post-Ṛgvedic age the Yajñas became extremely complicated. Their purpose also changed. The *Aitareya Brāhmaṇa* (8.1) says that when performing Yajña in company, the members of the company become brāhmaṇas and there is no distinction of castes. Its class-orientation is indicated in a legend in the same text (7.19), according to which once Yajña deserted the gods and the kṣatriyas and brāhmaṇas followed him to bring him back. The kṣatriyas, who symbolized ruling power, could not get hold of him through their weapons. But the brāhmaṇas could, because *yajña*, being confronted by them, saw in them his own power. So he agreed to return to the brāhmaṇas and said that he was ready to oblige the kṣatriyas, provided they depend on the brāhmaṇas. Very significantly this story throws light on the *entente* between the ruling and priestly classes and the subsequent sophistication of the Yajñas in which the two classes were involved. Among such Yajña the Aśvamedha (q.v.), Rājasūya (q.v.) and Vājapeya (q.v.) were most important. These belonged to the Somayāga category. There are three basic kinds of the Soma-Yāgas (q.v.), namely, *ekāha*, *ahīna* and *sattra*. The *ekāha* has only one *sutyā* day on which the *soma* juice is extracted and libations are made. All one-day sacrifices belong to this category. The *ahīna* has from two to twleve *sutyā* (separate) days. The *sattra* type lasts for more than twelve days, sometimes for a year or longer. There are seven fundamental forms of Soma-yāga, which are Agniṣṭoma (q.v.), Atyagniṣṭoma, Ukthya, Ṣoḍasin, Vājapeya (q.v.), Atirātra and Āptoryāma. They bear the generic title Jyotiṣṭoma (q.v.). A sacrifice performed by a sacrificer and his wife, with the help of four priests, is known as *iṣṭi*. The Darśapūrṇamāsa (q.v.), the *yajña* of the new-moon and full-moon, is the pattern or archetype of all other *iṣṭis*. Pākayajña, the offering of cooked food, are of seven types: *aṣṭakā, pārvaṇasthālīpāka, śrāddha, śrāvaṇī, agrahāyanī, caitrī* and *āśvayujī*. These are offerings to the ancestors, often having monthly compulsions (*GDS* 8.14-22). The *Baudhāyana Gṛhya Sūtra* (1.1) refers to seven Pākayajñas as *huta, prahuta, śūlagabha,* *baliharaṇa, pratyavarohaṇa* and *aṣṭakā-homa.* Vrātyastoma is a *yajña* through which those who lead the *vrātya* (fallen un-Vedic) life may be restored to superior status (*PB* 17.1-4, *KŚS* 22.4.1-28; *ĀpŚS* 22.5.4-14). Certain *yajñas* like Āgrayana are purely agricultural in character. Also see **Devayajña, Occasional Sacrifices, Soma Sacrifices, Śrauta Sacrifices, Viśvajit.**

**Yājñavalkya:** Yājñavalkya, 'descendant of Yajñavalkya, is repeatedly mentioned in the *Śatapatha Brāhmaṇa* (1.1.1.9; 1.3.1.21; 1.3.1.26; 1.9.3.16; 2.3.1.21; 2.4.3.2; 2.5.1.2) as an authority on questions of ritual. He is, however, also described as an authority on questions of philosophy in the *Bṛhadāraṇyaka Upaniṣad* (3.1.2). He is said to have been a pupil of Uddālaka Āruṇi, whom he opposed successfully in a dispute. His two wives, Maitreyī and Kātyāyanī, are mentioned in the *Bṛhadāraṇyaka Upaniṣad* (2.4.1, 4.5.1), which concludes with a passage ascribing to Yājñavalkya, Vājasaneya the 'White *Yajus*' (*śuklāni yajuṃsi*). It is remarkable that Yājñavalkya is never mentioned in any other Vedic text outside the *Śatapatha Brāhmaṇa* except the *Śāṅkhyāyana Āraṇyaka* (9.7; 13.1), where, however, both references are merely transcripts from the *Śatapatha Brāhmaṇa.* It has been supposed that Yājñavalkya belonged to Videha, but despite the legend of Janaka's patronage of him, his association with Uddālaka and the Kuru-Pañcālas, is worthy of consideration. In the *Bṛhadāraṇyaka Upaniṣad* the views of Yājñavalkya have been enunciated. He says that, 'As the sound of a drum cannot be seized until the drum is itself seized, or the beater of the drum . . .' similarly, nothing of any moment can be apprehended unless and until the Self itself is apprehended. Though Yājñavalkya believed in the identification of *ātman* with *Brhaman*, in reply to the ritualistic questions of Aśvala, he said that it was sacrifice alone which would enable the Yajamāna to free himself from the trammels of death. Regarding Jāratkārava's question, with reference to death and allied topics, Yājñavalkya said that when an ordinary man dies his *liṅgaśrīra*, or subtle body, leaves its former tenement; the *liṅgaśarīra* of the sage does not leave his body, and is entirely destroyed within him at the time of his death. Being asked what is the condition of the self when it leaves the human body. Yājñavalkya took Jāratkārava by the hand, led him out of the assembly, and there held some conversation with him. In reply to Bhujya's query about the face of the Pārikṣitas, the answer which Yājñavalkya gave was that the Pārikṣitas had gone of the place where all the sacrificers of Aśvamedha went. In reply to the questions of Usata and Kahola, Yājñavalkya said that the *ātman* is immanent in the whole world. Gārgī asked him what was it that supported the whole visible universe? Yājñavalkya's answer was that it was Ether or Akāśa. 'What is it,' asked Gārgī finally, 'that gives support to this Ether itself'. Yājñavalkya answered that it was what we might call the Akṣara or the Immutable *Brahman*, which he says, 'is neither dense nor subtle, neither short nor long, neither glowing nor humid; without shadow and without darkness, without air and without ether, without attachment and without taste or smell or sight or audition or thought; without light and without breath, without mouth and without measure; neither within nor without, neither devouring anything, nor having anything as the devourer of it.' Yājñavalkya's doctrine of the equation of *Brahman* and *ātman* also finds expression in his discourse with Uddālaka Āruṇi, in which he describes the *ātman* as 'existing within darkness as within light, within *prāṇa* as within all the organs of sense such as those of speech, vision, audition, and touch, as well as within the mind, the thinking faculty'. In fact, Yājñavalkya said that the *ātman* inhabits every existing object in the world, and that it is the *ātman* who is the 'unperceived perceiver, the unheard hearer, the unthought thinker,' and that everything else besides him is an illusion.

**Yajñopavīta:** Sacred thread worn by the *brahmacārin* during his Upanayana or initiation into student life. It is a symbol of *dvijatva* or rebirth (being consecrated), which is to be used throughout life. Consisting of nine strands in a set of three, its size varies according to the caste status. Each strand is a symbol of a deity. Religious acts done without wearing *yajñopavīta* are futile. Taking meal without wearing it makes one liable to expiation. *ĀGS* 1.19; *ĀpGS* 10.2; *ŚGS* 2.1; *BGS* 2.5.2; *BhGS* 1.1; *GGS* 2.10.1. See **Upanayana.**

**Yakṣu:** A tribe mentioned, once in the singular and once in the plural, in the hymn of the *Ṛgveda*, which celebrates Sudās's battle with the ten kings (*dāśarājña*). Who they were and what part they played in that conflict is quite uncertain. They seem, from the wording of the text, to have taken part in two conflicts, one on Paruṣṇī (Ravi), and one on the Yamunā (Jumna) with the aid of the Ajas, and Śigrus, under the leadership of Bheda. They were probably an eastern people.

**Yama:** The chief of the world of the dead is Yama. Only three hymns of the Ṛgveda (10.14; 10.135; 10.154) are addressed to him. The famous hymn (10.10), in which his sister Yamī urges him for an incestuous intercourse, has been the subject-matter of various mythological interpretations. Yama's name occurs about 50 times in the *Ṛgveda* but almost exclusively in the first and (far oftener) in the tenth book. He reveals with the gods (7.76.4; 10.135.1). Individual gods with whom he is referred to are Varuṇa (10.14.7), Bṛhaspati (10.13.4; 10.14.3), and especially Agni, who, as conductor of the dead, would naturally be in close relation with him. Agni is the friend (*kāmya*) of Yama (10.21.5) and his priest (10.52.3). A god (10.51.1) and Yama (who by implication are identical) found the hiding Agni

(10.51.3). Agni, Yama, Mātariśvan are mentioned together as three aspects of one reality (1.164.46). Yama is also mentioned in enumerations of other gods, including Agni (10.64.3; 10.92.11). He is, however, not expressly called a god, but only a king (9.113.8); 10.14 *passim*), who rules the dead (*yamarājña*: 10.16.9). Yama and Varuṇa are the two kings whom the dead man sees on reaching heaven (10.14.7). In one of the hymns devoted to his praise (10.14) he is associated with the Aṅgirases. Later texts (*TĀ* 6.5.2; *ĀSS* 16.6) make mention of the steeds of Yama, which are described as golden-eyed and iron-hoofed. He is the ultimate resort of the people (10.14.1), who gives the dead man a resting place (10.14.9; 10.18.13; *AV* 18.2.37).

**Yamunā:** Name of a river, so called as running parallel with the Ganges, is mentioned thrice in the *Ṛgveda* (5.52.17, 7.18.19, 10.75.5), and not rarely later. According to the *Ṛgveda* (8.18.19), the Tṛtsus and Sudās won a great victory against their foes on the Yamunā. In the *Aitareya Brāhmaṇa* (8.23) and the *Śatapatha Brāhmaṇa* (13.5.4.11) the Bharatas are famed as victorious on the Yamunā. Other Brāhmaṇas (*PB* 9.4.11, 25.10.24, 13.4; also *ŚŚS* 13.19.25.33; *KŚS* 24.6.10.29; *LŚS* 10.19.9.10; *ĀŚS* (12.6.28, etc.) also mention this river.

**Yati:** The word *yati* appears several times in the *Ṛgveda*. In 9.3.9, Indra is said to have given Bhṛgu the wealth snatched from the *yatis*. In the *Ṛgveda* 8.6.18 the *yatis* and the *bhṛgus* are said to have praised Indra. Here *yatis* are shown as devotees in Indra. But in the *Taittirīya Saṃhitā* (2.4.9.2; 6.2.75), *Kāṭhaka Saṃhitā* (8.5; 40.19) and *Aitareya Brāhmaṇa* (35.2) it is said that Indra threw *yatis* to the wolves. In these Saṃhitās the *yatis* appear to be hostile or alien to the Vedic rites, but what they did to deserve being slaughtered by Indra is not clear. In the *Atharvaveda* (2.5.3) Indra is said to have killed Vṛtra as he did in the case of *yatis*. Some of the Upaniṣads, however, show that *yati* was a person who had given up worldly affairs, practised *yoga* and endeavoured after the knowledge of *ātman* (cf. *Muṇḍaka* 3.1.5; 3.2.6).

**Yavyāvatī:** Name of a river in the *Ṛgveda* (6.27.6) and in the *Pañcaviṃśa Brāhmaṇa* (25.7.2). Sāyaṇa identifies it with Hariyupiya, while Hillebrandt thinks that the river is the same as the Djob (Zhob).

**Yātudhāna:** A class of black magicians mentioned in two hymns of the *Ṛgveda* (7.104; 10.87). The word *yātu* also appears in the *Avesta* in the sense of evil-doers. The Yātudhānas in the later texts are equated with the Rākṣasas and Piśācas. Apart from the practitioner of black magic, the term also denotes evil spirit and ghosts.

**Year:** Several Ṛgvedic hymns presuppose a considerable development of sacrificial ceremonies, the regulation whereof required an accurate knowledge of months, seasons, and the year. For example, the *sattras*, which lasted for one year, were an imitation of the sun's yearly course. In the *Ṛgveda* (10.62.2) and later, *Parivatsara* denotes a full year. *Saṃvatsara* and *parivatsara* were originally variants of the simple *vatsara* (year). The year was divided into two distinct parts, each consisting of six months of 30 days; in the midst of both was the *viṣuvat*, i.e. equatorial or central day, cutting the whole *sattra* into two halves. The identification of *saṃvatsara* (year) with sacrifice in many Brāhmaṇa passages and the etymology of the word '*ṛt-vij*' ( = *ṛtu* + *yaj*, 'season-sacrificer') require special consideration in this respect. *Saṃvatsara*, the whole year, is repeatedly mentioned from the *Ṛgveda* onwards (1.110.4; 1.140.2; 1.161.13, etc., *AV* 1.35.4; 2.6.1; 3.10.2; 4.35.4; 6.53.3, etc.). Its duration was, according to the concurrent evidence of the Saṃhitās and Brāhmaṇas, 360 days, divided into 12 months, exceeding in length by six days. The meaning of *saṃvatsara* shows that the year was equivalent to a complete cycle of seasons. The year was thus solar and at the same time sidereal, but not tropical. The month was determined and measured by the moon. The close affinity of the names for month and moon indicates a knowledge of lunar chronology. As a solar year, it appears only in the *Nidāna Sūtra* (5.12.2.5) of the *sāmaveda*, where the sun is stated to spend 13.3 days in each of the 27 nakṣatras. The year being obviously out of harmony with the solar year (whether sidereal or tropical), efforts were certainly made to effect an assimilation of the natural and the accepted year. The adjustment of the solar year to the lunar year was effected either by adding the intercalary month every two or three years, as the *Ṛgveda* 1.25.8 shows, by the insertion of twelve (intercalary) nights at the close of the lunar year, as is suggested by the *Ṛgveda* 4.33.7. This tells us that the Ṛbhus (the genii of the seasons) slacken their course and rest with the sun for twelve nights at the end of a year. The latter was, probably, the older device. The intercalation was not an easy matter in the Brāhmaṇa period, though there are traces of what may be regarded as a five-yearly or six-yearly intercalation. This is indicated by lists of years which are sometimes enumerated as five: *saṃvatsara, parivatsara, idāvatsara, idvatsara* (*anuvatsara* in *KS* 13.15; 39.6; 11.6) and *vatsara (VS* 27.45; *TS* 5.5; 7.3). But it must be noted that this fivefold list is not uniform. Only four are mentioned in some places (*PB* 17.13.17; *TB* 1.4.10.1), three (*AV* 6.55.3; *TS* 5.7.2.4), two (*AV* 8.8.23; *TB* 1.4.10.1), and six (*VS* 30.15; *TA* 4.19) in other places. In none of these enumeration is there any reference to the names being connected with system of intercalation. It is more probable that here we have no more than a mere series of priestly variations of *vatsara*, based on the older *saṃvatsara* and *prativatsara* variants. The key to the invention of the series is probably to be found in passages like that of the *Pañcaviṃśa Brāhmaṇa* (17.13.17), where several *cāturmāsya* sacrifices are equated with different years. The *devayāna* (*RV* 1.72.7; 10.2.7), equated by the *Bṛhadāraṇyaka Upaniṣad* and *Chāndogya Upaniṣad* to six months, when the sun is towards the north, seems to have commenced with the vernal equinox. The *Ṛgveda* 5.10 refers to an observation by the sage Atri of a total eclipse of the sun and in 2.3.2, the phases of the moon have not only received proper names, but are also invoked as deities. In the latter part of the *Atharvaveda* 19, the lunar mansions are enumerated by names, some of which are different from those in the *Taittirīya Saṃhitā*, the others appearing in a later form. The year-beginning seems to have been shifted from the vernal equinox to the winter solstice, at least before the *Taittirīya Saṃhitā*, in which there is a discussion as to whether the month should begin with the new or full moon. In the *Vājasaneyī Saṃhitā* (7.30; 22.31), the deity of the thirteenth month-the Aṃhasaspati-has an oblation offered to it, along with the deities of the twelve months. Again *nakṣatradarśa* and *gaṇaka* appear as names for an astronomer (30.10). The five-year time-unit called the *yuga*, accommodating two intercalary months, is mentioned for the first time in the *Taittirīya Brāhmaṇa*, giving the names of years as *saṃvatsara*, etc., with their overlords. The old names of the months were derived from the seasons such as Madhu, Mādhava, etc. The new names derived from 12 out of the 27 *nakṣatras* are found in the *Śatapatha, Kauṣītaki* and *Pañcaviṃśa* Brāhmaṇas. The number of the *nakṣatras* is put down as 27 in the *Taittirīya Saṃhitā*, but as 28 in the *Atharvaveda* and the *Maitrāyaṇī Saṃhitā*. The succession of 27 *nakṣatras*, which all lie not distant from the ecliptic, were combined into a kind of lunar zodiac, employed for the purpose of estimating the position of the moon for prescribing the time for a sacrificial act.

**Yoga:** The concept of Yoga has characterized the fabric of the later religious and philosophical systems of India. The word *yoga* is derived from the root *yuj*, to join or to unite. The *Ṛgveda* (5.81.1) reads, 'Wise men, priests and sacrificers concentrate their minds and join their prayers to the wise, the great Savitṛ'. The word *yoga* is often used with the word *kṣema* (separately as in the *Ṛgveda* 7.54.3, 7.86.8) or as a compound (as in *RV* 10.166.5). There is a striking description of sage (10.136.2-3) who differs entirely from the brāhmaṇa students or those undergoing consecration, for his ecstasy is not connected either with the sacrifice or with any of the rites ancillary to it, or to the entry of the youth into the full life of the community. His mortal body men see, but he himself fares on the path of the Apsaras, the Gandharvas, the beasts of the wild; he dwells in the eastern and the western ocean, the steed of Vāta, the friend of Vāyu, inspired by the gods. He knows secret desires; he is the dearest friend; he supports Agni and both the worlds; he is the heaven and the light, and, it seems his ecstasy is due to a potent draught which he drinks from a goblet with Rudra. Perhaps this is a reference to the use of some poison to produce exhilaration or hypnosis (cf. *AV* 2.27). His hair is long, his soiled garments are of yellow hue. In the *Atharvaveda* (15), the hymn dedicated to the Vrātyas shows some aspects of an incipient Yogic practitioner. It is, however, in the Upaniṣads that we come across the beginning of the science of Yoga. In the *Kaṭha* (6.18) we are distinctly told that it is necessary to suppress speech and mind, merging the latter in the knowledge of Self, the absolute. The highest stage is attained when the five sense cease to give knowledge, when the mind and the intellect are at rest; the firm restraint of the senses is Yoga. The *Śvetāśvatara* devotes its second chapter to the praise of Yoga, prefacing it with prayers adapted from the *Taittirīya Saṃhitā*, in which Savitṛ's help is sought to secure the application of the mind to the task set before the Yogin. He should hold erect his body, and cause his senses and mind to enter into the heart, check his movements, and breathe with diminished intensity through the nose, restraining from distraction of his mind. A clean, level spot by the presence of water, free from pebbles, fire or gravel, favourable to thought, not offensive to the eye, protected from the wind and secluded, is recommended. Lightness, healthiness, steadiness or freedom from desire, cleanliness of countenance, pleasantness of voice, sweetness of odour, and scantiness of excretions are the first stage in his progress. The revelation of the Absolute procures freedom from fetters and sorrow; sickness, old age, and death are overcome. The insistence on breathing as a matter of importance is noteworthy; restraint of breath not merely banishes evil influences; it tends to generate heat, thus producing *tapas*, and restraint serves to balance the activity of the brain, thus favouring the feeling of severance from the world and union with the absolute. The *Bṛhadāraṇyaka Upaniṣad* (1.5.23) appears to refer to *prāṇāyāma* (he should observe the one exhalation) while the *Chāndogya Upaniṣad* (8.15) refers to *pratyāhāra*. The *Maitrāyanīya* repeatedly develops the theme: the state to be aimed at is reaching the fourth stage (6.19). By the suppression of the organs, by pressing the tip of the tongue against the palate (6.20 f), by controlling voice, mind, and breath, one experiences the *Brahman*, the Self, and becomes selfless. Another device consists in making the sound of the ether within the heart audible by the control of breath (6.27). Or, again, by using the sound *Om* as an arrow, with mind as its point, the Yogin pierces the darkness and sees him who sparkles like a wheel of fire, the colour of the sun, *Brahman* that shines beyond the darkness, in the sun, the moon, the fire and the lightning (6.24). The oneness of the breath and mind and also of the senses and the relinquishment of all conditions of existence is declared to be the essence of *yoga*. A formal list of six elements of *yoga* appears in the *Maitrāyaṇī Upaniṣad* (6.18). These are *prāṇāyāma,* 'regulation of the breathing in and out', *pratyāhāra,* 'suppression' of the organs of sense, such as the mind, so as to prevent its activity from spoiling concentration', *dhyāna*, 'meditation', *dhāraṇā*, 'concentration of the attention' *tarka,* 'reflection', a term of doubtful sense in this context, and *samādhi,* 'absorption or complete union with the object of meditation'. This list differs, in the insertion of *tarka*, and in the placing of *dhyāna* before *dhāraṇā*, from the later list, which makes up the number of eight members by inserting as the first three items *yama*, 'discipline', refraining from doing injury, truthfulness, etc., *niyama*, 'self-restraint' such as purity, contentment, etc., and *āsana* 'postures in sitting'. Of all these the most important is the use of *Om* as a symbol of *Brahman* to meditate upon. It is recognized by the *Kaṭha* (2.17; cf. 1.1; *TU* 1.8; *MU* 2.2.4) but its importance belongs to the later Upaniṣads.

**Young Maidens:** *Kanīnakā* or *kanīnikā* denotes a maiden or young woman. So does the term *kanyā* (*RV* 1.123.10; 1.161.5; 3.23.10, etc.; *AV* 1.14.2; 11.5.18; 12.1.25, etc.) and also *kanā* (*RV* 10.61.5, etc.). There are rare forms, as *kanyanā* in the *Ṛgveda* (8.35.5) and *kanyalā* in the *Atharvaveda* (5.5.3; 14.2.52). There are other terms, i.e. *yoṣan, yoṣaṇā, yoṣā, yoṣit*, denoting 'young women, 'maiden' as an object of affection (*RV* 4.5.5; 3.52.3; 3.56.5; 3.62.8; 7.95.3; 1.48.5; 1.92.11; 3.38.8, etc. *Atharvaveda* 12.3.29; 14.1.56). The term *yoṣā* appears in the *Atharvaveda* (12.3.29) as a sense of wife, though it is treated as daughter in the *Ṛgveda* (1.117.20) and also merely as girl in the *Śatapatha Brāhmaṇa* (1.8.1.7). Maidens bowing before the youthful gallants come with love to them in the *Ṛgveda* (10.30.6). Maidens visited social and festive gatherings fully adorned (*RV* 7.2.5). A feature of the Ṛgvedic society implied wooing and seeking of young bachelors for marriage by young maidens. It also expresses a liberal attitude towards the free-mixing of opposite sexes. (*RV* 4.58.8). As an ordinary expression, *yuvatī* means a young woman or maiden in the *Ṛgveda* (1.118.5) and later (*AV* 14.2.61; *TB* 3.1.1.9; 3.1.2.4; *ŚB* 13.1.9.6; 13.4.3.8, etc.). Generally it denotes a woman attaining youth and as being at a stage of growing maidenhood, comments Sāyaṇa on *yauvanopetā* in the *Ṛgveda* 5.2.1.

**Yuga:** Yuga in the *Ṛgveda* (1.139.8; 3.26.3; 6.8.5; 6.15.8; 6.36.5; 9.94.12; 3.33.8; 10.10.10; 7.70.4; 10.72.1; 1.92.11; 1.103.4; 1.115.2; 1.124.2; 1.144.4) frequently denotes a 'generation'. The word *yuga* appears 33 times in the *Ṛgveda*. In several passages (e.g. 3.26.3) it appears to stand for a very brief period of time. In *Ṛgveda* (1.158.6) *dīrghatamā māmateyo jujurvan daśame yuga* means a short period while in other passages it denotes a longer one. There is no reference in the older Vedic texts to the five-year cycle, though in *Ṛgveda* (3.55.18) it is possible to recognize a recondite reference to the five-year units of time, each divided into six seasons. Nor do the older Vedic texts know of any series of *yugas* or ages such as are usual later. In the *Atharvaveda* (8.2.21) there are mentioned, in order, a hundred years, an *ayuta* (10,000), and then two, three, or four *yugas*. The inference from this seems to be that a *yuga* means more than an *ayuta*, but it is not very certain. The *Taittirīya Brāhmaṇa* (3.12.9.2) recognizes long periods of time, e.g. one of 100,000 years. To the four ages, Kali, Dvāpara, Tretā and Kṛta, there is no certain reference in Vedic literature, though the names appear as the designations of throws of dice. In the *Aitareya Brāhmaṇa* (7.15.4) the names do appear, but it is not clear that the ages are really meant. The later concepts *kalpa, manvantara* and *mahāyuga*, with their fabulous numbers of years, are elaborations of the original *yuga* concept. The word *kalpa* has its germ in the *Ṛgveda* (10.190.3), in which it is said *sūryā-candramasau dhātā yathāpūrvamakalpayat. divaṃ ca pṛthivīṃ cāntarīkṣamatho svaḥ*. The earliest datable reference to *kalpa*, denoting a vast span of time, is found in the inscriptions of Aśoka.

# Z

**Zodiac:** A belt of the heavens limited by lines about 80 from the ecliptic on each side, including all apparent positions of the sun and planets as known to the ancient astronomers and divided into 12 equal parts called signs of the Aries (*meṣa*), Taurus (*vṛṣa*), Gemini (*mithuna*), Cancer (*karkaṭa*), Leo (*siṃha*), Virgo (*kanyā*), Libra (*tulā*), Scorpio (*vṛścika*), Sagittarius (*dhanu*), Capricorn (*makara*), Aquarius (*kumbha*) and Pisces (*mīna*), each formerly containing the similarly named zodiacal constellations but now precession of equinoxes, coinciding with the constellation that bears the name of the preceding sign. The word zodiac is derived from the Greek word *zodion*, meaning 'little animals'. The Sanskrit equivalent of zodiac is *rāśicakra*. The concept might have originated in West Asia and the acquaintance of the Vedic Indians with it was marginal, though the latter had a good idea of the constellations. The twelve names of the *rāśis* mentioned above are found in later literature. Some signs of the zodiac are found drawn on the railing pillars of Buddha-Gayā, dated about the first century BC by which time the concept must have been popular in India. The twelve *nidānas* of the Buddha, the cycle of *pratītyasamutpāda,* the Buddhist symbolism of wheel, etc., have been interpreted by some scholars in terms of zodiacal function, but it is difficult at the present state of our knowledge to affirm this view with certainty. Some verses of the *Ṛgveda* may be cited in this connection. The *Ṛgveda* (1.164.11-13 and 48) says, 'The wheel of *ṛta* has twelve spokes; it revolves round the heavens; it does never wear out. O Agni, in this (wheel) seven hundred and twenty sons in pains abide. Some say that the father (Sun) who sends down water has five feet and twelve forms and remains endowed with fulness in the distant half (part) of heavens, while others say that he (the sun), the all seeing, is placed in a lower (place) that has seven wheels and six spokes; all the worlds abide in the revolving wheel with five spokes; one wheel and twelve rims (of the wheel) and the three naves-who is there to know these (thoroughly); in that (wheel, i.e. year) are placed together three hundred and sixty very unstable nails.' From this passage we learn of a year divided into three, five or six seasons, twelve months, 360 days and 720 days and nights. It is possible to hold that the wheel of *ṛta* means the zodiacal belt divided into twelve parts (*dvādaśāra*). But it is difficult to keep in view the twelve divisions correctly. The *Atharvaveda* (5.35.4) states that *saṃvatsara* has twelve spokes and the months have 30 spokes. The *rāśis* of the later period more or less coincide with the traditional names of the Indian months which were, however, designated after the names of the stars found in the Vedic literature, though the names of the Vedic months were different. In any case a correlation may be established between the stars and the zodiac, between months and the stars and between the zodiac and the months. See **Constellations, Months**.

**Zones:** Three zones-celestial, atmospheric and terrestrial-are frequently mentioned in the Vedic literature as divisions of the cosmos (*RV* 1.143.2; 1.159.1; 1.160.1; 4.14.12; 4.26.6; 4.53.5; 5.60.6; 5.69.1; *AV* 12.2.48, etc.). So far as the physical world is concerned, the four cardinal points are mentioned as four zones (*RV* 7.72.5; 10.36.14; 10.42.11; *AV* 15.2, etc.). The central zone is referred to as *dhruva* (*AV* 8.9.15; 13.3.6; 15.14.1-5, etc.). There is no mention of the geographical division of the earth in Vedic literature, but a division of the Indian subcontinent is found. There is a fivefold zonal division with the enumeration of residents therein, which we come across for the first time in the *Aitareya Brāhmaṇa* (8.14) though it has in a way been anticipated in the *Atharvaveda* (19.17.1.9). The *Aitareya Brāhmaṇa* division of the five zones are *Dhruvā Madhyamā Pratiṣṭhādiś* or Madhyadeśa or middle country, *Prācīdiś* or the eastern zone; *Dakṣiṇādiś* or the southern zone; *Praticīdiś* or the western zone; and *Udicyadiś* or the northern zone. The extent and limits of these zones cannot, however, be defined with any degree of plausibility.

**Zoology:** This branch of biology, dealing with the animal kingdom and the physiology, classification, characteristics, habits, etc., of its members, was not fully developed in the Vedic texts, though some kind of arrangement of animals in a series of groups is found in them, such as *amphibia, arthropoda, aves, chondrichthyes, mammalia, mollusca, orthoptera, osteichthyes, reptilia,* etc. The *Atharvaveda* (2.31.4; 3.27.1-6; 5.13.5-8, 9.12.1-18) mentions more than fifty anatomical parts of the ox and eighty of the horse, classifies snakes and some other creatures on the basis of colour, form and anatomical structure and distinguishes twenty-one varieties of adders (1.27.4). The *Taittirīya Saṃhitā* (2.6.2.2; 6.5.2.2) divides the animals into *invertebrata* and *vertebrata* on the basis of bones and makes another classification on the basis of teeth. The *Chāndogya Upaniṣad* (6.3.1) divides all living creatures on the basis of their mode of origin into *jīvaja* or *jarāyuja* (viviparous), *aṇḍaja* (oviparous) and *udbhijja* (born of vegetable organisms). The *amphibia* in the Vedas is represented by the *maṇḍukas*, or frogs

(*RV* 7.103, the famous frog hymn; 10.166.5; *AV* 7.112.2; *TS* 5.4.4.3; 5.7; *MS* 3.14.2; *VS* 24.36, etc.) having four pentadactyle limbs and a pelvic girdle joined to the vertebral column. The Vedic observation of the *arthropoda,* specially the *insecta* class, the *orthoptera,* etc., is indeed amazing. These include *āraṅgara* (bee), *indragopa* (cochineal insect), *upajihvikā* (ant), *ūrṇanābhi* (spider), *kaṅkata* and *kaṅkaparvan* (scorpion), *kṛkalāsa* (chameleon), *kṛmi* (annelida), *jabhya* and *tarda* (grain insect), *khadyota* (firefly), *tṛṇajalāyuka* (caterpillar), *tṛṇaskanda* (grasshopper), *daṃśa* (fly), *pipīla, pipīlikā* (ant), *bhṛṅgā, madhukara, makṣikā, saraghṛ, sarah,* (various kinds of bees), *maśaka* (mosquito) and various unidentified species, such as *alpaśayu, upakvasa, ejatka, prakaṅkata, pluṣi, magundī, sūcikā, adṛsta, alāṇḍu, avaskava, ejaraka, kepanā, kakṣaka, kīṭa,* (general term for worms), *kurūru, nilaṅgu, pataṅga* (general term for insects), *yavāṣa, vaghā, vṛkasarpi, saluna, śavarta, śipavitnuka, śvavrata, svavrata, samaṅka, stega,* etc. The Vedic list of *aves* is also elaborate. Among the carnivorous birds, mention is made of *gṛdhra* (vultures), *balākā* (crane), *śyena* (falcon), *saghan* (eagle), *suparṇa* (a kind of eagle), etc. The swiftness of their fight is specially recorded. Among other species, we have *aliklava* (carrion), *ulūka* (owl), *kapiñjala* (francoline patridge), *kapota* (pigeon), *kalaviṅka* (sparrow), *kikidīvi* (blue jay), *kukkuṭa, kuṭaru kṛkavāku* (cock), *kuṣītaka* (sea-crow), *kruñc, cakravāka* (curlew), *cāṣa* (heron), *khargalā* (owl), *darvidā* (woodpecker), *dātyauha* (gallinule), *dārvāghāta* (woodpecker), *dhvāṅkṣa* (crow), *pārāvata* (turtle dove), *pika* (cuckoo), *plava* (pelican), *madgu* (diver), *ropaṇākā* (thrush), *laba, varttikā* (quail), etc. Among the aquatic birds five species are mentioned, which are *āti, plava, madgu, haṃsa,* (gander) and *hāridrava* (water wagtail). Besides the Vedic texts refer to a number of species that cannot be identified with certainty. The *chondrichthyas* were probably represented by the Vedic *karvara, kalipāya, jhaṣa, rajasa, śakula,* etc., but there is doubt in regard to the identification of these creatures. The porpoise, belonging to the dolphine family is represented in the Vedic literature. *Kakutha* and *kakkaṭa* refer to crab while *śaṅkha* refers to conch. *Kūrma* or tortoise is, however, mentioned frequently along with its other name *kaśyapa.* It is also interesting to note that while the Vedic texts refer to numerous species of *mammalia,* almost all the varieties that are found in India even today, and describe their physical features and special characteristics, they do not tell us much about the *osteichthyes* and its varieties, *actinopterygii* and *choanichthyes.* We have mention only of *matsya* (fish) and *mahāmatsya* (great fish). Various carnivores (q.v.) and herbivores and their characteristics have been referred to. In some cases their habits are described metaphorically. For example, Agni, while entering the waters, has been compared with a lion (*RV* 3.9.4), which may be due to the lion's habit of springing on animals at their usual drinking places. As regards *reptalia,* the Vedic term for which is *sarisṛpa,* we have *makara* and *nākra* (crocodile), *godhā* (iguana), *vṛścika* (scorpion), *nakula* (ichneumon), and various kinds of serpents, such as *aghāśva, ajagara, āligī, āśīviṣa, kalmāṣagrīva, nāga, lohitāhi, śvitra, svaja,* etc. The classification as invertebrates and vertebrates was well known to the Vedic writers. There are references to animal anatomy, the constitution of their various limbs and the internal organism. This was due to the fact that the Vedic sacrificial cults required the slaughfering of the animals and various parts of their body were offered to the deities. The Vedic composers did not make any conscious attempt to create a science of zoology, but the way of its growth. It is in the Jain *Tattvārthādhigama,* and later medical treatises, that we come across an elaborate development of this branch of science. It also goes to the credit of the Vedic authors to trace the origin of all the species, genera, family, order, class and phyla of the animal kingdom to a single source and regard them as evolutes of an ongoing biological process. See **Animals, Birds, Carnivores, Herbivores, Insects, Reptiles, Serpents, Worms**.

**Zoolatry:** See **Animal Worship**.

**Zoomorphic Deities:** As typifying the forces of nature and supplying symbols or figures for the supernatural or the godhead, animals appear to have been known to the composers of the Vedic texts. Zoomorphism is not direct animal worship, but in this form of religious cult the deities are conceived of in the form of animals. Behind such conceptions primitive totemism must have played an important role. Thus, Indra and other powerful gods have been compared with bulls or rams, and Agni with the horse, and there is also the divine horse named Dadhikrāvan in the Veda. The god Pūṣan is invoked in the form of a goat. The name of the Aśvins is associated with the horse. But the extent to which zoomorphic deities came into prominence in the later Purāṇas is far greater than that in the Vedas which, in some cases, however, provide the nucleus of later developments. For example, Garuḍa as the vehicle of Viṣṇu has come out of the Vedic divine eagle, Garutman or Suparṇa. The great zoomorphic deity, Hanumant, the monkey-god, has some bearing on the Vedic Vṛṣākapi (*RV* 10.36). The Ṛgvedic Aja Ekapāda and Ahi Budhnya may also be regarded as zoomorphic deities. See **Animal Worship, Theriomorphism, Totemism**.

# Bibliography

## PRIMARY SOURCES


*Aitareya Āraṇyaka*, Text Ānandāśrama 37, Poona, 1898; ed. with Eng. trans. by A.B. Keith, Oxford 1909.

*Aitareya Brāhmaṇa*, ed. by Th. Aufrecht, Bonn 1879; by K.S. Agashe, Poona 1896; Eng. trans. by A.B. Keith, HOS, XXV, Cambridge Mass 1920, rpt. Delhi 1981; M. Haug, *The Aitareya Brāhmaṇa*, rpt. Delhi 1976-7.

*Āpastamba Dharmasūtra*, ed., G. Bühler, Bombay, 1892, 1894.

*Āpastamba Śrautasūtra*, ed., R. Garbe, Calcutta, 1892-1902.

*Ārṣeya Brāhmaṇa*, ed., A.C. Burnell, Mangalore, 1876; by B.R. Sharma, Tirupati 1984.

*Āśvalāyana Gṛhyasūtra*, ed., A.G. Stenzler, Leipzig 1864.

*Atharvaveda*, ed., R. Roth and W.D. Whitney, Berlin, 1856; ed., S.P. Pandit with Sāyaṇa's com. Bombay 1895-8; by Vishva Bandhu et al., Hoshiarpur, 1960-6, *Paipplāda*, tr., M. Bloomfield, SBE, XLII, Oxford 1897; ed., W.D. Whitney, Cambridge, Mass, 1905.

*Baudhyāna Dharmasūtra*, ed., E. Hultsch, Leipzig, 1884.

*Baudhāyana Gṛhyasūtra*, ed., R. Shamasastry, Mysore, 1920.

*Baudhāyana Śrautasūtra*, ed., W. Caland, Calcutta, 1904-23.

*Daivata Brāhmaṇa*, ed., J. Vidyasagar, Calcutta, 1881.

*Dharmasūtras*, tr., Āpastamba, Gautama, Vasiṣṭha and Baudhāyana by G. Bühler in SBE II and XIV.

*Gautama Dharmasūtra*, Text, Ānandāśrama, Poona, tr., G. Bühler, SBE II.

*Gopatha Brāhmaṇa*, ed., R.L. Mitra and H. Vidyabhusan, Calcutta, 1872; ed., V.P. Vidyāvāridhi, Calcutta, 1980.

*Gṛhyasūtras*, tr., Śāṅkhyāyana, Āśvalāyana, Pāraskara Khadira, Gobhila, Hiraṇyakeśin and Āpastamba by H. Oldenberg in SBE XXIX and XXX.

*Iśa Upaniṣad*, Eng. trans by R.E. Hume.

*Jaiminīya Brāhmaṇa*, ed. H.W. Bodezits, Leiden, 1973; ed. Raghu Vira and Lokesh Chandra, 2nd edn, Delhi, 1986.

*Kapiṣṭhala Kaṭha Saṃhitā*, ed., Raghu Vīra, Lahore, 1932; rpt, Delhi, 1968.

*Kāṭhaka Saṃhitā*, ed., Von Schroeder, Leipzig, 1900-11; ed., S.D. Satvalekar, Pardi, Svādhyāya Maṇḍala, 1983.

*Kātyāyana Śrauta Sūtra*, ed. V. Sarma, Benares 1933-7.

*Kauṣītaki Brāhmaṇa*, ed., E.B. Cowell, Calcutta 1861; Eng. tr., A.B. Keith, HOS, XXV, Cambridge, Mass, 1920; rpt, Delhi, 1981.

*Khadira Gṛhyasūtra*, ed., A. Mahadeva Sastri and L. Srinivasacharya, Mysore, 1913.

*Maitrāyaṇī Saṃhitā*, ed., Von Schroeder, Leipzig, 1881-6; ed., S.D. Satvalekar, Pardi, Svādhyāya Maṇḍala, New Delhi.

*Muṇḍaka Upaniṣad.* See under *Upaniṣads*.

*Nirukta*, ed., V.K. Rajavade, Poona, 1921-6; ed. and tr., L. Sarup, 2 Vols, Lahore.

*Pañcaviṃśa Brāhmaṇa*, ed., A Vedāntavagīśa, Calcutta, 1869-74; ed., W. Caland; rpt, 1982.

*Pāraskara Gṛhyasūtra*, ed., Gopal Sastri Nene, Benares, 1926.

*Ṛgveda*, Saṃhitā and Pada text with Sāyaṇa's com. ed. F. Max Müller, second ed., 1890-92; critically ed. N.S. Santakka, Vaidika Saṃśodhana Maṇḍala, 5 vols, Poona 1933 ff; trans. by R.T.H. Griffith, Benares 1896-7; in part by F. Max Müller, SBE XXXII, Oxford 1891 and H. Oldenberg, SBE Oxford, 1897.

*Ṣaḍviṃśa Brāhmaṇa*, ed., J. Vidyasagar, Calcutta, 1881; ed., H.F. Elsingh, Leiden, 1908; ed., B.R. Sharma, Tirupati, 1983.

*Sāmaveda*, ed., S. Samasrami, Calcutta, 1873; ed. and tr., Th. Benfey, Leipzig, 1848: rpt, New York, 1978.

*Sāmāvidhāna Brāhmaṇa*, ed., A.C. Burnell, London, 1873.

*Śāṅkhāyana Āraṇyaka*, ed., E.B. Cowell, Calcutta, 1861; ed., A.B. Keith, Oxford, 1909; ed., Bhim Dev, Hoshiarpur, 1980; Eng. tr., A.B. Keith, London, 1908: rpt, Delhi, 1975.

*Śāṅkhāyana Brāhmaṇa*, ed., and Eng. tr., Ganga Sagar Rai, Varanasi, 1987.

*Śāṅkhyāyana Śrautasūtra*, ed., A. Hillebrandt, Calcutta, 1886-89.

*Śatapatha Brāhmaṇa*, ed., A. Weber, London, 1885, rpt, Varanasi, 1864; Eng. tr., J. Eggeling, SBE XII, XXVI, XLI, XLIII, XLIV, Oxford, 1882-1900.

*Taittirīya Āraṇyaka*, Ex., B. Phadke, Ānandāśrama, Poona, 1981.

*Taittirīya Brāhmaṇa*, ed., R. Mitra, Calcutta, 1855-70; by N. Sastri, Ānadāśrama, Poona, 3rd edn., 1979.

*Taittirīya Saṃhitā*, ed., A. Weber, Berlin, 1871-2; with the Com. of Madhava, Calcutta 1854-99; by S.D. Satvalekar, Pardi, Svādhyāya Maṇḍala, New Delhi, 1983; A.B. Keith, *The Veda of the Black Yajus School*, rpt, Delhi, 1967.

*Upaniṣads*, J.L. Sastri, ed., *Upaniṣat Saṃgraha*, rpt., New Delhi, 1984; R.E. Hume, *Thirteen Principal Upanisads*, Oxford, 1921; S. Radhakrishnan, *Principal Upanisads*, rpt., Delhi, 1989.

*Vājasaneyī Saṃhitā*, ed., A. Weber, London, 1852; ed., S.D. Satavalekar, Pardi, Svādhyāya Maṇḍala, New Delhi, 1971; R.T.M. Griffith, *The Texts of the White Yajurveda* rpt, Varanasi, 1976.

*Vasiṣtha Dharmasūtra*, ed., A.A. Führer, Bombay, 1916.

## SECONDARY SOURCES

Abhyankar, K.D. and B.G. Siddharth, *Treasures of Ancient Indian Astronomy,* Delhi, 1993.

Aiyangar, K.V.R., *Ancient Indian Economic Thought,* Benaras, 1934.

Aiyangar, P.T.S., *Life in Ancient India,* Madras, 1912.

Altekar, A.S., *Education in Ancient India,* Benares, 1944.

——, *Position of Women in Hindu Civilization,* Benares, 1938.

——, *State and Government in Ancient India,* 3rd edn., Benares, 1958.

Anirvan, *Veda Mīmāṃsā*, Calcutta, 1965.

Apte, V.M., *Social and Religious Life in the Gṛhyasūtras,* Allahabad, 1939.

Arnold, E.V., *Vedic Metre*, Cambridge, 1905.

Aurobindo, Śrī, *On the Vedas,* Pondicherry, 1956.

Bandyopadhyaya, N.C., *Development of Hindu Polity and Political Theories,* ed., N.N. Bhattacharyya, New Delhi, 1980.

Bandyopadhyay, Santi, *Vaidik Yuger Yāgayajña,* Calcutta, 1395 B.S.

Banerjee, A.C., *Studies in the Brāhmaṇas,* Calcutta, 1963.

Banerjea, J.N., Development of Hindu Iconography Calcutta, 1956.

Banerjee, P., *Early Indian Religions,* New Delhi, 1973.

Banerjee, S., *Hindu Law of Marriage and Strīdhana*, Calcutta, 1896.

Banerji, S.C., *Dharmasūtras: A Study of Their Origin and Development,* Calcutta, 1962.

Banerji-Sastri, A., *Asura India,* Patna, 1926.

Basham, A.L., *The Wonder that was India,* Calcutta, 1988; ed., *A Cultural History of India,* Delhi, 1975.

Barth, A., *The Religions of India,* London, 1882.

Baruna, B.M., *A History of Pre-Buddhistic Indian Philosophy,* Calcutta, 1921.

Barn, J., *India in the Age of the Brāhmaṇas,* Calcutta, 1969.

Basu, P., *Indo-Aryan Polity,* London, 1925.

Belvalkar, S.K. and R.D. Ranade, *History of Indian Philosophy,* Vol. II, Poona, 1927.

Beni Prasad, *Theory of Government in Ancient India,* Allahabad, 1927.

Bentley, J., *A Historical View of Hindu Astronomy,* London, 1825.

Bergaigne, A., *La Religion Vedique*, Paris, 1878-83.

Bhargava, P.L., *India in the Vedic Age,* Delhi, 1970.

Bhatta, C.P., *Dice-Play in Sanskrit Literature,* Delhi, 1985.

Bhattacharyya, D., *Mythological and Ritual Symbolism: A Study with Reference to the Vedic and Tantric Agni,* Delhi, 1984.

Bhandarkar, D.R., *Some Aspects of Ancient Indian Culture*, Madras, 1940.

Bhattacharyya, N.N., *Historical of Indian Cosmogonical Ideas,* New Delhi, 1971.

——, *Ancient Indian Rituals,* 2nd edn., New Delhi, 1996.

——, *A Geographical Dictionary of Ancient Early Medieval India,* New Delhi, 1991.

——, *A Glossary of Indian Religious Historiography,* New Delhi, 1996.

——, *History of Tantric Religion,* New Delhi, 1982.

——, *Ancient Indian History and Civilization Trends and Perspectives,* New Delhi, 1988.

Bloomfield, M., *The Atharvaveda,* Strassburg, 1899; *The Religion of the Veda,* New York, 1908.

——, *Rig-veda Repetitious*, New Delhi, 1981.

——, *A Vedic Concordance,* rpt, Delhi, 1990.

Bongard-Levin, G.M., *A Complex Study of Ancient India,* Delhi, 1986.

Bregenhoj, C., *Ṛgveda as the Key to Folklore,* Eng. M.G. Abrahomsen, Helsinki 1987.

Caland, W., *Altindischer Ahnenkult,* Leyden, 1893.

Caland, W. and V. Henry, *L'Agniṣṭoma,* Paris, 1906-07.

Chakraborti, H.P., *Socio-Economic Life in India in the Vedic Period,* Calcutta 1986.

——, *Political and Legal Institutions in Vedic Literature*, Calcutta, 1981.

Chakravarti, C., *Common Life in the Ṛgvedic and Atharvaveda: An Account of Folklore of the Vedic Period,* Calcutta, 1977.

Chakrabarti, S.C., *Paribhāṣās in the Śrauta Sūtras,* Calcutta, 1980.

Chanda, R.P., Medieval Indian Sculpture in the British Museum, London, 1936.

Childe, V.G., *The Aryans,* New York, 1926.

Choudhuri, Usha, *Indra and Varuṇa in Indian Mythology,* Delhi, 1981.

Coomaraswamy, A.K., *A New Approach to the Vedas,* London, 1933.

——, *The Ṛgveda as Land-Nama-Bak,* rpt, Delhi 1980.

Cunningham, A., *The Ancient Geography of India,* ed. S.N. Majumdar, Calcutta, 1924.

Daṅdekar, R.N., ed., *Vedic Bibliography,* 5 vols., Poona, 1946 ff. *Vedic Mythological Tracts,* Delhi, 1979.

Dange, S.A., *Pastoral Symbolism from the Ṛgveda,* Delhi, 1970.

——, *Vedic Concept of Field and the Divine Fructification,* Delhi, 1971.

——, *Sexual Symbolism in Vedic Ritual*, Delhi, 1979.

Das, A.C., *Ṛgvedic India,* Calcutta, 1921.

——, *Ṛgvedic Culture,* Calcutta, 1925; rpt, Delhi, 1979.

Das, S.K., *Economic History of Ancient India,* 1925.

Dasgupta, S.N., *History of Indian Philosphy,* Vol. I, Cambridge, 1922; rpt, Delhi, 1975.

Date, V.H., *Upaniṣads Retold,* New Delhi, 1979.

Dayananda, Swami, *Vedatattvaprakāśa*, Delhi, 1935.

Deshmukh, P.S., *The Origin and Development of Religion in Vedic Literature,* London, 1933.

Deussen, P., *Philosophie des Veda,* Leipzig, 1894.

——, *Die Philosophie der Upaniṣads*, Leipzig, 1899; Eng. tr., Edinburgh, 1919.

——, *Sixty Upaniṣads of the Veda*, Eng. tr. *Sechzig Upaniṣads,* Delhi, 1980.

Devasthali, G.V., *Religion and Mythology of the Brāhmaṇas,* Pune, 1965.

Dhar, M.K. and R.L. Mehta, *Social and Economic History of Ancient India,* Delhi, 1991.

Dharmadhikari, T.N., ed., *Yajñāyudhāni,* Pune, 1989.

Dikshitar, V.R.R., *Hindu Administrative Institutions,* Madras, 1929.

——, *War in Ancient India,* rpt, Delhi, 1987.

Drury, N., *The Sacrificial Ritual in the Śatapatha Brāhmaṇa*, Delhi, 1981.

Dutt, N.K., *Aryanization of India,* Calcutta, 1925.

——, *Origin and Development of Caste in India,* 2 vols., London, 1931.

Edwards, M., *Everyday Life in Early India,* London, 1969.

Farquhar, J.N., *An Outline of Religious Literature of India,* London, 1920.

Furst, A., *Der Sprachgebrauch der alteren Upaniṣads,* Gottingen, 1915.

Geldner, K.F., *Kosmogonie des Ṛgveda,* Berlin, 1908.

Ghoshal, U.N., *A History of Hindu Political Theories,* London, 1923; *History of Hindu Public Life,* Calcutta, 1945.

Ghurye, G.S., *Vedic India,* Bombay, 1979.

Gonda, J., *De Vedische godsdienst,* The Hague, 1943; *Some Observations on the Relations between 'Gods' and 'Powers' in the Vedas,* Leiden, 1957.

——, *The Vision of the Vedic Gods.* The Hague, 1963.

——, *The Dual Divinities in the Religion of the Vedas.* Amsterdam, 1974.

——, *The Vedic God Mitra,* Leider, 1972.

——, *Selected Studies,* 5 vols, Leiden, 1975.

——, ed., *Vedic Literature* I, Wiesbaden, 1975.

——, *Ancient Indian Kingship from the Religious Point of View,* Leiden, 1969.

Gough, A.E., *The Philosophy of the Upaniṣads*, London, 1903.

Grassmann, H., *Worterbuch zum Ṛgveda*, 3rd edn., Wiesbaden 1955.

Grover, Usha, *Symbolism of the Āraṇyakas and Third Impact on the Upaniṣads,* New Delhi, 1987.

Gupta, Uma, *Materialism in the Vedas,* New Delhi, 1987.

Hale, W.E., *Asura in Early Vedic Religion,* New Delhi, 1986.

Heller, F., *Die Mystik in den Upaniṣaden,* Munchen, 1925.

Henry, V., *La Magie dans l'Inde Antique,* Paris, 1904.

Herzfeld, E., *Iran in the Ancient East,* London, 1941.

Hillebrandt, A., *Ritual-Literature,* Strassburg, 1910.

——, *Vedische Mythologie,* Breslau, 1891-1902.

——, *Veda Interpretation,* Breslau, 1895.

——, *Die Gotter der Ṛgveda*, Breslau, 1894.

Hopkins, E.W., *The Religions of India,* Boston, 1895.

Howard, W., *Vedic Recitations in Vārāṇasī*, Delhi, 1986.

Jane, S.D., *Studies in Early Indian Thought,* London, 1918.

Jayaswal, K.P., *Hindu Polity,* Calcutta, 1924.

Jolly, J., *Recht and Sitte,* Strassburg, 1896; Eng. trans. by B.K. Ghosh, *Hindu Law and Custom,* Calcutta, 1928.

Joshi, J.R., *Some Minor Deities in Vedic Mythology and Ritual,* Pune, 1977.

Joshi, Kireet, *The Veda and Indian Culture,* New Delhi, 1991.

Kaegi, Adolf, *The Ṛgveda*, New Delhi, 1975.

Kane, P.V., *History of Dharmaśāstra,* 5 vols., Poona, 1930-62.

Karambelkar, V.M., *The Atharvavedic Civilization,* Nagpur, 1959.

Karmarkar, A.P., *Religions of India,* vol. I, Lonavla, 1950.

Ketkar, S.V., *The History of Caste in India,* vol. I, New York, 1909, vol. II, London, 1911.

Keith, A.B., *The Religion and Philosophy of the Veda and Upaniṣads*, 2 vols., Cambridge Mass, 1925.

——, *Vedas of the Black Yajus School*, Cambridge, 1914.

——, *Rgveda Brāhmaṇas*, HOS XXV, Cambridge, 1920.

Kosambi, D.D., *The Culture and Civilization of Ancient India,* rpt, New Delhi, 1989.

Kulkarni, S.D., ed, *Beginnings of Life, Culture and History,* vol. I, Bombay 1988.

Kunhan, Raja C., *The Vedas: A Cultural Study*, Andhra University, 1957.

Lahiri, A.K., *Vedic Vṛtra,* Delhi, 1984.

Law, B.C., *Rivers of India,* Calcutta, 1944.

——, *Tribes in Ancient India,* Poona, 1943.

Law, N.N., *The Age of the Ṛgveda*, Calcutta, 1965.

Levi, S., *La Doctrine du Sacrifice dans les Brāhmaṇas,* Paris, 1898.

Linclon, B., *Priests, Warriors and Cattle,* Berkeley, 1981.

Macdonell, A.A., *Vedic Grammar,* Strassburg, 1910.

——, *Vedic Mythology,* Strassburg, 1887,

——, *History of Sanskrit Literature,* London, 1913.

——, *Bṛhaddevatā of Śauṇaka* Harvard, 1904.

Macdonell, A.A. and A.B. Keith, *Vedic Index of Names and Subjects,* 2 vols., London, 1912.

Majumdar, R.C., ed, *The Vedic Age,* London, 1951.

Max, Müller F., *History of Ancient Sanskrit Literature,* London, 1859, rpt, Allahabad, 1912.

Misra, P., *Evolution of the Brāhmaṇa Class,* Delhi, 1978.

Mitra, Prits, *Indian Culture and Society in the Vedas,* Calcutta, 1985.

Monier-Williams, M., *Religious Thought and life in India,* London, 1891; *Sanskrit-English Dictionary,* rpt, Delhi, 1989.

Mookerji, R.K., *Ancient Indian Education,* rpt, Delhi, 1989.

Muir, J., *Original Sanskrit Texts,* 5 vols, London, 1858-70.

Mukhopadhyay, P.C., *Journey of the Upaniṣads to the West,* Calcutta, 1987.

Nath, Vijaya, *Dāna: Gift System in Ancient India,* New Delhi, 1987.

O'Flaherty, W.D., *Sexual Metaphors and Animal Symbols in Indian Mythology,* Delhi, 1980.

——, *Tales of Sex and Violence (Folklore, Sacrifice in the Jaiminīya Brahmaṇa),* Delhi, 1987.

Oldenberg, H., *Die Religion des Veda,* Berlin, 1894.

——, *Ancient India,* Chicago, 1898.

——, *Die Weltanchanung der Brāhmaṇa Texte,* Gottingen, 1919.

Om Prakash, *Economy and Food in Ancient India,* Delhi, 1987.

——, *Religion and Society in Ancient India,* Delhi, 1985.

Pande, G.C., *Foundations of Indian Culture,* 2 vols., Delhi, 1900.

Pandey, I.P., *Dress and Ornaments in Ancient India,* Delhi, 1988.

Pandey, U.K., *Political Concepts and Institutions in the Śukla Yajurveda,* Patna, 1979.

Pannikar, R.P. et al., *The Vedic Experience, Mantra-mañjarī,* Delhi, 1983.

Pargiter, F.E., *Ancient Indian Historical Tradition, London 1922; Dynasties of Kali Age,* London, 1913.

Pischel, R. and K.P. Geldner, *Vedische Studien,* Stuttgart, 1889-1901.

Potdar, K.R., *Sacrifice in the Ṛgveda,* Bombay, 1953.

Pradhan, S.N., *Chronology of Ancient India,* Calcutta, 1927.

Pratt, J.B., *India and its Faiths,* Boston, 1915.

Radhakrishnan, S., *Indian Philosophy,* vol. I, London, 1923.

——, ed., *Cultural Heritage of India,* vol. I, Calcutta, 1958.

——, ed., *History of Philosophy: Eastern and Western,* London, 1952.

Ranade, R.D., *Constructive Survey of the Upaniṣadic Philosophy,* Poona, 1926.

Rapson, E.J., ed., *Cambridge History of India,* vol. I, Cambridge, 1922.

Ray, P.R. and S.N. Sen, eds., *The Cultural Heritage of India,* vol. VI, Calcutta, 1986.

Raychaudhuri, H.C., *Political History of Ancient India,* Calcutta University, 1972.

Reinach, S., *L'Origine des Aryens,* Paris, 1892.

Renou, L., *Religions of Ancient India,* tr., Sheila M. Fynn, London, 1953.

——, *Bibliographie Vedique,* Paris, 1931.

——, *Vṛtra et Verethragna,* Paris, 1935.

Samaddar, J.N., *Economic Condition of Ancient India,* Calcutta, 1922.

Sarasvati, V., *Vedic Concept of God,* Delhi, 1983.

Sarkar, S.C., *Some Aspects of Earliest Social History of India,* London, 1928.

Sastri, G.N., *Vedic Literature,* Calcutta, 1982.

Satya Sarva, *Comprehensive History of Vedic Literature,* Delhi, 1977.

Schrader, O, *Sprachvergleichung and Urgeschichte,* tr., F.B. Jevons, Jena, 1906-7.

——, *Antiquities of the Aryan Peoples,* Leipzig, 1908.

Schroeder, L.V., *Mysterium and Mimus em Ṛgveda,* Leipzig, 1908.

Senart, E., *Les Castes dans l'Inde,* Paris, 1896.

Sharma, R.N., *Culture and Civilization as Recorded in the Śrauta Sutra,* Delhi, 1977.

Sharma, R.S., *Perspectives in Social and Economic History of Early India,* 3rd edn., New Delhi, 1991.

——, *Aspects of Political Ideas and Institutions in Ancient India,* 3rd edn., New Delhi, 1991.

——, *Material Culture and Social Formations in Ancient India,* 4th rpt., New Delhi, 1992.

——, *Looking for the Aryans,* New Delhi, 1995.

Sharma, Subhra, *Life in the Upaniṣads,* New Delhi, 1985.

Shende, N.J., *The Religion and Philosophy of the Atharvaveda,* Poona, 1952.

——, *The Foundation of Atharvanic Religion,* Poona, 1949.

Singh, S.D., *Ancient Indian Warfare,* rpt., Delhi, 1989.

Skold, H., *The Nirukta: Its Place in Old Indian Literature, Its Etymologies,* Lund, 1926.

Spiegel, F., *Die arische Periode und ihre Zustande,* Leipzig, 1887.

Staal, F., *Agni: The Vedic Ritual of Fire,* Delhi, 1984.

Strauss, O., *Indische Philosophie,* Muchen, 1925.

Tamaskar, B.G., *Geographical Knowledge in Upaniṣads,* New Delhi, 1989.

Tatacharya, A., Ramanuja, *Vedakālinajanatantrasthānāni,* Tirupati, 1970.

Taylor, I., *The Origin of the Aryans,* London, 1889.

Thibaut, G., *Astronomie, Astrologie und Mathematik,* Strassburg, 1899.

Thieme, P., *Pāṇini and the Veda,* Allahabad, 1935.

Thite, G.U., *Medicine: The Magico-Religious Aspects According to the Vedic and Later Literature,* Pune, 1982.

Thite, U.K., *Sacrifice in the Brāhmaṇa Texts,* Pune, 1975.

Tilak, B.G., *The Arctic Home in the Vedas,* rpt., Poona, 1956.

——, *Vedic Chronology and Vedāṅga Jyotiṣa,* Poona, 1955.

Urquhart, W.S., *The Upaniṣads and Life,* Calcutta, 1916.

Vaidya, C.V., *History of Sanskrit Literature,* vol. I, Poona, 1930.

Vanenna, J., *La religion Vedique* (in Encl. de Pleiade Hist. des Reb), Paris, 1970.
Varma, S., *The Etymologies of Yāska,* Hoshiarpur, 1953.
Vesci, M., *Heat and Sacrifice in the Vedas,* Delhi, 1985.
Vatsyayan, K., ed, *Kalātattvakośa: A Lexicon of Fundamental Concepts of the Indian Arts,* 2 vols., New Delhi, 1988, 1992.
Wallis, H.W., *Cosmology of the Ṛgveda,* London, 1887.
Weber, A., *History of Indian Literature,* tr., J. Mann and Theodor Zachariae, London, 1882.
Winternitz, M., *History of Indian Literature,* vol. I, Calcutta University, 1927.
Wust, Walter, *Stilgeschichte und Chronologie des Ṛgveda,* Leipzig, 1928.